The Asset Securitization Handbook

The Asset Securitization Handbook

Phillip L. Zweig, Editor

DOW JONES-IRWIN
Homewood, Illinois 60430

Project editor: Jane Lightell
Production manager: Ann Cassady
Compositor: Publication Services, Inc.
Typeface: 11/13 Times Roman
Printer: Arcata Graphics/Kingsport

LIBRARY OF CONGRESS
Library of Congress Cataloging-in-Publication Data

The Asset securitization handbook/Phillip L. Zweig, editor.
   p. cm.
  Includes index.
  ISBN 1-556-23086-9
  1. Asset-backed financing I. Zweig, Phillip L.
HG4028.A84A87 1989
658.1'5224—dc19

88–15284
CIP

Printed in the United States of America
 2 3 4 5 6 7 8 0 K 5 4 3 2 1 0 9

PREFACE

Asset securitization is a rapidly evolving financial tool that enables depository institutions, finance companies, and other corporations to liquefy their balance sheets and develop new sources of capital.

This Handbook, which contains contributions from the nation's leading experts in this field, is aimed at corporate financial officers, accountants, lawyers, commercial and investment bankers, and other practitioners already playing a role or seeking to play one in applying this important new financial technology. The book does not take the position of advocating the use of securitization over other financing methods, but rather seeks to demonstrate its value as yet another tool for corporations and depository institutions as well as investors.

Since much has already been written on residential mortgage-backed securities, the predecessor of the asset-backed securities described in these pages, the Handbook avoids a lengthy discussion of these instruments. However, because commercial mortgages possess many of the characteristics of commercial loans, this subject is treated in detail.

Even though much effort was expended to eliminate outright duplication of material from chapter to chapter, this was not always possible and, indeed, some repetition was considered desirable for the sake of clarity. For example, several chapters contain different views and levels of technical detail on such key issues as credit enhancement, legal issues, and prepayments.

New applications of this methodology are constantly being devised, and the editors made every effort to include the most recent developments in the Handbook. Consequently, we believe it represents the most comprehensive examination of this market available today.

Phillip L. Zweig

LIST OF CONTRIBUTORS

Charles M. Adelman, Partner
Cadwalader, Wickersham & Taft,
New York

Tamara L. Adler, Vice President
Goldman, Sachs & Co., New York

Neil Baron, Partner
Booth & Baron, New York

Lowell L. Bryan, Director
McKinsey & Co., New York

Theodore V. Buerger,
Senior Vice President
Financial Security Assurance, New York

Owen Carney
Director, Investment Securities Division,
Office of the Comptroller of the Currency
Washington, D.C.

Asset Finance Group
Project Editor: Diana H. Strickler, Vice President
First Boston Corp., New York

William J. Haley, Vice President
Salomon Brothers Inc, New York

Wayne S. Hardenbrook,
Senior Vice President and Treasurer
Empire of America, Buffalo

Linda S. Iseley, Assistant Vice President
Financial Security Assurance, New York

Stephen Joynt, Managing Director
Standard & Poor's, New York

C. Thomas Kunz, Partner
Skadden, Arps, Slate, Meagher & Flom,
New York

Roger D. Lorence, Esq.
New York

Glenn B. McClelland Jr., Vice President
Citicorp, Harrison, New York

James W. McDonald Jr., Vice President
Citicorp, Harrison, New York

Benjamin S. Neuhausen, Partner
Arthur Andersen & Co., Chicago

John R. Price, Managing Director
Manufacturers Hanover Corp., New York

Robert I. Reich, President
Marine Midland Automotive
Financial Corp., Buffalo

Charles W. Sewright, Jr., President
Marine Midland Mortgage Corp., Buffalo

Christopher L. Snyder Jr., President
Loan Pricing Corp., New York

John E. Stewart, Partner
Arthur Andersen & Co., Chicago

M. Douglas Watson Jr.,
Vice President and Director
Moody's Investors Service, New York

Paul Willax, Chairman
Empire of America, Buffalo

CONTENTS

PART 1

ASSETS, STRUCTURES, AND RATING AGENCY CONSIDERATIONS

CHAPTER 1

INTRODUCTION

Lowell L. Bryan, Director
McKinsey & Co

BACKGROUND

Throughout most of history, lending money has been a relatively straight-forward business. Ever since medieval moneychangers and goldsmiths began accepting funds for safekeeping and lending out the idle cash to creditworthy borrowers, the fundamentals of lending have remained essentially the same. Banks have provided depositors with safe, liquid instruments in which to invest their funds and have taken those funds and lent them to borrowers under the agreement that they would be repaid with interest. In the process, banks absorbed the credit risk inherent in lending. Safety to depositors was provided by the bank's capital or by government backing in the form of deposit insurance or other federal support. Other lenders (e.g., consumer and commercial finance companies) have employed the same basic business system except they raised funds either by issuing securities or borrowing from banks instead of accepting deposits.

A new technology for lending called asset securitization is beginning to render this classic business system obsolete. Under the traditional system, the same institution (i.e., whether a commercial bank, a thrift, or a finance company) would originate the loan, structure the terms, absorb the credit risk, fund the asset, and service the collection of principal payments and interest. Under the new system, several different institutions might be involved, each of which might play different roles.

For example, in extending credit under the new system, one institution could originate the loan, a second (probably an investment bank) could structure the transaction, a third could insure the credit risk, a fourth could service the credit, and finally, an investor could purchase the credit enhanced asset.

Assets that have already been securitized include government insured mortgages, privately insured mortgages, automobile loans, credit card and lease receivables, commercial mortgages, and even commercial loan receivables. The volume of outstanding mortgage-passthrough securities, a product developed in the mid-1970s, is already very large (At the end of 1987 outstandings were approximately $682 billion or about 25 percent of total outstanding mortgage debt). To put this $682 billion figure in perspective, it exceeds the total loans made by all commercial banks to all the nation's businesses (i.e., as of June 1987, total commercial and industrial loans of the entire commercial banking system was about $500 billion). Although mortgage-backed securities originally were issued only by government related entities, private issuers are now becoming increasingly important. In 1987, roughly 3 percent of the total mortgage-backed securities outstanding (i.e., $20 billion) were issued by private institutions, although most of the underlying mortgages are guaranteed by an agency of the federal government. The private portion is expected to double to about 6 percent in 1988. In 1987, about half of new originations were securitized into passthroughs.

STATUS OF THE ASSET-BACKED SECURITIES MARKET

In the mid-1980s, this new technology was first applied to other non-mortgage loans: for example, car loans, commercial mortgages, credit cards, and lease receivables.

The public market for asset-backed securities (ABS) got underway in March 1985, when Sperry Lease Finance Corporation issued $192 million of lease-backed notes. Sperry Corporation (now Unisys) sold operating leases on computer equipment to SLFC, a newly formed subsidiary. SLFC then sold fixed-rate notes, collateralized by the leases, to institutional investors. The cash flow from the leases was sufficient to meet the debt service (i.e., principal and interest) on the notes. The structure resulted in a triple-A rating for the lease-backed notes, despite

Sperry's lower rating, and enabled Sperry to retain the tax benefits of the leases while achieving sale treatment for financial reporting purposes. Although a few asset-backed transactions had been placed privately prior to the SLFC issue, the Sperry offering marked the opening of a new, liquid sector in the capital markets.

In three years, the public ABS market has grown to $26.3 billion (see Exhibit 1-1). In 1985, the first year, only $1.2 billion of ABSs were offered. But, in 1986 issuance ballooned to over $10 billion. In 1987, ABS offerings totaled $10.0 billion, somewhat less than 1986. However, the participants in the market—both issuers and investment banks—broadened significantly in 1987. A large majority of the transactions to date have been collateralized by automotive loans, but an increasing number involve the securitization of credit card receivables (see Exhibit 1-1).

For example, the General Motors Acceptance Corporation (GMAC) alone sold about $8.0 billion of car loans, in seven separate transactions, in just 10 months (from December of 1985 to October of 1986). At the end of 1986, total new issuances of public securities backed by automotive loans were about $9.4 billion. By the end of 1987, the number of issuers had expanded from essentially just GMAC to include General Electric Credit (now General Electric Capital), RepublicBank, Marine Midland, Chrysler Financial, and Mack (Trucks) Financial. Securities backed by credit card receivables, introduced in the private market in 1986, reached about $2.4 billion in outstandings by year end 1987, with issuers including Bank of America, First Chicago, and Maryland National. And, in addition to First Boston and Salomon Brothers, the pioneers in underwriting these securities, Goldman Sachs, Drexel Burnham, Shearson Lehman, Kidder Peabody, and even some commercial banks are active in the investment banking part of the business.

POTENTIAL FOR GROWTH

Most knowledgeable observers believe that the asset-backed securities market has great growth potential. Standard & Poor's Corporation (S&P) has stated that the market (public and private) could reach $100 billion within five years.[1] To put this number in perspective, one should compare the volume of assets that could be securitized to the current size of the public ABS market. Exhibit 1-2 shows that total consumer

EXHIBIT 1-1
Asset-Backed Securities, U.S. Public Issues

1985

Date	Issuer	Collateral	Amount (thousands)	Manager(s)
03/07/85	Sperry Lease Finance, Series A	Computer Leases	$ 192,455	FBC
05/15/85	Valley National Financial	Autos	100,499	FBC
05/15/85	Marine Midland 1985-1 CARS Trust	Autos	60,171	SAL
08/01/85	Home Federal 1985-1 CARS Trust	Autos	103,205	SAL
09/12/85	Sperry Lease Finance, Series B	Computer Leases	145,805	FBC, BS
12/12/85	GMAC 1985-A Grantor Trust	Autos	524,684	FBC
12/13/85	Western Financial Auto Loans, Series 1985-A	Autos	110,000	DBL
	TOTAL 1985:		$1,236,819	

1986

Date	Issuer	Collateral	Amount (thousands)	Manager(s)
01/23/86	GMAC 1986-A Grantor Trust	Autos	$ 423,552	FBC
04/16/86	GMAC 1986-B Grantor Trust	Autos	1,049,491	FBC
06/18/86	Empire of America FSB 1986-A Grantor Trust	Autos	190,217	FBC
06/19/86	GMAC 1986-C Grantor Trust	Autos	755,074	FBC, ML, MS, SAL
07/15/86	Newmont First Capital	Affiliate Notes	50,000	SAL, KP
07/24/86	CARCO Series 1986-1	Autos	250,000	SAL
07/24/86	NMAC 1986-B1 Grantor Trust	Light Trucks	112,729	FBC
07/24/86	NMAC 1986-B2 Grantor Trust	Light Trucks	69,701	FBC
07/24/86	NMAC 1986-B3 Grantor Trust	Light Trucks	5,011	FBC
08/19/86	GMAC 1986-D Grantor Trust	Autos	354,750	FBC, ML, MS, SAL
08/19/86	GMAC 1986-E Grantor Trust	Autos	725,069	FBC, ML, MS, SAL
10/14/86	ABSC Class 1-A	Autos	2,095,000	FBC
10/14/86	ABSC Class 1-B	Autos	585,000	FBC
10/14/86	ABSC Class 1-C	Autos	1,320,000	DBL
11/13/86	Western Financial Auto Loans 2, Series 1986-A	Autos	191,930	DBL
11/18/86	Banco Central 1986-A Grantor Trust	Autos	66,614	FBC
11/18/86	GMAC 1986-F Grantor Trust	Autos	326,962	FBC, ML, MS, SAL

Date	Issuer	Collateral	Amount (thousands)	Manager(s)
12/02/86	ABSC Class 2-A	Autos	95,000	FBC
12/02/86	ABSC Class 2-B	Autos	25,050	FBC
12/02/86	ABSC Class 2-C	Autos	60,176	FBC
12/05/86	Goldome 1986-A Grantor Trust	Computer Leases	205,712	FBC
12/12/86	California CARS Grantor Trust 1986-A	Autos	514,222	SAL
12/17/86	GMAC 1986-G Grantor Trust	Autos	444,857	FBC, ML, MS, SAL
12/17/86	Sperry Lease Finance, Series C	Computer Leases	174,450	FBC

TOTAL 1986: $10,040,567

1987

Date	Issuer	Collateral	Amount (thousands)	Manager(s)
01/16/87	RepublicBank Delaware, Series A	Credit Cards	$ 200,000	GS, FBC
02/25/87	California Credit Card Trust 1987-A	Credit Cards	400,000	FBC
03/20/87	Western Financial Auto Loans 2, Series 1987-A	Autos	125,000	DBL
03/24/87	GMAC 1987-A Grantor Trust	Autos	163,639	FBC
04/22/87	GMAC 1987-B Grantor Trust	Autos	162,456	SAL
05/28/87	RepublicBank Dallas, Series A	Autos	230,000	GS, FBC, SAL
05/29/87	GMAC 1987-C Grantor Trust	Autos	166,140	FBC
06/03/87	GECC 1987-1 Grantor Trust	Autos	146,943	KP
06/04/87	Marine Midland 1987-1 CARS Trust	Autos	600,077	SAL, MMS
06/11/87	CFC-1 Grantor Trust	Autos	515,907	FBC, SAL
06/19/87	California Credit Card Trust 1987-B	Credit Cards	300,000	SAL, B of A
06/22/87	GMAC 1987-D Grantor Trust	Autos	323,361	SAL
06/23/87	Imperial CARDS Trust 1987-1	Credit Cards	100,000	SAL
06/30/87	Mack Trucks Receivables Class 1-A	Trucks	103,685	SLH, LF
06/30/87	Mack Trucks Receivables Class 1-B	Trucks	111,455	SLH, LF
07/02/87	ABSC Class 3-A	Autos	15,250	FBC
07/02/87	ABSC Class 3-B	Autos	10,425	FBC
07/16/87	Security Pacific Credit Corp. 1987-A Grantor Trust	Autos	103,010	FBC
07/29/87	ABSC Class 4-A	Autos	971,210	FBC
07/29/87	ABSC Class 4-B	Autos	439,630	FBC
07/29/87	Western Financial Auto Loans 2, Series 1987-B	Autos	110,000	DBL
08/24/87	Bank of Boston CARS Grantor Trust 1987-A	Autos	102,863	SAL
09/17/87	Mattel Funding	Trade Receivables	62,500	FBC, DBL
09/21/87	MEPC Capital	Affiliate Notes	100,000	SAL
09/23/87	Union Carbide Finance	Trade Receivables	249,000	FBC, GS, MS, SAL
09/24/87	Great American Credit Card Trust A	Credit Cards	110,000	GS, FBC
09/29/87	First Chicago CARDS Trust 1987-1	Credit Cards	800,000	SAL, FBC

EXHIBIT 1-1
Asset-Backed Securities, U.S. Public Issues (continued)

1987

Date	Issuer	Collateral	Amount (thousands)	Manager(s)
10/08/87	Volkswagen Lease Finance	Auto Leases	150,000	DBC, DR
10/09/87	UST FASTBACs 1987-A Grantor Trust	Autos	109,098	DBL
10/13/87	ABSC Series 5	Autos	142,675	FBC
10/23/87	Empire of America FSB 1987-A Grantor Trust	Autos	265,021	FBC
11/05/87	SBRI Class Y	Autos	176,750	SAL
11/05/87	SBRI Class A	Autos	265,825	SAL
11/12/87	CFC-2 Grantor Trust	Autos	1,002,254	FBC, SAL
11/12/87	Household Bank FSB Class A-1	Consumer Loans	151,700	GS
11/12/87	Household Bank FSB Class A-2	Consumer Loans	280,384	GS
11/18/87	ABSC Class 6-A	Autos	36,035	FBC
11/18/87	ABSC Class 6-B	Autos	88,500	FBC
11/20/87	UST FASTBACs 1987-B Grantor Trust	Autos	100,000	DBL
12/09/87	MBNA Credit Card Trust 1987-A	Credit Cards	500,000	FBC, GS
TOTAL 1987:			$ 9,990,793	

1988

Date	Issuer	Collateral	Amount (thousands)	Manager(s)
01/07/88	Westfield Finance	Affiliate Notes	$ 308,000	FBC, GS, ML
01/21/88	EOA Auto Funding	Autos	225,000	FBC, MS, SAL
02/19/88	Western Financial Auto Loans 2, Series 1988-A	Autos	155,000	DBL
02/26/88	Shawmut National 1988-A Grantor Trust	Autos	124,000	GS
03/04/88	BMWCC 1988 A1 Grantor Trust	Autos	39,798	KP
03/04/88	BMWCC 1988 A2 Grantor Trust	Autos	66,561	KP
03/14/88	CFC-3 Grantor Trust	Autos	753,109	SAL
03/16/88	Empire of America FSB 1988-A Grantor Trust	Autos	191,001	FBC
03/24/88	UST FASTBACs 1988-A Grantor Trust	Autos	87,500	DBL
03/25/88	Colonial Credit Card Trust 1988-A	Credit Cards	150,000	FBC, KP
04/20/88	Chemical Bank Grantor Trust 1988-A	Autos	257,415	CB, FBC
05/06/88	SLH ABS Corp. Class A-1	Autos	37,475	SLH
05/06/88	SLH ABS Corp. Class A-2	Autos	56,495	SLH
05/09/88	First Chicago Master Trust, Series A	Credit Cards	300,000	FBC, SAL, FNBC

1988

Date	Issuer	Collateral	Amount (thousands)	Manager(s)
05/12/88	MBNA Credit Card Trust 1988-A	Credit Cards	500,000	FBC
05/13/88	Mack Trucks Receivables Class 2-A	Trucks	47,540	SLH
05/13/88	Mack Trucks Receivables Class 2-B	Trucks	74,555	SLH
05/26/88	Western Financial Auto Loans 2, Series 1988-B	Autos	100,000	DBL
06/02/88	MEPC American Holdings	Affiliate Notes	180,000	GS, SAL
06/03/88	Household Bank FSB Series A	Consumer Loans/ Installment Contracts	439,500	GS
06/13/88	Marine Midland 1988-1 CARS Trust	Autos	254,059	SAL, MMS
06/15/88	First Chicago Master Trust, Series B	Credit Cards	600,000	SAL, FBC, FNBC
	TOTAL 1988:		$ 4,947,008	
	GRAND TOTAL 1985 TO DATE:		$26,265,185	

* KEY TO ABBREVIATIONS:

BS	= Bear Stearns		KP	= Kidder Peabody
CB	= Chemical Bank		LF	= Lazard Freres
DBC	= Deutsche Bank Capital		ML	= Merrill Lynch
DBL	= Drexel Burnham Lambert		MMS	= Marine Midland Securities
DR	= Dillon Read		MS	= Morgan Stanley
FNBC	= First National Bank of Chicago		SAL	= Salomon Brothers
FBC	= First Boston		SLH	= Shearson Lehman Hutton
GS	= Goldman Sachs			

installment credit is $625 billion. Only 4 percent of this amount has been securitized in the public market. In thinking about the potential for nonmortgage asset securitization, one should bear in mind that "consumer installment credit" does not include, for example, the billions of dollars of intercompany commercial trade receivables or commercial and industrial (C&I) loans held by banks. Further, consumer loans and commercial receivables have much shorter average lives than do mortgages, so that the pool of nonmortgage assets that could be securitized turns over frequently.

It is an understatement to say that the development of these new techniques of lending has major implications for lenders, particularly U.S. commercial banks and thrifts. Residential mortgages, automobile loans, and credit cards alone account for 40 percent of the total loans of the nation's depository institutions. In all, the potentially securitizable loans of all kinds in the United States are well over $4.5 trillion. The

EXHIBIT 1–2
Consumer Installment Credit ($ in Billions)

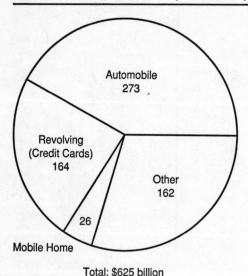

Automobile
273

Revolving
(Credit Cards)
164

Other
162

26

Mobile Home

Total: $625 billion

Source: Federal Reserve Statistical Release — "Consumer Installment Credit," April 8, 1988

---

[1]"Asset-Backed Securitization Credit Review," *Standard & Poor's CreditWeek*, March 16, 1987, p.1.

total volume of securitized debt now outstanding, in combination with the rapid growth in loans that have the liquidity of securities and securities that have the credit risk of loans, is enormous. It is a reasonable guess that within a decade some 80 percent of all new loans will be transformed into securities.

Why is asset securitization growing so rapidly? The answer will become clear if we step back and examine some of the marketplace forces at work. We also need to understand the principal innovations enabling the development of the technology and its advantages for the many different players who can participate in the new business system.

FORCES AT WORK

Let us begin by returning to securitization in the general sense of the word. It is important to understand why bank lending is continuing to lose ground to fundraising through the issue of securities in most markets. Debt securities inherently have many advantages over loans. Securities are liquid and tradeable, whereas loans are illiquid (i.e., there is only a very limited secondary market for most loans). The value of a debt security is determined by the market, whereas the value of a loan is based upon subjective valuation (i.e., What is the real value of a loan made to Mexico?—Book Value?—Eighty percent of book?—Forty percent of book?). Debt securities are also attractive to the large classes of investors (e.g., individuals and pension funds) who have little ability or appetite for assessing credit risks. Rating agencies exist to assess credit risk for investors; loans, on the other hand, have substantial credit risk and require significant in-house skill to assess creditworthiness and to work out problems that can lead to large losses.

Finally, debt securities have lower total costs than loans. For example, total costs of intermediating a collateralized mortgage obligation bond (one of the types of mortgage-backed securities) including underwriting costs, market making costs, and issuing costs (lawyers, accountants, rating agency fees) average about 1/4 of a percent per year, over the life of the bond. The same size portfolio of residential mortgages held by a commercial bank has a total annual average intermediary cost (e.g., equity costs, income taxes, reserves, insurance) of about 1.5 percent. In other words, in a commercial bank, significant costs must be incurred to pay commercial bank shareholders, the Internal Revenue Service, the

Federal Reserve system, and the Federal Deposit Insurance Corporation. These costs can be eliminated in securitized transactions, and the savings can be used to reduce costs to borrowers and increase yields paid to investors.

Traditionally, however, no matter how attractive it has been to issue debt securities, only a fraction of all potential borrowers have been able to tap into this market. Until recently, the only borrowers who were eligible players in the securities market were those whose creditworthiness could be assessed by outside rating agencies, or who had name recognition, and who were of a sufficient size to create issues large enough to meet investors' liquidity needs. (Even today, for example, an issue needs to be larger than $100 million to be called "liquid".) Indeed, almost all securities have historically been issued by governments (i.e., federal, state, and local) and by large "investment grade" corporations. This has meant that all borrowers requiring credit risk assessment and credit risk absorption by an intermediary, as well as all small borrowers, no matter how creditworthy, could not issue debt securities. Thus, individuals and small to midsized corporations have been foreclosed from participating in the advantages of financing through securities.

In recent years, investment grade private borrowers (i.e., large, high-quality corporations), have become active issuers of debt securities and have increasingly turned away from commercial banks as they have raised money through commercial paper and bonds.

The competitive advantages of debt securities over loans has also hastened the growth of loans that have the liquidity of securities. The excess capacity created by the large number of banks and investors willing to lend to large, high-grade corporations has created razor-thin spreads (i.e., under 1/4 of 1 percent). These low spreads, in combination with increasing capital requirements from regulators (who are worried about bad loans to developing nations, real estate developers, farmers, and energy companies) have made it impossible for commercial banks to lend money to high-grade corporations and earn reasonable returns on their shareholders' capital. As a result, banks have been looking for ways to satisfy their borrowers' credit needs without putting loans on their balance sheets. They have accomplished this largely through loan sales and note issuance facilities. Loan sales, the outright sale of a loan to another institution—have grown from almost nothing in 1982 to about $35 billion by the end of 1987. Note issuance facilities (the issuance of notes by a corporation in the Euromarket under a committed loan agreement from a bank) have grown from $4 billion outstanding to some $40 billion during the same time period.

Debt securities that have the credit risk of loans have also exhibited explosive growth. Led by investment bankers, the limits of the traditional system have been stretched to include borrowers that previously could never issue securities. For example, junk bonds grew from $3 billion in outstandings in 1982 to $159 billion by the end of 1987.

In combination, loans that have the liquidity of securities and securities that have the credit risk of loans have caused over $250 billion of large corporate borrowings to bypass bank balance sheets in the United States alone. In comparison, the total remaining large corporate borrowings from banks (much of which are acquisition loans) are no more than $50 to $75 billion.

All of this represents a trend toward financial assets being securities rather than loans. There are limits to how far securitization can proceed, however, through the displacement of loans by securities.

Traditional high-grade commercial and industrial loans still outstanding to large corporations in the United States now represent only about 1 percent of the $4.5 trillion of loans outstanding on the balance sheets of all U.S. depository institutions, finance companies, and corporations (i.e., even corporations make loans, largely through trade receivables). Most of these $4.5 trillion in loans are to individuals and small to midsized corporations. Before these loans can be removed from the balance sheets of depository institutions, finance companies, and corporations, they must be literally converted into securities through the new technology of asset securitization.

Of course, one important driver of the new technology over the last several years has been the U.S. investment banking industry, particularly First Boston and Salomon Brothers. Investment bankers first promoted the technology with government guaranteed mortgages and only later moved on to securitized privately issued residential mortgages, commercial mortgages, automobile loans, credit card receivables, and even commercial loans and lease receivables. From the beginning, however, the incentives for the investment banks have been the substantial underwriting fees and trading profits to be earned from the conversion of loans from individuals and small and midsized businesses (loans that would otherwise have been on the balance sheets of banks) into securities. Such conversion enables the investment houses to garner new revenue streams as they expand their business beyond the traditional debt securities issuers (namely large corporations, municipal and state governments, and the federal government) to smaller borrowers.

FINANCIAL INNOVATIONS

There are four financial innovations that investment bankers have used to convert loans into securities and to make the resulting securities more valuable. These developments will be discussed in greater detail in later chapters.

1. *Special-purpose vehicles.* A special-purpose vehicle is a trust or corporation that has been established for the sole purpose of owning the loans; the special-purpose vehicle then issues securities, which are bought by investors. The exact form of the special-purpose vehicle used depends upon the specific nature and risks of the assets, relevant legal, regulatory, and tax issues, and the objectives of the fundraiser. The purpose of the special-purpose vehicle is to isolate the risks inherent in the loans placed in the vehicle from all the other risks of the fundraiser.

2. *Pooling of borrowers.* Through the special-purpose vehicle, loans to different borrowers are pooled in order to reach the minimum size (i.e., roughly $100 million) necessary to be able to justify public securities issues. In addition, this pooling allows the credit risk to be diversified.

3. *Credit structuring and enhancement.* When a pool of loans and the collateral for the loans are segregated in a special-purpose vehicle, a credit underwriter (e.g., a commercial bank, a finance company, or an insurance company) can assess and underwrite the credit risk in that specific pool of loans and then guarantee the credit risk. Such a guarantee can raise the credit risk of the pool to investment grade levels. This in turn allows large classes of investors, such as individuals and pension funds who have neither the skill nor the desire to assess credit risk, to invest in the securities issued by the special purpose vehicle. In many cases, the careful structuring of the transaction is sufficient to allow the issue to be rated by a rating agency. In that case no additional credit guarantee is required.

4. *Repackaging of cash flows.* In some cases, the special-purpose vehicle has repackaged the cash flows from the loans. For example, a collateralized mortgage obligation (CMO) is a special-purpose vehicle structure that has been used to purchase mortgage loans and then issue tranches of varying maturity (e.g., a fast pay, a medium pay, and a slow pay tranche) backed by the underlying loans. Each of these tranches has a different expected life that reflects the expected repayment patterns of the underlying mortgages. As the loans are paid off by borrowers, the principal first goes to the first tranche until it is paid off, then the second tranche is paid off, and so forth.

This structure enables the packager (usually an investment bank) to tailor the cash flows of the different tranches to appeal to particular investor preferences. In the case of a CMO, a thrift might purchase a shorter tranche, while a long-term investor like a pension fund might purchase a longer tranche. This repackaging of cash flows also allows the packagers to create tranches with different prepayment risk characteristics.

Three examples, starting with a simple one and moving to more complex ones, illustrate how these financial innovations make the securitization of credit possible.

In September 1985, Franklin Savings Association of Ottawa, Ks. (in a transaction very similar to many other mortgaged-backed bonds issued by other thrifts) sold $100 million of U.S. government guaranteed loans to a special-purpose trust, which issued eight-year bonds. The bond was overcollateralized; Salomon Brothers underwrote the issue. In this case, the credit structuring (i.e., overcollateralization of the bond) enabled the issue to be rated triple-A.

In December 1985, Olympia & York (a large owner of commercial real estate properties) placed a mortgage on its building at 59 Maiden Lane in New York City in a special purpose trust. They issued a ten-year bond for $200 million, with annual interest payments with the principal payment due in a single payment, at the end of the tenth year. The mortgage and lease payments were used as collateral. The leases for 90 percent of the tenants (all of whom represented quasi-government risk) expired after the maturity of the bond. Aetna Life & Casualty guaranteed $30 million of interest payment to investors. The combination of the structuring of the credit and guaranty enabled the issue to be rated triple-A. The issue was underwritten by Salomon Brothers International.

In October of 1986, the automobile financing arm of General Motors, General Motors Acceptance Corporation (GMAC), completed the largest financial transaction ever by a single private issuer: a $4 billion new issue backed by low interest rate (under 5 percent) consumer loans that had been used by GM to promote the sale of new automobiles. In this transaction, First Boston, which packaged and underwrote the deal, created a new corporation, a special-purpose vehicle called the

Asset Backed Securities Corporation (ABSC). It was to purchase the automobile loans from GMAC and to issue notes to investors. The notes were issued in the three tranches: fast pay, medium pay, and slow pay. Morgan Guaranty provided a guaranteed investment contract that permitted the structuring of a fixed pay security, eliminating prepayment risk for investors. Investors were protected from the credit risk in several ways. First, GMAC provided a first loss guaranty of 5 percent (far in excess of GMAC's loss history on similar loans, which was under 1 percent). Also, the capital invested in ABSC by First Boston ($40 million) provided an additional 1 percent protection. Finally, Credit Suisse (a triple-A bank with higher credit rating than GMAC's double-A) put up a 6% stand-by letter of credit (a guaranty to ensure timely payment of principal and interest). This combination of credit enhancement enabled the security to be rated triple-A by Moody's and S&P.

The diversity of these issues is endless. Although these transactions seem complex, their complexity reflects the value of precisely tailoring terms. Indeed, one of the most appealing characteristics of this new technology is that it can be used to tailor the transaction to the particular needs of individual issuers and classes of investors.

Our discussion of innovations requires two other important points on the application of information technology to the process:

1. These kinds of transactions would be impossible without computers to keep track of cash flows and loan defaults from individual loans and to ensure that each participant receives the correct returns. To make this process work, each loan and interest must be tagged as it flows from the borrower to the intermediary who made the loan, to the special-purpose vehicles, and finally to the end investor who bought the security. Moreover, all of these transfers must be done in accordance with the complex legal documentation that is required to ensure that with each cash payment there is a proper transfer of both return and risk.

2. In addition, *computer-based analysis* of the cash flows is critical for understanding the expected returns for the participants and the credit and prepayment risks of the transactions. For example, some of the leading investment banks in this business have spent an enormous amount of energy analyzing the prepayment risks of different kinds of residential mortgages. Some of them, indeed, have analyzed the demographics of mortgage prepayments even down to the prepayment patterns by postal zip code. The analyses enable them to create the complex tranche structures that are often critical to the success of these types of transactions.

ADVANTAGES FOR PARTICIPANTS

The securitized asset, as befits any new technology that is replacing an old one, has many benefits for most of the participants.

1. *Benefits to issuing institutions.*   Issuing banks, thrifts, and finance companies that are selling loans to a special-purpose vehicle gain a number of immediate benefits. One of the principal immediate advantages is that they can free up equity capital that they would otherwise have to use to support the asset on their balance sheets. The actual credit risk implied by regulatory capital requirements for commercial banks (e.g., capital equal to 7 percent of the loan), or expected by rating agencies and the market for finance companies (e.g., 8 to 10 percent of the loan), is significantly higher than the actual expected credit losses inherent in many types of loans.

For example, actual loan losses on a pool of car loans or single-family mortgage loans are likely to be under 1 percent of the principal amount of the loans over the life of the pool. Selling the assets to a special-purpose vehicle, which in turn issues debt securities that are credit enhanced at a cost that reflects the actual credit risks of the loan, eliminates the excess capital. However, in the short term, as long as most of its competitors are still booking similar loans on their own balance sheets, the issuing intermediary is able to retain most of the remaining yield on the asset, less a modest loss in yield to induce the investor to try out the new instrument. Over the long term, however, more and more of the economic benefits of eliminating capital and other costs should migrate to borrowers and investors.

There are other advantages for issuing institutions. For example, with asset securitization an issuing institution is accessing a new funding source and some institutions, such as GMAC, issue in such volume that they get significant benefits from using new instruments to tap new markets. Moreover, securitization enables the issuing institution to eliminate any interest rate risk it might have from keeping the asset on its balance sheet. Securitization can be a cost-effective way of neutralizing the interest rate risk by having fixed-rate loans funded with floating-rate deposits or liabilities. Finally, asset securitization allows issuing institutions to expand the total volume of their business, since capital becomes less of a constraint on growth.

There are some other, less obvious, benefits. For example, in some cases, the securitized asset issue represents a better credit risk than the credit of the issuing institution by itself (such as in the case of a troubled commercial bank or thrift). Thus, the securitization provides the institution with access to credit with better terms and interest rates than it would have been able to get otherwise. Troubled Bank of America has been able to issue certificates backed by its credit card receivables at triple-A rates. In the process, Bank of America has saved 1.5 percent or more on its borrowing rates compared with what it would pay if it issued notes of a similar maturity directly. Here, the cash savings are more than enough to justify the new technology; the capital cost savings and transfer of interest rate risk are an extra bonus.

A final potential benefit of asset securitization is the ability to create new products by freeing the institution from the constraints of its own balance sheet. The boundaries of opportunity can be expanded. Commercial banks in the United States, for example, do not generally offer small businesses fixed-rate, medium-term loans. Small businesses, therefore, have to pay very high rates, even if they find someone to lend to them on a fixed-rate basis. However, if loans are securitized, interest rate risk is transferred and a bank may be able to create a product that still enables the lender to earn substantial interest-risk-free returns. As of this writing, a new company, Commercial Mortgage Corporation of America, is just beginning to offer securitized mortgages in amounts from $100,000 to $3,000,000 per loan.

2. *Benefits for investment banks.*The obvious gains for investment banks in the form of underwriting fees and trading profits in market segments previously outside their traditional business have already been noted. It has been estimated that as much as 40 to 50 percent of Salomon Brothers' and First Boston's earnings over the last three or four years are from underwriting, market making, and trading mortgage-backed securities. Remember that investment bankers played no significant role in the residential mortgage market before the mid-1970s.

3. *Benefits to guarantors of credit risk.* Guarantors of credit risk, with the appropriate skills, can charge fees greater than expected losses without actually having to extend loans. The primary guarantors of credit risks (excluding the federal government, which is the real guarantor behind most securitized mortgage debt) are commercial banks (primarily foreign banks) and special purpose insurance companies. In many cases (e.g., the GMAC transaction), the seller guarantees a portion of the debt.

4. *Benefits to borrowers.* In the short term, securitization offers little economic advantage to the underlying borrowers. In fact, the securitization of their loans is often not even apparent to the borrower.

In the early stages of securitization, lenders want to retain the savings from securitization for themselves.

However, over the longer term, as more and more assets are securitized, competition will force lenders to share the savings from securitization with borrowers, and the borrowers will eventually be able to borrow money more cheaply. Eventually, the real cost of borrowing could fall as much as 1 percent or more for many types of credit. If that happens, the eventual economic benefits to borrowers would be large.

One major benefit borrowers are already realizing from securitization is the increasing availability of credit with terms that lenders would not provide if they were forced to put the loans on their own balance sheet. This effect is more apparent with fixed-rate mortgage debt. Consumers greatly prefer fixed-rate mortgage debt over floating-rate debt but many institutions, particularly after the traumas of the early 1980s, have been reluctant to ever again carry fixed-rate loans on their books. (Several depository institutions, including a very large number of thrifts, actually failed due to interest rate mismatches during this time.) But with mortgage-backed securities, lenders can extend fixed-rate mortgage debt without taking any interest rate risk themselves. As a result, many more borrowers are obtaining fixed-rate mortgages than would have been possible without asset securitization.

5. *Benefits to investors.* For investors, the chief advantage of securitization is that it increases the volume and variety of their investment options. In the $4 billion ABSC transaction described earlier, one of the tranches was specifically designed to fit the needs of money market mutual funds. In general, there is a shortage today of triple-A, one-year paper, and one tranche was tailored to provide certain institutional investors with yields of 50 basis points more than they could earn on comparable investments. Given the intensity of the competition among investors for performance, even modest yield increases provide significant incentives for them to invest.

LIMITS TO GROWTH

There are, of course, some limits on how fast this new technology will render obsolete the classical credit system, even in the United States. One limitation is a shortage of people who are able to interact with investment bankers. Moreover, lawyers, accountants, and other professionals (such as computer programmers) with expertise in securitizing these instruments are equally scarce.

Another limitation is the time needed to develop the documentation for one of these deals. It can take up to six months' work with lawyers and accountants to iron out all the details before one of these complex financings can actually be underwritten and placed. Although the process does get easier over time, any institution that wants to raise money through a securitized asset issue for the first time must inevitably invest a lot of money and manpower in documentation and systems before the issue can be sold.

Finally, the necessary legal frameworks are far from clear. Given the newness of the instruments, neither regulators nor rating agencies nor potential guarantors are exactly sure what rules should be followed. The ambiguity over what is or is not possible is so great that many potentially securitizable transactions are being funded with conventional loans. Often the need to obtain financing is too great to await the resolution of all the uncertainties.

Overall, the growth in securitized asset volume has been explosive and has, perhaps, begun to outstrip the existing infrastructure. This is not surprising, since new technologies usually grow faster than the underlying infrastructure. For example, at the turn of the century would-be automobile purchasers had to operate with an infrastructure that had been designed for horses and buggies rather than cars. There were no service stations, automobile dealers, cost-effective manufacturers, and most roads were little more than cow paths.

In many ways, asset securitization is at a stage analogous to the turn-of-the-century automobile. In the United States, laws and regulations lag behind the new lending technology. Tax and accounting issues remain to be resolved. Legal documentation is not yet standardized. Correspondent banking services are required to involve community and local banks in the process. Still, there is clearly an interest in the market and the growing volume of issues suggests that the momentum of product development will only continue.

CHAPTER 2

OVERVIEW OF
ASSETS AND STRUCTURES

Asset Finance Group
The First Boston Corporation

ORIGINS OF ASSET-BACKED SECURITIES

Asset-backed securities (ABS or ABSs) have taken advantage of several important developments that became commonplace in the American financial markets through the growth of mortgage-related securities. Chief among these are legal structures, investor acceptance, and increased specialization of market participants.

The legal structures underlying asset-backed securities are the grantor trust, ownership of which is evidenced by pass-through certificates; the bankruptcyproof, special-purpose financing corporation, which issues single- or multi-tranche bonds; and the "credit card" trust.[1] These structures isolate the assets in such a way that the limited rights and obligations of all parties are clearly definable.

The pass-through certificate, first introduced to the public markets by Bank of America in 1977, is a deceptively simple concept. It represents the accommodation of the complexities of consumer lending to the

---

[1] The term "credit card" trust is used for convenience to distinguish such trusts from grantor trusts. See the glossary.

requirements of the securities market, all within the bounds of "passive" management prescribed by tax law for tax-free grantor trusts. The end result is the combination of many loans into a security that has a single aggregate face amount, a single monthly payment date, a single interest rate, and a single monthly principal payment.

This instrument was popularized in several variations through the issuance of over $600 billion of mortgage pass-through securities since 1977. The asset-backed securities market thus inherited a well established trading vehicle. New variations of asset pass-throughs later developed, such as the actuarial amortization of loans written on the Rule of 78s and the unique adjustment mechanisms for delinquencies and advance payments on simple interest loans (see Appendix B, Income Recognition Methods).

The mortgage pass-through has benefited from numerous special legislative provisions that do not apply to pass-throughs of nonmortgage loans. These include government agency issuance or guaranty of qualifying certificates, exemption from certain provisions of the Employee Retirement Income Security Act of 1974 (ERISA) to facilitate pension fund investment, exemption from many state securities regulations (Blue Sky laws), exemption from certain insurance regulations, exceptions to bank and thrift regulations on the sale of assets with recourse, and provision for multiclass pass-through securities.

The popularity of the mortgage market has increased familiarity with and acceptance of the characteristic that generally distinguishes pass-throughs from bonds—the principal retirement schedule, which is controlled by neither the seller nor the investor, but rather by the behavior of the individual borrowers. On any payment date, investors may receive any principal amount from a relatively minor sum up to the entire balance of the certificate, depending on the principal payments and prepayments on the underlying loans. Years of accumulated data and research have enabled participants in the pass-through market to make educated assumptions about the rates of prepayment that should be anticipated on their investments. Although the asset pass-through market has only begun to accumulate such data, early studies have shown that asset pass-throughs have a major advantage over mortgage pass-throughs. Prepayments on most nonmortgage asset pass-throughs appear to be relatively insensitive to movements in bond market yields. Thus, they appear more attractive in this respect than mortgage pass-throughs, whose prepayments are very sensitive to market yields.

The foundation of most structured financings, other than those using grantor trusts, is the bankruptcy proof, special-purpose financing corporation. Its purpose is to set the collateral apart from the general assets and obligations of the issuing parent. Subsidiary preferred stock, the mortgage pay-through bond and collateralized mortgage obligation (CMO) are vehicles that frequently use this form. These have given rise in fairly straightforward ways to asset-backed preferred stock and single- and multi-tranche asset-backed obligations (ABO).

Mortgage pay-through bonds were introduced to the public market by U.S. Home Finance in 1980 and quickly became the dominant means by which home builders financed their captive mortgage lending activities. The typical mortgage pay-through is structured to resemble a pass-through in terms of the economics to the investor, but to be sufficiently different from a pass-through ownership interest in the underlying pool of loans to be considered a debt financing for tax purposes. The primary motivation for such bonds has been to preserve installment sale treatment on the profits generated in the sale of homes. Issuers often preferred to give up yield to investors, relative to selling loans in pass-through form, because of this tax advantage. In the asset-backed securities market, the single-tranche, pay-through ABO first utilized in 1985 for Sperry Lease Finance Corporation (SLFC) can be thought of as a further development of the mortgage pay-through bond.

The CMO preserved the favorable tax treatment of pay-through bonds while adding the potential for improved pretax economics. After the introduction of the CMO by the Federal Home Loan Mortgage Corporation in 1983, it became commonplace for mortgage originators to consider all these structures for the sale or long-term funding of their loan production and to choose the most attractive opportunity under given market conditions. Additionally, various mortgage market participants were able to move between markets, buying pass-throughs and selling CMOs at prices that gave a high projected return on the equity invested. The extension of this CMO "arbitrage" activity was the development of a market for the equity, primarily in the form of certificates of beneficial interest in owner trusts.

The sale of the economic residual interest in special-purpose corporations was first used in connection with a CMO issue in 1985. It was followed by a host of similar transactions in the CMO market. Then, in 1986, Asset Backed Securities Corporation (ABSC), a wholly-owned, limited-purpose subsidiary of First Boston Securities Corporation, sold such certificates in connection with the first offering of ABOs, as shown in Exhibit 1–1(p. 6). The ABS market, taking advantage of these developments, can now provide loan originators the option to choose between pass-throughs and ABOs in order to obtain the most attractive funding.

The ABO, like the mortgage pay-through and CMO, was a structural adaptation partially motivated by the legal framework of the market. Many regulated financial institutions are prevented from investing in asset pass-through certificates because such investments are deemed to be ownership interests in the underlying assets. Unlike investments in mortgages, investments in automobile, credit card, or other consumer receivables are not specifically endorsed by regulations governing most financial institutions, and are impeded by numerous regulations. On the other hand, investment in highly rated corporate securities is specifically authorized for most investors. Therefore, ABOs reach a wider investor audience than asset pass-throughs.

Unlike asset pass-through certificates and ABOs, which draw extensively on mortgage market precedent, credit card asset-backed securities are an innovation of the ABS market itself. Credit card ABSs involve the securitization of credit card receivables, such as Visa and Master-Card receivables, which are unsecured and have no stated maturity or fixed installment terms (i.e., they are "revolving" accounts). The key is to increase the average life of a pool of assets that inherently has a very short average life (three to six months). The solution is to utilize a "revolving period" during which only interest is paid to investors. This revolving period is the major component of the average life of the typical credit card ABS (see section on types of asset-backed securities, p. 41).

The growth of mortgage-related securities is dependent upon the specialization of participants in the mortgage market. In the mortgage lending business, origination and servicing are generally viewed as businesses in themselves, separable from the funding of the portfolio and the management of the assets as a long-term investment. In contrast, in the consumer lending business all these functions are generally performed by individual, vertically integrated business units.

The success of the specialization strategies in the mortgage business has encouraged many firms in the consumer lending industry to reevaluate their strategic thinking and to consider the use of asset-backed securities to separate their lending activities from their portfolio management functions. Such separation has enabled mortgage lenders to adapt more quickly and efficiently to the increased volatility of the credit markets that has been a fact of business life since the shifts in Federal Reserve policy in October 1979. Similar needs exist in the consumer lending business: to economize on equity capital; to achieve high lending volumes even when achieving commensurately high funding volume is difficult; to maintain portfolio size and quality even when originations are slow; and to achieve balanced nationwide portfolio objectives in spite of regional and cyclical fluctuations.

ADVANTAGES OF ASSET-BACKED SECURITIES TO THE SELLER

There are several reasons why a company might decide to sell financial assets through an asset-backed security structure. These can be divided into strategic and financial benefits.

Strategic Benefits

• *Facilitate rapid asset growth and increase economies of scale.* Asset-backed securities enable companies to increase financing activity without inflating their balance sheets. In addition, greater economies of scale can be achieved in loan underwriting and servicing.
• *Decrease barriers to entry.* Securitization makes it easier for small entities to originate consumer loans.
• *Liquefy assets.* Securitization makes receivables more marketable and permits asset redeployment.
• *Manage earnings.* Receivable sales can be timed so that gains or losses can be recognized in the quarters or years desired, from both tax and financial reporting perspectives.

Financial Benefits

• *Improve asset/liability matching.*The interest rate, maturity, and duration risks associated with financing a specific pool of assets are completely removed when the assets are sold. For foreign currency-denominated assets, any currency risk is also eliminated. This attribute of an asset sale is particularly attractive in volatile capital markets.
• *Create riskless fee income.* ABSs change the nature of the earnings on a portfolio from spread income to fee income. Spread income is earned

by lending at a higher rate than borrowing, but is subject to the risk that funds cannot be borrowed over the life of the portfolio at rates sufficiently low to generate a profit. The fee income earned by the originator of ABSs is immune to subsequent interest rate changes, and can grow without capital constraints. In effect, the originator no longer is compensated for its ability to borrow funds at attractive rates and successfully to guess interest rate movements, but for its ability to originate assets at attractive rates and to provide cost-effective servicing.

• *Access new source of funds.* An ABS issue increases the company's financial flexibility. By separating the credit of the underlying assets from that of the company, access to the capital markets is enhanced regardless of the company's current or future credit ratings. Due to the distinction between the assets and the company, as well as differences in payment frequency and ratings, ABSs appeal to different sectors of investors than those that typically buy the company's securities.

• *Achieve sale treatment for financial reporting purposes.* Sold assets are off-balance sheet, except for any estimated liability associated with a recourse provision. This is particularly relevant in light of the Financial Accounting Standards Board's (FASB) recently issued Statement 94, which requires the consolidation of most captive finance companies for fiscal years ending after December 15, 1988.

• *Improve financial measurements.* Unlike asset financing, sold assets require little or no underpinning of equity. The reduction of assets and liabilities on the balance sheet, combined with the retention of servicing income, improves a variety of financial measurements such as returns on equity and assets and coverage and capitalization ratios.

• *Increase borrowing capacity.* A company can often leverage financial assets more through an ABS structure than through on balance sheet debt financing.

• *Achieve competitive financing cost.* ABSs generally compete with conventional debt financing on a cost basis. When the cost of the equity component needed to support debt financing is factored in, ABS structures can be significantly less expensive.

• *Increase utilization of foreign tax credits.* The Tax Reform Act of 1986 limits the ability of many companies to use foreign tax credits because interest expense of domestic finance subsidiaries is prorated on a worldwide basis. Asset-backed securities can be structured as a tax sale, rather than a borrowing, and thus do not generate interest expense.

ECONOMIC ANALYSIS

All-In Cost

Asset-backed securities are fixed-income securities. It is, therefore, tempting to analyze their cost in the same manner as traditional corporate debt securities. This approach, however, can lead a potential issuer to the wrong conclusion—that an ABS issue is more expensive than traditional financing alternatives, when in fact it may be cheaper.

The "all-in" cost of a traditional corporate debt issue can be expressed as a spread, in basis points, over a comparable maturity Treasury issue— the benchmark security. This spread consists of the number of basis points required to compensate the investor for the difference in credit quality between the riskless Treasury and the corporate issue, plus the underwriting commission on the corporate bond, expressed in basis points.

Consider the following example. Shown in Exhibit 2–1 is a two year "bullet" maturity issue by a double-A rated company and a double-A rated asset-backed security in which the company is the seller. The ABS issue, a pass-through, pays interest and principal monthly, is collateralized by automobile loans, and has a two-year average life.

Why does the ABS issue "cost" 25 basis points more than the corporate issue? There are three principal reasons. First, most investors demand a higher yield on monthly-pay securities than on semiannual-pay securities because of the administrative inconvenience presented by a greater number of reinvestment decisions. Second, there may be unscheduled principal repayments on the underlying automobile loans that would change the expected average life of the ABS—investors demand extra yield for

EXHIBIT 2–1

Security	Average Life	Rate*	Spread over Treasury
Treasury	2 years	8.06%	—
Double-A Corporate	2 years	8.73	67 basis points
Double-A ABS	2 years	8.98	92
Incremental Cost of ABS:			25 basis points

*Consists of the offering yield to investors plus the cost of the underwriting commission in the case of the corporate and ABS issues.

this uncertainty. And third, investors require a higher yield to compensate for the fact that while ABSs are, by convention, priced off average life, funding protection is being provided to the issuer until final maturity, which often far exceeds average life.

The above analysis is flawed, however, because it ignores the cost of equity. Inherent in an issuer's credit quality is the makeup of its capital structure. Every issue of debt must have some underpinning of equity to support it. An asset-backed security, on the other hand, derives its credit quality not from the company, but from the quality and diversity of the pool of assets backing it and from the credit enhancement supporting the assets. For most companies, the costs of structuring and credit enhancement are less than the cost of equity to support a debt issue.

For the ABS in the above example, suppose the credit enhancement consists of 7 percent recourse to the selling company. This means that, in the event of defaults on individual receivables in the pool, the seller is obligated to repurchase such receivables up to 7 percent of the initial principal amount of the ABS. This results in a debt to equity ratio for

EXHIBIT 2–2

Cost of Additional $100 Raised through Corporate Debt—

		Rate	Spread over Treasury
Debt	$100	8.73%	67 basis points
Equity	10	25.00	
Total	$110		
Weighted average cost of capital		10.21%	215 basis points

Cost of Additional $100 Raised through ABS—

		Rate	Spread over Treasury
Debt	$100	8.98%	92 basis points
Equity	7	25.00	
Total	$107		
Weighted average cost of capital		10.03%	197 basis points
Savings through ABS:			18 basis points

the ABS of approximately 14 to 1. Suppose further that the double-A corporate issuer has a 10 to 1 debt equity ratio and that the company's cost of equity is 25 percent on a pretax basis. An analysis of the weighted average cost of capital of each issue is shown in Exhibit 2-2. Thus, the all-in cost of the ABS issue, rather than being 25 basis points more than the traditional debt issue, is actually 18 basis points less.

Most ABS issues involve third party credit enhancement. For selling companies rated less than double-A, a letter of credit (LOC) from a highly rated commercial bank is often used to support the seller's recourse obligation. This is an ongoing cost for the life of the transaction and can be easily calculated. For example, if the seller's recourse is 7 percent, as in the previous example, and the LOC costs 1 percent, then the cost of the third party LOC is seven basis points $(.07 \times .01)$.

However, many ABS structures now being utilized, particularly for credit card transactions, do not involve recourse to the seller. Instead, a reserve account, created from "excess" servicing cash flows, reimburses a bank LOC. In this case, one can argue that no cost of equity should be assigned to the ABS transaction and the cost of credit enhancement is simply the cost of the LOC. An ABS with a nonrecourse, reserve account structure, therefore, compares even more favorably with a conventional issue.

Other Issuance Expenses

Other issuance costs that a company may wish to compare for ABS and conventional issues are shown in Exhibit 2–3, below. This comparison

EXHIBIT 2–3

Fee	ABS	Conventional
SEC registration fee	--------------------- Same ---------------------	
NASD filing fee	None	Maximum of $5,100
Printing and engraving	--------------------- Same ---------------------	
Legal	-------------- Higher for first ABS ---------------	
Accounting	------ Higher for ABS due to annual audits ------	
Trustee (acting as paying agent and registrar)	----------------- Higher for ABS -----------------	
Blue Sky	--------------------- Same ---------------------	
Rating agency fees	-----------------Higher for ABS -----------------	

shows that an ABS has somewhat higher structuring costs than a conventional financing alternative. In evaluating an ABS financing alternative, however, most issuers do not look at tangible costs alone. They also consider the many benefits of ABSs, which cannot be expressed in basis points.

INVESTMENT CHARACTERISTICS

The purchasers of asset-backed securities include all the major institutional investors in the fixed-income market. Outside the U.S., the primary investors have been European banks and money managers. In general, ABSs create incremental demand for a company's securities, since the credit of the company is separated from that of the underlying assets. Investors purchase ABSs on the basis of:

- Credit quality
- Cash flow consistency
- Positive convexity
- Yield premium
- Liquidity

Credit Quality

All public ABS offerings to date have been rated triple- or double-A. The assets used to back an ABS issue are typically of high quality in terms of delinquency and loss experience, the credit quality and diversity of the underlying obligors, and the experience of the servicer of the assets. In addition, asset-backed securities generally do not have the event risk characteristic of corporate debt. A number of companies with single-A or double-A rated securities outstanding, for example, have had setbacks and their debt securities have been downgraded. The grantor trusts or special-purpose subsidiaries typically used in ABSs are insulated from the selling company's or parent's problems.[2]

---

[2] Note, however, that ABSs may be subject to the risk that a credit provider may be downgraded.

Cash Flow Consistency

First Boston's Fixed Income Research Department has extensively analyzed the cash flow characteristics of ABSs. In 1986, First Boston published its findings on automobile asset-backed securities in a research report entitled "Prepayment Rates on Automobile Receivables." Using a new prepayment model, the "absolute" or ABS model (see Appendix A), First Boston demonstrated that such asset-backed securities exhibit:

• *Stable effective maturity.* Two common measurements of effective maturity—average life and duration—do not vary significantly with changes in prepayment rates. The reason for this prepayment insensitivity compared to that of mortgage pass-throughs or CMOs is that 36- to 60-month receivables have faster scheduled principal amortizations than 30-year mortgages and, therefore, the prepayments represent a smaller percentage of the total principal payment received. This gives every automobile pass-through the equivalent of a virtually guaranteed minimum sinking fund.

• *Predictable prepayment rates.* An analysis of prepayments speeds on automobile loans during different interest rate environments shows that such prepayment rates are relatively independent of market interest rate levels. Unlike mortgages, automobile loans and other short-term loans are not typically refinanced by the obligor if interest rates fall significantly. This is because cars generally depreciate quickly and the rates charged on used car loans are substantially higher than for new car loans. However, even if these factors did not come into play, refinancing would be unlikely because the reduction in the monthly payment would be quite small compared to the savings from refinancing a mortgage.

In addition, First Boston recently published a research report on credit card asset-backed securities. The typical credit card ABS has an interest-only period, the "revolving period," followed by an amortization period when the principal is paid down quickly. This structure tends to result in a relatively stable cash flow and average life—so much so that credit card ABSs have even greater cash flow consistency than automobile ABSs. The report also concludes that credit card ABS yields are relatively insensitive to changes in the monthly payment rate on the securitized receivables and that forecasts of monthly payment rates are less significant a factor in determining yields of such ABSs than those backed by automobile loans.

Positive Convexity

For a given decline in yield, the investor's profit is generally greater than the loss that would be created by an equal increase in yield. This favorable distribution of returns occurs because the prepayment rate on automobile receivables is relatively insensitive to market yield, and the effective maturity is relatively insensitive to the prepayment rate. ABSs closely resemble corporate noncallable debt in this respect. Exhibit 2–4 demonstrates the positive convexity of ABSs.

Yield Premium

Asset-backed securities in the primary and secondary markets are priced at a premium to benchmark Treasury securities. Moreover, most ABSs trade with a slightly higher yield than comparable short-term corporate debt. Given the high credit quality of ABSs and their other favorable

EXHIBIT 2–4
Positive Convexity

Interest Rate Environment	Instantaneous Returns		
	CMO	Corporate Debenture	ABS
+500 b.p.	−14.81%	−7.55%	−8.09%
+300	− 8.50	−4.64	−4.81
+100	− 2.63	−1.60	−1.59
Unchanged	—	—	—
−100	+ 2.00	+1.58	+1.69
−300	+ 2.50	+4.88	+5.09
−500	+ 3.28	+8.34	+8.41

Notes:
The CMO is CMSC E-1 9.95% due 1/1/96 (fast pay tranche).
The Corporate Debenture is an assumed double-A 9.25% two year note.
The ABS is an assumed double-A grantor trust offering of 9.375% automobile Asset Backed Certificates with a two year average life.

Source: The First Boston Corporation

investment characteristics, this premium adds to their appeal. For the reasons cited above, however, ABSs carry a smaller premium than CMOs of comparable average life. See Exhibit 2–5 for a comparison of trading levels.

Liquidity

With over $17 billion in public ABSs now outstanding,[3] secondary market liquidity has been substantially enhanced. First Boston estimates that average daily trading volume in ABSs is approximately $50 to $100 million. Moreover, ABSs generally trade with a bid/ask spread of approximately 1/8 of a point or less. This liquidity can be expected to accelerate as additional participants enter the market and issuance of asset-backed securities continues its rapid growth.

APPROPRIATE ASSETS

Ideal Asset Characteristics

A wide variety of financial assets can be utilized in ABS structures. Assets with the following characteristics are ideal for securitization:

- Predictable cash flows
- Consistently low delinquency and default experience
- Return higher than market ABS rates
- Total amortization of principal at maturity (i.e., no final balloon)
- Average life of more than one year
- Many demographically and geographically diverse obligors
- Underlying collateral with high liquidation value and utility to the obligors

Broad Applicability to Assets

ABS structures, however, can accommodate almost any type of asset, (e.g., assets with fixed amortization schedules or revolving credits), fixed or floating rates, and different levels of credit quality. The under-

---

[3] Over $26 billion of ABSs have been issued in the public market, but several billion of the aggregate initial principal amount has been repaid.

EXHIBIT 2-5
Trading Levels—Selected Securities

	7/87	8/87	9/87	10/87	11/87	12/87	1/88	2/88	3/88	4/88	5/88
New Issue Yield:											
2-Year Treasury	7.42%	7.80%	8.39%	8.40%	7.69%	7.88%	7.61%	7.13%	7.31%	7.58%	7.95%
2-Year Bullet Maturity Corporate New Issue	8.07	8.39	9.02	9.25	8.60	8.75	8.41	7.88	7.93	8.18	8.53
CMO "Fast Pay" Tranche 2-Year Average Life	8.62	8.89	9.62	9.71	9.02	9.03	8.78	8.28	8.44	8.74	9.14
Basis Point Spread to Treasury:											
2-Year Bullet Maturity Corporate New Issue	67	59	64	85	91	87	81	75	62	60	50
CMO "Fast Pay" Tranche 2-Year Average Life	120	109	124	131	133	115	118	115	114	116	119
ABSC Class 1-B, 2-B	58	57	56	81	93	88	71	60	64	65	60
California Credit Card Trust 1987-A	80	71	68	98	103	100	88	78	74	75	72
GMAC 1986-E Grantor Trust	81	68	66	96	106	105	88	78	75	77	74
Goldome 1986-A Grantor Trust	84	72	70	98	108	108	93	82	80	79	76
RepublicBank Delaware Credit Card Backed Notes, Series A	81	71	68	100	106	105	91	81	78	78	74
Sperry Series C	84	73	75	105	109	109	94	83	80	85	84

Notes:
Trading levels reflect those offering levels that First Boston makes and tries to maintain; however, actual trading levels away from First Boston may be different.
Figures reflect monthly averages of weekly levels.
Yields are corporate bond equivalent (CBE).

Source: The First Boston Corporation

lying assets can also utilize varying income recognition methods, including the Rule of 78s, simple interest, and effective interest methods (see Appendix B). Exhibit 1–1 (p. 6), shows the types of assets which have been used as collateral in the public transactions to date. In the private placement market, other types of assets have been securitized, including agricultural equipment receivables, insurance premiums and recreational vehicles. Future transactions should include an even greater variety of asset types.

Two Layers of Credit

This flexibility is primarily due to the two layers of credit characteristic of ABSs—the assets themselves and credit enhancement. A pool of receivables used to back an ABS must have a history of delinquencies and losses that is sufficient for the rating agencies to judge its credit quality. If a small number of receivables, each of which is of a relatively large amount, is used to back an issue (e.g., SLFC's lease-backed notes), the rating agencies will require information about each obligor in order to judge the credit quality of each receivable. The rating agencies must be satisfied that reliable estimates can be made of delinquencies and losses and, further, that credit support in an amount appropriate for the desired ratings and estimated levels is provided.

THE SECURITIZATION PROCESS

Basic Structure of an Asset-Backed Security

The essence of an asset-backed security is that it relies on structure and collateral to achieve its creditworthiness and therefore its marketability. An ABS utilizes a "bulletproof" or "bankruptcyproof" structure so that the ABS is effectively insulated from any misfortunes of the selling company. In addition, the credit risk of a single obligor (e.g., the issuing company of a conventional debt issue) is greatly reduced through the diversification provided by the large pool of assets typical of most ABSs.

Exhibit 2–6 shows the basic structure of an ABS. The issuer, which is also the registrant for purposes of any filing under the Securities Act of 1933 ('33 Act), offers ABSs to investors through an underwritten public offering or a private placement. The asset cash flows are remitted to the trustee, which pays scheduled interest and principal payments to the

EXHIBIT 2–6
Basic Structure of an Asset-Backed Security

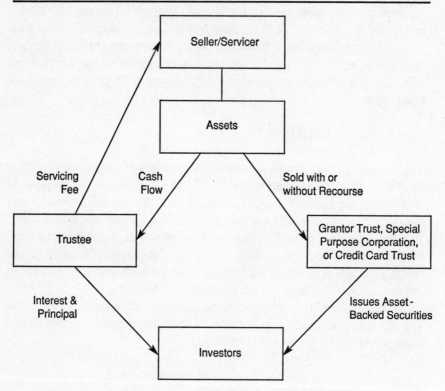

investors. In the typical ABS transaction, any prepayments on the assets are also paid by the trustee to investors. The aggregate cash flow from the assets is always equal to or greater than the required payments on the ABS. The difference, if any, is usually paid to the selling company as compensation for its role as servicer. (A portion may also be used for credit enhancement, including paying an LOC fee and/or funding a reserve account.)

The Role of the Rating Agencies

Background
In asset finance, the goal is almost always to create a double- or triple-A rated security. Most mortgage-related securities, the precursors of ABSs, are either triple-A or "agency" credits. In launching the public ABS

market, it was appropriate to create highly-rated ABSs in the mortgage security mold. ABS issues with the highest credit quality were likely to gain the most investor acceptance and achieve the greatest liquidity. This has proven to be the case. Seeking the highest ratings also makes sense for selling companies, almost all of which are rated less than triple-A.

Need for "Bulletproof" Structure

In order to obtain an ABS rating higher than that of the selling company, the rating agencies generally require an opinion from a nationally recognized law firm that a "true sale" of assets has occurred for bankruptcy purposes. The issuing entities shown in Exhibit 2–6—the grantor trust, credit card trust, and special purpose subsidiary—must in each case be bulletproof. In the event of bankruptcy or insolvency of the seller or parent, the pooled assets collateralizing the ABS would not be consolidated into the estate of the bankrupt entity. Without a true sale and/or "nonconsolidation" opinion, the rating agencies would take the position that the assets were not sold (for bankruptcy purposes), and the ABSs would likely be rated the same as the selling company's senior debt.[4]

Requirement for Credit Enhancement

Rating agencies require credit enhancement to the extent that cash flows on the underlying assets may be insufficient to pay the full amount of ABSs on a timely basis, based on conservative assumptions. Since a certain amount of loss is expected on most assets that might serve as collateral, one can expect the rating agencies always to require credit enhancement.

Types of Credit Enhancement

Credit enhancement can take many forms, including:

- Limited guaranty by (or recourse to) the seller or issuer (i.e., self insurance)
- Bank letter of credit
- Third-party insurance (surety bond)
- Reserve account (spread account)

---

[4]The hurdles are somewhat different for entities not subject to the Bankruptcy Code, such as banks and thrifts.

- Overcollateralization
- Senior/subordinated structure
- A combination of the above

The general rule is that the party or parties providing the credit enhancement must each have a credit rating at least as good as the rating sought for the ABS. For a selling company rated double-A or higher, self insurance in the form of recourse to the company for up to a certain percentage of the principal amount of the ABS may be most cost effective. In this case, the ABS would probably be rated the same as the senior debt of the selling company. For lower rated selling companies, credit support can be provided by enhancing the seller's limited guaranty with an LOC or surety bond from a highly rated bank or insurance company, and the ABS rating would be that of the third-party credit provider.

A reserve, or spread, account is most often used in commercial bank transactions where, for regulatory reasons, it is important to avoid recourse to the bank. A reserve account is funded by the excess finance charges on the assets, that is, the difference between the aggregate finance charges paid on the receivables and the sum of: (1) the coupon or pass-through rate on the ABS, (2) the servicing fees, and (3) any credit support fee to a third-party credit provider. The reserve account reimburses any losses incurred by a third party—such as an unaffiliated LOC bank—providing a guaranty against investor losses. In such a situation, the third party does not have recourse to any other assets of the seller.

Another form of credit enhancement is a senior/subordinated structure. In this case, the assets themselves provide the credit support. A separate, junior class of ABS is retained by the selling company or privately placed. Defaults up to a certain amount on the underlying assets would only reduce the payments to the party holding the junior class, and the investors, which hold the senior class, would be protected from defaults on the assets to that extent. In effect, this source of credit enhancement works the same as overcollateralization of a debt obligation.

Amount of Credit Enhancement

The amount of credit enhancement required by the rating agencies for a given ABS issue is based on conservative assumptions about the cash flows on the underlying pool of assets and is typically some multiple of the expected loss on the loans. For example, the 5 percent limited guaranty provided by General Motors Acceptance Corporation (GMAC) on the motor vehicle installment sale contracts in each GMAC grantor trust offering is roughly 10 times the historical net loss on such contracts. In general, the higher the desired rating, the greater will be the amount of credit support required.

Servicer and Trustee

The seller of receivables in an ABS transaction customarily retains an explicit role as the servicer of the pooled receivables on behalf of investors. In the common sense of the word, the seller services the receivables by sending invoices or coupon books, collecting payments from obligors on the underlying loans, and taking steps as appropriate to enforce delinquencies. The servicer's implicit role is to support the ABS structure itself.

As noted above, investors live in a principal-and-interest world— and constant-yield interest at that. However, an originator may not account for every asset suitable for securitization on an actuarial basis. Notably, trade receivables may bear no explicit interest, leases may be amortized on a straight-line basis, and the vast bulk of the automobile retail installment contracts amortize by the Rule of 78s. The servicer's first task is to allocate collections to principal and interest in keeping with the structure utilized for the ABS. (At the same time, the servicer should take care to exclude the earnings on the receivables from its own income stream.)

Just as investors prefer constant-yield securities, they prefer securities that pay predictably. The selling company may elect to undertake relatively cost-free responsibilities to smooth out the stream of collections and thereby create more attractive ABSs. The servicer often provides an advance mechanism to make payments otherwise expected from obligors. In the most common instance, the advance provides investors with the scheduled remittance when the obligor's own payment is collected after the close of the accounting cycle. The advance mechanism also bridges the period of an obligor's delinquency until the credit enhancement is called upon. Note that special care is taken to reimburse the servicer for any advances on accounts that default so that the advance mechanism cannot be construed as hidden additional recourse.

Finally, ABSs require an independent trustee to safeguard investors' interests. The trustee is either the legal owner of the securitized assets or the pledgee under the terms of an indenture. (The servicer often retains custody of the assets as agent of the trustee and in all events must amend its computer records to flag sold or pledged accounts.) The trustee also acts as a conduit for the remittances from the servicer to investors. Furthermore, the trustee is expected to assume the role of servicer if the seller becomes unable to act in that capacity.

Whole Asset Sales

Strictly speaking, whole asset sales are not asset-backed securities because no securitization is taking place. Smaller pools of assets (i.e., less than $50 million) may be sold directly to a single investor or a limited group of investors. The sale may take the form of a transfer of the asset documents and related files or a transfer of one or more certificates representing a participation interest in the assets. Servicing of the assets may be retained by the seller or transferred with the assets. Such sales may be with or without recourse to the selling company.

TYPES OF ASSET-BACKED SECURITIES

Asset-Backed Certificates—General

Asset-backed certificates are pass-through certificates issued by a grantor trust. Certificates are sold representing fractional undivided interests in one or more pools of financial assets. The selling company transfers assets with or without recourse to a grantor trust, which is deemed to be formed and owned by investors, in exchange for the proceeds from the issuance of the certificates. Thus, except for any recourse provision, the assets have been sold outright and the selling company has no obligation with respect to the repayment of the certificates. All collections of principal and interest (net of servicing fees) are deposited into an account maintained by a trustee. Interest payments are disbursed from this account by the trustee on the same business day of every month at the pass-through or "coupon" rate of interest. Principal payments, both scheduled payments and unscheduled payments that arise from prepayments on the assets are also disbursed on these payment dates. Examples of this type of structure are the 12 offerings of asset-backed certificates beginning in December 1985 by grantor trusts formed by GMAC.

Asset-Backed Certificates—Credit Cards

Credit card ABSs, structured as a sale of receivables, utilize a trust structure, which we refer to as a credit card trust, since the trust does not qualify as a grantor trust for federal tax purposes.[5] Because credit card receivables are revolving credits, the selling company agrees to convey to the trust all receivables generated by selected accounts for the life of the transaction. In general, more receivables are included in the transaction than those actually allocated to the credit card ABS investors. The additional receivables act as a buffer for seasonality and attrition, so that the total amount of receivables is always at least as great as the investors' interest in the receivables. For the revolving period, credit card ABSs do not amortize principal. Instead, principal payments received on the receivables are reinvested in additional receivables generated by the included accounts. The length of the revolving period largely determines the average life of the issue. The California Credit Card Trust 1987-A (Bank of America) offering of $400 million of asset-backed certificates is an example of this structure.

Asset-Backed Obligations

Asset-backed obligations are collateralized debt securities of a special-purpose corporation, either owned by the selling company or an unaffiliated third party or parties, secured by a pool of financial assets. Like CMOs, they are usually multi-tranche; that is, the cash flows from the underlying assets are divided and applied to classes of securities with varied maturities. Use of this concept enables the issuer to target the needs of specific investor groups more precisely. Second, interest and principal can be paid quarterly, for example, even though interest and principal on the underlying assets are received monthly. Most investors prefer these less frequent payments for their convenience. In addition, ABOs can be structured with or without prepayment uncertainty. Thus, they can be either pay-through or fixed-pay securities. Asset Backed Securities Corporation (ABSC) has offered $5.9 billion of ABOs in six transactions. In four of these transactions, the collateral was purchased

---

[5] The reinvestment of payments on the receivables, described below, is inconsistent with the passivity required of grantor trusts.

from GMAC. In one instance, the financial assets were purchased from General Electric Capital Corporation and in another, from BMW Credit Corporation.

Asset-backed notes are a single-tranche form of ABOs. Typically, an operating company, which holds the financial assets, forms a subsidiary that purchases a pool of assets from its parent and issues fixed-rate notes secured by the assets. The scheduled payments on the assets are sufficient to meet the debt service on the notes. Interest is paid monthly or quarterly. In addition, any prepayments on the underlying assets are usually paid to the noteholders, although a fixed-pay structure can also be used. Examples of asset-backed notes are Sperry Lease Finance Corporation's three series of lease-backed notes in 1985 and 1986 and RepublicBank Delaware's issue of credit card-backed notes in 1987.

Asset-Backed Preferred Stock

Asset-backed preferred stock (ABPS) is issued by a special-purpose, bankruptcy-proof subsidiary that purchases assets, such as trade and consumer receivables or intercompany notes, from its parent or affiliates. The assets are supported by a direct-pay LOC or surety bond in favor of the subsidiary issued by a triple-A rated commercial bank or insurance company, with the result that the subsidiary's preferred stock issue is rated triple-A. ABPS can enable companies in a low- or non-taxpaying position to obtain financing at significant savings over commercial paper.

Asset-backed preferred stock transactions require the issuer to meet asset coverage and liquidity tests to ensure that there is enough cash to pay the redemption price of the preferred stock and to pay dividends on an ongoing basis. In the event of a mandatory redemption, such transactions call for the institution providing credit support to pay the issuer the full face amount of the financial assets held by the issuer.

ABPS is attractive to corporate investors with high effective tax rates due to the 70 percent Intercorporate Dividends Received Deduction, which allows investors to deduct 70 percent of dividend income from federal taxable income. Examples of ABPS are the Short-Term Auction Rate preferred offerings in the fall of 1987 by Mattel Funding Corporation and Union Carbide Finance Corporation (see Exhibit 1–1, p. 6).

Asset-Backed Commercial Paper

This structure involves the sale of financial assets, usually at a discount, to a special-purpose corporation that, in turn, issues commercial paper. Proceeds from the issuance of the commercial paper finance the purchase of the assets. The commercial paper is paid by the cash flow from the assets, the issuance of new collateralized commercial paper or from borrowings under a liquidity facility. The special-purpose corporation (or partnership) may be a subsidiary of the originator of the assets or may be an independent entity owned by one or more third parties. The company or companies selling receivables to the special-purpose entity typically continues to service them.

The highest ratings are sought for the collateralized commercial paper. Although the credit quality of the collateralized commercial paper depends on the quality of the assets themselves and the type and level of credit enhancement, an additional factor is the bank liquidity facility. Unlike the "term" ABS structures, there must be assurance that the commercial paper can be rolled over or redeemed.

Asset-backed commercial paper programs can accommodate ongoing sales of receivables by originating companies. Properly structured, off-balance sheet, floating-rate financing can be achieved. In addition, asset/liability matching can be improved.

Public Offerings vs. Private Placements

Asset-backed security structures can be distributed through public or private offerings.[6] A private placement may make sense if the deal is relatively small (e.g., $50 million or less) or if there are reasons for wishing to avoid public disclosure. Also, investors in private placements tend to rely less on ratings and, in fact, ratings may not be required for some transactions. In a private placement, the "underwriter" may act either as agent—working on a best efforts basis—or as principal. One of the primary advantages of the public market is the liquidity it offers investors. For this reason, the public market can be expected over time to be a larger and more stable source of funding for issuers.

---

[6]In certain cases, such as asset-backed commercial paper, the offering is exempt from registration under the '33 Act.

ACCOUNTING AND TAX TREATMENT

Accounting Treatment

An objective of most ABSs is to qualify as an off-balance sheet transaction under the provisions of Statement of Financial Accounting Standards (SFAS) No. 77, "Reporting by Transferors for Transfers of Receivables with Recourse" (issued in December 1983). In general, SFAS No. 77 states that certain transactions that "purport" to be sales may be treated as such by the selling corporation, even if the seller offers recourse on the sold assets.

This financial accounting standard is not paralleled by regulatory accounting practices. For the purpose of reporting capital adequacy, commercial banks and bank holding companies must account for sales with recourse as secured financings—the assets stay on the books, and the ABS is recorded as debt of the seller. To obtain regulatory accounting sale treatment, bank transactions are structured "nonrecourse," where the inherent profit in the receivables themselves provides the credit enhancement (or reimbursement for a third-party credit enhancer). Although these structures are considered nonrecourse for regulatory accounting purposes, and thereby allow sale treatment, they are considered recourse transactions for financial reporting purposes and fall within the provisions of SFAS No. 77.

In most structures, the gross servicing fee equals the spread of the implicit rate of return on the collateral over the explicit rate to investors on the ABS. Under SFAS No. 77, the gross servicing fee is allocated first to basic servicing—the actual cost of staying in the servicing business, plus a fair return—and then to excess servicing. The present value of the excess servicing (adjusted to reflect any expected prepayments on the receivables) is booked as a gain on sale. Excess servicing received over the life of the receivable pool is applied to amortize the gain booked at the point of sale.

An alternative means of obtaining off-balance sheet treatment has been to sell assets into a special-purpose subsidiary. If the subsidiary is engaged in a different business than its parent, the subsidiary need not be consolidated for financial accounting purposes. Even if the subsidiary issues asset-backed notes (such as the three SLFC issues) and keeps the receivables on its balance sheet, they are off the balance sheet of the parent. Note, however, that the FASB has issued Statement 94, which requires consolidation of all majority-owned subsidiaries for fiscal years ending after December 15, 1988. In addition, the statement encourages earlier application of the new standards.

Tax Treatment

The large majority of ABSs enjoy symmetrical tax and accounting treatment, meaning that assets sold for accounting purposes are also sold for tax purposes. The income on the assets, or a substantial portion thereof, is no longer earned by the seller, but directly by the investors.

In a grantor trust structure, the investors are deemed to earn the entire gross income from the receivables, but are able to deduct servicing fees (to the extent that the fees are "reasonable"), leaving a net income equal to the stated coupon on the ABS. Some grantor trusts call for "strip" treatment, whereby an interest in the receivables is retained by the seller and the investor earns only the net, or investor, rate on the ABS. Of the two methods of investor taxation, the ongoing accounting requirements of a stripped ABS have proven to be more cumbersome. Furthermore, unless the seller is in a tax-loss position, stripping has a distinct tax cost resulting from the acceleration of taxable income.

The servicer's tax and accounting treatment of its fee can be quite different. Again, for accounting purposes, servicing in excess of basic servicing is booked as a gain at the point of sale, in expectation of its future receipt; the subsequent actual collection of excess servicing is applied to the previously booked gain. For tax purposes, though, the servicer recognizes income only as each payment accrues under the terms of the respective receivable.

"Asymmetrical" tax and accounting treatment allows the originator to eliminate the receivables from the balance sheet while retaining their tax ownership. For the tax purposes of both the issuer and the investor, the ABSs are considered debt. Asymmetrical treatment has appeared most often in credit card transactions where the substantial modification of the cash flows precludes the use of a grantor trust.

Expert Advice
Prospective issuers should be aware that the tax rules applying to ABSs are complex and that their application may vary based on the circumstances of a particular transaction. Companies should consult their own accounting and tax advisors on these matters.

LEGAL ISSUES

Bankruptcy

As stated above, each ABS structure is designed to achieve a sale for bankruptcy purposes. This ensures that the rating agencies assign ratings to an ABS commensurate with the quality of the asset pool, servicing, and credit enhancement facility. Some of the factors affecting the legal determination of whether a true sale has occurred are:

- Amount of recourse or limited guaranty—if the percentage is above a certain level, legal counsel may have difficulty opining that the transaction constitutes a sale rather than a secured financing.
- Tax treatment—a transaction that is a sale for tax purposes strengthens the true sale argument for bankruptcy purposes.
- Perfection of a security interest in the financial assets.
- For banks and thrifts, consideration of the positions of the FDIC and FSLIC concerning assets sold or pledged in an ABS.

Perfection of Security Interest

It is necessary to perfect a security interest (in favor of the trustee) in the financial assets backing the ABS. The exact nature of the assets determines whether perfection is accomplished by filing a financing statement under the Uniform Commercial Code, by notation on title documents, or by possession of the assets. In the case of secured receivables, a perfected and transferable security interest in the underlying assets themselves may be required.

SEC Registration

The '33 and '34 Acts
A public offering of ABSs must be registered with the Securities and Exchange Commission (SEC) under the '33 Act. Because the issuer is often a newly formed entity, Form S-1 is typically required. Registration may be effected on Form S-3 when certain requirements are met (e.g., the issuer is a majority-owned subsidiary of a company with a three-year reporting history under the Securities Exchange Act of 1934—known as

the '34 Act—and the security to be offered carries an investment grade rating).

Privately placed ABSs are exempt from registration under Section 4(2) of the '33 Act. In addition, public offerings made by commercial banks or thrifts, such as the RepublicBank issue of credit card-backed notes, are exempt from registration with the SEC. This exemption does not apply to bank holding companies or to grantor or owner trusts formed by banks or thrifts. Even for commercial banks and thrifts, however, an information memorandum or offering circular with disclosure substantially similar to a prospectus is made available to investors. Commercial paper is also exempt from registration pursuant to either Section 3(a)(2) or 3(a)(3) of the '33 Act.

Issuers of public ABSs are required to file periodic disclosure and financial statements with the SEC under the '34 Act.

Investment Company Act

A grantor trust, special-purpose corporation or credit card trust would be considered an investment company under the Investment Company Act of 1940 ('40 Act), unless a specific exemption applies. Fortunately, there is an exemption for certain types of pooled financial assets, such as automobile loans and credit card receivables. Registration under the '40 Act is not necessary in such cases. Where the assets are not exempt from the '40 Act (e.g., commercial and industrial bank loans), it should be possible to avoid '40 Act registration by utilizing the private placement exemption.

ERISA

The pooling of receivables and the sale of certificates backed by receivables to domestic pension plans could result in "prohibited transactions" under the Employee Retirement Income Security Act of 1974 (ERISA). This is due to the Department of Labor's characterization of a plan's purchase of such a certificate as an acquisition of an undivided interest in each of the pooled receivables, unless there are 100 independent investors in the securities or "benefit plan investors" that at all times own less than 25 percent of the value of such securities. This characterization applies to equity interests, such as those represented by pass-through ABSs, and is required to be disclosed in the prospectus covering the offering. The Department of Labor is considering whether to grant exemptions that would alleviate this concern in some cases.

Documentation

The documentation required for a public ABS offering falls into the following major categories:

- Sale or pledging of receivables
- Servicing
- Disclosure
- Underwriting
- Credit enhancement

Sale or Pledging of Receivables and Servicing

In general, the document that provides for the sale or pledging of receivables to the issuing entity also provides for servicing—the administration and collection of payments on the assets. This document is usually referred to as a pooling and servicing agreement. The seller makes certain representations and warranties which, if breached, give rise to repurchase or indemnification obligations. With respect to servicing, the agreement requires that the sold or pledged assets be serviced in a way consistent with the procedures utilized by the seller/servicer for its other assets not included in the transaction. In addition, certain other servicing procedures are enumerated to satisfy rating agency requirements.

The seller/servicer and the independent entity representing the interests of investors—typically a bank acting as either trustee or indenture trustee—are the parties to the agreement. When the ABSs represent debt obligations of the issuer, an indenture that qualifies under the Trust Indenture Act of 1939 is also required.

Underwriting

An underwriting agreement provides for the sale of the ABSs by the issuer to the underwriters and sets forth the terms and conditions of the purchase. The document also contains the representations and warranties of the issuer, certain covenants between the issuer and the underwriters, specific conditions on the obligations of the underwriters (which include delivery of opinions of counsel and "comfort letters"), and provisions for indemnity. Depending upon the transaction, the issuer's parent may also be a party to the underwriting agreement.

Disclosure and Credit Enhancement

Disclosure documentation consists of the requirements under the '33 and '34 Acts, as discussed above. Where third-party credit enhancement is used, such as a bank LOC or insurance company surety bond, appropriate disclosure and documentation will be required.

Due Diligence

The underwriters take certain steps to avoid liability under the '33 Act for any misstatements and omissions by establishing a due diligence defense. The underwriters and their counsel establish this defense by interviewing management and reviewing certain corporate documents, including corporate minutes. The underwriters also rely on the expertise of the client's public accountant, who ordinarily delivers comfort letters, both at signing and at closing. The issuance of asset-backed securities entails the same due diligence as any other public issue, as well as certain additional steps.

The due diligence considerations specific to ABSs can be divided into three general categories:

- Loan underwriting policies and procedures of the originator
- Systems requirements
- Loan file review (a periodic test of the completeness of the documents supporting the transaction)

The exact procedures will vary for each transaction.

APPENDIX A: PREPAYMENT MODELS

MEASURING PREPAYMENTS

Although prepayment of an automobile receivable occurs only once in its life, prepayments in a pool of many such receivables will tend to occur during each month of the pool's life. With each contract representing only a small fraction of the total pool balance, its prepayment in a given month reduces the remaining principal only slightly. The rate at which individual contract prepayments draw down the balance of a pool is called the prepayment rate or prepayment experience of the pool.

Contract balances are reduced not only by prepayment but also by scheduled monthly principal amortization. Accordingly, the fraction of a pool's original principal balance that remains at any given point in time (termed the "pool factor") may be expressed as the product of two other numbers: 1) the fraction of the original contracts remaining (not prepaid), or the "survival factor," and 2) the fraction of the representative contract that remains unamortized, or the "contract balance."

The aggregate prepayment rate over any given time interval from origination is defined as one minus the survival factor. Since the survival factor times the contract balance equals the pool factor, as stated above, it follows that the aggregate prepayment rate is one minus the ratio of the pool factor to the contract balance.

To state this algebraically, let

$$PF = \text{Pool Factor}$$
$$SF = \text{Survival Factor}$$
$$CB = \text{Contract Balance}$$
$$PR = \text{Prepayment Rate.}$$

All numbers are expressed as decimal fractions. For example, 15 percent is expressed as 0.15.

Since

$$PF = SF \times CB$$

it follows that

$$SF = PF/CB.$$

and since

$$PR = 1 - SF$$

it follows that

$$PR = 1 - PF/CB.$$

To illustrate these relationships, let us assume that a pool is originally composed of 10,000 contracts, each with an original balance of $10,000, giving an initial pool balance of $100,000,000. Each contract is fully amortizing over an original term of 60 months at an annual percentage rate of 14 percent. After 18 months the pool balance is \$58,914,274. What is the aggregate prepayment rate over that interval?

The pool factor is 0.58914 (remaining pool balance divided by initial pool balance, or \$58,914,274/\$100,000,000) and the contract balance is 0.76912 (from amortization tables). We can then calculate the survival factor:

$$\begin{aligned} SF &= PF/CB \\ &= 0.58914/0.76912 \\ &= 0.76600 \end{aligned}$$

and aggregate prepayment rate

$$\begin{aligned} PR &= 1 - SF \\ &= 1 - 0.76600 \\ &= 0.23400. \end{aligned}$$

Thus, the aggregate prepayment rate has been 23.4 percent over the 18 month interval.

Said differently, the pool is now composed of 7,660 contracts with a remaining balance of \$7,691.16 each, while 2,340 out of 10,000 contracts have prepaid.

ABS EXPERIENCE

It is convenient to state prepayment rates over a standard interval, such as monthly. In the previous example, 2,340 contracts have prepaid in 18 months. Therefore, on average 130 contracts have prepaid each month. As there were 10,000 contracts to begin with, this represents 1.3 percent of the *original* number of contracts which have prepaid on average each month. Said symbolically, let

ABS = Monthly ABS prepayment rate expressed as a decimal

n = Number of months in the interval over which the prepayment rate is measured

PR_n = Aggregate prepayment rate measured over the n months as illustrated above.

The cumulative ABS rate (monthly average prepayment rate since origination) is

$$ABS = PR_n/N$$

In this case,

$$N = 18$$
$$PR_n = 0.23400$$

so,

$$ABS = 0.23400/18$$
$$= 0.01300$$

or, 1.30 percent per month. The interim ABS rate for any given month within the interval is simply the difference between the beginning and ending survival factors for the month.

This measure of prepayment rates is termed the absolute model of prepayments because it measures prepayments in each month as an absolute number of receivables, expressed as a fraction of the original number. The model was designed by First Boston specifically to measure prepayments on pools of consumer installment sale contracts on automobiles. The model reflects historical experience on such assets better than do the prepayment models commonly used in the mortgage market. This observation has been confirmed in studies by First Boston of liquidation rates in several portfolios of automobile receivables. At First Boston, this model is denoted absolute or ABS, referring to both the absolute measure used and the asset-backed securities it was designed to analyze.

SMM EXPERIENCE

A prepayment measure commonly used in the analysis of mortgages is the SMM or Single Monthly Mortality model, which was developed by First Boston in 1977 specifically to measure prepayments on pools of home mortgages. This measure is a mortality rate, in which each month's prepayments are expressed as a fraction of the loans *remaining* at the end of the previous month. In this sense, it is a relative (or conditional) rather than an absolute rate—relative to the number of survivors remaining each month rather than to the fixed reference point of the original number of loans.

The SMM model regards the survival factor as the product of a series of monthly survival factors. For convenient notation, let

SMM $=$ Single Monthly Mortality rate (SMM prepayment rate)
SF_n $=$ Survival factor over an interval of N months from origination
SF_a $=$ Geometric average monthly survival factor over the N months.

SF_a is defined

$$SF_a = (SF_n)^{1/n}.$$

The cumulative SMM rate (average prepayment rate from origination) is

$$SMM = 1 - SF_a.$$

In this case,

$$\begin{aligned} SF_n &= 1 - PR_n \\ &= 1 - 0.23400 \\ &= 0.76600 \end{aligned}$$

so,

$$\begin{aligned} SF_a &= (SF_n)^{1/n} \\ &= (0.76600)^{1/18} \\ &= 0.98530 \end{aligned}$$

so,

$$\begin{aligned} SMM &= 1 - SF_a \\ &= 1 - 0.98530 \\ &= 0.01470 \end{aligned}$$

or, 1.47 percent per month.

For any given month within the interval, the interim SMM rate is the difference between the beginning and ending survival factors for the month (the interim ABS rate), divided by the beginning survival factor.

The cumulative and interim SMM rates will always be higher than the corresponding ABS rates, for a given interval of a given pool's life (except for the first month, during which they are equal), because the SMM rate is applied to a declining number of loans while the ABS rate is always applied to the original number.

The SMM model was developed because estimates of mortgage pool prepayment rates derived in SMM terms tended to be more accurate than those using previously available models. The ABS model is used for automobile receivables at First Boston because SMM rates tend to rise over time within the life of most pools of automobile receivables. The ABS rate tends to be more consistent over a pool's life, and is therefore a better indicator of future behavior than the SMM rate.

Exhibit 2-7 shows amortization and prepayment for a pool in which the ABS rate is held constant. Note how the interim SMM rate rises over time.

EXHIBIT 2-7
Cash Flow of a Hypothetical Pool of Automobile Receivables[1]

Month	Starting Balance (A)	Gross Interest (B)	Scheduled Principal (C)	Unscheduled Principal (D) $(L \times I \times A_1)$	Total Principal (E) $(C + D)$	Ending Balance (F) $(A - E)$
0						
1	$100,000,000	$1,166,667	$1,145,076	$1,300,000	$2,445,076	$97,554,924
2	97,554,924	1,138,141	1,143,178	1,284,918	2,428,096	95,126,828
3	95,126,828	1,109,813	1,141,079	1,269,660	2,410,739	92,716,090
4	92,716,090	1,081,688	1,138,775	1,254,224	2,392,999	90,323,091
5	90,323,091	1,053,769	1,136,262	1,238,608	2,374,870	87,948,220
6	87,948,220	1,026,063	1,133,536	1,222,809	2,356,346	85,591,875
7	85,591,875	998,572	1,130,592	1,206,827	2,337,419	83,254,456
8	83,254,456	971,302	1,127,424	1,190,658	2,318,082	80,936,374
9	80,936,374	944,258	1,124,029	1,174,300	2,298,329	78,638,045
10	78,638,045	917,444	1,120,401	1,157,752	2,278,153	76,359,892
11	76,359,892	890,865	1,116,535	1,141,010	2,257,545	74,102,347
12	74,102,347	864,527	1,112,427	1,124,073	2,236,500	71,865,847
13	71,865,847	838,435	1,108,071	1,106,938	2,215,009	69,650,837
14	69,650,837	812,593	1,103,462	1,089,604	2,193,066	67,457,771
15	67,457,771	787,007	1,098,594	1,072,067	2,170,662	65,287,110
16	65,287,110	761,683	1,093,463	1,054,326	2,147,789	63,139,321
17	63,139,321	736,625	1,088,062	1,036,378	2,124,440	61,014,881
18	61,014,881	711,840	1,082,387	1,018,220	2,100,607	58,914,274
19	58,914,274	687,333	1,076,431	999,851	2,076,282	56,837,992
20	56,837,992	663,110	1,070,189	981,267	2,051,456	54,786,537
21	54,786,537	639,176	1,063,654	962,466	2,026,121	52,760,416
22	52,760,416	615,538	1,056,822	943,446	2,000,268	50,760,148
23	50,760,148	592,202	1,049,685	924,204	1,973,889	48,786,259
24	48,786,259	569,173	1,042,238	904,738	1,946,976	46,839,283
25	46,839,283	546,458	1,034,474	885,045	1,919,519	44,919,764
26	44,919,764	524,064	1,026,387	865,121	1,891,509	43,028,255
27	43,028,255	501,996	1,017,971	844,966	1,862,937	41,165,318
28	41,165,318	480,262	1,009,219	824,575	1,833,794	39,331,525
29	39,331,525	458,868	1,000,124	803,946	1,804,070	37,527,455
30	37,527,455	437,820	990,679	783,077	1,773,756	35,753,699

[1]Assumes a pool of 10,000 receivables, each having a $10,000 initial principal balance, a 14% annual percentage rate and a 60 month term.

Pool Factor (G) (F/A_1)	Average Balance (H)	Contract Balance (I)	Number of Contracts (J)	Survival Factor (K) (G/I)	ABS[2] (L)	SMM[3] (M)
1.00000	$10,000.00	1.00000	10,000	1.00000		
0.97555	9,883.98'	0.98840	9,870	0.98700	0.01300	0.01300
0.95127	9,766.61	0.97666	9,740	0.97400	0.01300	0.01317
0.92716	9,647.88	0.96479	9,610	0.96100	0.01300	0.01335
0.90323	9,527.75	0.95278	9,480	0.94800	0.01300	0.01353
0.87948	9,406.23	0.94062	9,350	0.93500	0.01300	0.01371
0.85592	9,283.28	0.92833	9,220	0.92200	0.01300	0.01390
0.83254	9,158.91	0.91589	9,090	0.90900	0.01300	0.01410
0.80936	9,033.08	0.90331	8,960	0.89600	0.01300	0.01430
0.78638	8,905.78	0.89058	8,830	0.88300	0.01300	0.01451
0.76360	8,776.99	0.87770	8,700	0.87000	0.01300	0.01472
0.74102	8,646.71	0.86467	8,570	0.85700	0.01300	0.01494
0.71866	8,514.91	0.85149	8,440	0.84400	0.01300	0.01517
0.69651	8,381.57	0.83816	8,310	0.83100	0.01300	0.01540
0.67458	8,246.67	0.82467	8,180	0.81800	0.01300	0.01564
0.65287	8,110.20	0.81102	8,050	0.80500	0.01300	0.01589
0.63139	7,972.14	0.79721	7,920	0.79200	0.01300	0.01615
0.61015	7,832.46	0.78325	7,790	0.77900	0.01300	0.01641
0.58914	7,691.16	0.76912	7,660	0.76600	0.01300	0.01669
0.56838	7,548.21	0.75482	7,530	0.75300	0.01300	0.01697
0.54787	7,403.59	0.74036	7,400	0.74000	0.01300	0.01726
0.52760	7,257.28	0.72573	7,270	0.72700	0.01300	0.01757
0.50760	7,109.26	0.71093	7,140	0.71400	0.01300	0.01788
0.48786	6,959.52	0.69595	7,010	0.70100	0.01300	0.01821
0.46839	6,808.03	0.68080	6,880	0.68800	0.01300	0.01854
0.44920	6,654.78	0.66548	6,750	0.67500	0.01300	0.01890
0.43028	6,499.74	0.64997	6,620	0.66200	0.01300	0.01926
0.41165	6,342.88	0.63429	6,490	0.64900	0.01300	0.01964
0.39332	6,184.20	0.61842	6,360	0.63600	0.01300	0.02003
0.37527	6,023.67	0.60237	6,230	0.62300	0.01300	0.02044
0.35754	5,861.26	0.58613	6,100	0.61000	0.01300	0.02087

[2]"ABS" is the Absolute prepayment model: a constant percentage of the original number of contracts in the pool prepays monthly. It is the difference between the survival factor in the previous month and the survival factor in the current month.
[3]"SMM" is the Single Monthly Mortality prepayment model: a constant percentage of the remaining number of contracts in the pool prepays monthly. It is the ratio of the absolute prepayment rate in the current month to the survival factor in the previous month.

APPENDIX B: INCOME RECOGNITION METHODS

DESCRIPTION OF THE EFFECTIVE INTEREST, RULE OF 78s, AND SIMPLE INTEREST METHODS

A. *General.*
1. Precomputed methods
   a. Both effective interest and Rule of 78s contracts may be precomputed.
   b. Payment schedules and principal/interest breakdowns are known at the origination of the contract.
   c. Effective interest and Rule of 78s contracts may be combined in a pool bearing a constant pass-through rate (30/360 basis), through "behind the scenes" accounting adjustments.
   d. Advances of both interest and principal on delinquent installments are feasible because the principal/interest breakdowns may be precomputed.
2. Interest bearing methods
   a. Simple interest contracts are interest bearing (not precomputed).
   b. The principal/interest breakdown of each payment is not known until the payment is actually received.
   c. Simple interest contracts may be combined in a pool with a constant pass-through rate (actual/365 basis).
   d. Timing adjustments for interest payments are feasible, but advances of principal are not feasible, because the amount of principal to be paid each month is not known until the obligor's payment is actually received.

B. *Effective Interest.*
1. Results in economic accrual of interest assuming all intervals between payments are equal.
2. Current yield is constant.
3. $I = B \times CR/N$, where

   I = interest accrued in period
   B = principal balance of receivable as of the beginning of the current period
   CR = coupon rate (expressed as a decimal)
   N = number of periods in one year.

   Example: Automobile receivables, mortgage loans.

C. *Rule of 78s.*
1. Results in greater interest allocation to early periods than the effective interest method.

2. Current yield is higher in early periods and lower in later periods.
3. I = TFC × P/SOD, where

    I = interest accrued in period
  TFC = total finance charge during term of receivable
    P = number of periods remaining to term of receivable as of beginning of current period
  SOD = sum of digits for original term of receivable (e.g.,
      12 months: 1 + 2 + 3 + ... + 12 = 78;
      48 months: 1 + 2 + 3 + ... + 48 = 1176).

Example: Automobile receivables.

D. *Simple Interest.*
1. Results in economic accrual of interest taking into account the exact number of days between payments.
2. Current yield is constant.
3. I = B × CR × N/365 or 366, where

  I = interest accrued from preceding payment date to current payment date
  B = principal balance of receivable as of the preceding payment date
  CR = coupon rate (expressed as a decimal)
  N = number of days from preceding payment date to current payment date.

Example: Automobile receivables, credit card receivables.

COMPARISON OF THE EFFECTIVE INTEREST AND RULE OF 78s METHODS

A. *Monthly Current Yield.*
1. Exhibit 2–8 illustrates the difference between the Rule of 78s and the effective interest methods of income recognition with respect to monthly current yield for each month from the date of origination to the date of maturity.
2. The data presented were based upon a 48-month receivable with an original principal balance of $10,000 and an annual percentage rate of 12 percent.

B. *Outstanding Balance.*
1. Exhibit 2–9 illustrates the difference between the Rule of 78s and the effective interest methods of income recognition with respect to the outstanding balance for each month from the date of origination to the date of maturity.

EXHIBIT 2–8
Monthly Current Yield

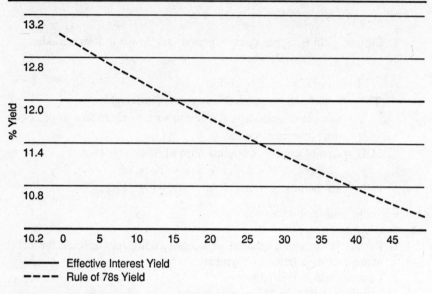

Source: The First Boston Corporation

EXHIBIT 2–9
Outstanding Balance

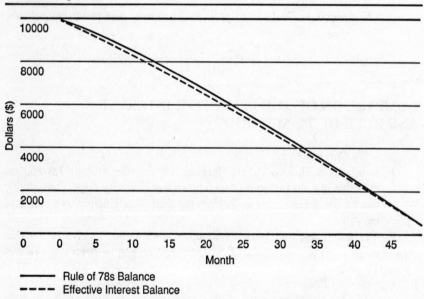

Source: The First Boston Corporation

EXHIBIT 2–10
Difference Between Outstanding Balances

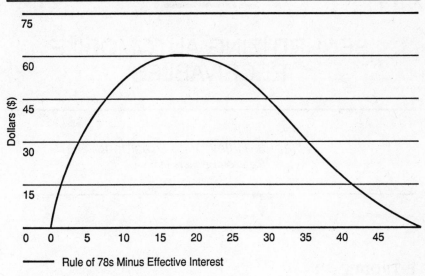

Rule of 78s Minus Effective Interest

Source: The First Boston Corporation

2. The data presented were based upon a receivable with the same characteristics as above.
3. The representation of the data has been exaggerated to illustrate the
   differences between the two methods of income recognition which otherwise would be obscured because of scale.
C. *Difference Between Outstanding Balances.*
   1. Exhibit 2–10 illustrates the difference between the outstanding principal
      balance calculated in accordance with the Rule of 78s income recognition
      method and the outstanding principal balance calculated in accordance
      with the effective interest income recognition method for each month
      from the date of origination to the date of maturity.
   2. The data presented were based upon a receivable with the same charac-
      teristics as above.

CHAPTER 3

SECURITIZING AUTOMOBILE RECEIVABLES

William J. Haley, Vice President
Salomon Brothers Inc

INTRODUCTION

Since its inception in May of 1985, the market for securities backed by automobile and truck receivables has grown rapidly. From the time the first CARS[1] security was issued—a $60 million offering by Marine Midland Banks, N.A.—a steady stream of CARS have come to the public market representing original issue volume through December 31, 1987 of $16.9 billion. Although the largest issuers have opted to issue CARS securities publicly (see Exhibit 3–1), there have been a number of large and small private placements that have added considerable volume to the market.

The purpose of this chapter is to highlight various components of a CARS transaction. Important participants in the development of the CARS market include: 1) originators of the automobile receivables, 2) underwriters that structure and sell the CARS securities, 3) the major rating agencies, 4) credit enhancers, and 5) investors who purchase and sell the securities in the secondary market.

---

[1]CARS, Salomon Brothers' abbreviation for Certificates for Automobile Receivables, will serve as a shorthand reference for all automobile and truck receivable-backed securities. ©Copyright 1988 Salomon Brothers Inc.

EXHIBIT 3–1
The Five Largest Public Issuers of CARS Securities, 1985-87

Issuer/Seller–Servicer	Number Of Issues	Principal Amount
General Motors Acceptance Corporation[1]	16	$11,430,096,000
Chrysler Financial Corporation	3	1,768,161,000
Marine Midland Bank N.A.[2]	3	1,102,823,000
Western Financial Savings Bank	4	536,930,000
Bank of America	1	514,222,000

[1]Total includes four issues in the name of Asset Backed Securities Corporation where GMAC was the originator of the assets.
[2]Total includes one issue in the name of Salomon Brothers Receivables Inc where Marine Midland was the originator of the assets.

Source: Salomon Brothers Inc

   This chapter is divided into five sections: 1) market potential, 2) primary characteristics of automobile loans, 3) advantages to issuers of CARS securities, 4) the secondary market for automobile loans, and 5) CARS investment properties. Appendix A provides a chronological listing of all public CARS securities through December 31, 1987, including pertinent facts about each issue.

MARKET POTENTIAL

Nonmortgage consumer debt, which includes automobile and truck lending activities, has grown rapidly in the United States. As of December 31, 1987, it totaled $612.1 billion or about 7.2 percent of credit usage in U.S. debt markets (see Exhibits 3–2 and 3–3). Automobile loans account for approximately 43 percent of the nonmortgage consumer debt market and have experienced a compound annual growth rate of 15 percent over the last ten years (see Exhibit 3–4).
   Although the automobile segment of the debt market is small compared with the $2.6 trillion in outstanding mortgage debt, its potential for growth is significant based upon the rapid turnover of automobile loan portfolios and the fast pace of originations.
   In the mortgage market, the weighted average life of a typical portfolio ranges from 10 to 12 years. In contrast, automobile loan portfolios

EXHIBIT 3–2
U.S. Consumer Installment Debt Outstanding[1]
(December 31, 1987, Dollars in Billions)

Automobile	$261.4
Revolving	145.9
Mobile Home	25.6
Other	179.1
Total	$612.1

[1]Seasonally adjusted

Source: Federal Reserve Board

have weighted average lives of about two years. Since automobile loans turn over five to six times faster than mortgage loans, originations in the two markets are almost identical at $225 billion a year.

The $682 billion in mortgage-backed securities now represent about 25 percent of mortgage debt outstanding. Although it is too early to

EXHIBIT 3–3
U.S. Credit Market Debt Outstanding by Type, December 1987

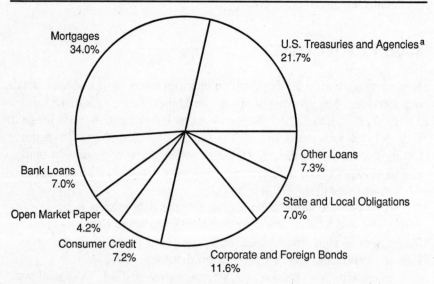

Mortgages 34.0%
U.S. Treasuries and Agencies[a] 21.7%
Other Loans 7.3%
Bank Loans 7.0%
State and Local Obligations 7.0%
Open Market Paper 4.2%
Consumer Credit 7.2%
Corporate and Foreign Bonds 11.6%

Privately held debt, marketable and nonmarketable.

Sources: Federal Reserve Board, Salomon Brothers Inc estimates.

EXHIBIT 3–4
Year-End Automobile Debt Outstanding[1] (1975–87, Dollars in Billions)

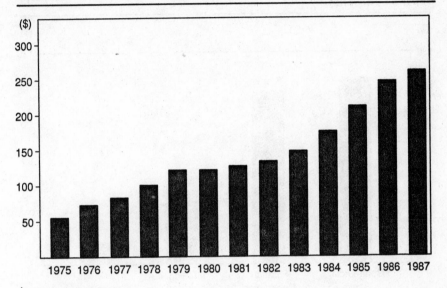

[1]Seasonally adjusted.

Source: Federal Reserve Board.

tell how large the CARS market will become, a similar 25 percent penetration level would produce more than $56 billion in annual CARS volume.

PRIMARY CHARACTERISTICS OF AUTOMOBILE LOANS

Automobile loans finance the purchase of automobiles and light duty trucks. Originations in the primary market for automobile loans are dominated by commericial banks and finance companies, although credit unions and savings institutions have also been active (see Exhibit 3–5).

Underwriting the Contract

Originators of automobile loan contracts underwrite each loan, process the necessary documentation, and advance funds to the obligor. Underwriting entails collecting and verifying information about the borrower's credit and ability to repay the loan. The process starts with an

EXHIBIT 3–5
Consumer Automobile Debt Outstanding by Lender[1] (December 31, 1987, Dollars in Billions)

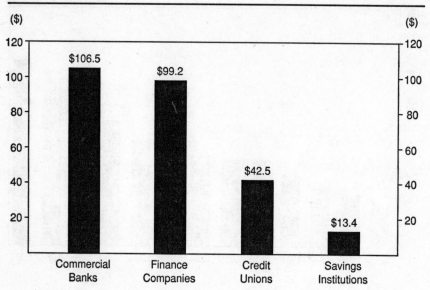

($)

$106.5	$99.2	$42.5	$13.4
Commercial Banks	Finance Companies	Credit Unions	Savings Institutions

[1]Seasonally adjusted.

Source: Federal Reserve Board.

application that lists liabilities, income, credit and employment history. This application is usually supplemented by a credit report issued by an independent credit reporting agency and, if necessary, a more thorough investigation of the applicant's employment and bank references.

Underwriters adopt a wide variety of standards in deciding whether or not to approve an application. Underwriting can be judgmental, or it can rely on a more mechanized credit scoring system. In either case, it is important to determine the potential obligor's ability to repay as well as the value of the vehicle.

The credit and underwriting policies followed by potential issuers of CARS securities are closely scrutinized by the underwriters of the CARS security, the credit enhancer and the rating agencies as part of their due diligence processes. Typically, an issuer will outline its credit and underwriting policies in the prospectus. This procedure is generally verified through on-site inspection of the originator's facilities and credit files, including a representative sampling of applications, credit reports and contracts.

It is common practice in the industry to advance the sum of the manufacturer's invoice costs to the dealer plus certain options, sales tax, insurance and license fees. Down payment requirements vary widely among underwriters but generally tend to protect lenders from overadvancing the collateral value of the underlying vehicle. Overadvancing can be a problem if a default occurs because automobiles depreciate rapidly once they leave the showroom.

To further protect collateral value, it is standard operating procedure among underwriters to require full insurance covering damage to the vehicle. Required insurance usually names the lender as loss payee and insures the vehicle against comprehensive loss. Most obligors will choose to pay their own insurance carrier since this coverage is cheaper than the insurance provided by the lender. Lenders generally employ mechanisms to protect themselves against a lapse in an obligor's insurance coverage. One such method is force-placed insurance whereby the lender, faced with a lapse in coverage, purchases a paid-up insurance policy and adds the cost to the obligor's loan balance. Alternatively, the lender can buy vendor secured insurance, which provides blanket protection on collateral in the event of loss due to lack of insurance.

Due diligence is an extremely important activity in a CARS underwriting since the lender's credit policy is the chief determinant of how the sold assets will perform. It is important to understand, prior to a CARS issue, how the loans were selected, documented and filed and whether the lender has perfected and conveyed a security interest in the vehicles. Collection activities are also scrutinized because a strong collection effort can help to mitigate underwriting mistakes.

Credit Quality

For the most part, cash flows associated with automobile loans are of high credit quality. The average loss experience on newly originated bank automobile loans varies among originators but generally ranges between 0.20 percent and 0.90 percent a year, a relatively low default rate compared with other types of consumer lending (see Exhibit 3–6).

Lending institutions generally measure credit quality by the level of delinquencies recorded on the portfolio and the actual loan losses incurred over time. A negative trend in delinquency numbers is a leading indicator of potential credit problems because an increase in delinquencies generally produces higher loan losses.

EXHIBIT 3–6

Bank Net Losses as a Percentage of Outstandings (Annual Data, 1967–1986)

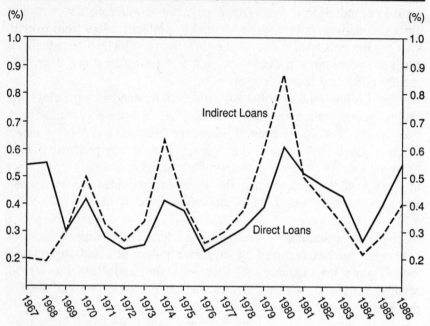

Source: American Bankers Association.

Lending institutions summarize losses on their automobile portfolios by "net charges-offs" (i.e., net of recoveries), expressed either as a percentage of liquidations or as a percentage of outstandings. In a rapidly growing portfolio, loss-to-liquidation ratios serve as a more accurate guide to credit quality because they eliminate the distortion that growth produces on the denominator of a net loss/total outstandings ratio. Notwithstanding this distortion, losses relative to total outstandings are a more common and widely accepted barometer of credit quality.

Net charge-offs on automobile contracts occur for a variety of reasons. The most common losses are due to: 1) repossessions, 2) a lack of insurance, and 3) "skips," where the servicer cannot or is unwilling for economic reasons to recover collateral when the borrower defaults. Not surprisingly, the most successful originators of automobile loans have reasonably defined underwriting standards and strong back office collection support.

In any CARS prospectus, potential investors will find a historical record of delinquency and net charge-offs on the lender's portfolio of automobile receivables. It is desirable to have at least three years of experience to judge the performance of the assets under various economic and interest rate environments. Lenders with shorter experience or a lack of data can also initiate CARS transactions, but they are subject to more thorough due diligence by underwriters, credit enhancers, and the rating agencies, all of whom are more comfortable working with a seasoned loan portfolio.

Exhibit 3–7 is a representative example of how delinquency and loan losses are disclosed in a typical CARS prospectus. The table reflects the disclosure made by Marine Midland Bank N.A. in the $442.5 million Salomon Brothers Receivables Inc CARS, Series I transaction dated November 5, 1987. In that transaction, Marine Midland was the originator and servicer of the sold assets.

As a guide to how well a particular portfolio of automobile receivables will perform under a CARS format, the delinquency and loan loss tables are an invaluable aid. Assuming that care has been taken to select a representative sample of loans, the performance of the CARS receivables should mirror the performance of the portfolio from which they came. In most cases, the loan files of the lender are not marked after the sale of the receivables to prevent bias in the servicing of the assets.

Rating Agency Perspective

In assigning a rating to a CARS security, the major rating agencies focus closely on the historical delinquency and loan loss data to determine the level of credit enhancement consistent with the rating being sought. Although there are many determinants in how a rating is assigned, it is clear that higher delinquencies and loan losses will lead to a higher credit enhancement requirement. Both of the major rating agencies generally look for at least 7 percent credit enhancement for a triple-A rating. The requirement moves upward from there depending upon the originator's overall risk profile, its level of experience as an originator and servicer of automobile loans, and the actual delinquency and loss experience on the target portfolio.

In general, it is the job of rating agencies to assess: 1) credit risk, 2) adequacy of cash flow, and 3) various legal issues important to the interests of CARS certificateholders. In assessing credit risk, each agency examines the originator's risk profile, as well as its underwriting and servicing procedures. The selection of an experienced trustee with demonstrated consumer loan experience is important because that entity

EXHIBIT 3–7
Delinquency and Loan Loss Information, 1983–87 Prospectus Disclosure — Marine Midland Bank N.A.

Delinquency and Loan Loss Information

The following tables set forth the delinquency experience and loan loss experience for the past four years, and for the nine months ended September 30, 1987, of the Servicer's New York State portfolio of indirect retail instalment loans for the purchase of consumer merchandise, including automobiles and light-duty trucks. In each period set forth below Motor Vehicle loans represented in excess of 91% of all indirect retail instalment loans in the Servicer's New York State portfolio.

Delinquency Experience
New York State Portfolio (1)

	At September 30, 1987		1986		1985		1984 (2)		1983 (2)	
	Number of Contracts	Amount	Number of Contracts	Amount	Number of Contracts	Amount	Number of Contracts	Amount	Number of Contracts	Amount
					(Dollars in thousands)	At December 31,				
Portfolio (Gross) (3)	185,794	$1,389,635	260,962	$1,837,600	218,871	$1,245,707	241,463	$1,390,312	202,167	$1,055,138
Delinquency (4)										
31-59 Days	3,563	22,322	5,060	31,284	5,080	26,196	5,499	29,189	4,191	19,651
60-89 days	1,038	5,599	1,492	6,630	1,540	8,533	1,453	7,562	1,106	4,962
90 Days or more	883	5,089	1,193	7,272	1,350	7,558	1,489	8,435	1,200	5,716
Total Retail Instalment Loans Delinquent	5,484	33,010	7,745	45,186	7,970	42,287	8,441	45,196	6,497	30,329
Delinquencies as a Percent of Amount Outstanding	2.95%	2.38%	2.97%	2.46%	3.64%	3.39%	3.50%	3.25%	3.21%	2.87%

(1) The table excludes retail instalment loans which the Servicer has sold but which it continues to service. The majority of such sold loans relates to a pool of Motor Vehicle Loans sold in June 1987 having an aggregate balance equal to approximately $600,000,000 (the "June Sold Loans"). The June Sold Loans were selected from the Servicer's New York State portfolio on substantially the same basis as the Contracts.

(2) 1983 and 1984 amounts include an immaterial amount of retail instalment loans which were not originated in New York State.

(3) Gross portfolio includes all amounts scheduled to be paid under indirect retail instalment loans, including unearned precomputed finance charges. Motor Vehicle Loans represented 92.3%, 92.5%, 91.8%, 94.9% and 93.3% of all amounts scheduled to be paid under indirect retail instalment loans in the Servicer's New York State portfolio at December 31, 1983, 1984, 1985 and 1986, and September 30, 1987, respectively.

(4) The period of delinquency is based on the number of days payments are contractually past due.

Loan Loss Experience
New York State Portfolio (1)

	Nine Months Ended September 30, 1987	1986	1985	1984 (2)	1983 (2)
			(Dollars in thousands)		
Portfolio:					
Period-end (net) (3)	$1,137,442	$1,533,323	$1,081,923	$1,131,942	$857,199
Daily Average During the Period (net)	1,389,301	1,277,647	1,057,274	1,002,386	737,258
Retail Instalment Loans Charged Off	10,090	12,748	10,481	9,081	7,145
Recoveries of Retail Instalment Loans Previously Charged Off	4,569	5,248	3,919	3,601	3,090
Net Charge-Offs	5,521	7,500	6,562	5,480	4,055
Net Charge-Offs as a Percent of Daily Average During the Period	.53%(5)	.59%	.62%	.55%	.55%

(1) The amounts in the table exclude retail instalment loans which the Servicer has sold but which it continues to service. Information for the Nine Months Ended September 30, 1987 (other than "Period-end (net)") is calculated including amounts with respect to the June Sold Loans through May 23, 1987, and excluding such amounts from May 23, 1987.

(2) 1983 and 1984 amounts include an immaterial amount of retail instalment loans which were not originated in New York State.

(3) "Period-end (net)" reflects the monthly average of amounts scheduled to be paid under indirect retail instalment loans for the applicable period.

(4) "Net Charge-Offs" means "Retail Instalment Loans Charged Off" minus "Recoveries of Retail Instalment Loans Previously Charged Off ."

(5) Annualized.

The data presented in the foregoing tables are for illustrative purposes only and there is no assurance that the delinquency, loan loss or repossession experience of the Contracts will be similar to that set forth above.

assumes successor servicer duties under most CARS structures. Both agencies will then subject expected cash flows under the CARS security to various theoretical stresses, including adverse economic conditions. Credit enhancement mechanisms are examined closely since they supplement cash flow. Finally, bankruptcy issues and perfected security interests are checked out to protect the integrity and value of the certificateholder's claim on the vehicles.

Common Characteristics

Typically, in an automobile lending arrangement, the vehicle is pledged as security for the contract. Most loans are fully amortizing and provide for level payment, despite the fact that different interest accrual mechanisms may be applicable on the underlying contracts.

Loans usually pay principal and interest on a monthly basis, although some quarterly and annual arrangements can be found. Final maturities on contracts can run as long as 72 months, although it is more common to find loan maturities of 36 to 60 months. Occasionally, a group of contracts will be originated with a balloon or bullet maturity. Most automobile loans have fixed rates (often called annual percentage rates or APRs) and finance purchases of new vehicles. Lenders also extend used car loans, but terms are more restrictive and maturities are shorter.

Automobile loans can be originated on a direct or indirect basis. Direct loans are booked by the bank or finance company without an intermediary. Indirect loans, which are becoming increasingly popular, are originated by dealers and sold to the ultimate lending institution. On some indirect contracts the dealer provides recourse to bolster the credit of the obligor. This practice is no longer common in the industry. Indirect loans with recourse have experienced lower loss levels than nonrecourse contracts, reflecting the extra level of dealer support.

Most of the CARS securities to date have been level pay and fully amortizing with five year final maturities. It is possible to pool loans with different interest accrual methods, although this frequently entails systems enhancement work. Indirect and direct loans, as well as new and used contracts, can be pooled. It is prudent, however, to keep the used portion below 30 percent of the total portfolio, since they produce higher delinquency and loan loss results. Most CARS securities carry a fixed rate since that is the basis on which most automobile loans are originated. Variable rate CARS securities are also feasible, although they are somewhat more difficult to structure.

Interest Charges

Automobile loans, like other forms of consumer installment credit, have historically carried high APRs compared with Treasury rates. As can be seen in Exhibit 3–8, the average APR for new and used car loans over the last 10 years has generally exceeded Treasury rates by spreads of 3.02 percent and 7.76 percent, respectively.

EXHIBIT 3–8
Auto Finance Companies: Average Finance Rates[1] (Jan. 78–Sept. 87)

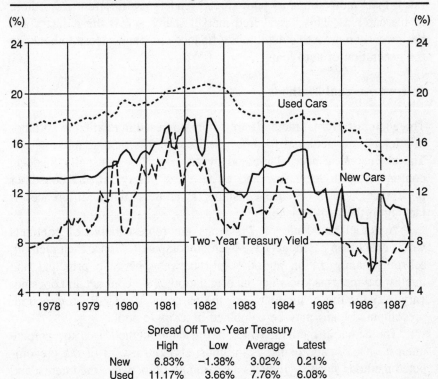

	High	Low	Average	Latest
New	6.83%	−1.38%	3.02%	0.21%
Used	11.17%	3.66%	7.76%	6.08%

Spread Off Two-Year Treasury

[1] Not seasonally adjusted.

Sources: Federal Reserve Board and Salomon Brothers Inc

New car APRs have been more volatile than used car rates because automobile manufacturers, particularly of late, have aggressively reduced the auto loan rates of their captive subsidiaries as a marketing tool to bolster the sales of their products. Used car rates, which are consistently high, have remained more stable than new car rates since they have not been used as a marketing tool. As recent statistics demonstrate, the incentive rate programs have altered the spread between new car APRs and Treasury rates. While the average spread between used car rates and Treasuries has been stable, new car rates on average have declined dramatically.

The incentive rate phenomena has not been broadly based. In fact, it is a trend that owes its existence to captive finance companies that have set the rates in conjunction with their parent organizations. Bank and thrift lenders have not been quick to follow the trend toward incentive rates; their motivations as pure spread lenders are different from those of the captives. This has altered market shares across the industry and has recently put captive automobile finance companies close to banks in the generation of auto loans.

Interest Accrual Methods

Three interest accrual methods are commonly used in relation to automobile loans—the actuarial method, the Rule of 78s, and simple interest. The choice of an accrual method by an originator is usually made in conformity with local law and custom and rarely reflects consumer preference. That's because consumer awareness of the differences is lacking in the marketplace.

Actuarial and Rule of 78s loans are representative of contracts where exact loan payments have been precomputed. Under each method, scheduled amortization and the split between periodic principal and interest payments is known at the origination of the contract and does not vary over the life of the loan. For the purposes of a CARS transaction, precomputed loans may be combined in a single pool.

The actuarial method, which is the same method used to compute interest on mortgage loans, is the most straightforward of the precomputed methods since it produces a constant ratio between the interest and principal components within each periodic payment. Under the actuarial method, current yield is always constant. This is an advantage in a

CARS transaction since there is a level amount of interest available in each monthly period to cover the interest coupon on the CARS security. Under the Rule of 78s method there is a greater interest allocation to early payments than to later payments. For the lender, Rule of 78s contracts produce a higher yield in the early periods than later in the life of the contract when interest payments relative to principal are proportionately smaller. This is not acceptable for a CARS transaction because it tends to create an interest coverage problem toward the final maturity of the security. Accordingly, Rule of 78s contracts are reamortized and converted to an actuarial basis for asset securitization purposes.

Because the periodic interest and principal components of an actuarial contract are constant over the life of an automobile loan contract, it is possible in a CARS transaction to have the servicer or the credit enhancer advance both interest and principal on delinquent payments to smooth and increase the predictabililty of cash flows.

Simple interest contracts are interest bearing and not precomputed. As a result, the timing of actual payment is important to the allocation between the interest and principal component of each payment. With a simple interest loan, the current yield to the lender is constant. Because the amount of interest due under a simple interest contract is dependent upon the date of payment, it is harder for a servicer to advance payments on a delinquent loan.

Prepayments

Prepayments under automobile loan contracts are normally allowed at any time without penalty.[2] Most automobile loans are due on sale, meaning that sale or trade-in of the vehicle results in a demand for repayment under the contract. This is the most common cause of prepayments. Other events leading to prepayment include: 1) repossession of the vehicle by the lender, which normally leads to a sale of the underlying collateral to satisfy the loan; 2) loss or destruction of the vehicle, which

---

[2] Outright prepayment penalties are extremely rare. In some parts of the country, it is permissible to calculate rebates of unearned finance charges on a Rule of 78s basis, thereby producing an implicit prepayment penalty. Such a penalty is seldom material, however, and rarely influences the obligor's decision to repay. That's because the Rule of 78s penalty is not well understood by consumers.

usually triggers insurance policies to satisfy outstanding indebtedness; 3) voluntary prepayment; 4) refinancing; and 5) death of the obligor.

Refinancing, which is common in the mortgage market when interest rates are declining, is not common for an automobile contract because loans on used cars carry higher APRs and shorter maturities. This combination usually produces a higher monthly payment. Although prepayments on automobile receivables are less sensistive to interest rates than prepayments on mortgage assets and therefore are more predictable statistically, there is still uncertainty in a CARS security about how prepayments affect investors. A great deal of attention has been focused on developing predictive models to measure the likelihood of prepayment. The two most common methods are the "absolute" or "asset-backed security" model (ABS) and the "constant prepayment rate" model (CPR).

The ABS measure expresses prepayments as a percentage of the original number of loans in the portfolio, whereas the CPR measure expresses prepayments as a percentage of currently outstanding loans. In the initial stages of a CARS transaction, there is little difference between comparable ABS and CPR measures. The difference can be pronounced, however, in the latter stages of a CARS transaction since the ABS measure is a constant function, whereas the CPR measure is a declining function. The ABS measurement assumes higher prepayment levels as the portfolio becomes more seasoned—a normal phenomenon in the automobile loan market.

An accurate prepayment estimate is important in that it defines the investor's time horizon with respect to the purchase of a CARS security. CARS are priced to a point on the yield curve that corresponds to the weighted average life of the portfolio. The determination of weighted average life takes into effect scheduled payments and the prepayment estimate.

Potential for Securitization

All of the characteristics of automobile loans noted in this section make them attractive raw material for securitization. Automobile receivables generally possess: 1) a documented history showing loss, delinquency and prepayment experience, 2) modest historical loss patterns, 3) standardized contracts, and 4) diversification of risk. These characteristics are important to any securitization effort.

ADVANTAGES TO ISSUERS OF CARS SECURITIES

Issuers securitize automobile receivables for many reasons. Generally, a prospective seller of automobile receivables will approach a CARS transaction with an agenda of strategic objectives that reflects its market position and financial structure. The most frequently cited reasons for securitization include: 1) cost of funds, 2) more efficient use of capital, 3) rapid portfolio growth, 4) asset-liability management, 5) enhanced financial performance, and 6) diversification of funding sources. A CARS issue will often be initiated for a combination of these reasons.

Cost of Funds

Cash flows of an automobile portfolio represent very high credit quality, with known loss experiences that can be credit enhanced to double- or triple-A credit quality. As a result, many issuers have found that CARS allow them to produce more attractive financing rates, through off-balance sheet segregation of the assets, than what they could produce in their own names. By segregating assets in support of a financing and adding a credit enhancement mechanism, many companies that are rated single-A or lower have taken advantage of triple-A ratings on their CARS securities to lower their overall funding costs. Large issuers that have taken advantage of this cost saving include Chrysler Financial, Bank of America and Western Financial, as well as a number of smaller issuers.

For higher rated entities, the funding advantage of a CARS transaction is not always as obvious because an alternative source of funds would be an on-balance sheet financing that might be more attractive than a CARS issue. However, one factor often overlooked by potential issuers of CARS in assessing alternative borrowing options is the cost of capital needed to support an on-balance sheet financing. For borrowers that allocate capital costs to borrowings, the weighted average cost of a CARS security, which requires no implicit equity support, is almost always superior to an on-balance sheet financing with full equity support.

More Efficient Use of Capital

CARS transactions are generally structured with the automobile receivables and a credit enhancement mechanism supporting the issue. Given the high quality of automobile receivables, this creates an opportunity where it is often acceptable to create higher leverage in a CARS transaction than what might be acceptable on the balance sheet of the originator. For example, General Motors Acceptance Corporation (GMAC) and Chrysler Financial Corporation (CFC) finance a large amount of auto receivable production on their own balance sheets, adhering to leverage ratios of approximately 8 or 10 to 1, ratios considered acceptable for the finance industry. With an on-balance sheet financing, these companies retain all risk of loss, including what would be considered catastrophic loss, thereby raising the required level of capital support.

Given their ability to originate and service high quality receivables, GMAC and CFC can reduce exposure on the assets that they sell through a CARS structure, retaining a 3 to 5 percent risk position on sold assets. Catastrophic risk passes to investors or credit enhancers or both, who accept it because it is considered to be a theoretical rather than practical risk. By shifting catastrophic risk, GMAC and CFC create an opportunity for themselves to leverage assets at a higher level than what is acceptable on-balance sheet, thereby improving their competitive positioning relative to banks, which are leveraged at a higher rate.

Rapid Portfolio Growth

Often, when a portfolio is growing at a rapid pace, new growth potential gets squeezed by the inability to increase capital quickly enough to support higher asset levels. Many financial institutions faced with this situation turn to securitization as a means of expanding their franchise without straining their balance sheets. A CARS transaction can use newly-originated assets as credit support in a stand-alone structure, thereby expanding the origination capacity of a well-positioned company like Marine Midland Bank. This strategy allows the bank, and others like it, to profitably leverage its outstanding origination and servicing network to expand into new markets.

Asset-Liability Management

Since automobile receivables are self-amortizing and allow prepayments at any time, it is often difficult for liability managers to choose an appropriate funding mechanism for these assets. One of the most attractive features of a CARS transaction is that it produces a perfectly matched financing, taking into effect the actual duration of the underlying assets.

Investors in CARS accept prepayment risk, thereby producing, for the liability manager, a funding vehicle that retires at the same time as the asset. This is a particularly attractive feature for banks and thrifts interested in better management of the gap between interest sensitive assets and interest sensitive liabilities.

Enhanced Financial Performance

When an automobile receivable is sold under a CARS structure, the certificateholder receives a rate of return based upon an agreed upon coupon rate. Excess interest, to the extent that the asset has been originated at a higher rate, generally is retained by the originator. The ability to retain both the customer relationship and the spread earnings on sold assets has proven to be an attractive combination for many issuers. The ability to earn spread earnings on assets that are off-balance sheet generally produces an immediate improvement on the originator's return on assets and, if the originator can generate asset growth at higher rates of return than the companion CARS issue, return on equity can also be improved.

Diversification of Funding Sources

Issuance of CARS securities creates new sources of funding since purchasers of CARS securities include asset-based lenders in addition to traditional buyers of medium-term notes and certificates of deposit. For lower rated originators, a triple-A CARS security is often attractive to investors that would not ordinarily buy their securities.

THE SECONDARY MARKET FOR AUTOMOBILE LOANS

Any transaction that involves the buying, selling, or packaging of an automobile loan after origination is a secondary market activity. When the secondary market for automobile loans is fully developed, it will create liquidity for high volume originators and will channel capital market funds into what has been a relatively illiquid market. Lenders facing a greater demand for automobile loans than they can meet using deposited funds will be able to sell loans into the secondary market to other lenders with an appetite for consumer assets, but without the ability to originate those assets. The process should lower the cost of funding to the consumer while rewarding the most efficient originators and servicers of automobile receivables.

Structure

Two basic structures have been employed in the secondary market for automobile receivables. The first is a "pass-through" structure analogous to GNMA, FNMA and FHLMC mortgage pass-through securities. To date, because of its wide usage by GMAC, the pass-through structure has been the most common format for securitizing automobile receivables, representing 57 percent of new issue volume. The second type of structure is a "pay-through" format analogous to cash flow bonds or collateralized mortgage obligations (CMO). Pay-through structures can be used to create collateralized borrowings or multiclass structures. They can also be used in conjunction with a guaranteed investment contract (GIC) to create a "fixed-payment" bond, a relatively recent and important innovation in the CARS market.

Structural decisions reflect how the issuer wants the transaction to be characterized and reported for accounting, regulatory, tax, and legal purposes. Important variables in the determination of structure, once the economic parameters have been decided, include: 1) the form and substance of the credit enhancement mechanism, 2) generally accepted accounting principals (GAAP), 3) regulatory accounting principals (RAP) for bank and thrift issuers, 4) tax considerations, and 5) legal considerations. These matters will be discussed in detail in later chapters.

Pass-Throughs

The pass-through, utilizing a grantor trust format, is the most common format for CARS securities, since it achieves sales treatment for GAAP, RAP, tax, and legal purposes. In a typical pass-through, auto receivables are sold to a grantor trust, which issues certificates representing undivided interests in the trust assets. The simplest pass-through structure uses collateral with higher APRs than the CARS coupon. Principal and interest are passed through monthly as received (usually on the fifteenth day of the succeeding month, with a 14-day interest-free delay).

EXHIBIT 3–9
Pass-Through Flow Chart

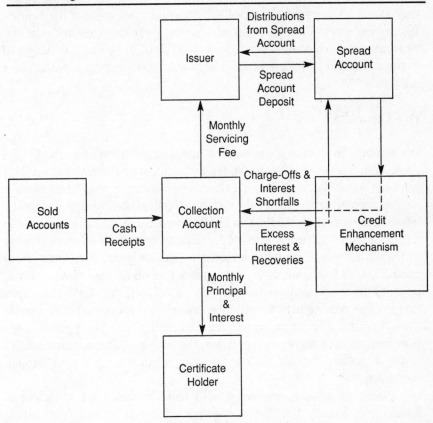

All principal received, together with interest at the pass-through rate, is paid to certificateholders as beneficial owners of the trust. The spread between the average loan rate and the CARS coupon is used to pay servicing fees (usually to the issuer), guarantee fees and other expenses. In addition, the spread is often used to support the credit enhancer under a mechanism known as the spread account. (For additional details on spread accounts, see recourse provisions below).

The trust is administered by an independent trustee acceptable to the issuer and the rating agencies. The trustee supervises the flow of funds under the structure and stands ready to provide backup servicing should the original servicer default on its obligations at any time during the life of the trust.

In a conventional pass-through, the trust is a passive vehicle. Since there is no active management of the cash flow, the performance of the trust assets are a mirror image of the portfolio from whence they came. Pricing on a pass-through is set at a spread over the Treasury rate that most nearly matches the weighted average life of the portfolio. Weighted average life takes into effect scheduled amortization plus a prepayment estimate.

Pay-Throughs

Pay-through structures have become increasingly popular in the CARS market because they allow for active managment of the cash flows. This has been particularly useful under certain yield curve conditions when it has been possible to create, through a multiclass structure, an arbitrage between the short and the long end of the yield curve. It is also possible in a pay-through structure to add enhancements that afford greater certainty to the cash flows. One such device is a GIC, or guaranteed investment contract, which guarantees a reinvestment rate on all cash flow received prior to its scheduled payment date. In effect, the GIC eliminates prepayment uncertainty and produces an investment opportunity similar in performance to a corporate sinking-fund obligation. Since greater cash flow certainty is attractive to investors, the pay-through structures usually result in tighter spreads to Treasuries than conventional pass-through securities.

Narrower spreads between CARS and Treasuries are attractive to issuers and have led to frequent usage of the pay-through structure. Because pay-throughs are more complex, however, higher setup and other costs, as well as potential opportunity costs associated with the GIC, need to be factored into the economic analysis. Sophisticated issuers, with enough asset volume to justify complex structuring, weigh all costs before determining whether a pay-through will produce a better all-in result than a pass-through.

Credit Enhancement

All CARS securities, public and private, have included some sort of credit enhancement to protect against losses on the underlying assets. Credit enhancement in the CARS market is different from that in the mortgage market, which has relied heavily on the full faith and credit

EXHIBIT 3–10
Pay-Through Flow Chart

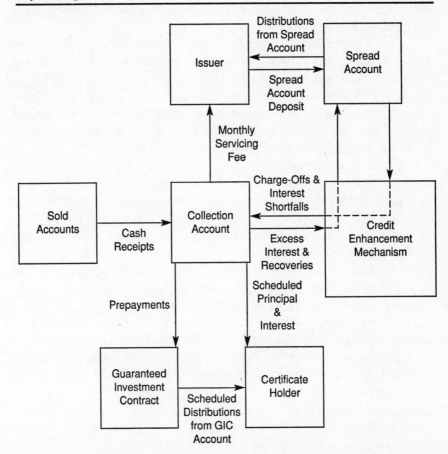

of the U.S. government. Credit protection for CARS is either provided by an issuer guarantee or a third-party credit facility, such as a letter of credit or a surety policy. Overcollateralization can also be used, although it has been more prevalent with mortgages than CARS.

The form of credit enhancement depends upon the issuer. Factors that guide the decision include: 1) the regulatory framework in which the issuer operates; and 2) its credit rating, since third-party credit enhancement can enable a CARS issue to have a higher rating than its sponsor. Banks, which are governed by regulatory accounting rules, must rely on third party credit enhancement because an issuer guarantee would disqualify the structure as a regulatory sale of assets. Finance companies or nonbank issuers can provide their own guarantees, as GMAC has done. Entities rated lower than double-A can generally justify the modest cost of credit enhancement because it improves the pricing on the CARS issue.

Credit protection, whether by issuer guarantee or third-party guarantee, usually takes a form analogous to a "pool policy" on pools of mortgages. It covers losses up to a fixed percentage that has ranged from a low of 5 percent to 100 percent (see Appendix A). The rating agencies determine the level of credit enhancement needed for the desired rating. Other determinants include the experience of the servicer and the historical performance characteristics of the assets.

Credit enhancement decisions are driven by the total cost saving they are likely to produce. Take, for example, the case of a single-A finance company that wants to securitize an automobile receivable portfolio with a historical loss pattern of 0.25 percent a year. To qualify for a triple-A rating, this would typically require 7 to 8 percent credit enhancement in the form of a letter of credit or a surety bond. Alternatively, it would be theoretically possible for the finance company to support the CARS issue with a 5 to 6 percent issuer guarantee to produce an overall single-A rating on the issue.

For analytical purposes, assume that a two-year single A-rated finance company CARS security could be issued at a yield to investors of 100 basis points over the treasury index and that spreads for triple-A rated CARS would be 75 basis points. Typically, credit enhancement costs run between 0.50 percent and 0.75 percent per year for a letter of credit or surety policy. Therefore, the implied cost of 7 to 8 percent credit enhancement would be, at worst, six basis points, thereby making the credit enhancement decision economically viable.

Recourse Provisions

When third-party credit enhancement is used in a CARS transaction, the credit enhancer generally looks to the issuer to back up its guarantee. The simplest and most straightforward mechanism is direct recourse. Direct recourse is acceptable in the case of reasonably good quality finance companies or thrift institutions. For banks, however, direct recourse is inconsistent with a regulatory sale of assets, thereby eliminating that option for them.

The spread account is a common mechanism for protecting third-party credit enhancers from loss. With a spread account, part or all of the interest earned on the auto receivable, in excess of the CARS coupon and monthly servicing fee, is placed in escrow to protect the credit enhancer's position. From a sales treatment standpoint, it is acceptable to bank regulators because the recourse provision is limited to a loss of future income on the sold assets, thereby protecting the bank's original capital position from loss on sold assets. Finance companies and thrift institutions have also found the spread account useful because it creates a stand-alone transaction in which the cash flow from the sold assets insulates security holders and credit enhancers from normal losses on the portfolio. It is generally acceptable to credit enhancers for the spread account cap to be lower than the actual level of credit enhancement provided. Spread account caps have ranged from 3 to 12 percent.

Another support mechanism that has been used in the CARS market has been overcollateralization. To date, very few issuers have used this option.

Investors in CARS securities and the rating agencies that protect them are not concerned with the mechanism through which the credit enhancer is protected. As a result, it is no longer common to detail these mechanisms in the prospectus. Instead, these are private arrangements negotiated in the reimbursement provisions of the letter of credit agreement or surety policy, or both.

CARS INVESTMENT PROPERTIES

Comparative Yield Analysis

CARS represent high quality (usually double-A or better), short-term investment opportunities with weighted average lives of about 1 to 2 years and final maturities of five years. Because they are backed by amortizing assets, with either a monthly or quarterly pay, CARS are often compared to short-term investment alternatives, including medium-term notes and CMO-A pieces.

CARS consistently offer substantial yield premiums compared with similarly rated medium-term notes. Conversely, collateralized mortgage obligation A pieces offer higher yields to investors than comparable CARS issues because CMOs carry a higher degree of refinancing risk. On a fully risk adjusted basis, CARS offer exceptional value compared to both medium-term notes and CMO-A pieces.

Structure

Most CARS securities have been structured as grantor trust pass-throughs or as pay-through notes. The most recent innovation in the CARS market has been to add a guaranteed investment contract to the pay-through structure to produce a fixed amortization schedule impervious to prepayment levels, thereby creating a security that resembles a corporate sinking fund obligation. It is also possible in a pay-through structure to create a multiclass security to satisfy various investor maturity preferences. Multiclass structures with GICs are more prevalent with large issues (over $250 million) then they are with smaller CARS offerings.

Secondary Market Activity

By the end of 1987, there were 42 public CARS issues totalling $16.9 billion. Trading activity in CARS securities is moderate, although the secondary market is becoming increasingly liquid. CARS typically trade with bid-offer spreads of 4/32 of a point or less, and there are a number of bellwether issues to guide marketmakers (see Exhibit 3–11).

Prepayments

Cash flows on fixed payment CARS are certain. Cash flows on other types of CARS issues depend on the prepayment rate of the underlying automobile loans.

Presently, there are two measures of prepayments in common usage in the CARS market: The "constant prepayment rate" model (CPR) and the "asset-backed securities" model or "absolute" rate (ABS), both of which are discussed earlier in this chapter. A great deal of attention has been focused on these models in an effort to improve their statistical validity. The importance of a reliable measurement technique, from an investor's perspective, is that the models help to predict weighted average life, which in turn set the pricing parameters relative to the Treasury yield curve.

EXHIBIT 3–11

Secondary Market Prices on Actively Traded CARS Issues, December 22, 1987

ASSET SALES REPORT'S BELLWETHER GROUP

Prices On Actively Traded Asset-Backed Securities (At close of business, Tuesday, Dec. 22, 1987)

	Coupon rate	Final Scheduled Payment	Rating Moody's /S&P	Amount Issued ($ mil.)	Current Pool Factor	Expected Avg. Life (years)	Prepmt. Rate	Price	C.B.E Yield (%)	Interpolated Treasury Yield (%)	Spread Over Treasury (Basis pts)	
											Latest	Week Ago
California Credit Card Trust 1987-B [1]	8.20	5/15/92	Aaa/–	300	1.0*	1.3	–	99.52	8.48	7.65	83	83
CFC-1 Grantor Trust [2]	8.30	5/15/92	Aaa/AAA	516	.873	1.8	1.3 ABS	99.31	8.68	7.82	86	86
Marine Midland 1987-I CARS Trust [3]	8.45	4/15/92	Aaa/AAA	600	.785	1.4	17.0 CPR	99.75	8.54	7.69	85	85
California CARS Grantor Trust 1986-A [4]	6.80	12/16/91	Aaa/AAA	514	.518	1.1	20.0 CPR	98.16	8.44	7.58	86	86
GMAC 1986-E Grantor Trust [5]	6.90	8/15/91	Aa1/AA	725	.621	1.5	1.0 ABS	97.44	8.69	7.72	97	95
GMAC 1986-C Grantor Trust [6]	7.80	6/17/91	Aa1/AA	755	.567	1.4	1.0 ABS	98.77	8.66	7.69	97	95

Current Pool Factor: Percentage of dollar amount issued that remains outstanding. ABS estimates the expected monthly prepayment rate as a percentage of the original number of pooled loans. CPF estimates the expected annual prepayment rate as a percentage of the current number of pooled loans. CBE Yield: Corporate Bond Equivalent yield allows investors to compare all fixed-income securites to corporate bonds, which pay interest semi-annually and are based on a 360-day year.

*Entire issue amount expected to remain outstanding until principal payments begin in January 1989.

[1] Sold by Bank of America on 6/15/87.
[2] Sold by Chrysler Financial Corp. on 6/11/87.
[3] Sold by Marine Midland Automotive Financial Corp. on 6/4/87.
[4] Sold by Bank of America on 12/12/86.
[5] Sold by General Motors Acceptance Corp. on 8/19/86.
[6] Sold by General Motors Acceptance Corp. on 6/19/86.
Interpolated Treasury Yields based on 7.55% yield for 1 year, 7.89% yield for 2 years.

Source: Salomon Brothers Inc

Legal Investment Criteria

Most CARS securities are not eligible liquid assets for thrift investment purposes. To qualify, the following criteria must be met: 1) the CARS security must be a corporate debt obligation (pay-through versus pass-through), 2) the stated final maturity must be three years or less, 3) the securities must be registered and freely transferable, and 4) the securities must be investment grade. Occasionally, an issue of CARS securities will be structured specifically to meet the first two requirements, although that is not common.

Employee benefit plans subject to the Employment Retirement Income Security Act of 1974 (ERISA) and individual retirement accounts may not purchase CARS securities structured as asset sales if the conveyed assets are deemed to be "plan assets" as defined by the U.S. Department of Labor in November 1986. Receivables that backup a CARS issue are plan assets if the investment represents an equity interest. Thus, if a participant in the benefit plan takes out a CARS loan that might conceivably serve as collateral for the CARS issue, the benefit plan cannot purchase the security.

There are certain exceptions to the rules governing benefit plans. First, CARS securities are not deemed to be plan assets if the issue is held by at least 100 independent investors, and are publicly offered for sale. It must also be registered with the Securities and Exchange Commission and freely transferable. Second, if the equity participation by benefit plans, including those not subject to ERISA, is less than 25 percent of the value of beneficial interests not held by the trustee, the collateral also escapes characterization as a plan asset.

APPENDIX A
Outstanding CARS Securities (Dollars in Millions) through June 1988

Issue	Offering Date	Principal Amount	Coupon	Stated Final Maturity	Rating	Credit Support	Lead Manager
CARS							
The Marine Midland 1985-1 CARS Trust	May 85	$ 60	9.625%	15 May 89	AAA/-	10% Insurance Bond	SAL
Valley National Financial, Series 1985-A	May 85	100	9.500	15 Jun 90	–/Aa1	7% LOC	FBC
The Home Federal 1985-1 CARS Trust	Aug 85	103	9.750	15 Jul 90	AAA/Aaa	9% Insurance Bond	SAL
GMAC 1985-A Grantor Trust	Dec 85	525	8.450	15 Dec 90	AA/Aa1	5% Limited Guaranty	FBC
Western Financial Auto Loans, Series 1985-A	Dec 85	110	8.375	1 Dec 90	–/Aa1	Reserve Fund	DBL
GMAC 1986-A Grantor Trust	Jan 86	424	8.550	15 Jan 91	AA/Aa1	5% Limited Guaranty	FBC
GMAC 1986-B Grantor Trust	Apr 86	1,050	7.100	15 Apr 91	AA/Aa1	5% Limited Guaranty	FBC
Empire of America FSB, 1986-A Grantor Trust	Jun 86	190	7.700	17 Jun 91	–/Aaa	10% LOC	FBC
GMAC 1986-C Grantor Trust	Jun 86	755	7.800	17 Jun 91	AA/Aa1	5% Limited Guaranty	FBC
CARCO Series 1986-1	Jul 86	250	7.500	15 Jul 91	AAA/Aaa	7% LOC	SAL
NMAC 1986-B1 Grantor Trust	Jul 86	113	7.250	15 Dec 89	AAA/Aaa	8% LOC	FBC
NMAC 1986-B2 Grantor Trust	Jul 86	70	6.700	15 Aug 90	AAA/Aaa	9% LOC	FBC
NMAC 1986-B3 Grantor Trust	Jul 86	5	5.700	15 Aug 89	AAA/Aaa	9% LOC	FBC
GMAC 1986-D Grantor Trust	Aug 86	355	6.500	15 Aug 89	AA/Aa1	5% Limited Guaranty	FBC
GMAC 1986-E Grantor Trust	Aug 86	725	6.900	15 Aug 91	AA/Aa1	5% Limited Guaranty	FBC
GMAC 1986 Euro-A Grantor Trust	Sep 86	276	7.250	16 Sep 91	AA/Aa1	5% Limited Guaranty	SAL
Asset Backed Securities Corp., Series 1	Oct 86	2,095	6.250	17 Oct 88	AAA/Aaa	6% LOC; GIC 5%	FBC
		585	6.900	15 Apr 89		GMAC Limited Guaranty	
		1,320	6.950	15 Oct 90			
Banco Central 1986-A Grantor Trust	Nov 86	67	6.150	25 Oct 91	AA +/–	14% Limited Guaranty; 14% Standby LOC	FBC
GMAC 1986-F Grantor Trust	Nov 86	327	6.850	15 Nov 91	AA/Aa1	5% Limited Guaranty	FBC

APPENDIX A
Outstanding CARS Securities (Dollars in Millions) through June 1988 (continued)

Issue	Offering Date	Principal Amount	Coupon	Stated Final Maturity	Rating	Credit Support	Lead Manager
California CARS Grantor Trust 1986-A	Dec 86	514	6.800	16 Dec 91	AAA/Aaa	17% LOC	SAL
GMAC 1986-G Grantor Trust	Dec 86	445	6.850	16 Dec 91	AA/Aa1	5% Limited Guaranty	FBC
Western Financial Auto Loans 2, Series 1986-A	Dec 86	192	6.625	1 Dec 89	AAA/Aaa	100% Insurance Bond, Reserve Fund	DBL
Asset Backed Securities Corp., Series 2	Nov 86	95 25 60	6.250 6.650 6.850	15 Dec 91 15 Jun 89 15 Dec 90	AA/Aaa	6% LOC, GIC, 5% GMAC Limited Guaranty	FBC
GMAC 1987-A Grantor Trust	Mar 87	164	7.000	16 Mar 92	AA/Aa1	5% Limited Guaranty	FBC
Western Financial Auto Loans 2, Series 1987-A	Mar 87	125	6.750	1 Mar 90	AAA/Aaa	100% Insurance Bond, Reserve Fund	DBL
GMAC 1987-B Grantor Trust	Apr 87	162	7.700	14 Apr 92	AA/Aa1	5% Limited Guaranty	SAL
GMAC 1987-C Grantor Trust	May 87	166	8.350	15 May 92	AA/Aa1	5% Limited Guaranty	FBC
RepublicBank Dallas, Series A	May 87	230	8.500	15 May 92	AAA/Aaa	12% LOC	GS
CFC-1 Grantor Trust	Jun 87	516	8.300	15 May 92	AAA/Aaa	7% LOC	FBC
GECC 1987-1 Grantor Trust	Jun 87	147	8.500	15 Jun 92	–/Aaa	8% Limited Guaranty	KP
GMAC 1987-D Grantor Trust	Jun 87	323	8.150	15 Jun 92	AA/Aa1	5% Limited Guaranty	SAL
Marine Midland 1987-1 CARS Trust	Jun 87	600	8.450	15 Apr 92	AAA/Aaa	7% LOC	SAL
Asset Backed Securities Corp., Series 3	Jul 87	15 10	7.400 7.450	15 Jun 90 15 Jun 92	AAA/–	GIC, 8% GECC Limited Guaranty	FBC
Security Pacific Credit Corp. 1987-A Grantor Trust	Jul 87	103	7.700	15 Jun 92	–/Aaa	10% LOC	FBC
Asset Backed Securities Corp., Series 4	Jul 87	971 440	7.400 8.300	15 Oct 89 15 Apr 92	AAA/Aaa	6% LOC, GIC, 5% GMAC Limited Guaranty, Minimum Principal Payment Agreement	FBC

Issuer	Date	Amount ($mil)	Coupon	Maturity	Rating (S&P/Moody's)	Credit Enhancement	Underwriter
Western Financial Auto Loans 2, Series 1987-B	Jul 87	110	7.800	1 Sep 90	AAA/Aaa	100% Insurance Bond	DBL
Bank of Boston CARS Grantor Trust 1987-A	Aug 87	103	8.250	15 Aug 92	–/Aaa	8% LOC	SAL
Volkswagen Lease Finance	Oct 87	150	9.750	15 Oct 92	AAA/–	18% LOC	DR
UST 1987-A Grantor Trust	Oct 87	109	9.200	15 Oct 92	AAA/Aaa	100% Insurance Bond	DBL
Asset Backed Securities Corp., Series 5	Oct 87	36	7.550	15 Nov 88	AAA/Aaa	5% LOC	FBC
		89	8.650	15 Nov 92			
Salomon Brothers Receivables Inc	Nov 87	177	8.150	15 Nov 89	AAA/Aaa	8.5% LOC, GIC	SAL
		250	8.500	15 Nov 90			
CFC-2 Grantor Trust	Nov 87	1,002	8.550	15 Oct 92	AAA/Aaa	7.5% LOC	FBC
Asset Backed Securities Corp. Class A	Nov 87	36	7.550	15 Nov 92	NR/Aaa	NA	FBC
Asset Backed Securities Corp. Class B	Nov 87	89	8.650	15 Nov 88	NR/Aaa	NA	FBC
BMW Credit Corp., Montvale, N. J.	Nov 87	100	8.550	NA	AAA/Aaa	100% Surety Bond	DBL
UST FASTBACs 1987-B Grantor Trust US Trust, Norfolk					FSA		
Volvo 1987-B Lease Finance Corp.	Jan 88	149	8.900	15 Dec 92	NA	NA	FBC
Volvo Finance North America Inc.	Jan 88	225	NM	NM	AAA/Aaa	Asset Transfer Agreement/ E Finance Corp.	FBC
EOA Auto Funding Series A						100% Surety Bond	
EOA Auto Funding Series B						100% Surety Bond	
EOA Auto Funding Series C							
Empire of America FSB, Buffalo	Feb 88	155	7.750	1 Mar 91	AAA/Aaa	100% Surety Bond	DBL
Western Fiancial Auto Loans 2							
Western Financial Auto Loans 2, Inc.							
Shawmut National 1988-A	Feb 88	124	7.450	15 Oct 92	NR/Aaa	7% LOC	GS
Connecticut National Bank							
BMWCC 1988 A-1 Grantor Trust	Mar 88	40	7.500	15 Mar 93	NA/Aaa	50% Limited Guaranty	KP
BMWCC 1988 A-2 Grantor Trust	Mar 88	67	6.900	15 Mar 93	AAA/Aaa		
BMW Credit Corp.							
CFC-3 Grantor Trust	Mar 88	753	7.700	15 Feb 93	AAA/Aaa	7.5% LOC	SAL
Chrysler Financial Corp.							

APPENDIX A
Outstanding CARS Securities (Dollars in Millions) through June 1988 (continued)

Issue	Offering Date	Principal Amount	Coupon	Stated Final Maturity	Rating	Credit Support	Lead Manager
Empire of America 1988-A Empire of America FSB	Mar 88	190	7.750	15 Sept 93	NR/Aaa	11% LOC	FBC
UST FASTBACS 1988-A Grantor Trust US Trust-Norfolk	Mar 88	88	7.850	20 Apr 91	AAA/Aaa	100% Surety Bond	DBL
Chemical Bank Grantor Trust 1988-A Chemical Bank	Apr 88	257	8.100	15 Apr 93	NR/Aaa	8% LOC	Chem FBC SLH
Shearson Lehman Hutton ABS Corp. Westamerica Bank	May 88	38 57	7.400 8.300	15 Apr 89 15 Apr 93	NR/Aaa NR/Aaa	NA	SLH
Mack Trucks Receivables Corp. 2 Mack Financial Corp.	May 88	48 75	7.450 8.350	15 Nov 89 15 May 93	AAA/Aaa	14% LOC	SLH/LF
Western Financial Auto Loans 2, Inc. Western Financial Savings Bank	May 88	100	8.500	1 Jun 91	AAA/Aaa	100% Surety Bond	DBL
Marine Midland 1988-1 CARS Trust Marine Midland Automotive Financial Corp.	Jun 88	254	8.500	15 Jun 93	AAA/Aaa	9% LOC	SAL MMS

Key to Abbreviations:
Chem = Chemical bank
DBL = Drexel Burnham Lambert
DR = Dillon Read
FBC = First Boston Corp.
GS = Goldman Sachs
KP = Kidder Peabody
LF = Lazard Freres

LOC = Letter of Credit
MMS = Marine Midland Securities
NA = Not Available
NM = Not Meaningful
NR = Not Rated
SAL = Salomon Brothers
SLH = Shearson Lehman Hutton

Source: Salomon Brothers Inc

CHAPTER 4

SECURITIZING CREDIT CARD RECEIVABLES

Asset Finance Group
The First Boston Corporation

INTRODUCTION

From their beginnings in the 1950s, credit cards have become a major consumer payment mechanism as well as a major form of consumer borrowing. Credit cards now account for an estimated 61.9 percent of all retail store purchases (see Exhibit 4–1) and, together with other forms of revolving debt, 23.4 percent of nonmortgage consumer debt.

In spite of the enormous volume of these assets, the development of credit card asset-backed securities (credit card ABSs) had been constrained by the complexity of credit card receivables, relative to installment receivables such as automobile loans, and the fact that even a sold portfolio of credit card receivables is affected by the ongoing condition of the issuer and the industry. But with the offering of credit card ABSs by the California Credit Card Trust 1987-A, an efficient mechanism for the securitized sale of credit card receivables became available.

STRUCTURES

Common Features

There are two basic forms of credit card ABSs: sales using certificates of ownership of the credit card receivables and borrowings using notes collateralized by receivables.

EXHIBIT 4–1
Method of Consumer Payment—Retail Stores

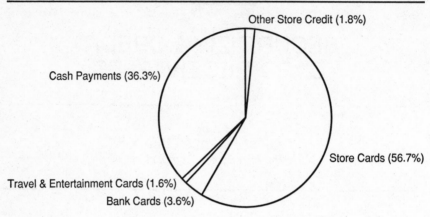

Notes:
Method of payment reflects the means of payment by retail store customers, as evidenced through the experience of 20 major retail stores in 1984.
Other Store Credit includes 30-day and installment credit granted by the retail store.

Source: Based on data from National Retail Merchants Association, *Economic Characteristics of Retail Store Credit*, August 1986.

The two structures have many common features.

• The credit card ABS issuer continues to service the receivables and is paid a servicing fee. Generally, no notification is given to cardholders that their accounts are included in the transaction.

• The receivables of a specified set of accounts are included in the transaction. Generally, more receivables are included than those actually allocated to the credit card ABS investors. The additional receivables supply a buffer for seasonality and attrition, so that the total amount of receivables is always at least as great as the investors' interest in the receivables.

• For a specified period, the "revolving period," credit card ABSs do not amortize principal. Instead, principal from the receivables is retained by the issuer to reinvest in additional receivables. The length of the revolving period largely determines the average life of the issue.

• Interest on the credit card ABSs is paid monthly on the fifteenth day of the following month to give the servicer time to process reports on the receivables.

• Principal repayments on the credit card ABSs are distributed monthly with the interest payment during the amortization period, which follows the end of the revolving period. The amount of principal distribution is determined as cardholder payments are received on the receivables. Because cardholder monthly payment rates are relatively stable, principal is repaid in approximately equal installments.

• Credit card ABSs depend, in part, on the rapid pay-out of investor principal to protect the investor against loss in the event of a deterioration in the receivables portfolio. Prescribed pay-out events result in the credit card ABSs amortizing prematurely. Pay-out triggers include such events as delinquencies or losses above prescribed levels, insolvency of the issuer, or a significant decline in portfolio yield.

• A guaranty, which may be from a third party or from the seller, except in the case of nonrecourse asset sales by banks, is provided to protect against credit loss. Fraud losses are generally borne by the seller as a cost of servicing.

• Since credit cards constitute "accounts" or "general intangibles" under the Uniform Commercial Code, there is no need for a trustee to take physical possession of any account documents to perfect a security interest in the receivables. The administrative burden is therefore less than with many other asset-backed transactions.

Sale of Receivables

In a sale of receivables, the receivables are typically sold to a trust owned by the investors. All new receivables originated from the securitized portfolio of accounts are automatically sold at the time of their creation. Because of possible fluctuations in the total amount of receivables in the accounts, a second ownership class is retained by the seller that increases or decreases in size to absorb the fluctuation. The trust does not qualify as a grantor trust because payments received on trust receivables are reinvested in new receivables generated by the included accounts during the revolving period. The credit card ABSs are usually treated as debt for tax purposes.

The advantages of a sale structure are:

• Sale for financial reporting purposes. A gain may be recognized at the time of sale.
• Sale for regulatory accounting purposes (banks and thrifts).
• Sale for Regulation D. Depositary institutions, such as banks and thrifts, do not need to maintain reserves against the transaction.

- May be structured to be nonrecourse to the seller
- May be possible to structure a sale for tax purposes

The disadvantages of a sale structure are:

- Limited modification of cash flows
- No direct recourse or overcollateralization is permitted; third party credit enhancement is required (banks).

Collateralized Notes

In a collateralized note offering, the issuer, either directly or through a special-purpose corporation, issues notes secured by the receivables and, possibly, credit support, such as a reserve account or letter of credit.

The advantages of collateralized notes are:

- Substantial modification of cash flows is possible.
- Direct recourse and overcollateralization may eliminate need for third party credit enhancement.

The disadvantages of collateralized notes are:

- Require equity support, which raises the all-in cost to the issuer
- Not off-balance sheet for financial reporting purposes
- Not off-balance sheet for most regulatory reporting purposes (banks and thrifts)
- May be reservable for purposes of Regulation D

Most companies wish to sell assets when they enter into a credit card ABS transaction because of the advantages enumerated above. Indeed, RepublicBank Delaware has been to date the only issuer of collateralized notes. Exhibit 4–2 shows all outstanding U.S. public issues of credit card asset-backed securities. The offering by Imperial CARDS Trust 1987-1 in June 1987 was the first public credit card transaction by a thrift. In addition, the first retailer offerings were filed with the SEC in April and May of 1988 for Montgomery Ward, J.C. Penney and Sears. These are the first credit card ABSs to be collateralized by private label credit card receivables, as opposed to Visa and MasterCard receivables.

New Developments

Recently, some new features have been introduced in the credit card ABS market: controlled amortization of principal, a bullet principal payment, and the master trust.

EXHIBIT 4–2
Credit Card Asset-Backed Securities—U.S. Public Issues

Date	Seller/Servicer	Issuer	Type	Amount (Thousands)	Manager(s)
01/16/87	RepublicBank Delaware	RepublicBank Delaware	Credit Card-Backed Notes	$200,000	GS, FBC
02/25/87	Bank of America	California Credit Card Trust 1987-A	Asset-Backed Certificates	400,000	FBC
06/19/87	Bank of America	California Credit Card Trust 1987-B	Receivable-Backed Certificates	300,000	SAL, B of A
06/23/87	Imperial Savings Association	Imperial CARDS Trust 1987-1	CARDS	100,000	SAL
09/24/87	Great American First Savings Bank	Great American Credit Card Trust A	Credit Card Pass-Through Certificates	110,000	GS, FBC
09/29/87	The First National Bank of Chicago; FCC National Bank[1]	First Chicago CARDS Trust 1987-1	CARDS	800,000	SAL, FBC
12/09/87	Maryland Bank, N.A.	MBNA Credit Card Trust 1987-A	Asset-Backed Certificates	500,000	FBC, GS

EXHIBIT 4–2 (continued)

Date	Seller/Servicer	Issuer	Type	Amount (Thousands)	Manager(s)
03/25/88	Colonial National Bank USA	Colonial Credit Card Trust 1988-A	Asset-Backed Certificates	150,000	FBC, KP
05/09/88	The First National Bank of Chicago; FCC National Bank[1]	First Chicago Master Trust	Asset-Backed Certificates, Series A	300,000	FBC, SAL, FNBC
05/12/88	Maryland Bank, N.A.	MBNA Credit Card Trust 1988-A	Asset-Backed Certificates	500,000	FBC
06/15/88	The First National Bank of Chicago; FCC National Bank[1]	First Chicago Master Trust	CARDS, Series B,	600,000	SAL, FBC, FNBC

Notes:

[1] FCC National Bank is servicer.

Key:

B of A = Bank of America

FBC = First Boston Corp.

FNBC = First National Bank of Chicago

GS = Goldman Sachs & Co.

KP = Kidder Peabody

SAL = Salomon Brothers

- Controlled amortization results in level monthly payments of principal during the amortization period. A predetermined amount of cardholder principal payments received during the amortization period is paid to investors, while the remainder, as in the revolving period, is reinvested in new receivables. This level monthly principal payment is a fraction of the cardholder principal payments expected to be received during the month. This fraction represents a small enough portion of historical monthly cardholder principal payments that its receipt is considered highly likely. The two offerings by Maryland Bank utilize controlled amortization (see Exhibit 4–2).
- In the case of a bullet payment, principal is returned to investors in one lump sum at maturity, instead of being amortized monthly. To achieve this, the structure must incorporate a high credit quality funding source to guarantee the bullet payment. The planned offering of credit card ABSs by MWCC Receivables Trust One, collateralized by Montgomery Ward Credit Corporation receivables, is an example of a bullet payment credit card ABS.
- A master trust allows an issuer to place into a trust credit card accounts with an aggregate balance that exceeds—or where the portfolio is expected to grow, will exceed—the amount necessary to support the issuer's immediate financing needs. At the same time, it offers the ability to securitize the excess at a later date through subsequent series as funding needs or market conditions warrant. The master trust was first used in First Chicago's offering of asset-backed certificates in May 1988. First Chicago placed approximately $1.6 billion of receivables into the master trust and issued Series A, which included $300 million of these receivables. Additional series, such as the subsequent Series B, can be issued from the remaining $1.3 billion as First Chicago desires. The planned offering by J.C. Penney also employs the master trust structure.

CASE STUDIES

Case studies of the RepublicBank Delaware and Bank of America transactions are shown because they were the first two public issues of credit card asset-backed securities and are representative of collateralized notes and a sale of receivables.

California Credit Card Trust 1987-A

Background

Bank of America is the third largest bank in the United States and has the second largest bank card portfolio. The bank has had considerable experience with securitization of its assets and had originated several mortgage and automobile loan pass-throughs prior to its credit card ABSs. The bank uses asset-backed securities as a way of reducing assets without losing the related servicing and customer relationship benefits. Bank of America's objectives were to obtain sale treatment for financial reporting and regulatory accounting purposes, to have the security be nonrecourse to the bank, and to avoid any disruption in the bank-customer relationship.

The credit card ABSs were issued by the California Credit Card Trust 1987-A and consisted of $400 million of 6.9 percent asset-backed certificates rated triple-A by Moody's and Standard & Poor's. The securitized receivables came from approximately 840,000 accounts from the bank's Northern California Classic Visa portfolio. These accounts were seasoned at least two years and were delinquent less than one month.

Structure

Bank of America originated the trust and gave it the right to purchase automatically all receivables generated by the selected accounts at the time the receivables are posted to the accounts. Because the amount of receivables fluctuates daily, the value of the trust also fluctuates. Since the investor amount is fixed at $400 million, the bank retains certificates representing the remaining value of the receivables in the trust. Thus, the bank's investment in the trust fluctuates with the size of the trust's receivables. Although the bank's interest absorbs the fluctuation, it is not subordinate to the investors' interest in terms of credit or other risk.

Investors are protected against losses by a letter of credit issued by Union Bank of Switzerland (UBS). Finance charges received by the trust in excess of 12.79 percent, the sum of the certificate rate plus servicing fees, are paid to UBS. UBS, in return, agrees to reimburse the trust for the amount of all receivables charged off. UBS's liability is limited to $60 million—15 percent of the offering. If UBS makes a payment, the liability decreases by that amount. However, it is increased by the amount of finance charges paid to UBS by the trust, but not above the initial $60 million level. Thus, investors are protected both by the UBS guaranty and by the excess finance charges on the receivables.

For its protection, UBS deposits excess finance charges received into a reserve account, which builds to a maintenance level equal to a fraction of UBS' liability under the letter of credit. Amounts in excess of the maintenance level are paid to Bank of America, as are all amounts remaining in the reserve account at the end of the transaction.

Exhibit 4–3 shows the investor cash flow from the California Credit Card Trust 1987-A.

RepublicBank Delaware

Background
RepublicBank Delaware is a wholly-owned subsidiary of RepublicBank Corporation, the largest bank holding company in Texas.[1] RepublicBank Delaware was organized as a Delaware consumer credit bank for the purpose of issuing credit cards. The bank issues Visa, MasterCard, and American Express Gold Cards. Prior to July 1986, the bank's credit card portfolio was owned by RepublicBank Dallas, a Texas-based banking affiliate. The bank's objective was a lower all-in cost of funds rather than sale treatment for financial or regulatory accounting.

The credit card ABSs consisted of $200 million of 7.15 percent credit card-backed notes rated triple-A by Standard & Poor's Corporation. The notes are general obligations of the bank collateralized by the receivables of approximately 227,000 Visa and MasterCard accounts that, at the time of selection, were seasoned at least three months, were delinquent less than one month, and had made at least one payment. Most of the accounts have Texas billing addresses.

Structure
The collateral for the notes is approximately $240 million of receivables, a cash reserve account, and a letter of credit. The receivables are the entire receivable balances of the accounts selected by the bank. The $40 million of excess receivables, 20 percent of the offering, is provided as a buffer to protect against fluctuation in the amount of receivables and also

---

[1] RepublicBank Delaware became First RepublicBank Delaware through RepublicBank Corporation's acquisition of Interfirst Corp. in June 1987. In August 1988, the Federal Deposit Insurance Corp. was appointed receiver of First RepublicBank Delaware, causing a default under the terms of indenture for the credit card backed notes. Accordingly, amortization of principal, which had been scheduled to begin October 15, 1989, began September 15, 1988. Principal and interest on the notes are fully protected by the FDIC.

EXHIBIT 4-3
Sample Credit Card ABS Cash Flow

California Credit Card Trust 1987-A
6.9% Asset-Backed Certificates

Investor Cash Flow Report

Month	Beginning Investor Amount (A)	Investor Principal Distributions (B)	Investor Earned Finance Charges (C)	Additional Payment by the LOC Bank (D)	Investor Servicing Fee (E)	Guaranty Fee (F)	Payment to the LOC Bank (G)	Investor Interest Distributions (H)	Total Investor Distributions (I)
03/87	$400,000,000	$ 0	$ 6,170,000	$0	$ 1,433,333	$ 31,250	$ 2,405,417	$ 2,300,000	$ 2,300,000
04/87	400,000,000	0	6,170,000	0	1,433,333	31,250	2,405,417	2,300,000	2,300,000
05/87	400,000,000	0	6,170,000	0	1,433,333	31,250	2,405,417	2,300,000	2,300,000
06/87	400,000,000	0	6,170,000	0	1,433,333	31,250	2,405,417	2,300,000	2,300,000
07/87	400,000,000	0	6,170,000	0	1,433,333	31,250	2,405,417	2,300,000	2,300,000
08/87	400,000,000	0	6,170,000	0	1,433,333	31,250	2,405,417	2,300,000	2,300,000
09/87	400,000,000	0	6,170,000	0	1,433,333	31,250	2,405,417	2,300,000	2,300,000
10/87	400,000,000	0	6,170,000	0	1,433,333	31,250	2,405,417	2,300,000	2,300,000
11/87	400,000,000	0	6,170,000	0	1,433,333	31,250	2,405,417	2,300,000	2,300,000
12/87	400,000,000	0	6,170,000	0	1,433,333	31,250	2,405,417	2,300,000	2,300,000
01/88	400,000,000	0	6,170,000	0	1,433,333	31,250	2,405,417	2,300,000	2,300,000
02/88	400,000,000	0	6,170,000	0	1,433,333	31,250	2,405,417	2,300,000	2,300,000
03/88	400,000,000	0	6,170,000	0	1,433,333	31,250	2,405,417	2,300,000	2,300,000
04/88	400,000,000	0	6,170,000	0	1,433,333	31,250	2,405,417	2,300,000	2,300,000

	(A)	(B)	(C)	(D)	(E)	(F)	(G)	(H)	(I)
05/88	400,000,000	0	6,170,000	0	1,433,333	31,250	2,405,417	2,300,000	2,300,000
06/88	400,000,000	0	6,170,000	0	1,433,333	31,250	2,405,417	2,300,000	2,300,000
07/88	400,000,000	0	6,170,000	0	1,433,333	31,250	2,405,417	2,300,000	2,300,000
08/88	400,000,000	0	6,170,000	0	1,433,333	31,250	2,405,417	2,300,000	2,300,000
09/88	400,000,000	81,529,941	6,170,000	0	1,433,333	31,250	2,405,417	2,300,000	83,829,941
10/88	318,470,059	81,529,940	4,912,401	0	1,141,184	31,250	1,908,763	1,831,203	83,361,143
11/88	236,940,118	81,529,941	3,654,801	0	849,035	31,250	1,412,110	1,362,406	82,892,346
12/88	155,410,178	81,529,941	2,397,202	0	556,886	31,250	915,457	893,609	82,423,549
01/89	73,880,237	73,880,237	1,139,603	0	264,738	31,250	418,250	424,811	74,305,049
02/89	0	0	0	0	0	0	0	0	0
Totals	$400,000,000		$129,334,007	$0	$30,045,177	$718,750	$50,358,051	$48,212,028	$448,212,028

Notes:
(A) Outstanding certificate principal balance.
(B) Investor principal liquidations plus payments under the guaranty minus principal reinvestment.
(C) Investors' share of portfolio finance charges.
(D) Any additional payments by the Letter of Credit Bank, Union Bank of Switzerland (UBS), to protect the certificate yield.
(E) Investors' share of the servicing fee paid to servicer.
(F) Payment by the trust to UBS for the guaranty.
(G) Investor finance charges less the investor servicing fee, the guaranty fee and certificate interest.
(H) (C) + (D) − (E) − (F) − (G).
(I) (B) + (H).

Source: The First Boston Corporation

provides extra credit enhancement. The reserve account is funded from gross cardholder payments and builds to a maximum of $14 million, 7 percent of the offering. The letter of credit, from Union Bank of Switzerland, provides an additional 5 percent protection.

Since the notes are general obligations of RepublicBank Delaware, the bank absorbs any credit losses directly. As general obligations, the other assets of the bank, including the accounts themselves, may be available to note investors as general creditors of the bank. No draws can be made on either the reserve account or the letter of credit except in the event of a default by the bank to make a payment.

Exhibit 4–4 compares several of the principal terms of the California Credit Card Trust 1987-A asset-backed certificates and RepublicBank Delaware credit card-backed notes.

VALUATION

Asset-backed securities in general are valued on the basis of the timing and certainty of the cash flows to investors compared to similar average life investments. For credit card ABSs, analyzing the timing and certainty of cash flow involves an evaluation of the underlying portfolio's credit quality and historical cardholder monthly payment rate and the security's structure with regard to principal payment patterns and the possibility of early termination through pay-out events.

The credit quality of credit card ABSs is derived from the quality of the accounts from which the securitized receivables are drawn and from the amount and source of credit support. Credit support must be sufficient to insulate investors from any reasonable risk of loss. The amount of credit support is determined from the historical performance of the securitized portfolio as well as from an evaluation of the servicer's effectiveness. Credit support is ordinarily provided by a highly rated bank or insurance company, overcollateralization or a seller guaranty.

Timing of principal payments on credit card ABSs depends on the length of the revolving period and the schedule for returning principal to investors. Issuers have flexibility in selecting the length of the revolving period, and therefore the average life of the security, limited only by uncertainty about the future direction of the credit card industry and performance of the securitized portfolio. Schedules for principal repayment utilized to date include: the basic structure where principal is paid through to investors as received from cardholders (e.g., California Credit Card Trust 1987-A); controlled amortization where the investor receives

EXHIBIT 4–4
Comparison of California Credit Card Trust 1987–A Asset-Backed Certificates and RepublicBank Delaware Credit Card-Backed Notes

California Credit Card Trust 1987-A Asset-Backed Certificates	*RepublicBank Delaware Credit Card-Backed Notes*
Average Life and Maturity 18 months interest only 1.8 year average life 2.0 year expected maturity	*Average Life and Maturity* 32 months interest only 3.0 year average life 3.3 year expected maturity
Ratings Aaa/AAA by Moody's/S&P	*Rating* AAA by S&P
Structure The receivables are sold by Bank of America for both GAAP and regulatory accounting. The Trust holds the receivables and a 15% letter of credit which is reimbursed by the excess spread on the investor participation. Certificates are issued by the Trust, with no recourse to the bank.	*Structure* The receivables are not sold, but pledged as collateral for Credit Card-Backed Notes issued by RepublicBank. The Notes are general obligations of the bank.
Credit Enhancement The certificates' credit quality is dependent only on the assets, which are separated from the seller. Credit enhancement is provided by the 15% non-declining letter of credit and the excess spread on the receivables which is available to reimburse and reinstate the letter of credit.	*Credit Enhancement* RepublicBank maintains the receivables as collateral for the Notes and absorbs the losses on the receivables. Under the collateralized note structure, the investor looks to the 7% cash reserve account and the 5% letter of credit only if RepublicBank defaults on its obligations.
Approach to Portfolio Size Variation A Seller Certificate exists that represents the principal amount of receivables held by the Trust in excess of the $400 million amount issued as Investor Certificates. The Seller Certificate amount fluctuates with variations in the aggregate amount of the cardholder balances. As of the cut-off date, the Seller Certificate was for approximately $225 million or 39% of the amount of receivables held by the Trust. If the amount of receivables outstanding drops to $500 million or less during the revolving period (causing the investor percentage ownership of the Trust receivables to increase to 80% or more), an early pay-out would occur.	*Approach to Portfolio Size Variation* Room for fluctuation in the aggregate amount of receivables outstanding in the portfolio is provided by over-collateralization of the Notes. At issuance, $240 million of receivables collateralized $200 million of Notes. If, at any point during the revolving period, the amount of receivables drops below 90% of the $200 million of Notes outstanding (i.e. $180 million) or drops below $200 million for a significant period of time, an early pay-out would occur.
Collateral Bank of America included well-seasoned accounts in the Trust. Each account was at least two years of age.	*Collateral* RepublicBank Delaware's portfolio consists primarily of accounts recently transferred from RepublicBank Dallas. Minimum account seasoning is 90 days, and at least one payment must have been made on the account.

level monthly payments (e.g., MBNA Credit Card Trusts 1987-A and 1988-A); and the bullet payment of principal in a lump sum at maturity (e.g., MWCC Receivables Trust One).

In the case of the basic structure, the monthly payment rate has the effect, during the amortization period, of increasing or decreasing the amortization speed of the security. If payments are received faster, principal is paid faster, and the security is retired sooner. During the revolving period, the monthly payment rate has no effect on cash flow timing. As can be seen from Exhibit 4-5, even extreme changes in the monthly payment rate have little effect on the price of a credit card ABS, although this effect increases as the transaction becomes more seasoned. Historically, monthly payment rates have been quite stable over time and should not play a major role in credit card ABS valuation.

The amortization period is expected to begin at the end of the scheduled revolving period and the security should be fully amortized shortly thereafter. The revolving period may end, and the security may

EXHIBIT 4-5
Sensitivity to Monthly Payment Rates—California Credit Card Trust 1987-A

Price[1]	Monthly Payment Rate					
	10%	15%	18%	21.72%[2]	25%	100%
98.50	7.67%	7.73%	7.75%	7.77%	7.78%	7.84%
98.75	7.53	7.58	7.60	7.61	7.62	7.67
99.00	7.40	7.43	7.44	7.45	7.46	7.50
99.25	7.26	7.28	7.29	7.30	7.30	7.33
99.50	7.13	7.14	7.14	7.14	7.15	7.16
99.75	6.99	6.99	6.99	6.99	6.99	6.99
100.00	6.86	6.84	6.84	6.84	6.84	6.82
100.25	6.72	6.70	6.69	6.68	6.68	6.65
100.50	6.59	6.55	6.54	6.53	6.52	6.48
100.75	6.45	6.41	6.39	6.38	6.37	6.31
101.00	6.32	6.26	6.24	6.23	6.21	6.14
Average Life	2.06 yrs.	1.89 yrs.	1.83 yrs.	1.79 yrs.	1.76 yrs.	1.62 yrs.

Notes:
[1] Assumes a standard 14-day payment delay.
[2] Pricing assumption for California Credit Card Trust 1987-A, 6.9% Asset-Backed Certificates.

Source: The First Boston Corporation

amortize sooner than scheduled if a pay-out event occurs. Pay-out events are events that may weaken the transaction and increase the risk of investor loss. Examples of such pay-out events are: a significant increase in loss rates, which may exhaust the guaranty; the bankruptcy or receivership of the card issuer, which could affect the quality of the servicing; and a reduction in portfolio yield, which would lessen the money available to pay credit card ABS interest and other expenses.

For the investor, pay-out events are a two-edged sword. They provide investor protection against loss or delay in payment of amounts due on the credit card ABSs, but also create the possibility that credit card ABSs will amortize sooner than expected. Pay-out events are unlikely and should not occur unexpectedly because loss, delinquency, and other pay-out event characteristics change slowly. Investors should, nonetheless, assess the possibility of a pay-out event in their valuation of a credit card ABS.

The timing and certainty of credit card ABS cash flows should cause them to trade between high-grade corporate debt and ABSs that amortize monthly, such as those secured by automobile loans. In fact, credit card ABSs should be an attractive investment for investors who seek yield pick-up but who traditionally have been restricted to high-grade corporate debt or Treasury securities.

TOTAL RETURN ANALYSIS

Total return is an all-inclusive measurement of the yield a security will return over a specified holding period. It consists of the return on several components including the coupon cash flows, principal cash flows, capital gain or loss, and reinvestment income. For example, if a security is purchased at a price of $100 and an interest rate of 10 percent, the investor yield, ignoring reinvestment income and if held to maturity, would be 10 percent. If the investor instead sold the security after one year at a price of $105, his *total return* for the investment would be 15 percent.

ABSs fluctuate in value with changes in market conditions. Unlike conventional debt of comparable duration, however, ABSs typically pay principal during the life of the transaction. As a result, even if the price rises from $100 to $105, the *size* of the investors' position is smaller and they are unable to fully participate in the gain (or loss) on the price movement.

Exhibit 4–6 shows this effect on total return. Using recent pricing information on a new issue basis and prices one year later, determined

EXHIBIT 4–6
Comparisons of Yield, Price, and Total Return—Selected Securities

	Current			In One Year			
	Yield	Price	Avg. Life	Yield	Price	Avg. Life	Total Return
Term CD	8.33%	100.00	2.0 yrs.	8.01%	100.30	1.0 yrs.	8.59%
ABSC 2-B[1]	8.27	96.86	2.2	7.95	98.56	1.2	8.60
Automobile Asset-Backed Security[2]	8.47	97.29	1.9	8.30	97.91	1.5	8.55
California Credit Card Trust 1987-A	8.42	97.50	1.8	7.90	99.06	.8	8.70

Notes:
[1] Asset Backed Securities Corporation, Class 2-B.
[2] GMAC 1986-G.
Yields are corporate bond equivalent (CBE).
Assumes 7.0% reinvestment rate.

by using the securities' current spreads and the current yield curve, the total return for a one-year holding period has been calculated for each of four securities. Note that the average life of each security has been reduced by one year, except in the case of the automobile ABS, which has been reduced by only .4 years. This is because automobile loans amortize principal each month. Amortization during the holding period causes the average life to decrease by less than the elapsed time. As can be seen from the exhibit, although credit card ABSs have a yield give-up of 5 basis points to the automobile ABS on a current basis, the total return is 15 basis points higher if held for the one-year period. This is because the automobile ABS does not roll down the yield curve as much as the credit card ABS and, therefore, does not benefit from the lower yield at the short end of the yield curve.

Exhibit 4–7 shows that credit card ABSs have a greater expected total return than the other securities shown, even though the fixed-payment securities have a greater total return for negative yield shifts. Expected total return refers to the total return in a given yield scenario weighted by the probability the scenario will occur. Credit card ABSs have a greater total return than fixed-payment securities for all bearish

EXHIBIT 4–7
Comparison of Total Return—Selected Securities

Yield Shift	California Credit Card Trust 1987-A	Automobile Asset-Backed Security[1]	ABSC 2-B[2]	Term CD
+300 b.p.	6.66%	6.84%	5.35%	5.97%
+200	7.33	7.41	6.42	6.84
+100	8.01	7.99	7.50	7.71
0	8.70	8.55	8.60	8.59
−100	9.39	9.17	9.71	9.48
−200	10.09	9.78	10.83	10.38
−300	10.80	10.43	11.97	11.29
Expected Total Return	8.70%	8.57%	8.61%	8.60%

Notes:
[1] GMAC 1986-G.
[2] Asset Backed Securities Corporation, Class 2–B.
Yields are corporate bond equivalent (CBE).
Assumes 7.0% reinvestment rate.

Source: The First Boston Corporation

interest rate scenarios shown and a greater total return than automobile ABSs in all but the most bearish scenarios. The ability of automobile ABSs to provide a greater total return in a severe bearish environment is a result of the amortization of principal during the holding period, whereas the credit card ABS acts more like conventional debt. Exhibit 4–8 shows the change in total return from the base scenario for the yield shifts shown in Exhibit 4–7.

EXHIBIT 4–8
Change in Total Return—Selected Securities

Yield Shift	California Credit Card Trust 1987-A	Automobile Asset-Backed Security	ABSC 2-B	Term CD
+300 b.p.	−204 b.p.	−171 b.p.	−325 b.p.	−262 b.p.
+200	−137	−114	−218	−175
+100	− 69	− 56	−110	− 88
0	0	0	0	0
−100	+ 69	+ 62	+111	+ 89
−200	+139	+123	+223	+179
−300	+210	+188	+337	+270

TOTAL RETURN AND CONVEXITY

Cardholders do not vary their payment patterns significantly when general interest rate levels change. Since the monthly payment rate is relatively insensitive to interest rates and because the amortization period is condensed, credit card ABSs do not have the negative convexity problem found in mortgage-backed securities. Negative convexity refers to a security having less upside potential than downside risk for a given shift in interest rates. It results from the tendency of some prepayable assets, such as mortgages, to prepay faster when interest rates decline (and the security backed by the assets may be at a premium) than when interest rates rise.

Exhibit 4–9 shows the total return for the California Credit Card Trust 1987-A, 6.9 percent asset-backed certificates for various holding periods under different interest rate scenarios. Exhibit 4–10 shows the change in total return for the yield shifts shown in Exhibit 4–9.

OUTLOOK

Credit card receivables as assets for securitization have had an explosive start. Their unique characteristics and the unique needs of credit card issuers are likely to foster innovations of many different forms and

EXHIBIT 4–9
Comparison of Total Return — California Credit Card Trust 1987–A

	Holding Period			
Yield Shift	3 Months	6 Months	12 Months	18 Months
+300 b.p.	−7.29%	2.10%	6.66%	8.10%
+200	−1.97	4.39	7.33	8.23
+100	3.53	6.71	8.01	8.35
0	9.21	9.08	8.70	8.48
−100	15.09	11.49	9.39	8.61
−200	21.16	13.93	10.09	8.74
−300	27.44	16.43	10.80	8.87

Notes:
Purchase price is 97.50% with a yield of 8.42%.
Yields are corporate bond equivalent (CBE).
Assumes 7.0% reinvestment rate.

Source: The First Boston Corporation

EXHIBIT 4–10
Change in Total Return—California Credit Card Trust 1987–A

	Holding Period			
Yield Shift	3 Months	6 Months	12 Months	18 Months
+300 b.p.	−1650 b.p.	−698 b.p.	−204 b.p.	−38 b.p.
+200	−1118	−469	−137	−25
+100	−568	−237	− 69	−13
0	0	0	0	0
−100	+588	+241	+ 69	+13
−200	+1195	+485	+139	+26
−300	+1823	+735	+210	+39

structures over the next several years. This will happen in the context of rapid change in all areas of asset finance, including accounting, law, finance and taxation.

Market opportunities will continue to expand as these changes evolve and investors throughout the financial community become more familiar with credit card receivables. The number and diversity of credit card ABS issuers will increase not just among banks and thrifts but also among finance companies such as retailers and oil companies. Furthermore, the market for credit card asset-backed securities—now confined to the United States—will become global in scope.

APPENDIX A:
THE CREDIT CARD INDUSTRY

GENERAL

The credit card industry is highly complex with both internal and external competition. Credit cards compete directly with personal checks, traveler's checks, money orders, cash and other types of payment. There are various types of credit cards and, in the case of banks and retailers, thousands of competing issuers offering the same card type. Even with all the existing cards, new cards are being introduced (e.g., the Sears Discover card and the American Express Optima card). A user of credit cards can choose from a wide variety of service options with many different pricing structures.

Credit card accounts are consumer revolving credit facilities and generally are unsecured. General purpose cards, such as Visa or American Express, place few restrictions on what can be purchased and participating merchants are numerous. In the more limited case, such as retail cards and airline travel cards, use may be restricted either in the number of participating merchants or in the types of goods and services obtainable.

Credits cards are a multiuse service. They principally provide a convenient method for making payment and serve as a borrowing vehicle for the cardholder. They also provide other services such as aiding in identification. Cardholders value each service according to individual needs. The issuer's cost of providing these services can change as cardholder usage patterns change. The profit on any individual cardholder account, even ignoring credit losses, can be negligible or nonexistent. Only when viewed in aggregate can the effectiveness of a card issuer's pricing structure be evaluated.

The credit card industry is affected by many external events such as technological innovation in telecommunications and computers, tax and other legislation, and consumer trends. Technological innovation decreases the marginal cost of providing cardholder services even as recent tax legislation increased the cardholder's aftertax cost.

It is possible to divide the credit card industry into three parts: 1) a cardholder base that uses the cards to make purchases or cash advances and subsequently makes payments on the accounts; 2) a merchant base that accepts the cards, and 3) clearing operations that provide transaction processing and advance funds. Cardholders who use a card's revolving credit facility to pay their account balance in installments are known as "revolvers." Cardholders who pay in full each month without incurring finance charges are known as "convenience users."

TYPES OF CREDIT CARDS

Bank Cards

The most common type of credit card is the bank card, almost all of which are either MasterCard or Visa. Although the MasterCard and Visa associations establish uniform designs and logos for their respective cards, the cards themselves are actually issued by card-issuing member banks of the Visa or MasterCard systems. Merchants are enrolled into the system by merchant-signing ("acquiring") member banks.

The arrangement of having individual banks responsible for marketing both to the consumer and merchant bases, together with the generally lower annual cardholder and merchant discount fees of bank cards relative to other charge and credit cards, results in greater penetration of both the cardholder and merchant bases and in greater volume than any other card type. Although the Visa and MasterCard associations are fiercely competitive, most major banks offer both cards to their cardholder customers and merchant clients—a situation known as duality. Duality has made it possible for the two giants to cooperate on matters of common interest to their members, such as common merchant numbers, joint listing of lost and stolen cards, and competition with American Express.

The bank cards recently began to pursue the traditional customers of the more prestigious Travel & Entertainment cards. Both Visa and MasterCard launched premium (gold) cards in 1981 and are currently engaged in a joint effort to enroll more prestigious merchants.

Travel and Entertainment (T&E) Cards

T&E cards, by far the most common being American Express, are offered primarily as a payment service. Until its introduction of the Optima card, American Express avoided the cardholder option of revolving the regular account balance. American Express offers three T&E cards: the standard green card; the Gold Card, which comes with a revolving line of credit issued by a "participating financial institution"; and The Platinum Card, introduced in 1984.

American Express, like the other T&E cards, traditionally has been widely used by upscale business travelers because it has no preset credit limit. The merchant base, though smaller than that of the bank cards, includes more prestigious merchants because these cards are likely to be carried by out-of-town travelers and because they do not compete with the individual merchant's card programs for revolvers. Although bank cards have gained market share from the T&E cards, American Express is still the overwhelming favorite for business travel, particularly among foreign travelers.

In response to the recent inroads by bank cards, American Express is targeting more retail merchants and repositioning as more a general purpose card than solely a T&E card. American Express also introduced its series of Optima cards, which corresponds to the three T&E cards but, like bank cards, have a revolving credit option. Optima is available to current American Express cardholders who have been members in good standing for at least one year. The revolving credit feature is separated from the T&E cards to protect their image, yet provides a defense against the continuing gains of the premium bank cards. Optima appears to be competing on the basis of price for the upper end bank cardholders.

The two other T&E cards, Carte Blanche and Diners Club, now both issued by subsidiaries of Citicorp, have smaller cardholder and merchant bases and are still used primarily for travel and entertainment.

Retail Cards

Retail credit cards are offered by retailers both to facilitate purchases by their customers and to generate revenue otherwise lost to other credit cards as finance charges or merchant fees. Retail cards typically charge higher annual percentage rates than do bank cards but have no annual cardholder fee. Most programs are relatively small, although several, notably Sears, J.C. Penney, Montgomery Ward, and several oil companies, number their accounts in the millions.

Oil and other specialty cards are offered to consumers of a single line of products or services. Examples include oil company credit cards, used for tires, batteries and accessories, and the UATP card, used for airline tickets.

Financial Services Cards

Financial services cards are a comparatively recent development. They combine traditional credit card features with the ability to access savings, money market, and other investment accounts. Financial services cards are hampered in their consumer acceptance by their currently low penetration of the merchant base. They have the advantage of being backed by institutions with substantial assets (e.g., the Discover card is offered by a Sears subsidiary and the Choice card is offered by Citicorp). Sears has invested hundreds of millions of dollars in Discover and appears committed to its success.

THE MERCHANT BASE

The depth of the merchant base is a major factor in consumer acceptance of a credit card. Consumer acceptance is critical to generating volume since cardholders tend to concentrate their use in one or two cards. Because economies of scale are so important, any general purpose card must have the broadest possible merchant acceptance.

Both Visa and MasterCard have approximately equal merchant bases of about 2.5 million. A result of duality is that a bank offering either Visa or MasterCard to its merchants will generally offer the other. American Express has approximately 1 million merchants, Diners Club 800,000, and Discover about 550,000.

For merchants, credit cards offer convenience and ease of payment for their customers. They may also give the customer float on the transaction. Merchants who do not accept the credit cards their customers carry make shopping more difficult, less attractive and more expensive. Third-party credit cards (i.e., other than the merchant's own retail card) also eliminate fraud and credit risk. The merchant's cost in accepting a card is the inconvenience of administering the card program, the cost of training the merchant's personnel and the merchant discount fee paid for the use of the card.

Merchants issuing their own retail cards save the merchant discount fee, usually 2 to 7 percent of the transaction amount, and generate finance charge income, but incur the overhead cost, credit and fraud risk, and receivables financing cost. These costs can be considerable. Several surveys have indicated that most retail card programs are unprofitable largely because of the high receivables financing cost associated with the expensive equity component in retailers' cost of capital. To the extent that the merchants' own credit cards can help generate incremental sales, the loss may be recovered in other profit centers. Furthermore, if retailers are able to finance their accounts receivable without tying up equity, such as by using a credit card ABS structured as a sale, they may obtain additional financial benefits from their retail card programs.

Industry Concentration

The bank card market is becoming increasingly concentrated as a result of the acquisition of smaller portfolios by larger issuers. In 1985 the market share of the top 100 commercial bank card issuers increased from 73 to 78 percent. Consolidation will continue, in part, as a result of the trend toward consolidation in the banking, thrift, and other industries. Portfolio acquisitions, such as the sales of the credit card operations of Beneficial National Bank USA and MBank USA, are likely to continue.

The Battle for "Wallet Share"

As the market for credit cards becomes increasingly saturated and the propensity to acquire and use multiple cards (especially those with annual cardholder fees) declines, the battle has shifted to one of "wallet share" as each card issuer attempts to make its card the cardholder's preferred card and the last to be canceled. To achieve this, many card issuers are offering incentives tied to use, such as rebates to the cardholder or the cardholder's affinity group or free travel insurance. These incentives are likely to increase further the instability of the industry pricing structure as consumers choose between "no frills" and "full service" cards.

Trend Toward National Banking

The larger card issuers are using bank cards to extend a national presence. Competition is made keener by their aggressive marketing, which may take some of the profitability out of the industry. Currently, they are competing on the basis of the lower quality credits. Should rate wars develop, smaller issuers may be hurt.

APPENDIX B:
CREDIT CARD RECEIVABLES

YIELD CONSIDERATIONS

Card issuers generate revenue both from the cardholder and from the participating merchants. Merchant revenues are principally the merchant discount fees discussed in Appendix A.

Cardholder revenue is generated from two primary sources, finance charges and annual cardholder fees. Finance charges are assessed based either on the amount of credit extended, such as the fee on cash advances, or the amount outstanding, or both. Finance charges are the principal component of portfolio yield for most issuers, although annual cardholder fees and merchant discount fees can also be very significant, especially for T&E cards. The annual cardholder fee is a fixed amount, though it may be paid monthly. Additional fees include late penalty fees, lost-card fees, over-limit fees, extra-card fees, per transaction fees and service fees for such things as checks returned for insufficient funds.

The portfolio yield realized from the annual percentage rate (APR) on the receivables is usually less than the APR since most issuers have an interest-free grace period. The relationship between the APR and the portfolio yield for issuers with grace periods depends on such factors as the incidence of convenience use and the length of the grace period. The portfolio yield, however, tends to be about 90 percent of the APR for credit cards with grace periods. Because cardholders can pay off their account balances at any time, usually without penalty, the APR charged is a market rate. The competitive effect, however, is mitigated by several factors:

• When selecting a credit card, many cardholders do not expect to be revolvers. They accept the card expecting to be convenience users. Only after they have a card does the revolving behavior develop. Once cardholders become revolvers, however, they often consolidate their card debt with a lower cost card. Some card issuers target these highly profitable accounts by offering incentives, such as tiered pricing for large balances, to acquire or retain them.

• Most cardholders are unaware of the APR charged on their account. In a recent American Bankers Association survey, 40 percent of bank cardholders questioned were unaware of their card's APR, although the awareness level may be increasing.

• The finance charges assessed are normally quite small, since the balance outstanding is usually small. The savings from moving from a 19 percent finance charge to a 14 percent finance charge is only $50 per year for any account with a $1,000 average balance. Since most revolvers do not revolve all year, the savings are even less. Much of these savings are offset in the first year by the annual cardholder fee on the new card.

Annual cardholder fees are usually assessed once a year in advance, although they may also be assessed monthly. The fee is usually assessed whether or not the card is used. When a cardholder payment is received by the card issuer, any unpaid annual cardholder fee is satisfied prior to unpaid finance charges or principal. The portfolio yield effect of the annual cardholder fee, therefore, is relatively stable.

State and Consumer Group Activity

Many states have usury laws, which limit the finance charges and annual cardholder fees that may be assessed on credit cards. Recently, with profits on credit card portfolios at record highs, several states, including Texas and Connecticut, have enacted or lowered interest rate and fee ceilings. In Texas, many of the major banks moved their card operations to Delaware. Other states (e.g., Illinois, Georgia, Oregon, South Carolina, and Indiana) have also considered ceilings. The Georgia Legislature, however, recently enacted legislation that removed all interest rate and annual cardholder fee caps in an effort to attract more card issuers to the state and boost employment.

The practical effect of state usury laws is limited as a result of the 1978 U.S. Supreme Court decision in the suit brought by Marquette National Bank of Minneapolis against First National Bank of Omaha. Marquette sought to enforce a Minnesota usury law against First National, a Nebraska bank. The Court found that federal law granted banks the right to export the rate of interest permitted under the laws of their home state. As a result of this decision, banks in several states with restrictive usury laws relocated their operations, including their portfolios of credit card accounts, to states with a more favorable business climate. State usury laws still apply to issuers located within the state.

Consumer groups are increasingly active in encouraging consumers to be more conscious of high credit card finance charge rates. Furthermore, a number of politicians use high finance charge rates as a political issue. In Illinois, the State Treasurer withdrew state funds from First National Bank of Chicago because of its refusal to lower interest rates charged on its cards. The introduction of Optima by American Express, with its 13.5 percent initial APR, intensified consumer group and political pressure on bank card issuers to lower rates.

Federal Usury Legislation

In recent years, a number of bills have been proposed in Congress that would restrict the amount of finance charges and annual cardholder fees charged on credit cards. Most of these bills propose a ceiling based upon a spread to some floating index, such as 4 percent plus the IRS interest on overdue tax payments or 5 percent plus the Federal Reserve discount rate at the time of the transaction. Although the legislation's benefits for consumers are uncertain, the motivation is apparent. In a statement on his introduction of an early version of the Credit Cardholder Protection Act, Senator D'Amato wrote:

> Lenders are taking advantage of consumer dependence on credit cards. The average interest rate charged on credit card purchases is currently 19.2 percent, with some companies charging as high as 21.6 percent, even though banks now lend much of their money at a mere 9.5 percent. I am hard pressed to believe that the average credit card issuer requires a 9.7 percent margin over the prime rate to cover the risk and costs involved in issuing a credit card.[2]

A study by the staff of the Federal Reserve, however, estimates that earlier versions of both legislative proposals, had they been in effect from 1972 to 1985, would have resulted in losses on bank card portfolios in 10 of those 14 years and only marginal profits in 2 years. Since retail cards have generally higher interest rates than bank cards and already appear to operate at a loss, retailers would be affected even more substantially than banks by any applicable usury laws.

Although many card issuers may be hurt, the effects on cardholders may be even more severe. Card issuers, in response to national usury ceilings, may take several actions which, from the investor's perspective, would have the effect of lowering portfolio yield but increasing portfolio quality. Such actions may include the following:

- Tightening credit standards on issuing cards, renewing cards, and raising credit limits—making it more difficult for younger or low-income families and marginal credit risk consumers to qualify
- More strictly enforcing policies on delinquencies
- Reducing or eliminating the interest-free grace period for convenience users
- Raising merchant discount fees, possibly increasing the cost of goods and services typically bought using credit cards

---

[2] Press release, Office of Sen. Alphonse D'Amato, January 6, 1987.

- Increasing minimum payment terms
- Raising the annual cardholder fee and other fees (e.g., late fee, per transaction fee)

Passage of federal usury legislation in the near future is improbable, despite recent activity in the House Banking Subcommittee on Consumer Affairs, because of the effect of interest rate caps on both card issuers and consumers. It is more likely, however, that legislation may be passed requiring fuller and more frequent disclosure of the payment terms and fees on credit card accounts.

CREDIT QUALITY CONSIDERATIONS

As with other consumer receivables, the primary determinants of the credit quality of a credit card receivables portfolio are the credit guidelines and procedures used to select the cardholders. Unlike other forms of consumer debt, credit cards involve periodic credit reviews. Credit reviews can occur with each use of the card and with each renewal of the credit card account. This credit review can be based on the actual behavior of the cardholder, which is a better determinant of credit quality than prescreening.

Issuers market their credit card products by targeting groups defined to increase the likelihood of a targeted consumer applying for, or accepting, the issuer's card and minimizing the number of credit rejects. The type of marketing program is indicative of the portfolio credit quality likely to ensue, particularly for less seasoned accounts.

- *Preapproved applications.* The Truth in Lending Act prohibits the mailing of unsolicited credit cards to prospective cardholders. Issuers, however, may mail preapproved account applications conditioned only upon the prospective cardholder signing and returning the application. Generally, the credit quality of such portfolios is lower until seasoning selects out the bad accounts. It is, however, an effective way to gain market share.
- *Prescreened applications.* By targeting specific groups of consumers, card issuers are able to identify selected information about prospective cardholders that can be used to shorten the application process. If the issuer correctly identifies the cardholder information, the credit evaluation should be as valid as a full application review. Since the targeted group has some common characteristics, however, the performance of the resulting portfolio, even if a full credit check is used, may differ, for better or worse, from a random solicitation. Therefore, an evaluation of prescreened marketing programs is helpful in evaluating a portfolio.

• *Affinity groups.* Affinity group marketing programs, which may also be preapproved, involve soliciting prospective cardholders who share an affiliation, such as having graduated from the same university, with the affinity group's endorsement. As with prescreened programs, the respondents are likely to perform in a manner that differs statistically from a random solicitation of accounts. By using the affinity group's endorsement—often secured by card issuer payments to the affinity group in an amount based upon cardholder usage—a card issuer can obtain otherwise unavailable membership lists and may achieve greater card volume if the cardholders/affinity group members see this as a way of supporting their organization.

Delinquencies and outstandings are seasonal, peaking after the holiday period. Delinquencies correspond to the level of cardholders' debt burden: because this is unsecured debt and cardholders probably have other credit cards available to them, the immediate effects to the cardholder of delinquency are less severe than with other forms of debt.

Losses on newly-issued credit cards go through a loss cycle with two peaks. The first peak occurs when the accounts first reach the age when they can be charged off, typically four to six months. The second peak occurs at about one and a half years. Losses on more seasoned accounts are often associated with major events in the cardholder's life, such as unemployment or divorce. For this reason, loss rates correspond to the unemployment rate. Both yield and credit performance on an account tend to increase with each year of seasoning. Although the seasoning effect on yield and credit performance is minor after the second year, the combined effect on credit-adjusted yield can be significant.

Recoveries on charge-offs tend to be received long after charge-off and in relatively small amounts. This is largely because as unsecured debt there is no collateral to repossess. Issuers can look only to recoveries from the cardholder. Further, because of their unsecured status, card issuers have a greater interest than secured lenders in working with the cardholder in a debt work-out situation rather than forcing a bankruptcy, which could result in a complete loss for the issuer.

Exhibits 4–11 and 4–12 show losses as a percent of charge volume and outstanding receivables respectively. These exhibits illustrate the effect of monthly payment rates on loss rates. For example, although American Express has the lowest loss rate as a percentage of gross sales volume, its monthly payment rate, and therefore receivable turnover, is much higher than that of the bank cards and results in higher losses as a percentage of outstandings. For this reason, many card issuers, including American Express, quote loss data in terms of volume, especially when the principal component of income is also based on volume (i.e., merchant discount fees).

EXHIBIT 4–11
Net Charge-Offs as a Percentage of Gross Sales Volume

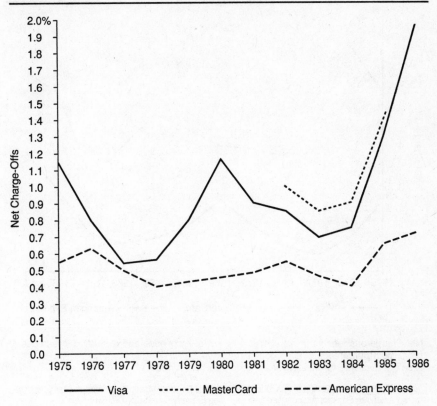

Notes:
Net Charge-offs reflects gross charge-offs, net of recoveries and excluding losses due to fraud, as a percentage of gross sales volume.
Data not available for MasterCard prior to 1982 or for 1986.

  Sources: Based on data from Visa Quarterly Statistical Reports, MasterCard International as reported by the American Bankers Association, and American Express Credit Corporation Forms 10-K.

Roll Rate Analysis

Roll rate analysis may be performed by a credit card issuer to project future portfolio credit losses by using current portfolio performance data. Roll rate analysis traces from month to month the percentage of receivables that are in the various stages of delinquency. It has a high level of reliability because

EXHIBIT 4–12
Net Charge-Offs as a Percentage of Outstandings

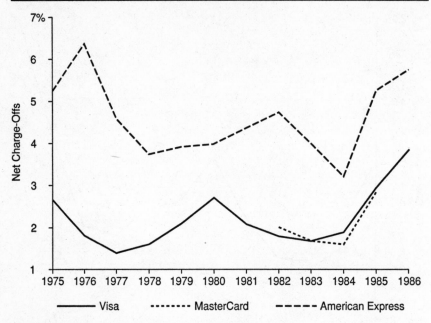

Notes:
Net Charge-offs reflects gross charge-offs, net of recoveries and excluding losses due to fraud, as a percentage of average outstandings.
Data not available for MasterCard prior to 1982 or for 1986.

Sources: Based on data from Visa Quarterly Statistical Reports, MasterCard International as reported by the American Bankers Association, and American Express Credit Corporation Forms 10-K.

of the statistical accuracy that large numbers of small account balances provide.

Roll rate analysis relies on the practice of most card issuers of not charging off accounts until they are several months delinquent, usually six months. Using actual portfolio data, the percentage of one month delinquent receivables that subsequently become two or more months delinquent can be calculated for each delinquency category. Using these aging or roll rates, it is possible to forecast the amount of receivables originated this month that will be charged off six months from now. Additional adjustments are made for events, such as bankruptcy or death of the cardholder, that can occur at any time during this delinquency aging process.

CARDHOLDER PAYMENT PATTERNS

The cardholder monthly payment rate determines the speed at which credit card ABSs amortize during the amortization period. Although this rate varies industry-wide, over time it tends to remain within a fairly narrow range. Changes to a specific portfolio's monthly payment rate can be more dramatic and result from changes in the card's payment terms, such as removal of a card's grace period.

A portfolio's monthly payment rate is dependent on the amount of convenience use and the payment terms of the card. Convenience use is independent of general interest rates. It is largely a function of the existence and length of the grace period and whether the card carries a revolving option. For credit cards with a revolving option, the minimum monthly payment is intended to ensure compliance with the loan terms and generally bears little relationship to

EXHIBIT 4–13
Monthly Payment Rate—Visa

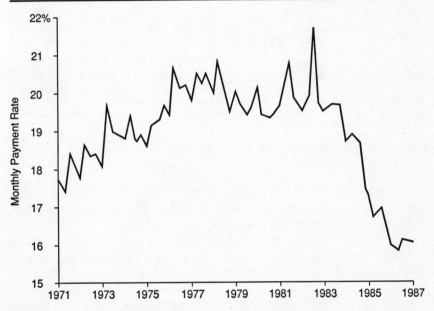

Note:
Monthly Payment Rate per quarter by Visa cardholders in the U.S.

Source: Based on data from Visa Quarterly Statistical Reports.

EXHIBIT 4–14
Monthly Payment Rate—American Express

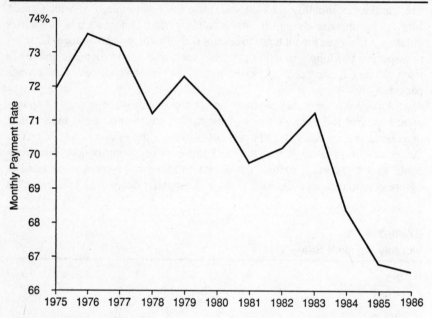

Note:
Monthly Payment Rate per annum by American Express cardholders in the U.S. Derived from the average life of cardmember receivables per annum, assuming a 360-day year. American Express figures reflect those receivables primarily from U.S. cardholders and, to a small degree, from Canadian cardholders, purchased by American Express Credit Corporation from American Express Company.

Source: Based on data from American Express Credit Corporation Forms 10-K.

what is actually received, on average, by the portfolio. Thus, the card issuer's payment terms for its cards, rather than the APR or general interest rate levels, is the primary determinant of the monthly payment rate.

Exhibit 4–13 shows trends for Visa—bank cards generally have a minimum monthly payment of 3 to 5 percent of the balance outstanding. Exhibit 4–14 shows the corresponding trend for American Express—T&E cards require payment in full each month.

CHAPTER 5

SECURITIZING TRADE AND LEASE RECEIVABLES

Glenn B. McClelland, Jr., Vice President
James W. McDonald, Jr., Vice President
Citicorp North America

INTRODUCTION

The focus of this chapter is on some of the problems faced by corporate clients and investors in issuing and purchasing securitized assets and on the benefits they can realize from securitization. In a broad sense, this chapter deals with the use of a new financial tool as a means of assisting corporate management in better shaping its balance sheet, allocating its scarce equity resources and increasing shareholder value. It is a means of helping management tailor the capital structures of their different businesses to achieve these businesses' full potential for growth and returns.

While it is a relatively new corporate finance technique, securitization has emerged as a flexible and useful tool that has moved rapidly into the mainstream of financial technology.

Perhaps at a more technical level, the most important concept relating to asset securitization from the standpoint of the seller is that a securitization decision is really an investment decision and not simply a financing alternative. When an asset is allowed to remain on the balance sheet, in effect, a decision has been made to invest capital in this asset for a period of time. This means that both debt and equity have been allocated to support this asset. Therefore, the hold versus securitize decision should always entail an evaluation of the alternative uses to which that capital could be put if it could be freed up through securitization, and the cost of securitization should be compared to a firm's cost of capital.

In its simplest form, the concept of allocating some combination of debt and equity to support each asset is apparent from an examination of the most basic form of a balance sheet (see Exhibit 5-1).

This is particularly evident when one pictures the development of a balance sheet from the startup of a company. From this perspective, the acquisition of each asset is an investment decision and each asset acquired must somehow be financed. As a balance sheet matures into the assets, liabilities, and equity that will support an ongoing business, a particular target capital structure emerges as a desirable objective. It then becomes meaningful to talk about the cost of owning assets in terms of the weighted average cost of capital of the firm.

As a further refinement to this process, an argument is often made that each investment decision should be made by comparing cost of capital to returns on equivalent-risk investments traded in the capital market (i.e., using different hurdle rates to evaluate each category of investment) and not simply to a firm's overall weighted average cost of capital. In this way, different return expectations for individual types of businesses can be matched against the perceived amount of risk of the undertaking in question. One can also argue that the net present value of an investment computed in this way should be further adjusted by the net present value of the financing decision associated with making the investment. In other words, each investment decision thus becomes

EXHIBIT 5–1

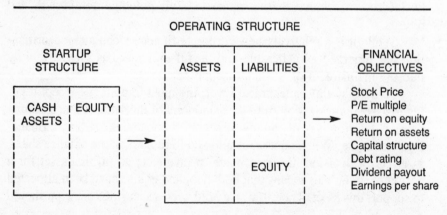

interactive with the means used to finance it. And what should really be measured is the combined impact of both the investment and financing decision on a firm's overall financial structure and its aggregate cost of capital:

$$^1\text{Adjusted NPV} = \text{Investment NPV} + \text{NPV of financing decisions}$$
$$\text{caused by project acceptance.}$$

To a large degree, the argument for asset securitizaton is that it promotes diversification of risk, which benefits asset originators by giving them more financial flexibility and access to investors. This chapter is written for the practitioner interested in understanding practical applications of asset securitization from the point of view of originator and investor.

THE INVESTOR

From a debt investor's perspective, buying a securitized financial instrument offers an opportunity to diversify obligor risk and to substantially isolate the financial risk of the portfolio of assets supporting the security from the operating risks of the asset originator. From an equity investor's point of view, securitization provides an opportunity for improved value if the companies whose shares they hold use the cash proceeds from assets sold to retire stock or to reinvest into assets that yield a higher return.

THE SELLER

Today's technology for the securitization of accounts receivable and lease assets offers management of financial and industrial companies the ability to significantly enhance shareholder value if it is used judiciously

---

[1]A good description of what is referred to as an "Adjusted-Present-Value Rule" is contained in Brealey and Myers *Principals of Corporate Finance*. For purposes of this discussion, it is sufficient to say that the net present value of an investment in an asset can be improved if it can be shown that the net present value of financing decisions associated with financing the investment is also positive. At a minimum, a negative net present value of any financing decision should not be greater than the positive net present value of the investment. The mathematics of this calculation are not overly complicated. The most difficult aspect of this methodology is describing the impact of financing decisions on the debt capacity and overall cost of capital of the firm. A simple debt to debt cost comparison is insufficient.

as part of an integrated financial plan. To be most effective, these techniques should be used in a way that is consistent with a firm's overall operating strategy and with a knowledge of the cash flow dynamics and risk characteristics associated with the firm's business. Just as each seller or originator of receivables may have a different financial reason for using asset securitization, the ratings of sellers in various Citicorp-managed receivables securitizations also span a wide range (see Exhibit 5–2).

THE OPERATING CYCLE

Every business ultimately faces the test of whether, over time, the revenue generated from its operations will exceed its expenses. In addition, survivability and financial and operating independence often hinges on such fundamentals as ensuring that adequate cash is available when required and in protecting against catastrophic loss. In its simplest form, a firm can be understood by focusing on its operating cycle or, in more complex cases, by focusing on the operating cycles of each of its component businesses. A firm must also demonstrate an ability to achieve competitive growth rates while achieving returns on equity substantially higher than its cost of capital. Failure to do so often results in market to book ratios of less than 1:1, poor returns to investors, and vulnerability to hostile takeovers.

EXHIBIT 5–2
Profile of Participants

	Combined Citicorp Programs		
S&P	Number	Size ($mm)	Percent
AAA	9	$1,210	16%
AA	6	1,674	22%
A	13	1,587	21%
BBB	17	2,175	29%
Nonrated	10	895	12%
	55	$7,541	100%

MEASUREMENT

An "operating cycle" is the interval between the purchase of essential materials used in production, inventory items, and their ultimate conversion into cash. For a business operating on an ongoing basis, the cycle emerges from the pattern of its cash transactions and the interplay of its own marketing and production activities and those of its competition, customers, and suppliers. This becomes clear in a practical sense when one considers the components of an operating cycle and how these vary under different circumstances.

A normal operating cycle consists of:

- A purchase date
- An adjustment for contractual payment terms (days accounts payable)
- A manufacturing and/or warehousing period
- The date of sale
- Actual liquidation of customer accounts receivable

Thus, from a study of how this pattern changes over time, one can get an insight into the business of a firm and a feeling for the "cash intensity" of its operation—a measure of the cash needed to fund growth. In practice, this picture gets vastly more complicated as actual settlement of payables and collections of receivables vary from contractual terms. It is also complicated by variations in nonoperating cash flows, such as those required for investments in capital equipment and research and development, and by changing levels of expenses for administration, taxes, and dividend payments.

VARIATIONS IN CIRCUMSTANCE

Nevertheless, an analysis of the operating cycle of a firm provides important clues to changes in its operation and its relative dependence on external sources of cash to finance its growth. Consider the following simplified examples:

1. A generic case (see Exhibit 5–3). In this example, the firm has a relatively balanced relationship between the credit extended to it by its suppliers and the payment terms it gives its customers. Thus, this

EXHIBIT 5–3

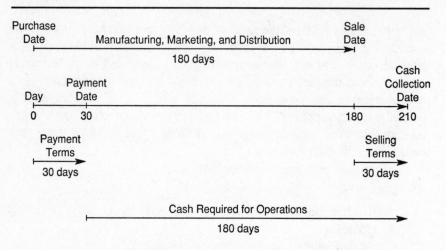

firm's operating cash requirements are principally determined by its manufacturing, marketing, and distribution efficiency and it will generally have to fund its operating requirements for only 180 days.

2. Improved purchasing terms (see Exhibit 5–4). In this second example, the firm has been able to cut its operating cash requirements

EXHIBIT 5–4

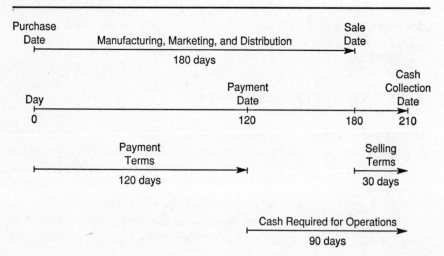

in half by negotiating more favorable payment terms from its suppliers without changing the terms of credit it grants its customers. In extreme cases, sellers may grant payment terms that fully cover the firm's working capital requirements. This may be done for several reasons: the firm in the middle is a service firm with a relatively simple production process that adds value and a markup; or the recipient of credit is in a relatively more powerful bargaining position; or, the firm granting the credit is deliberately attempting to use the granting of credit to improve the competitiveness of its customers and thereby benefit itself.

This brings us to our next examples:

3. Extended production period (see Exhibit 5–5).

4. Extended payment terms (see Exhibit 5–6).

Both examples 3 and 4 suggest that generating cash for working capital may present a significant competitive challenge, particularly if the cash requirements that arise out of an extended operating cycle increase dramatically. This situation can arise from any number of circumstances that extend production times or force the granting of extended credit terms for competitive reasons. Variations of the operating cycle of a firm together with the requirements for cash investments in nonoperating items, such as capital or technological equipment and research and

EXHIBIT 5–5

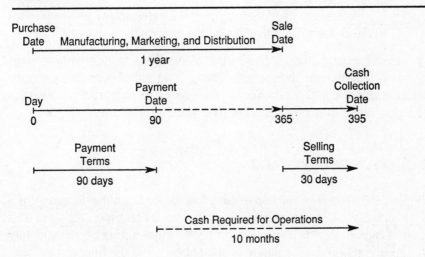

EXHIBIT 5–6

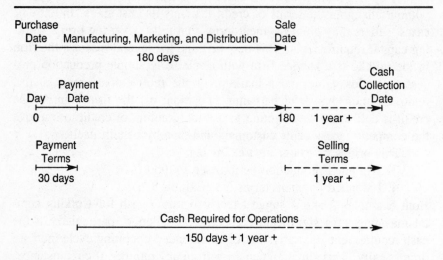

development, are principal determinants of the "asset intensity" of a business. Asset intensity is defined as the level of sales that can be generated with a given level of assets. In each case, the following questions must be asked:

- Is the operating margin sufficient to cover the cost of financing the firm's operating cycle?
- Is it possible to charge enough for the extension of payment terms to cover the relevant return on investment?

Asset securitization activities that allow firms to efficiently manage the cash requirements businesses need to fund growth can add a significant competitive weapon to the arsenal needed to support management's struggle for sales growth, market share, and profitability.

EQUITY AND LEVERAGE

In part, the answer to the above questions depends on the adequacy of a firm's equity and on the relationship between its return on equity and its cost of capital. Another question is whether the resulting capital structure is appropriate, given the nature of the industry and the financial strategy of the competition.

To illustrate this dilemma, let's consider some of the differences between finance companies and operating companies (see Exhibit 5–7).

In fact, we know that in the real world it is often increasingly difficult to distinguish between so-called finance and operating companies. Some industrial companies have built large captive finance entities and many large financial service firms are performing a wide range of activities beyond the realm of traditional banking. In the past, attempts to lessen the resulting confusion of investors included the reporting of captive finance companies on an unconsolidated basis. Proposed changes in consolidation accounting scheduled to take effect in 1988 (Statement of Financial Accounting Standards No. 94; consolidation of all majority-owned subsidiaries) will add to this confusion by requiring these to be consolidated. As it is, current bankruptcy law makes it difficult to isolate the bankruptcy risk of a parent company from captive finance subsidiaries.

The result:

• Credit rating agencies often must disaggregate a firm's activities to determine appropriate levels of equity and leverage for each type of business and then recombine them to produce a rating for the corporation as a whole.

• Debt investors often have to make investment choices involving firms in a complex array of businesses possessing some of the disadvantages of leverage and some of the uncertainties of operating risk, product liability, and vulnerability to environmental hazard litigation.

EXHIBIT 5–7

Finance Companies	*Operating Companies*
Assets fundamentally liquid	Assets fundamentally illiquid
Lower operating risk—focus on "collectability"	High operating risk—focus on design, production, and marketing
Assets large in relation to "sales"	Sales large relative to assets
Profitability mainly a function of managing financial risk and the development of a comparative advantage in credit and services	Profitability mainly a function of managing operating risk and the development of product and marketing expertise
Low margin	High margin
High leverage	Moderate leverage

• Equity investors with equally specific investment preferences also often find their choices complicated by firms whose overall return on equity is reduced by the need to support relatively large portfolios of financial assets yielding returns below their overall ROE objectives.

• Firms seeking to raise capital may thus find themselves confronted by a situation where the complexity of their operations and their inability to fully separate financial and operating risk results in higher than acceptable costs of debt and equity, as investors charge them a premium to offset perceived complexities.

POLICY CHOICES

Attempted solutions to the above dilemma have encompassed a wide range of options:

- A spinoff of dissimilar operating companies
- Asset sales
- Sale and lease-back activities
- The use of captive finance companies
- Stock repurchases
- Franchising of successful operations
- Joint ventures
- Third-party financed vendor leasing operations
- Large minority investments in affiliated businesses

In one way or another, these activities can achieve the following results:

- Simplify third-party analysis
- Improve overall returns to shareholders
- Substitute third-party equity for self funding
- Improve sustainable growth rates
- Improve investor perceptions of management strategy

SEPARATION OF FINANCIAL AND OPERATING RISK

Recently, asset securitization has become an important tool for many major corporations because it may achieve many of the above objectives and also make it easier for management to separate elements of financial and operating risk.

SUSTAINABLE GROWTH RATES

Before examining examples of the use of asset securitization for specific portfolios of financial assets, it is helpful to review some familiar analytical tools and to suggest ways in which these may be useful in measuring corporate financial performance and improving shareholder value.

A sustainable growth rate is the growth rate in earnings that can be maintained over time. This ability to sustain growth is in part a function of what a firm earns and what it reinvests in its business. As a simplification, if one considers earnings as a proxy for cash generation, this concept can be expressed by considering sustainable growth as a function of a firm's return on equity (ROE) and the rate at which earnings are reinvested in the business (the reinvestment rate).

Hence,

$$\text{Sustainable growth} = \text{ROE} \times \text{Reinvestment Rate}$$
$$\text{or SG} = \text{ROE} \times (1 - \text{Dividend Rate})$$

Return of equity may be defined as

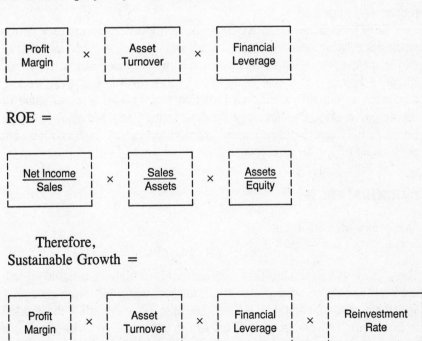

ROE =

Therefore,
Sustainable Growth =

SG =

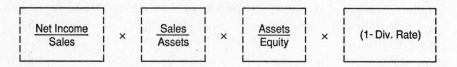

$$\boxed{\frac{\text{Net Income}}{\text{Sales}}} \times \boxed{\frac{\text{Sales}}{\text{Assets}}} \times \boxed{\frac{\text{Assets}}{\text{Equity}}} \times \boxed{(1 - \text{Div. Rate})}$$

Thus, it follows that sustainable growth rates can be increased by:

- Increasing profit margins
- Improving asset turnover
- Increasing financial leverage
- Increasing the reinvestment rate (lowering the dividend pay-out rate)

These considerations are particularly important because a firm's market value and return to shareholders are in part a function of its sustainable growth rate and its relative performance or operating efficiency. Asset securitization can have a positive impact on sustainable growth by helping improve profit margins by lowering interest costs and freeing up cash for higher yielding investments. This in turn can boost ROE and reduce asset intensity.

Both growth rates and ROE can have important effects on a firm's stock price, which can be demonstrated when ROE, growth, and cost of capital measures are combined as a measure of performance. Increased financial leverage can also be helpful in this regard. However, securitization is a valuable additional tool that can be used without some of the negative effects of leverage on debt ratings and financial coverage ratios. It may also be useful when borrowing to retire high coupon debt as restricted by indenture covenants.

PERFORMANCE

One proxy for performance is:

$$\text{ROE} - \text{Cost of Capital}$$

Thus, markets will reward firms that can achieve high sustainable growth rates and relatively large positive spreads between their return on equity and their cost of capital. This can be seen by comparing the market to book ratios of competitive firms in the same industry. In general, it can be shown that favorable performance and relatively high sustainable growth rates will be rewarded with relatively higher market value.

In principle, the relationships between a company's market-to-book ratio and its sustainable growth rate and performance can be expressed as follows:

$$\frac{\text{Market Value}}{\text{Book Value}} = \frac{\text{ROE} - \text{Growth}}{\text{Cost of Capital} - \text{Growth}}$$

Thus, for a firm with a ROE of 16 percent, a cost of capital of 16 percent, and a sustainable growth rate of 12 percent, the firm's theoretical market-to-book ratio would be calculated:

$$\frac{16\% - 12\%}{16\% - 12\%} = \frac{4}{4} = 1$$

An improved ROE to 18 percent, would have the following results:

$$\frac{18\% - 12\%}{16\% - 12\%} = \frac{6}{4} = 1.5{:}1$$

Therefore, it is possible to show that a 2 percent change in ROE in this scenario can increase a company's market-to-book ratio by 50 percent. Correspondingly, a decrease in ROE to 14 percent—less than the cost of capital—would have the following result:

$$\frac{14\% - 12\%}{16\% - 12\%} = \frac{2}{4} = 0.5$$

Thus, holding the sustainable growth rate constant, it can be shown that a company whose book value per share is $20 should have a market value between $30 and $10 per share, depending on whether ROE gains 2 percent or shrinks 2 percent. Increased sustainable growth rates accentuate this result. Consequently, a firm's accumulation of shareholder wealth or ultimate "decapitalization" can depend significantly on such basic ratios as profit margin, asset turnover, financial leverage, and dividend policy. Therefore, asset securitization activities can be valuable tools in managing these results toward corporate objectives.

BENEFITS OF ASSET SECURITIZATION

Securitization involves structuring portfolios of financial assets in such a way that enables them to be sold as a package to investors. Investors provide funding for this process by purchasing notes or securities, the repayment of which is backed by the acquired assets and their associated cash flows. Asset securitization transactions typically involve the use of a trust or third-party investor who acquires and holds ownership interests in these pools for the benefit of the noteholders. Investors typically look primarily to the asset cash flows for repayment of their notes and have only limited recourse to the seller. Debt investors diversify their risk and usually improve their yields from these transactions. In addition, in the case of true sales and most limited recourse transactions, investors gain a substantial separation between financial risk of their cash flows and the seller's operating risks.

Sellers potentially obtain greater access to a broader base of investors, improved returns on assets, higher asset turnover ratios, reserve debt capacity, and a resulting improved return on equity. In addition, depending on the use of proceeds and the fit of asset securitization within an overall operating and financial strategy, an asset securitization program may significantly enhance the company's ability to increase sales and provide competitive funding for their customers, at given levels of equity. Equity investors in turn may benefit from the firm's increased operating efficiency and perceived lower risk due to the company's reduced need to hold high levels of financial assets. These benefits are considerably magnified when a company's operating cycle requires a substantial infusion of cash to finance growth. Banks and investment banks may earn substantial fee income by structuring and distributing asset-backed securities.

SECURITIZATION OF ACCOUNTS RECEIVABLE

Accounts receivable, such as trade and lease receivables, are often ideal candidates for asset securitization. Trade accounts receivable are typically noninterest bearing or are interest bearing at rates that do not meet internal hurdle rates. Various forms of term receivables, including leases, may be interest bearing but are often of long enough tenor so that a substantial allocation of corporate equity is required to support their rapid growth in relation to sales.

Typical Investment Criteria

Considerations that are generally important to prospective investors in securities backed by receivables include:
• Has the underlying pool's performance been strong, with low loss levels and consistency over a number of years?

Although loss experience is historic and may not be relied on exclusively as a predictor of future performance, it is one of the key indicators of the quality of a receivables pool. Before deciding to acquire a portfolio, a trade receivables investment company analyzes both the level and consistency of loss experience for each pool over a number of years. For each pool, an appropriate loss reserve is established at a significant multiple of this loss experience.

• Does the seller have a *sound credit and collection process* and is the data generated sufficient to provide the investor with the information he needs to monitor the portfolio?

Originating companies are usually appointed servicing agent and the ability of these companies to manage receivables collection is scrutinized before a securitization program is completed; this collection process must be audited regularly thereafter.

• Is there a provision for a backup servicer in the event of liquidation?

TRADE RECEIVABLES

Trade receivables generally are both low risk and highly liquid. These obligations arise from the sale of merchandise, insurance, or services to manufacturers, distributors, retailers, or consumers and represent claims for goods already sold and services already performed. Therefore, the payment obligation of and cash flow from obligors does not depend on future earnings of the seller. Loss experience on typical nonconsumer receivables tends to be very low. These low loss rates are evidence of the mutually beneficial relationship between a commercial/industrial buyer and a seller of goods. Losses on consumer receivables do tend to be higher, but this experience is typically quite stable and predictable because of the actuarial base contained in this type of receivables pool.

Most trade receivables are payable within 30 to 60 days of invoicing and, as a result, a portfolio of receivable pools tends to have a rapid turnover.

These portfolios include a diversity of obligors, pools and sellers in 22 industries. Exhibit 5–12 shows the composition of Citicorp-managed trade receivables securitization programs as of Dec. 31, 1987.

Types of Receivable Pools

There are basically three types of trade receivable pools. They are retail, commercial and wholesale.

EXHIBIT 5–12

Basic Elements	Combined Citicorp Programs
Diversification	
Obligors	19,774,000
Pools	68
Sellers	55
Inherent Liquidity	
Turnover	6.5X/56 Days
Annual Volume	$43.6 Billion

Retail
• Those arising from sales to a large number of customers, typically 100,000 or more, where balances due per customer are modest.

Retail receivable pools are statistically homogeneous due to the large number of obligors and the relatively low variation in individual account exposure. There is an actuarial basis for prediction of losses, permitting substantial credit protection from a reserve that is a relatively low multiple of loss experience. In establishing reserves for this type of receivable, it's important to protect investors if future loss experience should increase to several times the historical norm.

Department stores, oil companies, or financial institutions with retail credit card portfolios have receivable pools with these characteristics.

Commercial
• Those arising from commercial or industrial sales to a broad base of customers, usually 5,000 or more, with typical balances due per customer ranging from about $10,000 to $40,000.

These commercial receivable pools have a greater variation in individual obligor exposure. Because these pools frequently include a limited number of obligors with larger than average account balances, loss reserves for these pools are established at levels that provide adequate credit protection against any concentration risk that may arise as a result.

Manufacturers that sell through a large number of distribution outlets or capital goods manufacturers that sell large ticket items to consumers or other companies are examples of companies that generate commercial receivables.

Wholesale

- Those arising from sales to a limited number (less than 100) of customers with balances due per customer typically being over $1 million.

In industries with this type of receivables profile, customer relationships tend to be relatively stable over a long period of time with suppliers and customers getting to know each other well. In this case, it is not uncommon for losses to be extremely low and sometimes nonexistent. A review of a portfolio with large obligor concentrations includes a performance review and an in-depth credit review of each large obligor.

Receivables in this category are often created when the seller's products are used as a part of a buyer's manufacturing process—either as raw materials or as capital equipment used in manufacturing.

Others

In addition to these types of receivables, there are also many other streams of predictable financial payments that may be securitizable even if they are subject to future performance for payment.

In all cases, the strength of the credit process of the financial intermediary structuring a transaction and its ability to provide ongoing monitoring and reporting services are critical to gaining investor confidence and making the transaction work. This is true in part because certain receivables are not good candidates for securitization where future payment is unpredictable, subject to offset or cancellation, or where the payment history is erratic or subject to change in the future. Knowing what to measure and how to structure adequate protection for investors is a skill developed from years of experience. Thus, the experience of firms structuring securitized transactions, the strength of their credit process, and their commitment to asset monitoring and follow up auditing are critical to investor confidence.

REPRESENTATIVE TRANSACTIONS

The previous section described various categories of receivable pools. In actuality, receivable pools of commercial and industrial companies vary widely. They are typically much more heterogeneous than the automobile (CARS) and consumer credit card receivables (CARDS) currently being securitized in public markets.

We have already seen that firms may wish to securitize receivables to meet stock price or return on asset objectives, improve sustainable growth rates, and to supply additional equity. These decisions are essentially investment decisions, not just financing decisions.

The flexibility of these transactions is illustrated in these examples:

• A triple-A rated company with a high ROE may want to maintain a high stock price and need to continuously ensure that funds are freed up from low yielding assets and reinvested in uses with higher returns.

• A triple-B rated company may need additional access to investors without damaging its debt ratings.

• Some companies may want an additional source of funds to meet special needs, such as acquisitions and other major capital expenditures.

• A highly-leveraged company with an undervalued stock may want to take itself out of leveraged buy out (LBO) contention by buying back shares without incurring additional debt, or by increasing the dividend or issuing a special dividend. In addition, selling receivables removes a near cash asset from the balance sheet, effectively eliminating it from a raider's list of post-LBO funding sources.

• Many companies use funds from a receivables sale to retire high cost debt and thereby improve their profitability.

• Assets may also be securitized to meet tax planning objectives.

Specific examples of such transactions include the following:

• The U.S. holding company of an international conglomerate entered into a $750 million program for securitization of the trade receivables of several of its manufacturing and retailing subsidiaries. It was able to generate a significant amount of capital at competitive pricing without separate SEC debt filings, a parental guarantee, or acceleration of taxable income.

• The financing subsidiary of a leading international luxury automobile manufacturer securitized $100 million in lease payment receivables, enabling it to offer competitive marketing programs without upsetting the company's financial targets.

• A major tire manufacturer sold $250 million of open account trade receivables to finance a major capital expenditure project. The company obtained the funds at a cost that was competitive with its own commercial paper. By utilizing this securitized offering, the company preserved the financial flexibility to expand its commercial paper program for other uses.

• A global advertising and corporate communications firm with over $2 billion in billings securitized $35 million of media services receivables to provide funding for a three-year headquarters relocation program. The receivables sale avoided potential difficulty with tax regulations regarding the status of the firm's tax-exempt investment portfolio that might have occurred with a direct loan.

• A European-based chemical firm, with annual sales in excess of $10 billion, sold $80 million in subsidiaries' trade receivables that reduced capital employed by the subsidiaries and provided immediate financial reporting advantages in its headquarters country. It subsequently securitized an additional $108 million of receivables utilizing receivable sales as an ongoing corporate finance technique.

• A U.S. transportation company securitized $100 million of trade accounts receivable in order to redeploy the assets to tax-favored investments and thereby improve returns.

FUNDING ASSET SECURITIZATION ACTIVITIES

Public market funding devices include a wide variety of single-purchase liquidating facilities and revolving purchase structures. To be economically feasible, these typically need to be relatively large ($100 million minimum) and have maturities long enough to amortize initial costs. Nevertheless, for certain types of homogeneous assets that can be packaged in large enough quantities, this can be an efficient way to fund asset securitization transactions. However, high initial costs and long delays due to SEC registration requirements may accompany public transactions.

For trade receivable transactions, which generally fund assets in the 30 to 60 day range, revolving purchase structures, funded using bankers acceptances or commercial paper, tend to be most efficient. Depending on the kinds of pools funded and the credit of the seller, bank funded deals may also be efficient. Minimum efficient size is in the $20 million range, and transactions in the $300 to $400 million range are not uncommon. Heterogeneous term receivables and complex contractual payment flows extending beyond one year may still be efficiently funded by commercial paper—alone or in conjunction with an interest rate swap. Private placements can also be quite competitive in many cases where asset structures need to be custom tailored to investor needs or where regulatory requirements and costs of a public deal may make it less flexible and more expensive on an all-in basis.

A typical funding structure involves a trust or other bankruptcy remote issuer, an asset pool with excess collateralization large enough to represent a significant multiple of historical loss experience, and some form of third-party credit and liquidity support. True asset securitization structures are designed so that investors can evaluate their creditworthiness principally on the basis of the asset pools, their associated cash flows, and the servicing capability of the asset originator. Credit and structuring skills of the financial institution doing the securitization are also critically important, as is the follow-up and monitoring ability of the trustee or "program manager." In addition, some form of bank credit and liquidity support is also required for assurance of timely payment. However, these securitization activities are fundamentally different from traditional letter of credit-backed commercial paper programs, where investor decisions rely heavily on credit arbitrage rather than asset-backed cash flows.

SECURITIZATION OF LEASES

Leasing can be a fairly complex form of financing. In some respects, it is similar to an installment sale where a seller extends credit to a buyer and accepts payment over an extended period of time. But there are important differences related to the ownership of the underlying assets, tax and accounting treatment, and the presence of lease residuals. Nevertheless, from the lessor's perspective, leasing activity may increase the operating cycle of a company substantially and put a severe strain on equity as assets grow. In this sense, leasing and installment sales can have a similar effect on a company's balance sheet.

For a leasing company, asset securitization can be a very attractive way to free up equity to allow more origination and thus facilitate higher sustainable growth rates. This same advantage can accrue to industrial companies that also need to be concerned about excessive growth in financial assets that could negatively impact their price earning ratios and cost of capital.

The following account of the first Sperry (now a part of Unisys) lease securitization was written by James McDonald, Sperry's Director of Corporate Finance at the time. This transaction was one of the pioneering lease securitization deals, and this account of the thinking behind it shows how one company reacted to some of the issues discussed earlier.

THE SPERRY LEASE SECURITIZATION:
A CASE STUDY

This case study illustrates the evolution of one of the earliest public non-mortgage securitization financings as it progressed from a perceived need to an innovative solution that met the financial needs of both the originator and investors. The concepts that underlie it have become an important part of current asset securitization technology.

The origin of the asset-backed note offering by Sperry can be traced to decisions made by its senior management early in 1983 to redeploy its capital away from leasing and customer finance and into its core manufacturing business. Among the mainframe computer manufacturers, Sperry had been the leader in using its capital for customer finance. In fact, Salomon Brothers analyst Stephen T. McCleelan, in his book, *The Computer Shakeout*, referred to Sperry as a "bank." Besides making computers, Sperry manufactured farm equipment through its New Holland subsidiary. This activity also required customer finance. The rise in interest rates in the late 1970s and early 1980s required Sperry to increase its borrowing to support its customer finance programs. By 1981, this burden had reached $2.2 billion. Although a portion of this burden could be managed by using an off-balance sheet finance company, the market was showing increasing resistance to Sperry debt. The rating agencies and debt investors were no longer willing to consider Sperry and Sperry Financial, the captive off-balance sheet finance company, as separate credits. The result was the lowering of the Sperry credit rating to triple-B plus from single-A. It became clear to management that a manufacturing company could not leverage itself enough to support the levels of customer finance required in Sperry's market.

Capital Redeployment

The solution to the computer finance problem was equally complex. The first task was to provide customer financing for future sales. This was done by establishing a series of third-party programs and raising the rates for direct Sperry leases. These changes did not hurt sales since there was no shortage of leasing companies willing to finance the Sperry customer. The more complex problem was how to dispose of the more than $1 billion of lease receivables already on the balance sheet. Senior management was committed to redeploying capital and was not content to let the existing receivables balance decline over time. The goal was quite simple—remove the existing finance receivables from the balance sheet and replace them with cash. The transaction had to be done with minimal impact on financial and tax accounting and minimal, if any, recourse to Sperry.

Earnings Impact

When the project started in the first quarter of 1984, receivable sales were being executed at a significant discount or with some form of recourse. Because Sperry wanted to improve its balance sheet and redeploy assets, doing the transaction either as a sale with recourse or at rates above market was unacceptable. At the time, Sperry had adopted the accounting practice of reporting its leases as sales and placing the finance lease receivables as an asset on the balance sheet. This was achieved by present valuing the lease receivables using 11 percent. Consequently, any sale of lease receivables at a discount in excess of 11 percent would create an earnings loss, since the lease at the 11 percent present value had previously been taken into income.

It is important to note that discount rates for receivables with average lives ranging from 2 to 3 years were well in excess of 11 percent in 1984. Sperry had done some small sales of receivables in 1984 and accepted the negative earnings impact. Although any proposed structure would be evaluated on its economic merits, it was clear that there would be no significant volume of transactions under a structure that created a negative earnings impact.

Tax

Besides supporting equipment sales, Sperry's customer finance programs had provided a significant tax shelter. The leases for tax purposes were reported as operating leases so that the lease payments were reported as income as they accrued. This created a favorable mismatch with the financial books, where the lease was shown as a sale. In addition to creating the mismatch, Sperry was able to depreciate the computers and claim the investment tax credit. A sale of the receivables would accelerate income and cause depreciation and investment tax credit recapture. If Sperry had planned to continue leasing, the tax shelter from that activity would have lessened the tax impact of sales. However, since future leasing was being dramatically reduced, they no longer anticipated any tax shelter.

Structure

An investment banking firm had approached Sperry and suggested the sale of the lease receivable to a nonaffiliated special purpose finance company, which would in turn issue public debt to finance the purchase. The firm suggested using the collateralized mortgage obligation structure for lease receivables. The debt would achieve investment grade status through an escrow account to be funded by a "hold back" of a portion of the purchase price that was to be paid to Sperry. The exact mechanics of the escrow fund were not clear and, after several weeks of analysis, it did not appear that it would work. In addition, the analysis indicated that a "hold back" would make the funding uneconomical. Finally, the sale to an unaffiliated company would have a negative earnings and tax impact.

A New Security

The concept of a debt offering modeled after mortgage-backed securities was appealing. Consequently, Sperry worked with several of its commercial and investment bankers to develop a viable structure. A private placement was considered, but later a public offering was chosen to achieve economies of scale. Originally, it appeared that 100 percent credit enhancement would be required, but research showed the market would be willing to take part of the risk and accept a lower level of credit enhancement. This position was consistent with the grid that Standard & Poor's had developed that based the required amount of credit enhancement upon the credit rating of the underlying assets. One of Sperry's bankers developed the concept of using an affiliated special purpose company. The special purpose company would be bankruptcyproof to allow its public debt to achieve a higher credit rating than that of its parent. The new company would be consolidated for tax purposes and consequently there would be no tax acceleration or recapture when the receivables were sold. Finally, since the special purpose company would be an affiliate of Sperry, there could not be either a gain or loss upon the sale. Rather, the gain or loss depended upon whether the sale was at a discount above or below 11 percent and this gain or loss would be amortized over the life of the debt issued to finance the purchase of the receivables. The structure solved two of Sperry's major tax and accounting concerns.

When the concept of an asset-backed security was being developed, there were no credit enhancers, insurance companies, or banks issuing letters of credit that were willing to assume the first loss. It became clear that Sperry would have to provide the credit enhancement and take the first loss.

A financial guarantee either in the form of a letter of credit or surety bond would be used as a backup to the Sperry guarantor. It would be issued by a triple-A bank or insurance company so that the note could achieve a triple-A rating.

Special Purpose Company

Making the decision to form the special purpose company, Sperry Lease Finance Corporation (SLFC), and to issue asset-backed notes turned out to be the easiest part of the transaction. The execution would truly test the patience, nerve, creativity and endurance of lawyers, accountants, bankers, credit enhancers, and the Sperry staff. Fortunately, the group was able to work well as a team and endure the months of drafting and negotiating. The first step was to develop accurate cash flows for the leases involved. All of this information was contained in the Sperry computer system, but it had to be extracted in a form that was useful for a public sale. The next step was to review the lease documents. It is important to remember that the leases were manufacturing leases that were not originally drafted to permit later resale. They contained many of the provisions common to computer leases, such as downtime credits and upgrade provisions. They were not the "hell or high water" leases commonly used today.

Debt Rating

The negotiations with Standard & Poor's (S&P) were fruitful and resulted in a triple-A rating. Two significant issues emerged from the negotiations with S&P. First, S&P was willing to let Sperry indemnify the investors for any provisions in the lease documents that would squeeze cash flow. This solved the problem of how to deal with lease clauses that allowed downtime credits.

Credit Enhancement

The other issue concerned the amount of credit enhancement. In order to achieve a triple-A rating, S&P required 20 percent credit enhancement. However, the S&P bankruptcy attorney felt that 20 percent recourse to Sperry would destroy the clean sale between Sperry and its special purpose subsidiary. This in turn would prevent the subsidiary from being bankruptcyproof, thus breaching the distinction between a pledge and a sale and jeopardizing the desirable separation of Sperry's operating risk form the financial portfolio being securitized. As a result, the credit enhancement was split into two pieces: 5 percent recourse to Sperry and 15 percent recourse to SLFC. Since SLFC would have few assets available to meet its recourse obligations, the letter of credit bank (Union Bank of Switzerland or UBS) would be in essence taking a first loss position. The bank was protected to the extent that Sperry's 5 percent recourse would have to be exhausted before the SLFC recourse could be called upon. Fortunately for Sperry, UBS was willing to split the letter of credit because they felt that the first recourse of 5 percent to Sperry was enough to cover any potential risk. After S&P indicated that it would give the structure a triple-A rating, the transaction moved smoothly since the SEC had no comments. The sale of the notes by SLFC in February of 1985 represented five months of planning and nine months of structuring and implementation (See Exhibit 5–13).

EXHIBIT 5–13
The Sperry Lease Securitization

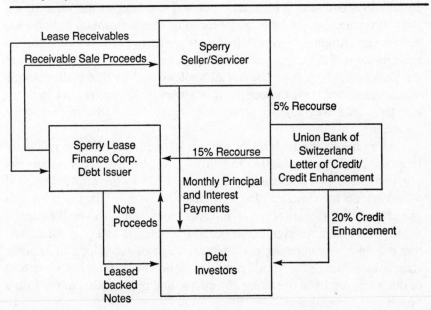

Summary

The project started out as a means of redeploying assets on Sperry's balance sheet when it decided to shift away from direct leasing. The lease-backed note concept developed into a vehicle that would permit indirect support of customer finance with minimal impact on the company's balance sheet.

CONCLUSION

The securitization decision is both an investment decision and a financing decision. It also is an attempt to efficiently reconcile needs of investors with those of asset originators. As an alternative or substitute for equity, securitization has important implications for balance sheet management, capital structure and the overall strategy of a firm. The use of sustainable growth rate analysis and a focus on the market value of the firm are critical to understanding the potential of this new and powerful corporate finance tool. Incremental access to investors, added financial flexibility, and improved communications with the financial marketplace are important potential benefits of this technology.

One of the most important roles of chief financial officers of public corporations is that of a communicator and marketer of the value of the firm. Having the right ideas and executing sound financial policies are not enough. Routine, periodic disclosures of required financial information are not sufficient to enable a firm to fully realize its market potential for shareholders. A broad financial strategy and evidence of strategic vision consistent with the operating realities of a firm and its industry can go a long way toward preserving shareholder value in periods of uncertainty.

In addition, the realities of today's marketplace and the relatively large pools of funds available to skillful financial managers, other corporations, and potential raiders have given life to the concern that "if you don't do it, someone else may do it for you." Thus, a judicious use of asset securitization within the context of a firm's overall financial strategy may achieve significant economic benefits and play an important role in communicating management's aggressive efforts to improve shareholder value. The result can be a higher stock price, achievement of other financial and operating objectives, and preservation of the firm's operating independence.

Acknowledgment

This chapter draws heavily on the work and ideas of many other Citicorp personnel, particularly John Bryan, Laura Leach, David McCollum, and Bill Stengel. The authors gratefully acknowledge their contributions.

CHAPTER 6

SECURITIZING COMMERCIAL MORTGAGES

Tamara L. Adler, Vice President
Goldman, Sachs & Co.

THE EVOLUTION OF COMMERCIAL MORTGAGE-BACKED SECURITIES

The development of commercial mortgage-backed securities ("CMBSs") has provided tremendous opportunities to real estate owners/developers, mortgage bankers, lenders, and securities investors. Although a broad range of market participants are interested in CMBSs, only 3 to 4 percent of outstanding income-property mortgages are securitized—far below the 33 percent share of single-family home mortgages. With the development of rating criteria for commerical mortgages, the adoption of capital market techniques to create synthetic securities, and the promulgation of new regulations under the Tax Reform Act of 1986, however, the barriers to securitizing commercial real estate debt have been tumbling.

Currently more than $900 billion of outstanding loans are secured by income-producing properties located in the United States (see Exhibit 6–1). The size of this market is roughly equivalent to the municipal or corporate bond markets. Annual trading activity for municipal and corporate bonds is approximately 20 percent and 60 percent, respectively. In contrast, only about 1 to 2 percent of outstanding commercial mortgages are traded annually.

Commercial mortgages comprise a significant portion of the investment portfolios of many life insurance companies, thrift institutions,

EXHIBIT 6–1
Commercial Mortgage Market as of December 1987 ($Billions)

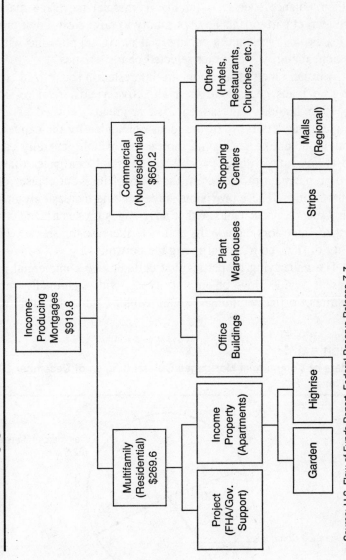

Source: U.S. Flow of Funds Report, Federal Reserve Release Z.7.

commercial banks, pension funds, and money managers (see Exhibit 6–2). Traditionally, holders of commercial mortgages have not been able to utilize their commercial mortgages as fully or as easily as other assets on their balance sheets. A liquid commercial mortgage market offers these market participants an opportunity to raise cash, book profits, take tax losses, and structure a commercial mortgage portfolio with specific duration, maturity, and other selected characteristics.

A broad range of investors are interested in securitized commercial mortgage loans because of their attractive yields, relative safety, and increasing liquidity. Investment risk is greatly reduced as a result of the quality underwriting of the loans demanded by the capital markets. In addition, unlike residential mortgages, which generally can be prepaid at any time without penalty, commercial mortgages often provide some prepayment protection in the form of lock-out clauses or prepayment penalties. These provisions have become increasingly important to capital market participants. Other advantages for securitized commercial mortgage investors include the ability to increase the size, diversity, and quality of their commercial mortgage portfolios.

The underlying properties that collateralize commercial mortgages represent a wide range of property types, with high-quality multifamily properties, office buildings, retail centers, and industrial/warehouse

EXHIBIT 6–2
Holders of Commercial Mortgages Outstanding as of December 1987 ($Billions)

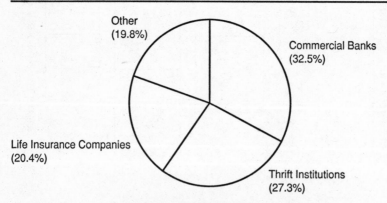

Other
(19.8%)

Commercial Banks
(32.5%)

Life Insurance Companies
(20.4%)

Thrift Institutions
(27.3%)

Includes Commercial and Multifamily Mortgages
Total = 919.8 Billion

Source: U.S. Flow of Funds Report, Federal Reserve Release Z.7.

properties being among the most desirable. Securitized commercial mortgage loans may be originated specifically for capital market investors or may be seasoned loans that are attractive to the secondary market due to property value appreciation, amortization of principal, and clean payment histories.

The lack of standard documentation and underwriting criteria, the wideranging loan sizes, the unique characteristics of each property, and the lack of actual data on default and prepayment experience have presented obstacles to the development of a securitized commercial mortgage market. Continued expansion of this market is dependent upon the ability to eliminate—or at least reduce—the need for potential investors to reunderwrite the loans. The development of the secondary

EXHIBIT 6–3
U.S. Mortgage Market Outstanding as of December 1987

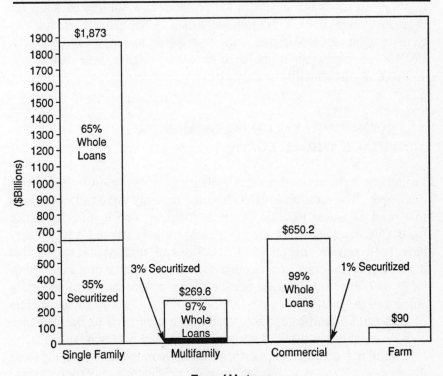

Type of Mortgage

Source: U.S. Flow of Funds Report, Federal Reserve Release Z.7.

commercial mortgage market thus received a boost when the rating agencies (Duff & Phelps Inc., Moody's Investors Service, and Standard & Poor's Corp.) developed criteria for rating commercial mortgage loans and pools. The availability of ratings for CMBSs has facilitated investment by those who desire a benchmark against which to evaluate the security and by those who need an investment grade rating in order to participate in the issue.

While a number of barriers to the development of CMBSs remain, the benefits of securitized commercial mortgages are considerable. The establishment of a secondary commercial mortgage market improves the supply and cost of capital. Moreover, transaction costs associated with underwriting real estate can be reduced, making evaluation and pricing of real estate investments more efficient. By reallocating cash flows and increasing liquidity, commercial mortgage securitization enables mortgage originators and investors to better match their assets and liabilities, thereby reducing interest rate, maturity and other portfolio risks. Commercial mortgage securitization provides new sources of funds for those institutions that choose to liquefy their balance sheets and releases equity capital that would otherwise be required to support those assets. CMBSs create new opportunities to increase yields, manage cash flows, and control asset/liability imbalances.

ANALYZING AND VALUING COMMERCIAL MORTGAGE WHOLE LOANS

Institutions have utilized various structures for the sale of commercial mortgages. The most basic structure, and the only one available until a few years ago, was the sale of whole loans or participations in whole loans. Purchases and sales of commercial mortgage whole loans typically have been private, negotiated transactions of unrated mortgages that have been credit-enhanced through the use of a letter of credit, third-party or issuer (mortgagee) guarantees, or subordination of a certain amount of the mortgage's cash flow. The primary purchasers and sellers of commercial mortgage whole loans have continued to be insurance companies, thrift institutions, pension funds, and commercial banks.

Valuing a commercial mortgage whole loan requires an analysis of the mortgage loan terms, the quality of the originator's underwriting, and the quality of the real estate. The risk profile of a single mortgage loan is generally quite different from that of a pool of mortgage loans primarily because casualty, condemnation, default, and prepayment can disrupt the cash flow from a single mortgage more dramatically than the cash flow from a pool of mortgages. Consequently, the pricing of a commercial mortgage whole loan tends to be at yields that are substantially higher than those demanded by the market for commercial mortgage pools.

The primary mortgage loan terms that affect value are interest rate, payment terms, and prepayment provisions. The interest rate, or contract rate, that is paid by the borrower on a commercial mortgage loan usually differs from the mortgage yield or internal rate of return, which is the actual yield to the lender or investor. The difference between the interest rate and the mortgage yield can usually be attributed to 1) servicing fees charged by the originator or third-party for monitoring the debt, 2) loan fees charged by the lender or investor, and 3) prepayment proceeds and any prepayment penalties or yield maintenance charges.

Based on its contract rate, a mortgage can be priced at a premium or a discount. Investors are reluctant to pay premiums that are significantly in excess of par primarily because in the event of casualty, condemnation, or default, the premium paid is unlikely to be recovered. Even if a penalty is associated with any of these events, investors are wary that the property value recovered as a result of casualty, condemnation, or default may not be sufficient to provide for payment of the penalty. In contrast, mortgages that are priced at a slight or substantial discount to par are very attractive to investors because investors are more likely to realize par value in the event of casualty, condemnation, or default even though their investment was in an amount less than par.

Four methods of principal and interest payment are typically found in commercial mortgages: balloon loans, constant payment loans, constant maturity loans, and participating loans. Balloon loans can be either interest-only loans with the full principal amount due at maturity or level amortization loans whose payment schedule is abbreviated to provide for a "bullet payment" at a certain date. Typical terms may provide for a 10-year loan with a 25- or 30-year amortization schedule. Interest-only (or "bullet") loans tend to be seven years or less. Constant payment loans provide for a periodic loan payment of a fixed amount that is to be applied first to the payment of interest and second to the repayment of principal. As the loan balance is reduced, the portion of the payment required to pay interest declines, and consequently, the portion applied to the repayment of principal increases. In contrast, constant maturity loans provide for the payment of interest and principal in a fixed period of time. Payment may be irregular (e.g., due to floating interest rates or annual payment caps or both), but the term will be fixed. In participating mortgage loans, the lender receives, in addition to the contract rate of interest and repayment of principal, cash flow in the form of a participation, usually in ground rent, gross rent, net income, or resale price.

Unlike residential mortgages, which are prepayable at any time generally without penalty, commercial mortgages generally have some restrictions on prepayment. Borrowers can be prohibited or "locked-out" from prepaying the loan for the entire term of the loan or for a shorter period. Additionally, a prepayment penalty may be assessed or yield maintenance or cash flow maintenance provisions may be stipulated. These provisions usually provide that the lender receive the same cash flow payments originally contracted for or the present value of the difference between the remaining scheduled payments and the remaining principal balance, using a discount rate that is usually based on the yield of the U.S. Treasury issue having a maturity equal to the remaining maturity of the mortgage. Lock-out periods and prepayment penalties are important to capital market investors, especially those purchasing mortgages at a premium to par.

The pricing of commercial mortgage loans is influenced not only by interest rate, payment terms, and prepayment provisions, but also by the quality of the mortgage originator's underwriting. Particularly important are the loan-to-value and debt service coverage ratios. The loan-to-value ratio refers to the ratio of the original mortgage balance to the appraised value of the property. Typical loan-to-value ratios range between 70 and 80 percent. Obviously in noncredit situations, the lower the loan-to-value ratio, the more conservative the underwriting by the lender. Debt service coverage ratios refer to the ratio of net operating income of the property to debt service required under the terms of the mortgage. Debt service coverage ratios usually range between 1.05–1.25:1; the higher the ratio, the more conservative the mortgage loan underwriting. For secondary market investors, a clean payment history is also essential. Typical standards (and those required by the rating agencies) include no late payment within the immediately preceding 12 months and only two late payments within the preceding three years.

Since almost all commercial mortgages are nonrecourse mortgages, that is, secured only by the property, the quality of the real estate must be analyzed in order to accurately value the mortgage. In the event of casualty, condemnation, or default, the value of the real estate is the sole source of repayment to the lender. Thus, value is affected by the location of the real estate, the property type, seasoning of the property, tenant quality, lease terms, property management, and construction quality. The existence of asbestos and any other environmental hazard will also affect value.

The analysis of commercial whole loans provides the basis for understanding how CMBSs are structured, rated, priced, and traded. While market conditions heavily influence the attractiveness of particular structures, the importance of understanding and evaluating the basic terms of the mortgages and the quality of the underlying real estate remains constant.

SELECTED STRUCTURES: RATED COMMERCIAL MORTGAGE BONDS

The first structure in which real estate debt was rated on the basis of the underlying real estate rather than on the basis of the issuer's guarantee utilized a property-specific analysis. Known as rated commercial mortgage bonds (RCMBs), these securities carry investment grade ratings based on the strength of the real estate's cash flow and are secured by a first mortgage lien on the real estate and an assignment of the property's cash flows. Determining how to value this security requires an understanding of the benefits and risks of both RCMBs and comparably rated securities outstanding in the capital markets. Although RCMBs are structured to closely resemble corporate bonds and are given similar credit ratings by the rating agencies, RCMBs are priced at a premium to comparably rated corporate bonds. This premium can be attributed to several factors: 1) RCMBs are relatively new securities; 2) the RCMB market is not as liquid as the corporate bond market; 3) prepayment risk may be perceived to be slightly higher due to the risks of casualty and condemnation; 4) mortgage lending rates have traditionally been higher than corporate lending rates; and 5) the market is generally not as familiar with commercial real estate debt.

Historically, mortgage lending rates have been higher than corporate lending rates because, among other things, real estate lending has not offered the same liquidity or diversity as corporate lending, real estate underwriting (i.e., credit analysis and due diligence) has been more costly than corporate underwriting in terms of time and expense, and commercial real estate lending has been perceived to be riskier than corporate lending. The development of the RCMB market, however, should provide more liquidity and diversity than traditionally has been available to real estate lenders and, to the extent lenders understand and rely on the ratings, should reduce real estate underwriting expenses. Although RCMB spreads should therefore narrow, RCMBs will, in all likelihood, continue to trade at a premium to corporate bonds, reflecting the increased risk that the market associates with commercial real estate lending.

RCMBs are structured financings designed to be rated by the rating agencies. To finance commercial real estate by issuing RCMBs, a special-purpose entity, formed by the real estate owner, simultaneously issues the RCMBs, transfers the proceeds received (less expenses) to the owner in exchange for a first mortgage lien on the property and an assignment of the property's cash flows, and assigns this collateral to a trustee that acts on behalf of the RCMB investors (see Exhibit 6–4).

Ratings are critical for RCMBs because, as in structured financings generally, RCMBs are not directly issued by the entity that owns the asset or is seeking the funds. Unlike traditional corporate debt where ratings are based on the general financial health of the issuer, ratings for

EXHIBIT 6–4
The Components of Rated Commercial Mortgage Bond Transactions

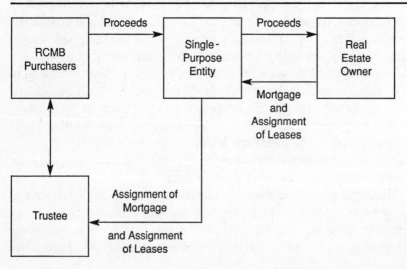

RCMB-structured financings are based on the quality of the underlying real estate as well as the legal and structural basis upon which the RCMB financing is created. RCMBs, however, are similar to traditional corporate debt in that the underlying asset (i.e., income-producing real estate) can, in effect, be viewed as an operating company, with the lease payment stream (typically derived from multiple lessees) being comparable to revenues received from various corporate product lines. Unlike an operating company, however, pricing can be changed only in accordance with lease terms.

Standard & Poor's, Moody's, and Duff & Phelps have each issued criteria for rating property-specific, nonrecourse commercial real estate structured financings.[1] Each agency analyzes the cash flow expectations from the property under various scenarios or "stress tests" and the evaluates the certainty of timely and ultimate payment of RCMB interest and principal.

Standard & Poor's Property-Specific Rating Criteria

S&P's threshold criteria for rating nonrecourse commercial real estate debt securities require the underlying asset to be seasoned, fully occupied, prime-quality commercial real estate. Property-specific investment grade ratings can be obtained for notes that secure either multi-tenanted or single-tenanted property, provided however, that in the latter case there is a long-term lease in place from a tenant rated "A" or better. S&P requires that nonrecourse commercial real estate financings secured by construction projects or buildings that are not fully occupied be guaranteed if the bonds are to be rated. Such a rating will then be determined on the basis of the rating of the guarantor. If, however, the real estate meets S&P's threshold requirements, S&P employs a two-part, interrelated analysis to evaluate the likelihood of timely and ultimate payment to bondholders. First, S&P analyzes the property and its income stream to determine its creditworthiness as mortgage collateral for a rated bond issue. A recent MAI (Member of the Appraisal Institute) appraisal of the property and cash flow pro formas extending at least ten years beyond the term of the RCMBs are required for this analysis. Then, S&P eval-

---

[1]See Standard & Poor's Corp., *Credit Review*, April 25, 1988 and November 24,1986; Moody's Investors Service, *Structured Finance Research & Commentary*, March 1987 and December 1986; Duff & Phelps Inc., *Rating of Commercial Real Estate Securities*, Fall 1986.

uates the debt structure payment mechanisms to ensure that the structure of the financing assures timely and ultimate receipt of, and trustee access to, the collateral's cash flow and value. Differences between cash flow from the property and debt service and between bonds outstanding and refinancing proceeds are required to be covered with credit enhancements which, in some cases, are required to last for the full term of the bonds. S&P's objective is for the sum of the property's cash flows, refinancing proceeds, and credit enhancements to be sufficient to repay bondholders in a timely fashion.

Cash Flow Analysis

In order to evaluate both the strength of the property's income stream for debt service coverage and the property's market value for principal repayment, S&P prepares a projection of cash flow and a current determination of value for the property, as well as current loan-to-value and debt service coverage ratios based on the proposed financing. S&P's projections may differ from those used by the MAI appraiser if S&P determines that different assumptions should be utilized.

S&P then assesses the risks of the property and the payment mechanism. Although S&P does not rate the physical real estate, these risk assessments are specific to the property and are measured in terms of how they could affect the market projections. Thus, RCMBs having the same rating could be secured by properties having different loan-to-value and debt service coverage ratios. After evaluating these risks, S&P "stresses" the cash flow to ensure that the RCMBs will continue to pay timely interest and principal notwithstanding economic downturns. The severity of the cash flow stress tests will depend upon the risk analysis of the property, the payment structure, and the rating requested. The higher the rating requested, the tougher the stress test applied to the cash flows.

If the RCMBs are not fully amortizing, S&P determines whether the refinancing proceeds that would be available under the stressed cash flow analysis would be sufficient to repay the entire principal outstanding. This analysis is central to evaluating the risk of repayment of principal at maturity. If the bonds are not fully amortizing, the likelihood of bondholders to receive full and timely principal repayment is dependent upon the ability of the borrower to refinance the property or to realize sufficient proceeds from a sale of the property. Foreclosure does not alleviate this risk since foreclosure proceedings can significantly impair the timeliness of payment to bondholders. S&P, therefore, emphasizes the amount of equity a mortgagor has in the property at the time of issuance of the RCMBs. Although some consideration may be given to property appreciation, much more weight is given to conservative loan-to-value ratios on properties for which balloon financing is sought.

Moody's Property-Specific Rating Criteria

In December 1986, Moody's introduced its credit rating system for debt securities collateralized by commercial real estate. Moody's analysis begins with an evaluation of the strengths and weaknesses of the real estate market in which the property is located. Moody's assesses both the market's inherent vulnerabilities to sharp declines in demand for office space (the "demand-side risk") and the market's susceptibility to overbuilding (the "supply-side risk"). The demand-side and supply-side classifications for the market are then used to derive an overall long-term market classification.

Moody's then evaluates the project risk to gauge the competitive advantage or disadvantage of the building against comparable buildings in the same market. As part of the project risk analysis, Moody's reviews, among other things, location, amenities, construction quality, functional layout, energy efficiency, ownership, building management, lease structure, and credit quality of the tenants.

The foregoing data is used in sensitivity models to project cash flow under various adverse circumstances that account for specific market and project risks. Moody's then assesses the financial market risk to determine the discount rates to be applied to cash flow in estimating the building's market value over the life of the security. Moody's does not publish specific debt service coverage or loan-to-value ratios. Instead, Moody's uses region-specific worst-case scenarios; each property's minimum debt service coverage and maximum loan-to-value ratios are based on individually specified characteristics. As in S&P's method, loan-to-value ratios are calculated on a discounted cash flow approach to value, and debt service coverage tests are based on the stressed income stream.

Cash Flow Analysis

Moody's cash flow analysis segregates its base-case projections of cash flows into three income streams, each of which represents a different level of risk. The first income stream is derived from existing leases. The second is derived from anticipated rents under projected lease renewals and new leases, assuming no growth in rental rates, and the third is derived from inflation. Each component is then stressed to determine its reaction to adverse economic conditions.

• *Existing leases*. The income stream derived from existing leases is subjected to the least stress on the basis that the primary risk is the inability of the tenants to pay rent. To the extent that Moody's determines that the tenants are creditworthy, the stress factor will be low. The stress factor used is based on projected defaults that are, in turn, based on Moody's evaluation of the particular real estate market.

• *Projected rents*. The income stream derived from projected rents under new leases is stressed according to assumptions regarding vacancy prior to releasing and rent concessions. Since this income stream is based on projections, it will be subjected to greater stress than the income stream derived from existing leases.

• *Inflation*. Income derived from inflation is subjected to the greatest stress on the theory that, because of the compounding effect, any small error in the growth rate assumptions can have a large impact near the end of the bond term.

From the stressed income streams, annual operating expenses and debt service are estimated and then deducted, and any shortfall between the stressed annual income and the sum of the annual expenses and debt service is made up with credit enhancements.

Duff & Phelps' Property-Specific Rating Criteria

D&P's rating criteria is similar to that established by S&P and Moody's. D&P examines ten qualitative factors that it believes may impact timely payment of principal and interest on the bonds:

- Market and site area
- Leases and tenants
- Economy of the area
- Project seasoning
- Construction quality
- Management and leasing
- The owner or developer
- Bullet mortgage payment terms
- Hazards such as earthquakes and asbestos
- Any default history

If D&P determines that one or more of these qualitative factors are significantly more important than the others, then those factors will be given the weight deemed appropriate by the firm's staff.

To obtain a D&P rating of "2" (comparable to S&P's "AA" or Moody's "Aa"), the property's cash flows must support a minimum debt service coverage ratio of 1.25:1 and a maximum loan-to-value ratio of 70 percent after being stressed to take into account deterioration of rents and increases in expenses. Credit enhancement, in the form of letters of credit, surety bonds, or cash, will be required to make up for any shortfall. In addition, D&P requires all financings to have minimum credit enhancement to insure against the potential uncertainty of timely payment of rent due to tenant defaults and delinquencies and the occurrence of unanticipated capital expenditures. The amount of this minimum credit enhancement, however, will not exceed one year of debt service.

The RCMB Perspective

Since the first RCMB was issued in 1985, the rating agencies have rated RCMBs secured by office buildings and multifamily properties. The first four issues were publicly sold in the Euromarket at relatively wide spreads; the remainder have been privately placed in the United States. Until May 1988, no RCMBs had been rated higher than double-A. In May 1988, however, Goldman, Sachs & Co. privately placed the first triple-A rated RCMB, which was secured by a 1.1 million-square-foot headquarters building 100 percent leased by IBM Corporation and located in Westchester County, New York. Obtaining a property-specific rating for notes secured by a single-tenant property was a novel approach for the rating agencies (in this case, S&P and Moody's) which had historically rated only multi-tenanted properties located in major cities.

Pricing RCMBs depends, to a large degree, on an analysis of the benefits, risks, and similarities of RCMBs relative to comparably rated corporate bonds. Like corporate bonds, RCMBs carry investment grade ratings, are evidenced by senior notes, are partially amortizing or bullet loans, have a similar range of maturities, can contain call options and lockout periods, and have semi-annual interest payments or, if they are Eurodollar financings, annual interest payments.

Unlike a typical corporate bond that is an unsecured obligation of the issuer, however, RCMBs are secured by a first mortgage lien on the real estate and an assignment of the property's leases and rents. In addition, since the rating agencies require that RCMB issuers be bankruptcy-remote, RCMB issuers must be single-purpose entities. Thus, unlike typical corporate bond structures, cash flow for RCMB interest and principal payments cannot be hindered by other liabilities. This rating agency requirement also ensures that RCMB issuers will not be subject to hostile takeovers, leveraged buyouts, or share repurchase programs, each of which can result in sudden credit deterioration.

In further contrast to corporate bonds, event risk for RCMBs is limited to the unlikely occurrence of casualty to the building or condemnation by a government entity. Yet, in both of these instances, bondholders are protected in terms of principal repayment by insurance proceeds or condemnation awards. The investors' bargained-for yield, however, is unprotected. Unlike corporate bonds, total or partial prepayment can occur in the event of total or partial casualty or condemnation. This perceived increased risk for the investor is one of the factors that contributes to the increased yield that RCMB investors demand. This risk of unanticipated prepayment, however, should be balanced by investors against the reduced risk of bankruptcy and other events that may cause an unexpected prepayment under typical corporate bond structures.

RCMBs secured by single properties are not comparable to conventional residential mortgage-backed securities in terms of structure, collateral, liquidity, or yield. Conventional residential mortgage-backed securities are secured by pools of residential mortgages, are typically rated triple-A and are traded in a strong secondary market. Spreads on comparably rated residential mortgage-backed securities, however, are higher than those offered for RCMBs. This yield differential can be largely attributed to the greater prepayment risk for residential mortgages and the source of debt service payment on conventional residential mortgage-backed securities.

A common feature of almost every residential mortgage is the ability to prepay at any time with little or, most frequently, no penalty. Thus, investors who purchase residential mortgage-backed securities run a high risk of not getting their bargained-for yield. This risk is translated into a higher yield spread on residential mortgage- backed securities. In addition, unlike RCMBs collateralized by commercial office buildings where debt service payments are derived from lease payments made by commercial real estate tenants, payments on conventional residential mortgage-backed securities are derived from payments made by individual homeowners. The rate of default of tenants in buildings that secure comparably rated RCMBs may be perceived to be lower than the rate of default by individual homeowners. The higher yield spread on conventional residential mortgage-backed securities is thus also attributable to this perceived higher rate of default.

Although RCMBs may be a less costly source of financing for owners and developers, the capital markets may not be the appropriate financing source for all commercial real estate borrowers. The lower cost of funds that can be found in the capital markets is accompanied by tougher underwriting criteria and covenants. Conversely, the higher interest rates offered by traditional institutional lenders are accompanied by less restrictions. Thus, contrary to what some believe, the advent of RCMBs and their accompanying lower interest rates may not ultimately equalize the costs of funds in the capital and institutional markets if the lending criteria remain distinct. Instead, financing commercial real estate in the capital markets will be accomplished by owners and developers whose properties have strong enough cash flows to achieve a rating that will enable the marketplace to offer interest rates low enough to compensate for the rating agency restrictions and structuring requirements. For these capital market participants, pricing that is already favorable should become more efficient as the secondary market develops and investors become more familiar with the RCMB structure.

SELECTED STRUCTURES: RATED
COMMERCIAL MORTGAGE PASS-THROUGHS

Three years after the first rating criteria for commercial mortgage pools were published by S&P and two years after the first RCMB was issued, the first publicly registered and rated commercial mortgage pool was lead managed by Goldman, Sachs & Co. Meritor Mortgage Securities Corporation, a wholly-owned subsidiary of Philadelphia-based Meritor Savings Bank, used a senior/subordinated structure to issue three tranches of senior certificates that were rated triple-A by S&P and Moody's. The offering consisted of three classes of senior certificates aggregating $212.9 million .[2] Credit support for the senior certificates was provided

---

	Class A-1	Class A-2	Class A-3
[2]Initial Outstanding Amount	$87.1 million	$71.8 million	$54 million
Interest Rate	8.75%	9.40%	9.40%
Last Scheduled Distribution Date	8/1/92	12/1/94	6/1/99
Weighted Average Life	2.3 years	5.2 years	7.7 years

by a subordinated, unrated $28.5 million tranche retained by Meritor (representing approximately 11.75 percent of the principal balance of the mortgage pool) and a cash reserve fund of approximately one million dollars established to provide liquidity in the event of payment delays.

The pass-through certificates represented ownership interests in 141 fixed-rate mortgages secured by office buildings (30 percent), apartments (29 percent), retail facilities (22 percent), warehouses (17 percent), and miscellaneous property types (2 percent) located in 28 states. No one loan represented more than 3.3 percent of the pool, and no one borrower represented more than 5 percent of the pool.

The loans included in the pool had an aggregate outstanding principal balance of approximately $242 million, an average loan balance of $1.7 million, a weighted average annual interest rate of approximately 10.2 percent, and a weighted average remaining term to stated maturity of approximately 6.3 years. The loans were highly seasoned, having a weighted average mortgage age of 6.4 years. The weighted average original loan-to-value ratio of the pool was approximately 68 percent; the weighted average adjusted loan-to-value ratio of the pool (i.e., current principal balance divided by original appraised value) was approximately 56 percent. Approximately 97 percent of the loans were balloon loans, and approximately 99 percent of the loans had some type of prepayment penalty after the expiration of any lock-out period. The weighted average remaining lock-out period was 10.4 months.

Meritor Savings Bank sold its interest in the mortgage loans to Meritor Mortgage Securities Corporation which in turn sold its interest to a REMIC trust.[3] Monthly payments of principal and interest on the underlying mortgage loans were determined to be sufficient to fund a trust expense reserve and to make scheduled payments of interest and principal on the senior certificates (see Exhibit 6–5).

A modified discounted cash flow analysis was used to ensure that mortgage payments would be sufficient to pay scheduled distributions. Scheduled payments on each loan having a net coupon lower than the highest certificate rate were discounted monthly at that rate to determine cash flow value. For net coupons on mortgage loans that were above the highest certificate rate, the amount of certificates issues was limited to the face amount of the mortgage loan. The subordinated amount,

---

[3]See page 176 *infra*.

EXHIBIT 6–5
Meritor Mortgage Securities Corporation Cash Flow Structure

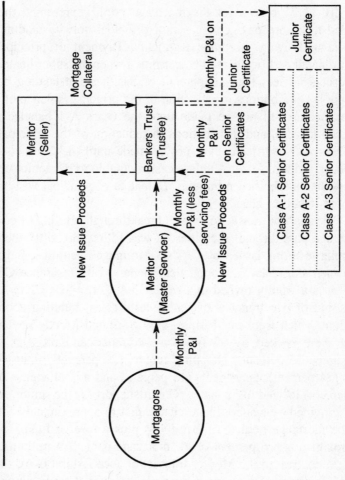

initially 11.75 percent of the mortgage pool, represented the amount needed to ensure payment of senior principal notwithstanding defaults on the underlying mortgage payments. Payment of principal on the subordinated certificates will be permitted when the subordinated amount represents no less than 16 percent of the then outstanding balance of the pool. Distributions in reduction of the principal balance of Class A-2 certificates will not be made until the Class A-1 balance has been reduced to zero, and distributions in reduction of the principal balance of Class A-3 certificates will not be made until the Class A-2 balance has been reduced to zero, unless cash available to the senior certificates is less than a specified minimum. In that case, principal will be reduced without regard to class.

The Meritor transaction was a breakthrough offering of commercial mortgage pass-through securities. It was followed shortly thereafter by a similar offering issued by CIGNA Mortgage Securities, Inc., a wholly-owned subsidiary of Connecticut General Life Insurance Co., which in turn is a wholly-owned unit of CIGNA Corp. The CIGNA offering consisted of two tranches of senior certificates, totalling about $236.6 million, which were rated triple-A by S&P and Moody's.[4] The certificates were backed by 93 fixed-rate commerical mortgages on office buildings (35 percent), shopping centers (26 percent), industrial buildings (24 percent), apartments (13 percent) and miscellaneous properties (2 percent) located in 32 states. Credit support for the senior certificates was provided by a subordinate class equal to approximately 5.5 percent of the mortgage pool ($13.7 million) plus a reserve fund representing approximately 5.6 percent of the mortgage pool ($14 million).

In contrast to the Meritor transaction (see Exhibit 6–6), the reserve fund was designed to maintain the dollar amount of credit support needed to absorb the losses expected under the triple-A stress scenario rather than to provide only liquidity in the event of payment delays. The cash flow subordination provided in the CIGNA issue was not limited to a specified dollar amount. As the CIGNA payment priority diagram indicates (see Exhibit 6–7), the reserve fund is replenished from principal and interest

---

	Class A-1	Class A-2
[4]Initial Outstanding Amount	$144.3 million	$92.3 million
Interest Rate	8.75%	9.40%
Last Scheduled Distribution Date	4/15/96	1/15/02
Weighted Average Life	5.4 years	9.4 years

EXHIBIT 6–6
Meritor Mortgage Securities Corporation Payment Priority

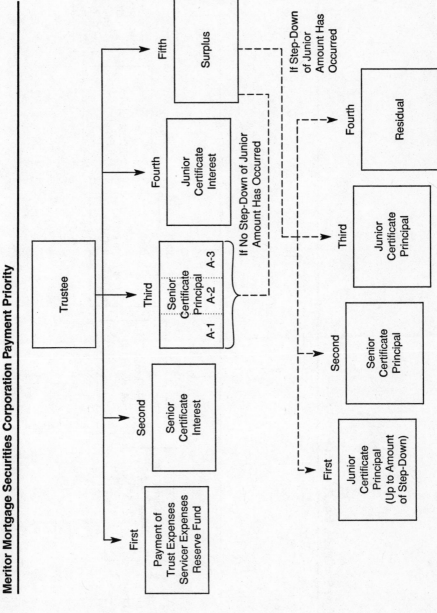

EXHIBIT 6–7
CIGNA Mortgage Securities, Inc. Payment Priority

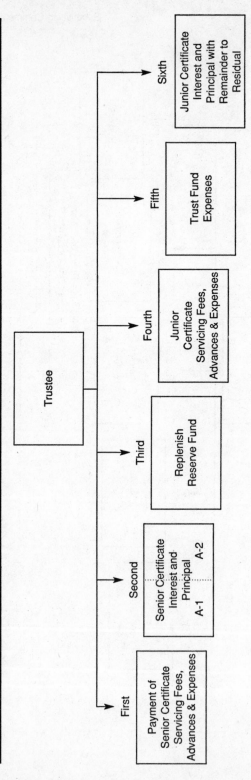

otherwise allocated to the initially 11.75 percent of the mortgage pool, represented the amount needed to ensure payment of senior principal notwithstanding defaults on the underlying subordinate class. Consequently, the dollar amount of credit support over the life of the transaction could exceed the sum of the initial reserve fund plus the aggregate principal value of the subordinate class.

The Rating Agencies' Analysis of Commercial Mortgage Pools

Standard & Poor's
In rating both the Meritor and CIGNA structures, S&P utilized an actuarial analysis. Using this approach, the credit quality of the commercial mortgage portfolio was assessed without addressing each loan on a property-specific basis. S&P's actuarial approach is comprised of three components.[5]

First, an on-site review of the lending institution's loan origination and servicing is conducted. S&P uses this review to determine the credit quality of the portfolio and the performance of the overall portfolio. Second, loan eligibility guidelines are used to ensure minimum pool quality and to achieve some certainty in specific loan characteristics. Data for each pooled loan is obtained through the use of comprehensive fact sheets. Particular attention is paid to loan payment type, payment history, debt service coverage, property seasoning, and particular credit risks, such as ground leases and natural hazard risks.

The third stage involves calculation of credit loss assumptions for the pool and an analysis of the securities' structure to determine whether there is sufficient cash flow available to meet defined payments. The pool is then assigned factors reflecting foreclosure frequency (an assumed percentage of loans that may become delinquent or may default over the life of the issue) and loss severity (the assumed total losses on defaulting loans). The base case credit loss numbers, which are modified to reflect the results of S&P's underwriting and servicing review, are calculated using a stratification of the pool by loan-to-value, seasoning, payment type, geographic concentration, and other pool-specific concerns.

The credit loss assumptions are used to evaluate the pool's ability to support the principal and interest payments on the securities notwith-

---

[5] *See* Standard & Poor's Corporation, *Credit Week*, Edith H. Shwalb and Andrew Berman, December 21,1987, p.23.

standing reduced cash flow. Two tests are then applied: 1) a liquidity test to determine whether amounts available from mortgage cash flow, reserves, or advance obligations of a rated entity are sufficient to pay current debt service, notwithstanding mortgagor delinquencies and recoveries, and 2) a default test to determine the pool's ability to withstand mortgagor defaults and subsequent recovery of foreclosure proceeds. S&P's selection of the loans within the pool to undergo these scenarios depends upon a variety of factors, including loan coupon, the number of loans in the pool, and variability in loan size. The timing of the losses assumed depends upon the schedule of loan maturities (particularly balloon loans) and whether the structure provides for contractual final maturity dates.

Moody's

Unlike S&P, Moody's assesses each loan on an individual basis by assigning a quality rating (QR) to each mortgage in the pool.[6] The strength of the QR is determined on the basis of various factors, including loan-to-value and debt service ratios, mortgage and property seasoning, borrower payment records, occupancy, and refinancing risk. Moody's also considers the strength of the regional market for each mortgage in the pool, which is classified as strong, average, or weak based primarily on industry diversification. Moody's also analyzes credit risks related to the collateral's exposure to toxic waste and asbestos. The primary concern regarding environmental hazards is the pool's exposure to super liens in those states that have super lien legislation and to refinancing risk on balloon mortgages.

Even though the two agencies use different approaches for rating large pools of commercial mortgages, the credit support levels they arrive at tend to complement each other. S&P and Moody's as well Duff & Phelps concentrate on the property type, geographic diversification and other mortgage loan characteristics of the pool, the strength and experience of the originator and servicer, and the amount of credit enhancement provided by the reserve fund and the subordinate certificates. Consequently, both the Meritor and CIGNA transactions qualified for a triple-A rating. They were well-diversified geographically and within

---

[6] Moody's Investors Service, *Structured Finance*, Ezra P. Grossman and Jeffery F. Fastov, May 1988, p. 37.

each of the four basic property types, carried conservative loan-to-value ratios, and were issued by subsidiaries of experienced commercial real estate lenders and servicers.

SELECTED STRUCTURES: GUARANTEED COMMERCIAL MORTGAGE PASS-THROUGHS

In addition to rated commercial mortgage pass-throughs, guaranteed commercial mortgage pass-throughs have been structured and sold in the public markets. These securities have been structured with full recourse to the issuer and have been rated based on the rating of the issuer, or they have involved "swapping" an institutions's multifamily mortgages for Federal National Mortgage Association ("FannieMae") or Federal Home Loan Mortgage Corp. ("FreddieMac") pass-through securities, which are backed by the mortgages swapped. In effect, through this "swap" FannieMae and FreddieMac provide a guarantee for which they receive a fee. To support their guarantee, these agencies require the institution to provide limited recourse credit support in the form of agency securities, recourse to the issuer, or third-party letters of credit. As of July 1988, FannieMae had issued $2.5 billion of guaranteed multifamily pass-throughs through limited recourse swaps. Unlike rated commercial mortgage pass-throughs, FannieMae and FreddieMac are restricted by their charters to buying or guaranteeing only residential or multifamily loans. Consequently, this structure can be more limiting in terms of collateral type than a rated commercial mortgage pass-through.

DEVELOPING STRUCTURES

While commercial mortgage pass-throughs, whether guaranteed or rated, have become the most widely used structures for securitizing commercial mortgages, mortgage-backed bonds, medium-term notes, and auction preferred stock collateralized by commercial mortgages are also being developed for this purpose. Improved understanding of commercial mortgages and the development by the rating agencies of criteria for rating overcollateralized (or "market value") structures have clearly facilitated this broadening of the securitized commercial mortgage market. As a result, holders of commercial mortgages will continue to have more and more sale and financing alternatives available to them.

MAJOR TAX AND ACCOUNTING ISSUES

Whole Loans

A mortgagee will generally be treated for tax purposes as having sold a mortgage loan, or an interest in such a loan, if the burdens and benefits of ownership have effectively been transferred to the purchaser. Thus, a transfer of a mortgage loan in which the loan originator retains the entire risk of loss (e.g., by indemnifying the "purchaser" against default) will not be regarded as a sale for tax purposes. A sale of a senior participation in a mortgage loan will, however, receive sale treatment for tax purposes even though the seller retains a subordinated interest.

If a sale of a mortgage loan occurs, the seller will recognize a tax gain or loss equal to the difference between the amount received and the seller's basis in the mortgage (generally, its original principal amount less any principal previously repaid). A mortgage originator will generally recognize a tax gain or loss on the sale of a whole mortgage loan, even if the originator retains servicing rights and receives normal servicing fees, provided the burdens and benefits of the mortgage loan have been shifted to the purchaser. A mortgage originator will generally recognize a tax gain or loss on the sale of a participation interest. Such interest may be either pari passu (all payments by the mortgator shared pro rata) or on a senior/subordinated basis (any shortfall first reduces payments to the holder of the subordinated interest).

If the mortgage originator receives a normal servicing fee on the transferred mortgages, the form of the transaction will not affect tax treatment; the fee will generally be ordinary income. If, however, the object of the transaction is to capture the "spread" between the interest rate on the mortgage loans and the rate payable to holders of the participations, or if a whole loan is sold at a premium representing such spread, the tax effects of the transaction will vary depending on its form.

If a whole loan or a participation in a whole loan with an interest rate of, for example, 12 percent is sold at a premium, such that the yield to the purchaser is 10 percent, the amount of such premium will be includible by the seller for tax purposes as gain in the year of the sale. In any structure where the originator retains an excess servicing fee, the ownership of the excess interest will be treated as retained by the seller, and both the sold and retained interests will be reported under the coupon stripping rules of the Internal Revenue Code.

Financial institutions such as banks, thrifts, and insurance companies that need to actively manage their asset (and/or liability) size, vis-à-vis their regulatory capital positions, and institutions that need to restructure their portfolios will find that it can be advantageous from an accounting standpoint to sell commercial mortgages either outright or in conjunction with the issuance of whole loan participations. Under generally accepted accounting principles ("GAAP"), regulatory accounting principles applicable to FDIC-insured banks and FSLIC-insured thrift institutions, and statutory accounting principles applicable to insurance companies, the transfer of a whole loan and the issuance of a whole loan participation, without recourse to the seller, constitute a "sale," and thereby enable the transferor to remove from its balance sheet the principal amount of such a loan or the principal amount underlying such a participation. Similarly, properly structured transfers of commercial mortgages that allow for some recourse, either to the transferor or to the holder of a junior interest in a pool of mortgages, as in the case of "senior/subordinated" whole loan participations, result in the sale of the mortgages or the principal amount underlying the *senior* participation under generally accepted, FSLIC and statutory accounting principles.

When structuring a sale of whole loans, either outright or in connection with the issuance of participations, from the transferor's viewpoint the principal accounting objective is usually to recognize in the period the loan is sold the economic gain or loss from the sale. Gain or loss is equal to the sum of net cash proceeds plus the present value of the excess servicing, minus the sum of the book value of the mortgage and any reserves for losses under recourse provisions. Under most circumstances in which the seller does not retain servicing, GAAP and statutory accounting principles would require that gain or loss be recognized at the time the loan is sold.

When loans are sold without the servicing rights, and such rights are retained by the seller, Statement of Financial Accounting Standards No. 65, "Accounting for Certain Mortgage Banking Activities ("SFAS No. 65"), is applied to determine whether, and to what extent, the sale encompasses "excess servicing" fees. SFAS No. 65 instructs that, if the stated servicing fee rate differs materially from a "normal" servicing fee rate, the sales price should be adjusted, for purposes of determining gain or loss on the sale, to provide for the recognition of a normal servicing fee in each subsequent year. The amount of the adjustment is the present value of the so-called "excess servicing" fee, or the difference between normal and stated servicing fees, amortized over the estimated life of the mortgage loans. The same guidance can be found in SFAS No. 77, paragraph (6).

The seller must determine an appropriate estimate for what constitutes a "normal" fee, based upon an examination of the characteristics of the loan or pool and a comparison of the accounting, reporting, and remitting requirements of the servicing agreement with those of other servicing agreements used in connection with similar loans or pools. Further, the seller must determine an appropriate discount rate and prepayment rate to apply to the excess servicing fees. SFAS No. 65 provides no guidance for making such a determination. Although a number of alternatives exist, this matter is currently under discussion at the FASB. Accordingly, institutions would be well-advised to consult with their accounting firm in making these determinations.

Commercial Mortgage Pools

If mortgages are contributed to a trust that issues participation certificates, the mortgage originator will receive sale treatment for tax purposes to the extent that participation interests in the trust are actually sold. Under current Treasury regulations, all interests in such a trust must be substantially identical, except that one class of interests (e.g., those retained by the originator) may be subordinated to another class. In addition, the trustee may not be given power to vary the investment in the trust; all payments received from mortgagors must be distributed to holders of participation interests and may not be reinvested.

If mortgages are contributed to an "owner trust" (the structure often used for issuance of CMO debt), assuming no REMIC election, there will generally not be a sale of the mortgages by the originator until the owner trust certificates are sold. If the residual interest is sold, the originator will recognize a gain or loss on such a sale. Interest paid on the CMO bonds will be allowable as a deduction to the holders of the owner trust certificates and all interest payments received on the mortgages will be gross income to such holders.

A REMIC ("Real Estate Mortgage Investment Conduit") is a tax-passive pass-through entity (trust, pool, partnership, or corporation) that can hold mortgages secured by any type of real property and can issue multiple classes of ownership interests in those mortgages to investors. These interests can be purchased and sold in the form of pass-through certificates, bonds, or other legal forms. The creation of REMICs removes, as of January 1, 1987, many of the tax provisions that have prevented issuers and investors in residential and commercial mortgage-backed securities from structuring more economically efficient securities.

A REMIC must consist of one or more classes of "regular interests" and a single class of "residual interests." No other types of REMIC interests are permitted. Regular interests may have a fixed or floating interest rate and a specified principal amount.

Regular interests can be issued in multiple classes. Therefore, in a mortgage pool where prepayments are experienced, the cash flow from the earliest mortgages to prepay can be assigned to a short-term regular interest class while the cash flow from the last mortgages to pay off can be assigned to a long-term regular interest class, as is done in the case of a CMO.

Regular interests also can be issued with differing priorities in the event of defaults or prepayments on the underlying mortgages. Senior and subordinated participations in mortgage pools can be created and issued as classes of regular interests. The advantage of a REMIC senior/subordinated arrangement (as compared with similar arrangements under the grantor trust rules) is that the new tax law explicitly allows both the senior and subordinated classes to be freely traded. The IRS's position has been that multiple classes of interests in a traditional grantor trust participation or pass-through results in the trust being taxed as a corporation.

Residual interests are defined simply as interests that are not regular interests. Residual interests generally are intended to include rights to payments that are contingent on a certain speed of prepayments. Excess servicing income and "excess" mortgage principal in an overcollateralized structure are examples of items accruing to the residual interest holders.

In addition, residual interests can include the right to earnings on qualified reserve funds or cash flow investments that are not needed to pay the amounts guaranteed to holders of regular interests. There are no restrictions on the size of residual interests, but there must always be one residual interest in a REMIC. Only one class of residual interests is allowed, but more than one investor can share in the residual interest.

The contribution of mortgages to a REMIC will not result in sale treatment, but a sale will be recognized for tax purposes when and to the extent that interests in the REMIC are sold to third parties. The originator/sponsor of the REMIC will recognize gain or loss on such sale equal to the difference between the sale price of the REMIC interest and that portion of the originator's tax basis in the contributed mortgages allocated to such interest.

Existence of an excess servicing fee distinct from the residual interest in a REMIC would create the possibility that the structure would be in violation of statutory requirements. Thus, in a REMIC, the originator may retain the benefit of the spread only by retaining the residual interest.

The REMIC provisions provide flexibility in structuring transactions to allow issuers to treat the REMIC issue either as a sale of assets or a financing for accounting purposes, provided that they satisfy applicable GAAP and regulatory accounting principles (RAP). If the transaction is a sale of assets for accounting purposes, the assets are treated as if transferred to a third party and, as such, are removed from the issuer's balance sheet. Any gain or loss on disposition is immediately recognized. If an issuer does not wish to recognize the accounting gain or loss in the year issued, a financing structure should be developed. In this case, the gain or loss is reported over the life of the financing, primarily as the difference between interest income and interest expense.

Commercial mortgage pass-through certificates will normally be issued by a grantor trust, which is not taxable as a separate entity; instead, income, deductions, gains, and losses arising from the mortgages are taxable to the owners of the trust. Initially, this owner will be the mortgage originator or depositor. As participation certificates are sold to investors (assuming that there is a real transfer of the benefits and burdens of owning the mortgage), the originator will realize gain or loss for tax purposes on such a sale. The amount of gain or loss for tax realized on the sale, prorated for the percentage interest that is sold.

Senior/subordinated pass-through securities will be treated in the same manner as nonsubordinated securities, provided the requirements of the "Sears Regulations," discussed below, are met. The mortgage originator, acting through a grantor trust, will recognize gain or loss on the sale of beneficial interests in the trust, equal to the difference between the originator's basis in the portion of the mortgages sold and the amount realized on the sale.

Treasury Regulation 301.7701-4 (c) permits grantor trust pass-through treatment for a trust that issues senior and subordinated certificates only if the trust qualifies as a "fixed investment trust." In practice, this means that the trustee should have no power to vary the investment (e.g., by substituting mortgages), and should be required to distribute all interest and principal payments on the mortgages to the certificateholders, and not reinvest the proceeds. The regulations allow a subordination feature as the only permissible difference among classes of interest in the trust, although a "shifting interest" subordination structure as provided in the Meritor transaction would not be permitted.

Commercial mortgage pass-through certificates will generally have the same characteristics as the underlying mortgages. Thus, the certificates will be "qualifying real property loans" for purposes of the thrift bad debt deduction, "real estate assets" for real estate investment trusts, and "loans secured by an interest in real property" for the purpose of the rules governing permitted assets of domestic building and loan societies, assuming in each case that the underlying mortgages so qualify and, in the case of senior/subordinated certificates, that the "Sears Regulations" standards are met.

Each commercial mortgage pass-through certificate represents an undivided interest in the unpaid principal balance of each mortgage in the pool, plus interest payments on the outstanding principal balances at the mortgage interest rate, typically coupled with a corresponding obligation to pay a servicing fee (usually in the form of an interest rate "spread") to the servicer. Holders will be required to report as income their proportionate share of interest income and will be entitled to deductions for servicing fees and other expenses (subject to the later discussion of excess servicing fees). Holders will recognize gain or loss on the sale or other disposition of their certificates equal to the difference between the amount realized on the disposition and their basis in the certificates (generally, their cost, less any repayments of principal received while they held the certificates).

Holders of either senior or subordinated certificates will generally recognize interest income on the underlying mortgages as it is received or accrued, with offsetting deductions for servicing fees (subject to the discussion of "excess servicing fees" covered later). Holders will recognize gain or loss on the sale or other disposition of certificates equal to the difference between the amount realized on such disposition and the holders' basis (generally cost less any principal payments received) in the certificates.

There is little authority as to what level of "spread" constitutes reasonable servicing compensation for tax purposes. If the spread is reasonable, the mortgage seller/servicer would report the servicing spread as ordinary income as received and would have a corresponding deduction for actual servicing costs. If, however, the servicing compensation is determined to be in excess of a reasonable amount, purchasers may be required to report income according to the coupon stripping rules of the Internal Revenue Code. If the participations are sold at a price not equal to the aggregate principal amount, holders may have either original issue discount (if the mortgages are sold for a price less than their face amount) or amortizable premium (if sold at a price exceeding the face amount), with corresponding adjustments to the holders' income over the life of the certificates.

When mortgage pass-through certificates representing undivided ownership interests in a pool of mortgages are issued entirely without recourse to the sponsor, the sponsor should properly account for the transfer of the underlying mortgage assets as a sale of such assets. However, even when mortgage pass-through certificates are issued with recourse to the sponsor, the transfer of the underlying mortgages may be treated as a sale of such assets under GAAP, provided that the requirements of FASB Statement of Financial Accounting Standards No.77, "Reporting by Transferors for Transfers of Receivables with Recourse" ("SFAS No.77") are complied with. SFAS No.77 provides that sale treatment is not appropriate unless the structure of the transaction is such that:

• The transferor surrenders control of the future economic benefits embodied in the receivables. Control has not been surrendered if the transferor has an option to repurchase the receivables at a later date.
• The transferor's obligation under the recourse provisions can be reasonably estimated. Lack of experience with receivables with characteristics similar to those being transferred or other factors that affect a determination at the transfer date of the collectibility of the receivables may impair the ability to make a reasonable estimate of the probable bad debt losses and related cost of collections and repossessions. A transfer of receivables shall not be recognized as a sale if collectibility of the receivables and related costs of collection and repossession are not subject to reasonable estimation.
• The transferee cannot require the transferor to repurchase the receivables except according to the recourse provisions.

Conceivably, a sponsor could retain 100 percent of the recourse risk and still obtain sale treatment provided the recourse can be reasonably estimated and an appropriate reserve is provided when the receivables are sold. Estimation of recourse risk, not usually a problem when pooling residential mortgages, is more difficult with pools of commercial mortgages due to their lack of homogeneity and historical loss data.

The American Institute of Certified Public Accountants Savings and

Loan Associations Committee has recently considered the accounting treatment for transfers with recourse of receivables involving commercial mortgages or securities collateralized by commercial mortgages. Recognizing that recourse estimation is more difficult for commercial mortgages, the Committee believes that it may be possible for transfers of commercial mortgages with recourse to be treated as sales in accordance with the provisions of SFAS No. 77, *provided* that appropriate data is available at the date of transfer to estimate the recourse provision. Specifically, the Committee has stated that sufficient information should be available on the individual properties to indicate whether there is any current doubt about the ultimate collectibility of the receivables. If a specific mortgage is believed to have a current loss exposure, the Committee has stated that there is a presumption that the ultimate loss exposure cannot be reasonably estimated in accordance with SFAS No. 77, and that the transaction therefore should not be treated as a sale.

Although the requirement that the transferor "surrender control of the future economic benefits embodied in the receivables" would appear to defeat sale treatment where a seller retains excess servicing fees, this provision is generally interpreted as permitting the retention of such fees under the theory that they are not "embodied" in the receivables sold. Similarly, the right to receive prepayment penalties on a pool of commercial mortgages would seem to run counter to the concept of surrendering control of the "future economic benefits embodied in the receivables." However, the benefit of the prepayment penalty, like servicing, is generally deemed to have been stripped from the assets prior to sale and is, therefore, not viewed as being "embodied" in the receivables sold. Conversely, pass-through participations by which the sponsor may benefit from an increase in the value of the mortgaged property through retention of an "equity kicker" are much more difficult to characterize as benefits not "embodied in the receivables." Hence, sponsors seeking to retain such interests may have difficulty fitting within the parameters of SFAS No. 77.

SFAS No. 77 indicates that although the first factor generally prohibits options to repurchase by the sponsor, it would not prevent the sponsor from retaining an option to repurchase assets when the amount of outstanding receivables is only minor. Thus, a so-called "clean-up" call, which allows the sponsor to repurchase the receivables when the cost of servicing becomes unreasonable, may be structured into the transaction. Sponsors that are not seeking to account for the transaction as a sale can structure a substantial call or take-out provision into the transfer, since such a call might cause the transfer to fail to meet SFAS No.77 criteria.[7]

Pass-through transactions may also be structured with senior and subordinated interests in a "senior/subordinated" structure where principal and interest payments to the holders of the junior certificates are subordinated to the interests of the senior class. This structure provides credit enhancement to the senior certificateholders without the need for third-party credit enhancements. In a senior/subordinated transaction, SFAS No. 77 is interpreted to permit the retention of a subordinated residual piece by the sponsor. Thus, provided all other criteria are met, if a subordinated class is retained, sale treatment for GAAP purposes should be possible with respect to the senior interests in the mortgages sold. The subordinated class retained by the sponsor would continue to be accounted for by the sponsor as an asset (unless it is sold) and treated accordingly.

Sponsors of mortgage pass-through transactions that are thrifts or commercial banks reporting to the FSLIC or FDIC must also be concerned about the proper accounting for a transaction under regulatory accounting principles; treatment will depend upon whether the sponsor is insured by the FSLIC or the FDIC. Regulatory accounting principles governing reports to the FSLIC permit an insured institution to account for the transaction as it would under GAAP. That is, the FSLIC recognizes the principles of SFAS No. 77 in determining whether sale treatment is appropriate.

However, the federal banking agencies follow the guidelines of the Federal Financial Institutions Examination Council ("FFIEC"), which specifies how sales of assets (other than residential mortgages, which are treated differently) should be accounted for on call reports of banks they regulate. FFIEC guidelines reject the more liberal SFAS No. 77 standards and establish their own standards, which disallow sale treatment in any transaction where the bank retains *any* risk of loss on the assets transferred. Although there are exceptions to this general standard, they do not generally assist in the structuring of asset securitizations. However, the FFIEC has determined for call report purposes that retention (by a bank that transfers loans "without recourse") of a residual interest in an escrow account established to absorb losses on the transferred loans does not, in and of itself, constitute a risk of loss or obli-

---

[7]See paragraph 34 of SFAS No. 77.

gation for payment. Thus, escrow accounts have been used successfully in asset securitization transactions (e.g., for credit card receivables) to assure sale treatment of the underlying assets. The escrow account is generally funded with the spread between the interest received from the underlying receivables (minus servicing fees) and the interest paid to certificateholders, and thereby serves as a credit enhancement. Typically, however, the spreads associated with commercial mortgages are not wide enough to establish a spread account in an amount currently acceptable to the rating agencies for a triple-A or double-A rated security.

OUTLOOK

While many barriers to securitized commercial mortgage transactions have been eliminated, a number of hurdles still remain. Lack of standardization of commercial mortgages continues to be the biggest impediment to the rapid development of this market. Creative structuring, however, can offset this lack of conformity, and the availability of rating criteria and other benchmarks can be used to establish consistency.

Securitized commerical mortgage transactions constitute one of the most far–reaching structural changes occurring in the real estate capital markets. By increasing the supply of capital, decreasing the cost of assembling debt, and improving the efficiencies of evaluating and pricing real estate investments, commercial mortgage securitization has significantly altered the relationships between borrowers, lenders, and investors. As a result, securitized commercial real estate transactions should continue to take over a growing portion of the real estate debt markets.

Credit: Several pages of this chapter appeared in an article by the author in the Summer 1987 issue of the *Real Estate Finance Journal*.

CHAPTER 7

SECURITIZING
FEDERAL ASSETS

John R. Price, Managing Director
Manufacturers Hanover Investment Banking Group

INTRODUCTION

September 1987 witnessed the dramatic entry into the capital markets of a cluster of issues backed by a diverse array of loans originally made by federal government agencies and held until that time in their portfolios. Just days before the end of the government's fiscal year, underwriters and advisors finished structuring the securities and placing them with investors to satisfy the requirements of the Omnibus Budget Reconciliation Act, which had become law nearly a year earlier.

The federal government is not a newcomer to asset securitization. In fact, nearly two decades earlier it had pioneered the field by creating the Government National Mortgage Association (GNMA). GNMA had built upon the efforts of some thrifts to tap the capital markets for mortgage financing and had been the principal mechanism for transforming the mortgage business. What separated this new effort from the federal government's earlier forays into securitization was the fact that these sales were successfully concluded *without recourse* to the government, either directly or indirectly, by giving agency status to the issuing entities. Although pricing of the earlier GNMA issues was affected to some degree by the novelty of the instrument and to a great degree by interest rate moves and prepayment rate assumptions, it was affected most by the government's guarantee of principal and interest to the holder.

Indeed, the assets underlying the GNMA guaranteed issues were themselves either guaranteed or insured by the Federal Housing Administration or the Veterans Administration. In contrast, the 1987 sales contained
no federal agency guarantee and the participants went to great lengths
to avoid government backing.

For some time, the Reagan Administration had been interested
in the selling of government assets. There were several reasons for
this. Some were related to the drive to privatization. Thus, the sale
of government assets was a first cousin of the move to enlist private
suppliers to perform services previously done by government employees.
In several successive budgets there had been proposals to sell many
varieties of assets, ranging from the Tennessee Valley Authority itself to
Rural Housing loans. Politically, this effort had encountered heavy seas,
despite the fact that some moves in this direction had finally become
acceptable enough to warrant implementation. These included giving
housing allowances to low-income users of housing instead of awarding
subsidies to the builders of low-income housing.

A second reason for the Administration's eagerness to sell loans
was that it wanted to try to pinpoint the amount or nature of the "true
subsidy" in many of the government's loan programs. Although a below-
market interest rate is a subsidy that is fairly easy to determine, many
government lending programs in fact place the government in the position
of being a lender of last resort. In these cases, there is no source of funds
for the borrowers other than government agency "public policy" loans.
To qualify for these loans, the borrower must usually demonstrate an
inability to obtain credit from conventional sources.

This means that there is not a ready "market" rate for these loans
that will permit an easy calculation of the real cost to the government
of making, servicing, and holding them. A market rate, or price, it
was reasoned, would really include an assessment by the marketplace
of the underlying credit quality of the loans. This assessment would be
reached through disciplined analyses of delinquency and default rates.
The market might also impose a penalty (which rating agencies and
investors would have to calculate) for transplanting the loans and their
servicing to the private sector, on the expectation that servicing standards
might be more exacting, and therefore reveal more delinquencies.

A third desire, closely related to the last one, was to improve the
overall quality of credit management. This, it was hoped, would not
only help determine subsidy levels but also reduce them. It was also

hoped that helpful lessons might emerge by examining the way the loans were originated, the degree of uniformity of documentation, and the application of qualification criteria. The Administration believed that although there was room for disagreement over whether certain public policy loans should be made in the first place, no one could argue with the need for good data, complete documentation, and clear credit standards if the loans were going to be made.

Many of these ideas had been around for some time, however, and the federal asset sales program only became a reality due to the convergence of accounting and politics. By the end of fiscal year (FY) 1986, the continuation of record budget deficits was leading to a bipartisan consensus that ways had to be found to reduce those deficits. The fact that the federal government operates on a cash accounting basis meant that the sales of loans from its portfolio would generate funds that could be used immediately to reduce the deficit. Most accountants agreed this would occur only if the sales were made on a nonrecourse basis; arguably, the sales would resemble borrowings if the federal government provided recourse. Despite many misgivings, enough bipartisan support was garnered to include loan asset sales in the law reconciling the budget for Fiscal Year 1987 and beyond. Even some of those who opposed the sale of existing loan assets and favored only sales of newly originated loans went along reluctantly with the "budget fix".

THE SECURITIES

In order to structure the securities for an asset-backed offering, many policy and technical obstacles had to be overcome. Even before the passage of OBRA (Omnibus Budget Reconciliation Act) and some further sales requirements contained in the Continuing Resolution, the Office of Management and Budget had identified several portfolios in certain departments for pilot programs and had created a Federal Credit Policy Working Group made up of senior level representatives of Agriculture, Education, and Housing and Urban Development, in addition to the omnipresent OMB and Treasury. Representatives of other agencies joined later. Seeking to deflect any statutory requirements for sale, the Working Group wanted to assure that the pilot sales were conducted under rules and in a manner that would reflect the Administration's intentions. Accordingly, the group drafted loan sale "Guidelines" that became the focus of most of the early discussions with financial advisors and investment bankers trying to find common ground with the government. The Guidelines reflected the Administration's distaste for recourse to the Federal Government, whether explicit or implied. All loans were to be sold without recourse and the servicing of the loans was to be turned over to private sector servicers as well.

Secondly, both Treasury and OMB insisted that the loans be sold with income from them being subject to federal income tax. This reflected Treasury's long standing opposition to tax-exempt financing, a view that had found its way at last into the Tax Reform Act of 1986. Fresh from this victory, Treasury and OMB were determined that the tide would not recede when it came to the disposition of federal government loans where the obligors were entities whose notes or bonds would ordinarily carry interest exempt from federal tax.

The Guidelines therefore provided that the loans must be sold in such a way that the payment of interest or dividends on them would be taxable. Although the Guidelines also allowed some sales of loans on a whole loan basis, the Working Group viewed that as an exception and not the rule. The Working Group would have to approve any whole loan sales, loan-by-loan. (See Appendix A for Guidelines for Loan Asset Sales, as modified following the FY 1987 loan sales and promulgated on February 9, 1988).

The Working Group turned to the Department of Agriculture and supported efforts of the Department to bring to market first a portfolio that all felt would be an auspicious beginning for the program. The Farmers Home Administration (FmHA), like many government lending agencies, had gone through many changes of emphasis and levels of sophistication of management in its decades of operation. By the time it became the focus of the new loan sales program, it was an agency with $70 billion in loans on its books, divided unequally among three principal programs. By this time, the top management of the FmHA had banking and financial experience. In addition, while the FmHA had placed its liabilities for 15 years with the Federal Financing Bank, it had earlier placed notes in the private capital markets. Most importantly, the FmHA data suggested that the delinquency rates for its borrowers in one of its programs were very low. For these reasons, the government began with a sale from the Rural Development Insurance Fund of its

Community Program loans. This sale was to be the "minesweeper" and FmHA, its advisor, and its underwriters were to identify and resolve most of the questions that would face sales from all agencies.

Tax Issues

Taxing the Untaxable—Alchemy in Federal Finance
One result of the selection of the Community Program loans at FmHA was that the issue of selling taxable or tax-exempt was immediately on the table. The sale of obligations bearing a tax-exempt coupon could realize higher cash proceeds at the time of sale than if interest on the obligations were taxable. For this reason, some firms interested in the asset sales program had initially suggested to FmHA that the portfolio should be analyzed on a tax-exempt basis.

The Community Program loans consisted of a variety of obligations, and they could be characterized for tax purposes as exempt or taxable depending on who the obligors were and the use to which the original proceeds were put. The loans had been made to meet essential community purposes in rural areas, such as water and waste treatment. Loans for such purposes would ordinarily be tax-exempt when issued by local government units regardless of whether the loans were general obligations payable from tax revenues of the obligor or only from revenues by the financed project. The remainder were the obligations of local not-for-profit entities, such as volunteer firemens' associations and libraries. Such obligations also would ordinarily be tax-exempt only if they were viewed for tax purposes as issued on behalf of a local government unit. A change after 1968 in the regulation governing the FmHA program requires opinions of bond counsel on the tax status of the loan, but the loans closed before then were thought able to sustain characterization as tax-exempt to the same extent as subsequent ones would have.

A very similar question was being confronted simultaneously at another government department whose loans were candidates for sale. The Department of Education had inherited two higher education loan programs from the Department of Housing and Urban Development and the Department of Health, Education and Welfare. The two portfolios whose loans were to be combined and sold were the College Housing Loan Program (CHLP) and the Academic Facilities Loan Program (AFLP). Generally, the loans had been extended to private colleges and universities. Yet some of the obligors were public universities, and the security for the loans varied from mortgages and pledges of project revenues to bonds that were issued by state units or their agents.

In light of these characteristics in both the Education and FmHA portfolios, firms could not be blamed for thinking how to aggregate, or disaggregate the loans, whether on a functional, regional, or a general obligation and pooled basis.

However, the momentum behind the adoption of the Guidelines was sufficient to assure that the sale would have to be on a taxable basis. Furthermore, while the immediate proceeds received by the government would be higher if the obligations were structured to pass through their underlying tax exempt character, Treasury and OMB were convinced they could demand taxable financing on a present value basis. This depended upon assumptions about the taxable nature of ultimate holders of any obligations being sold in this program. If the bulk of the ultimate holders were themselves taxable entities or individuals, the stream of tax payments Treasury would receive in the future would, on a present value basis, offset the increase in current proceeds realized if the loans were sold on a tax-exempt basis.

Therefore, structuring was to proceed on the premise that the untaxed was to be converted into the taxable. If a stream of payments was to be taxable, the makers of the payments could not be the original obligors on many of these loans. There was no way to arbitrarily recharacterize the payments made to a holder by one of the municipalities or the facilities whose revenues were pledged to the holder of the note. Converting the stream of payments into taxable payments required an entity that would receive the stream of payments from the underlying obligors, but which would be the issuer of new obligations. The entity could not simply be a surrogate for the underlying communities. Likewise, it could not be a surrogate for, or an agent of, the current holder of the underlying debt, namely the federal government. These two premises shaped the final form of the transaction.

For this reason, a pass-through security could not be used for sale of either the FmHA or the Education Department portfolios (it was for the Rural Housing portfolio, which did not have tax-exempt issuers, but home owners as the obligors). Even though, in both portfolios, there would be streams of payments that would be taxable, the presence of large percentages of the periodic payments ultimately deriving from local government units would taint the pass-through security at least to the extent of such payments. The government's determination to impede the flow of tax-exempt income would alone have barred a pass-through. A firm determination of which loans' payments could be flowed through to purchasers of a pass-through security as either exempt or taxable would have been a difficult task as well. This would have been particularly true of the FmHA Community Program portfolio, because bond opinions had been required relatively late in the program's history. Moreover, the scrutiny and new bond counsel opinions required would have been even more costly than the due diligence on the portfolio proved to be.

Even the use of pay-through securities issued by a grantor trust raised difficulties. Although the trust would likely be able to issue its own debt secured by the underlying loans, and although the interest on the newly issued obligations of the trust would be taxable, there was still an impediment. In the grantor trust, an equity position would be needed, so that the debt issued by the trust would not be deemed by the Internal Revenue Service to be equity in the absence of a qualifying equity interest. With the grantor trust, the holder of the equity, or ownership position or the holder of the beneficial interest, would be deemed to hold an interest in the underlying assets. Pass-through securities would ordinarily have represented an equity interest in a grantor trust. Therefore, to a greater or lesser degree, the holding of these interests, which would constitute the residual value of the trust after payment of debt service, would mean that tax-exempt income would be recognized in their hands. Once more, the Guidelines for the asset sales would be interpreted to preclude this. At this stage, the government was being advised to retain the residual interests for a while. But, assuming that the residuals would eventually be sold, this difficulty would remain. As long as the government agency held the beneficial interest, the presence of the tax-exempt income in its hands would leave it in the same position it was in as a portfolio lender, before the inception of the loan sales program. Once it did sell the beneficial interests in the grantor trust, the new owner's tax-exempt income would closely match his stream of revenue. Although the purchaser would presumably pay a higher price for a stream of tax-exempt income on the residual, the government (for the same reasons it would not want to sell the underlying loans on a tax-exempt basis) would not want to sell the residual with the same results.

Taxing the Issuing Entity
Treasury seemed most concerned about taxation of the stream of income received by the holder of the instrument. We have noted that the proceeds

would have differed on the sale had Treasury agreed to the sale of tax-exempt assets. Since Treasury knew they would earn back the differential over time by taxing the recipients of income from the new bonds, they imposed their preference for taxable securities. Already faced with a pricing that would yield the selling agencies less in cash proceeds at closing than they might have otherwise obtained, program officials were very concerned about any other factors that would further reduce the proceeds. In the case of the two portfolios that contained the large quantities of tax-exempt loans, there was another factor that could have dramatically reduced the proceeds. This was the fact that the loans in both the Community Program portfolio at FmHA and the loans in the College Housing and Academic Facilities Loan programs at the Department of Education, bore coupon rates that were considerably below market. The weighted average interest rate in the Education portfolio was 3.16 percent, with a fairly narrow range of coupons from 2.75 to 3.75 percent. The Farmers Home Administration Community Program loan portfolio had a weighted average interest rate of just over 5 percent, with most loans bunched there (although coupons ranged from 3 percent to over 14 percent).

These rates were well below market even if the loans were to be bought from the government on a tax-exempt basis. Assuming they would be bought by an entity that would issue taxable debt to buy them, the market discount would be even greater to produce yields at current market levels. The loans were originally issued at par and repayments of principal to the government would result in a tax-free return of capital since the government is not a taxpayer. But a sale of the loans, even tax-exempt ones, at a discount to face (because of changes of interest rates, for example) would create market discount in the hands of the holders so that payment of principal on the loans would only in part represent a tax-free return on capital and in part the receipt of taxable income. This was a period in which the Treasury long bond range was over 8 percent, climbed to 9.25 percent at closing, and higher shortly thereafter. Unless otherwise sheltered, a market discount on loans bought by the entity issuing debt would cause the entity to recognize income on which tax would have to be paid.

Initially, the pricing of the sale would be adversely affected. If the entity were unable to meet the cash requirements for tax payments, the cash flows and the pricing would have to be adjusted in a way that would dramatically affect the proceeds the government could receive on the loan sale. Cash flow that otherwise could go for debt service would have to be diverted to the payment of taxes. Thus the overcollateralization level would have to be increased to support the senior debt, and the proceeds to the government at closing would be reduced. Also, the residual might have no value in the marketplace at all because there would be no cash flow at some point, and it would be accompanied by a growing tax liability. Thus, not only would less value have been obtained up front in the sale of the loans, but there would be no value to the residual. Both on grounds of policy and statute, it appeared unlikely that the government would allow the sale of the residual for its tax loss value. No doubt a purchaser, using whatever assumptions he wished about future tax rates, might have assigned a value to the use of the tax liabilities contained in the residual due to the mismatch between deductions and recognizable market discount. But the government, and the IRS in particular, had or would have had, severe difficulties with finding value in the residual by permitting its use in this way.

This came about in the following manner. Of course, the existence of market discount, with respect to the loans, would not increase the tax liability of the issuing entity, when this entity was capitalized previously with debt that paid deductible interest (including original issue discount) at approximately the same rate as the effective rate of interest on the loans (taking into account the discount on the loans). The deductions for interest on the debt, which would be greater in early years, would measurably reduce the potential tax liability for the market discount by effectively sheltering such discount.

Yet, in another of the fascinating peculiarities of this transaction, the value of the shelter was minimized because a large portion of the underlying assets (the loans held in FmHA's portfolio) was itself tax-exempt. By statute, one is not permitted to borrow on a taxable (and deductible) basis to purchase or carry securities or obligations on whose stream of payments one pays no tax. In other words, double dipping at the expense of the IRS is prohibited. Therefore, there could be no interest deduction on that portion of the underlying portfolio of loans deemed to be tax-exempt. As a result the value of the shelter from the issuance of debt was effectively eliminated.

Tax considerations now became paramount. As a result, the question became, how can we reduce or eliminate tax at the entity level? Three possibilities emerged, each with its own complications.

First, the cleanest approach was based on the idea that these sales had a public policy purpose: to reduce the federal budget deficit and improve the management of the credit quality of federal loan programs. That appeared to argue in favor of giving a selling entity not-for-profit status. If the issuer were a nonprofit obligor under Sections 501(C)(3) or 501(C)(4) of the Internal Revenue Code, there would be no tax imposed on it as a result of the recognition of market discount, or for that matter, any other provision of the Code.

A second approach was derived from corporate tax law and seemed to be particularly suited to a transaction where a taxable exchange would otherwise result in recognition of market discount. This was the application of the nonrecognition exchange sections of the Internal Revenue Code. The tax law provides certain situations in which gain is not recognized on transfers to corporations by their shareholders. Under Section 351 of the Code, if a person exchanges an asset or group of assets for stock (or debt securities) in a company to which the assets are transferred, and immediately following the exchange such person controls at least 80 percent of the stocks of the transferee, no gain or loss is recognized on the exchange for tax purposes, and the tax basis of the assets is carried over to the transferee.

In our example, this meant that if the loans could be transferred to the issuing entity in a Section 351 exchange, it would not be necessary to deal with the market discount question, with its dramatic impact on pricing, because no discount would be created in connection with such a tax-free exchange. In order to qualify as a Section 351 exchange, the selling agency, in this case the Farmers Home Administration, would receive both cash and all of the stock in the issuing entity in exchange for the loans it transferred.

The new entity would raise cash by issuing taxable debt, both senior and subordinated securities, to be discussed later. The stock would be the "equity" interest in the issuing entity—the equivalent to the stock that a transferor taking advantage of Section 351 of the Revenue Code would get back, with or without cash, when his assets were transferred to the newly formed corporation. In our case, the presence of cash as part of (the largest part by far) the value received by the transferor was not a problem. Ordinarily, the receipt by the transferor of cash or "boot" will result in a partial taxation of the transaction. Because the transferor in this transaction was the federal government, there was no taxable party to the transfer.

The holding, even briefly, of an interest characterized as "equity" presented difficulties for the government. This related once more to the desire to avoid any appearance of recourse to the government. The holding of "stock" in a "corporation" concerned many of the government's lawyers who were anxious to avoid a connection with an issuing entity that might lead it to be characterized as an agency of the government.

Here we were caught between the legislative and policy needs of various federal agencies. For this approach to be useful, therefore, another step was required. Instead of creating a corporation whose stock would be distributed to the transferor of the assets, a business trust would be formed. This placed with the selling agency an appropriately different type of interest, namely a certificate of beneficial interest in the trust and not stock or equity in a corporation. The tax objectives could be realized because the trust could be taxed as a corporation and enjoy the advantages of the Section 351 transfer. Yet the important distance that the government sought to place between itself and the issuer/purchaser could be created.

In fact, this section of the Code did not insulate the issuer as much as a nonprofit entity would. In the latter case, there were no tax liabilities. With the business trust, there were still possible scenarios where alternative minimum tax results could adversely impact the trust. It was not certain, at the time the sale was to take place, what changes there might be in the alternative minimum tax law. So, a substantial tax reserve would have to be created at closing from the proceeds.

Yet a third approach was used in the Department of Education sale. Faced with the same need to avoid market discount and the unwillingness to hold an "equity" interest, underwriters sought to avoid tax liability at the issuer level by establishing a Regulated Investment Company under the Investment Company Act of 1940 that is not subject to an entity level tax provided certain distribution and other requirements are satisfied. It was debatable whether the business trusts being created for these two sales would fit the definition of the Investment Company Act. If they were, and if there were not relief from the regulatory provisions of that Act, it was going to be difficult to bring off a successful sale. For one thing, the economics would have been severely affected. Unlike issues supported by pools of mortgages, where amendments to the Act had kept pace with market developments in the world of collateralized mortgage obligations, the issues contemplated here were supported by a wide range of nonmortgage assets, including general obligation and revenue bonds. Although issues secured by mortgages were exempt from some of the onerous provisions of the Act, these issues might have been subject, for example, to a 300 percent overcollateralization requirement. At this point, the tactics of two of the sales diverged. Each depended on a favorable attitude by the Securities and Exchange Commission, which was forthcoming in both instances.

In the first, the FmHA sought and received a blanket exemption from the provisions of the 1940 Act. Certain requirements were imposed on the transaction, but only a couple had even a slight impact on marketing. On the other hand, the Education Department sought numerous exemptions from what otherwise would have been required of its Regulated Investment Company. By doing so it avoided taxation at the entity level.

Thus, all three approaches appear to be practical. The nonprofit entity approach was not specifically used in any of the sales because it would have required more time to secure the approval of the Revenue Service.

The largest of all the sales, the Rural Housing loans from FmHA, did not have to wind its way through the labyrinth of tax laws, since it relied on a recently passed statute that afforded tax freedom for mortgage loan sales. The REMIC or Real Estate Mortgage Investment Conduit had been exempted by Congress from taxation, even though the regulations were still being drafted as the sale was being prepared. This legislation was asset specific and did afford the necessary relief for the sale structure.

Issues of Recourse

Nothing was more important to the federal government than to assure the finality of sales and to avoid recourse to the government. The initial instinct was to have purchasers "put the money on the stump and run." In fact, during the fiscal year, the Administration encouraged an effort by one federal agency to put out its loans for bid at auction, but the offer was withdrawn when it became clear that the prices offered for a loan pool of uncertain credit quality were going to be unacceptable. However, the aborted auction procedure did convince the government that the two Departments required to conduct sales in the fiscal year were proceeding correctly. Each had retained financial advisors to determine what sort of structure would be the most practicable for the sale of the types of loans held by the Departments. The cancelled auction helped to solidify another notion. Rather than simply sell whole loans, about which little was known, into the marketplace, and point to (perhaps) low offering prices as a means of showing how much inherent subsidy there was in the programs, it was felt desirable to structure the sales to maximize proceeds to the selling agencies, develop the data and procedural changes the private sector wanted, and improve the management of credit programs.

Senior-Subordinate Structures and Overcollateralization

One of the first things apparent to those examining the loans to be sold was that the loans had been originated according to public policy criteria rather than standard commercial criteria. In the case of the FmHA Community Program borrowers, few of the communities had credit ratings. Without exception, the community, or the water district or community facility, in order to qualify for the FmHA loan, had to be unable to obtain the funds on commercial borrowing terms. It was true that the delinquency data maintained by FmHA indicated that the overall credit quality of the portfolio was good, and that delinquencies were low, one reason this portfolio had been selected for a pilot sale in the first place. Still, there was no aging of delinquencies according to commercial practice, and the kinds of data associated with rated securities were absent. As a result, on a private sector comparable basis, the credit quality was uncertain.

The government advisors believed that they should not give up any value and were initially wary of structures that did not provide upfront cash. The task was to work within, or if necessary, get modifications of, the Guidelines. The first of the Guidelines reads as follows:

> Loan asset sales shall be made without future recourse to the federal government. For the purposes of these guidelines, recourse includes any federal guarantees of principal and interest payments, repurchase contracts, agreements to replace bad loans with good loans, warranties relating to collateral value, or any other agreements requiring continued federal involvement or contingent liability. Any credit enhancement measures, such as reserve funds, over collateralization, or insurance, shall be the responsibility of the purchaser.

Given the other constraints on the sale, it seemed to FmHA's advisors and underwriters on this first portfolio that a senior-subordinate pay-through structure would capture the most value for the selling agencies. One of the first steps was to give tapes of the FmHA portfolio to the rating agencies to help them in their analysis. Meanwhile, representatives of the principal bond insurance firms were invited to consider taking part in the transactions. Because of the potential size of the offerings, an ironic relationship developed between the rating agencies and the bond insurers. If the insurers were overly ambitious in their approach to these untested portfolios and were improperly to price guarantees of principal and interest payments, the ratings of the bond insurance firms themselves might be in jeopardy from the same rating agencies that would be depending upon their policies to upgrade the ratings on these issues.

In any case, and particularly before there were solid numbers on the cash likely to be generated by the sales, it was clear that some overcollateralization or coverage ratio would be required for any bonds to obtain an investment-grade rating. The cash flow in excess of that needed to support principal and interest payments on the senior debt could itself be structured as a junior or subordinate interest in the cash flow. That cash flow could in turn be sold as debt, discounted admittedly at some steeper price by the market.

As with similar asset-backed issues and CMOs, there would be some "dregs" or possible residual cash flow after servicing both senior and junior debt. These would be the possible result of reserve funds or overly pessimistic estimates of the cash flows from the collateral. Again, the government was told that the residual interest itself would have some value, although it would be discounted even more aggressively than junk bonds. The government's advisors initially preferred to hold the junior, or subordinate interests, and the residuals. That was because the rating agencies and the investing public would all find these securities novel and would demand a premium for the uncertainty about repayment. This would be reflected in the level of overcollateralization or coverage ratio the rating agencies would insist on to give the issue the highest rating, or the rating where the government maximized its return. The advisors believed that as the aging of the underlying portfolio proceeded, and as a delinquency record was compiled, the perception of the credit quality would improve. That in turn would likely bring the government a higher market price for the subordinate interest and the residual. Arguably, this potential increase in value could be frustrated by interest rate moves. An uptick of one or two points in the Treasury's long bond yield might more than offset a conviction that one or two fewer percentage points of coverage ratio were enough to support a triple-A rating.

Yet, this market argument was not the one which caused the government to delay for some time approving a rather standard senior/subordinate structure. Rather, the concern of policymakers was for the government to take back, even for a short time, a subordinate or residual interest, or both. A point in need of clarification arose from concern that the government was not receiving all cash at the closing in full payment of the value of the loans it had sold. Any lingering interest in the form of retention of securities that were part of the payment for the loans might be construed as a continuing government presence in the transaction, giving rise to the concern that a court could determine that the issuing entity's paper was equivalent to government agency paper.

The crucial point was finally accepted. Once the government had sold loans and received cash and security interests, the purchaser and the rating agencies did not look to the seller of the assets collateralizing the new issue (with the exception of the curing of any defects explicitly discussed in any representations and warranties made by the seller, discussed later). Rather, it was eventually understood that the credit enhancement techniques referred to earlier were a part of structuring the transaction. They impose a cost on the transaction because they add to the price that can be obtained on the sale of the senior portion of the cash flow. Yet once structured, as with similar commercial sales, there is no recourse back to the seller.

Even after that conceptual hurdle was cleared, some officials were still uneasy about whether that conclusion would be reversed if the government were to continue in perpetuity to hold a residual interest. Although the same conclusion was appropriate, the members of the Working Group initially placed a 36-month time limit on the duration of holding a residual or subordinate interest in any of the issuing entities to be created. This required one further modification. For the tax reasons discussed above, the potential use of a not-for-profit trust as an issuing entity raised another novel twist on the retention of interests. For Internal Revenue Service approval of Section 501(c)(3) or (c)(4) status, some form of "equity" in the issuing entity was needed. This was because the trust would be issuing debt supported by the cash flow from the loans it would be purchasing from the government and no entity, not even a nonprofit one, can escape the IRS's requirement that a substantial level of equity be maintained.

In an ordinary business trust, the equity interest would, of course, be freely transferable. That is the case with the issuing vehicles used finally in 1987 by both the FmHA Community Program and the Education sales. However, in the case of the nonprofit issuer there was a clash of purposes. The government favored an alienation of any interest within

36 months. Yet, to allow a nonprofit issuer, the IRS felt that there had to be some continued residual interest in favor of the federal government throughout the entire duration of the trust. Thus, the government itself would have to be an ultimate beneficiary or charitable remainderman under the terms of the trust. It needed to have a permanent position as beneficiary to allow the public purpose nature of the trust to stand. It could be disastrous if the characterization were to change down the road, due to the imposition of tax liability. Given this clash of public purposes, the OMB and the Working Group agreed that if the nonprofit issuer appeared to be the best vehicle to serve the government's purposes, the retention for the entire life of the trust of a charitable remainderman interest would not violate the Guidelines and would not be deemed to indicate recourse to the federal government.

It was never resolved whether the government could "retain" ownership of the remainder interest, but hypothecate it in such a way as to "cash out" the interest. Time simply overcame things, and the three sales moved down the routes of business trust, Regulated Investment Company, and REMIC, all with subordinate and residual interests.

Representations and Warranties, and Recourse

Another issue that threatened to be interpreted as recourse was the making of representations and warranties by any of the federal agencies about the loans they were selling. The federal government is not accustomed to making representations and warranties and was concerned about both the nature of the specific representations and warranties, and their duration beyond the closing. The greatest concern was that representations might be made that would cause the issuing entity to be viewed as a federal agency. Initially, there was difficulty making any representations and warranties much beyond the validity of the loans and the legal description of the program under which the loans had been originated. Gradually, acceptance was won for statements about the authority of the agencies to sell the loans, execute the loan sale agreements, transfer servicing to the private sector, and confer good title for each note being sold. Once this bridge was crossed, the next question had to do with the loans themselves, and dealt with such things as rights of set offs, insolvencies of borrowers, rights of rescission, and delinquency data.

The government finally did agree to make legal representations like those commonly found in sales agreements. It was a bit more reluctant to represent the exact characteristics of the loans themselves. This was due largely to the data on the loans, as was discussed earlier. For loan information on the FmHA sale to be viewed as accurate enough, full file reviews ultimately became necessary, and representations and warranties in the prospectus reflected this. Initially, the government had generally assumed that all loans from a given portfolio would be sold, including those delinquent and those in default. In fact, one piece of legislation dictated that the Commerce Department's Economic Development Administration could sell only the delinquent or defaulted loans, if any were sold at all.

It was true that the portfolio quality at FmHA was very high, with around 1 percent delinquencies as the government's information indicated, and as due diligence affirmed. Nonetheless, and because there were plenty of current loans in the $8 billion Community Program portfolio, the government was persuaded to adhere to the commercial practice of keeping delinquent loans out of the portfolio to be sold. This was one of those points in the process in which the private sector felt strongly that replicable and acceptable structures and practices had to be used to achieve market acceptance. The government ultimately agreed to commercial-type representations and warranties, as well as remedies for the breach of them. The remedies were for substitution or a cash payment equivalent to the bond value of the deficient loans. In the case of the sales from the FmHA portfolio of Community Program loans and of the Education Department loans, substitution would begin right after closing. In the case of the Rural Housing portfolio, the process would be extended because the file by file due diligence process on more than 140,000 loans had to be deferred until after the closing, due to the closeness of the fiscal year-end deadline.

Building Cash Flows

Modelling the cash flows for these portfolios was one of the more daunting tasks investment bankers were asked to perform in 1987. The Community Program portfolio, the first to be explored, turned out to have an interesting array of loan payments. Because the underlying obligations were often made by municipalities, the frequency stated in the bond instruments was annual or semiannual. Aside from the fact that some were amortizing loans and some were principal plus loans, the original payment schedules had often been modified by supplemental agreements between the obligors and the Farmers Home field office that serviced their loans. These agreements often converted annual pay loans into monthly payments to FmHA. The maturities and coupon interest rates also varied widely. Initially, it was hoped that reliance upon data on the entire portfolio of loans compiled from answers to a questionnaire sent to all FmHA district offices would be sufficient. However, when the accountants began to compare the accounting tape generated by the financial arm of the agency with the data delivered from the field, there was still enough doubt to warrant a complete file review of the loans tentatively selected for sale. Thus, instead of reviewing 2,000 loans, as originally contemplated, over 8,200 loans were fully reviewed, and just over 6,400 were included in the sale. Based on the loan characteristics and cash flows, underwriters decided to structure the securities as discount bonds and to create a series of five tranches of pay-through bonds, mirroring to some extent the underlying maturities and flows on the loans. The average lives of the tranches ranged from $3\frac{1}{2}$ to around 32 years. This was to become the first issue of multiclass pay-through bonds.

Meanwhile the rating agencies had been analyzing the loans and the proposed bond structure. Due to the interpolation in the financing structure of several reserve funds, the rating agencies were satisfied with a lower coverage ratio (107 percent) than had been anticipated and awarded the issue triple-A ratings. With this structure and ratings, the first sale was ready to be priced and brought to market.

The Department of Education offering, with a somewhat similar collateral portfolio and bond structure, soon followed.

Although the Rural Housing portfolio did not raise the question of tax-exempt income, it did pose some difficulties that sometimes made it appear that it could not be successfully structured. The Rural Housing portfolio was made up of loans to the owners of homes who had few assets and little income and could not get a conventional or even a government insured mortgage. The rates charged to the borrowers were market rates at the time the loans were made, under the program as it had operated until recent years. At one point, the policy decision was made to offer loans only to borrowers who needed a subsidy. From that time, a subsidy could be offered to buy down the actual debt service requirement of the borrower from the market rate of interest to as little as 1 percent. This amount could fluctuate from year to year, as FmHA personnel adjusted the subsidy based on need.

Clearly, modelling the cash flows on these loans would be difficult.

The law also required interest subsidies for any borrowers who became eligible, even though they had borrowed at market rates when they initially incurred the obligation. Unless the federal government absorbed the risk of the need for interest subsidy or "interest credit" and thus gave the cash flows some level of predictability, the portfolio would be unsaleable. A similar problem concerned the rights of borrowers to a moratorium on payments in certain hardship situations. The stage was set for a clash between the desire to see a sale—as mandated by statute— and the interpretation of the guideline barring recourse to the federal gorvernment. If the rights of borrowers under the statute were to be observed and the loans were to be sold, the federal government had little choice other than to preserve the rights of borrowers to an interest credit. The solution was to use the Rural Housing Insurance Fund to backstop the need to substitute loans or provide for the interest credit. In anticipation of the possibility some future statute would expand the rights of Rural Housing borrowers, even those whose loans had been sold, the Insurance Fund insulated the issuing trusts from any reductions in payments due to such developments.

The payment characteristics of the loans again posed difficulties for the cash flows. As noted in the prospectus, the mortgage interest is calculated according to a simple interest method. This means that the borrower's payment will be allocated between principal and interest based on when he makes his payment. If the payment is ahead of schedule, more of it will be allocated to principal, and the reverse if the payment is late. Because this would have some impact on yields, the securities were structured to modify that impact. Another portfolio characteristic that would affect credit quality perceptions (and consequently the coverage ratios required by the rating agencies), was the fact that loans were originally made for 100 percent of appraised valuation. In other words, there was no owner's equity in the transaction at first, and there were no recent appraisals that could be used to calculate what sort of equity cushion there might be. Furthermore, no escrow was ever required of the borrowers for the payment of taxes or hazard insurance premiums. From time to time FmHA would make supplemental loans to borrowers for payment of these types of expenses, and the monthly payments by borrowers to FmHA to repay these advances were not unlike payments into an escrow fund.

A senior subordinated structure, involving a series of trusts with cross support features, was chosen to make these cash flows most marketable. The portfolio of loans was going to be striated or grouped by interest rate (excluding any interest credit loans, loans in delinquent status, or loans on which there was an outstanding loan being repaid to FmHA for any tax or insurance premium payment). A class of certificates was issued based on a grouping of underlying loans with a characteristic interest rate; the class would receive a fixed pass-through rate of interest on the underlying principal balance for the class. Shortfalls would be taken from amounts otherwise payable to subordinated interests. If there was insufficient payment from the mortgagors to pay the amount of interest and principal owed to the senior security holders, a policy written by the American Loan Guarantee Association would provide for payment. The underwriters calculated that the bond insurance premium was going to impose less of a penalty on the transaction to obtain a triple-A rating than would the full amount of cash flow coverage in the form of overcollateralization. It was estimated that nearly 130 percent coverage would be required in the absence of bond insurance, and the coverage requirement to obtain those triple-A ratings was reduced to 120 percent once the insurance policy was obtained.

PRICING THE SECURITIES

The FmHA sale of Community Program loans was attractive because of a discount coupon bond and the novel characteristics of the issue, and it began to resemble a corporate with an original issue discount coupon. There was strong interest found by the underwriters in an issue that paid like a corporate, but lacked the usual corporate risks. For example, due to the low coupon rate of the underlying loans, there was not a high risk at all of prepayment. Similarly, due to the nature of the trust and the underlying assets, there was not the kind of "event" risk that dominates many corporate issues—such as the risk of a takeover and the subsequent burdening of an issuer with additional debt service.

These characteristics, and the strong ratings given the issuer, permitted the Community Program Trust to go out at a relatively tight spread to Treasuries of comparable maturities. One tranche—a 20-year tranche in which much of the issue was concentrated—was priced off the 30-year Treasury and, at a final pricing of 105 over, was extremely popular. All series bore a 4.5 percent coupon. In the sale of the College and University Facility Loan Trust, the five series of bonds bore a coupon ranging from 8.5 to 10.55 percent. The Rural Housing sale resulted in the unusual phenomenon of one tranche (the short maturity first tranche) being priced at a lower interest rate than Treasuries. The summary by issue follows:

1. Sale of the Farmers Home Administration RDIF Loans

The bonds have five different stated maturities, and all series bear a 4.5 percent coupon rate. The bonds were priced as follows:

Series	Amt.	Stated Maturity (Average Life)	Price	Yield	Spread over Treasury
A-1	$245 mil	4/1/96 (3.47 years)	87.848	8.77%	+48 basis points
A-2	$116 mil	10/1/97 (7.47 years)	73.650	9.52%	+65 basis points
A-3	$204 mil	4/1/02 (10.47 years)	65.540	9.87%	+80 basis points
A-4	$1.031 mil	10/1/18 (20.47 years)	51.734	10.3%	+105 basis points
A-5	$203 mil	4/1/29 (31.95 years)	46.249	10.25%	+100 basis points

Source Congressional Budget Office

2. Sale of the Department of Education College Housing and Academic Facilities Loans

Series	Amount	Coupon	Stated Maturity (Average Life)	Price	Yield	Spread above Treasury
1	$12 mil	8.5	12/1/89	99.84	8.59	+35
2	$10.2 mil	9.2	12/1/91	99.875	9.24	+50
3	$12.3 mil	9.7	12/1/93	99.65	9.78	+75
4	$55 mil	10.2	6/1/02 (Avg. Life 10.44)	99.25	10.32	+95
5	37.6 mil	10.55	12/1/14 (Avg. Life 20.87)	99.375	10.63	+110

Source: Congressional Budget Office

3. Sale of Farmers Home Administration Rural Housing Insurance Fund Loans

Series	Amount	Coupon	Stated Maturity (Average Life)	Price	Yield	Spread over Treasury
1-A	184.316	6.33	6/1/94	93.6	8.63	− 1
1-B	126.661	6.33	6/1/97	83.15	9.52	+ 28
1-C	170.185	6.33	8/1/00	75.25	10.26	+ 85
1-D	616.414	6.33	4/1/26	67.15	10.76	+119
2-A	105.198	6.83	5/1/94	94.75	8.72	+ 8
2-B	263.806	6.83	10/1/02	78.5	10.31	+ 90
2-C	283.842	6.83	4/1/26	70	10.82	+125
3-A	153.896	7.33	2/1/01	87.625	9.865	+ 62.5
3-B	202.550	7.33	4/1/26	73.25	10.97	+140
4-A	135.436	8.33	2/1/05	88.4	10.36	+ 95
4-B	132.829	8.33	4/1/26	79.94	10.97	+140

Source: Congressional Budget Office

Valuing the Subordinate Interests

As noted earlier, the Federal Credit Policy Working Group favored retaining only briefly any subordinate or residual interests arising from the structuring of the transactions. Undoubtedly the recourse concerns were partly accountable for this attitude. However, another reason for wanting to realize cash was that the legislation had been passed with the expectation that the sales would receive proceeds at closing. It was going to be easier to tell the Congress that you got cash and not just a security that your banker tells you may be worth "X" in the current interest rate environment. The contrary argument was to hold onto the securities until they had realized their potential value and not sell them now at a steep discount to a speculator, who would later reap a windfall benefit when the "real value" of the underlying loans was demonstrated.

To establish for the government loan sales program as a whole that a subordinate interest did have some immediate tangible value and could be counted as proceeds now for deficit reduction purposes, the Farmers Home Administration elected to sell its subordinate debenture in the Community Program Trust. Since the collateral was the same as for the senior securities, a rating was sought. The paper obtained a single-

A rating and was of a single maturity, October 1, 2029. The pricing was at 170 over the 30-year Treasury, and brought about 53 percent of par (4.5 percent coupon once more), yielding 11.35 percent to maturity. The government, therefore, had cash proceeds and could argue that the residual interest, in which markets are made, had tangible value as well. The other sales have not yet liquidated the subordinate interests but are expected to do so within 36 months of the closing on the original sales.

BORROWER RELATIONS

Virtually all of the loans in the asset-backed offerings stemmed from public policy. That fact impinged most dramatically in the Rural Housing sales, where the obligors on the mortgages sold were to be granted the following: 1) a moratorium on their obligations for a statutorily specified time; 2) an interest credit; and 3) assurance that future changes in the law that would give to other borrowers whose loans had not been sold rights that had not existed at the time of sale, would apply to them as well.

In the FmHA Community Development loan sale attention was given to the way in which the borrowers were serviced, but it was not felt that future changes in servicing requirements, more advantageous to borrowers, should be transported into the private sector servicing environment. Therefore, to a greater or lesser extent, a loan servicing structure in the private sector was going to have to replicate the kind of servicing that the borrowers enjoyed when the government was the servicer. For example, in the FmHA Community Program sale, the servicing structure was organized so that the water districts would continue to deal with an organization that provided substantial assistance to the borrowers already. Payment practices would not be changed, even though they differed from the regular delinquency aging practices in the commercial sector. The structure even included a protective advance reserve fund so that if certain advances were required to keep machinery functioning, it would be available as it had been from FmHA. In these regards, attempts were made to make a servicing environment familiar and helpful. This was important as well in securing a favorable response from the rating agencies. Since these loans were "hot house plants" and had never been serviced before other than by the government, there was naturally concern about how rating agencies would analyze the possible impact of changed servicing environments on the expected performance of the obligations. The retention of the National Rural Water Association as a subservicer in the FmHA Community Program was, in part, to allay this concern.

Interestingly, here in the servicing area, there was once again a clash of purposes in the loan sales program. On the one hand, there were those who viewed private sector servicing as potentially more demanding than public sector servicing. It was thought that if stricter standards were imposed, a clearer picture of true delinquencies and defaults might emerge. This in turn would clarify the real amount of subsidy in the program, as indicated by the more lax credit management this might imply about the current servicing.

On the other hand, there were those who wished to derive the greatest or maximum proceeds at sale. To them, the recreation of a servicing environment closest to that in which the loans had been handled would mean the delinquency data ought not to worsen. This, it was thought, would give greatest comfort to the rating agencies.

In the end, the rating agencies ran an aggressive series of stress tests on the portfolios, using worst case assumptions about performance. These assumptions were really independent of the servicing environment and ran all the way to Depression economic scenarios.

Moreover, in the end, some servicing requirements (in Rural Housing) were deemed necessary because statute accorded the rights to borrowers, even if their loans were sold. Private sector servicers will observe these borrowers' rights, and borrowers may appeal to the FmHA if there are disputes.

FUTURE SALES

The foundations have been laid for more sales of federal loans. The private capital markets have embraced issues of securities which, while they are backed by assets with alien characteristics, are structured in such a way as to give comfort on payment speeds and repayment. It was vitally important that the first of the sales be properly structured and marketed. The underwriting firms made a strong marketing effort in these sales, and the new familiarity with the underlying portfolios will be helpful for future sales. Similarly, the servicing mechanisms of the loans have now been put in place.

The sheer bulk of the federal lending programs suggests this may be an area in which pilot programs really do portend a future of scale and consequence. To be sure, concern about the budget deficit was the glue that bound together the supporters of asset sales, who were its champions for such disparate reasons. It is entirely possible that a similar concern, with much of the partisanship bleached from it, could be the engine that drives voluminous government asset-backed security sales in the future. If there is any basis for objecting to asset sales from existing portfolios on the grounds that they are an artificial offset to expenditures in the unified budget, that objection evaporates when newly originated loans are sold. Just as mortgage bankers originate mortgages according to origination criteria and documentation that are acceptable in the marketplace, federal departments and agencies can originate new loans in a more standardized format that will allow their sale into the capital markets. The impact this will have on the budget is positive and dramatic. Today, every dollar of disbursement on a newly originated loan is a budget outlay in the unified budget. But, if the loans were sold as securities in the public market, only that part of the loan that really represents the government subsidy would not be picked up by the payment by the private markets. Thus, whether the subsidy is in the form of below market interest rate, or credit quality, its cost would be borne by the federal government. But the rest of the loan would be laid off on and funded by the private markets.

Just as the capital markets were opened for the national financing of the housing industry, the capital markets have now been opened to the funding of public policy lending, without federal guarantees that distort the moves of the marketplace. When compared with strong corporate issues or other asset-backed security issues, the issues that saw the light of day in September 1987 will be competitive and will become widely accepted as sound portfolio investments.

APPENDIX A

Fiscal year 87 Loan Asset Sale & Prepayment Receipts (in millions of dollars)

Agency	Target Amts.	1987 CBO Baseline Receipts	Face Value Loans Sold	Sale Receipts	Face Value Loans Prepaid	Pre-Pmnt Receipts	Authority
EDA	$ 50	$ 50	$ 28	$ 15	$ 12	$ 12	Reconciliation
DOEd	$ 579	$ 579	$ 237	$ 119[1]	$ 792	$ 482	Higher Ed Act
EXIMBANK	$1,500	$1,500	N/A	N/A	$1,900	$1,900	Reconciliation
FmHA:RDIF							
Class A	$1,025	$1,117	$1,799	$1,017	$ 291	$ 221	$1 bil/Recon
Class B (not sold)			$ 135	$ 71			$25.5 mil/CR.
FmHA:RHIF							
Class A	$1,715	$1,727	$2,375	$1,746	N/A	N/A	Reconciliation
Class B			$ 593				
GNMA	0	$ 437	0	0	0	0	Existing
HUD Pub. Fac.	$ 35	0	N/A	N/A	$10	$ 9	Pilot Program
HUD Multi Fam	$ 200	0	N/A	N/A	N/A	N/A	Pilot Program
SBA Disaster	$ 144	0	N/A	N/A	$ 4	$ 3	Pilot Program
VA Vendee	None	$ 673	$ 905	$ 849	N/A	N/A	Existing
TOTAL	$5,248	$6,083	$6,072	$3,817	$3,009	$2,627	

[1]Receipts from the DOEd loan sale included approximately $21 million in net receipts which were received after October 1st and intended to be credited toward fiscal 1988.

Source: Congressional Budget Office

APPENDIX B

LOAN ASSET SALES GUIDELINES

February 9, 1988

I. Introduction

The following guidelines for the sale of loan assets and prepayments have been established and approved by the Federal Credit Policy Working Group. The guidelines are designed to insure that agencies will meet the objectives of the loan asset sale program which have been derived from the Administration's stated priority to reform federal credit. These objectives are set forth as follows:

- Reduce the Government's cost of administering credit by transferring servicing, collection, and other administrative activities to the private sector.
- Provide an incentive for agencies to improve loan origination and documentation.
- Determine the actual subsidy of a federal credit program.
- Increase unified budget offsetting collections in the year of sale.

II. Guidelines for Loan Asset Sales

The following guidelines shall be adhered to by each agency in its approach to, and implementation of, all loan asset sales. However, the Federal Credit Policy Working Group realizes that there are or will be occasions for which changes to the guidelines will be necessary. Agencies are encouraged to bring problems to the Working Group for discussion. The guidelines have been amended to reflect modifications already authorized by the Working Group and will be modified periodically in the future to reflect additional changes.

A. Loan asset sales shall be made without future recourse to the federal government. For the purposes of these guidelines, recourse includes any federal guarantee of principal or interest payments; agreements to repurchase loans or to replace delinquent loans with current loans; warranties as to collateral value; and other agreements entailing continued federal involvement that could create contingent liability. Recourse does not include: representation and warranty obligations in accordance with Guideline B; changes in internal agency policy or regulations needed to satisfy the agency's legal obligations to borrowers; arrangements made by the purchaser of the loans to provide for credit enhancement measures (such as overcollateralization, reserve funds, or insurance) that do not impose contingent liability on the agency or the government; or retention by the federal government of a junior security representing a residual interest in the income produced by the loans after the sale. Agencies planning to retain a junior interest for more than 18 months or for an indefinite period must submit to OMB a plan for disposition.

B. If necessary, agencies may include in a loan sale agreement representations and warranties to the purchaser of loan assets concerning matters of fact and law, such as the characteristics of loans, the agency's authority to sell loans, and the legal enforceability of loans and security interests. Agencies may not warrant as to the future creditworthiness of borrowers. The duration of warranty periods will be based on reasonable time periods for verification and will be determined on a case-by-case basis. The remedy for a branch of warranty may include substitution of an alternative loan not initially included in the sale pool or cash payment by an agency up to the value of the defective loan. Each agency is responsible for ensuring that it has the resources needed to satisfy warranty obligations. Loan sale agreements incorporating warranties shall be signed by an agency official of appropriate rank and shall name the individual agency as the warrantor. The text of warranties should be reviewed by OMB and Treasury.

C. Loans of tax-exempt entities shall be sold only if the future interest payments on the loans are subject to full federal income tax. This does not preclude sales of securities representing pooled loans or whole loans to tax-exempt investors for portfolio or trading accounts in the normal course of business but *is* meant to preclude purchases by such investors from the proceeds of tax-exempt borrowings made for that purpose. Further, the financing of prepayments of loans shall be on a taxable basis; that is, borrowers should not issue tax-exempt bonds to prepay their outstanding loan balances.

D. Agencies should seek to contract out the servicing of loan assets prior to sale. If for valid reasons agencies are not able to do so before sale, collection and servicing shall be transferred to the purchaser with the sale of a loan asset.

E. Agencies shall sell loans and prepare to sell loans in the amounts stated in the budget for FY 1988 and FY 1989. Agencies shall sell newly issued loans and seasoned loans from their portfolios after approval of their sale plan.

F. Where appropriate, each agency shall choose, through a competitive process, a professional financial consultant to provide expertise on its loan asset sale program. Consultants will not be permitted to purchase loans from programs on which they are advising.

G. Loan asset sales may be conducted on a competitive bid or negotiated basis. In the latter case, the invitation to negotiate should be disseminated widely and negotiations conducted as competitively as possible.

H. In limited circumstances where the borrower is not an individual, agencies may offer current borrowers the right to purchase their loans if that seems likely to achieve the highest price; borrowers who are not current on their principal and interest payments shall not be allowed to purchase their loans.

I. Loan asset sales shall be sufficiently large to assure market interest. This is particularly important when developing markets for new types of securitized loans. In such cases, we would expect sales to be over $100 million. Other details, including timing of sales, the composition and size of loan pools, and other marketing issues, shall be handled individually by each agency and will vary from portfolio to portfolio depending on market conditions.

J. Agencies may sell loan assets held by the FFB.

K. Agencies should not sell loan assets directly to government-sponsored enterprises or to entities acting on their behalf for their own account.

L. To the extent possible, newly made loans should be sold on a regular basis within six months of when the loan was closed. It is recommended that when newly made loans are scheduled for sale, agencies arrange for private servicing from the beginning. All proceeds from the sale of newly made loans will flow into the Treasury General Fund, absent legislation to the contrary.

M. In competitive bid situations, agencies should be prepared to analyze bids for minimum price acceptability against an established valuation methodology. It is not likely that there will be good reason to disclose the methodology or price floors to bidders. Any such minimum price valuation methodology should be reviewed by OMB and Treasury.

CHAPTER 8

RATING ASSET-BACKED TRANSACTIONS

M. Douglas Watson, Jr. , Vice President & Director
Moody's Investors Service
Stephen Joynt, Managing Director
Standard & Poor's

Editor's Note: The two major rating agencies, Moody's Investors Service and Standard & Poor's, are key participants in the securitization process. This chapter presents the views of each agency in two separate sections.

SECTION I. THE MOODY'S VIEW

INTRODUCTION

The process for rating a structured transaction such as a receivable-backed security and rating a corporation's debt issue is very different. In the analysis of a corporation seeking a rating, Moody's analysts review and study the financial condition and performance of a company, assess management's input on this performance and their prospects, and arrive at a rating conclusion. There is virtually nothing that management of a company can do to change a rating conclusion in the short run.

With a structured transaction, the process typically starts with the rating desired; in other words, the issuer or investment banker will tell us that to successfully market the issue a triple-A or double-A is needed. The question then becomes what legal, structural, and credit supports are necessary to achieve that rating. Of course, in those cases where the risk to investors is greater than that represented by the desired rating, Moody's expresses its opinion whenever possible.

Naturally, in this type of environment, Moody's cannot simply react to input but must take a more active role in these transactions representing the interests of investors. In short, Moody's attempts to make sure that the structure, the legal risks, and the credit risks result in a composite risk level to the investor that is consistent with the rating requested. In this role Moody's is an advocate for the investor.

This advocacy role is becoming more important today for several reasons. First, today's transactions, in a structural sense, are tighter than they were two years ago. Second, the transactions today are legally more complex. Finally, there are more credit issues to consider today in view of the rapidly changing credit quality of those entities that typically provide incremental support, such as mortgage insurers, sureties, and banks. Under this rubric of growing credit concerns, we also have to consider the deterioration in credit quality of the nongovernment-supported assets used in these transactions.

THE RATING PROCESS

In assigning its ratings, Moody's will work with the issuer, attorneys, investment bankers, and other participants involved in the transaction—in most cases from its very early stages. Generally, one or more analysts are assigned to each transaction. If the issue involves residential mortgage loans or receivables, Moody's analysts will usually visit the originator and servicer to examine the underwriting and collection operations thoroughly. Each analyst is responsible for review and analysis of all documents and legal opinions, as well as any necessary financial data. At the time of the pricing or offering of the security, a "prospective" rating is typically issued. When the draft documents are in final form, the analyst presents the transaction to the Rating Committee. After review of the transaction and consideration, the Committee assigns the appropriate rating.

RATING RECEIVABLE-BACKED TRANSACTIONS

There are two basic types of receivable-backed structures in the market today. First, there is the pass-through or pay-through structure, where the cash flow from the receivables will be utilized to pay all principal and interest to the security holders. These transactions generally follow one of two formats. In the first, the receivables are sold to a grantor trust, which in turn issues participation certificates representing undivided ownership interests in the receivables. In the second form, the originator sells the receivables to a "bankruptcy remote" entity, which may be a subsidiary, which in turn issues debt securities collateralized by the sold receivables.

In the second type of receivable structure, the liquidation value of the receivables assures the ultimate payment of the debt instruments issued. This structure has been used for commercial paper programs and can be used for intermediate-term note programs. In this structure, the originator sells the receivables to a "bankruptcy remote" issuer, which must maintain the liquidation value of the receivables in the event of a default. In these programs, cash flow is typically used to purchase new receivables to maintain the liquidation value. Consequently, to assure timely payment of the notes secured by the receivables, a liquidity facility is generally required.

For pass-through/pay-through transactions, we must be satisfied that under any prepayment scenario the receivables will throw off sufficient principal and interest to pay principal and interest on the rated securities. This analysis can be complex, because interest is often computed on a different basis for the receivables than it is for the rated securities. Computer runs are a necessity here to demonstrate the integrity of the program.

For liquidation value deals, we must be satisfied that the liquidation value of the collateral is always maintained at the required level to assure ultimate payment. Furthermore, the liquidity facility must be available even in the event of the originator's insolvency.

Quality of Receivables

The goal of this analysis is to determine the predictability of the cash flow generated by the receivables pool and thereby determine how much variance from the scheduled cash flow will occur in a stressful environment.

The first step of this process is to examine the track record of the originator by looking at its history of delinquencies, defaults, repossessions (if applicable), and recoveries.

To understand the statistics provided in this review, we study the originator's policies on providing extensions, rewriting contracts, holiday grace periods, and curing methods.

The most accurate way to analyze a receivables portfolio is by using a "static pool" approach. A static pool analysis uses data either from a pool of receivables previously sold or historical repossession and severity data which is then modeled simulating a pool of sold receivables. The idea is to capture the actual losses that would occur in a pool of receivables once they have been securitized. This provides a proxy for expected loss and is a much more accurate indicator than losses to liquidations, which can be heavily influenced by how fast outstandings are growing.

The next step in our analysis of the quality of the originator's receivables is to determine whether the track record is necessarily a good indicator for future performance. The predictive value of the track record is directly related to the consistency of the originator's underwriting standards and collection procedures.

The final step in this process is to apply a stress test to the receivables in question, with the severity of the test depending on the rating level.

In those cases where the receivables or leases are generated in conjunction with the manufacture of a product—and assuming the rating of that manufacturer is less than the rating requested for the transaction—we must consider the impact on the quality of the receivables pool in the event the manufacturer becomes insolvent.

Servicer Credit Quality

In rating a receivable-backed transaction, we are very concerned about the servicer's quality from two perspectives: first, the servicer's operational quality, that is, how well equipped is the servicer to carry out its day-to-day responsibilities; and second, the servicer's credit quality, that is, its capability to fulfill the financial responsibilities it takes on as servicer.

To assess the operational quality of the servicer, Moody's usually visits the offices of the servicer to get a firsthand impression of its procedures and professionalism.

In assessing the operational quality of the servicer, we look at the degree to which the process is automated, what capacity constraints exist, audit and review systems, and finally, the systems and procedures used to prevent fraud in the process.

Of critical importance is the servicer's collection methods. Clearly, if the servicer has efficient and effective collection procedures, both frequency and severity factors will be favorably influenced.

The credit quality of the servicer is also crucial, because the servicer is usually responsible for making advances on delinquent receivables, repurchasing defective receivables, and collecting and holding payments on the receivables until they are turned over to the trustee.

We generally look for investment-grade servicers for highly rated receivables-backed deals. For all transactions rated at a level higher than the servicer, there must be a substitute servicer available to assume the responsibilities if the servicer fails. The substitute servicer is often the trustee in the transaction.

The minimum credit quality of the servicer that we would look for depends upon several factors:

1. The maximum maturity of the deal. Clearly, the shorter the maturity, the greater the differential can be between the rating of the servicer and the rating of the transaction.

2. The availability of regulatory protections. In the case of thrift institutions, for example, the regulators have indicated to us that it is likely a servicing contract would be honored after the institution came under the control of the liquidator.

3. The capability of the substitute servicer to take on the operational responsibilities of the contract.

4. The strength of the legal structure. In other words, how likely is it that a portion of the cash flow would be tied up in the event of the servicer's insolvency?

5. The amount of cash flow that could be adversely affected by the servicer's insolvency.

After analyzing these variables, if the servicer is not of sufficient credit quality, we determine the maximum amount of cash flow that could be adversely affected by the servicer's insolvency and insist that that amount be put up either in reserves or assured through a letter of credit available to the trustee.

Legal Concerns

There are a number of legal concerns that must be addressed in rating a receivables-backed transaction. First, it is important that a true sale has occurred from the originator to the issuer. In other words, the issuer should own the receivables free and clear of any liens. If the transfer of receivables to the issuer were considered a pledge of collateral rather than a sale, the receivables and their proceeds would be tied up by the automatic stay in the event of the originator's insolvency. Of course, this is not a concern if the rating requested is the same as that of the originator.

Another critical legal issue is that the trustee for the security holder must have a perfected interest in the receivables and the proceeds from the receivables. Typically, Uniform Commercial Code (UCC) filings on the receivables are done, the receivables are segregated and marked, and they are held by a custodian for the trustee, thus avoiding any commingling of the proceeds from the sold receivables with those retained by the servicer. In most transactions, payments are segregated or at least identifiable.

Next, we are interested in preserving the "sanctity" of the issuer. If a debt issue is the form of the security, the issuer—whether a subsidiary or independent corporate entity—must be structured so as to minimize the possibility of bankruptcy; in other words, no other debt or other businesses can be permitted. Furthermore, the issuer must conduct its business in such a way as to minimize the possibility it would be substantively consolidated into the affairs of the originator if the originator failed.

We must also be satisfied that the transfer of receivables would not be considered a fraudulent transfer, that the trustee has a security interest in the vehicles if it's an automobile deal, and that potentially preferential payments by obligors or the servicer are addressed in the structure.

Auto Receivables

In assessing the credit quality of auto receivable-backed (ARB) securities, Moody's examines the quality of the underlying receivables and the structural features of each transaction to determine the degree to which the scheduled payments on the certificates are assured. The following is a brief overview of the primary credit features upon which we base our analysis.

Structure

In ARB transactions, the certificate trustee owns the receivables, free and clear of any liens of the originator and is entitled to all future cash flow derived therefrom.

Furthermore, the trustee has a security interest in each automobile pledged as collateral. The trustee for the certificate holders enters into a servicing contract under which another entity (most likely an affiliate of the originator of the loan) services the receivables. The servicer is responsible for maintaining the file for each receivable and for collecting the monthly payments from each underlying borrower.

For the ARB certificates' rating to be above those assigned to either the originator of the receivables or the servicer, the legal structure of each transaction will have to provide for the timely pass-through of all amounts due with respect to the underlying receivables, regardless of the financial condition of either party.

Asset Quality—Insurance Coverage

Credit enhancement in an ARB certificate program is usually provided by a guarantee or repurchase commitment of a highly rated entity. The agreement commits the guarantor to repurchase defaulted receivable contracts at a price equal to their remaining principal balances, up to a specified maximum amount. The maximum amount of the commitment will be a major determinant of the rating assigned to the certificates.

In examining the adequacy of the proposed credit loss coverage, Moody's focuses on the following key statistics:

- The frequency with which contracts may be expected to go into default in the future
- The loss that will be realized, net of all collection costs, on the repossession and sale of the automobile
- The likelihood of any significant recovery of such losses following legal action against the borrower
- The potential size of any other claims against the credit loss policy, such as required servicer advances

Typically, default frequency of auto loans is greatest in the first 18 months of a contract. While we do not expect this pattern to vary dramatically from one lender to another, lenders with different underwriting standards will have significantly different expected-default frequencies.

Our analysis will focus on the stability of the underwriting standards and the originator's delinquency and default record over the past 5 to 10 years. We adjust these numbers based on a review of the loans supporting the certificates. In particular, we evaluate the seasoning of the pool, the expected effect of any change in underwriting standards, the types of automobiles in the pool (new or used), the sensitivity of the pool to changes in the economic climate, and the policies of the servicer limiting modifications of contracts.

In analyzing the expected loss from a defaulted receivable, we re-examine the portfolio's historical loss experience. The actual loss rate is a function of several factors, including the speed and cost of repossession, the quality of the servicer's sale procedures for repossessed cars, and the market for used cars of the type in the portfolio. Furthermore, some receivable contracts provide for recourse to the auto dealer if the underlying borrower defaults. When it is relevant, we will examine the health of the dealer network in general and raise or lower the expected loss rate accordingly.

Credit Card Receivables

Structure
A securitized pool of credit card receivables is composed of a discrete set of cardholders' accounts. Except under limited circumstances, there will not be additions to this initial set of accounts. This is important when evaluating a pool's potential performance because the underwriting and payment history of the accounts are known at the outset.

The securitized credit card receivables include those receivables initially existing under the cardholder accounts as well as the receivables arising under the accounts from time to time thereafter. Receivables will consist of principal balances and finance charge balances; the latter may include such items as interest charges, annual fees, and service fees.

We believe that unsecured credit card receivables carry greater loss risk than do auto receivables. In addition, industry losses are growing and vary widely by issuer. Just as important, historical loss performance may understate future loss potential depending upon a variety of factors. Consequently, it is important for investors to gain a full understanding of the key characteristics that are predictive of future losses on credit card portfolios.

This section presents the primary variables that Moody's has found to be predictive of charge-offs in credit card portfolios and focuses on Moody's assessment of these variables when evaluating securities backed by credit card receivables.

Key Predictive Variables
The following is a list of key predictive variables and some of the specific questions and concerns that Moody's might have relating to each variable when assessing a particular credit card portfolio.

Type of Credit Card

Is the card a retailer's card, a travel and entertainment card, or a bank card? Since charge-off performance may vary significantly depending on both the relationship between the cardholder and issuer and on the type of credit card, we segment and analyze each separately.

Cardholder Concentrations

What cardholder concentrations exist by state and, where significant, by regions within a state? Moody's recognizes that some regions are more stable than others.

Are there affinity groups (endorsements by fraternal, professional, or business organizations) or marketing programs in the portfolio that produce portfolio concentrations in certain cardholder characteristics, such as occupation or level of income? Demographic concentrations may also increase credit risk.

Historical Loss Performance

Loss performance of the accounts in the portfolio may be an excellent indicator of credit quality, particularly for the more seasoned accounts.

Portfolio Seasoning

What is the seasoning distribution of the accounts in the existing portfolio? Portfolio seasoning is a critical element in predicting future loss performance on a portfolio as it reduces credit risk in portfolios both by eliminating weaker credits through attrition (primarily charge-offs) and by establishing a track record of performance.

Portfolio Underwriting

Moody's determines when and how the present portfolio was underwritten. Some of our questions include the following: Does the portfolio contain preapproved accounts? If so, when and how were they originated and what percentage of the portfolio do they represent? Preapproved accounts are generated from issuer mass mailings and are inexpensive ways to build volume. However, except for an initial screening to determine the mailing list, these accounts are not underwritten. Although this type of marketing approach may be valid for business reasons, it generally increases credit risk and Moody's will assess each mailing separately.

What percentage of the portfolio is composed of solicited or "take-one" accounts? Moody's will be concerned as to how these "take one" accounts were underwritten. Is there a credit scoring model in place? If so, what is its predictive validity and reliability? How does the verification process work? Does it include credit bureau checks, income confirmation, and employment verification?

Does the portfolio contain accounts from another issuer? If so, when were they acquired, what percentage of the portfolio do they represent, and how do they differ from in-house originations?

What underwriting changes have been implemented by management during the portfolio's history? Significant changes in underwriting tend to invalidate previous loss history.

Servicing/Collection Quality
The ability of the servicer to effectively "work" the portfolio is critical in minimizing credit losses. Moody's focuses on the credit strength of the servicer and the quality of the servicer's collection system.

Credit Enhancement Evaluation
Once Moody's completes its analysis of the key predictive variables, an evaluation is made of the credit enhancement features protecting investors against credit losses on the portfolio.

The approach for evaluating these credit enhancement features is prospective in nature and is a function of Moody's view as to how the particular portfolio would perform under a variety of stressful economic environments. Based upon Moody's analysis of the underwriting process, seasoning, and loss history associated with each segmented category, initial estimates of future portfolio performance are developed in a stressed economic environment with the degree of stress varied by rating category.

These initial estimates of portfolio performance assume a highly diversified portfolio. The next step is Moody's analysis of actual portfolio diversification.

Geographic and demographic concentrations are assessed as to their potential impact on future portfolio charge-offs. To the extent that portfolios are geographically or demographically concentrated, they need greater credit enhancement for a given rating category.

Finally, Moody's concludes its assessment, based on its evaluation of both the servicer and the relationship between the servicer (as issuer) and the cardholders. Moody's determines the likelihood of a servicer (issuer) default and the resulting impact on charge-offs.

RATING COMMERCIAL MORTGAGE-BACKED SECURITIES

The rating system for commercial mortgage-backed securities is composed of four parts. Analysis begins with an assessment of the stability of the local commercial real estate markets. This involves an intensive and ongoing analysis of demand-side and supply-side risk and results in classification of each market on a scale of one to four. In the second phase of the analysis, Moody's commercial real estate unit meets with building owners and management, visits the site and reviews appraisals, engineering reports, rent rolls and other documents to assess risks associated with the project and its lease structure. Simultaneously, Moody's assesses financial market risk to determine the discount rates to be applied to cash flow in estimating the building's market value over the life of the security.

In the third phase of the analysis, Moody's uses a computer-based sensitivity model to analyze cash flow and market value projections, which provide the basis for calculating the amount of credit enhancement needed. In the fourth phase, analysts assess the legal and structural risks associated with the security itself. The final rating results from the above analysis.

The Real Estate Market

Demand-Side Risk
The objective of Moody's demand-side analysis is to evaluate the potential risk of a significant decrease in demand for office space over the bond term. This is accomplished through an examination of vulnerabilities within the local economic base.

Specifically, the economic base is judged in terms of 1) secular growth performance, 2) volatility characteristics, and 3) diversification of industries. These attributes are then compared with those of other cities and serve as the basis for classifying these cities into four risk groups.

Supply-Side Risk

The objective of the supply-side analysis is to determine the degree to which a local market is prone to overbuilding. This analysis, like the demand side, is designed to uncover the particular vulnerability of each real estate market to depressed conditions in the future. Based on the historical development pattern, current market conditions, and vulnerabilities to overexpansion in the future, Moody's again has classified major cities into four risk groups. These supply-side classifications are then considered in constructing the assumptions used to project cash flow.

Building-Specific Factors

Project Risk

The objective of the project risk analysis is to gauge the competitive advantage or disadvantage of the building under rating review against comparable buildings in the same market. Market data support the premise that, under adverse economic conditions, a building that possesses superior attributes should maintain a higher level of occupancy and effective rental rates than competing buildings. Therefore, such a building will be subject to less severe assumptions in forecasting cash flows. On the other hand, a building that is judged to be inferior will require an increase in the degree of stress applied to projected cash flows. The project risk analysis entails a review of engineering and other reports, construction quality, presence of asbestos, asbestos abatement/removal programs, functional layout, amenities, location, ownership, and building management, among other factors.

Lease Structure Risk

The objective of the lease structure analysis is to highlight potential shortfalls in debt service coverage resulting from the actual mix of terms under existing lease contracts. After the application of Moody's assumptions, projected cash flow is compared to debt service. Where a shortfall exists in any year, Moody's looks for credit enhancement from an acceptable source to be in place at the time of closing to cover the shortfall.

Moody's views the lease structure from a portfolio perspective and from an individual lease perspective.

Sensitivity Analysis and Calculation of Credit Enhancement

Factoring in all the foregoing analysis, a sensitivity model is used to calculate the amount of credit enhancement, if any, that is needed to help ensure full and timely payment of principal and interest on the bonds. The sensitivity model involves a two-pronged approach. The first part is a cash flow analysis. The second focuses on the relationship of the building's market value to the amount of outstanding debt. Moody's sensitivity model essentially gauges the capacity of a building to withstand extremely soft market conditions and a simultaneous increase in interest rates while continuing to meet the contractual obligation under the bond.

SECTION II. THE STANDARD & POOR'S VIEW

Standard & Poor's applies the same basic rating criteria to various types of asset-backed structured transactions, be they asset credit card receivables, automobile receivables, manufactured housing receivables, unsecured consumer loan receivables, equipment leases, receivables-backed commercial paper, and so on. The earliest form of asset-based securitization was mortgage pass-throughs, and the market has evolved through collateralized mortgage obligations to where it is today.

Once a rating application is received, S&P analyzes the issue's structure and then determines the equity support needed to enhance credit quality to the level sought by the issuer.

S&P evaluates three key areas: credit risk, cash flow, and legal issues.

When assessing the credit risk, the originator's overall risk profile is examined. Portfolio quality is analyzed using various performance statistics and a complete review of the originator's credit and underwriting guidelines is undertaken. Last, but certainly not of least importance, is an evaluation of the servicer and trustee.

In examining cash flow, specific risks inherent in the payment structure are identified and collateral composition and sufficiency are evaluated.

On legal issues, two key concerns are the perfection of lien or asset ownership and evaluation of risks associated with the bankruptcy of the seller/servicer.

Credit and legal analysis are closely interrelated so that when the receivables seller is of sufficient credit quality, legal concerns over possible bankruptcy are moderated.

Once a transaction's risks in the three areas are identified, S&P assesses the adequacy of available equity support. Support may be in the form of a letter of credit, overcollateralization, reserve fund, subordination, guaranty or excess cash flow.

At the time of this writing, in early 1988, the major issuers are auto finance subsidiaries of auto manufacturers, commercial banks and thrifts writing auto loans, credit card issuers, leasing and finance units of manufacturers, and leasing finance companies. Products and services underlying the issues are: automobile, credit card and manufactured housing receivables, computer leases, unsecured consumer loans, and corporate loans. The most recent type of issue is receivables-backed commercial paper typically issued through a special-purpose corporation (issuer) organized by an investment banker; the sole business of the special-purpose corporation is to finance the company's receivables. Products on the horizon are home equity loans and boat loans.

EVALUATING CREDIT RISKS

The principal credit risk in asset-backed financings is impairment of cash flows from delinquency or loss on pledged or acquired assets. Such impairment, depending on the issue structure and the certificate contract, may cause liquidity risks, if cash flows from receivables are not sufficient to cover debt service on a timely basis—or losses, if cash flows are not sufficient to retire the outstanding debt. Credit (equity) support may be pledged to the transaction to mitigate these risks.

In determining the risks of delinquency or loss on the receivables, S&P uses a qualitative and quantitative approach, supported by on-site management meetings. S&P evaluates the originator's overall risk profile, underwriting standards, collection procedures, and pool selection process. This requires a review of the originator's historic and expected financial performance, organizational strengths and weaknesses, and the competitive position and strategy in the business line from which the assets are sold. S&P meets with management to review the underwriting, operations, and controls of the specific business unit. Elements of that review are: historic and current lending criteria; portfolio characteristics, including any relevant customer concentrations; historic and prospective value of the underlying assets backing the receivables; historic portfolio origination and repayment statistics; delinquency and loss statistics of the receivables portfolio; and audit procedures and accounting systems.

Selection of the Pool from the Portfolio Is a Critical Step in Determining Credit Risk

The pool should represent either a random or a quality oriented sampling of the entire portfolio—not predominantly lesser quality receivables left over after previous pool selections. How the selection process addresses risk concentrations, lending criteria, current or historic delinquency, rewrites and extensions, and aging of accounts also may affect pool performance. S&P reviews the selection process for the current financing and previous financings from the same portfolio. An overly conservative selection process in a previous financing may cause this financing to have a lower portfolio quality.

S&P expects a wide disparity in portfolio performance among originates because of differences in underwriting, servicing, underlying asset protection, and the character and degree of risk concentration. Differences in the pool selection process are also expected to have a varying impact on receivable quality. Thus, credit support levels will vary significantly on an issuer-by-issuer basis—even for the same type of receivable.

EQUITY SUPPORT

Under S&P's weak link approach, a transaction is not rated higher than the rating applicable to the credit support component. Therefore, a transaction supported by a double-A rated credit support is typically rated double-A or lower.

Equity support for an issue is expressed as a fixed percentage of the notes outstanding or a fixed dollar amount. In transactions where the receivable pool amortizes, it's generally possible to decrease the credit support proportionately to the notes outstanding down to a minimum coverage level. This minimum coverage level or "floor" is designed to support the greater cash flow uncertainty existing at and near the issue's maturity. This reflects the uncertainty regarding the statistical validity of the original portfolio analysis for a declining and possibly less diversified pool—plus the impact of certain credit policies, such as extensions and force placed insurance, which may hurt cash flow availability to redeem notes at maturity. Minimum credit coverage in most issues has been 5 to 8 percent of the original dollar amount of the certificates or notes oustanding for automobile receivable transactions and 1 to 17 percent for credit card receivable transactions. In open pool credit card transactions, characterized by an initial nonamortization period, the credit support generally remains at a fixed dollar amount for the life of the deal.

Adequate credit support reflects the amount and timing of potential charges for losses against assets. Coverage under the credit support decreases when the support is drawn on. The credit support will reinstate up to a given percentage of notes outstanding or dollar amount, whichever applies, when reimbursed through excess cash flow off the receivables, recoveries on defaulted or delinquent receivables, or other reimbursement mechanisms. Where an issue is structured for cash flow to either reimburse the equity support or provide direct support via a reserve fund, S&P analyzes the certainty of receiving sufficient excess cash flow. Depending on the structure and availability of a reserve fund used in conjunction with a third-party credit support, the reserve fund may or may not add to the coverage provided by the equity support.

LOOKING AT PASS-THROUGHS
AND PAY-THROUGHS

A primary challenge in rating receivable transactions is accurate valuation of the receivables. In these structured financings, cash flows generated by receivables support certificates or note payments. Receivables must be valued to ensure that their payments are sufficient to meet certificate or note obligations. Valuation of underlying receivables is similar in both pass-throughs and pay-throughs, the two most common types of receivable transactions.

The pass-through structure essentially gives certificate holders an equity interest in the receivables. The structure establishes a grantor trust as the issuer into which receivable collateral is sold. Certificate holders of the trust are entitled to all cash flow from the receivables.

A pay-through is the issuer's liability, for which the receivables serve as security. The receivables' cash flow is the primary source of debt service. Pay-throughs can be structured as single-class notes or multiple-class notes. With multiple-class structures, principal is repaid by class, beginning with the earliest stated maturity.

Both pass-throughs and pay-throughs can use various methods to value the underlying receivables. Once the discounting method is chosen, each receivables collateral piece must be valued. The sum of these values for the receivable collateral pool is the dollar amount of certificates or notes issued.

COLLATERAL VALUATION

Collateral for pass-throughs and pay-throughs are valued similarly so noteholders are paid what they are promised. To ensure this, the note value for each piece of collateral must equal the lesser of:

- The principal amount of the notes that the collateral piece can support if it were to prepay.
- The present value of the future scheduled cash flows (assuming no prepayments) discounted at the highest note interest rate.

With *premium collateral*, the receivable collateral rate is greater than the rate on the notes plus the servicing fee and other expenses. Notes must then be valued at the principal amount (at par) of the receivables. By valuing the collateral at par, receivable prepayments do not hurt the deal's cash flows. With a full prepayment, the amount paid is at least equal to the principal plus one month's interest on that principal amount.

With *discount collateral*, the receivable collateral rate is less than the rate on the notes plus the servicing fee and other expenses. Notes can then be issued only at a discount. Without discounting, receivable payments would not meet the debt service obligations of the notes.

PRESENT VALUE METHODS

The present value method chosen is an important rating consideration. Three methods are used:

- Gross-to-gross
- Constant-to-net
- Net-to-net

The methods are not equivalent from a ratings perspective, nor do they generate equal note values. However, each method assumes no prepayments on the receivables for the life of the receivables or the scheduled maturity of the notes, whichever is earlier.

Gross-to-Gross

This method discounts gross cash flows at a gross rate. Gross cash flows are cash flows generated by the receivables assuming no prepayments. The gross rate is the note rate plus the servicing fee and other expenses,. Cash flows are discounted at the same frequency as note payments.

The gross-to-gross method is only representative of a conservative valuation under certain circumstances. The method is generally not acceptable because it overstates receivable cash flows and slows receivable amortization. The notes would not fully amortize by the due date if the servicing fee and other expenses were calculated as a percentage of the outstanding collateral balance. However, this method would be acceptable if the servicing fee and other expenses were calculated as a percentage of the outstanding note balance (the alternate gross-to-gross method) rather than the outstanding collateral balance.

Constant-to-Net

Net cash flow is discounted at the note rate using this method. Cash flows are calculated net of the servicing fee and other expenses which are calculated as a percentage of the outstanding collateral balance. The fee is assumed to be a constant dollar based on the initial outstanding collateral balance. Cash flows are discounted at the note rate, at the same frequency as note payment.

The constant-to-net method is conservative from a rating perspective, but it generates lower note values relative to the other two methods. Constant-to-net understates the cash flows due noteholders by assuming that fees and expenses are a fixed dollar amount. This is often a conservative assumption because servicing and other fees are usually a fixed percentage of the declining outstanding collateral balance.

Net-to-Net

The net-to-net method discounts cash flows net of the servicing fees and other expenses, assuming that those fees and expenses decline with the outstanding collateral balance. Cash flows are discounted at the note rate, at the same frequency as note payments.

This method is acceptable because it accurately reflects cash flows and debt service requirements. Net-to-net generates a higher note value than the constant-to-net method.

These computations ensure that the corresponding note value of each piece of collateral can always be supported regardless of how that receivable actually pays.

VALUATION ASSUMPTIONS

The assumptions behind the valuation method are extremely important. Present value methods require assumptions about the rate and frequency of discounting and the determination of future scheduled cash flows.

In the multiple-class pay-through structure, the rate at which the cash flows are discounted must be the highest note rate of any of the bond classes. Discounting at the highest note rate is necessary because the debt service requirement will increase as classes with lower rates are repaid. If, during the early years of the transaction, the higher rate collateral were to prepay, only the lower rate collateral will be left to pay down the higher rate notes, resulting in a potential shortfall.

The frequency of discounting must correspond to the frequency of note payment dates. This is the longest time period for which cash flow from the collateral can be invested. If notes are repaid quarterly the cash flows must be discounted on a quarterly basis.

Future scheduled cash flows are comprised of cash flows, net of servicing and other fees, expected to be received if no prepayments occur as well as reinvestment income.

If receivables collateral has a maturity longer than the maturity of the notes, cash flow from the receivables expected after the maturity of the notes cannot be included. For a triple-A rating, the reinvestment income assumed to be received must be calculated assuming an annual rate of 4.5 percent for the first year of the transaction, 4 percent for the second year, and 3 percent from the third year to the maturity of the notes.

For an issue rated double-A, the reinvestment scenario is 4.5 percent, 4.0 percent and 3.5 percent; for a single-A rated issue, the percentages are 4.5 percent, 4.5 percent and 4.0 percent, while a triple-B rating calls for 4.5 percent throughout the life of the transaction.

Instead of using these reinvestment rate assumptions, some issuers negotiate a guaranteed investment contract to lock in a higher reinvestment rate. The number of days of investment income that can be assumed is a function of when cash flow is remitted to the trustee. If cash is remitted on the 20th day of a month, reinvestment income can be assumed from the 22nd day of that month to the next payment date. The two-day lag allows for delays incurred by remittance dates falling on weekends and holidays.

AMORTIZATION OF COLLATERAL

Industry standards and accounting procedures provide different methods of amortizing receivable collateral. Many auto receivable contracts are amortized using the Rule of 78's method instead of the actuarial method that is used in most mortgages. The monthly payments due on any loan are the same under both methods, however, they allocate interest and principal in different proportions.

Initially, the Rule of 78's applies more of the monthly payment to interest, thus amortization of collateral is slower than under the actuarial method. The interest portion of receivable payments might not match the interest requirement of the notes. Without this matching, a shortfall in cash flows is possible. To correct this mismatch, accounting systems usually are developed to convert the Rule of 78's to the actuarial amortization method.

ADDITIONAL PAY-THROUGH CONCERNS

Pay-throughs usually cause concerns not present in pass-throughs because of legal and structural differences—particularly reinvestment risk, stated maturity determination, and default/collateral sale restrictions.

Reinvestment risk arises when note payment dates occur less frequently than collateral payment dates. The risk is that the collateral would be prepaid and then invested at a rate lower than the highest note rate (negative carry). Options that can cover this risk are establishment of a reserve fund or an interperiod call provision, which can be written into the transaction documents so that the notes can be called on dates other than note payment dates.

In a case where a transaction closed December 31 and the first quarterly note payment date was April 1, the reserve fund would have to equal the cash available from all the collateral prepaying on January 1, plus reinvestment income, at the assumed reinvestment rates to April 1, less debt service required on the notes on April 1.

If an interperiod call provision is used to cover reinvestment risk, the transaction documents provide for a test to be performed by the trustee each month (other than months in which a note payment date occurs). The test shows that cash flow received to date, plus assumed cash flows expected to be received before the next note payment date, plus reinvestment income, is greater than the debt service required to be paid on the next note payment date.

All stated maturity calculations include assumptions to ensure that notes will be retired by the stated maturity. Excess cash flow (above the amount needed to pay debt service on the notes) may be available to pay down notes. However, availability of excess cash is usually uncertain so it is not typically used to determine stated maturities. Excess cash flow may come from:

- Excess reinvestment income from investments yielding rates higher than those assumed, and/or from more days of reinvestment than assumed;
- Discounting the highest note rate when determining note value;
- Interest income from premium collateral;
- Recaptured discount if the discount collateral prepays.

To determine the stated maturity date, calculations typically assume that only scheduled cash flows are received (no prepayments) and that only the change in note value is paid as principal on each payment date.

One exception is the stated maturity calculation for credit card receivable transactions. Credit card receivables are unique when compared to other receivable assets because their revolving nature creates new outstanding balances and fluctuations in minimum payments. S&P determines an assumed payment rate based on historical portfolio performance, industry trends, terms of the credit card agreement, and the desired rating.

Cash flows based on the assumed payment rate and any credit enhancement should be sufficient to retire the notes on or before stated maturity. Cash flow and credit criteria reduce any concern that default in payment of principal and/or interest will occur. The single-purpose rating criteria and applicable legal opinions reduce any concern over the issuer being involved in a bankruptcy proceeding (voluntary or involuntary). However, the rating criteria anticipates the possibility of a technical default.

If a technical default occurs and is not cured, most transactions call for: the trustee to either sell the collateral (if sale proceeds are sufficient to pay noteholders all principal and interest due or if 100 percent of noteholders approve the sale), or to continue to pay the notes under the terms of the documents because no payment default has or is expected to occur. The latter option is referred to as the optional preservation of the trust estate, and it relies on the presence of sufficient collateral cash flow to pay noteholders by the stated maturity of the notes. Collateral valuation assures cash flow adequacy, making this option viable for the trustee.

SERVICER/TRUSTEE EVALUATION

Both the trustee and servicer play key roles in asset-backed receivables transactions. S&P assesses whether both entities can perform their individual job functions in the best interests of the certificate holders.

The obligation of the servicer to manage and maintain control of the assets and its payment stream is of utmost importance, as is the servicer's potential obligation to support the transaction through a cash advance mechanism.

The method of evaluating a servicer's capability in the management of assets depends on the actual role the servicer plays in the receivable transaction. In most cases, the servicer is also the originator and underwriter of the receivables. In such cases, S&P's evaluation is part of the due diligence process and is reflected in the credit support required or the rating given the transaction. S&P's evaluation usually involves a site visit, including an in-depth review of the company's operations and a meeting with management to discuss procedures, methods, history, and future outlook. If the servicer is not also the originator or underwriter,

S&P still completes a certain amount of due diligence on the servicer. In such cases, due diligence focuses more on management and company operations.

The servicer's role is also important in terms of protecting asset proceeds. If the servicer is not rated as high as the bonds, the servicer must remit cash flow to the trustee as soon as possible within a maximum of 48 hours. S&P sees this time exposure as a risk. However, it is considered to be adequately covered via the credit support and the floor amount that is maintained.

Evaluation of the servicer's capabilities inevitably is limited in scope and duration. It is of utmost importance that a servicer support all its representations and warranties and provide coverage against potential employee error. As a result, S&P requests the servicer to obtain errors and omission insurance equal to 5 percent of the outstanding obligation or show that other existing insurance can cover the same inherent risks. The servicer should not be allowed to resign until a suitable successor is appointed. The servicing fee should be within industry standards to ensure willingness of a substitute servicer should the original servicer withdraw or be withdrawn for any reason. The servicer's fee should be a percentage of the principal balance outstanding and should be subordinated to the certificate holder's right to receive principal and interest. Payment of such fees should be demonstrated in the submitted cash flows, and the pooling and servicing agreement or other applicable financing document should specify this.

In most transactions, servicers have a cash advance obligation. Therefore, the credit strength and financial capability of the servicer is considered. The cash advance role is typically one that provides timely payment on a portion of debt service. In most asset-backed financings the credit support (either letter of credit, insurance policy, or guarantee) is also available to cover timing shortfalls. If the credit support does not backstop the cash advance need, S&P expects the rating of the servicer to be within one category of the rating of the financing (e.g., single-A servicer for a double-A issue).

The trustee's function begins on receipt of the asset proceeds from the servicer. Under the financing documents, the trustee should be instructed to deposit the revenues immediately into the trust account designated for the transaction. The funds should not be commingled with other funds of the trust department. The account should be held in trust for the benefit of certificate holders. If funds are to be invested, they should be in high-quality permitted investments specified in the transaction. Investments should mature no later than the date such funds are needed to pay certificate holders. Investing the funds this way reduces potential credit and interest rate risks to certificate holders.

The trustee is also responsible for performing monthly calculations of payments received as well as future cash flow. These reports must be audited regularly. The transaction's complexity will determine frequency and scope of the independent audits, which should be completed at least annually. More complex deals may require quarterly or semiannual audits.

Like the servicer, the trustee cannot resign without prior appointment of an equally capable successor. The trustee should be willing to take over the servicer's obligations should the servicer withdraw or be unable to perform. Minimum capital and surplus requirements and experience in similar structures is suggested. Provisions for payment of the trustee's fees and expenses should also be provided and such ongoing fees subordinated to payment to certificate holders. These fees should also be reflected in submitted cash flows.

LEGAL ISSUES

Debt secured by nonmortgage receivables must satisfy essentially two legal concerns—bankruptcy by the seller and the issuer. Debt is typically secured by receivables sold by one company (seller) to another company that issues the debt (issuer). Bankruptcy by the seller could impair timely payment of debt service—a major concern—and bankruptcy by either party must be avoided in structuring of the transaction. These issues are addressed in a separate chapter.

AUTOMOBILE RECEIVABLE CRITERIA

At the time of this writing, S&P rates $16.3 billion of automobile receivable-backed debt plus $600 million of auto lease paper. All issues have been fixed rate, level pay, fully amortizing contracts. S&P relies on an actuarial approach, supported by on-site management meetings to evaluate portfolio quality. The likelihood of credit losses is determined by analyzing historical performance of the portfolio from which pooled receivables are drawn. Performance and characteristics of pooled receivables are examined in relation to industry norms, total portfolio characteristics, the structural characteristics of the transaction, and any legal risks.

Unlike mortgage lending, auto finance does not have standardized underwriting and servicing. Consequently, portfolio quality and performance will vary widely. Through an analysis of auto receivable data, S&P has determined that as a benchmark, an 8 percent credit support would normally be sufficient for a prime pool for a triple-A rating. Lower credit support levels will result in lower ratings.

A prime pool will have relatively conservative underwriting standards, new vehicles backing the notes, maturities of less than 60 months, and an originator that demonstrated consistently low relative delinquency and loss performance. The 8 percent benchmark reflects a significant multiple of historic frequency and severity of losses in auto lending as measured by repossession, gross loss, recovery and net loss statistics. This coverage is strengthened by the relatively short maturity of these issues, which lessens the risk of dramatic or prolonged economic weakness and consequent negative impact on portfolio quality.

Actual credit supports for triple-A rated auto receivables transactions have ranged from 5 to 17 percent due to differences in portfolios, and hence, pool quality. Characteristic of structured financings, ratings on auto receivables transactions are clustered in the highest rating categories. But since pool quality and the financial rationale for securitizations vary widely, S&P expects future transactions to have ratings all across the rating spectrum. S&P's evaluation of the credit support takes into account the stress on the transactions from liquidity needs due to delinquency and the permanent impairment of cash flow resulting from actual credit losses. The structural characteristics will also impact support levels by affecting what portions of receivable cash flow will be available to cover note obligations.

S&P does a comparative analysis on the portfolio from which the pooled receivables will be drawn, based on the following ratios:

1. *Repossession.* Repossessions as a percentage of gross contracts is a good indicator of loss frequency.

2. *Gross losses.* Gross losses as a percentage of gross receivables.

3. *Recoveries.* The extent and timing of recoveries are reviewed to detect liquidity stress on the credit support.

4. *Net losses.* Net losses as a percentage of gross receivables is a good indicator of loss severity that takes into account the servicer's collection ability.

5. *Delinquency.* The percentage of delinquencies to gross receivables is the best indicator of both liquidity stress on the deal and potential future losses that could occur. S&P requests delinquency reports on a 30-, 60-, and 90-plus-day basis. These numbers have varied widely.

6. *Prepayments*. Although prepayments do not have a direct effect on collateral quality, they are important in determining the deal's estimated life and the time period during which the credit support must be available. The amount of prepayments also is important in pay-through structures where note payments do not directly reflect payments on receivables.

7. *Insurance*. The auto contract obligor should be required to maintain physical damage insurance on the vehicle in at least the actual amount financed and outstanding. The insurance policy and any proceeds thereof should be assigned to the trustee. If the insurance lapses, the servicer may force place insurance on the vehicle and include the premium balance in the pooled receivable amount—such amount may need to be covered under the credit support.

There are many servicing policy elements that may affect the realized credit performance of the rated pool. The most important are "charge-off policy" and "extensions."

Without a firm charge-off policy, the failure to declare a delinquent receivable in default on a timely basis could delay recognition of losses and ultimately distort the performance statistics. Most issuers charge the receivable off when it is delinquent 90 to 180 days.

A liberal extension policy may have a negative impact if the receivable's maturity is extended beyond the note's stated maturity causing a shortfall of principal available to pay down the notes at maturity.

AUTO RECEIVABLE CHARACTERISTICS

S&P examines the characteristics of the specific receivables and how they were originated to determine if the pooled receivables will differ materially from the total portfolio. S&P must adjust the performance statistics of the portfolio accordingly. To do that, S&P looks at the following lending criteria and portfolio statistics:

1. *Loan-to-value ratios*. Loan-to-value ratios differ significantly among issuers within ranges of 90 to 115 percent of dealer cost on new vehicles. Greater total loan-to-value ratios generally require higher levels of credit support.

2. *Dealer recourse*. While overall net losses on recourse versus nonrecourse receivables generally are not significantly different, some portfolios, due to a high quality dealer network, indicate that lending on a nonrecourse basis results in greater losses than lending on a recourse basis.

3. *Maturity*. Original maturity appears to have a modest impact on receivable quality, with longer maturities performing slightly worse than shorter maturities.

4. *New versus used*. General Motors Acceptance Corporation data indicates that loss severity and cumulative net losses on used vehicles are 2 to 3 times higher than on new vehicles. This distinction hasn't been demonstrated consistently by all issuers.

5. *Seasoning*. Receivable seasoning has a positive impact on quality. A more mature receivable has more equity and a more established payment history. Most losses tend to occur between 6 and 18 months following receivable origination.

6. *Risk concentration*. Heavy concentration in one geographic region, industry, or type of asset may have a negative impact on credit quality.

An important aspect of auto receivables concerns perfecting a security interest in the receivable. A security interest in an auto receivable may be perfected by taking possession of the document representing the receivable or by filing a financing statement under the Uniform Commercial Code. Perfection of the interest in the vehicle itself requires compliance with state certificate of title laws. Under these laws, the security interest created in an auto must be noted on the certificate of title to perfect such security interest against possible claims of other parties. Due to the large number of vehicles involved, however, the certificate of title to each vehicle usually is not amended to reflect the assignment to the trustee of the seller's security interest in each vehicle. S&P's analysis of the receivables will take into account the possibility that recoveries on repossessed vehicles may not, in some cases, be available to the issuer.

CREDIT CARD-BACKED SECURITIES CRITERIA

S&P's analysis of credit card-backed securities is similar to that of the more common mortgage and auto receivable-backed issues. However, analysis reflects differences in the nature of the collateral and structure of the securities.

Bank credit cards are unsecured revolving debt obligations, supported only by the customer's contractual promise to pay. Since there is no tangible asset to repossess in the event of cardholder default, recoveries are relatively low, typically below 30 percent. In addition, customers who cannot pay all their debts tend to pay their secured loans first. Concern with the unsecured revolving nature of credit card loans is reflected in conservative loan loss assumptions.

Unlike the Federal National Mortgage Association, Federal Home Loan Mortgage Corporation, or Government National Mortgage Association, the MasterCard and Visa organizations do not require adherence to specific underwriting standards. Diversity in account solicitation methods and underwriting standards among issuers cause significant variations in portfolio charge-off experiences. The recent upward trend in industry losses is attributed to aggressive growth, relaxed underwriting standards and an increase in consumer bankruptcies. Preapproved mass mailings tend to yield higher risk accounts because accounts are selected based on relatively limited information.

New accounts typically carry higher loss ratios than mature or seasoned accounts in a portfolio. As accounts mature, only strong credits remain on file by avoiding charge-off. Seasoning of the pool of selected accounts will minimize this concern. Geographic distribution is also considered in the charge-off risk assessment. Portfolios that are concentrated in high-risk regions, due to a lack of industry diversification, will be evaluated accordingly.

Based on an assessment of a bank's credit policies and procedures, historic charge-offs and delinquencies, and portfolio characteristics, S&P will assume a future charge-off rate of 3 to 5 times historic levels. Conservative pool selection criteria may mitigate credit concerns and reduce charge-off assumptions.

To minimize credit concerns, high risk accounts can be eliminated from the pool of selected accounts. Accounts may be declared ineligible based on age, method of acquisition, geographic location, payment history, current status, or size of credit limits.

Annual percentage rate income is the major component of portfolio yield. Few issuers charge annual percentage rates below 15 percent and some charge rates as high as 21 percent. Although convenience use will reduce portfolio yield, issuers may increase the available portfolio yield by including annual membership and other fees. Excess yield, or available yield after required payments of investor interest, servicing fees, and letter of credit bank fees, is an important consideration in rating credit card-backed securities. Excess yield, if any, may be available to cover loan losses. If a reserve account is established, excess yield may also fund this account. If excess yield is available to cover losses, a high yielding portfolio should provide a considerable amount of loss protection. However, portfolio yield is subject to outside influences such as competition, legislative action, and convenience use and, as a result, could decline.

In response to competitive pressure, the issuer may choose to lower its credit card rates. Banks have aggressively expanded the highly profitable credit card market and, for the most part, have resisted competing directly on price. However, the industry is approaching saturation and consumer awareness of credit card rates is increasing. The next phase of competition may include price reduction to maintain and increase market share. A number of bank card issuers have recently lowered their rates and the trend may continue. Competition may also come from alternative sources of credit. S&P believes it is highly unlikely banks will reduce rates below that required to cover debt service on the securitized receivables.

Ceilings on credit card rates have been proposed at the federal and state legislative levels. A rate ceiling could reduce the bank's annual percentage rate and have an immediate effect on a portfolio's ability to absorb losses. Issuers have avoided state-imposed ceilings by locating their operations in nonrestrictive states. Banks may also be able to increase fees to counteract legislated annual percentage rate ceilings.

The recent federal tax law change that phases out the deduction of credit card finance charges effectively increased the cost of credit card borrowing for those who itemize deductions. This may significantly alter cash flows by accelerating payments, reducing the amount of reborrowing, or increasing convenience use.

Not all bank credit card receivables are subject to finance charges. Many issuers let customers avoid interest by paying off the entire balance each month. About 30 percent of all monthly Visa statements do not include finance charges. Although these "convenience users" are a small percentage of outstandings (below 10 percent for some issuers), they account for a high percentage of payment volume and new purchases. As convenience use rises, the portfolio yield will decline and payment rates increase.

Minimum and average monthly payment rates vary by portfolio. Most banks require a minimum monthly payment of the greater of a percentage of outstandings (generally below 5 percent) or a minimum dollar payment amount. Since payment terms vary by bank and cardholders have the option to pay any amount above the minimum, portfolio payment rates vary significantly.

In 1985, monthly payment rates for Bank of America's Northern California Classic Visa portfolio and Republic Bank's total bank card portfolio averaged 21 percent and 17 percent respectively. During the same year the estimated industry average payment rate, based on Visa statistics, was approximately 14%. Payment rate will directly influence the timing of cash flows to the investors. If cash flows are delayed due to a decline in payment rate, investor loss exposure is increased. S&P recognizes the uncertainty of payment rates due to the product's payment flexibility. For purposes of cash flow analyses, portfolio historic payment rates are conservatively discounted by more than 50 percent. Expected cash flows, based on assumed payment rate and credit enhancement, must be sufficient to retire investor principal prior to the issue's stated maturity.

Credit card balances have historically paid down at a rapid rate. The expected life of credit card receivables, based on experience, is about 6 to 8 months. Issuers converted these historically short-term credit card receivables into long-term securities by incorporating a revolving non-amortization period. During this period, only interest is paid the investor and principal payments are, in effect, reinvested. Investor principal payments begin after the nonamortization period, which has a scheduled duration and may be prematurely discontinued by the occurrence of a payout event.

Protective payout events are designed to end the nonamortization period before scheduled termination if the portfolio quality deteriorates significantly. Payout events may be seen as safety valves that let the deal wind down early if certain potentially adverse events occur. Payout events may occur if there is a substantial decline in yield, a significant increase in losses, or a change in cardholder payment or borrowing habits that could hurt portfolio performance. Also, certain occurrences of an issuer, servicer, or trustee default may be payout events. An issue structured with conservative payout events will minimize credit concerns.

The revolving nonamortization period is followed by an amortization period during which applicable cardholder principal payments are passed-through to retire investor principal. Credit card receivables are expected to pay down at 10 to 20 percent per month. Thus, the expected life for credit card receivables should be less than one year. Minimum payments are generally below 5 percent so theoretically, it could take more than five years for credit card-backed securities to amortize. The level of credit enhancement needed to cover liquidity concerns at final maturity will be inversely related to the length of the issue's scheduled amortization period.

Cardholder reborrowing, or new purchase and advance volume, is important in determining cash flows. The reborrowing rate is determined by the individual's approved borrowing capacity and the degree of debt the cardholder is willing to accept. Customer reborrowing rates vary by portfolio and may be influenced by economic conditions and the availability of alternative sources of credit. Normally, the trustee will have a security interest in new receivables (reborrowings) originating from the selected accounts. The conveyance of new receivables to the trust may cease if the issuing bank becomes insolvent.

The amount of cardholder reborrowing is significant. If the rate of reborrowing declines significantly during the nonamortization period, an early payout event could occur and shorten the life of the issue. Depending on the structure of the transaction, growth in the portfolio will influence principal cash flows during the amortization period. A drop in cardholder reborrowing may hurt cash flow by extending the issue's life. Extending final maturity increases loss exposure and liquidity concerns. Positive growth in the amortization period could have the opposite effect on cash flows.

Growth in new borrowings is evidenced by the upward trend in card-holder balances. As with other industry data, this information may be distorted by the tremendous growth in new accounts. Limited static pool data is available to support positive growth assumptions.

In addition to conservative selection criteria and pay-out events, credit quality may also be enhanced by letter of credit support, a reserve account, or overcollateralization. The adequacy of the level and type of cash flow support is measured by the issue's ability to withstand worst-case scenarios.

The market for credit card-backed issues is just beginning to emerge and a standard security structure is evolving. Each structure has a different degree of sensitivity to portfolio performance. The key variables to portfolio performance are yield, charge-offs, payment rate, and reborrowing rate. Each variable is interrelated and subject to outside influences. Before issuing a rating, S&P subjects each cash flow structure to a sensitivity analysis to study the effect of extreme adverse conditions, including a dramatic increase in loan losses, combined with substantial declines in portfolio yield, payments, and new volume. Conservative assumptions are developed, based on an analysis of the issuer, portfolio, and industry.

RECEIVABLES-BACKED COMMERCIAL PAPER

S&P rates over $10 billion in receivables-backed commercial paper and expects this to grow substantially. This type of commercial paper offers an additional financing outlet and increased liquidity. In most cases, the program's rating is higher than that of the company that originates the receivables, reducing financing costs. The receivables in the programs issued through early 1988 include credit cards, auto leases, trade receivables, and utility leases.

Receivables-backed commercial paper typically is issued through a special-purpose corporation (issuer) organized by an investment bank whose sole business is to finance the company's receivables. Repayment is supported by payments on the receivables. Shortfalls due to losses and delinquencies are covered by credit support, typically an irrevocable letter of credit. Liquidity lines are also in place as receivable payments are not usually matched with commercial paper maturities.

Each issuer is a bankruptcy-remote entity legally unaffiliated with the company originating the receivables, and the issuer's business is limited in the following ways: borrowing from bank(s) under the credit agreement; issuing commercial paper; engaging in certain incidental activities; and using commercial paper proceeds to lend to the company (a pledge transaction) or to buy receivables from the company (a sale transaction).

The issuer is barred from incurring additional debt. All parties other than commercial paper holders must agree not to file the issuer into bankruptcy for one year and one day after all commercial paper is paid. The overall intent is to insulate the issuer from Chapter 11 bankruptcy code proceedings.

The CP programs are legally structured to avoid a "credit link" with the originator of the receivables. A pool of accounts receivables is transferred to an independent third party, which issues the CP. As a special-purpose unaffiliated corporation, the issuer cannot be drawn into bankruptcy if the originating company filed for bankruptcy. The rating is based on the program's structure and the receivables' credit quality, not the originator's creditworthiness.

In a pledge transaction, the company pledges its interest in the receivables to the issuer as security. In a sale transaction, the issuer uses its funds to buy accounts receivable from the company. In both transactions, the issuer grants a perfected security interest in the receivables to the banks and the paper holders equally.

Receivables payments may not be available on any particular day to pay maturing CP. "Match funding" the cash flow of the receivables with CP maturities is generally difficult. Cash flow in a pledge transaction may also be subject to an automatic stay in a company bankruptcy. For these reasons, irrevocable bank lines must be available to ensure timely payment of maturing CP. The lines must equal 100 percent of the value of the receivables and must be provided by banks with ratings as high as the program's rating. Exceptions to the 100 percent bank line requirement are limited to companies with adequate liquidity and with ratings at least equal to those of the issuer.

Losses and delinquencies lower the value of the receivables and the liquidity lines. To protect against a potential repayment shortfall, each program provides for credit support, the size of which is determined primarily by the credit risk inherent to the receivable.

The support can come from overcollateralization, third-party credit support, or a combination of both. Overcollateralization is a pledge of receivables greater than a dollar-for-dollar pledge against outstanding paper. Third-party support is usually an irrevocable bank letter of credit. However, this support could also be a secondary market repurchase agreement, a surety bond, or some other type of facility. If an institution provides the support, the institution must be rated at least as high as the CP program's rating.

The criteria for evaluating the credit quality of receivables-backed CP is the same as with long-term asset-backed financings discussed early in the chapter. Five years of pool data are generally required, including delinquencies and total write-offs. These are sometimes modified, based on the industry, particular pool, and availability of data. In some issues, 100 percent credit support was needed due to an inability to fully analyze the receivables' credit quality.

The short exposure of CP (generally 270 days maximum maturity) and potential "pay down" of issuance arrangements if the credit quality of the receivables declines, reduces credit support requirements.

No CP program can be rated higher than the institution that provides the liquidity and credit support facilities. All but certain "match-funding" programs must count on liquidity facilities to provide funds for timely payments of maturing CP. All programs must rely on credit support to cover CP backed by nonperforming receivables. Credit and liquidity support ensures CP payment. The program's rating is based on the credit quality of both the receivables and the support.

DIFFERENCES IN STRESS TEST ASSUMPTIONS

There is an important difference between mortgage-backed and asset-backed criteria. With mortgages, we assume a long-term financing with an average life of 12 years. So the time period over which changes in the economy and interest rates affecting mortgages is substantial and the stress assumptions must be very conservative.

In other asset-backed transactions, we have to assess what maturity exposure the assets represent and develop individual stress assumptions.

For auto loans, maturities are usually 3 to 5 years. Average maturity is probably closer to 1 1/2 to 2 years due to prepayments, a much shorter period than for mortgage loans and a period we can more accurately predict.

When we analyze the credit going into a mortgage pool, we use a depression scenario because there is a possibility of a severe recession or even depression over the 12 year average life of a mortgage. When dealing with much shorter-term auto loans, we can eliminate depression and use, in some transactions, a mild or even slight recession scenario.

With credit cards, if a credit card receivable pool had repayments paid through as cardholder payments came in, the investor would typically be paid off in six months. Because issuers have created a credit card security structure that allows for an individually determined non-amortization period (two, three, or four years), S&P needs to analyze each transaction to determine the "assumed maturity" on which to stress test the dependent credit variables and, therefore, base the rating.

PART 2

ACCOUNTING, TAX, AND LEGAL CONSIDERATIONS

CHAPTER 9

ACCOUNTING
CONSIDERATIONS

John E. Stewart, Partner
Benjamin S. Neuhausen, Partner
Arthur Andersen & Co., Chicago

INTRODUCTION

The recent explosion in the number and volume of asset-backed financings, including securitization transactions, has created many accounting issues. Some of these have arisen because the new financial products are not specifically addressed in the accounting literature, and others because the literature itself provides conflicting guidance.

This chapter will discuss the following accounting considerations faced by sellers/issuers:

1. An overview of U.S. generally accepted accounting principles (GAAP).
2. A detailed discussion of GAAP for basic transaction structures, including relevant pronouncements of the Financial Accounting Standards Board (FASB), its Emerging Issues Task Force (EITF), and the Securities and Exchange Commission (SEC).
3. Application of GAAP to specific transaction structures.
4. Discussion of what the future might have in store insofar as accounting is concerned.

The chapter will not cover regulatory accounting practices or accounting issues faced by buyers/investors.

In addition to the many finance-related factors that have contributed to the growth of asset-backed securities, two accounting developments also have led to increased interest in, and volume of, transactions, and a third may indirectly create further interest. First, there was the issuance of FASB Statement No. 77, *Reporting by Transferors for Transfers of Receivables with Recourse* (December 1983). As will be discussed later, the criteria included in Statement 77 for sale accounting (removal of the assets from the balance sheet with gain or loss recognition) are frequently not difficult to meet. In fact, sellers/issuers can retain the credit and interest rate risks inherent in the receivables transferred and still achieve sale accounting.

Second, in October 1987 the FASB issued Statement No. 94, *Consolidation of All Majority-owned Subsidiaries*, which requires that all finance subsidiaries be consolidated for financial reporting purposes beginning for annual financial statements in calendar year 1988. As a result, this frequently-used vehicle for off-balance sheet treatment of receivables and related debt by commercial companies is eliminated. Some companies are looking to other means to achieve off-balance sheet treatment for their receivables, namely, certain forms of securitization.

Third, the opportunity to recognize a sale of receivables and resulting gain or loss takes on added significance because of FASB Statement No. 91, *Accounting for Nonrefundable Fees and Costs Associated with Originating or Acquiring Loans and Initial Direct Costs of Leases* (December 1986). The Statement, which is effective in calendar year 1988, generally requires that loan origination and commitment fees (and certain related costs) be deferred and amortized over the life of the related loan or receivable rather than being recognized at the time of origination or over the commitment period. Upon sale, gain or loss is recognized taking into account the deferred items, thereby triggering more rapid recognition of fees than Statement 91 would otherwise allow.

OVERVIEW OF GENERALLY ACCEPTED ACCOUNTING PRINCIPLES

Securitization transactions cover a wide spectrum. At one extreme are outright sales of assets or interests in assets. At the other are borrowings collateralized by assets. In between are sales of assets with recourse to the seller and nonrecourse borrowings collateralized by assets. The transactions at the ends of the spectrum usually are easy to account for because their substance follows their form; it is the transactions in the middle that create accounting issues. That is, transactions in the middle have characteristics of both sales and borrowings and raise questions of whether the seller/issuer should continue to include the receivables on its balance sheet or record gains and losses.

Before discussing in detail the accounting considerations faced by sellers/issuers, it is worthwhile to provide an overview of the authoritative literature affecting securitization transactions. This overview helps set the stage for the complexities and potential controversies in accounting for these transactions.

The FASB has issued two accounting standards that are specifically relevant: Statement 77 and Technical Bulletin 85-2, *Accounting for Collateralized Mortgage Obligations (CMOs)* (March 1985).[1]

Transfers (Sales) of Receivables With Recourse

In a sale of receivables with recourse, the seller is obligated to make payments to the buyer or to repurchase receivables sold under certain circumstances, typically for defaults up to a specified percentage that sometimes greatly exceeds likely credit losses. The amount of recourse can vary from a small percentage of the receivable balances to 100 percent. The form of the recourse also varies. In addition, the seller often guarantees to the buyer a specified return or yield during the term of the receivables.

Statement 77 allows receivables to be removed from the balance sheet (with gain or loss recognition) if they are irrevocably transferred in a transaction that "purports to be a sale or a participation agreement." The seller can have no options or obligations to repurchase nondelinquent receivables (calls and puts). Off-balance sheet treatment is allowed even though it is probable that the seller/transferor will make future payments to the buyer/transferee for credit losses, the effects of prepayments, or changes in interest rates—as long as the credit losses and the effects of prepayments can be reasonably estimated. Statement 77 also allows off-balance sheet treatment of transfers of partial interests in receivables.

---

[1]Also relevant are the accounting rules on consolidation of subsidiaries and special-purpose entities, which are discussed later in this chapter.

Any interests retained are recorded (or remain) as assets on the seller/-transferor's balance sheet.

In practice, it has often not been difficult to achieve sale accounting under Statement 77, particularly for large pools of homogeneous receivables.

Collateralized Mortgage Obligations

A collateralized mortgage obligation (CMO) is a debt security collateralized by a pool of mortgage loan receivables. The interest and principal payments of the mortgagors are accumulated, then used to pay interest and principal to the CMO holders. The CMOs are frequently nonrecourse to the general credit of the borrower/issuer; the holders may look only to the cash flow from the mortgage collateral for their interest and principal payments. Although the FASB had mortgage receivables in mind when it issued Technical Bulletin 85-2, the FASB staff has indicated that it is appropriate to apply the Technical Bulletin by analogy to other types of receivables. The purpose of the Technical Bulletin was to give guidance on when transactions that are in legal form debt instruments may be treated as sales for accounting purposes.

Technical Bulletin 85-2 allows assets and debt to be removed from the balance sheet (with gain or loss recognition) in a CMO transaction if virtually all of the cash flows from the assets are irrevocably passed to the creditors and if the borrower/issuer cannot be required to make any future payments to the creditors other than from cash flows from the collateral. The borrower may not retain even secondary liability to pay the obligations. The Technical Bulletin does not allow off-balance sheet treatment for passage of partial interests in the assets' future cash flows to creditors unless the interest retained by the borrower is "trifling." Further, if a CMO transaction qualifies for off-balance sheet treatment under the Technical Bulletin, the "trifling" interests retained by the borrower (if any) may not be recorded as assets; these interests are recorded as they accrue to the benefit of the borrower.

Before the introduction of the REMIC provisions of the 1986 Tax Reform Act, tax and other constraints made it quite difficult to achieve sale accounting under the Technical Bulletin. However, it has been possible to achieve sale accounting and postREMIC sale accounting may become more prevalent for transactions involving mortgages. Although the Technical Bulletin sets stringent criteria, it is unique in the accounting literature by permitting sale treatment even though the legal form is debt.

Conflicting Guidance

Statement 77 and Technical Bulletin 85-2 provide conflicting guidance. Receivables transferred in a transaction that purports to be a sale or a participation may be removed from the balance sheet under Statement 77 even though there is 100 percent recourse to the seller/transferor for credit losses and the effects of changing interest rates. Further, the interests transferred may be removed from the balance sheet even if the seller/transferor retains a substantial interest in the transferred receivables. In addition, the seller/transferor may retain the benefits of favorable interest rate movements and the effects of prepayments.

If the transaction is structured as a borrowing, however (with the receivables pledged as collateral, as in a CMO transaction), Technical Bulletin 85-2 provides that even lack of recourse to the borrower ("seller") for credit losses and a fixed interest rate on the borrowing are not sufficient to remove the assets from the balance sheet. Stated differently, a transfer of receivables structured as a borrowing may be required to be accounted for as a liability even though there is no recourse to the seller/transferor for credit losses and there is no interest rate risk. Further, CMOs cannot be removed from the balance sheet if the seller retains more than a "trifling" interest in the future cash flows from the receivables.

Statement 77 and Technical Bulletin 85-2 are also inconsistent in that Statement 77 permits the initial recording of a residual interest in a sales transaction (e.g., due to a positive spread of receivable interest rates over investor pass-through rates) while Technical Bulletin 85-2 does not.

Ambiguous Transactions

The scope of Statement 77, as noted, limits it to transactions that purport to be sales or participations, as opposed to collateralized borrowings, which may be an issue of legal form. Thus, the FASB appears to place importance on legal form in an unsettled area of law.

As discussed in Chapter 11, the legal line between a sale of assets and a pledge of assets to secure a loan is not always clear. Some "buyers" have been unpleasantly surprised to learn that they may be classified as secured creditors in bankruptcy proceedings, in which case they could be forced to share their "collateral." For example, some attorneys believe that a sale of receivables with 100 percent recourse would be treated as a secured borrowing upon bankruptcy of the issuer, yet Statement 77 clearly contemplates sale treatment for some transactions with 100 percent recourse.

These ambiguities, as well as other matters, have given rise to "scope" questions: How is one to determine whether Statement 77, Technical Bulletin 85-2, or some other pronouncement applies. These scope questions as well as other matters sometimes make accounting for transactions in the middle of the spectrum difficult.

Issuer Objectives

To summarize, the criteria included in the accounting literature for removing assets and liabilities from the balance sheet produce different accounting results for transactions in which the substance is similar or identical but the form is different. If the receivables transaction purports to be a sale or a participation, one standard applies; if the receivables transaction purports to be a borrowing, another, and radically different, standard applies, regardless of the seller/transferor/debtor's rights and obligations in the two transactions. Further, for some transactions the form is ambiguous.

Because the financial reporting treatment of a securitization transaction is, in large part, dependent on its form, the transaction form selected by an issuer may be influenced by his accounting objectives. Does he desire off-balance sheet treatment and gain or loss recognition? Or does he desire to monetize receivables whose fair value is less than their carrying amount ("underwater") without loss recognition and thus prefer financing (on balance sheet) treatment?

This background sets the stage for the detailed discussion that follows.

DETAILED DISCUSSION OF GENERALLY ACCEPTED ACCOUNTING PRINCIPLES

This section discusses existing generally accepted accounting principles in more detail and is organized as follows:

- Sales without recourse
- Sales with recourse

- Collateralized mortgage obligation-type structures
- Other nonrecourse borrowings
- Recourse borrowings
- Consolidation (transactions through subsidiaries or special-purpose companies)
- Income tax accounting

Sales Without Recourse

In a sale of receivables *without* recourse, the buyer has no claim against the seller for failure of debtors to pay when due. Accounting for sales without recourse is based on general asset sale accounting principles (including Statement 77) and is similar to transfers of receivables with recourse that qualify for sale accounting. Therefore, that part of this chapter should be referred to for additional guidance. For example, for all sales, with or without recourse, if the seller will service the receivables and the stated servicing fee differs materially from a normal servicing fee (or if no servicing fee is specified), the sales price and, therefore, the gain or loss are adjusted to provide a normal servicing fee in each future period. Also, for all sales with or without recourse, a difference between the coupon interest rate on the receivables and the rate of interest passed through to investors can cause an adjustment of the sale price and the gain or loss.

The sale transactions described here (as well as those with recourse) may involve creation of a trust into which a pool of assets is sold. Certificate holders are entitled to cash flows from the assets (e.g., a pass-through structure) and have an ownership interest in the assets. It is also possible in these transactions for various independent originators of receivables to pool their receivables in a single transaction to increase the size of the offering and thus gain access to, for example, the public markets or otherwise save on transaction costs. The originators may receive cash or an interest in the total pool.

Nonrecourse Sale of Whole Receivables
A nonrecourse sale of whole receivables is accounted for like any other outright sale. The receivables are removed from the balance sheet and gain or loss is recognized for the difference between the sales proceeds received and the carrying amount of the receivables sold.

Nonrecourse Sale of Undivided Interests

A nonrecourse sale of undivided interests in a receivable or pool of receivables (e.g., a participation) is accounted for as a partial sale of the receivables. The percentage interest sold is removed from the balance sheet and gain or loss is recognized for the difference between the sales proceeds received and the carrying amount of the interests sold. The percentage interest retained continues to be recorded as an asset. Stated differently, sale accounting is applied to the interests transferred but not to the interests retained.

Nonrecourse Sale of Interest or Principal Strips

Assuming the transaction is structured in form as a sale (as opposed to a debt issue), a nonrecourse sale of interest or principal strips in a pool of receivables is accounted for as a partial sale of the receivables. The seller should allocate the carrying amount of the receivable pool between the strips sold and the strips retained and recognize gain or loss on the strips sold.

One method of allocating the carrying amount of the receivable pool between the strips sold and the strips retained is based on a computation of the present value of the future estimated cash flows for each component using as a discount rate the original yield on the receivables (i.e., use the *same* discount rate for both the principal and the interest cash flow). In 1982, this method was supported by the Accounting Standards Executive Committee (AcSEC) of the American Institute of CPAs. The problem with this method is that financial markets do not price that way. For example, say a 10-year receivable pays interest every six months and principal at maturity. If the interest coupons and principal were separated, the market would discount the principal at a 10-year rate. The market would discount the first interest coupon at a 6-month rate, the second interest coupon at the 12-month rate, and so on. The market discount rates for the two elements would rarely, if ever, be equal. Thus, this method could result in an immediate gain in a positively-sloped yield curve environment if the originator of the receivables sold an interest strip immediately after originating the receivables.

In 1988, AcSEC withdrew its support for the method described in the previous paragraph. In addition, in 1988, the EITF addressed the matter (Issue 88-11) and reached a consensus that the seller should allocate the carrying amount of the receivable pool between the strip sold and the strip retained based on their relative fair values on the date that the receivable pool was acquired and recognize gain or loss on the strip sold. If it is not practicable to determine fair values on the date of acquisition, the allocation should be based on the relative fair values of the strip sold and the strip retained on the date of the sale. The EITF agreed to deal with some implementation issues with respect to this consensus at a future meeting.

The carrying amount allocated to the strips retained should continue to be accounted for as it was previously, that is, it continues to be recorded as an asset and should not result in a current gain or loss. An amount of premium or discount should be determined on the strips retained and amortized to income using the interest method.

Nonrecourse Sale of Multiclass Pass-Throughs

Multiclass pass-through certificates representing interests in pools of mortgages became feasible under the REMIC provisions of the Tax Reform Act of 1986. Multiclass pass-throughs differ from interest and principal strips in that the investor's interest through a multiclass pass-through is identifiable only at the level of the pool; the investor does not have an identifiable interest in any individual receivable. The classes behave like the tranches in a CMO (i.e., with different expected lives). However, the structure is different—each class represents a specified ownership/participation interest in the cash flows of a pool of receivables rather than a class of a debt issue.

Many accountants would account for the sale of multiclass pass-throughs similarly to sale of strips—allocate the carrying amount of the mortgage pool between the interests sold and the interests retained based on their relative fair values (see previous discussion) and recognize gain or loss on the interests sold. If all of the principal is sold via the multiclass pass-throughs, the "excess servicing" method of computing gain or loss may also be used. Under the excess servicing method, the entire pool of receivables is considered sold for a price equal to the sum of: 1) the proceeds received from investors and 2) the current fair value of the residual interest retained by the seller (adjusted, if necessary, for a normal servicing fee if the issuer is the servicer). If the residual interest retained represents a small fraction of the receivables, the excess servicing method and the allocation of carrying amount based on relative values will result in similar gains or losses.

Some accountants differ on sales recognition. They believe that the inability to identify the investor's interest in the individual receivables indicates that the multiclass pass-through is actually a pledging of cash flows—a nonrecourse borrowing collateralized by mortgages—and would apply Technical Bulletin 85-2 (see later discussion). These accountants note that multiclass pass-throughs may be economically identical to CMO type structures and believe the same accounting should be applied.

Sales With Recourse

In a sale of receivables *with* recourse, the buyer has a right to receive payment from the seller for failure of debtors to pay when due and, in some cases, for the effects of debtor prepayments. As discussed below, the form of recourse can vary. "Recourse" is defined in Statement 77 as "the right of a transferee of receivables to receive payment from the transferor of those receivables for (a) failure of the debtors to pay when due, (b) the effects of prepayments, or (c) adjustments resulting from defects in the eligibility of the transferred receivables."

Statement 77 applies to all types of receivables—trade receivables, installment receivables, residential mortgage loans, second mortgage loans, commercial loans (including commercial mortgages), finance lease receivables (auto, computer, airplane and so on), credit card receivables, insurance premium loans, student loans, mobile home loans, manufactured home loans, multifamily mortgage loans, receivables denominated in foreign currencies, and so on.

Under Statement 77, a sale of receivables with recourse is recorded as a sale if all of the following three conditions are satisfied:

1. The seller surrenders control over the receivables; he has no option to repurchase receivables, and he cannot substitute new receivables for receivables previously sold except in accordance with recourse provisions (i.e., no call).
2. The seller's obligation under the recourse provisions can be reasonably estimated.
3. The buyer cannot require the seller to repurchase the receivables except in accordance with the recourse provisions (i.e., no put).

If all three conditions are satisfied, the transaction is accounted for as a full or partial sale, similar to a nonrecourse sale. In addition, the seller's estimated recourse obligation is recorded at the date of sale. A sale of receivables with recourse may follow any of the four forms discussed for nonrecourse sales—whole receivables, undivided interests (e.g., participations), principal or interest strips, or multiclass pass-throughs–and the accounting is basically the same.

If any of the three conditions is not satisfied, the transaction is accounted for like a full recourse borrowing collateralized by receivables (see later discussion).

Concerning conditions 1 and 3 above, Statement 77 provides some additional guidance. First, the existence of a right of first refusal based on a bona fide offer by an unrelated party ordinarily will not preclude sale accounting. Further, some transfer agreements require or permit the seller to repurchase transferred receivables when the amount of outstanding receivables is minor to keep the cost of servicing those receivables from becoming unreasonable ("clean-up call"). If those reversionary interests are not significant to the transferor—interpreted in practice as no more than 5 to 10 percent of the original balances transferred—their existence alone does not preclude sale treatment. However, a clean-up call based solely on passage of time rather than on the uncollected balance would preclude sale accounting (because of uncertainty concerning the amount of receivables outstanding at the time the call becomes exercisable), unless the amount scheduled to be outstanding based on *contractual* maturities is less than 5 to 10 percent of the original balances transferred.

A put or call for any reason not in accordance with the recourse provisions of the agreement or a clean-up call would violate the sale criteria in Statement 77. For example, a repurchase option, even if at fair market value, is inconsistent with sale accounting. Further, a provision allowing the purchaser of the receivables to put the receivables back to the seller if the seller is not meeting certain defined servicing performance criteria would preclude sale accounting. A put triggered by declining creditworthiness of the *seller* or market value declines due to interest rate increases would also preclude sale accounting.

For a transaction to be covered by Statement 77, the transaction must "purport to be a sale or participation." A discussion of this condition, as well as other implementation matters, follows.

Purport To Be a Sale

Because, as indicated above, Statement 77 is a fairly permissive accounting standard, sellers frequently want to have the transaction covered by Statement 77, particularly if the receivables are not "underwater" (i.e., sale accounting would not give rise to loss recognition) and the objective is off-balance sheet treatment. Off-balance sheet treatment may be desired to improve reported debt/equity ratios, to avoid violating existing debt covenants and for other reasons. If covered by Statement 77, sale accounting (with resulting gain or loss) is frequently not difficult to achieve. This is in contrast to the requirements of Technical Bulletin 85-2 or other accounting literature, for example, in accounting for recourse debt securities. As a result, a frequent question—a scope question—is whether Statement 77 applies.

Statement 77 establishes accounting standards for "transfers of receivables with recourse that *purport* to be sales of receivables. It also applies to *participation agreements* (that is, transfers of specified interests in a particular receivable or pool of receivables) that provide for recourse, factoring agreements that provide for recourse, and sales or assignments with recourse of leases or property subject to leases that were accounted for as sales-type or direct financing leases." Statement 77 "does not address accounting and reporting of loans collateralized by receivables, for which the receivables and the loan are reported on the borrower's balance sheet."

The FASB has provided limited additional guidance on the scope of Statement 77. Technical Bulletin 85-2 notes that its scope relates to "*bonds* secured by mortgage(s) . . . *structured* so that all or substantially all of the collections . . . are paid through to the holders . . . " (emphasis added). Technical Bulletin 85-2 also notes:

> In specifying the scope of Statement 77, the phrase *purport to be sales* and all the transactions enumerated in paragraph 3 refer only to those transfers structured as sales agreements. As a result, the provisions of Statement 77 do not apply to CMOs because they are not structured as sales agreements; rather, CMOs are debt instruments collateralized by mortgage-backed securities or mortgage loans.

Questions arise as to whether a transaction must be a legal sale (a true sale for bankruptcy purposes—see Chapter 11) or a sale for tax purposes (see Chapter 10) to be covered by Statement 77. In practice, the answer is generally no. Each discipline has its own rules or guidelines in determining whether a transaction is a sale or a financing. For accountants, as indicated in Technical Bulletin 85-2, the structure or form determines which accounting literature applies. In practice, disclosure document descriptions or other documentation of the transaction have typically been used to decide whether a transaction purports to be a sale (participation) or a borrowing. Descriptions such as "sale," "participation," or "transfer of rights, title and interest" typically indicate that the transaction purports to be a sale.

However, representations by the parties to the agreement in the documentation that they will treat the transaction as a borrowing for tax purposes are troublesome to some accountants because those representations call into question what the transaction purports to be.

It is also possible that a transaction may represent a sale for tax purposes but a financing (borrowing) for financial reporting purposes because of the different criteria used to evaluate the transaction.

Forms of Recourse

Recourse in the transaction may take different forms. Determining whether recourse exists is important for two reasons. First, if it exists, the seller/issuer must be able to make a reasonable estimate of the obligation to achieve sale accounting. Second, if the recourse obligation can be estimated and sale accounting is achieved, the seller needs to record the estimated obligation as a liability. The amount of any such liability should be determined based on the seller's normal policies for estimating the allowance for uncollectible accounts (and collection and repossession costs) for similar, wholly-owned assets taking into consideration the nature of and limits on the recourse.

Various forms of recourse are as follows:

- In the most straightforward form, the seller makes cash payments to the buyer to reimburse the buyer for losses caused by debtor defaults or delinquencies. The buyer's recourse to the seller may be unlimited or capped. Under some recourse agreements, the buyer may be required to repossess any collateral before it can exercise its recourse rights.
- Another form of recourse requires the seller to replace defaulted receivables with good receivables.
- Still another form is a holdback reserve. The buyer pays only part of the purchase price at the date of sale. The remainder is held back until the receivables are collected and is reduced by defaults on the receivables. After the receivables are collected, the balance remaining in the holdback reserve is paid to the seller. Until then, the estimated holdback is reflected by the seller as a receivable from the buyer.
- One of the newer forms of recourse is a senior/junior (subordinated) participation. The seller creates senior and junior participation interests in a pool of receivables, sells the senior participations and retains the junior participations. Defaults and other losses are charged first against

the junior participations. The holders of the senior participations are protected against the loss until the junior participations are completely eliminated. (Note that if the seller sells both the senior and junior participations, the sale would be nonrecourse.)

• Still another form of recourse that has been developed to deal with certain bank regulatory constraints involves depositing so-called excess servicing fees (excess of interest earned on the receivables transferred over the sum of interest passed through to investors and a normal servicing fee) in an escrow account. The recourse to the seller is limited to the amounts in the escrow account. The seller is entitled to any unused funds in the escrow account and may be able to withdraw funds from the escrow account before all receivables are collected if the account exceeds specified levels. This escrow account is also referred to as a reserve fund or spread account.

Many securitization transactions also involve third-party letters of credit or surety bonds that support the issuer's recourse obligations and provide additional assurances to the investors. Other than fees involved in gain or loss computations, the existence of third-party credit enhancement generally has no effect on the seller/issuer's accounting. Likewise, the seller/issuer may collateralize its promise under the recourse provisions (using other assets) without precluding sale accounting.

Estimating Losses under Recourse Provisions

With respect to meeting the second condition for sale accounting, Statement 77 states that:

> Lack of experience with receivables with characteristics similar to those being transferred or other factors that affect a determination at the transfer date of the collectibility of the receivables may impair the ability to make a reasonable estimate of the probable bad debt losses and related costs of collections and repossessions. A transfer of receivables shall not be recognized as a sale if collectibility of the receivables and related costs of collection and repossession are not subject to reasonable estimation.

The ability to estimate just the maximum exposure is not sufficient to meet the condition. The seller must be able to make a reasonable estimate of the actual exposure.

It is not possible to state any single criterion to be used as a guideline to determine whether recourse obligations can be reasonably estimated.

There are, however, a number of factors that bear on this determination. They include the following:

1. Type of loan—Transactions in the marketplace today involve a wide range of commercial or consumer receivables and loans. Consumer loans such as automobile and credit card receivables are common and the related recourse provisions generally are more susceptible to loss estimation.

2. Number of loans—The larger the number of loans involved in a transaction, the easier it is to estimate losses on the portfolio as a whole. In other words, the range of probable loss percentages typically is narrower in larger populations.

3. Nature of recourse obligation—The nature of the formula for determining recourse is a factor in estimation. For example, recourse up to a stated ceiling is easier to estimate than a complex, multifactored formula under which recourse is unlimited.

4. Quality of the loans—Generally speaking, the better the quality of the loans, the easier it is to estimate losses. For example, loss estimation is easier in the case of performing loans (versus nonperforming), third-party guaranteed receivables (versus unguaranteed loans), and low loan-to-value loans (versus high loan-to-value loans).

5. Homogeneity—Loss estimation is generally simpler when all of the receivables in the transaction have similar characteristics.

6. Track record—If the type of receivable involved in the transaction is well established in the marketplace, there may be significant track records with regard to past losses. Loss estimation is easier in this case than in a transaction in which the type of receivable is novel and little or no track record exists.

7. Seasoning—Loss estimation is typically easier for seasoned receivables than new receivables.

If a transaction involves a large number of receivables of a common variety, and if a significant track record on losses exists for receivables of a type that is representative of the subject receivables, there generally should be no problem with regard to loss estimation under the recourse provisions for accounting purposes. Receivables in this category typically include automobile loans and credit cards. At the other end of the spectrum, a transaction involving a single commercial loan may not qualify for sale accounting because the loss on a single loan may not be reasonably estimable.

Interest Rate Changes and Prepayment Penalties

Some sales or participations of fixed-rate receivables provide that the seller will pay a floating rate to the investors. Thus, if the fixed rate exceeds the floating pass-through rate, the seller retains the excess. If the floating pass-through rate exceeds the fixed rate, the seller makes up the deficiency. The converse, of course, is also possible (i.e., the underlying receivables are floating rate, but the investors desire a fixed rate).

Statement 77 specifically indicates that a floating rate provision does not preclude sale accounting treatment if a transaction otherwise qualifies as a sale. This is true regardless of whether the floating-rate provision is traditional or "inverted." The sale is recorded based on market interest rates in effect at the date of sale. Subsequent changes in interest rates are accounted for as changes in the sales price, that is, recorded as current gains or losses as the negative or positive spread accrues.

Statement 77 also does not preclude sale accounting if the seller guarantees the buyer a yield. Such a guarantee, however, could impact gain or loss computations.

Last, Statement 77 has been interpreted in practice not to preclude sale accounting if the seller retains the right to receive any prepayment penalties.

Guarantees of Prepayment Experience

Some receivables transactions require the seller/transferor/debtor to make payments to the buyer/transferee/lender on a fixed schedule regardless of when the transferred receivables are collected. For example, the purported seller may guarantee a specified prepayment pattern or a minimum or maximum prepayment pattern on the receivables because the investor does not want to assume the risk of prepayments. While the transactions are described as sales or participations in the legal documents, an issue arises as to whether a fixed payment schedule is consistent with the notion of a sale or participation. Part of the reason for this issue is that Statement 77 defines "recourse" to include the "effects of prepayments" but never describes what those effects are. Does it include a seller guarantee of the timing of the collection of the receivables?

In practice, the resolution of this issue by most accountants has been that a commitment by the seller to pay cash to the buyer on a fixed schedule indicates that either 1) the transfer is structured as a loan and falls outside the scope of Statement 77, or 2) the transaction is covered by Statement 77 but must be accounted for as a borrowing because the commitment represents an effective put or call option and thus violates the Statement 77 criteria for sale accounting. This is the case even if the projections of prepayment experience approximately coincide with the guarantees. Stated differently, to achieve sale accounting the receivables should be sold through their maturity, whether that is earlier or later than anticipated or hoped for. Thus, while the seller can guarantee a yield or rate of return to the buyer, it cannot guarantee a maturity and achieve sale accounting.

Sale accounting is allowed if the seller pays a bona fide third party to provide a guarantee of the timing of payments to the investor, provided that the third party has no recourse to the seller and the seller will not finance the third party with regard to the guarantee.

Servicing Activities

Another issue arises when receivables pay monthly but payments to investors are made less frequently, for example, quarterly. When a seller acts as servicer on a pass-through, it administers payments and reinvests temporarily retained excess cash. In addition, it commits to pay the stated pass-through rate to investors and faces the risk that reinvestment income will fall short of that commitment. In return for taking this risk and performing the stipulated administrative functions, the seller enjoys the possible benefit of reinvestment rates in excess of the pass-through rate on funds temporarily held.

The fact that the seller in the pass-through retains funds temporarily generally does not preclude sale accounting because accumulating small payments on individual receivables and remitting larger periodic payments to investors is a normal function performed by sellers. Moreover, the compensation paid to the seller is in consideration of the services performed and the risk assumed. If the seller/service retains funds for extended periods before making payments to investors, however, the arrangement may take on many of the characteristics of a borrowing and the compensation to the seller may exceed the value of the services performed; therefore, sale accounting may not be appropriate. In practice, some accountants believe that quarterly periods are reasonable for monthly pay receivables and do not preclude sale accounting.

Gain or Loss Computations

Statement 77 provides that if a transfer of receivables qualifies as a sale, all "probable adjustments" in connection with the recourse obligations to the seller should be accrued in accordance with FASB Statement No. 5, *Accounting for Contingencies* (1975).[2] Probable adjustments are defined as:

> Adjustments for (a) failure of the debtors to pay when due, for example, estimated bad debt losses and related costs of collections and repossessions accounted for in accordance with Statement 5, (b) estimated effects of prepayments, and (c) defects in the eligibility of the transferred receivables—for example, defects in the legal title of the transferred receivables.

The difference between 1) the sales price (adjusted for the accrual for probable adjustments) and 2) the net receivables (gross receivables plus accrued interest less unearned finance and service charges and fees net of deferred origination costs) should be recognized as a gain or loss on the sale. Investment or commercial banking fees, legal fees, and so on, incurred to consummate the transaction should be accrued as a reduction of the gain or increase in the loss.

If receivables are sold with servicing retained and the stated servicing fee rate differs materially from a "current (normal) servicing fee rate" or no servicing fee is specified, the sales price should be adjusted to provide for a normal servicing fee in each subsequent servicing period. This normal servicing fee should not be less than the estimated servicing costs. If the specified servicing fee is greater (less) than the normal servicing fee rate, the sales price should be adjusted upward (downward) by the present value of the difference over the estimated life of the receivables. Estimates of excess (or deficient) servicing fees should be based on realistic projections of prepayments and should be reflected as their discounted present values using interest rates commensurate with the risk and maturities involved. In essence, the objective is to adjust the actual sales price to an estimated sales price that would have been obtained had a normal servicing fee been specified. (Note that if the seller is not the servicer, it still will need to adjust the gain or loss

---

[2]Statement 5 requires loss or expense recognition when both of the following conditions are met:

a) Information available prior to issuance of the financial statements indicates that it is probable that an asset had been impaired or a liability had been incurred at the date of the financial statements .

b) The amount of loss can be reasonably estimated.

for the present value of any difference between the coupon rate on the receivables and the pass-through rate to the investors.)

If the excess of the coupon interest rate on the receivables sold over the pass-through rate to the investors exceeds a normal servicing fee (so-called "excess servicing"), but that excess over the receivables' lives cannot be reasonably estimated, the initial gain or loss on sale should not be adjusted. Rather, the excess should be recorded as income as received. A situation of this type might be the sale of a single receivable that can be prepaid at any time without penalty.

Statement 77 defines current (normal) servicing fee rate as "a servicing fee rate that is representative of servicing fee rates most commonly used in comparable servicing agreements covering similar types of receivables." In practice, this definition has been the subject of varied interpretation. The FASB has recently issued Technical Bulletin No. 87-3 (December 1987), *Accounting for Mortgage Servicing Fees and Rights*, to provide more explicit guidance for residential mortgages. Specifically, the Technical Bulletin indicates that the normal servicing fee rate that should be used for mortgages is that set by the Government National Mortgage Association, the Federal Home Loan Mortgage Corporation, and the Federal National Mortgage Association (unless a higher rate is needed to cover the cost of servicing). That rate should generally be used whether the loans are sold to those organizations or to private sector investors.

The FASB has not provided guidance for other types of receivables, but the Technical Bulletin might be looked to as an analogy. Further, in discussing measurements of normal servicing fees for residential mortgages, the FASB's EITF reached a consensus in Issue 85-26 that use of a normal fee developed as a function of the servicer's cost is not appropriate. Determining normal service fee rates for nonmortgage receivables, such as automobile loans and credit card receivables, may be more difficult than mortgages. Some studies performed by investment banking and other firms exist and should be referred to.

Questions have also arisen about accounting for the impact of changes in estimates due to prepayments on the net excess servicing fee receivable or net servicing fee deficiency payable initially established at the time of sale. Two approaches have been suggested:

1. If prepayment experience is unfavorable, the net excess servicing fee receivable (or deficiency payable) would be decreased (or increased) currently to the present value of the estimated remaining future excess (or deficient) service fee revenue, with the adjustment charged to income. The same discount rate used to calculate the original receivable or payable would be used to calculate the change. If prepayment experience is favorable, the receivable (or payable) would not be adjusted currently; however, amortization would be adjusted prospectively.

2. The seller would compute a new interest rate from the date of the initial sale based on the initial net receivable or payable balance recorded, but using the new estimate of the timing and amount of net cash flows for the excess (or deficient) servicing. The net receivable or payable would be adjusted to the amount at which it would have been stated had the current estimate of cash flows been used since inception. The catch-up adjustment (gain or loss) would be reflected in income currently.

In December 1986, the FASB's EITF addressed this issue for mortgages and reached a consensus that the first approach should be used (Issue 86–38). The second approach is based on Statement 91, which was issued after the EITF consensus. The EITF has not changed its consensus, and both approaches are used in practice. To address the inconsistency, the FASB has authorized its staff to draft a proposed Technical Bulletin on amortization of mortgage servicing rights, excess servicing fees and interest-only certificates.

Questions also arise with regard to income recognition for servicing activities. Assuming the fees can be reliably measured, they should be recognized on the accrual method as the servicing is performed, not on a cash basis. In transactions using an escrow account (see page 262), receipt of cash may be delayed until later in the term of the transaction.

Third-Party CMO Transactions

During 1986, the EITF addressed a transaction involving mortgages that could also be accomplished with other receivables (Issue 86-24). In the transaction, an enterprise sells receivables with or without recourse to an unrelated third party that then uses the receivables as collateral for debt issued through a special-purpose entity owned and controlled by the unrelated third party. The enterprise does not have the right to repurchase the receivables nor can the receivables be put back to the enterprise other than through the recourse provisions, if any. As part of the transaction, the enterprise acquires the right to receive a defined portion of the total payments received from the receivables in excess of the amount required to service the collateralized debt (the residual interest).

The accounting issue is whether Statement 77 or Technical Bulletin 85-2 applies to the enterprise—a scope question. (Technical Bulletin 85-2 would apply to the third party.) While the FASB and SEC staffs expressed concerns because the enterprise is in approximately the same economic position as if it sponsored its own debt issue, the EITF reached a consensus that because there was a legal sale, the transaction should be accounted for in accordance with Statement 77. Any gain or loss from the sale, including the present value of the residual interest if it can be reliably estimated, should be recognized in the period in which the transaction occurs.

A third-party CMO transaction should be distinguished from a situation in which the enterprise that originated the receivables uses the special purpose entity of an unrelated third party to obtain existing SEC registration rights but simultaneously the enterprise originating the receivables becomes the legal owner of the special purpose entity. This transaction should be accounted for under Technical Bulletin 85-2.

Disclosure

For transfers of receivables with recourse reported as sales, the transferor's financial statements should disclose 1) the sales proceeds to the transferor during each period for which an income statement is presented, 2) if the information is available, the balance of the receivables transferred that remain uncollected at the date of each balance sheet presented, and 3) the nature and amount of the recourse provisions.

Collateralized Mortgage Obligation-Type Structures

As indicated previously, Technical Bulletin 85-2 is the other major pronouncement of the FASB affecting securitization transactions. The FASB developed the Technical Bulletin when CMO transactions began to grow in volume, but before securitization of other receivables became more common. While the FASB had mortgage receivables in mind when it issued the Technical Bulletin, the FASB staff has since indicated that it is appropriate to apply Technical Bulletin 85-2 to other types of receivable transactions by analogy.

CMO transactions are in form borrowings by the issuer (often a special-purpose subsidiary of the sponsor) secured by mortgage receivables. The borrowings (bonds) are structured so that all or substantially all of the collections of principal and interest from the underlying mortgage collateral are paid through to holders of the bonds. The CMOs are frequently nonrecourse to the general credit of the borrower; the holders may look only to the cash flow from the mortgage collateral for their interest and principal payments. The bonds are typically issued with two or more maturity classes (tranches); the actual maturity of each bond class may vary depending upon prepayment experience on the underlying mortgage collateral. One or more of the classes may provide a variable rate to investors even though the underlying receivables are fixed rate, and one or more of the classes may guarantee a specified schedule of cash flows to investors. The sponsor of the CMO often retains the mortgage servicing rights.

Originators of receivables can participate in the issuance of the CMOs in two ways: 1) by sponsoring a CMO entity using only receivables previously originated or purchased by the company, or 2) by participating with other independent enterprises who also contribute receivables into one overall bond issue.

Technical Bulletin 85-2
Technical Bulletin 85-2 provides that CMO transactions should be recorded as a liability and the mortgages should continue to be recorded as assets unless all of the following conditions are satisfied:

1. Neither the issuer nor its affiliates have the right or obligation to substitute collateral or to obtain it by calling the obligations.
2. The expected residual interest, if any, in the collateral is nominal.
3. The investor can look only to the issuer's assets or to third parties (insurers or guarantors) for repayment of both principal and interest on the obligation, and neither the sponsor nor its other affiliates are even secondarily liable.
4. There is no requirement to redeem the obligations before their stated maturity other than through normal pay-through of collections on the mortgage collateral.

If all four conditions are satisfied, the transaction is recorded as a sale of the mortgage collateral for the proceeds received on the obligations, with gain or loss recognized for the difference between the initial proceeds and the full carrying amount of the underlying collateral. If the issuer retains any residual interest, the residual interest is not recorded as an asset; instead the residual is recorded as it accrues to the benefit of the issuer.

If the CMO transaction does not qualify for sales accounting, off-setting of the assets and liabilities is not appropriate.

CMOs usually are issued by special-purpose corporations or trusts. The sponsor should consolidate its majority-owned special purpose CMO entities. Thus, if the CMO transaction is recorded by the issuer as a borrowing, the mortgage assets and CMO liabilities are reflected on the sponsor's consolidated balance sheet. No gain or loss is recognized upon issuance of the CMO debt.

Some CMOs require or permit the issuer to call the obligation when the amount of the outstanding bonds is minor to keep the cost of servicing the underlying mortgage loans relative to their remaining outstanding balances from becoming unreasonable. With respect to condition 1 listed previously, if the amount of reacquired collateral is expected to be minor (no more than 5 to 10 percent in practice), the existence of this type of call provision alone does not preclude sale accounting. Further, a provision calling for substitution of collateral in the event of faulty title for a limited period after inception of the transaction (e.g., 90 days) typically would not preclude sale accounting.

With regard to condition 2, the expected residual is defined as the present value of all amounts expected to revert to the issuer or its affiliates (including reinvestment earnings). Excess (above normal) servicing fees and any overcollateralization should be considered to be part of the expected residual interest. In practice, "nominal" has been interpreted as 1 to 2 percent of the fair market value of the collateral. Further, condition 2 would not be met if an affiliate of the issuer retained one of the CMO tranches (even if the residual cash flows are not retained). However, the retention of servicing rights does not, in itself, preclude sale accounting.

Prior to the introduction of the REMIC provisions of the 1986 Tax Reform Act, tax law constraints caused CMO transactions to be structured in such a way that they typically failed the sale recognition criteria of Technical Bulletin 85-2. With REMIC, this will change. However, REMIC applies only to real estate mortgage transactions, not to other types of receivables.

Sales of Interests
To avoid recording the mortgage collateral and the CMOs on their consolidated balance sheets, sponsors sell either ownership interests in the CMO entity or residual interests in the mortgage collateral. The

sale of ownership interests typically is accomplished by issuing CMOs through a trust. The sponsor creates a trust entity and deposits the underlying mortgage collateral into the trust. The trust then issues CMOs. The issuance would be accounted for as a financing at the trust level. The sponsor then sells ownership interests in the trust to third party investors currently or at later date.

If the sponsor retains more than a 50 percent ownership interest in the trust, consolidation of the trust (including balance sheet presentation of all the mortgages and debt payable) would be required under Technical Bulletin 85-2, as the trust is considered to be a conduit for the sponsor. If the sponsor retains less than a 50 percent ownership interest in the trust, the trust would not be consolidated (or would be deconsolidated). Rather, the equity method of accounting (one line, net treatment) would generally be appropriate for the interest retained, and the mortgages and debt would not appear on the sponsor's consolidated balance sheet.

An issuer might sell the contractual right to residual cash flows, rather than selling ownership interests. In such instances, if the issuer sells sufficient residual cash flows to reduce its retained interest in the residual cash flows to a nominal level and the other conditions of Technical Bulletin 85-2 are satisfied, the issuance of CMOs would be accounted for as a sale. The sale of the residual cash flows must occur at inception since that is the only time the original accounting—sale versus financing—is determined (although some accountants may permit a grace period of up to one month). A later sale of the contractual right to residual interests does not change the original accounting.

Other Nonrecourse Borrowings

While CMO transactions are often structured as nonrecourse borrowings (at least pre-REMIC), other securitization-type transactions have also made use of a nonrecourse borrowing structure. A discussion of developments in the accounting profession for these structures follows. Also discussed is the notion of right of offset. If a right of offset exists, transactions can be netted in the balance sheet.

Lease Receivables

One of the more widely discussed accounting issues in the leasing industry in the last several years has concerned the accounting for nonrecourse debt collateralized by direct financing or sales-type lease receivables or property leased under such leases.

Some accountants believed that borrowing nonrecourse effectively represented a sale of the pledged asset or receivables or otherwise reduced the borrower/lessor's risk and thus should be treated, for financial reporting purposes, as a sale or netted against the related asset. Others believed a right of setoff effectively exists and thus permits netting on the balance sheet. Still others believed that borrowing nonrecourse should be treated like any other borrowing—not netted against the related asset and without any immediate income statement impact. They believed that, except for leveraged lease accounting under FASB Statement No. 13 (*Accounting for Leases*, 1976), in certain CMO transactions under FASB Technical Bulletin 85-2, or when an explicit right of setoff exists as defined in APB Opinion No. 10 (*Omnibus Opinion*, 1966), the authoritative accounting literature permits no other treatment. As a result of these different views, there was a diversity in accounting practices over the years.

Recently, however, this issue has been resolved. In December 1986, the FASB issued Technical Bulletin 86-2, *Accounting for an Interest in the Residual Value of a Leased Asset: Acquired by a Third Party or Retained by a Lessor That Sells the Related Minimum Rental Payments*. The Technical Bulletin indicates that nonrecourse debt associated with directed finance and sales-type leases should be shown as debt on the lessor's balance sheet (i.e., not netted). Nonrecourse financing is not considered an in-substance sale, and Opinion 10 prohibits the offsetting of assets and liabilities unless a legal right of setoff exists.

In June 1987, the SEC staff issued a Staff Accounting Bulletin (SAB 70) to clarify its position on the issue. In summary, the SAB contains the following points:

1. It is inappropriate to remove direct finance or sales-type lease receivables and nonrecourse debt from the balance sheet either by accounting for the transaction as a sale or assignment or offsetting the lease receivables and nonrecourse debt.

2. Nonrecourse borrowing arrangements by lessors (which may be structured as sales with repurchase options) involving operating lease rentals and/or the underlying leased asset do not result in the recognition of a sale of the leased asset.

3. The concept of right of setoff embodied in Opinion 10 and Topic 11-D of the SEC's Staff Accounting Bulletins refers to "the existence of a right between *two* parties, owing ascertainable amounts to each other, to set off their respective debts by way of mutual deduction so that in any action brought for the larger debt, only the remainder after the deduction may be recovered. The debts must, therefore, be to and from the same parties acting on their own behalf" (emphasis added). The pledging of lease receivables or leased assets as security for nonrecourse debt involves *three* parties—lessee, lessor, and nonrecourse lender—and thus does not qualify for offsetting in the financial statements.

Further, in April 1988, the FASB issued two proposed Technical Bulletins that are relevant. The first proposes to clarify "right of set off" in Opinion 10 by indicating that a right of set off 1) exists when each of *two* parties owes the other determinable amounts, 2) allows each party to offset the amount owed *by* the other against the amount owed *to* the other, and it is the intent of each party to offset, 3) is enforceable by law, and 4) will be recognized and protected in the event of the bankruptcy of either of the debtors. The second proposed Technical Bulletin, dealing with several lease accounting issues, generally reinforces the notion that nonrecourse debt should not be netted against the related asset.

The FASB and SEC's actions do *not* affect the accounting for nonrecourse debt applicable to leveraged leases. That accounting is specifically covered by FASB Statement 13, which permits netting nonrecourse debt against the leased asset if specified criteria are met.

Note Monetization
Another transaction involving nonrecourse debt called "note monetization" was addressed by the EITF in 1984 (Issue 84-11). In connection with the bona fide sale of property, the seller accepts a note receivable from the buyer and treats the transaction as an installment sale for tax purposes. The property serves as collateral for the note. Wishing to convert the note to cash, the seller obtains from a bank a loan on essentially the same terms as the note. The bank officially has full recourse to the seller to avoid jeopardizing the seller's installment sales treatment for tax purposes; however, the seller has an unconditional put option that enables it to satisfy the loan in full by transferring the note to the bank, thereby effectively making the loan a secured nonrecourse borrowing from the seller's perspective. The put option typically is exercisable at any time; however, in some cases, the put option may expire if not exercised within a specified short period following a default on the note by the buyer (to protect the bank's interest in the note and related collateral). Usually the seller intends to exercise the put option only in the event of default on the note.

The accounting issue is whether the seller can offset in the balance sheet its liability on the bank loan against its notes receivable and offset in the income statement the interest expense on the bank loan against the interest income on the note. The EITF reached a consensus that setoff in these circumstances was not permitted by the existing authoritative literature. As in the leasing transaction discussed earlier, a right of offset does not exist because three parties are involved—the bank, seller, and buyer.

General Comment

These recent activities make it clear that, except for leveraged leases and qualifying CMO-type transactions, nonrecourse debt should be reflected as debt in the balance sheet and not offset against any related asset. Further, if these transactions are accomplished through a special-purpose subsidiary, the subsidiary should be viewed as a conduit and consolidated with its parent sponsor (Technical Bulletin 85-2).

Recourse Borrowings

A recourse borrowing collateralized by a pool of receivables is a liability of the issuer for which the lender (noteholder) has recourse not only to the collateral but also to the general credit of the issuer. The instrument is an obligation of the issuing entity and not an ownership interest in the receivables. These transactions can take a variety of forms or possess various characteristics, including the following:

• Obligations for which scheduled payments on the receivables (collateral) are sufficient to meet the debt service on the obligations and any prepayments on the underlying assets are paid to the noteholders (so-called pay-through bonds).
• Multiclass obligations similar to CMOs, for which principal is paid by class, beginning with the class with the earliest stated maturity.
• Obligations that guarantee the noteholders a fixed maturity irrespective of the prepayment experience of the underlying assets (so-called fixed-pay bonds).
• Overcollateralized obligations (i.e., the expected cash flows from the pledged assets exceed expected debt service or, stated differently, the fair market value of the pledged assets exceeds the amount of the obligations).

In any of these structures, the obligations may call for quarterly principal and interest payments even though the payment schedule for the underlying assets is monthly.

A recourse borrowing collateralized by assets is recorded as a liability like any other debt. The assets continue to be recorded as assets on the issuer's balance sheet and continue to be reported at their existing carrying amount (i.e., no immediate gain or loss is recognized). Debt issuance costs should be deferred and amortized over the term of the borrowing. (This is also the case for nonrecourse borrowings and Statement 77 transactions accounted for as financings.)

Sometimes these structures provide for the debt to be issued by a special-purpose subsidiary. Typically, the operating parent company forms the subsidiary, which purchases the pool of receivables from its parent (or the receivables are otherwise transferred to the subsidiary) and issues the obligations secured by the receivables. This structure, which can also exist in nonrecourse debt arrangements as mentioned earlier, helps protect the investors by helping to isolate the receivables from bankruptcy concerns related to the parent. This structure also raises financial reporting issues concerning consolidation, which are discussed in the next section of this chapter.

Consolidation

The rules that deal with consolidation of subsidiaries with their parent companies for financial reporting purposes are contained in the following promulgations:

1. FASB Statement No. 94, *Consolidation of All Majority-owned Subsidiaries*.
2. FASB Technical Bulletin 85-2.
3. SEC Regulation S-X Rule 3A-02.

FASB Statement No. 94

As part of its major project on consolidation and the reporting entity (see discussion later in this chapter), the FASB issued Statement 94 in October 1987. The Statement, which is effective for fiscal years ending after December 15, 1988, requires consolidation of all majority-owned subsidiaries unless:

• Control is expected to be temporary.

- Control does not rest with the majority owner (e.g., a subsidiary in bankruptcy or a subsidiary subject to severe foreign exchange restrictions).

Prior to the issuance of Statement 94, the accounting rules also permitted nonconsolidation of subsidiaries that were "heterogeneous in character" relative to the rest of the companies controlled by the parent company. The most common application of this provision was the nonconsolidation of finance subsidiaries of commercial/industrial parent companies. Beginning for annual financial statements in 1988, this practice is no longer acceptable. Financial statements for prior periods presented with current period financial statements must be restated to conform with Statement 94.

As a result, a frequently used form of off-balance sheet treatment of receivables and related debt by commercial companies is eliminated. Finance subsidiaries of financial institution parents (e.g., banks, savings and loans, insurance companies, brokers and dealers in securities, investment banks, and so on) are presently consolidated by their parents (no argument exists for heterogeneity) and thus are not generally affected.

While Statement 94 specifically applies only to corporate subsidiaries, most accountants would apply the same rules to noncorporate entities (e.g., trusts and partnerships) in which a parent company holds a controlling ownership interest.

Statement 94 continues the existing requirement of providing summarized information about previously unconsolidated subsidiaries—specifically, summarized information about assets, liabilities, and results of operations (or separate statements) for each subsidiary or in groups, as appropriate.

FASB Technical Bulletin 85-2

As indicated previously, Technical Bulletin 85-2, which addresses collateralized mortgage obligations (but can be applied to other receivable transactions by analogy), concludes that a majority-owned entity formed to issue the CMO is merely a conduit for the sponsor and the financial statements of that entity should be consolidated with those of its sponsor. Thus, the exception for heterogeneous subsidiaries prior to Statement 94 (see previous discussion) has not been available for such a special-purpose subsidiary. If the sponsor is an existing unconsolidated finance subsidiary that has other substantive operations, the CMO entity must be consolidated with its direct parent, but under GAAP prior to Statement 94, the finance subsidiary did not need to be consolidated by its commercial parent. However, as noted earlier, Statement 94 changes that practice and does so retroactively.

If a controlling share of the ownership interest of the issuer is sold to independent third parties, the issuer's financial statements should not be consolidated with those of its original parent or sponsor. If a securitization transaction is consummated through a trust or other entity whose financial statements are consolidated by its parent or sponsor, the consolidated financial statements will contain the assets and liabilities of the issuer. However, if substantially all of the receivable interests are transferred to others in transactions accounted for as sales, consolidation will generally have minimal effect on the balance sheet of the parent or sponsor.

SEC Regulation S-X

The SEC's rules in Regulation S-X Rule 3A-02 generally are consistent with official promulgations of the FASB. In addition, the rule states that "consolidation of an entity, *notwithstanding the lack of technical majority ownership*, is necessary to present fairly the financial position and results of operations of the registrant, because of the existence of a parent-subsidiary relationship by means other than record ownership of voting stock" (emphasis added). Thus, the SEC requires consideration of indications of control other than ownership of a majority interest in deciding whether a parent-subsidiary relationship exists requiring financial statement consolidation.

Special-Purpose Entities

As indicated earlier, some securitization transactions entail establishment of a special-purpose entity, e.g., a corporation that is organized solely to issue debt and purchase receivables from its sponsor. The purpose is to isolate the receivables from bankruptcy concerns relating to the originator or to achieve some other objective (e.g., regulatory). If these entities are owned by their sponsors, Technical Bulletin 85-2 and Statement 94 provide guidance—they should be consolidated by their parents.

If, however, these special-purpose entities are not owned by their sponsor but by another party (so-called orphan subsidiaries or nonsubsidiary subsidiaries), the accounting rules are not clear. This other party might be a not-for-profit entity, or an individual such as an employee of the investment banking organization hired to broker the transaction. In accordance with SEC Rule 3A-02, many accountants would require consolidation of the orphan subsidiary by the sponsor when: 1) the residual risks and rewards of the receivables and/or the debt reside with the sponsor (e.g., a sale of receivables with recourse to the special-purpose entity, which then issues debt or a guarantee of the debt by the sponsor who retains the interest spreads or excess value in the entity), 2) the only activities of the special-purpose entity involve receivables of the sponsor, and 3) the legal owner is the owner as an accommodation to the sponsor and has made a nominal capital investment. Frequently in these cases, the sponsor controls and manages the activities of the special-purpose entity.

EITF

The EITF addressed the issue of consolidation of 50 percent or more owned special-purpose CMO entities when ownership is considered to be temporary. The transaction (Issue 85-28) involves a majority-owned entity (the "issuer") that is formed by a financial institution to issue collateralized mortgage obligations. The collateralized mortgage obligations are to be accounted for as borrowings and remain on the balance sheet of the issuer. The question is whether the financial institution is required to consolidate the issuer if a sale of ownership of the issuer is expected, although a specific sale has not yet been arranged.

A consensus was reached that consolidation would always be required if the entity was formed by an institution that normally originates mortgages and then transfers those mortgages to the entity. Also discussed was the question of whether an investment banker that does not normally originate mortgages and that establishes a special-purpose entity to house the mortgages would be required to consolidate if control is likely to be temporary. There were mixed views on the latter question and no consensus was reached.

FASB Consolidation Project

As previously mentioned, the FASB is presently working on a major long-term project on consolidation and the reporting entity. The project also involves restudying the equity method (APB Opinion No. 18, *The Equity Method of Accounting for Investments in Common Stock*, 1971), including accounting for joint ventures, partnerships, other 50 percent-

or-less owned affiliates, and so on. Further, the project will address trusts and special-purpose entities. As the first part of the project, the Board issued Statement 94.

As part of the project, the Board has been considering a concept of the reporting entity for business enterprises that is based primarily on a concept of control, rather than on majority stock ownership (i.e., legal ownership). Under this concept, 1) the boundaries of a reporting entity would be determined on the basis of a parent company's control of an entity's operating and financing policies (not legal ownership), and 2) all controlled entities would be included in consolidated financial statements. The Board has expressed support for the general thrust of this concept, but has expressed concerns about some aspects, and the FASB staff is working to resolve those matters.

The timing for completion of the remaining parts of the project is uncertain.

Income Tax Accounting

Differing treatment for financial reporting and tax purposes for securitization transactions may give rise to timing (temporary) differences and thus to the need to account for deferred taxes. APB Opinion No. 11, *Accounting for Income Taxes* (1967), provides guidance in this area. Further, in December 1987, the FASB issued FASB Statement No. 96, *Accounting for Income Taxes,* that supersedes Opinion 11. Statement 96 is effective for fiscal years beginning after December 15, 1988, with earlier application encouraged.

APPLICATION OF GAAP TO SPECIFIC TRANSACTION STRUCTURES

This section of the chapter discusses the application of GAAP as outlined above to specific transaction structures. The preceding sections have discussed the accounting issues pertinent to several of the common structures presently being used to securitize nonmortgages receivables, including automobile and truck receivables, credit card receivables, lease receivables, and so on. This section emphasizes some of the accounting issues raised by certain unique structural features.

Automobile and Truck Receivables

Securitization transactions involving automobile and truck receivables have taken the following forms or have the following features:

1. Sale structures:
   a. Sale of whole loans with full or limited recourse (e.g., in a private placement transaction).
   b. Sale of pass-through certificates under which a pool of receivables is held by a passive trust and the investor owns an interest in the trust. The sale may be with full or limited recourse (including senior/subordinated structures).
   c. Same as 1.b. except that participation interests in the pool of receivables are transferred directly to the investor (i.e., no trust).
   d. For banks that are sellers of receivables, as in 1.a. through 1.c., the structure may involve an escrow account as described on page 262 to satisfy regulatory accounting requirements necessary to achieve sale treatment. The escrow structure can also be used by nonbank sellers.
   e. The seller in 1.a. through 1.d. may be the originator of the receivables (e.g., the operating parent company), an existing finance subsidiary of the parent company, or a special-purpose subsidiary (or orphan subsidiary) designed to provide bankruptcy protection.
   f. In 1.a. through 1.d., the investor is entitled to receive his pro rata interest in all payments received on the underlying receivables (i.e., pass-through). Thus, the investors have the risks of prepayments. The investor may receive payments quarterly even though the underlying assets call for monthly payments. (Note that if investors are guaranteed a specified prepayment experience or a minimum or maximum prepayment pattern, an issue arises as to whether the transaction fails the sales criteria of Statement 77—see pages 264-265.)
2. Borrowing structures:
   a. A borrowing by an operating company with full or limited recourse secured by the receivables.
   b. A borrowing by a special-purpose subsidiary (or orphan subsidiary) of an operating company, with full or limited recourse, secured by the receivables.

c. In structures 2.a. and 2.b., the investor may be guaranteed a fixed maturity (guaranteed investment contracts or other funding arrangements may be involved) or prepayments may be passed through as debt service payments. Further, the structures may be multiclass and provide for quarterly payments even though the assets call for monthly payments.
3. Common features:
   a. In all the structures above, the investor interests may provide a fixed or variable (floating) return.
   b. In all the structures, the originator/seller typically continues to service the receivables for a stated or unstated fee.
   c. All of the structures above may provide for credit enhancement from a third party (for example, letter of credit, surety bond, and so on).

The accounting issues raised by the structures or features described above have been discussed in the preceding sections of this chapter.

One variant of the sale structure, however, raises some unique issues for the investment banker. In this structure, the receivables are sold, as in 1.a. through 1.d., to a wholly-owned special-purpose subsidiary of an investment banker. The special-purpose subsidiary issues multiclass debt secured by the receivables. The structure's purpose is to reduce for investors the uncertainty with regard to the timing of cash flows caused by prepayment rates. In this respect, it is similar to a CMO. In some forms of this structure, the maturity of the debt is guaranteed and thus the investment banker assumes the risk of prepayments, although it may contract with a third party to assume a portion of that risk through a funding arrangement to compensate for irregularities in cash flows caused by unexpectedly fast or slow payments.

In this structure, the seller follows Statement 77 and no unique problems are raised. However, the investment banker is faced with some accounting issues. First, the special-purpose subsidiary may need to be consolidated by the investment banker (see earlier discussion of consolidation). Second, unless the transaction meets the tests for sale accounting in Technical Bulletin 85-2 (which is unlikely), the receivables and debt will be reflected on the balance sheet of the investment banker.

Because the investment banker often prefers not to reflect the transaction on its balance sheet, additional transactions are consummated. First, the receivables and debt are transferred to a trust owned by the special-purpose subsidiary. The special-purpose subsidiary may remain a secondary obligor with respect to the debt. Second, more than 50 percent ownership interest in the trust is sold to third-party investors. Typically, no investor acquires an ownership interest greater than 50 percent so that no investor consolidates the trust. After the sale of ownership interests, the investment banker owns less than 50 percent of the trust and thus need not consolidate it. This arrangement is similar to the CMO trusts described on pages 271-272.

The accounting rationale for the investment banker removing the assets and debt from its balance sheet is based on one or all of the following: 1) the sale of the ownership interests to the investors represents a sale of a wholly-owned entity and thus should be so treated (deconsolidated), 2) the sale to the investors represents a sale of receivables for cash and assumption of indebtedness by the investors (if the subsidiary guarantees the debt, the sale is with recourse and is covered by Statement 77), or 3) from the perspective of the investment banker, the debt has been extinguished as defined in FASB Statement No. 76, *Extinguishment of Debt* (November 1983), because the investment banker has been legally released from being the primary obligor under the debt, and it is probable that the investment banker will not be required to make future payments with respect to the debt under any guarantees. Reference should also be made to page 279 for issues raised when the investment banker intends to sell interests in the trust but has not consummated the transaction by the balance sheet date.

Credit Card Receivables

Securitization of credit card receivables has taken the form of two general structures:

1. A sale of ownership interests in the receivables (participation) or in a trust that owns the pool of receivables.
2. A full or limited recourse borrowing secured by the receivables. A special-purpose subsidiary (or orphan subsidiary) may be used to accomplish the transaction. The maturity of the debt is tied directly or indirectly to the credit card receivable cash flows. The investors may be guaranteed a fixed maturity.

These structures usually 1) provide for credit enhancement by a third party, 2) call for the originator to continue to service the receivables, and 3) for a bank under structure No. 1, make use of an escrow account arrangement (see page 262). Most of the accounting issues raised by these structures are covered in the preceding sections of this chapter.

Structure No. 1, however, typically involves further complications not discussed previously. These complications arise from the revolving nature of credit cards—that is, in a revolving receivables pool, customers are continually making new purchases and paying down old balances. As long as a customer continues to meet the seller's credit criteria, he is entitled to make new purchases up to his credit limit. This revolving nature leads to the following transaction structure:

1. The transferor sells a participation in an existing pool of receivables (a selected closed group of accounts). Generally, more receivable balances are included than the investors' interest, with the transferor retaining an ownership interest in the excess. The additional amount provides a buffer so that the total receivables balance always exceeds the investors' interest in the receivables. In certain instances, additional credit card accounts may be added to the pool at a later date and in certain instances accounts are deleted from the pool.

2. The investors receive an agreed pass-through rate of interest (fixed or variable) on their outstanding participation balance. Any difference between the finance charge paid by customers and the interest paid to the investors is retained by the transferor similar to other receivable sales with servicing retained.

3. For a specified period (the revolving period), the investors' participation principal balance does not amortize as payments are made on the receivables. Instead, principal payments received on the receivables are retained by the transferor on behalf of the investors to reinvest in additional undivided interests in new receivables (i.e., new borrowings by the credit cardholders). The length of the revolving period is selected by the transferor. During the revolving period, the investors maintain a constant dollar investment. However, because the total dollar balance in the pool may increase or decrease, the investors' *percentage* interest in the pool is constantly changing. The seller retains the remaining interest (100 percent less investors' percentage interest).

4. Portfolio charge-offs will be passed through to the investors based upon the participation interest. However, the investors are typically protected against loss because there is recourse a) directly to the transferor (including senior/subordinated structures), b) to an escrow account (see page 262), and/or c) to third-party credit enhancement.

5. At the end of the revolving period, the amortization period begins. During that period, principal repayments on the credit card receivables are distributed to the investors.

The revolving period may end (and the amortization period begin) sooner than scheduled if certain events occur.[3] These so-called payout events are intended to protect investors against severe deterioration in the credit quality or payment characteristics of the underlying assets. Payout events can include a large decline in portfolio yield, a significant increase in losses or changes in cardholder repayment or borrowing patterns that could adversely affect portfolio performance.

The accounting issues center around the revolving period, the amortization period, and gain or loss computations.

During the revolving period, the investors' *dollar* investment remains constant, but their *percentage* interest is constantly changing. For example, assume that a group of investors buys a $100 participation in a $400 pool of credit card receivables. During the first month, cardholders pay $100 on prior charges and incur $150 of new charges. The activity in the receivables pool is as follows:

	Total Pool	Investors' Share	
		Amount	Percent
Beginning of Month 1	$400	$100	25.0
Collections	(100)	(25)	25.0
New charges	150	25*	16.7
End of Month 1	$450	$100	22.2

*Investors' share of collections is reinvested.

---

[3] This feature is not an outright put of the then existing investors' balance (which, if present, would preclude sale accounting under Statement 77), but rather merely provides for an earlier start to the amortization period and a payout to investors on the then-existing receivables.

A recap of receivables at the end of Month 1 is as follows:

	Total Pool	Investors' Share before Substitution	Substitution of New for Old	Investors' Share after Substitution
Old receivables	$300	$ 75 (25.0%)	$(8)	$ 67 (22.2%)
New receivables	150	25 (16.7%)	8	33 (22.2%)
	$450	$100	$ –	$100

An issue arises as to whether, in effect, the investors are putting $8 of receivable interests back to the transferor or the transferor has a call to reacquire $8 of receivable interests. If so, the provisions of Statement 77 for sale accounting would be violated and off-balance sheet treatment of the transaction, a frequent objective of structure No. 1, not achieved. While the matter is not free from doubt, most accountants who have faced this matter in practice have concluded that sale accounting is not precluded. In part, their rationale has been that the changing percentage interest in the pool occurs automatically. Neither the investors nor the transferor can control the extent to which customers make new purchases within their credit limits. Neither party has an option; both parties are locked into a particular course of action as defined at the outset of the transaction.

The amortization period also raises accounting issues. A number of formulas or methodologies have been devised to determine the amount of principal payments allocable to investors.[4] One method calls for a continuation of the constantly changing percentage approach, i.e., a portion of the monthly principal payments received on the entire pool will be passed through to the investors based on the percentage, at the beginning of the month, of their remaining participation balance to the entire pool balance. A second method calls for fixing the percentage at the end of the revolving period based on the then determined relationship

---

[4]Note that within these methodologies, the amortization techniques may call for "controlled amortization," which attempts to increase the predictability in cash flows allocated to investors during the amortization period. This submethod, however, does not guarantee the investors a minimum or maximum not otherwise dependent on the cash flows of the pool.

of the investors' balance to the total balance of the pool. Principal collections on the pool are allocated to investors based on this fixed percentage until the investors' balance is reduced to zero (variations of this method, but having similar economic effects, are possible). A third method calls for an arbitrary or formula-driven percentage or percentages (e.g., 99 percent) of all principal payments of the pool to be allocated to investors even though their percentage ownership in the pool at the end of the revolving period is significantly lower.[5] While the first and second methods appear to have some logic to them (i.e., they attempt to approximate actual payments on the investors' balance), some accountants believe the third method conflicts with the notion that the transaction is a participation in a pool of receivables and thus find it inappropriate if sale accounting is to be achieved.

The third unique accounting issue involving credit card receivable sales is the gain or loss computation. As indicated in a previous section of this chapter, if the excess of the earnings on the pool over the pass-through rate to the investors exceeds a normal servicing fee, the present value of the difference, assuming it is reliably estimable, may be imputed as gain at the outset of the transaction. These computations involve difficult estimates and, in some cases, no such upfront gain exists.

In those cases when such gain does exist, an issue arises for what period the difference can be computed. As described previously, during the revolving period, collections of principal balances on receivables existing at the time of sale are reinvested in new receivables on behalf of the investors. Some believe that the difference can be computed for the entire contemplated period of the transaction, including the total revolving and amortization periods. Others, however, believe that this position is inconsistent with what the transaction purports to be (i.e., a purchase of a specified interest in the cash flows from a pool of existing and future receivables). They believe that any gain computed at the inception of the transaction should be limited to the gain (spread) on the receivables that then exist. Gain should not be imputed on receivables that do not yet exist. Any gain on yet to be originated receivables should be recognized when those receivables arise and are sold to the investors via reinvestment.

---

[5] Although this third method has been encountered frequently with credit card receivables, it can exist in structures involving other receivable pools as well.

For example, assume a bank sells a $100 participation in a pool of credit card receivables. The investors will reinvest their share of collections for 18 months. At the end of 18 months, the investors will begin to receive their share of collections. The pool at any point in time has a weighted average expected life of six months. Further, the excess spread is 4 percent per year. Under the first approach, the bank would estimate that investors will hold $100 of receivables for a weighted average of 24 months (18-month revolving period plus weighted average run off of six months). The gain from excess spread is $100 × 4 percent/year × 24 months = $8, all recognized at the date of the initial sale. Under the second approach, the $100 of receivables sold initially has a weighted average life of six months, so gain on the initial sale is computed as $100 × 4 percent/year × 6 months = $2. Additional gain would be computed as investors apply their share of collections to buy additional receivables.

Securitization of credit card receivables is a relatively new phenomenon and is still evolving. The accounting issues raised have not been definitively resolved by the accounting profession. As a result, the views of accountants may differ in the interim more so in this area than other securitization transactions.

Trade and Other Short-Term Receivables

Securitization transactions involving pools of trade (and other short-term) receivables raise some of the same issues as credit card receivables because of their revolving nature. Some structures developed to sell interests in trade receivable pools have made use of a revolving phase and an amortization phase. Others are optionally renewable for receivables that arise later. In these various structures, the yield to investors may float or otherwise bear no relationship to the stated interest rate (if any) on the receivables pool. These transactions are covered by Statement 77, the accounting for which has been discussed previously.

Trade receivable transactions have also frequently made use of special-purpose companies (either subsidiaries or orphan subsidiaries). In one structure, the special-purpose company purchases receivables from the seller, frequently with recourse, and finances the purchase by issuing commercial paper, often credit enhanced by a letter of credit, in addition to the sponsor's responsibility to repurchase defaulted receivables. The seller bears all the transaction costs and benefits from, or is at risk for, any positive or negative spread between the interest rate, if any, earned on the receivables and the commercial paper rates. This is accomplished through a floating-rate provision in the receivable sales agreement or through a management fee. The structure raises issues concerning consolidation by the seller whether the special-purpose company is a subsidiary or orphan subsidiary. These issues have been discussed in a preceding section of this chapter.

Another structure involving a special-purpose entity raises accounting issues for the bank (or other sponsor) providing the credit enhancement. This structure has been followed for trade receivables as well as other types of receivables. In this structure, the thinly-capitalized special-purpose company is established by the bank, but is owned by a not-for-profit entity as an accommodation to the bank (or other sponsor). The special-purpose company acquires receivables from several unrelated sellers, financing their acquisition with commercial paper. The sellers account for their transaction under Statement 77. The sponsoring bank provides a back-up letter of credit, or it may arrange for several banks to provide back-up capabilities. The sponsoring bank retains the benefits of any positive spread between the effective yield on the receivables and the commercial paper rates (through payment of fees and so on). The not-for-profit entity receives a small fee.

An issue exists of who, if anyone, should consolidate the special-purpose company. The not-for-profit entity is the legal owner but has no day-to-day control, no risk of ownership, and no substantive rewards of ownership (it receives only a small fee); its ownership has no substance. No single seller of receivables would consolidate the special-purpose company, because the special-purpose company owns receivables of several sellers, and it is the sponsoring bank that enjoys the positive financing spread. However, the bank may be required to consolidate the special-purpose company depending on the circumstances. The bank exercises day-to-day control over the special-purpose company and enjoys the positive financing spread. If, in addition, the bank bears more than 50 percent of the credit risk through its issuance of letters of credit or other credit enhancement, a strong case exists that the bank should consolidate the special-purpose company. If, on the other hand, the special-purpose company is a free standing entity that is not thinly capitalized, is owned by an independent third party that controls the entity, and has risks and rewards of ownership and a business purpose for that ownership, the presumption to consolidate by the bank may be overcome.

Lease Receivables

Lease receivables arise from transactions accounted for as direct finance or sales-type leases under FASB Statement 13. Structures that involve the securitization of lease receivables have involved the following.

1. The lessor discounts the lease receivables at a bank or other financial institution and assigns the receivables as collateral. The proceeds received equal the present value of the receivables discounted at the bank's lending rate. The lessor signs a *nonrecourse* note payable secured by the lease receivables and, perhaps, by the equipment being leased. The nonrecourse note may or may not contain a prepayment option (with or without penalty) on the part of the lessor. The lessee may pay rent directly to the bank or to the lessor, who then disburses funds to the bank. The transaction may be done on a lease-by-lease basis or a pool of lease receivables. The lessor is the owner of the equipment and retains the residual value.

While this transaction is not a classic "securitization" transaction because no traded securities are created, it is a popular asset-based financing.

2. A special-purpose subsidiary of a parent company is formed that acquires a pool of lease receivables originated by its parent and issues debt securities collateralized by the lease receivables and a limited guarantee of the receivables by the parent. Third party credit enhancement may also be present. As receivables are collected, the proceeds are used to pay down the obligation. Either the parent or the special-purpose subsidiary retains the leased equipment's residual value. The special-purpose subsidiary is used to provide bankruptcy protection to the investors.

These transactions have been structured as borrowings (versus outright sales) to avoid potentially unfavorable tax treatment—i.e., immediate taxation of the financing proceeds.

In the recent past, the accounting treatment of structure No. 1 has varied in practice, with some accountants accepting sale treatment and others not. The FASB and SEC have recently issued promulgations that clarify the accounting—they should generally be treated as on-balance sheet borrowings as discussed in a preceding section of this chapter.

Structure No. 2 raises consolidation issues that have previously been addressed in this chapter. In summary, special-purpose subsidiaries should be consolidated by their parent companies. If the special-purpose subsidiary is a subsidiary of a previously unconsolidated finance subsidiary with substantive operations, the special-purpose subsidiary should be consolidated by its immediate parent, but further consolidation with the ultimate parent may not have been required under GAAP prior to Statement 94. However, as mentioned previously, beginning in 1988 Statement 94 calls for consolidation of all majority-owned subsidiaries irrespective of their degree of homogeneity with their parent companies. This change in accounting rules may give rise to other structures that achieve off-balance sheet treatment—including formations of joint ventures and transactions structured as sales.

Commercial Loans

Accounting for sales by banks and other financial institutions of commercial loans (including commercial mortgages) involves many of the same considerations that other receivable transactions do. Particularly difficult judgmental assessments under Statement 77 arise if the loans are sold with recourse, since commercial loans are typically not homogeneous in character. Some believe that only commercial loans of the highest quality can qualify as sales. AcSEC is presently considering whether to issue guidance on commercial mortgages. Gain recognition, if any, due to "excess servicing" also involves difficult determinations (as to a normal servicing fee, prepayment experience, and so on). Also important to the structuring of transactions for banks that are sellers are certain regulatory accounting requirements, which are more stringent than current GAAP.

Various transaction structures have been employed in selling commercial loans, including outright sales without recourse, sales with recourse (including those involving senior/subordinated structures), participations, pools, and sales with recourse to special-purpose companies funded by commercial paper. These special-purpose companies are not owned by the selling financial institution, but may be managed by that institution (orphan subsidiaries). The accounting issues thus raised have been discussed elsewhere in this chapter and are not repeated here.

One transaction for which the accounting has been recently addressed is called a strip participation or a sales of loans under committed facilities. In this transaction, a financial institution or group of financial institutions engaged in commercial lending (lender/seller) makes short-term loans under a long-term credit commitment (e.g., a 90-day loan issued under a five-year revolving credit commitment). The lenders sell the short-term loans to third parties, for example, other banks. The sale is for the maturity of the short-term loan and is without recourse. However, the equivalent of a repurchase agreement may exist if the lender/seller is unconditionally committed to relend to the borrower under the credit commitment at the maturity of the short-term loan. Thus, in the event of the deterioration of the credit quality of the borrower, the lender/seller could be required to honor its credit commitment to the borrower and advance funds, which would permit the repayment of the short-term loan sold to the purchaser. Other arrangements provide that the original lender is not obligated to honor its credit commitment if there has been a deterioration in the borrower's financial position (e.g., "no material adverse changes" clause or other covenants or provisions requiring the maintenance of financial ratios).

The accounting for this transaction has been discussed by the EITF (Issue 87-30). The EITF reached a consensus that the sale of a short-term loan under a long-term credit commitment that contains a substantive subjective convenant (e.g., "no material adverse change" clause) should be accounted for as a sale. The EITF also reached a consensus that the sale of a short-term loan under a long-term credit commitment that contains only objective covenants (e.g., financial ratios and other data) should be accounted for as a sale only if the objective covenants are substantive; that is, they are specific to the borrower and are expected to be meaningful and relevant in determining whether the financial institution will be obligated by the long-term credit commitment to relend to the borrower.

This EITF consensus is in the context of generally accepted accounting principles, and the bank regulatory agencies may not agree for regulatory reporting.

Other Special-Purpose Company Structures

Preceding sections of this chapter have discussed the accounting issues raised by various structures involving special-purpose entities—in particular, whether the entity should be consolidated by its sponsor irrespective of the legal owner. The discussion that follows touches on a few other structures involving special-purpose entities not discussed previously. One transaction in effect permits companies, for example savings and loan associations, access to the commercial paper market or other publicly-traded debt markets, which often provide for less expensive sources of funds than other markets. To accomplish this objective, the following is done:

1. A special-purpose company *not* owned by the sponsor, say an S&L, is established (to protect the investors in the event of bankruptcy). The special-purpose company may be owned by a charity or an affiliate of the investment banker who is the commercial paper dealer.

2. The special-purpose company purchases longer-term receivables from the S&L under an agreement to resell them to the S&L on a short-term basis (i.e., a collateralized financing transaction). Thus, unlike the structures discussed previously, the S&L is *borrowing* from the special-purpose company secured by the receivable rather than *selling* the receivables.

3. The special-purpose company finances the purchase by issuing commercial paper, which may be backed up by credit support agreements from insurers or banks (e.g., an irrevocable line of credit).

4. The receivables underlying the repurchase agreement effectively serve as collateral for the commercial paper.

The primary accounting issues involves whether the S&L should consolidate the special-purpose entity. However, whether or not the entity is consolidated, the S&L will retain the receivables on its balance sheet (the repurchase agreement is a financing transaction) and reflect a liability. If the special-purpose entity is not consolidated, the liability of the S&L will be labeled a repurchase agreement. If the special-purpose company is consolidated by the S&L, the liability will be labeled commercial paper outstanding.

Another structure calls for the special-purpose entity to issue preferred stock rather than some form of debt security. It then purchases receivables from the sponsor. The receivables may be mortgages, automobile loans, trade receivables, and so on. In this structure, the special-purpose entity is typically a subsidiary and would be consolidated by its parent. The preferred stock is sold to corporate investors who, under present tax law, enjoy a tax-advantaged investment because of the partial tax exemption associated with corporate dividends to corporate investors. The sponsoring enterprise foregoes interest deductions, but this may not be a problem if it has net operating losses. Because of the investor's tax advantage on the preferred stock, it can be offered at relatively low dividend rates, thus providing the sponsor a relatively low cost of funds. In effect, the investor has purchased collateralized preferred stock.

In consolidation, the receivables of the special-purpose subsidiary will remain on the parent's balance sheet. The preferred stock will be reflected as "minority interest," *not* included in consolidated stockholders' equity. The preferred stock dividends (including any related accretion or amortization of discount or premium) are charged to income as minority interest in determining consolidated net income.

THE FUTURE

The FASB is in the early stages of a major project dealing with financial instruments and off-balance sheet financing. The project may create sweeping changes in accounting, particularly for financial institutions, but the project is not limited to financial institutions. The FASB decided to add this project to its agenda primarily for five reasons: proliferation of financial instruments, lack of guidance in the existing accounting standards, inconsistent guidance in the existing accounting standards, SEC concerns, and Emerging Issues Task Force concerns.

The FASB decided early on that they could not possibly deal with this issue on an instrument-by-instrument basis. The number of existing financial instruments is far too great for that to be feasible, and there is no way that such an approach could ever keep up with the creativity of capital market participants in devising new instruments. Instead, the FASB has adopted the only feasible approach of identifying broad common accounting issues that underlie many of the new financial instruments and financial transactions and addressing them on a general basis. In doing so, the FASB has divided the project into six phases.

For purposes of the project, the FASB has tentatively defined "financial instruments" broadly to encompass all of the traditional instruments—bonds, stocks, loans, deposits, leases (as lessor and lessee), repurchase agreements, acceptances, trade receivables and payables—as well as the newer or more exotic ones. As a result, each aspect of the project could have a pervasive effect.

Disclosure

The first phase of the project deals with improving disclosures about on- and off-balance sheet financial instruments. An FASB exposure draft of proposed disclosure requirements was issued in November 1987. The proposed disclosures cover five broad areas of risk—credit, liquidity, interest rates, current market values, and foreign currency.

The FASB is proposing to require these disclosures for both on- and off-balance sheet transactions. If enacted as proposed, these requirements may significantly increase disclosure for securitization transactions.

Recognition (On/Off Balance Sheet Issues)

The second phase of the project deals with issues of when assets and liabilities affected by financial transactions should be removed from the balance sheet. For example, should receivables be considered sold and removed from the balance sheet if the seller has recourse or other continuing involvement with them? Also, should liabilities be considered settled and removed from the balance sheet when assets are dedicated to settle them, such as in an in-substance defeasance? This phase of the project also will deal with offsetting of assets and liabilities.

This phase of the project has the potential to significantly change the accounting for asset securitization transactions and thus could change the market, or at least the structures, for these transactions. It involves a reconsideration of Statement 77 and Technical Bulletin 85-2 among other things.

Accounting for Instruments That Transfer
Market and Credit Risks

This phase of the project will deal with accounting for futures contracts, interest rate and currency swaps, options, forward commitments, non-recourse arrangements, and financial guarantees and for the underlying assets or liabilities to which the risk-transferring instruments are related. This phase would appear to have little direct impact on securitization transactions, although the accounting issues raised by financial instruments designed to transfer credit risk may be of importance.

Measurement

The fourth phase of the project will deal with how financial instruments should be measured in the financial statements, for example, at market value, amortized original cost, or the lower of cost or market. This phase of the project could have tremendous ramifications for financial institutions as well as many other enterprises. The accounting standards currently permit investments in fixed income assets to be accounted for at amortized cost if the entity has both the intent and the ability to hold them to maturity. Liabilities—both deposits and debt—are accounted for at amortized cost. Investments in equity securities are generally accounted for at the lower of cost or market unless they are in trading accounts.

Any movement toward market value accounting for fixed-income assets would have an indirect effect on securitization transactions. Ignoring the on- or off-balance sheet considerations (debt-equity and capital ratios), it could reduce the incentive to sell appreciated assets because unrealized appreciation could be recognized without a sale, and it could remove the disincentive to sell "underwater" assets because unrealized depreciation would be recognized anyway. Further, more market value accounting for assets and liabilities may increase the incentive to securitize assets so as to achieve better asset and liability maturity matchings or otherwise reduce interest rate risk and thus reduce volatility in reported income and stockholders' equity.

Accounting for Securities With Debt and Equity Characteristics

Many securities have characteristics of both debt and equity, for example, convertible debt, redeemable preferred stock, adjustable rate and auction rate preferred stock, equity commitment notes, and so forth. This phase of the project will deal with the issuer's accounting for these instruments, specifically, whether they should be classified as liabilities or as equity on the balance sheet. This phase is not likely to have a significant impact on securitization transactions, but it could affect structures involving, for example, preferred stock.

Special-Purpose Companies and Trusts

The final phase of the project will deal with whether the creation of separate legal entities or trusts affects the accounting for financial instruments and transactions. This phase of the project is closely related to the FASB's ongoing project on the reporting entity (consolidation and the equity method) and may be addressed as part of that other project rather than separately in the financial instruments project. This phase may well impact securitization transactions involving special-purpose entities.

Summary

The project on financial instruments and off-balance sheet financing is a major and long-term undertaking. Some believe it may be the most complicated project the FASB has even assumed. Work on the project could easily extend over five years or more because of the complexities of the issues and the controversies that are likely to emerge. Further, it can be expected that the various phases of the project will change as the FASB progresses. But conclusions ultimately reached in this project could have a significant effect on asset securitization transactions and the enterprises that participate in them. Until the FASB develops guidance, the EITF may address specific issues as they arise.

CHAPTER 10

TAX CONSIDERATIONS

Charles M. Adelman, Partner
Cadwalader, Wickersham & Taft
Roger D. Lorence, Esq.
New York, N.Y.

INTRODUCTION

This chapter analyzes the principal U.S. federal income tax considerations involved in creating and investing in asset-backed securities. As can be gleaned from the other subjects covered in this book, "asset-backed securities" involve pools of financial assets that generally provide streams of cash flow that can be packaged in various ways and sold to investors as securities. It is the hallmark of a "securitized" pool that no one investor receives all of the payments on any discrete asset. The way in which such payments are divided among investors in a given case is the primary determinant of the tax consequences of the transaction.

The tax principles applicable to asset-backed securities are largely derived from those developed in the mortgage-backed securities field.[1] The earlier development of mortgage-backed securities stemmed from the housing shortage of the late 1960s, which led to the need for creative solutions for generating liquidity in the secondary mortgage market. The roles of the Government National Mortgage Association (GNMA), the Federal Home Loan Mortgage Corporation (FHLMC), and Federal National Mortgage Association (FNMA) were facilitated by the

---

[1]The principal differences stem from 1986 tax legislation that governs mortgage-backed, but not asset-backed, securities. *See* discussion on pp. 301-302 *infra*.

issuance of a series of rulings published by the Internal Revenue Service that established the pattern for sales of pools of mortgage loans in the form of "pass-through" certificates.[2]

Just as mortgage-backed securities were preceded by sales and financings of whole pools of mortgage loans, usually to a single purchaser who was also a mortgage lender, asset-backed securities were preceded by an even longer history of financing or factoring (selling) whole pools of accounts receivable. Such transactions generated most of the case law that forms the foundation for the current tax analysis that distinguishes between sales and financings of assets.[3]

Basic Tax Issues

Three interrelated themes run through the tax analysis of asset-backed securities transactions. First, ownership of the assets must be determined for federal income tax purposes. Have the assets been sold to the investors or pledged to secure debt of the issuer? The answer to this question generally determines whether the seller realizes gain or loss upon issuance and, if appropriate, the manner in which the seller continues to report income from the transaction over time. The investor's ownership of the assets themselves, as compared with debt of the issuer, affects the timing of reporting of income and recovery of capital by the investor and can have other consequences.[4]

---

[2]*See Rev. Rul.* 70-544, 1970-2 C.B. 6, and *Rev. Rul.* 70–545, 1970-2 C.B. 7 (GNMA program), *as modified by Rev. Rul.* 74-169, 1974-1 C.B. 147; *Rev. Rul.* 71-399, 1971-2 C.B. 433 (FHLMC program), *as amplified by Rev. Rul.* 72-376, 1972-2 C.B. 647, *Rev. Rul.* 74-221, 1974-1 C.B. 365, *Rev. Rul.* 74-300, 1974-1 C.B. 169, *Rev. Rul.* 80-96, 1980-1 C.B. 317, and *Rev. Rul.* 81-203, 1981-2 C.B. 137; and *Rev. Rul.* 84-10, 1984-1 C.B. 155 (FNMA program). The extension of the consequences of the "government" programs to pass-throughs sponsored by commercial banks was described in *Rev. Rul.* 77-349, 1977-2 C.B. 20.

[3]*See, e.g., Elmer v. Commissioner,* 65 F.2d 568 (2d Cir. 1933); *Southeastern Finance Co. v. Commissioner,* 4 T.C. 1069 (1945), *acq.,* 1945 C.B. 6, *aff'd,* 153 F.2d 205 (5th Cir. 1946); *Alworth-Washburn Co. v. Helvering,* 67 F.2d 694 (D.C. Cir. 1933).

[4]For example, ownership of mortgage loans (as opposed to debt secured by mortgage loans) is desired by thrift institutions to maximize deductions for additions to their bad debt reserves for "qualifying real property loans" under applicable provisions of the Internal Revenue Code of 1986 (the "Code"). *See* sections 593(a)(2), 593(d)(1), and 7701(a)(19)(C)(v). As another example, a lessor of automobiles or equipment may wish to pledge the leases and the assets to secure an issuance of bonds but would not want to be treated as selling the assets, since this may result in a recapture of depreciation deductions previously taken. *See* section 1245. All section references herein are to the Code unless otherwise indicated.

The second basic tax theme in analyzing these transactions is the "entity classification" of the arrangement chosen for issuing the securities. In a transaction where the issuer is treated as having sold the assets to the holders of the securities (as with pass-through certificates), the holders do not have legal title to the assets. The Internal Revenue Code of 1986 and regulations of the U.S. Department of the Treasury ("Treasury") describe three arrangements with distinct tax treatments in which investors may own assets beneficially, but in which legal title is held on their behalf by an agent: 1) a partnership in which the investors are partners,[5] 2) a corporation in which the investors are shareholders,[6] or 3) a trust in which the investors are beneficiaries.[7] Investors who purchase assets assume that they will be taxed directly on the income from the assets, without any intervening level of tax. Treatment as an association taxable as a corporation would result in the imposition of a corporate tax (currently at a maximum 34 percent rate) and the distribution of nondeductible "dividends" to investors. Unless partnership treatment is available, ordinarily only a trust, in particular a "grantor trust",[8] would provide a tax-free vehicle for investors.[9]

In debt issuances, the classification of the entity that owns the assets and issues the debt will determine how the "residual" interest remaining after payment of the debt is taxed. This issue is of prime importance to investors in the developing market for residuals from asset-backed debt transactions.

Third, how do the seller and investors report income from the transaction? The applicable rules for determining the timing of income and return of capital on an investment for tax purposes can be exceedingly complex. The reporting of interest income on financial instruments is

---

[5]Treas. Reg. § 301.7701-3.

[6]Treas. Reg. § 301.7701-2.

[7]Treas. Reg. § 301.7701-4. For tax purposes, ownership arrangements are classified in accordance with their substance. State law classification is important but will not control over the substantive tests in the applicable regulations.

[8]*See* discussion on pp. 316-317, *infra*.

[9]The Code also provides special vehicles that may be formed as corporations but are not subject to tax. For example, a regulated investment company (RIC) (sections 851-855) or a real estate investment trust (REIT) (sections 856-859) could be used to issue mortgage-backed securities; a RIC also could issue other asset-backed securities. Investors are taxed on distributions from these entities. However, the various qualification requirements for these entities make them not as well-suited to the issuance of pass-through securities as a grantor trust.

straightforward. But many uncertainties arise in reporting income when the asset is purchased for less than its face amount (that is, at an original issue discount[10] or market discount[11]), or when the purchase price exceeds the face amount (that is, at a premium).[12] This is particularly true for obligations that are payable in installments and prepayable in whole or in part. These rules provide challenges both for issuers, who must disclose certain of this information in connection with the issuance of the securities and report annually to investors, and for investors themselves (or their advisors), who must make sure that their income from these transactions is reflected in their returns according to applicable rules.

REMICS

The Tax Reform Act of 1986 introduced a new device for issuing mortgage-backed securities: the "real estate mortgage investment conduit," or "REMIC."[13] Insofar as they relate to traditional residential mortgage-backed securities, REMICs are beyond the scope of this book, but commercial mortgages are often considered to be asset-backed transactions. Therefore, the use of REMICs in such transactions deserves mention.

The REMIC provisions of the Code provide an essentially tax-free vehicle for issuing mortgage-backed securities and prescribe the tax treatment of investors and the conditions for qualification. A REMIC can be formed as a corporation, partnership, or trust, or even a segregated pool of assets for local law purposes, but the tax treatment provided in the statute is not affected by the choice of entity. Two types of interests are permitted: 1) one or more classes of "regular interests," which have debt-like features and are in fact treated as debt under the REMIC rules, whether issued in the form of debt or pass-through certificates; and 2) one class of "residual interests," which may have stated principal and interest payments, as well as all remaining cash flow after payment of the regular interests. The residual interests are taxed on their pro rata share of the taxable income computed at the REMIC level, and special rules

---

[10]*See* discussion on pp. 321-323 and pp. 326-327, *infra.*

[11]*See* discussion on pp. 323-325, *infra.*

[12]*See* discussion on p. 328, *infra.*

[13]Pub. L. No. 99-514, § 671(a), 100 Stat. 2085, 2308-2317, (1986), adding sections 860A-860G to the Code.

are provided to ensure taxation of a component of such taxable income representing "noneconomic" income that may be offset by noneconomic losses in later years.[14] Special rules are provided for qualifying assets (primarily mortgage loans, temporary investments of cash flows, and reserve funds) and a 100 percent excise tax is imposed on income from "prohibited" transactions that generally would be inconsistent with "fixed investment trust" status.[15] The REMIC rules contain a "sunset" provision allowing other vehicles that issue multi-class mortgage-backed securities to be used without incurring a corporate tax until December 31, 1991.[16] Despite the popularity of REMICs, their long run viability will depend largely on how they are administered by the Treasury Department and the Internal Revenue Service.

CLASSIFICATION OF THE TRANSACTION

Determination of Sale Treatment

Risks and Benefits
When treatment of a transaction as a sale is the desired result for tax purposes, the parties must have transferred economic ownership of the assets.

The tax law has a long history of viewing assets in a monolithic way, seeking to find "the owner" of the assets. Under this view, when the seller gives up ownership, it transfers all it owns to a trust (or partnership or association) beneficially owned by investors. Only since 1982 has the Code prescribed rules for the sale of interest payments separated from the underlying principal of an obligation ("coupon stripping").[17] More recent

---

[14]Income due to these timing differences is referred to as "phantom income." *See* footnote 59 and discussion on p. 314, *infra*. The imposition of a "hell-or-high-water" tax on this income was the major *quid pro quo* for Treasury's agreement to support the tax-free REMIC vehicle.

[15]*See* discussion on pp. 14-15, *infra*.

[16]Pub. L. No. 99-514, § 675(c), 100 Stat. 2085, 2320 (1986).

[17]Former section 1232(c), as added by Pub. L. No. 97-248, § 232(b), 96 Stat. 324, 499 (1982), *amended by* Pub. L. No. 98-369, § 41(a), 98 Stat. 494, 551-552 (1984), adding section 1286 to the Code. *See* discussion on pp. 307-308 and pp. 329-330, *infra*.

market innovations in dividing up cash flows generally have not been matched by new legislation or regulations, except for REMICs. This has led to restraints on the flexibility of issuers in structuring transactions without having the resulting arrangement treated as an association taxable as a corporation.[18]

Thus, most asset sales are structured as undivided beneficial interests in the assets (*e.g.*, interest and principal or rent under a lease) in the form of pass-through certificates, based on the precedents involving mortgage pass-throughs. In general, structuring the transaction as a sale (*i.e.*, having the terms of the documents reflect an outright sale) will go a long way toward accomplishing the tax goal. Thus, the courts have held both the form and the intent of the parties to be important factors in determining sale characterization.[19] However, the true economic indicators of ownership must complement and not contradict the form.

The general principal expressed in the case law is that the seller must transfer to the purchaser the "substantial incidents of ownership" of the assets.[20] This includes the relevant risks and benefits of the ownership of the assets. These risks and benefits fall primarily into four categories: 1) credit risk, 2) risk of changes in value, 3) interest-rate risk, and 4) prepayment or reinvestment risk.

First, credit risk is the risk least often transferred to investors, due to investors' concern about the assurance of repayment of their investment. However, long-standing tax treatment recognizes that receivables are often sold "with recourse," and the Internal Revenue Service agrees that this factor alone will not jeopardize sale treatment.[21] Thus, both third-party guarantees[22] and direct guarantees of the seller[23] have been approved as consistent with a sale.

Second, the risk of changes in the fair market value of the assets can

---

[18] *See* discussion on pp. 318-319, *infra*.

[19] *See, e.g., Schaeffer v. Commissioner*, 41 Tax Ct. Mem. 752 (1981).

[20] *See, e.g., Town & Country Food Co. v. Commissioner*, 51 T.C. 1049 (1969), *acq.*, 1969-2 C.B. xxv; *United Surgical Steel Co. v. Commissioner*, 54 T.C. 1215 (1970), *acq.*, 1971-2 C.B. 3.

[21] *See, e.g., Rev. Rul.* 81-251, 1981-2 C.B. 156; *but see Rev. Rul.* 78-118, 1978-1 C.B. 219 (retained credit risk plus interest rate risk resulted in debt treatment). Unfortunately, securitized arrangements are inherently more ambiguous than a mere sale with recourse.

[22] *See Rev. Rul.* 70-545, *supra* (GNMA); *Rev. Rul.* 77-349, *supra* (letter of credit).

[23] *See Rev. Rul.* 71-399, *supra* (FHLMC); *Rev. Rul.* 84-10, *supra* (FNMA).

be borne by the investors only if they are given the right to dispose of their beneficial interests. This right is usually granted in the underlying documents. On the other hand, the right of the seller to call the securities and recover the assets when they have paid down to a small fraction (usually 10 percent) of their size on transfer, often termed a "clean-up call," has been held not to be inconsistent with sale treatment.[24]

Third, payment characteristics of the security that differ from the characteristics of the underlying assets that cause the seller to be subject to fluctuations in market rates of interest indicate a debt, rather than a sale.[25] This can occur, for example, when the assets bear a fixed rate of interest but a floating rate measured by an independent index is "passed through."

In the absence of the third factor, the fourth is most often looked to for a determination of pass-through status. As owners, the investors should bear the risk of reinvesting principal cash flows (prepayment or reinvestment risk) through the matching of the assets' payment characteristics to those of the pass-through security. In theory, purchasers in the aggregate should step into the shoes of the seller with respect to the seller's rights under the assets. This means that when obligors make monthly payments on the assets there should ordinarily be a monthly pass-through of such payments with little or no manipulation of cash flows so that the seller is not at risk for reinvestment earnings on the amounts generated by the assets.[26] This factor is related to the discussion below of the very limited powers of the trustee of the grantor trust holding the assets to deal with the assets.[27]

It is not inconsistent with sale treatment for the seller to continue to service the assets as the purchasers' agent. The seller's retention of the physical accounting records or documents and its role as collection agent for the purchasers have long been held to be consistent with sale treatment.[28]

---

[24]*See, e.g., Rev. Rul.* 84-10, *supra.*

[25]*See, e.g., Rev. Rul.* 78-118, *supra.*

[26]Where obligors pay only a partial month's interest on prepayments in full, seller/servicers should be able to pay a full month's interest to purchasers as an adjustment to servicing compensation. In addition, quarterly pass-through of monthly pay assets may be possible where the seller/servicer does not incur reinvestment risk or benefit. *See, e.g., Rev. Rul.* 75-192, 1975-1 C.B. 384.

[27]*See* footnote 69 and accompanying text, *infra.*

[28]*See, e.g., Rev. Rul.* 54-43, 1954-1 C.B. 119.

Tax Consequences to the Seller

A seller of assets recognizes gain or loss for tax purposes measured by the difference between the amount realized (the sale price) and the seller's adjusted basis in the assets.[29] In some instances, the seller has no further tax consequences from the transaction. When the seller is also the servicer of the asset pool, however, it will receive compensation for such services, usually in the form of a percentage of the outstanding principal balance of the assets, payable monthly and retained by the servicer out of interest flows in the assets.[30] In general, this servicing income is all ordinary income to the seller as it is received over time. But if the servicing fee is determined to exceed "reasonable" compensation for the services rendered, under ill-defined standards, the seller will be treated as having retained the "unreasonable" portion of the spread as a beneficial ownership interest in that portion of the interest payments. This would lead to an analysis of the transaction under the "coupon stripping" rules, discussed on pages 307–309 and 329–330.

Tax Consequences to the Investors

If the transaction has been structured properly to ensure grantor trust status,[31] each investor, as the owner of an individual beneficial interest in the assets, will be treated in the same way as if it directly acquired a group of assets of the type included in the pool and paid an agent to service them on its behalf. This has several ramifications. First, the investor must report its share of the entire income from the assets (gross interest at the rate paid by the obligors on the underlying receivables[32]) and may generally deduct the reasonable servicing fees paid to the seller/servicer.[33] These items must be reported according to

---

[29]Section 1001(a).

[30]As a result, the pass-through rate on a pass-through certificate is generally the interest rate on the asset minus the servicing fee. *See, e.g., Rev. Rul.* 77-349, *supra.*

[31]*See* discussion on pp. 316-317, *infra.*

[32]*See* discussion on pp. 331-332, *infra*, concerning imputed interest on an obligation that carries a below-market rate.

[33]Investors who are individuals, estates, or trusts (either directly or indirectly through certain pass-through entities) may be subject to limitation under section 67 on their miscellaneous itemized deductions, including deduction under section 212, for expenses incurred in the production of income. This rule, a response in part to inflated "investment" expenses, which are difficult to audit, seems harsh in the context of bona fide expenses charged by a fiduciary on an investment priced at a net yield.

the investor's own tax accounting method and taxable year.[34] Because the trustee of the pool is the investors' agent, investors who use the cash method of accounting must report income as it is *received* by the trustee, whereas accrual method holders must report amounts as they become *due to* the trustee. These amounts are thus frequently reportable in the same month that investors receive their checks. Reporting only net income on the basis of the pass-through rate on the certificate is inconsistent with the tax characterization of the security.

Second, the receivables may be purchased for less than their face amount, giving rise to market discount income[35] or, less frequently, for more than their face amount, giving rise to premium expense.[36] Theoretically, these determinations should be made on a receivable-by-receivable basis by allocating the price paid for the pass-through certificate among the receivables based on their relative fair market values on the date of sale. As a practical matter, investors are unlikely to have information on every receivable in a pool. Moreover, treating the certificate in the aggregate to compute market discount income, premium expense, or gain or loss on sale would probably not result in large distortions of income or expense. The Internal Revenue Service itself has ruled that homogeneous mortgage pools should be treated as "mass assets" for purposes of determining whether a swap of such pools results in recognition of gain or loss.[37]

---

[34]Treasury Regulations § 1.671-4 requires the trustee of a grantor trust to file annual information returns on Form 1041 but to report items of income and deductions attributable to each owner on a separate statement attached to that form. The annual filing is imposed by section 6012(a)(4) and is required by section 6072(a) to be filed on or before April 15 following the close of the calendar year.

[35]Sections 1276-1278. These provisions apply to obligations issued after July 18, 1984, and will thus apply to most receivables. *See* discussion on pp. 323-325, *infra*.

[36]Section 171. Deductions for amortization of premium on obligations of individuals is permitted only for obligations issued after September 27, 1985. *See* discussion on p. 328, *infra*.

[37]*Rev. Rul.* 81-204, 1981-2 C.B. 157, *amplified by Rev. Rul.* 85-125, 1985-2 C.B. 180. The United States Tax Court has recently adopted the view that an exchange of pools of mortgage loans does not result in the exchange of property that differs materially in kind or extent. *See Cottage Savings Association v. Commissioner*, 90 T.C. 732 (1988); *Federal National Mortgage Association v. Commissioner*, 90 T.C. 405 (1988); *San Antonio Savings Association v. Commissioner*, 55 Tax Ct. Mem. (CCH) 813 (1988); *but see Centennial Savings Bank FSB v. United States*, 682 F. Supp. 1389 (N.D. Tex. 1988), *appeal docketed*, No. 88-1297 (5th Cir. May 4, 1988), *cross-appeal docketed*, No. 88-1297 (5th Cir. May 5, 1988). Whether pooled receivables should be considered in the aggregate or individually is not easily resolved. Different rules can apply depending on when the receivables were originated (*see* footnotes 35 and 36, *supra*), or whether the obligor is a corporation, partnership, or individual.

Third, as noted previously,[38] any special treatment of the assets for tax purposes, such as the treatment of certain loans secured by real property, will flow through to the beneficial owners of the assets. Any uncertainties in the tax treatment of certain assets will also be reflected by investors in pass-through certificates. For example, it is not clear how investors would report income and return of capital on a purchase of undivided beneficial interests in leases. Although leases are obligations in a broad sense, they are probably not evidence of indebtedness under the market discount and premium rules. Thus, it is not clear whether discount income could or should accrue on a constant interest basis, on a straight-line basis over time, or on some other method. Likewise, it is possible that any premium purchase price may not be deducted over time, as with bond premiums, but rather taken as a loss only after all payments have been received.

Coupon Stripping and "Excess Servicing"

As noted previously, tax law until recently did not have a coherent approach to the sale of interests in obligations representing different percentages of the interest and principal payments on the obligations. The absence of applicable rules for reporting gain or loss where interest payments were sold separately from principal led to abusive transactions in which an owner of obligations sold off all the principal in year one, allocated its entire tax basis to the sold principal, and claimed losses based on the discounted price received. In year two, the taxpayer sold the interest stream and reported capital gain on the proceeds of the sale.[39] The predecessor of section 1286 of the Code was adopted in 1982[40] to provide rules for allocating tax basis between the sold principal (termed a "stripped bond") and retained interest ("stripped coupon") and for the reporting of income on such interests by the seller and purchaser.[41] The two (or more) stripped ownership interests are treated as obligations

---

[38] *See* footnote 4, *supra.*

[39] *See* Staff, Joint Comm. on Taxation, *General Explanation of the Revenue Provisions of the Tax Equity and Fiscal Responsibility Act of 1982*, at 164 (1982).

[40] See footnote 17, *supra.* These rules apply only to assets that are "evidences of indebtedness," so that leases are excluded. *See* section 1286(e)(1). Most likely, lease cash flows are treated as homogeneous for these purposes, so that a sale of any portion carries with it a proportionate share of the seller's basis. It is not clear how the investor would report income and recovery of basis on the acquired lease interest.

[41] Any combination of stripped interest and/or principal payments may be sold or retained.

issued with original issue discount on the date the stripping occurs.[42] This brings the tax treatment into harmony with the economics of the transaction, since the stripped cash flows are similar to zero coupon instruments that are, by definition, issued with original issue discount.

The enactment of the coupon stripping rules presented both an opportunity and a "risk" for tax purposes. The opportunity was the introduction in the capital markets of new types of securities representing the rights to stripped bonds and stripped coupons, based in large measure on the relative certainty provided by the new tax (and by extension, accounting) rules. Originally applied to Treasury securities, strips have expanded significantly into the mortgage-backed securities field.[43] The "risk" was that the statutory recognition of non-pro rata beneficial interests in mortgage loans could lead to application of those rules to transactions that fit them in substance but not in form. The primary area in which this phenomenon may occur is with the "spread" between the interest rate on the underlying obligations and the pass-through rate that is retained by a seller of pass-throughs.

The spread paid by the pass-through investor as servicing compensation has traditionally been deductible as long as it is "reasonable."[44] There is support, at least prior to the enactment of section 1286, for treating the spread in excess of "reasonable" compensation as an additional purchase price paid by the investor to the seller/servicer over

---

[42] The original discount rules and their application to stripped bonds and stripped coupons are discussed on pp. 329-330, *infra*.

[43] As discussed on pp. 318-319, *infra*, an entity holding stripped obligations in the form of pass-through certificates can qualify as a grantor trust and not as association taxable as a corporation. In addition, although not free from doubt, the component interests in mortgage loans should be treated as qualifying real property loans for thrift bad debt reserve purposes. *See* footnote 4, *supra*.

[44] The reason that this area is fraught with uncertainty is that, unlike accounting notions of "normal" and "excess" servicing, there is very little guidance on what constitutes "reasonable" servicing for tax purposes. Industry norms for servicing various assets other than mortgage loans are difficult to ascertain. Although the form of the transaction is generally not determinative, a shift of the entire spread to a new servicer if the original servicer is terminated is partial evidence that the servicing is true compensation for services and not disguised additional purchase price or the seller's retention of an interest in the assets. In many cases, however, the magnitude of the spread makes this characterization uncertain. On the other hand, if the terms provide for a portion of the spread as a fee for servicing and the balance as a "retained yield" or "retained spread" that may be sold separately by the seller, a retained beneficial ownership by the seller of the nonservicing portion would be the likely characterization.

time.[45] However, it is likely that the transaction would now be characterized under the coupon stripping rules. The confusion on this issue is not expected to be resolved until Treasury regulations are promulgated under section 1286.[46]

Determination of Debt Treatment

The counterpart to pass-through treatment for a securitized pool of assets is treatment as debt of the issuer secured by the assets. This type of debt is called "pay-through" debt, because it matches, more or less, the cash flows on the asset pool.

When securities are structured as a debt offering secured by a pledge of a pool of assets, two issues must be addressed for federal income tax purposes: 1) beneficial ownership of the assets must remain with the issuer and not be sold to the investors, and 2) the securities must be treated as bona fide indebtedness of the issuer and not as the equivalent of an equity investment.

Debt Versus Sale

In a properly structured transaction, the issuer will continue to be the tax law owner of the assets and will receive the income thereon and bear the costs related to their servicing and will pay and deduct interest expense and original issue discount, if any, expense to the debtholders.

As with the determination of sale treatment, a number of economic factors must be weighed to determine whether the issuer has pledged assets to secure indebtedness. The proper conclusion is not based on a mere reversal of one or more of the risk/benefit factors considered previously in determining whether a transaction that appears to be a sale is so treated for tax purposes. The multi-factor analysis creates a sizable "grey area" between the two possible conclusions, making the outcome

---

[45] *See Rev. Rul.* 71-399, *supra*, holding 9. Under this characterization, however, the computation of the seller's gain or loss and the method of amortizing the premium purchase price paid by the investors are complex. The seller would most likely be required to estimate the value of the future payments and report the entire gain or loss as of the sale date. Income or loss could be recognized in the future if actual spread payments were greater or less, respectively, than the estimates.

[46] The three alternative characterizations of the "excess servicing" case are discussed in C. Adelman and R. Lorence, *Tax Considerations for Asset-Backed Securities,* in *The Securitization of Assets,* at 9-19 (Inst. Int'l Research, 1985).

of any controversy difficult to predict. In any given transaction, the economic interest of the seller can be demonstrated both by a combination of debt-like factors and the relative magnitude of any one or more of such factors.

First, retention of credit risk on the assets is a positive debt factor. However, it alone will not suffice, and one or more additional risks must be retained by the issuer to find a debt.[47] Moreover, except in unusual cases, third-party credit support, such as pool insurance or a letter of credit, will tend to neutralize the significance of nominal credit risk on the issuer, especially if the third-party arrangement is necessary to obtain the rating with which the debt is issued.

Second, retention of reinvestment risk by varying the frequency of payment on the debt from that on the assets is indicative of debt. Such a variation could take the form of debt payable quarterly backed by collateral payable monthly. Having a fixed payment schedule on the debt that requires reinvestment of prepayments on the collateral that are faster than the schedule is even more indicative of debt treatment. In either case, the presence of a guaranteed investment contract to absorb reinvestment risk weakens the importance of the variation in payments, although it is not inconsistent with the issuer's decision to manage its risk by entering into such a contract. The matching of payment schedules on the collateral and the nominal debt is more indicative of a sale than a pledge.[48] The use of monthly pay assets as collateral for a debt that pays monthly is supportable if other factors strongly support pledge treatment.

A third factor is the ability of the issuer to call the debt when a significant portion of the collateral remains outstanding by selling or refinancing such collateral, thereby benefitting from its increased market value. Since pass-throughs are typically found to be sales even with "clean-up" calls of 10 percent, a call must be more significant than this to carry much weight toward a finding of debt.[49]

---

[47] *Rev. Rul.* 81-251, *supra. See Rev. Rul.* 78-118, *supra*, where a transaction that was in form a sale of certain fixed-interest loans was held to be a secured debt because the issuer retained credit risk and promised to pay a floating rate of interest tied to an index, thereby bearing interest rate risk.

[48] *See, e.g., Rev. Rul.* 65-185, 1965-2 C.B. 153.

[49] *Cf. Rev. Proc.* 75-21, 1975-1 C.B. 715, *as modified by Rev. Proc.* 76-30, 1976-2 C.B. 647, *Rev. Proc.* 79-48, 1979-2 C.B. 529, and *Rev. Proc.* 81-71, 1981-2 C.B. 731, in which the Internal Revenue Service's guidelines for finding ownership of property subject to a "true lease" prescribe a retained economic interest after expiration of the lease equal to 20 percent of the value

A fourth factor is the ability of the issuer to withdraw collateral and substitute new collateral of either the same or a different type and of equal or greater value. The inability to substitute collateral is some evidence of a sale, whereas the ability to substitute collateral beyond a relatively short initial period is inconsistent with sale treatment, since it tends to negate beneficial ownership by the investor.

A fifth factor, which does not have an exact counterpart in determining sale treatment, is the present value of the collateral cash flows (including reinvestment income) in excess of anticipated debt service.[50] When the terms of the debt permit the issuer to withdraw excess cash flow not required for debt service, the residual value includes both the amount of such withdrawn excess cash flow and any collateral expected to remain after the debt has been paid. If the collateral has little or no residual value, then it may be argued that the issuer had disposed of substantially all of its ownership interests in the collateral.[51]

Under these guidelines, debt treatment should be appropriate for a pledge of monthly pay collateral to secure an instrument that 1) is in form a debt with quarterly payments, 2) permits a call when 15 to 20 percent of the collateral is expected to be outstanding, and 3) leaves a residual value of between one and two percent of the value of the pool. If monthly debt payments are substituted for quarterly or the call is reduced to 10 percent, other features, such as a fixed payment schedule or a floating interest rate, could help achieve the same result. Each case calls for careful judgment by issuer's tax counsel to ensure proper treatment.

Debt Versus Equity

It is critical to the transaction that the asset-backed debt be treated for tax purposes as the indebtedness of the issuer and not as an equity interest

---

of the property and at a point when 20 percent of the economic life of such property remains. This is not directly translatable to the debt/sale context, but suggests that a 20 percent call would aid a finding of debt.

[50] To determine present value, a discount rate equal to a current, arm's-length equity rate of return should be applied to the cash flows anticipated by the parties under a reasonable prepayment assumption.

[51] This test is similar to the concept of a "normal" residual for accounting purposes. *See* Financial Accounting Standards Board, Technical Bulletin 85-2. Although not well-defined, counsel can ordinarily find comfort in the range of 1 to 2 percent of the total value of the collateral at closing. For very large transactions (*e.g.*, in excess of $500 million), economically significant residuals may be present at lower percentages of total value.

in the issuer. If it is debt, the issuer may deduct interest (or original issue discount, if any) under section 163, offsetting in whole or part the issuer's income received on the assets. If treated as stock, payments on the security would be nondeductible dividends, and a double tax would thus be imposed on the income on the assets.[52] Whether the security would be debt or equity depends on the circumstances of each case.

Section 385 of the Code, adopted by the Tax Reform Act of 1969,[53] authorizes the Treasury Department to promulgate regulations to determine whether an instrument is debt or equity. Section 385 lists the following factors that such regulations may include: 1) whether there is an unconditional promise to pay a fixed sum on a specified date and to pay a fixed interest rate in return for adequate consideration; 2) whether the instrument is subordinated or preferred to other debt; 3) the ratio of debt to equity; 4) whether the instrument is convertible into stock; and 5) the relationship between holdings of debt and equity. Three sets of proposed regulations were issued between 1980 and 1982 and all three have been withdrawn.[54] In the absence of Treasury Department interpretations of section 385, the multi-factor test set forth in the case law must be applied.

Although the formal characteristics of indebtedness are an important factor, the form alone does not determine the proper characterization of the asset-backed security as debt or equity for federal income tax purposes. Rather, the courts look to the economics of the transaction.[55] Although many aspects have been considered, court decisions have focused primarily on the following features: 1) whether the purported debtholders are also equity owners and whether they hold the debt in proportion to their equity; 2) whether the corporation's nominal equity is sufficient to satisfy its working capital needs; 3) whether the nominal debt is placed at the risk of the business; and 4) the ratio between nominal debt and nominal equity.

---

[52]Dividends received by security holders who are corporations are generally 70 percent deductible if the shareholder owns less than 20 percent of the voting stock of the issuing corporation, thus reducing the double tax to 10.2 percent (*i.e.*, the top corporate rate of 34 percent reduced by 70 percent of such rate). This incremental cost is almost always considered significant enough to be avoided.

[53]Pub. L. No. 91-172, § 415, 83 Stat. 487, 613-614 (1969).

[54]*See* 45 Fed. Reg. 18957 (Mar. 24, 1980) (first set); T.D. 7747, 1981-1 C.B. 141 (second set); 47 Fed. Reg. 163 (Jan. 5, 1982) (third set); *revoked by* T.D. 7920, 1983-2 C.B. 69.

[55]*E.g., Fin Hay Realty Co. v. United States*, 398 F.2d 694 (3d Cir. 1968).

In the case of the typical corporate or owner-trust issuer, the debt would not be held by the equity investors. In such a case, the debtholders can be expected to enforce their rights as creditors.[56] The second factor looks to whether the issuer has enough equity to meet working capital needs, so that the nominal debt is not placed at the risk of the business.[57] The typical asset-backed bond issuer will be formed solely for purposes of the issuance of one or more series of bonds and generally will have minimal working capital needs. Further, this factor would appear to be less significant when the debt is secured and thus superior to general creditors. Nevertheless, it is recommended that even though those working capital needs are relatively low, the issuer should be adequately capitalized at the outset so that the initial equity plus retained earnings will be sufficient to meet anticipated working capital needs.

A third factor examined by the courts is whether the purported loan has been placed at the risk of the business.[58] If the nominal debt is "secured" only by the prospects of the issuer's future success, the securities resemble equity more than debt. The typical asset-backed notes represent an unsubordinated obligation fully secured by high quality collateral. There is no reported case in which nominal debt that was fully secured and held by persons who were not nominal shareholders or related to such shareholders has been recharacterized as equity.

The fourth factor examines the ratio of nominal debt to nominal equity of the issuer. The adequacy of the debt-to-equity ratio may depend on the kind of business the corporation is engaged in. A finance subsidiary with minimal working capital needs may support a comparatively high debt-to-equity ratio.[59] Although the typical limited purpose finance subsidiary or owner-trust might appear to have a comparatively high debt-to-equity ratio, this ratio may not be inconsistent with debt characterization. There is no case-law standard for any specific numerical debt-to-equity ratio. Accordingly, each counsel must determine a ratio

---

[56]*See, e.g., New England Lime Co. v. Commissioner*, 13 T.C. 799 (1949) (publicly-held debentures with interest payments dependent upon adequate income levels of the issuer held to be debt).

[57]*See, e.g., Stinnett's Pontiac Service, Inc. v. Commissioner*, 730 F.2d 634 (11th Cir. 1984).

[58]*See, e.g., Motel Corp. v. Commissioner*, 54 T.C. 1433 (1970).

[59]*See, e.g., Jaeger Auto Finance Co. v. Nelson*, 191 F. Supp. 693 (E.D. Wis. 1961).

that is not unreasonably high in light of the overall transaction. As with the size of the retained beneficial ownership of the residual interest in the collateral,[60] many transactions reflect the view that one to two percent equity should be sufficient in this type of security, with even higher ratios possible as the size of the transaction, and thus the absolute dollar amount of equity, increases.

Tax Consequences to the Issuer

If the asset-backed security is treated as debt for federal income tax purposes, the issuer will determine its taxable income by reporting all items of gross income (or expense) on the assets and deducting all applicable bond and other expenses. Gross income items include interest and original issue discount or market discount income on assets that represent indebtedness, as well as reinvestment income on temporary investment of cash flows. If the assets are leases, gross income is reportable for amounts received in excess of the basis allocable to a particular period, subject to the uncertainties noted on page 307. Deductions include premium expense on obligations acquired at a cost in excess of par, interest and original issue discount expense, if any, on the debt, amortization of debt issuance costs, and operating expenses.

To the extent the issuer's items of income exceed its deductions for a given taxable year, it will be subject to tax on the difference if it is a corporation.[61] Since most corporate issuers are special-purpose subsidiaries within a corporate group, earnings are generally subject to only one level of tax. In addition, members of an affiliated group may file consolidated tax returns and thereby utilize losses of other group members in determining consolidated taxable income.[62]

---

[60]*See* footnote 51 and accompanying text, *supra*.

[61]This difference may be due to overcollateralization and therefore represented by corresponding cash flow, or it may be due to timing differences in the reporting of income on the assets and expenses on the debt. Such differences can arise if income is received on the assets at a uniform rate of interest or yield, but the debt is divided into serial maturities ("tranches") with interest rates or yields that increase with each succeeding maturity. Noncash income can also arise if collections of principal on assets acquired at a discount (giving rise to discount income) are used to retire a class of bonds that was issued with little or no discount. Noncash income in these transactions is frequently referred to as "phantom" income, because it is noneconomic and, therefore, matched by noncash losses in later years.

[62]Sections 1501-1504; Treas. Reg. § 1.1502-11.

If the issuer is formed as an owner-trust, the organizational documents should be drafted to ensure that the issuer will not be treated as an association taxable as a corporation but rather as a grantor trust or a partnership.[63] In either event, the issuer would not be subject to tax, but rather the owners would be taxable on their pro rata shares of the owner-trust's income and expenses. Treatment as a grantor trust would have consequences similar to those described on page 317, while treatment as a partnership would be subject to the rules of subchapter K of the Code.[64]

Tax Treatment of Investors

Tax treatment of investors in debt instruments is conceptually much more straightforward than treatment of holders of pass-through certificates. Rather than report to investors the gross income and corresponding servicing expenses on a pool of hundreds or perhaps thousands of receivables, the issuer need only report with respect to the debt itself. This includes stated interest and original issue discount income, if any.[65] Secondary market purchasers must also determine the extent of any market discount income or premium expense.[66] While these rules are fairly easy to apply to obligations that pay all of their principal in

---

[63]*See* discussion on pp. 316-317, *infra*. The owner-trust vehicle was designed as a means of financing the equity or residual interest in a secured debt transaction by selling it, as well as the debt, to investors. Since more than one investor is contemplated, consolidated returns would not be possible if the entity were treated as an association taxable as a corporation.

[64] Sections 701-761. Unlike a grantor trust, a partnership has its own accounting method and taxable year (usually a calendar year in these types of transactions) and is subject to special rules for determining an owner's basis in its interest and the partnership's basis in its assets, among others. Differences also exist in annual reporting to the Internal Revenue Service and the residual investors.

[65]Issuers of publicly-offered obligations must set forth on the bond's face information relating to how the original issue discount is computed and must file Form 8281 with the Internal Revenue Service within 30 days of the closing setting forth similar information. Prop. Treas. Reg. § 1.1275-3. Stripped bonds and stripped coupons are exempt from these reporting rules unless the Treasury provides otherwise in the future. Prop. Treas. Reg. § 1.1275-3(b)(1)(iii). Further, prepayable installment obligations are not subject to the Form 8281 requirement until so required by the Internal Revenue Service. Temp. Treas. Reg. § 1.6049-7T(d)(2).

[66]*See* discussion on pp. 323-325 and p. 328, *infra*. Market discount can also arise upon original issuance of a publicly-offered obligation if, due to a delay in selling, market prices have dropped relative to the initial sale price to investors.

one payment at maturity, more complex rules apply if principal on the obligation is payable in installments or is prepayable, or both. Certain aspects of these rules are discussed on pages 326-327.

Classification of the Issuing Entity

While issuers and investors have the full range of entities available to them under state law, their choice will generally be governed by two considerations: 1) marketing, primarily investor familiarity with a particular vehicle, and 2) how the entity will be viewed for tax purposes.

General Principles

The guiding principle of entity classification is that arrangements for ownership of property are classified in accordance with their economic substance, not necessarily their chosen form. Applicable Treasury regulations set forth tests that help distinguish among corporations, trusts, and partnerships. In general, corporations and partnerships share the characteristics of "associates" that are jointly engaged in business for profit. However, the characteristics of continuity of life, management by a centralized agent acting in a representative capacity and not as an owner, limited liability, and free transferability of interests are typical of a corporation and not a partnership.[67] The regulations generally provide that an entity that has no more than two of these four characteristics will not be classified as an association taxable as a corporation, but rather as a partnership or a trust.

In contrast, a trust is formed for the "protection and conservation of property" by a trustee on behalf of its beneficiaries.[68] The status of

---

[67]Treas. Reg. § 301.7701-2(b). A general partnership, by contrast, lacks: 1) continuity of life because the death, insanity, or bankruptcy of a partner terminates the legal relationship among the partners; 2) centralization of management because all partners can bind the partnership to third parties; 3) limited liability because partners are jointly and severally liable for obligations of the enterprise; and 4) free transferability of interests because under local law a transfer of a member's interest technically results in a dissolution of the old organization and the formation of a new one. Limited, as opposed to general, partnerships can encounter classification problems because of the resemblance of limited partnership interests to corporate stock.

[68]Treas. Reg. § 301.7701-4(a).

investors who purchase interests in a trust as "associates" is not altogether clear. But if the trust, with certain exceptions noted below, has a single class of ownership interests, representing undivided beneficial interests in the assets of the trust, the investors will not be treated as engaged in a joint enterprise for the conduct of business for profit.[69] Rather, the trust will be treated as a "fixed investment trust," the most common vehicle for pass-through certificates.

Grantor Trusts

Fixed investment trusts have traditionally been classified as "grantor trusts" under applicable Code rules.[70] Unlike "normal" trusts, which are taxable on income that is not distributed to beneficiaries,[71] grantor trusts result in taxation of the person or persons who exercise various controls over the trust's assets or income. Thus, for example, retention of beneficial control over both income and principal on the trust's assets results in taxation of the entire trust income and gains to the beneficiary.[72] This is, in fact, the common conclusion of all of the pass-through rulings issued by the Internal Revenue Service.[73] The pass-through investors, as "grantors" through their up-front cash investment, are taxed on their pro rata share of their beneficial interest in the trust.[74]

---

[69]Treas. Reg. § 301.7701-4(c). In addition, the trust must be passive, distributing all payments as received with reinvestment only to the next distribution date. *See, e.g.,* the revenue rulings cited in footnote 2, *supra.*

[70]Sections 671-679. It is not clear when this connection became broadly applicable to pooled investments. *See, e.g., Rev. Rul.* 61-175, 1961-2 C.B. 128 (joint investment by thrift institutions in a pool of mortgage loans treated as a grantor trust). While the grantor trust provisions were adopted as part of the Internal Revenue Code of 1954, fixed investment trusts have a much longer history, and it is quite clear that no tax was imposed on them at the trust level. *See, e.g., Commissioner v. North American Bond Trust,* 122 F.2d 545 (2d Cir. 1941), *cert. denied,* 314 U.S. 701 (1942).

[71]Section 641.

[72]Section 677; Treas. Reg. § 1.671-3(a)(1).

[73]*See* footnote 2, *supra.*

[74]*See* discussion at pp. 305-306, *supra.* The Code does not provide, and the Internal Revenue Service has never articulated, a clear mechanism for how one investor/grantor becomes substituted for another by a sale of a pass-through certificate. This is further evidence that the Code provisions were designed with family trusts and not publicly traded investment vehicles in mind. However, the system seems to work fairly well even without such a rationale.

The "Sears Regs."

The fixed investment trust regulations were amended in 1986, courtesy of the mortgage-backed securities industry,[75] to provide that trusts with multiple classes of interests will ordinarily be classified as an association or a partnership, not as a trust. The Treasury Department's concern was the lack of a coherent system for taxing beneficial interests in pooled assets that were divided up in unusual ways, such as in serially maturing classes. Treasury's concern reflected the fear that the "phantom" income component of the serial structure, representing differences in the timing of reporting taxable income (or loss) and economic income, would not be taxed under the traditional grantor trust format,[76] and thus required computation as if the assets were owned by a legal entity like a corporation. While this is achieved in either the partnership or association format, the former classification is unlikely in a publicly traded investment pool.

At the same time, the so-called Sears Regulations provide that a trust with multiple classes nevertheless will be classified as a trust "if the trust is formed to facilitate direct investment in the assets of the trust and the existence of multiple classes of ownership interests is incidental to that purpose."[77] The regulations provide two examples that meet this requirement: 1) "senior/subordinated" offerings and 2) coupon strips. In a senior/subordinated offering, assets that do not have the benefit of a government guarantee are pooled and two classes of pass-throughs are issued: a senior class and a subordinated class. The first class (typically representing from 90 to 95 percent of the undivided interests in the trust) is sold to investors whose rights are senior to the subordinated class, which represents the remaining undivided interests in the trust and functions as credit support for payment of the senior

---

[75]T.D. 8080 (March 21, 1986), *amending* Treas. Reg. § 301.7701-4(c). These regulations are known as the "Sears Regs." because they were issued in proposed form on April 27, 1984, on the eve of an offering by Sears Mortgage Securities Corporation of a four-class mortgage pass-through arrangement in which the cash flow on the assets was modified on a "fast pay/slow pay" basis (*i.e.*, serially maturing certificates). The investors, by dividing up the cash flow according to their different objectives, were held to be associated in a profit-making business. That transaction can now be done under the REMIC rules, but only if the assets are mortgage loans secured by real property.

[76]*See* footnote 61, *supra*.

[77]Treas Reg. § 301.7701-4(c)(1).

investors' interests.[78] In stripped pass-through offerings,[79] the sponsor may create two or more classes entitled to all principal, all interest, or some proportion of both. For example, Class A may receive all of the rights to principal and none of the interest, which goes to Class B (termed an "interest only/principal only" or "IO/PO" strip).[80] The two exceptions may be combined in a single transaction by dividing the senior class of a senior/subordinated offering into two subclasses (*e.g.*, Subclass A-1 receives all of Class A's rights to principal and Subclass A-2 receives all of Class A's rights to interest).

Owner-Trusts

For the first several years after the introduction in 1983 of mortgage-backed pay-through debt in the form of collateralized mortgage obligations, issuers bridled under the tax requirements for some level of equity and residual cash flows necessary to ensure debt treatment for tax purposes.[81] This situation was ameliorated by the introduction of owner-trusts sponsored by investment banks, mortgage bankers, thrifts, and others. Owner-trusts either could act as direct issuers of asset-backed debt or could assume assets and the related debt from special-purpose subsidiary issuers.[82] The key to their success was the ability to sell off the residual cash flows to the new equity investors, the purchasers of the certificates representing beneficial ownership of the trust.

Structured as trusts for local law purpose, owner-trusts have only one class of beneficial interest and, therefore, should be classified as fixed investment trusts for tax purposes. However, the possibility that the trust may be viewed as engaging in business for profit[83] has made it

---

[78]Treas. Reg. § 301.7701-4(c)(2), Ex. (2).

[79]Either intentional or unintentional, as may occur with "excess servicing." *See* discussion at pp. 307-309, *supra*.

[80]*See* Treas. Reg. § 301.7701-4(c)(2), Ex. (4).

[81]*See* discussion on pp. 312-314, *supra*.

[82]Owner-trust vehicles came to prominence in the areas of leveraged equipment leasing transactions. *See* Flowers, *Federal Income Tax Considerations in Leasing Transactions*, in *Equipment Leasing 1987*, at 57, 168-73 (Practicing Law Institute 1987).

[83]The trust could be deemed to be engaged in profitable business activities by virtue of limited reinvestment of cash flows or reserve funds or by its very nature as a leveraged vehicle. The Internal Revenue Service is itself uncertain how to resolve this issue and will not rule on the classification of a leveraged leasing trust. *See Rev. Proc.* 88-3, I.R.B. 1988-1, at 29, § 5.36.

advisable to provide in the trust documents for sufficient partnership-like characteristics so as to preclude characterization as an association taxable as a corporation under Treasury regulations. Thus, the owner-trust generally will not have the corporate characteristics of free transferability of interests (by restricting the owners' ability to sell their trust certificates without consent), centralized management (by giving the trust owners control over all matters of trust administration that require management discretion) or limited liability (trust owners are generally jointly and severally liable for expenses of and claims against the trust, other than the liability on the asset-backed debt).[84] By using the owner-trust structure, the party structuring the transaction can sell off its entire interest in the assets to two groups of investors (debtholders and trust certificate-holders) and provide the optimal tax results for each group.

TAX TREATMENT OF PARTICULAR ITEMS

The Code and the Treasury regulations provide complex rules for computing and reporting the income of the investors in asset-backed securities. These securities are particularly difficult to analyze under rules that were initially designed to cover relatively straightforward instruments (*e.g.*, 10-year corporate "bullet" bonds with semiannual interest payments). Just as the economics of asset-backed securities are made complex by such issues as prepayments, the tax analysis is no less complicated.

The rules considered in this section relate to: 1) the timing of reporting of certain items of income and expense; 2) special rules applicable to certain types of receivables, and 3) applicable rules for foreign investors.

General Rules for Computing and Reporting "Time Value of Money" Items

The applicable rules of the Code for reporting income from financial instruments were extensively amended, first in 1982, then again in 1984 and 1986, to place investors more closely on an economic accrual basis

---

[84]The fourth characteristic that distinguishes a corporation from a partnership is continuity of life. The ability to defeat this characteristic by making the trust terminable upon the death, insanity, insolvency, or bankruptcy of any owner is generally precluded under state trust law and by concerns

with regard to their yield on such instruments. The cash method of accounting in this area has been preserved largely with respect to stated interest and, to the extent described below, market discount.

Original Issue Discount

The original issue discount rules are designed to differentiate the principal amount of an obligation between a return of the investor's capital and any yield component (other than uniform payments of stated interest) and thereby 1) to measure accurately the investor's yield to maturity and to require periodic reporting of the income resulting from that yield and 2) to treat that portion of principal payments that represents the yield component as ordinary income rather than capital gain. Original issue discount, governed by sections 1271 through 1275 of the Code, is the excess of the obligation's "stated redemption price at maturity" over its "issue price." The stated redemption price at maturity of an obligation includes all principal payments as well as payments designated as interest other than "qualified periodic interest payments." Qualified periodic interest payments are made at fixed, periodic intervals at least annually over the obligation's term at either a fixed interest rate or a variable rate keyed to a qualifying index.[85] The issue price in the case of a loan is essentially the price paid for the obligation,[86] and in the case of a sale or exchange of property is the value of the property sold or exchanged. The original issue discount rules are the subject of an extensive set of proposed regulations published on April 8, 1986.[87] Original issue discount must be included in the investor's income if it is not *de minimis*, as discussed below, and is deductible by the obligor on a constant interest method. The issuer's and holder's methods of tax accounting for interest (*i.e.*, cash vs. accrual) are irrelevant. The original issue discount rules place all taxpayers on the accrual method of accounting for such amounts.

---

of the rating agencies that have rated the debt securities based on the continued validity of the issuer. However, corporate status exists only if at least three corporate characteristics are present. Treas. Reg. § 301.7701-2(a)(2).

[85]Inclusion of irregular nonqualifying, interest payments in the stated redemption price at maturity prevents the deferral of income by back-loading stated interest payments.

[86]In the case of publicly offered obligations, the initial offering price at which a substantial amount of the obligations is sold, and in the case of a private offering, the price paid by the first buyer of each debt instrument. Sections 1273(b)(1) and (2).

[87]51 Fed. Reg. 12022-98 (April 8, 1986).

For example, original issue discount on a zero coupon bond (all payments of interest and principal due at maturity) with a five-year term and a stated redemption price at maturity (face amount) of $100,000 issued for $55,840 has a yield to maturity of 12 percent, compounded semiannually. The portion of the $44,160 of original issue discount reportable as income each year increases as maturity approaches. This is because the obligor owes the holder an accrued but unpaid interest-equivalent on the yield accrued in earlier periods but not paid until maturity, rising from $3,350 in the first six-month accrual period to $5,660 in the last period.[88] Similar computations must be made for obligations that provide for qualifying periodic interest payments, but that are issued at a discount. For example, a 15-year note with a face amount of $100,000 and semiannual interest payments of 10 percent per annum that is issued for $86,235 bears $13,765 of original issue discount, as the note's yield is 12 percent, and the parties must account for both stated interest and original issue discount.[89]

The types of assets discussed here are generally more complex than the examples described above, because payments of principal on pay-through debt are due in installments, rather than in a "bullet" at maturity. Such obligations are classified as "installment obligations" under proposed Treasury regulations.[90] They are required to accrue original issue discount for the interval between installment dates in an amount equal to the yield to maturity of the obligation times its "adjusted issue price" at the beginning of the period, less payments of qualified periodic interest during that period. For this purpose, the adjusted issue price is the obligation's issue price plus previously accrued original issue discount, less payments of stated redemption price previously received. Further complicating matters is the fact that principal payments may be accelerated by prepayments, which may be estimated at original issuance but which will be determined by actual experience.

Original issue discount will be considered to be zero to an investor if it is *de minimis*, that is, generally less than 1/4 percent times the number of complete years to maturity of the obligation.[91] For installment

---

[88] *See* Prop. Treas. Reg. § 1.1272-1(k), Ex. (1).

[89] *See* Prop. Treas. Reg. § 1.1272-1(k), Ex. (4).

[90] *See* Prop. Treas. Reg. § 1.1272-1(b)(2).

[91] Section 1273(a)(3).

obligations, original issue discount is considered *de minimis* if it is less than 1/4 percent of the stated redemption price at maturity times the number of complete years to maturity, using the bond's weighted average maturity. This is determined by multiplying the number of full years (rounding down partial years) from the issue date until each payment is scheduled to be made by a fraction whose numerator is the amount of each principal payment and whose denominator is the original face amount, and adding the resulting products.[92]

There are special rules that determine the issue price of obligations offered in exchange for property when the seller has not charged the buyer a sufficient rate of interest. The stated interest payable on the obligation is tested under section 1274 to determine whether the parties have converted interest into principal by setting an artificially low interest rate. This determination is made by comparing the rate on the obligation with the rate on Treasury obligations of similar maturities (called the "applicable Federal rate"). If the testing rate is not met, the issue price would be reduced so as to impute original issue discount. A number of statutory exceptions are provided.[93] For sales or exchanges involving total payments that are $250,000 or less but exceed $3,000, a similar rule for imputing interest is provided by section 483, except that the amount of principal recharacterized as imputed interest is not currently included as original issue discount. Rather it is reported on a straight-line basis as principal payments are received in an amount not exceeding such payments.[94]

Market Discount
If the assets are debt instruments that are purchased at a price less than their face amount,[95] the difference is subject to treatment as market discount under the rules of sections 1276 through 1278, enacted by the

---

[92] *See* Prop. Treas. Reg. § 1.1273-1(a)(3)(ii)(A). If the obligation pays equal payments comprised of principal and qualified periodic interest at intervals of one year or less for the entire term of the obligation, a simplified *de minimis* rule of 1/6 percent times the number of full years to final maturity is provided. *See* Prop. Treas. Reg. § 1.1271-1(a)(3)(ii)(B).

[93] The exceptions include sales involving total payments of $250,000 or less, sales of principal residences, and sales involving debt instruments that are publicly traded or are issued for publicly traded property. *See* Code section 1274(c)(3).

[94] *See* discussion on p. 331-332, *infra*.

[95] In the case of instruments issued with original issue discount, the price must be less than their original issue price plus previously accrued original issue discount.

Tax Reform Act of 1984.[96] These rules are intended to provide for recognition of the time value inherent in market discount, on the theory that "the discount is a substitute for stated interest, and the holder of the obligation receives some of his return in the form of price appreciation when the bond is redeemed at par upon maturity."[97] The rules were also designed to combat leveraged purchases of market discount obligations, which result in current deductions of interest expense and deferral of what was then preferentially-taxed capital gains.[98]

The market discount rules do not apply to: 1) obligations issued before July 18, 1984 (although the rules for deferring related interest deductions discussed below will apply); 2) obligations issued in an installment sale under section 453 in the hands of the original holder or certain related transferees; 3) short-term obligations (which are subject to their own rules, discussed below); and 4) obligations bearing *de minimis* market discount.[99]

The rules for accruing market discount are complex. In general, market discount accrues on a ratable (straight-line) basis, as provided in section 1278(b)(1). The holder may elect, on an obligation-by-obligation basis, to accrue market discount on the constant interest method. The holder generally must recognize accrued market discount as ordinary income upon receipt of payments includible in the stated redemption price at maturity (generally, principal amounts), in an amount not exceeding such payments. Any remaining market discount must be recognized upon disposition of the obligation to the extent of the gain thereon.

The Tax Reform Act of 1986 introduced rules governing obligations whose principal is payable in installments. The method of accrual for such obligations is to be specified in forthcoming Treasury regulations; in the absence of such regulations, the market discount would accrue either on the constant interest method or in the proportion that interest paid

---

[96]Pub. L. No. 98-369, § 41(a); 98 Stat. 494, 543-548 (1984).

[97]Staff of the Joint Comm. on Taxation, *General Explanation of the Tax Reform Act of 1984*, at 93 (1984).

[98]*Id.*

[99]The *de minimis* rules are similar to the original issue discount provisions. *See* sections 1278(a)(2)(C) and (5). It is likely that Treasury regulations, when issued, will provide rules for computing *de minimis* market discount on installment obligations that are similar to those discussed above for original issue discount obligations.

or accrued in the current accrual period bears to total remaining stated interest.[100]

Under section 1277, holders are required to defer a portion of the interest deductions on any debt used to purchase or carry a market discount obligation, to the extent such deductions would exceed the sum of the interest income and accrued market discount for the year. The deferred interest expense is generally allowed as a deduction in the year the related market discount income is recognized by receipt of principal payments or upon disposition of the obligation. The investor may avoid the interest expense deferral rule by electing to include market discount in current income as it accrues on all market discount obligations acquired by the investor in that year or thereafter.[101] Amounts representing gain on sale or exchange (including retirement) of the obligation in excess of the accrued market discount generally would be capital gain or ordinary income, depending upon whether the asset is held as a capital asset under section 1221.

Acquisition Discount on Short-Term Obligations

Assets that are short-term obligations (any obligation having a fixed maturity date not more than one year from the issue date) are subject to sections 1281 through 1283. Acquisition discount is the excess of the obligation's stated redemption price at maturity (which for this purpose includes both principal payments and any stated interest payments, whether or not payable at maturity or over the obligation's term[102]) over the holder's basis in the obligation.[103] Unless the taxpayer elects otherwise, acquisition discount on an obligation that is not a "short-term Government obligation" (the assets discussed here would not be such obligations) includes only original issue discount in lieu of mar-

---

[100]Sections 1276(a)(3) and (b)(3); H. Conf. Rep. No. 99-841, 99th Cong., 2d Sess. (to accompany H.R. 3838), at II-842 (hereinafter "Conference Report"). Where the obligation was issued with original issue discount, the current period's accrued market discount would be in the proportion that the current period's accrued original issue discount bears to total remaining original issue discount. *Id.*

[101]Section 1278(b)(2).

[102]Under Prop. Treas. Reg. § 1.1273-1(b)(1)(ii)(D), no payments of interest on short-term obligations constitute qualifying periodic interest payments. Any payments of interest are therefore included in the stated redemption price at maturity and give rise to acquisition discount.

[103]Section 1283(a)(2).

ket discount. Although section 1281 generally provides for deferral of acquisition discount, exceptions are provided for certain holders, including accrual method taxpayers, banks, regulated investment companies, and common trust funds. In the case of asset-backed securities, most investors are likely to be covered by the exception and must accrue any such acquisition discount currently. As for the method of accrual, however, the holder must include the acquisition discount on the obligation in gross income ratably (or, at his election, on an obligation-by-obligation basis, may accrue on the basis of a constant interest method). Holders not subject to current inclusion rules are subject to an interest expense deferral rule under section 1281 that is similar to the market discount rule.

New Rules for Prepayable Obligations

To resolve uncertainties under prior law, the Tax Reform Act of 1986 introduced new rules regarding the computation of original issue discount and market discount on certain obligations whose principal is subject to prepayment.[104] Under prior law, it was not clear whether discount should accrue based on scheduled payments (which generally would result in slower accrual by spreading the discount over the stated term) or using a reasonable prepayment assumption (to accrue the discount based on the anticipated receipt of the payments to which the discount relates). Section 1272(a)(6) now governs debt instruments whose payments "may be accelerated by reason of prepayments of other obligations securing such debt instrument (or, to the extent provided in regulations, because of other events)."[105] Although these rules clearly may apply to asset-backed debt, it is not certain whether they apply to asset-backed pass-throughs, because pass-throughs represent an undivided ownership interest in the underlying assets, whose prepayment experience does not depend on that of another obligation. Because the economic characteristics of pass-throughs are similar to those of pay-through bonds, and because prepayment rates are significant in the pricing of pass-throughs, Treasury regulations nevertheless may provide that prepayment rules of section 1272(a)(6) should apply to pass-throughs as well. Until such

---

[104]Pub. L. No. 99-514, § 672, 100 Stat. 2085, 2320 (1986) adding section 1272(a)(6).

[105]Section 1272(a)(6)(C)(ii). The prepayment rules also apply to a "regular interest" in a REMIC or a "qualified [real property] mortgage" held by a REMIC.

regulations are issued, taxpayers are probably justified in using either the scheduled payment or reasonable prepayment approach with respect to pass-throughs, as long as a consistent practice is followed.

Section 1272(a)(6) provides that the original issue discount accruing in each accrual period on prepayable obligations issued after December 31, 1986 will be calculated based on the increase in the present value of the obligation's remaining payments, taking into account payments includible in the stated redemption price that were received during the period. The present value calculations are based on: 1) the yield to maturity of the obligation as of the closing date; 2) the prepayment rates and assumed rates for earnings on the assets reinvested between payment dates (the "reinvestment rate") used in pricing the obligation; and 3) events (including actual prepayments) that have occurred before the end of the accrual period.[106] This method, referred to as the "level yield" method, will accelerate the inclusion of original issue discount income as compared with the scheduled payment method and will convert into ordinary income what could otherwise be capital gain on a repayment of principal.[107]

Rules similar to those found in section 1272(a)(6) for prepayable obligations should also apply to obligations purchased at a market discount, whether or not the obligation is issued with original issue discount. It is likely that a prepayment assumption should be used in computing the anticipated payment schedule on the security. This is similar to the assumption that would be made in computing original issue discount, but using the anticipated prepayment rate at the time of purchase, whether or not the holder elects to accrue on the basis of a constant interest rate.[108] Thus, to the extent that pay-through bonds (and similar debt to the extent specified in regulations) prepay, recognition of market discount income will be accelerated or deferred, depending upon whether actual prepayments are faster or slower than the prepayment rate assumed for pricing purposes.

---

[106]Conference Report at II-238.

[107]An original issue discount obligation which prepays, but which is not subject to the special rules of section 1272(a)(6), will, under section 1271(a)(1), be treated as having been sold or exchanged. If the obligation is held as a capital asset, any unaccrued original issue discount attributable to the prepaid principal would, therefore, be capital gain. The foregoing treatment does not apply to an obligation of a natural person. Section 1271(b).

[108]Conference Report at II-843.

Premium

To the extent that the investor pays more for a security than its face amount (or in the case of a pass-through security, more than the face amount of the investor's share of the underlying obligations), the difference is "premium."[109] The Tax Reform Act of 1986 extended the rules of Code section 171, discussed below, to the amortization of premium on obligation of all issuers originated after September 27, 1985.[110] Prior statutory rules governed only bonds issued by corporations and governmental issuers, leaving uncertain the deductibility of premium paid for the obligations of noncorporate obligors, such as individuals borrowing to purchase a residence or an automobile. The new statutory provisions are intended to make the rules for amortization of premium consistent with those for inclusion of discount income.[111]

Section 171 provides that a taxpayer who holds an obligation as a "capital asset" (within the meaning of section 1221) may elect to amortize premium (whether the premium is paid on issuance or upon acquisition in the secondary market) under the constant interest method. The same rules that apply to accrual of market discount on prepayable installment obligations will also apply to amortizing premium on such obligations,[112] although it is unclear in the absence of Treasury regulations whether the alternatives to the constant interest method that may apply to accrual of market discount will be available. A reasonable prepayment assumption should be used in determining the anticipated payment schedule on the obligations, similar to that used in accruing original issue discount.[113]

---

[109]Where the stated redemption price at maturity of an obligation includes both principal payments and some or all of the interest payments (*see* discussion at pp. 321-322, *supra*), amortizable bond premium does not exist unless it exceeds the entire amount of unaccrued original issue discount. However, section 1272(a)(7) provides special rules for obligations issued with original issue discount that are purchased in the secondary market for a price greater than the issue price plus the amount of original issue discount that has accrued to that date (termed "acquisition premium"). In effect, the premium reduces the amount of original issue discount accrued in each future accrual period.

[110]Pub. L. No. 99-514, § 1803(a)(11)(A), 100 Stat. 2085, 2795(1986).

[111]*See* Staff, Joint Comm. on Taxation, *Explanation of Technical Corrections to the Tax Reform Act of 1986 and Other Recent Tax Legislation*, at 14 (1987). The view precluding current deduction of premium stems from *New York Life Ins. Co. v. Edwards*, 271 U.S. 109 (1926), so that the problem was not resolved for 60 years (and many uncertainties remain to be resolved by legislation or regulations).

[112]*See* Conference Report at II-842.

[113]*Id.* at II-843.

Stripped Bonds and Stripped Coupons

As discussed previously, section 1286 provides rules for the tax treatment of both issuers and investors in stripped bonds (principal payments) and stripped coupons (interest payments). The seller must allocate its adjusted basis in each whole asset between the interests retained and those interests sold on the basis of the fair market value of each.[114] The seller would then recognize gain or loss on the interests sold equal to the difference between the purchase price and the adjusted basis for the interests sold. The seller would be treated as having purchased on the date of sale each interest retained for an amount equal to the basis allocated to that item. The seller would then report the difference between the purchase price and the aggregate expected interest payments as it accrues under the original issue discount rules.

Purchasers of stripped bonds and stripped coupons would be treated as the beneficial owners of their pro rata share of each asset *less* that portion in which the seller retained a beneficial interest (*e.g.*, the excess servicing spread). Like the sellers, purchasers would report original issue discount income over time, equal to the difference between their purchase price and the cash flows they expect to receive from their interests in the same assets. Purchasers would include such original discount as it accrues under a constant yield based on the yield to maturity of the pass-through.[115] Each secondary market purchaser must report its own amount of original issue discount on the security equal to the difference between its purchase price and the remaining cash flows on the date of purchase, presumably using a reasonable prepayment assumption. Purchasers would report such original issue discount income in lieu of reporting interest or market discount income and return of principal under their applicable method of accounting for such assets. The strip owned by purchasers would include their allocable share of the reasonable servicing fees paid to the servicer, and each purchaser would be entitled to deduct its pro rata share of such servicing fees, subject to the limitations on holders that are individuals, estates or trusts.[116]

---

[114]It is problematical whether the seller would have to compute gain or loss separately for each asset or could take an aggregate approach. Proposed regulations for original issue discount (Prop. Treas. Reg. § 1.1275-2(d)) appear to permit an aggregate approach for a *purchaser* of obligations in a simultaneous transaction, but no comparable authority exists for a seller.

[115]*See* discussion on pp. 320-321, *supra*.

[116]*See* footnote 33, *supra*.

Where a pass-through certificate is recharacterized as a strip because the servicer retains "excess" servicing compensation, the net tax consequences to the investors should not differ greatly from those for pass-throughs, except that: 1) if the purchase price is less than the assets' remaining unpaid principal balance, the difference, which would otherwise be treated under the market discount rules, would be converted into original issue discount, and 2) cash method holders would in effect be placed on the accrual method of tax accounting, with resulting acceleration of reporting of income. Neither of these two effects is likely to be great. However, administrative burdens are placed on the seller/servicer in terms of recordkeeping and reporting of transactions under the original issue discount rules.

Special Problems in Computing Interest on Certain Receivables

Certain consumer receivables, such as automobile loans, may present special problems in properly computing interest reportable by investors if stated interest does not conform to the general tax models of interest (based on compounding of interest principles).

Rule of 78s

Many installment obligations either: 1) allocate scheduled payments between principal and interest or 2) calculate the rebate of unearned finance charges upon a prepayment in full under the so-called "Rule of 78s."[117] The Rule of 78s is a sum-of-the-digits method that allocates interest to each scheduled monthly payment by multiplying the total interest payable over the loan's scheduled life by a fraction, whose numerator is the number of months remaining on the loan at the time the calculation is made and whose denominator is the sum of the months' digits for the entire term of the loan. For example, the denominator for a 12-month loan is 78, which is the sum of 1 through 12, so that the first month's interest would be the total interest times 12/78. The effect is to "front-load" interest, in contrast to the constant interest method.

The Internal Revenue Service has held that the Rule of 78s lacks

---

[117]*See* New York State Bar Assn. Tax Section, *Report of Ad Hoc Committee on the Proposed Original Issue Discount Regs.*, Tax Notes (Jan. 26, 1987) at 417-18, 424-25. The Rule of 78s is not authorized for consumer loans under the laws of many states.

economic substance and, as a general rule, may not be used for federal income tax purposes.[118] However, the IRS permits both "borrowers" or "lenders" (presumably including secondary market purchasers) to use the Rule of 78s method for typical level-payment consumer installment loans with maturities of 60 months or shorter that contractually provide for the Rule of 78s.[119]

Proposed Treasury regulations, however, appear to provide treatment that is inconsistent with IRS rulings.[120] The proposed regulations would require the investor to report the front-loaded Rule of 78s interest as "prepaid" interest (because it exceeds the interest that accrues under the constant interest method) based on the parties' allocations but would allow the borrower to deduct only the interest that accrues under the constant interest method. Until the Treasury Department clarifies the treatment of the Rule of 78s, reliance on the Internal Revenue Service's announced exception under Revenue Procedure 83-40 appears to be reasonable.

Incentive Rate Automobile Loans ·

Sellers of personal property, most typically automobile dealers under manufacturers' programs, may offer purchasers an "incentive rate" loan as a sales promotional device. The purchaser may usually choose between a cash rebate or a below market-rate loan. Section 483 provides that the tax treatment correspond to this economic reality; a portion of each principal payment is recharacterized as interest as each payment is received to the extent that the receivable bears "unstated interest" (that is, does not bear total stated interest equal to the interest that would be due if the dealer charged a specified "test" rate of interest).[121] The unstated interest is allocated among the payments based on a compounding of interest method. The test rate is intended to set a minimum rate of interest (the "applicable Federal rate") equal to the rate paid by the Treasury on obligations of a similar maturity and is gener-

---

[118]*Rev. Rul.* 83-84, 1983-1 C.B. 97.

[119]*Rev. Proc.* 83-40, 1983-1 C.B. 774. This exception was reaffirmed in *Rev. Rul.* 86-42, 1986-1 C.B. 82.

[120]Prop. Treas. Reg. § 1.446-2 (proposed to be retroactive to transactions occurring after May 8, 1986).

[121]Principal payments due up to six months from the issue date are excluded form this recharacterization rule.

ally substantially lower than the market rate that would be charged to the obligor, especially on consumer debt. Unlike original issue discount arising on sales of property under section 1274,[122] unstated interest is reported as income under section 483 only as principal payments are made or become due.[123]

The treatment of such receivables when they are sold as pass-throughs in the secondary market is uncertain, because the security typically will bear a yield higher than the imputed interest rate. For example, assume that a 36-month consumer obligation with a $10,000 face amount issued at a nominal 1.9 percent interest rate (compounded monthly) bears $738 of imputed interest because the test rate is 7 percent compounded monthly. When the receivable is sold to investors through a pass-through arrangement, the investors pay not the restated $9,262 imputed principal amount, but $9,126 because the yield on the pass-through is 8 percent, compounded monthly. The market discount provisions clearly would treat $136 of the $874 discount (the difference between $9,262 and $9,126) as market discount; the treatment of the original $738 of imputed interest is uncertain. Although not clearly intended by Congress, the imputed interest may be converted into market discount by operation of the terms used to define market discount.[124] This treatment would result in a more straightforward computation of income (because the secondary market investor treats the entire excess of the nominal face amount over cost as market discount) than separate computations of section 483 imputed interest and section 1278 market discount. Ultimate resolution of this issue may require either guidance from Treasury or legislation.

---

[122]*See* discussion on p. 323, *supra*.

[123]On the other hand, consumers who purchase the property as "personal use property," as defined in Code section 1275(b) (property that is not substantially for investment or business use), may deduct only stated interest.

[124]Market discount is the difference between the "stated redemption price at maturity" of the obligation and its basis to the purchaser. Section 1278(a)(2). Because stated redemption price at maturity has the same meaning as under the original issue discount provisions (*see* section 1278(a)(5)), such amount includes interest that is not "qualified periodic interest." *See* discussion on p. 321, *supra*. Since section 483 imputed interest is not payable for the first six monthly payments, it is not qualified periodic interest and is thus restored to principal as part of the stated redemption price at maturity.

Foreign Investors

Asset-backed securities can be attractive to foreign investors, provided
the interest payable thereon qualifies as "portfolio interest" that is exempt
from 30 percent U.S. withholding tax on U.S.-source interest income.[125]
Generally, this requires that the obligation be in registered form and that
certain certification procedures designed to substantiate the status of the
investor as a non-U.S. citizen, resident, or entity are complied with.[126]
In general, any interest-bearing (or original issue discount-bearing) obligation originated after July 18, 1984 may qualify for treatment as portfolio interest; however, leases may not so qualify because they generate
rental income, not interest. In the case of asset-backed debt, the date
of issuance is the relevant date. In the case of pass-through certificates,
however, each underlying obligation must have been issued after the
foregoing effective date to qualify for the withholding exemption.

The treatment of foreign investors who acquire residual interests
in owner-trusts is uncertain and depends upon the proper treatment of
the trust and the residual interest. If trust classification is correct, then
an entity-level tax is avoided and income on the assets (assuming they
are debt obligations originated after July 18, 1984) should be portfolio
interest whose tax treatment flows through to the investor. However,
the trust could be classified as engaged in a trade or business and
classified as a partnership,[127] with a resulting 20 percent withholding
tax on distributions and the loss of portfolio investment treatment for
distributions.[128] These potential results are sufficiently unattractive such
that, even if reduced rates under a treaty may be applicable, foreign
investors should approach any contemplated purchase of residuals with
caution.

---

[125] Code sections 871(h), 881(c). Market discount income and gain upon sale of an asset generally
would not be subject to withholding tax, provided the foreign investor does not hold the asset in
connection with the conduct of a U.S. trade or business (*i.e.*, the asset must be a "portfolio" asset).
See B. Hirsh and R. Lorence, *Foreign Investment in Asset-Backed Financial Instruments—Part I,*
in 9 *Investment/USA* (Sept. 1987) at 2-3.

[126] *See* Code sections 871(h); 881(c); Treas. Reg. § 35a.9999-5.

[127] *See* discussion on pp. 319-320, *supra.*

[128] *See* B. Hirsh and R. Lorence, *Foreign Investment in Asset-Backed Financial Instruments—
Part II,* in 9 *Investment/USA* (Oct. 1987) at 2, 4.

FUTURE DIRECTIONS

This chapter's discussion demonstrates that the Congress and the Treasury Department have not yet provided an understandable and coherent framework for the taxation of the ever-increasingly diverse and complex universe of asset-backed financial instruments. Although a more or less workable regime for taxing *real property* mortgage-backed securities was enacted in 1986, the treatment of other asset-backed securities remains mired in complex, ambiguous and often contradictory rules. The result of this unclear tax treatment is economic inefficiency, leading to higher transaction costs and, ultimately, higher interest costs to the users of the assets (such as automobiles and computers), which are the collateral for the securities.

The authors hope that the Treasury Department will promptly supply regulatory guidance under the REMIC, original issue discount, market discount, and coupon stripping rules and that Congress will extend the REMIC regime to the asset-backed financial products that are the subject of this book.

CHAPTER 11

INSOLVENCY CONSIDERATIONS

Neil Baron, Partner
Booth & Baron, New York

Asset-backed securities are generally sold on the credit of the asset pools that secure them as opposed to the credit of the originator (which originates, sells, or pledges the assets). Indeed, these securities receive ratings that are higher than the rating on the originator's unsecured debt. It is, therefore, necessary to structure these transactions so that the insolvency, receivership, or bankruptcy (collectively an "insolvency proceeding") of the originator would neither impair the timely application of proceeds from the receivables or the bank facility to make payments on the asset-backed securities nor result in a recapture of payments made to the holders of such securities prior to an insolvency proceeding.

Moreover, although the cash flow from the bank facility or receivables and the credit enhancement may be more than adequate to make payments on the asset-backed securities, an insolvency proceeding of the issuer (which issues securities backed by receivables) resulting from the inability to pay other obligations is likely to result in a default on such securities. Therefore, in addition to structuring these financings in a manner that would insulate the receivables from the originator's insolvency proceeding, the issuer's activities should be limited to minimize the likelihood that it would become subject to an insolvency proceeding.

CASH FLOW DEBT

Most asset-backed securities are "cash flow debt" or cash flow certificates where cash flow from receivables plus a relatively small credit enhancement (a letter of credit to cover the first 7% of losses) is sufficient to make payment on the asset-backed securities.

The structure of cash flow debt will differ depending on whether the originator is the type of entity that is eligible to become a debtor under the United States Bankruptcy Code (the "Bankruptcy Code").

Originators Subject To Bankruptcy Code

For originators that can become debtors under the Bankruptcy Code, the transfer of receivables from the originator to the issuer should constitute an absolute sale or other absolute disposition of the receivables necessary to remove the receivables from the estate of the originator in the event of its bankruptcy. When such transfer constitutes a pledge as opposed to a sale, the receivables would constitute property of the originator. As a result, the originator's bankruptcy is likely to result in a default on the cash flow debt.

Generally, a creditor cannot exercise its rights on pledged collateral in a timely manner when the originator (pledgor) has become the subject of a proceeding under the Bankruptcy Code. Although legally a creditor ultimately should be able to realize the benefits of pledged collateral, it is likely to experience delays in payment. For example, under Section 362(a) of the Bankruptcy Code, the filing of a bankruptcy petition automatically stays all creditors from exercising their rights to pledged collateral. The stay would affect creditors holding security interests in asset pools and any other collateral pledged by an originator that has become a debtor under the Bankruptcy Code. Although the bankruptcy court is required to provide relief from the stay under certain circumstances, including those where the creditor is not adequately protected, it is difficult to determine whether those circumstances will exist or to estimate the duration of the stay. The adequate protection concept would not require timely payment. Moreover, creditors are likely to be viewed as adequately protected when the value of or cash flow on their collateral exceeds the amount of their claims.

Under Section 363 of the Bankruptcy Code, a bankruptcy court, under certain circumstances and subject to the adequate protection requirement, can permit a debtor to use pledged collateral, including cash collateral, to aid in the debtor's reorganization. For example, in the Continental Airlines and Air Florida bankruptcies, the bankruptcy courts permitted both airlines to use proceeds on receivables pledged to bank creditors who were viewed as adequately protected by their liens on certain aircraft.

Under Section 364 of the Bankruptcy Code, a bankruptcy court, subject to the adequate protection requirement, can permit a debtor to incur new debt that has a lien on assets that is prior to the lien of existing creditors. Under Section 542 a secured creditor in possession of its collateral may be required to return such collateral to a debtor. Thus, Section 542 could require an issuer holding receivables as pledgee to return them to a bankrupt originator that had pledged such receivables to secure asset-backed securities. (Nevertheless, the existence of a first perfected security interest should result in ultimate—but not necessarily timely—payment to holders of asset-backed securities.)

True Sale

As a result, when the originator is seeking a cost of funds or rating more favorable than the cost of funds or rating associated with the general unsecured debt of the originator, the transfer of the receivables should, for bankruptcy law purposes, constitute a true sale or other absolute disposition as opposed to a pledge of the receivables. Under bankruptcy law, a primary basis for recharacterizing a sale of receivables as a pledge is the existence of substantial recourse by the buyer (i.e., issuer) against the seller (i.e., originator) for defaults on the receivables. Case law indicates that such recourse results in retention by the originator of the risk of loss on the assets purportedly sold and that such retention is inconsistent with the notion of a sale. All cases known to the author that recharacterized sales as pledges involved full recourse for defaults on sold receivables. It is arguable, however, that when the originator agrees to reimburse the issuer for the first, say, seven percent of defaults on a receivable pool that has an historic default rate of .5 percent, the originator has retained all the risk on the pool. Therefore, a conservative approach would require that the sale of receivables by the originator to the issuer not involve recourse against the originator for defaulted receivables beyond a reasonably anticipated default rate based primarily on an historical analysis. The level of recourse might, however, reflect other factors that might result in defaults that are higher than history would indicate, such as a high concentration of receivables in a few account obligors. Because there is no precedent indicating that recourse of less than 100 percent but materially beyond the historic default rate would result in a pledge, law firms are split on their ability to provide true sale opinions when recourse materially exceeds historic rates.)

Moreover, recourse against the originator on the part of the providers of partial credit enhancement (e.g., pool insurance and letters of credit) also should be limited to such a reasonably anticipated default rate. Insurers and letter of credit providers may, of course, be subrogated to the issuer's rights against defaulting account debtors and have recourse against any spread between the yields on the receivables and payments on the asset-backed securities, provided that the originator does not report such spread until it is no longer available to fund defaults on the receivables. Otherwise, if the originator were to report the spread before it ceased to be available to cover defaults, defaults on the receivables would result in a loss to the originator and, as a result, might be viewed as recourse against the originator. Counsel has been comfortable, however, in opining as to the true sale nature of the transfer of the receivables to the issuer when the issuer, not the originator, books the spread. Because the spread generally is booked as an excess servicing fee, the issuer will serve as master servicer and appoint the originator as subservicer, and the issuer would not pay subservicing fees to the originator until the spread is no longer available to fund defaults. As a result, defaults on the receivables would no longer result in a loss to the originator.

Courts have also indicated that free use of collections on the receivables by the purported seller is inconsistent with the notion that the proceeds and, perhaps, the receivables are no longer property of the originator. More precisely, the originator's use of proceeds for, say, 30 days prior to remittance to the issuer may be a basis for viewing the proceeds as property of the originator and, therefore, an argument for recharacterizing the transaction as a pledge (although, this alone should not result in such a recharacterization). A conservative approach, therefore, would require proceeds to be remitted to the issuer promptly and the originator to be precluded from using such proceeds unless there is an express agreement to lend proceeds to the originator and to permit the issuer to terminate such loans in the event of an adverse credit event with respect to the originator.

In order to support further the true sale nature of the transactions, the transfer of the receivables should be accounted for as a sale on the originator's financial statements.

Finally, outside counsel to the originator should be prepared to provide an unqualified opinion indicating that the transfer of the receivables by the originator to the issuer is sufficient to remove the receivables from the originator's estate for purposes of Section 541 of the Bankruptcy Code, and that Sections 362(a), 363, and 542 of the Bankruptcy Code would not apply to receivables or proceeds thereon in the event of the originator's bankruptcy.

Substantive Consolidation

In many instances the issuer will be a subsidiary of the originator. Even assuming a true sale to such a subsidiary, if the subsidiary's assets and liabilities were substantively consolidated with those of its bankrupt parent, the receivables would be viewed as property of the bankrupt parent. More precisely, when the issuer has issued debt collateralized by receivables sold to it by its parent-originator, the issuer and the bankrupt originator would be viewed as a single debtor that has pledged collateral to the holders of the asset-backed securities. As a result, timely payment of proceeds to holders of the asset-backed securities is likely to be impaired.

To allay this concern, the subsidiary should be established as a separate corporate entity. Among factors that can demonstrate this separation are an independent officer and director, separate books and records, and board of directors meetings to authorize corporate action of the subsidiary. Additionally, as confirmation of such separateness, the parent's counsel should provide an unqualified opinion indicating that the assets and liabilities of the subsidiary could not be consolidated with the parent's if the parent becomes bankrupt.

Perfection

Purchasers of receivables must perfect their rights by complying with the Uniform Commercial Code regardless of whether the transfer is a pledge or a sale. When the originator commingles proceeds of sold receivables with the originator's own funds for more than 10 days, the rights of the purchaser of the receivables (i.e., the issuer) may become unperfected. As a result, the issuer purchasing the receivables could be an unsecured creditor with respect to funds contained in the originator's commingled account on the date of the latter's bankruptcy, and payments made from such commingled account during the preference period preceding such bankruptcy might be recaptured as preferences. Although the risk of recapture as a preference is remote when the transfer constitutes a true sale, there exists indirect precedent that provides some support for such recapture. Moreover, when the originator commingles for less than 10 days, the issuer continues to be perfected in such an account up to the full amount of its claim; but the issuer would not have priority over purchasers of receivables or other creditors that also have claims to such an account.

These concerns may be addressed in one of the following ways:

• Proceeds could be collected by the issuer. In such a case, the issuer may collect and commingle proceeds of receivables not sold by the originator with proceeds of receivables sold by the originator and remit the latter's proceeds to it.
• The collecting bank may collect proceeds as agent for the originator and purchasers of receivables (including the issuer) as their interests appear. In this case, the bank should not be permitted to remit any proceeds to the originator without the issuer's written instruction, which may be given at the closing of the transaction. Moreover, the issuer should enter into a written agency agreement with the bank to establish a true agency relationship.
• The originator may collect proceeds of sold receivables in its own account if this account does not contain any of the originator's funds, including proceeds of receivables that the originator has not sold. Moreover, the originator should not have the right to withdraw funds from this account.

Additional Disincentives

The foregoing would provide comfort upon a legal determination on the merits that the transfer of receivables would be viewed as a sale, substantive consolidation would not occur, proceeds on the receivables that have not been paid to holders of the asset-backed securities would not be property of the bankruptcy estate of the originator, and proceeds that have been paid to such holders could not be recaptured as preferences.

Nevertheless, recently bankrupt parent companies have caused seemingly healthy subsidiaries to file petitions under the Bankruptcy Code. This raises a concern that when the issuer is a subsidiary of the originator, a bankrupt originator might cause the bankruptcy filing of the issuer as an attempt to seize the subsidiary's assets for the originator or its creditors by one of the means described earlier or by other means. Such an attempt would be facilitated if the bankruptcy court in which the originator's case were pending had jurisdiction over the subsidiary.

During the issuer's subsidiary's bankruptcy proceedings, debt service could not be paid without a court order. To address this concern, the boards of directors of both the parent and subsidiary might adopt resolutions indicating that it is not the intent of either company to file or cause the filing of a voluntary bankruptcy petition with respect to the subsidiary so long as the subsidiary is solvent and does not reasonably expect insolvency. Although such a resolution could be rescinded, it would discourage such a filing.

Moreover, as additional disincentive, the prospectus might disclose, in substance, the following:

• The financing is structured to assure investors that the voluntary or involuntary application for relief under the Bankruptcy Code or any similar applicable law (insolvency laws) with respect to the originator will not result in a similar voluntary application with respect to the issuer as long as the issuer is solvent and does not reasonably foresee becoming insolvent as a result of the originator's insolvency or otherwise.

• Counsel has advised the issuer and its parent that in counsel's opinion the assets and liabilities of the issuer could not be substantively consolidated with the assets and liabilities of its parent in the event of an application for relief under the insolvency laws with respect to the issuer or its parent or both.

• In counsel's opinion, the transfer of receivables by the originator to the issuer constitutes a sale and, therefore, such receivables would not be property of the originator in the event of the filing of an application for relief by or against the originator under the insolvency laws.

• Counsel knows of no other legal theory under which the receivables could be made available to the bankrupt originator or its creditors.

• The issuer and its parent believe that, as long as the issuer is solvent and does not reasonably foresee becoming insolvent, the filing of a voluntary application under the insolvency laws by the issuer to make such assets available to its parent or its parent's creditors would be an inappropriate use of the insolvency laws that could be successfully contested by the holders of the issuer's asset-backed securities.

• The issuer has no intent to file, and its parent has no intent to cause the filing of, a voluntary application under the insolvency laws with respect to the issuer so long as the issuer is solvent and does not reasonably foresee becoming insolvent.

Special Purpose Issuers

The foregoing should provide ample assurance that the rights of the issuer and access by the issuer and the holders of the asset-backed securities to the receivables and proceeds thereon would not be impaired by the originator's bankruptcy.

When the issuer issues debt secured by receivables, a bankruptcy of the issuer is likely to result in a default notwithstanding strong performance of the receivables pool due to Sections 362(a), 363, 364, and 542 of the Bankruptcy Code. When, however, proceeds on the receivables and credit enhancement proceeds are sufficient to pay all the issuer's liabilities (not just the asset-backed securities) there should be no reason for the issuer to become subject to a bankruptcy proceeding. Therefore, to ameliorate the risk that the issuer would become subject to such a proceeding, the following special purpose criteria are required:

• The issuer's business should be restricted to the purchase of the receivables and the issuance of the asset-backed securities.
• The issuer should be prohibited from incurring any additional debt other than debt that 1) is fully subordinated to the subject debt, 2) is nonrecourse other than with respect to proceeds in excess of the proceeds necessary to pay the subject debt ("excess proceeds"), and 3) does not constitute a claim against the issuer to the extent that excess proceeds are insufficient to pay such debt.
• The issuer should be prohibited from selling or assigning the receivables to any entity unless such entity meets the above criteria and such sale or assignment is subject to the lien of the holders of the asset-backed securities.

Banks and Thrifts

Originators that are not subject to the Bankruptcy Code, such as banks and thrift institutions, may pledge—instead of sell—the receivables to the issuer or directly to the debtholders. Both the Federal Savings and Loan Insurance Corporation and the Federal Deposit Insurance Corporation (the receivers for insolvent thrifts and banks, respectively) have concurred with opinions that, as a matter of law, perfected security interests are generally enforceable against insolvent thrifts and banks. Nevertheless, counsel should provide an opinion that the securities holders' rights with respect to the receivables and proceeds thereon would be valid, binding, and enforceable notwithstanding the insolvency, receivership, or similar proceeding of the originator of the receivables. Concerns regarding substantive consolidation and the filing of healthy subsidiaries are inapplicable; but the concerns about commingling described earlier are relevant.

When a finance vehicle is used by a bank or thrift to issue the asset-backed securities, the special purpose criteria should be satisfied with respect to such an issuer. Also, counsel should be asked to provide opinions that the transfer by the originator to the issuer is a true sale or that the issuer or debtholders have a perfected security interest subject to no prior or equal liens in the receivables.

PREFERRED STOCK

Some issuers that have purchased receivables, whole residential mortgages, and GNMA, FNMA, and FHLMC securities, and securities from their parents have issued preferred stock instead securities of secured debt. The dividend rate on the preferred stock is generally lower than the interest rate on debt collateralized by receivables due to the intercorporate dividend exclusion presently enjoyed by purchasers of preferred stock. This exclusion is now under review by Congress. Because dividends on the preferred stock are not tax deductible, however, the originator/parent must have a net operating loss to absorb the subsidiary's income. The pricing is based largely on conclusions that proceeds on the receivables are sufficient to pay dividends and the sale price or market value of such assets is sufficient to pay the redemption price. Again, the transaction must be structured so that the bankruptcy of the originator would not impair the timely availability of the receivables and proceeds thereon (including proceeds from the sale thereof) to pay dividends on and the redemption price of the preferred stock. Because there is no conventional market for traditional receivables, preferred stock supported by such receivables has involved a commitment to the issuer to purchase such receivables at an amount sufficient to pay the redemption price. Such commitment must be either issued or guaranteed by an entity with a rating at least as high as the rating sought on the preferred stock.

Substantive consolidation of a subsidiary with its parent would have substantially more onerous results where the subsidiary had issued preferred stock than if it had issued debt. In the former situation, the rights of the preferred shareholders to the subsidiary's assets would be subordinate to the rights of the parent's unsecured creditors in such assets. Because filing a voluntary petition by the subsidiary would facilitate such consolidation, the certificate of incorporation and by-laws should provide that a vote by the holders of two-thirds of the outstanding preferred stock would be required to authorize the filing of a voluntary bankruptcy petition with respect to the subsidiary while the subsidiary was not insolvent and that such provisions could not be changed without a similar vote. Moreover, counsel should provide an opinion on the validity and enforceability of these provisions in case of the parent/originator's bankruptcy. Also, neither the parent nor the subsidiary should be able to vote on any preferred stock purchased by them.

As an additional disincentive against the parent/originator inappropriately causing the subsidiary to file a voluntary bankruptcy petition, the dividend rate could substantially increase as a result of a missed dividend or failed auction (in the case of auction rate preferred stock). The increased dividend accrual should be enforceable notwithstanding the subsidiary's bankruptcy, assuming the voluntary filing is successfully contested by the preferred shareholders—an assumption supported by counsel's opinion regarding enforceability of the preferred shareholders right to vote on a voluntary bankruptcy and the inability of the subsidiary to be consolidated with the estate of its bankrupt parent. In this connection, counsel should provide an opinion that, assuming such proceeding would be successfully contested by the preferred shareholders, the increased dividend would accrue during the bankruptcy of the subsidiary. Moreover, the elements described previously regarding debt secured by the receivables (i.e., criteria regarding "pledge versus sale," substantive consolidation, commingling, opinions regarding other theories of law, and additional disincentives) are applicable to the issuance of preferred stock.

DEBT DEPENDENT ON LIQUIDITY FACILITY: COMMERCIAL PAPER

These types of commercial paper financings, while rated based in large part on the receivables, are also dependent on a bank liquidity facility provided to the issuer (such as a revolving credit agreement) to pay debt service. Therefore, the bank should be rated at least as high as the rating sought on the commercial paper.

The need for a liquidity facility stems from the fact that the maturities of the receivables do not match the maturities of the commercial paper. For example, commercial paper might mature every 15, 30, or 90 days, while receivables might be paid at different intervals. Therefore, a liquidity facility is necessary to pay commercial paper as it matures.

Typically, the bank is required to lend to the issuer an amount equal to the receivable pool, but this amount is reduced by receivable defaults. An analysis of the receivable pool is, therefore, necessary to determine that receivable defaults will not reduce the bank's obligation to fund maturing commercial paper to a level below the amount of outstanding commercial paper.

The issuer's bankruptcy could result in two problems. First, it is questionable whether under Section 365(e)(2) of the Bankruptcy Code the bank's obligation to fund would be enforceable in the event of the issuer's bankruptcy. Second, payments made by the issuer to the commercial paper holders within the 90 day period (one year for commercial paper holders that are insiders) preceding the issuer's bankruptcy might be recaptured as preferences.

In order to address these concerns, the financing should be structured to provide assurance that 1) the issuer's bankruptcy will not occur for at least one year and one day after all the commercial paper has been retired, and 2) the insolvency or bankruptcy of the originator does not impair either the timely use of the liquidity facility to pay maturing commercial paper or the ability of commercial paper holders to retain payments made to them. The following guidelines are helpful:

• The issuer should satisfy the criteria regarding the issuer's bankruptcy-remote nature.

• The issuer should be prohibited from incurring any debt other than the commercial paper and the obligation to repay the bank for advances under the liquidity facility.

• The bank should be obligated to fund under the liquidity facility (up to the amount of nondefaulting receivables) in all events other than an issuer bankruptcy. An originator bankruptcy should not excuse the bank from its obligations to fund.

• All creditors of the issuer other than the commercial paper holders (typically the bank and depositary) should enter into an agreement with the issuer and the depositary or trustee acting on behalf of the commercial paper holders prohibiting such creditors from filing an involuntary bankruptcy petition against the issuer for one year and one day after all the commercial paper is retired.

• The depositary or trustee should be irrevocably instructed and have the right to draw on the liquidity facility on behalf of the commercial paper holders in the event that there are insufficient funds in the commercial paper account to pay the commercial paper holders, or in the event that such funds become subject to a restraining order due to the originator's bankruptcy.

• No outstanding stock of the issuer should be owned by the originator. Instead, such stock should be owned by an entity, such as a charity or an affiliate of the commercial paper dealer, that has no incentive to cause the issuer to file a voluntary petition in bankruptcy.

• The amount of the liquidity facility should not be reduced by proceeds paid on the receivables until such proceeds are applied to the payment of commercial paper.

• As confirmation, a legal opinion should be provided to the effect that the liquidity facility is valid, binding, and enforceable notwithstanding the originator's bankruptcy.

CHAPTER 12

SECURITIES LAW CONSIDERATIONS

C. Thomas Kunz, Partner
Skadden, Arps, Slate, Meagher & Flom

INTRODUCTION

This chapter addresses the principal securities law considerations applicable to asset securitization.

The first section of the chapter briefly describes the three principal structures that have been most frequently used in public and private securities offerings to securitize assets such as automobile installment purchase obligations, credit card receivables, and lease receivables. The first section also describes certain of the features of asset securitization structures that raise securities law concerns.

The second section of the chapter analyzes the principal securities law considerations applicable to securities issued in the three structures. Particular emphasis is placed on the considerations applicable under the Securities Act of 1933, the Securities Exchange Act of 1934, and the Investment Company Act of 1940.

ALTERNATIVE METHODS OF STRUCTURING AN ASSET SECURITIZATION

There are three basic methods that have been most frequently used to structure the issuance of asset-backed obligations. These methods are 1) the issuance of certificates by a grantor trust, the assets of which consist of the assets to be securitized, 2) the issuance of debt securities collateralized by the assets to be securitized by a limited-purpose subsidiary established by the originator of such assets, and 3) the issuance by a "conduit" issuing corporation of debt securities collateralized by the assets to be securitized. A brief description of certain of the material features of each of the methods follows.

Additional methods of securitizing assets have been employed in certain circumstances. For example, certain commercial banks and savings and loan associations have directly issued debt securities collateralized by the assets to be securitized. In addition, asset owners have sold participations in pools of their assets to institutional purchasers. Because none of these alternative methods are utilized to accomplish the same goals generally sought through asset securitization, and because the securities law considerations applicable to these methods are not unique to asset securitization, they are not discussed in this chapter.

Choosing which of the three principal structures will be utilized in a particular transaction involves a weighing of a number of factors, including tax considerations, accounting considerations, and securities marketing concepts. The analysis of these factors is considered elsewhere in this book.

Grantor Trust

In asset securitization transactions, a grantor trust is a trust (the "trust") in which the beneficiaries are considered to be the holders of an undivided beneficial interest in the assets of the trust as evidenced by certificates (the "certificates"). The trust is generally formed by the asset owner (the "seller") and a commercial bank or trust company (the "trustee") pursuant to a pooling and servicing agreement (the "pooling and servicing agreement"). According to the pooling and servicing agreement, the seller conveys the assets to be securitized to the trustee in exchange for the certificates. The seller offers and sells all of the certificates to investors directly or through underwriters or dealers in a public or private offering. The certificates entitle the holders to their pro rata share of collections of principal and interest on their unpaid principal at a designated rate (the "pass-through rate").

Generally, the seller will be appointed pursuant to the pooling and servicing agreement as the servicer of the assets (in such capacity, the "servicer") as agent for the trust. All collections of proceeds of the assets are allocated in accordance with the pooling and servicing agreement.

Customarily, collections will be applied principally to pay principal and interest at the pass-through rate to the holders of the certificates, to pay the servicer a specified servicing fee, and to make such other allocations as are set forth in the pooling and servicing agreement, including any remittances to any provider of credit enhancement such as a letter of credit bank.

The structure of a grantor trust transaction is in part driven by federal income tax considerations. As discussed in more detail elsewhere in this book, entities that exercise more than a modicum of managerial discretion over their assets may be considered associations taxable as corporations. If a grantor trust were considered an association taxable as a corporation, significantly adverse federal income tax consequences could occur. Simply put, the grantor trust would have taxable income on the income derived by it from its assets. However, payments to the holders of the certificates of interest at the pass-through rate might not be deductible from the trust's income for purposes of determining its taxable income. As the beneficial owners of the trust's assets, the holders of the certificates would probably be found to have an equity interest in the trust and payments to them of interest could, therefore, be considered payments of nondeductible dividends.

To avoid this result, the trust is structured as a fixed investment trust. This can only be achieved if there is little or no modification of the cash flow from the trust's assets. Consequently, the holders of the certificates normally receive a pro rata portion of principal and interest payments received on the trust's assets soon after it is paid to the trust. The trust is, therefore, a "look through" or "conduit" entity. Consequently, the trust cannot issue different classes of certificates with different interest rates, different maturities, and different rights and priorities with respect to the cash flow, such as are typically issued in collateralized mortgage obligations transactions.

Limited Purpose Finance Subsidiary

In asset securitization transactions, a limited purpose finance subsidiary is a corporation established as a wholly-owned subsidiary of the seller (the "finance subsidiary"). The finance subsidiary's activities are expressly limited by its charter to the issuance of debt securities (the "finance subsidiary debt securities") collateralized by the assets to be securitized. The finance subsidiary offers and sells the finance subsidiary debt securities in a public or private offering and utilizes the net proceeds of the sale simultaneously to acquire the assets to be securitized from the seller. The finance subsidiary debt securities are generally issued according to a trust indenture (the "trust indenture") entered into by the finance subsidiary with a commercial bank or trust company (the "indenture trustee").

The finance subsidiary debt securities may be issued in a single series or a multiple series with different interest rates and maturities and different priority rights to cash flow from the assets securitized. The assets to be securitized and all proceeds thereof are assigned and pledged by the finance subsidiary to the indenture trustee. The cash flow from the assets is expected to provide for the payment of principal of and interest on the finance subsidiary debt securities.

As noted previously, the finance subsidiary, unlike a grantor trust, can issue finance subsidiary debt securities in series with different maturities and interest rates. This ability is premised on a conclusion that for tax purposes the finance company debt securities will be treated as a debt and not as equity. As discussed elsewhere in this book, classification of the finance subsidiary debt securities as debt for tax purposes will depend upon, among other things, whether the finance subsidiary is structured with an appropriate ratio of debt to equity.

Conduit Issuing Corporation

In asset securitization transactions, a "conduit" issuing corporation or asset-backed securities corporation ("asset-backed securities issuer") generally refers to a corporation established as a wholly-owned subsidiary of an entity not affiliated with the seller of the assets to be securitized. Generally, the unaffiliated entity has been an investment banking firm active in the underwriting of asset-backed securities. The asset-backed securities issuer stands ready to purchase assets to be securitized from a number of different sellers.

This issuer finances its purchases of the assets to be securitized through the issuance of a series of debt securities (the "asset-backed securities issuer debt securities") collateralized by the assets to be securitized. The issuer offers and sells its securities in a public or private offering and utilizes the net proceeds of sale to acquire the assets from the seller. These securities are generally issued according to a trust indenture entered into by the asset-backed securities issuer and an indenture trustee.

The securities may be issued in a single class or in multiple classes with different interest and maturities. The assets to be securitized and all proceed thereof are assigned and pledged by the asset-backed securities issuer to the indenture trustee. The cash flow from the assets is expected to provide for the payment of principal of and interest on the debt securities.

There are three principal purposes sought to be achieved by the establishment of an asset-backed securities issuer. First, the issuer generally has an effective shelf registration statement filed with the Securities and Exchange Commission (SEC). Consequently, sellers can utilize the asset-backed securities issuer as a vehicle to securitize their assets in a public offering without themselves going through the sometimes lengthy securities registration process for a trust or a finance subsidiary.

Second, because the asset-backed securities issuer is unaffiliated with the seller, the seller may be able to obtain accounting, tax, and other benefits that might not be available if the seller transferred the assets to be securitized to a finance subsidiary.

Third, as in the case of a finance subsidiary, an asset-backed securities issuer is permitted to issue debt securities having different maturities and interest rates and priority rights to cash flow from the assets securitized so long as the issuer is appropriately structured. Consequently, the issuer offers a seller more flexibility in securitizing assets than does a grantor trust.

Other Structuring Considerations

A company contemplating an asset securitization will choose which of the three principal methods of structuring the transaction it will utilize. Certain customary components of an asset securitization that are relevant to the securities law aspects of asset securitization will, however, be present no matter which method is employed. Other such components may or may not be present depending upon the method chosen. A brief description of common features of asset-backed securities issuances that require consideration under the securities laws appears later in the chapter.

Credit Enhancement

As discussed elsewhere in this book, in order to sell the asset-backed securities and obtain a rating from one of the nationally recognized statistical rating agencies, it may be necessary either for the assets to be securitized or for the asset-backed securities themselves to be the beneficiary of a form of credit enhancement.

The most common methods of providing credit enhancement in asset-backed securities issuances have included the issuance of a letter of credit (the "letter of credit") by a banking institution, the issuance of a surety bond (the "surety bond") by a surety company, "overcollateralization," that is, assigning and pledging for the benefit of the asset-backed securities assets having a value in excess of the principal and interest owing on such securities, and a limited guaranty (the "limited guaranty") issued by the seller.

Although in certain transactions the credit enhancement directly supports payment of the certificates, the finance subsidiary debt securities, or the asset-backed securities issuer debt securities, in most cases the letter of credit, the surety bond, or the limited guaranty is designed to support the assets to be securitized. The beneficiary of the credit enhancement (generally the trustee in a transaction involving a grantor trust and the indenture trustee in cases involving a finance subsidiary or an asset-backed securities issuer) is entitled to draw on the letter of credit, the surety bond, or the limited guaranty for the value of any asset that has become defaulted in accordance with the operative documentation. The credit enhancement, though most often limited to a percentage of the entire principal amount of the asset-backed securities, is a material factor in an investor's willingness to purchase the asset-backed securities.

Guaranteed Investment Contracts

In asset securitization transactions involving the issuance of debt securities by a finance subsidiary or an asset-backed securities issuer, the timing of receipt of payments on the assets securitized may have important consequences for the ability of the finance subsidiary or the asset-backed securities issuer to make timely and full payment of scheduled interest payments on the finance subsidiary debt securities or asset-backed securities issuer debt securities. If the interest rate available for investments made with monies received on the assets is less than the interest rate payable on the debt securities, investment of payments on the assets until the time needed for application to the scheduled interest payment could result in a shortfall in the amount needed to make the interest payment.

To protect against this risk, the finance subsidiary or the asset-backed securities issuer may enter into a guaranteed investment contract (a "guaranteed investment contract"). Generally referred to as a "GIC," the guaranteed investment contract is generally entered into with a banking institution or an insurance company. The provider of the guaranteed investment contract agrees, for a fee, to pay a specified interest rate on funds invested with it by the finance subsidiary or the asset-backed securities issuer. The risk of falling interest rates relative to the interest rates payable on the finance subsidiary debt securities or the asset-backed securities issuer debt securities is thus shifted to the provider of the guaranteed investment contract.

Minimum Principal Payment Agreements

Grantor trust transactions and most issuances of asset-backed debt securities by finance subsidiaries and asset-backed securities issuers place the risk of prepayment or faster-than-expected prepayment of the assets on the holder of the certificates, the finance subsidiary debt securities, or asset-backed securities issuer debt securities. This result occurs, in the case of the certificates, because all payments or prepayments of the principal of the assets owned by the trust are "passed-through" currently to the holders of the certificates. In the case of debt securities issued by a finance subsidiary or an asset-backed securities issuer, this result occurs because the amount of principal periodically payable to the holders of the debt securities is often measured by the aggregate principal payments or prepayments made on the assets during the particular period.

Because of the restrictions inherent in the nature of a grantor trust as an inactive pass-through vehicle, it is not possible in the normal grantor trust transaction to eliminate the possibility of prepayment risk to the holders of the certificates. In the case of finance subsidiary debt securities and asset-backed securities issuer debt securities, however, it is possible to remove from the holders of the debt securities the risk of faster-than-anticipated prepayment of the assets.

The risk is removed by the finance subsidiary or the asset-backed securities issuer entering into a minimum principal payment agreement (the "minimum principal payment agreement") with a banking institution or other provider. Under the minimum principal payment agreement, an assumed rate of prepayment is specified. The assumed rate is determined on the basis of a review of the historical prepayment history of the assets to be securitized. If prepayments on the assets for a specific period are less than expected, the minimum principal payment agreement obligates the provider to advance the deficiency to the finance subsidiary or the asset-backed securities issuer. If prepayments of the assets for a specified period are greater than expected, the "excess" prepayments are invested with the provider, which pays a specified rate of interest to the finance subsidiary or the asset-backed securities issuer.

SECURITIES LAW CONSIDERATIONS

The Securities Act of 1933

Section 5 of the Securities Act of 1933 (the "Securities Act") provides in substance that, unless a registration statement is in effect for a security, it is unlawful to sell or deliver such a security and, unless a registration statement has been filed with the SEC for a security, it shall be unlawful to offer to sell or offer to buy such a security through the use of any prospectus or otherwise. In addition, Section 5 of the Securities Act imposes certain prospectus delivery requirements.

The Securities Act provides for two broad categories of exemptions from the provisions of Section 5. The first, the so-called securities exemption, exempts certain types of securities from the provisions of Section 5. These exemptions are contained in Section 3 of the Securities Act and provide exemptions for, among other categories of securities: 1) any security issued or guaranteed by the United States, any territory thereof, the District of Columbia, any state of the United States, or any political subdivision or political instrumentality thereof (Section 3(a)(2)); 2) any security issued or guaranteed by any bank (Section 3(a)(2)); 3) any security issued by a savings and loan association, building and loan association or similar institution (Section 3(a)(5)); and 4) any insurance or endowment policy or annuity contract issued by a corporation subject to the supervision of the insurance commissioner, bank commissioner, or any agency providing like functions of any state (Section 3(a)(8)).

The second broad category of exemptions, the "transactional exemption," exempts certain types of transactions from the provisions of Section 5. These exemptions are contained in Section 4 of the Securities Act and provide exemptions for, among other types of transactions: 1) transactions by any person other than an issuer, underwriter, or dealer (Section 4(1)); and 2) transactions by an issuer not involving any public offering, that is, "private placements" (Section 4(2)).

Two other introductory concepts under the Securities Acts are relevant to asset securitization—the definitions of the terms "security" and "issuer."

The term "security" is broadly defined under Section 2(1) of the Securities Act to include any note, stock, bond, debenture, certificate of interest or participation in any profit-sharing agreement or, in general, any interest or instrument commonly known as a "security."

The term "issuer" is defined under Section 2(4) of the Securities Act to mean every person who issues or proposes to issue any security. With respect to certificates of deposit, voting-trust certificates or collateral-trust certificates, or with respect to certificates of interest or shares in an unincorporated investment trust not having a board of directors, the term "issuer" means the person performing the acts and assuming the duties of depositor or manager according to the provisions of the trust or other agreement under which such securities are issued.

A final introductory concern under the Securities Act is the choice of the appropriate form of registration statement.

The most attractive form for a registered offering of securities issued in an asset securitization transaction is Form S-3. This form is generally available only to "seasoned" companies that file periodic reports with the SEC under the Securities and Exchange Act of 1934 (the "Exchange Act") and for majority-owned subsidiaries of such companies.

Form S-3 is a short form registration statement that permits a "free form" approach to the preparation of the prospectus. It allows the incorporation by reference of annual reports and other materials previously filed under the Exchange Act, along with any such materials subsequently filed. In order to be eligible to utilize Form S-3, the registrant must meet certain registrant and transaction requirements and, in the case of a majority-owned subsidiary, certain majority-owned subsidiary requirements. In general, the primary transaction requirement relevant to this chapter is that Form S-3 is available for offerings of debt securities or nonconvertible preferred stock, but not, except in limited circumstances, for the offering of equity securities.

A form not available for transactions involving asset securitization is Form S-11. This form is quite commonly utilized in securitizations involving mortgages and other interests in real estate. It is, however, only available for use by real estate investment trusts and other issuers whose business is primarily that of acquiring and holding for investment real estate or interests in real estate such as mortgages. It is not, therefore, available for asset securitization transactions.

Form S-1 is the general form of registration statement used for offerings of securities for which no other form of registration statement is prescribed. The Form S-1 disclosure requirements prescribed by the SEC provide for fuller disclosure and less incorporation by reference than do the requirements of Form S-3. The SEC has, however, been quite willing to recognize that a number of the required disclosure items specified by Form S-1 are inapplicable to asset securitization transactions.

Another consideration when determining which form of registration statement is appropriate in an asset securitization is whether a shelf registration is possible under Rule 415 under the Securities Act. A "shelf" offering is an offering of securities made on a "delayed or continuous basis in the future." That is, the securities are registered, put on the shelf and taken down off the shelf at some point in the future. Shelf offerings may provide distinct advantages over discrete one-time offerings, primarily from the point of view of cost and response to market conditions. Because the securities are registered and "on the shelf," an issuer can take advantage of favorable securities marketing conditions without being concerned with the substantial time it may take to file and have declared effective a new registration statement.

Although Rule 415 is available to permit delayed or continuous offerings of securities of a number of different types, in the asset securitization area it is generally available only for securities registered on Form S-3. As noted previously, this generally means only debt securities and nonconvertible preferred stock of seasoned reporting companies and their majority-owned subsidiaries, including an asset-backed securities issuer owned by a seasoned reporting company.

APPLICATION OF THE SECURITIES ACT TO ASSET SECURITIZATION TRANSACTIONS

Grantor Trust Transactions

Initial Analytical Concerns

As discussed earlier, in a grantor trust transaction, certificates issued by the trust evidence a fractional undivided interest in the trust's assets. For initial analytical purposes under the Securities Act, two issues are relevant: 1) are the certificates "securities?" and 2) if the certificates are "securities" who is the "issuer?" The first issue is relevant because the Section 5 requirements apply only to "securities." The second is relevant because in a public offering, the "issuer" signs the registration statement and accordingly assumes the liabilities imposed on issuers under Section 11 of the Securities Act.

It is clear that the certificates are "securities" as defined in the Securities Act. Accordingly, the offer and sale of the certificates will be subject to the registration statement and prospectus delivery requirements of Section 5 unless the certificates are "exempt securities" under one of the provisions of Section 3 of the Securities Act or are offered and sold in an "exempt transaction" under Section 4 of the Securities Act.

Exempt Security Status

In most cases the certificates will not be "exempt securities" under Section 3 of the Securities Act. The certificates are issued by the trust, for which a Section 3 exemption is unavailable. There are certain no-action letters of the staff of the SEC that allow an issuer to forego registration of a security if the security offered mirrors precisely a security that is an exempt security and the security offered permits the holder thereof to proceed against the obligor on the underlying security.

The certificates in a typical grantor trust context would not fulfill the criteria of these no-action letters. First, the assets normally securitized through grantor trust transactions are not themselves "exempt securities" under Section 3. The assets generally securitized such as automobile loan installment obligations, consumer credit card receivables, and consumer or business lease receivables are generally obligations of individuals or corporations to pay periodic payments. They do not generally fall within any of the categories of exempt securities. Second, even if the assets securitized did fall within one of the categories of exempt securities, the certificates issued by the trust generally do not precisely mirror the underlying assets nor do the certificates give the holder the right to proceed directly against the underlying obligor.

Private Placement Alternative

The certificates issued in a grantor trust transaction may be offered and sold in an "exempt transaction." Numerous grantor trust asset securitizations have been accomplished by "private placements" exempt by virtue of Section 4(2) of the Securities Act from the registration and prospectus delivery requirements of Section 5.

A detailed analysis of the private placement exemption is beyond the scope of this chapter. It is sufficient to note that the offer and sale of the certificates should be entitled to the private placement exemption if the following conditions are met: 1) the certificates are offered and sold solely to sophisticated investors, 2) the offerees by virtue of their status have access to or are provided with and can evaluate the type of information that would be provided in a registration statement, 3) steps are taken to confirm that the purchasers are not buying with a view to distribute the certificates, 4) the certificates are not offered by any form of general solicitation or general advertising, and 5) steps are taken to restrict the transferability of the certificates unless they are registered or sold in another transaction exempt from registration. Regulation D promulgated by the SEC provides a "safe harbor" for the availability of Section 4(2). By complying with the terms of Regulation D (which are set forth in Rules 501 through 506 under the Securities Act), the offer and sale of certificates would conclusively be an exempt private placement.

Registered Offerings

If the certificates in a grantor trust transaction are not sold in an exempt private placement or other exempt transaction, they would have to be sold in a registered offering. In order to comply with Section 5 of the Securities Act, a registration statement for the certificates will have to be filed with, and be declared effective by, the SEC and a prospectus meeting the requirements of the Securities Act will have to be prepared and utilized.

The initial concern is defining who the "issuer" of the certificate is under the Securities Act. As discussed earlier, this characterization will determine who has to sign the registration statement and who takes on issuer liability under the Securities Act.

Although, as previously noted, Section 2(4) of the Securities Act defines an "issuer" generally as every person who issues or proposes to issue any security, an exception is created for certificates of interest in an unincorporated investment trust not having a board of directors. In such a case, the "issuer" will be the person performing the acts and assuming the duties of depositor or manager according to the provisions of the trust or other agreement or instrument under which such securities are issued. This exception precisely fits a grantor trust transaction. The certificates are interests in the trust—an unincorporated entity not having a board of directors. Consequently, the seller as the person who deposited the assets into the trust and who assumes the duties of servicer to "manage" the trust's assets would be considered the "issuer" of the certificates under Section 2(4) of the Securities Act. The board of directors and appropriate officers of the seller will, therefore, be the persons required to sign the registration statement for the certificates, and the seller, rather than the trust, will have the liabilities imposed on issuers under Section 11 of the Securities Act.

It should be noted that, although the person who deposits the assets into the trust will be considered the "issuer" of the certificates for purposes of signing the registration statement and assuming issuer liability under the Securities Act, the SEC is not willing to accept the position that the certificates are "issued by" such person if such position would lead to the certificates being treated as an "exempt security" under Section 3 of the Act. For example, if a bank is the seller of a pool of automobile loan installment contracts to the trust, the bank will be the "issuer" of the certificates for purposes of the definition of "issuer" in Section 2(4) of the Securities Act. The SEC will not, however, accept an argument that the certificates are securities "issued or guaranteed" by a bank and, therefore, exempt from the registration and prospectus delivery requirements of Section 5 of the Securities Act. The SEC's position is premised on the certificates representing an interest solely in the assets owned by the trust. Because the bank is not obligated to make principal or interest payments on the certificates, the SEC is unwilling to treat the certificates as "issued" by the bank for purposes of Section 3(a)(2).

A registered offering of the certificates of a grantor trust will have to be registered on Form S-1. The certificates may not be registered on Form S-3 for two reasons. First, for purposes of determining the registrant requirements, even though the seller will be considered the "issuer" of the certificates under the Section 2(4) definition of "issuer," the trust, rather than the seller, is considered the registrant for purposes of the registrant requirement. The trust is not a "seasoned" reporting company under the Exchange Act and thus the registrant requirement is not met. Second, because the certificates represent an ownership interest in the assets of the trust, the certificates are considered equity securities. Because Form S-3 is generally only available for debt securities and nonconvertible preferred stock, the form will not be available for the certificates.

Although the certificates will have to be registered on Form S-1 as noted above, the SEC has been willing to allow elimination of disclosure items required by the form when the item is not applicable to an asset securitization transaction. For example, Form S-1 generally requires the inclusion of financial statements of the issuer. Although the seller is considered the issuer for purposes of signing the registration statement and assuming issuer liability under Section 11 of the Securities Act, the SEC has not required inclusion of the seller's financial statements in the registration statement. This position recognizes that the certificates evidence a right to payment from the assets of the trust and are not an obligation of the seller.

In preparing and filing the registration statement for the certificates, consideration should be given to the question whether any "separate security" is being offered. The issue is whether, in addition to the certificates, investors are being asked to invest in the risk of another security. Generally, in asset securitization transactions, a separate security will be offered. As discussed previously, asset securitization transactions customarily are structured so that the investor relies on the credit of the assets to be securitized and upon certain other credit components, such as the credit enhancement provided by a limited guaranty of the seller, a letter of credit or a surety bond, the reinvestment certainty of a guaranteed investment contract, or the prepayment risk assurance of a minimum principal payment agreement. To the extent that any of these items are present in a transaction, their status as a possible "separate security" must be considered. If it is determined that the item is a separate security, the separate security will itself be subject to the same type of Securities Act concerns as the certificates; that is, the separate security must also be registered unless it is an exempt security or is offered in an exempt transaction.

In a grantor trust asset securitization, because of the constraints imposed on the transaction to assure that the trust is a passive conduit entity, it is generally not possible to have significant timing differences between receipt of cash flow on the assets and the passing through of such cash flow to investors. Therefore, the investors take the risk of greater than anticipated prepayments. Consequently, there is no need for a guaranteed investment contract or a minimum principal payment agreement. On the other hand, in order for the certificates to be rated by one or more statistical rating agencies and to be marketed to investors at an interest rate level that is attractive to the seller, it is generally necessary to obtain a degree of credit enhancement to relieve the investors of credit risk with respect to the trust's assets. This customarily has meant that a letter of credit or surety bond of a prime quality banking institution, surety company, or financial guaranty company is issued in favor of the trust permitting the trustee to obtain funds thereunder equal to the value of any asset that becomes defaulted as defined in the pooling and servicing agreement, up to the amount of such letter of credit or surety bond. In cases where the seller is itself a prime quality institution, the seller may issue a limited guaranty (instead of a letter of credit or surety bond) providing the trust with a guaranty against default on a portion of the assets.

It is well established that a letter of credit or surety bond is a "separate security" for purposes of the Securities Act. Generally, this will not mean, however, that the letter of credit or the surety bond needs to be registered or sold in an exempt private placement. Instead, the letter of credit or the surety bond will likely be an "exempt security" under Section 3 of the Securities Act. If the letter of credit is issued by a "bank" or by a political subdivision of the United States (such as one of the Federal Home Loan Banks) it will be an exempt security under Section 3(a)(2) of the Securities Act; if it is issued by a savings and loan institution, it will be an exempt security under Section 3(a)(5). If the surety bond is issued by a surety company or a financial guaranty company subject to the supervision of a state insurance commissioner, bank commissioner, or any officer performing similar functions, it will be an exempt security under Section 3(a)(8).

For purposes of Section 3(a)(2), the term "bank" means any "national bank or any banking institution organized under the laws of any state, territory, or the District of Columbia, the business of which is substantially confined to banking and is supervised by the state or territorial banking commission or similar official." Accordingly, any letter of credit issued by a national bank or state chartered bank will be an exempt security under Section 3(a)(2). A number of letters of credit issued in asset securitization transactions are, however, issued by foreign banking institutions through branches based in the United States. For a number of years, the staff of the SEC had a consistent no-action letter position that, as long as the branch was subject to regulation by a banking regulatory body substantially equivalent to that which would be applicable to a similarly situated national or state bank, the staff would not recommend enforcement action against branch issuers of letters of credit that did not register them. Numerous foreign banking institutions have applied for and received no-action responses on the letters of credit of their U.S. branches. In September 1986, this no-action position was formalized into an interpretive release of the SEC. In the release, the SEC took the position that a U.S. branch or agency of a foreign bank will be considered a "bank" for purposes of Section 3(a)(2) "provided that the nature and extent of federal and/or state regulation and supervision of the particular branch or agency is substantially equivalent to that applicable to federal or state-chartered domestic banks doing business in the same jurisdiction." As a result of the interpretive release, it is no longer necessary to obtain a staff no-action letter for a letter of credit.

It is also well established that a limited guaranty is a "separate security" for purposes of the Security Act. Unless the limited guaranty is issued by a seller such as a bank whose securities are "exempt securities" under Section 3, or unless the limited guaranty is offered together with the certificates in an exempt private offering, the limited guaranty will have to be registered.

If the limited guaranty is to be registered together with the certificates, generally one document will be filed with the SEC. The document will consist of a combined Form S-1 registration statement for the certificates and whichever form of registration statement is appropriate for the limited guaranty. In selecting a registration statement form upon which to register the limited guaranty, more flexibility is possible than with the certificates. Specifically, the limited guaranty will probably meet the transaction requirement for use of Form S-3. Accordingly, if the seller meets the registrant requirement of Form S-3, the limited guaranty may be registered on Form S-3. In such circumstances, the document filed with the SEC would be a combination registration statement that would register the certificates on Form S-1 and the limited guaranty on Form S-3. If the seller does not, however, meet the registrant requirement for use of Form S-3, it would be necessary to register the limited guaranty on Form S-1. Consequently, the document filed with the SEC would be a combination registration statement that would register the certificates on Form S-1 and the limited guaranty on Form S-1.

Finance Subsidiary Transactions

Initial Analytical Concerns

As discussed previously, in a finance subsidiary transaction, the seller generally forms a wholly-owned finance subsidiary that issues finance subsidiary debt securities. The proceeds of the finance subsidiary debt securities are used to acquire the assets to be securitized from the seller, and these assets are assigned and pledged to the indenture trustee to secure the finance subsidiary debt securities.

For initial analytical purposes, it appears clear that the finance subsidiary debt securities are "securities" under the Securities Act and that the "issuer" of the finance subsidiary debt securities is the finance subsidiary. It is also clear that, because the finance subsidiary is generally a newly-formed, limited purpose subsidiary of the seller, in virtually all foreseeable circumstances the finance subsidiary will not be an entity whose securities are "exempt securities" under Section 3 of the Securities Act. Accordingly, the offer and sale of the finance subsidiary debt securities will be subject to the registration statement and prospectus delivery requirements of Section 5 of the Securities Act unless the finance subsidiary debt securities are sold in an exempt transaction under the Securities Act.

Private Placement Alternative

Like grantor trust certificates, the finance subsidiary debt securities may be offered and sold in an "exempt transaction." A number of finance subsidiary asset securitizations have been accomplished by private placements exempt by virtue of Section 4(2) of the Securities Act from the registration and prospectus delivery requirements of Section 5.

The steps that must be taken to assure that the offering and sale of the finance subsidiary debt securities is an exempt private placement are the same as those for private placement alternatives in the context of certificates issued by a grantor trust. The Regulation D "safe harbor" would also be available for the offering and sale of the finance subsidiary debt securities.

One note of caution is in order when considering a private placement: to the extent that the seller contemplates a number of asset securitizations through the same finance subsidiary, the doctrine of "integration" must be considered if certain of these transactions are made through one or more public offerings and one or more private placements. The doctrine should also be considered by a seller who effects asset securitizations through separate grantor trust transactions where certificates of the trusts are offered in both registered and private offerings. The doctrine of integration is an interpretive policy announced by the SEC. Under this policy, two otherwise distinct offerings of securities may, under certain circumstances, be considered as one offering. If all parts of the integrated offering have not been made in accordance with or an exemption from the registration and prospectus delivery provisions of Section 5, the offering would violate the Securities Act. For example, if an issuer does a registered public offering of its securities and closely follows such an offering with the private placement of similar securities, the doctrine of integration might apply to combine the two offerings into one. In that case, part of the integrated offering was made to the public in accordance with a registration statement, and part was made in a "private placement." The doctrine of integration would, however, destroy reliance on the private placement exemption because not all the securities offered in the integrated offering (that is, the publicly offered ones) would have been effected in compliance with the private placement requirements. Thus, since the entire integrated offering was neither made in accordance with an effective registration statement or an effective private placement, the offering would be in violation of Section 5 of the Securities Act.

Generally, the factors that should be considered in determining whether offers and sales of securities should be integrated are:

- Whether the sales of the separate securities are part of a single plan of financing
- Whether the sales involve issuance of the same class of securities
- Whether the sales have been made at or about the same time
- Whether the same type of consideration is received
- Whether the sales are made for the same general purpose

The SEC has, however, in Rule 152 specifically provided that an otherwise exempt private placement will remain exempt notwithstanding the subsequent decision of the issuer to make a public offering or to file a registration statement. Rule 152, by its terms, would only apply to a public offering that preceded a private placement

The precise scope of the application of the doctrine of integration to asset securitization transactions is not settled. There is some significant support for the notion that because the holders of separate issuances of asset-backed securities are relying on separate pools of assets, they are not buying the same class of securities. Where separate trusts are involved, it is also possible to argue that while the "issuer" of the certificates for purposes of signing the registration statement and for purposes of issuer liability under Section 11 of the Securities Act is the seller, for purposes of the doctrine of integration, the separate trusts should be respected as separate issuers and the doctrine should, therefore, be inapplicable. Until there is further guidance on this issue, sellers should be prudent and consider the application of the doctrine to their proposed transactions.

Registered Offerings

If the finance subsidiary debt securities are not sold in an exempt private placement or other exempt transaction, they will have to be sold in a registered offering. In order to comply with Section 5 of the Securities Act, a registration statement for the finance subsidiary debt securities will have to be filed with, and been declared effective by, the SEC and a prospectus meeting the requirements of the Securities Act will have to be prepared and utilized.

Unlike the grantor trust context, there is no difficulty determining who is the "issuer" of the finance subsidiary debt securities for purposes of the Securities Act. The finance subsidiary is clearly the issuer. Consequently, the principal issues will be which form of registration statement to use and whether any "separate" securities are present in the proposed transaction.

A registered offering of finance subsidiary debt securities will have to be registered on either Form S-3 or Form S-1. Form S-3 will be available to the finance subsidiary if the holder of its stock (the seller or an affiliate of the seller) meets the requirements for use of Form S-3. If the parent of the finance subsidiary meets the Form S-3 requirement of "seasoned" reporting company under the Exchange Act, the finance subsidiary will qualify for use of this form as a majority-owned subsidiary of such Form S-3 eligible parent for purposes of registering the finance subsidiary debt securities. The only significant condition that must be met prior to use by the finance subsidiary of Form S-3 is that the owner of the finance subsidiary's stock will have to be registered under the Exchange Act by filing Form 10.

Utilization of Form S-3 will have certain benefits. As discussed above, the form is a shorter form registration statement than Form S-1 and allows more flexibility in drafting the prospectus. The finance subsidiary would also be permitted to file the Form S-3 registration statement as a "shelf" registration statement under Rule 415. Whether a particular finance subsidiary involved in asset securitization transactions will utilize the shelf registration approach depends on a number of factors. If the finance subsidiary proposes to do a discrete "one time" offering of finance subsidiary debt securities, the "shelf" registration alternative does not offer any advantage. On the other hand, if the finance subsidiary contemplates a number of offerings of finance subsidiary debt securities collateralized by the same or similar types of assets, filing the Form S-3 registration statement and complying with Rule 415 would streamline the registration process and permit the finance subsidiary to respond quickly to securities market conditions.

In preparing and filing the registration statement for the finance subsidiary debt securities, consideration should be given to whether any "separate security" is being offered. As discussed earlier in the case of the certificates of a grantor trust, the issue is whether investors are being asked to invest in a security in addition to the finance subsidiary debt securities.

If the transaction involves a letter of credit, a surety bond, or a limited guaranty, the issue and the analysis are substantially the same as discussed above in the case of grantor trust asset securitization. An issuance of finance subsidiary debt securities may, however, also involve a guaranteed investment contract or a minimum principal payment agreement.

Although it might be argued that a guaranteed investment contract or a minimum principal payment agreement does not constitute a "security" for purposes of the Securities Act, the more prudent approach is to conclude that they are "securities" under the act and proceed to determine if they are "exempt" securities or if they have to be registered.

Whether a guaranteed investment contract or a minimum principal payment agreement is an exempt security under Section 3 of the Securities Act will depend principally on who is the provider of the agreement. If the provider of the guaranteed investment contract or the minimum principal payment agreement is a "bank" as defined in Section 3(a)(2) or a U.S. branch or agency of a foreign bank meeting the conditions of the interpretive release, the guaranteed investment contract or the minimum principal payment agreement will be an exempt security under Section 3(a)(2) and may be offered along with the finance subsidiary debt securities without registration.

If the provider of the guaranteed investment contract or the minimum principal payment agreement is a U.S. insurance company, the guaranteed investment contract or the minimum principal payment agreement should be an exempt security under Section 3(a)(8) of the Securities Act, provided the contract is considered an "insurance policy" within the meaning of Section 3(a)(8) of the Securities Act. In the case of guaranteed investment contracts, the SEC has issued an interpretive release defining the circumstances in which a guaranteed investment contract issued by an insurance company will be considered to be within the meaning of Section 3(a)(8). The type of guaranteed investment contract usually entered into in asset securitization transactions should qualify under the interpretive release and should, therefore, be an exempt security under Section 3(a)(8). Although there is no similar interpretation for minimum principal payment agreements issued by an insurance company, the same type of analysis should apply as set forth in the interpretation for guaranteed investment contracts. Because the parties intend the minimum principal payment agreement to be a kind of insurance against an unanticipated rate of prepayment and do not intend the agreement to be an investment in the insurance company providing the agreement, the minimum principal payment agreement should be regarded as an exempt security under Section 3(a)(8).

If the provider of the guaranteed investment contract or the minimum principal payment agreement is not an entity whose securities are exempt securities under Section 3 of the Securities Act, the guaranteed investment contract or the minimum principal payment agreement would either have to be issued in an exempt private placement of the finance subsidiary debt securities or be registered. The considerations applicable to the registration of a guaranteed investment contract or a minimum principal payment agreement, such as which registration statement to use, would be substantially identical to those applicable to the registration of a limited guaranty.

Asset-Backed Securities Issuer

As discussed earlier, in an asset-backed securities issuer transaction, a number of sellers generally sell assets to be securitized to a limited-purpose company that is unaffiliated with the sellers. The asset-backed securities issuer is generally owned by an investment banking firm that is active in the sale of asset-backed securities. The proceeds of the securities are used to acquire the assets to be securitized from the seller and such assets are assigned and pledged by the issuer to the indenture trustee to back the debt securities.

For initial analytical purposes, it is clear that the asset-backed securities issuer debt securities are "securities" under the Securities Act and that the "issuer" of the securities is the asset-backed securities issuer.

It is also clear that, because the issuer is generally a limited-purpose subsidiary of an investment banking firm, in virtually all foreseeable circumstances the issuer will not be an entity whose securities are "exempt securities" under Section 3 of the Securities Act. Accordingly, the offer and sale of the securities will be subject to the registration statement and prospectus delivery requirements of Section 5 of the Securities Act unless they are sold in an exempt transaction under the Securities Act.

Private Placement Alternative
As in the case of grantor trust certificates and finance subsidiary debt securities, the asset-backed securities issuer debt securities may be offered and sold in an exempt private placement.

The steps that must be taken in order to assume that the offering and sale of the asset-backed securities issued debt securities is an exempt private placement, including consideration of the doctrine of integration, are the same as for certificates and finance subsidiary debt securities. The Regulation D "safe harbor" would also be available for the offering of the asset-backed securities issuer debt securities.

Registered Offering
If the asset-backed securities issuer debt securities are not sold in an exempt private placement or other exempt transaction, they would have to be sold in a registered offering. In order to comply with Section 5 of the Securities Act, a registration statement for the securities will have to be filed with and be declared effective by the SEC, and a prospectus meeting the requirements of the Securities Act will have to be prepared and utilized.

The asset-backed securities issuer will be the "issuer" of the securities. The principal issues to be considered in registering its securities are the form of registration statement to use and whether any "separate" securities are present in the proposed transaction.

A registered offering of asset-backed securities issuer debt securities will have to be registered on Form S-3 or Form S-1. Form S-3 will be available to the issuer if the holder of its stock meets the requirements for use of Form S-3. If the parent of the asset-backed securities issuer meets the Form S-3 requirement of a "seasoned" reporting company under the Exchange Act, the issuer will qualify for use of the form as a majority-owned subsidiary of such Form S-3 eligible parent for purposes of registering the securities. The only significant condition that must be met prior to use by the asset-backed securities issuer of Form S-3 is that the owner of the issuer's stock will be required to register the stock under the Exchange Act by filing Form 10.

Utilization of Form S-3 will have certain benefits. As discussed previously, the form is a shorter form registration statement and the issuer would also be permitted to file the Form S-3 registration statement as a "shelf" registration statement under Rule 415.

It should be noted that the flexibility permitted through use of a shelf registration on Form S-3 has resulted in the establishment of a number of asset-backed securities issuers. The First Boston Corporation, Salomon Brothers, Inc, Merrill Lynch Capital Markets, and Shearson Lehman Hutton Inc have each established an asset-backed securities issuer, which has filed a shelf registration statement on Form S-3. These issuers offer clients of the investment bank sponsors a ready method by which the clients can access the asset-backed securities market. Because the issuers have effective shelf registration statements, sellers of assets can access the market through these issuers without themselves going through the registration process.

As in the case of asset-backed securities issued by a grantor trust or a finance subsidiary, in preparing and filing the registration statement for the asset-backed securities issuer debt securities, consideration should be given to whether any "separate" security is being offered. If the transaction involves a letter of credit, a surety bond, a limited guaranty, a guaranteed investment contract, or a minimum principal payment agreement, the issues and analysis are substantially the same as discussed earlier in the case of a trust or finance subsidiary asset securitization.

The Securities Exchange Act of 1934

Introduction

Section 12 of the Securities Exchange Act of 1934, as amended provides for the registration of securities traded on national securities exchanges and of securities of issuers whose equity securities are "widely held." Issuers whose securities are registered under Section 12 of the Exchange Act must file with the SEC the periodic reports required according to Section 13 of the Exchange Act.

Generally, the provisions of Section 12 will not be applicable to the trust, finance subsidiary, or asset-backed securities issuer. First, the certificates, finance subsidiary debt securities, or asset-backed securities issuer debt securities are generally not listed on a national securities exchange. Second, the equity securities of the trust, the finance subsidiary, or the asset-backed securities issuer are generally not held by the number of holders required under Section 12 to subject it to the registration requirements as a "publicly held" company.

Section 15(d) of the Exchange Act, however, provides that each issuer that has filed a registration statement that has become effective under the Securities Act shall file with the SEC the periodic reports required under Section 13 of the Exchange Act for a security registered according to Section 12. Consequently, when a trust, finance subsidiary, or asset-backed securities issuer offers registered asset-backed securities, the provisions of Section 15 require that it file periodic reports with the SEC under Section 13 of the Exchange Act. If the offering of asset-backed securities is a nonregistered private placement, the issuer does not need to file reports under the Exchange Act.

Reporting Requirements

Section 13 requires the trust, the finance subsidiary, or the asset-backed securities issuer to file annual, quarterly, and sometimes monthly reports. The SEC has prescribed three forms to be filed to comply with the periodic reporting requirement—Form 10-K for the annual reporting requirement, Form 10-Q for the quarterly reporting requirement, and Form 8-K for the monthly reporting requirement.

Forms 10-K, 10-Q, and 8-K provide detailed instructions on the information required in the annual, quarterly, and monthly reports. A review of the forms and the instructions that accompany them reveals that much of the information required does not apply to an asset-backed securities issuer. In the case of certificates issued by a trust, the trust is not engaged in any business activity other than the passive holding of the assets to be securitized and the "passing-through" to the holders of the certificates payments from the assets held by the trust. In the case of a finance subsidiary, such companies are generally special purpose companies whose activities are limited solely to the issuance of the finance subsidiary debt securities backed by the assets to be securitized. Although an asset-backed securities issuer may issue more than one series of asset-backed securities issuer debt securities, its activities are specifically limited to the issuance of such securities and the acquisition of the assets to be securitized. In addition, the holders of a series of securities issued by the asset-backed securities issuer are generally entitled to look solely to the assets purchased with the proceeds of such securities.

Because the business activity of the trust, the finance subsidiary, and the asset-backed securities issuer is limited, and because the holders of securities issued by such entities look to the creditworthiness of the assets to be securitized and to any credit enhancement, most items required in Forms 10-K, 10-Q, and 8-K are largely irrelevant to securities issued by such entities. Accordingly, the SEC has routinely granted requests for modification of the Section 13 reporting requirements for issuers of asset-backed securities. Such requests have been filed according to Section 12(h) of the Exchange Act or as "no-action" requests.

Section 12(h) permits the SEC to exempt in whole or in part any issuer from the provisions of Section 13 or 15(d) of the Exchange Act. Beginning with the first mortgage-pass-through certificate offering by Bank of America in 1978, a number of issuers have filed exemptive requests under Section 12(h). In these requests, the issuers have asked to be relieved from a number of the items required in the annual report on Form 10-K. In addition, issuers that are trusts have often requested relief from the obligation to file quarterly reports on Form 10-Q and have instead agreed to file on Form 8-K the monthly servicer reports relating to the assets held by the trust. Issuers that are finance subsidiaries or asset-backed securities issuers have generally also requested relief under Section 12(h) of the Exchange Act from compliance with a number of the items required in the quarterly reports on Form 10-Q.

Currently, the practice of exempting asset-backed securities issuers from compliance with a number of the reporting requirements of Forms 10-K and 10-Q is firmly accepted by the SEC. Consequently, a number of recent issuers of asset-backed securities have not filed exemptive requests under Section 12(h). Such issuers have instead filed "no-action" letters with the staff of the SEC. In such requests, the issuers have indicated the modifications they propose to make to the periodic reports they will file and have requested that the staff advise them that it would not recommend enforcement action if the issuers comply with their reporting obligations. A number of such "no-action" requests have been granted.

Termination of Reporting Obligation
Section 15(d) of the Exchange Act provides that the issuer's obligation to file periodic reports with the SEC shall be automatically suspended for any fiscal year other than the fiscal year within which the registration

statement is filed if, at the beginning of such fiscal year, the securities of each class to which the registration statement relates are held of record by fewer than 300 persons. Accordingly, if the certificates, the finance subsidiary debt securities or the asset-backed securities issuer debt securities are owned of record by fewer than 300 persons as of the commencement of the fiscal year of the trust, the finance subsidiary, or the asset-backed securities issuer, the duty to continue filing periodic reports will be suspended. In most asset securitizations, the securities are held by fewer than 300 persons.

The Investment Company Act

Introduction

Section 7 of the Investment Company Act of 1940, as amended (the "Investment Company Act"), provides that it shall be unlawful for any investment company having a board of directors, or any depositor or trustee of or underwriter for an investment company not having a board of directors, to offer for sale, sell, or deliver after sale, any security or interest in a security, if such security or interest will be made the subject of a public offering, unless the investment company is registered with the SEC pursuant to Section 8 of the Investment Company Act. Registration requires continuous compliance with the relevant provisions of the Investment Company Act and the rules and regulations thereunder. Because such compliance is costly and time consuming, the critical inquiry under the Investment Company Act in the context of an asset securitization transaction is not whether or how to comply with the statute, as is the case under the Securities Act and the Exchange Act, but how best to avoid compliance. The Investment Company Act, as it relates to asset securitization transactions, is, therefore, best understood in terms of its exemptions and "safe harbors."

Of course, the need to find an exemption from compliance with the Investment Company Act or a "safe harbor" thereunder is necessarily premised on a conclusion that the issuing entity is, in fact, an "investment" company. Accordingly, a few definitions are in order.

The Investment Company Act defines an "investment company" as one of two types of entities relevant to this discussion. Section 3(a)(1) of the Investment Company Act defines an investment company generally as any issuer that "is or holds itself out as engaged primarily, or proposes to engage primarily, in the business of investing, reinvesting, or trading in securities." Section 3(a)(3) of the Investment Company Act defines an investment company as any issuer that "is engaged or proposes to engage in the business of investing, reinvesting, owning, holding, or trading in securities and owns or proposes to acquire investment securities having a value exceeding 40 percent of the value of its total assets (exclusive of government securities and cash items) on an unconsolidated basis." "Investment securities" are defined, for purposes of Section 3(a)(3), as any "security" other than a government security, a security issued by an employees' securities company or a security issued by majority-owned subsidiaries of the owner (issuer) that are not investment companies.

A Section 3(a)(1) investment company must be "primarily engaged" in some form of investment activity. Although it could be said that a grantor trust, finance subsidiary, or asset-backed securities issuer had "invested" in securities, the activities of these entities would not likely satisfy this test. It is more likely that such an issuer would be considered a "prima facie" investment company, that is, an investment company under Section 3(a)(3).

An issuer may be considered a "prima facie" investment company even if it engages in no activity other than the issuance of a security. Unlike the activity test imposed by Section 3(a)(1), Section 3(a)(3) imposes an "asset" test that can be satisfied by the mere "holding" of securities. As a result, an entity owning a static pool of "investment securities," such as a grantor trust, or an entity pledging a static pool to an indenture trustee, such as a finance subsidiary or an asset-backed securities issuer, would be considered a "prima facie" investment company, provided that it was an "issuer" of a "security" and held "investment securities" with a sufficient value relative to the value of its total assets. Accordingly, two additional introductory concepts under the Investment Company Act are relevant to asset securitization—the definition of the terms "issuer" and "security." It is also important to notice that these terms have a somewhat broader scope under the Investment Company Act than under the Securities Act.

"Security" is defined in Section 2(a)(36) of the Investment Company Act and is given the same broad definition as in the Securities Act. Significantly, however, the Investment Company Act does not "exempt" securities. Because the nature of what constitutes a security differs, an "exempt security" under the Securities Act would often be considered a security and, as a result, an investment security for purposes of the Investment Company Act. It is crucial to an understanding of the Investment Company Act to realize that this statute is concerned primarily with the nature of the issuing entity's activity and assets, rather than with the nature of the security issued, as is the case under the Securities Act.

The term "issuer" is defined in Section 2(a)(22) of the Investment Company Act as "every person who issues or proposes to issue any security, or has outstanding any security which it has issued." The definition differs in two significant ways from that in the Securities Act: 1) it does not incorporate the references to depositor or manager of a trust, as in the Securities Act, a fact that assumes importance when considering the availability of exemptions; and 2) it maintains issuer status after the security has been issued, which indicates the Investment Company Act's concern with activity and asset base on an ongoing basis rather than at a single point in time.

What emerges from an understanding of the relevant definitions under the Investment Company Act is the fact that, because the issuer in an asset securitization transaction (whether a grantor trust, a finance subsidiary, or an asset-backed securities issuer) issues a "security" and holds "receivables" of some kind, which are both "securities" and "investment securities" within the Investment Company Act, an exemption from compliance therewith or a "safe-harbor" thereunder must be sought.

The Investment Company Act provides for a number of exemptions and "safe harbors." Section 3(b) generally exempts issuers that are "primarily engaged" in an activity other than investment activity. Rule 3a-1 provides a "safe harbor" from compliance with the Investment Company Act for prima facie investment companies. Section 3(c)(1) generally exempts issuers of privately-placed securities. Section 3(c)(2) exempts entities engaged in underwriting or operating as brokers or dealers. Section 3(c)(3) exempts, among others, banks, insurance companies, and savings and loan associations. Section 3(c)(5) exempts any issuer "primarily engaged" in "sales financing" activity and not engaged in the business of issuing redeemable securities. Section 6(c) provides for an exemptive order process whereby the SEC is empowered to exempt an issuer otherwise subject to compliance with the Investment Company Act on the terms and conditions set forth in the exemptive order. Rule 3a-5 provides a "safe harbor" to a finance subsidiary, provided that the security issued by such finance subsidiary is unconditionally guaranteed by its parent. Each exemption and "safe harbor" will now be considered in context of an asset securitization transaction.

The 3(b) Exemption and the Rule 3a-1 Safe Harbor

The 3(b) exemption is available to issuers presumed to be investment companies under Section 3(a)(3), and provides, essentially that, in spite of the fact that more than 40 percent of the value of an issuer's assets consist of investment securities, such an issuer will not be considered an investment company if it is "primarily engaged," directly or indirectly, in other activities. For purposes of the Section 3(b) exemption, the SEC considers five factors in applying the "primarily engaged" test. The agency focuses principally on the issuer's asset base, sources of income, historical development, public representations of policy, and present activity to determine if the issuer's primary activity is not investment activity. Generally, if at least 55 percent of an issuer's income is derived from sources other than investment securities and the other factors indicate significant operations other than investment activity, the Section 3(b) exemption will be available, despite the fact that a significant portion of the issuer's assets consists of investment securities. The "safe harbor" under Rule 3a-1 Investment Company Act tightens this test, by providing that no more than 45 percent of the issuer's asset base may consist of investment securities. The Section 3(b) exemption and the Rule 3a-1 "safe harbor" are primarily utilized by operating companies that have significant securities portfolios and would be unavailable in a grantor trust transaction due to the restraints imposed by federal tax law upon the trust's activities. The argument would also be unavailable to a finance subsidiary or an asset-backed securities issuer due to the limited nature of their assets and sources of income as well as their limited purpose.

The (3)(c)(2) and 3(c)(3) Exemptions

The 3(c)(2) and 3(c)(3) exemptions are also of limited utility in asset securitization transactions. Section 3(c)(2) exempts underwriters and broker-dealers, who typically hold large positions in investment securities and would otherwise be considered investment companies. Section 3(c)(3) exempts, among others, banks, insurance companies, and savings and loans, which are otherwise subject to regulation. However, such exemptions would not be available to an asset-backed securities issuer formed by an underwriter, a finance subsidiary formed by a bank, or a grantor trust formed by either of them. This is because each entity is a separate issuer, and an exemption available to a sponsor or parent is not available to an issuer by attribution. Although an exemption would be available to a direct issuance of securitized assets by an underwriter or bank, accounting, tax, regulatory, and rating agency considerations often make this an undesirable alternative.

The "Receivables" Exemption

The exemption under the Investment Company Act most frequently sought by issuers of securitized assets is provided by Sections 3(c)(5)(A) and (B), the so-called "receivables" exemption. The "receivables" exemption generally exempts an issuer that is not engaged in the business of issuing "redeemable" securities and is "primarily engaged" in the business of "purchasing or otherwise acquiring notes, drafts, acceptances, open accounts receivable, and other obligations representing all or a part of the sales price of merchandise, insurance or services," or "making loans to manufacturers, wholesalers and retailers of, and to prospective purchasers of, specified merchandise, insurance or services."

The exemption first requires that the security issued not be "redeemable." A "redeemable security" is defined in Section 2(a)(32) of the Investment Company Act as "any security, other than short-term paper, under the terms of which the holder, upon its presentation to the issuer, is entitled (whether absolutely or only out of surplus) to receive approximately his proportionate share of the issuer's current net assets, or the cash equivalent thereof." Most asset securitization transactions, whether involving the issuance of a certificate, a finance subsidiary debt security, or an asset-backed securities issuer debt security, are structured to provide for redeemable security. The redemption feature is often referred to as a "clean-up call," that is, a redemption at the issuer's option, when the principal balance of either the assets securitized or the security issued declines to a specified percentage (typically 5 to 10 percent) of the initial balance. However, because the security is not redeemable at the option of the holder, the existence of a clean-up call does not destroy the availability of the exemption.

The second and more complicated requirement is that the issuer be "primarily engaged" in "sales financing" activity; that is, the business of purchasing or acquiring "receivables." This requirement involves the composition and nature of the issuer's assets and the nature of the issuer's activities.

Deciding whether the issuer of a securitized asset satisfies the "sales financing" requirement involves a determination that the asset to be securitized is, in fact, a "receivable." As previously discussed, the majority of asset securitizations to date have involved assets such as installment obligations for the purchase of motor vehicles, credit card receivables, and lease receivables, and the determination has most often been made in that context.

There is little dispute that installment obligations for the purchase of motor vehicles constitute "receivables" within the meaning of the "receivables exemption"; however, the refinancing of such an obligation may not qualify as a receivable, unless the loan can be traced to the repayment of a receivable. The same is true of credit card receivables, which are typically generated with a purchase of merchandise; however, if cash advances represent a significant percentage of the overall portfolio, it may be difficult, if not impossible, to relate the application of the cash advance to the purchase of merchandise.

There is also little dispute that a "sales-type" or "financing" lease[1] qualifies as a receivable and that an "operating" or "true" lease,[2] in the absence of other factors evidencing sales financing activity, does not.

A detailed discussion of the distinction between leases that qualify as "receivables" and those that do not is beyond the scope of this chapter. What is important is to understand that the analysis of a lease as a "receivable" is a complicated one and that, unless the parties to a lease securitization transaction have been satisfied that the lease operates to "sell" the leased property or is otherwise related to sales financing activity, another exemption must be sought. As a result, a number of lease receivable transactions have been done as private placements.

If the issuer satisfies the "sales financing" requirement, the determination must then be made that the issuer is "primarily engaged" in such activity. The "primarily engaged" test under Section 3(c)(5) differs

---

[1] A sales-type or financing lease is, generally, a lease that either transfers ownership of the leased property to the lessee by the end of the lease term, contains provisions for a purchase option at nominal consideration at the end of the lease term for a price less than the booked residual value of the leased property, is for a term equal to or greater than 75 percent of the estimated useful life of the leased property, or provides for rental and other minimum loan payments equal to or greater than 90 percent of the fair value of the leased property less any investment tax credit retained by the lessor.

[2] An operating or true lease is generally a lease that does not contain any of the characteristics of the "sales-type" or "financing" lease and typically provides for a purchase option at a price equal to the booked residual value of the leased property at a time other than at or near the end of the property's estimated useful life.

somewhat from the test under Section 3(b) and Rule 3a-1 in that it looks to the assets that are related to "sales financing" activity as a percentage of total assets, rather than to the overall activity and the sources of income of the issuing entity.

The SEC has held that an issuer is "primarily engaged" in "sales financing" activity for purposes of Section 3(c)(5) if at least 55 percent of its assets are "receivables" of the type discussed above. The 55 percent test applies to an asset base, rather than to a transaction. Accordingly, a finance subsidiary or asset-backed securities issuer would not become an investment company because the "receivables" included in the collateral securing a particular series of debt were less than 55 percent of the total value of the collateral securing the obligation. However, because the assets of trusts formed by the same depositor are not integrated for purposes of the 55 percent test, the assets of each grantor trust would be separately considered.

The "primarily engaged" test is also concerned with the composition of the remaining 45 percent of an issuer's assets, which must be, if not "receivables," at least "receivables-related"—that is, related to the overall "sales financing" activity of the issuer. Although the criteria for what constitutes a "receivables-related" asset have never been clearly established, it is generally believed that the temporary investment of receivable proceeds (for instance, under a guaranteed investment contract) pending distribution or reinvestment in additional receivables and the existence of credit enhancement, such as a letter of credit, limited guaranty, or surety bond, are sufficiently related to the issuer's overall "sales financing" activity as not to destroy the availability of the "receivables" exemption.

There are a number of assets, such as franchise fees and syndication payments that have been or are being securitized. However, it is often determined that assets of this kind are insufficiently related to sales financing activity to qualify as "receivables" under the "receivables" exemption. Assets of this type are most often securitized under the "private placement" exemption.

The "Private Placement" Exemption

The exemption provided by Section 3(c)(1) under the Investment Company Act—the "private placement" exemption—is the exemption typically sought when it has been determined that no other exemption or safe harbor is available. Compliance with the Securities Act private placement exemption is important to ensure the availability of the Investment Company Act private placement exemption; however, as discussed more fully below, the Investment Company Act exemption is more limited. As a result, an asset securitization transaction that qualified as a private placement under the Securities Act might not qualify as such under the Investment Company Act.

Section 3(c)(1) of the Investment Company Act exempts "any issuer whose outstanding securities (other than short-term paper) are beneficially owned by not more than one hundred persons and which is not making and does not presently propose to make a public offering of its securities. . . ." As a result, a private placement under the Investment Company Act must satisfy two requirements: 1) there must be a "nonpublic" offering, and 2) 100 or fewer holders must beneficially own the issuer's outstanding securities. However, as is often the case, what appears simple is often complicated.

The "nonpublic" offering requirement is not difficult to satisfy. Generally, a transaction structured to comply with the private placement exemption under the Securities Act will qualify as a "nonpublic" offering under Section 3(c)(1). However, as a result of the "100 or fewer beneficial owners" test and the ongoing nature of the "outstanding securities" test, the test is somewhat tighter. As discussed in more detail below, care must be taken to ensure that the sale or subsequent transfer of a security to a sophisticated investor does not trigger the "attribution" rules in Sections 3(c)(1)(A) and (B).

It is important to stress what has been implied before: the "private placement" exemptions under the Securities Act and the Investment Company Act are not coterminous. A security may often be privately placed under the Securities Act even though an exemption under the Investment Company Act (most often the "receivables" exemption) is available. However, if another exemption from compliance under the Investment Company Act is not available, a security cannot be offered and sold to the public, or subsequently transferred, in accordance with an effective registration statement under the Securities Act. A public offering at any point in time would destroy the Section 3(c)(1) exemption.

The "100 or fewer beneficial owners" requirement is somewhat more complicated as a result of the application of the attribution rules. A careful examination of this requirement is essential to an understanding of the "private placement" exemption under the Investment Company

Act. It is also important to realize that integration and aggregation rules are applicable as well, which may influence the choice of the issuing entity in an asset securitization transaction.

The "100 or fewer beneficial owners" requirement first tests "outstanding" securities. The "outstanding" test is not especially worrisome in the case of a grantor trust transaction, unless offerings by discrete issuers are integrated for purposes of the test. However, in the case of an offering of securities by a finance subsidiary or an asset-backed securities issuer, discrete series of outstanding debt would be aggregated. In addition, the holders of the issuer's equity securities would be included in the computation. In either case, unless *all* the issuer's outstanding securities are beneficially owned by 100 or fewer persons, the inquiry need go no further. The "private placement" exemption will be unavailable. Unfortunately, the "100 or fewer beneficial owners" test is not always a matter of counting to one hundred. If it appears, at first glance, that the requirement will be satisfied, the attribution rules should then be applied.

The attribution rules under Section 3(c)(1)(A) provide generally that beneficial ownership of an issuer's securities by an entity is deemed to be beneficial ownership by one person unless the subject entity owns 10 percent or more of the outstanding voting securities of the issuer. In such a case, beneficial ownership by the subject company is attributed to the holders of the entity's outstanding securities, and, for purposes of the "100 or fewer beneficial owners" requirement, each holder of the subject entity's securities would be deemed to be a holder of the issuer's securities. The result, if the entity was widely held and the "value" exception described below was not satisifed, would be the loss of the private placement exemption.

The attribution rules do contain an exception, however. Attribution does not apply, if, as of the date of the most recent acquisition by the subject entity of securities of the issuer, the value (generally the fair market value) of all securities privately placed under the Investment Company Act (securities of issuers that have qualified for the "private placement" exemption under the Investment Company Act) held by the entity constitutes 10 percent or less of the value of such entity's total assets.

A final word about the operation of the attribution rules is in order. The basic test under Section 3(c)(1) is that of ownership of an issuer's "securities." The attribution rules test ownership of "voting securities." A "voting security" is defined in Section 2(a)(42) of the

Investment Company Act as "any security presently entitling the owner or holder thereof to vote for the election of directors of the Company." The definition has little meaning in the case of an issuance of certificates by a grantor trust, which in reality, is nothing but a pool of assets and therefore has no board of directors. For this reason, a certificate is not generally viewed as a "voting security" for purposes of the attribution rules. The definition has more meaning in the case of an issuance of debt by a finance subsidiary or an asset-backed securities issuer, which are both typically limited purpose corporations, have boards of directors, and issue voting securities. The attribution rules would apply to the issuer's voting stock. As the number of issuers formed by a sponsor increases, the likelihood of the application of the attribution rules does as well.

A private placement has certain inefficiencies, and because of the illiquid nature of a privately placed security, pricing is often adversely affected. As a result, if an exemption is otherwise unavailable, or if there is doubt as to an exemption's availability, a Section 6(c) exemptive order may be sought.

The Section 6(c) Exemption

Section 6(c) of the Investment Company Act provides that the SEC, by rules and regulations or by order upon application, may grant an exemption from compliance with part or all of the Investment Company Act. The SEC has promulgated a number of rules according to this statutory grant of authority, none of which are applicable to an asset securitization transaction. As a result, an issuer to which an exemption is otherwise unavailable must apply for 6(c) exemptive order.

For several reasons, the Section 6(c) exemptive order process is of limited use in asset securitization transactions. The process requires extensive negotiation with the SEC and, as a result, is time consuming. In addition, even if an exemptive order is granted, the order benefits only the applicant and typically places severe restraints on its flexibility. Because the final structure of an asset securitization is often not determined until immediately prior to pricing, 6(c) exemptions are not applied for unless it is believed to be absolutely necessary.

More importantly, there is presently little assurance that a 6(c) application will be granted. The SEC has recently taken the position that as a result of the promulgation of Rule 3a-5 under the Investment Company Act, the granting of a 6(c) exemptive order will be conditioned upon the presence of an unconditional guaranty of the security to be issued by the entity sponsoring the issuer. The policy seems to reflect a conservative position and evidences a desire to proceed cautiously in the case of asset securitization. It is unclear whether the SEC will change its position in the near future. As a result, the filing of a Section 6(c) application should be considered only as a last resort. The same could be said of the Rule 3a-5 safe harbor.

The Rule 3a-5 Safe Harbor

Rule 3a-5 provides a safe harbor for finance subsidiaries organized to finance the operations of domestic or foreign companies. At first glance, it would appear to be of great utility to an issuer of a securitized asset. However, a number of features of the rule make it of little, if any, use to an issuer of a securitized asset.

"Finance subsidiaries" are defined generally under Rule 3a-5 as corporations that are wholly-owned subsidiaries of a parent company. As a result, the Rule 3a-5 safe harbor would not appear to be available to a grantor trust. The safe harbor would be available to a finance subsidiary or an asset-backed securities issuer. However, the rule severely restricts the assets that are eligible investments for a finance subsidiary to government securities, securities of its parent or if entities controlled by its parent, and debt securities exempted under Section 3(a)(3) of the Securities Act (generally, commercial paper and other short-term debt obligations arising from current transactions). Because most assets securitized to date would be ineligible under this requirement, the safe harbor provided by Rule 3a-5 would be unavailable. Even if an asset of the nature permitted under Rule 3a-5 were to be securitized, the requirement that the security be supported by a full recourse guaranty of its parent has potentially adverse tax, regulatory, and accounting implications. Moreover, a security backed by such a guaranty would likely be rated on the basis of the parent's credit rating rather than on the credit quality of the assets to be securitized. As a result, the Rule 3a-5 safe harbor is not likely to find any issuers seeking its shelter.

Acknowledgment

The author is grateful to Salvatore Palazzolo, an associate at Skadden, Arps, Slate, Meagher & Flom, for his assistance in the preparation of this chapter.

PART 3

THE ROLE OF DEPOSITORY INSTITUTIONS

CHAPTER 13

THE BANK ROLE

Robert I. Reich
President, Marine Midland Automotive Financial Corp.
Charles W. Sewright, Jr.
President, Marine Midland Mortgage Corp.

THE EVOLUTION OF THE BANK ROLE

There was a time when the role of banks as deposit gatherers and lenders was relatively easy for the consumer to grasp. Banks held the funds of depositors for safe keeping and quite often paid the depositor a fee or interest for the right to loan those funds to others. To generate a profit they charged borrowers interest at a spread over the interest they paid depositors. However, the role of banks has evolved over the years to where they are presently major sellers of assets or loans through securitization.

Banks have traditionally been "portfolio lenders." That is, they made loans and held them in their own portfolios as assets to earn the interest being paid by borrowers. The loans were typically generated within the banks themselves or through their branch offices. Since the primary responsibility of the banks was to safeguard the funds of their depositors, their livelihood and survival depended on their ability to make quality loans that would be repaid, thereby avoiding defaults, charge-offs, and erosion of their deposit bases. To minimize credit risk, the banking industry developed skills and systems to evaluate creditworthiness. Even with the evolution of improved credit underwriting skills, portfolio lenders still kept loans on their books. In so doing, banks were also retaining the credit risk for as long as the loan was outstanding. Therefore, banks improved their collection skills to control and manage the outstanding risk as much as possible. This has resulted in collection systems that not only recorded the repayment of a loan, but also aged portfolios and tracked information such as late payments and delinquencies. Such information helps to monitor the payment habits of individual borrowers and allows bank management to aggressively pursue delinquent payments in a timely and consistent manner so as to better control default exposure.

The development of credit collection information also had the side effect of allowing the depositors, stockholders, and investment community to begin measuring the effectiveness of banks in the critical areas of credit risk assessment and management. Since the safety of the funds of depositors and the perceived effectiveness of management could be significantly affected by the ability of banks to manage credit risk and collect outstanding loan balances, banks began to develop intricate and very effective servicing capabilities. The evolution of servicing obviously included the development of collection systems, extensive databases of borrower and payment information, and tracking reports. They also developed the ability to better protect collateral securing the loans using security perfection techniques, document control systems, collateral repossession, and resale. Banks became experts not only in evaluating credit risk, but also in managing collections and servicing the loan portfolio. This evolution set the stage for a new development in banking: the ability not just to sell loans to accelerate the collection of cash prior to the scheduled maturity date, but to sell loans receivable for the principal balance outstanding while continuing to service or collect them for a fee.

Although banks have bought loan portfolios when acquiring other banks during expansion or have sold loans to free-up cash in order to avoid liquidity crises, the wholesale selling of consumer loan portfolios accelerated after bank deregulation. Deregulation invited new competition, giving increased access to the relatively low-cost source of funds that had previously been the competitive bastion of the banking industry. With increased competition for depositor wealth, banks have found it increasingly difficult to attract enough deposits to maintain regulatory liqudity and reserve levels required to support lending activities. One solution to this problem is to decrease or discontinue lending during periods of insufficient deposits. A better choice, however, may be to sell loans to obtain cash for continued lending, while retaining the right to service the loans for the investor or purchaser for fee income. This "asset sale" approach was first popularized in mortgage banking and since the early 1970s has developed into a major, efficient source of funds and servicing fees. Similarly, banks began to sell other loan assets or receivables to liquefy their balance sheets. By selling loans and other assets, banks have been able to reduce their outstanding balance sheet loan levels (and therefore capitalization and reserve requirements), giving them the ability to continue their lending capability without the need for additional deposits or capital infusion.

Banks first began selling nonmortgage receivables via the traditional whole loan route. This approach typically required banks to locate an interested buyer of the portfolio, quite often with the help of a broker or a merchant banker. Extensive pricing and contract negotiations were usually involved, with each transaction being somewhat unique, given the needs of both the purchaser and seller. With increased sale activity came the need for "settlement reporting" by the seller/servicer to the investing or purchasing institution. The settlement reports supplied appropriate information and reports to allow investors to track the performance of portfolio collections, delinquencies, defaults, and recoveries, enabling them to assure themselves that their investment and attendant credit risk were being properly managed. Because of the unique structure being used for each asset sale, it became apparent that development of a more standardized product structure was needed to provide consistent, cost effective settlement reporting requirements for institutions that were frequent sellers. In addition, and perhaps more importantly, a more standardized product was needed if the nonmortgage receivables market was ever to gain the market efficiencies and investor confidence enjoyed by its more established cousin, the mortgage-backed securities market.

With whole loan sales and attendant settlement reporting systems becoming more prevalent, the stage was set for the next step in the evolution of banks as marketers and sellers of loans and servicing skills: the securitization of asset sales. It became apparent to those institutions in the forefront of the asset sales revolution that if such an active secondary market could develop for mortgages, the same thing could happen for nonmortgage receivables. In 1985, nonmortgage receivable-backed securities were born. The year started with the sale of Sperry equipment leases in a structured securitized transaction. However, an even more significant event in the development of asset securitization also occurred in early 1985. Marine Midland Bank, in partnership with Salomon Brothers, created the CARS (Certificates of Automobile Receivables) grantor trust securitized structure in a private placement that opened up consumer receivables to securitization. In mid-1985, Marine Midland Bank, together with Salomon Brothers, issued the first public CARS security, and Valley National Financial issued a public securitized automotive receivable-backed grantor trust with First Boston. Since those two public issues, the asset-backed market has exploded with billions of dollars in automotive loans and credit card receivables being sold in structured securitized transactions through both private and public placements. Numerous banks, as well as thrifts and major corporations, have sold nonmortgage receivables through asset-backed issues. The assets sold have included receivables related to equipment leases, automotive loans, recreational vehicle loans, credit cards, and commercial real estate. In a very short time the role of the bank has evolved from being a "portfolio lender" to that of a "portfolio seller." Its role can be multifaceted as an active loan originator, credit underwriter, seller, securities issuer, dealmaker or structure developer, and portfolio servicer.

THE BANK AS A SELLER OF ASSETS

Not every bank should pursue securitization. Although securitization indeed offers many advantages to bank participants, there are also pitfalls. How then should a bank decide whether the sale of assets or securitization is right for it? This section establishes a framework for making securitization decisions and identifies the key determinants from several viewpoints.

Banking institutions typically have many financial objectives. These may range from all-encompassing goals such as building capital and maximizing net income growth to very detailed statements of key operating ratios, such as limiting charge-offs to a certain percentage of outstanding assets or maintaining certain liquidity levels in the balance sheet. It is critical that the linkage between a bank's strategic objectives and its decision to securitize be an explicit one. Consideration of securitization in the absence of this linkage can be unhealthy and lead to serious balance sheet problems.

Although many banks are experimenting with securitization, it is important to understand one's motivations or objectives before opting for this technique. Exhibit 13–1 defines the primary motivations/benefits behind a securitization program. These are grouped into regulatory, risk/exposure management, and financial categories. Let's discuss each of them in greater detail:

EXHIBIT 13–1
Motivation for Securitization

Category	Issue
Regulatory	Capital Adequacy
Risk/Exposure Management	Funding
	Asset Liability Management Flexibility
	Rate Risk Management
	Asset Concentration
	Credit Risk
	Industry Risk
	Geographic Risk
Financial	Earnings
	Accelerate Recognition
	Margin Optimization
	Return
	Fee Income Development

• *Regulatory*—Clearly a banking institution's overriding concern is to ensure adequate capital resources to support its lending activities. Without this level of capital, not only will the institution be out of compliance with regulations, but it will jeopardize its ability to safeguard the cash of its depositors. Securitization can be viewed as yet another source of capital. This buoying of capital through securitization occurs through the removal of assets from the balance sheet and the resulting infusion of cash. This cash arising from reduced loan loss reserves, principal recovery, and gain on sale of assets can be injected directly into the bank's capital base.

• *Risk/Exposure Management*—Flexibility in funding and making asset/liability decisions are central to informed balance sheet management. To obtain maximum flexibility, bank management should have the option to fund either on or off the balance sheet. This flexibility should apply to both new originations and existing portfolios on the bank's books. In this fashion, the institution can take advantage of market dislocations in the funding yield curve and sudden shifts in interest rates. The fundamental desire is to obtain the lowest possible cost of funding, and securitization indeed represents another way to pursue this objective.

Beyond the notion of "funding cost" alone, securitization provides a way of passing interest rate risk to a third party. While matched funding is a well understood concept, it is difficult to apply. In practice, the projected asset balances used to establish matched funding requirements are typically different than the actual balances realized over the life of the assets. As discussed above, securitization enables the bank's asset/liability manager to match fund virtually 100 percent by exporting the funding and rate risk to the ultimate investor. Although funding risk is an important driver of securitization, so is lending or credit risk. For banks seeking to reduce credit risk, securitization offers the ability to limit exposure with a "spread account." Simply stated, the spread account is a mechanism for providing the investor some multiple of coverage for historical losses, but a multiple well below 100 percent. The spread account is funded by the assets' cash flow, which is held in trust to satisfy credit losses and delinquency. Other dimensions of lending risk can also be better managed through securitization. These include reducing concentrations of the balance sheet in particular asset types or industry segments and providing geographic balance to a portfolio by securitizing loans from regions with unusually heavy concentrations.

• *Financial*—Yet another impetus for securitization is financial. If there is sufficient spread, the seller bank may be able to accelerate its recognition of future excess servicing income as gain on sale in the current period. This not only enhances current year earnings but builds a stream of fees into the future for the continued servicing of the sold loans. These servicing fees, if continuously increased through additional securitization transactions, provide an annuity for the bank without attendant rate risk. Earnings may also be increased in the future by consciously securitizing a pool of loans to lock in spreads when rates are low and the interest rate forecast calls for higher rates. In addition, the fees earned in both the current year and in the future improve the overall return on assets of the institution as income is generated while assets on the balance sheet are reduced. At a time when shareholder return is of overriding importance, the ability to generate fee income is essential.

Strategic objectives notwithstanding, there are often multiple and sometimes conflicting motivations for a bank to securitize or sell assets. Often the notion of securitization will be broadly discussed in various quarters of the bank from a variety of differing functional viewpoints. However, the depth and breadth of their understanding can have a dramatic and lasting impact on the desired results of the asset sale. Therefore, it is important that various interests within the institution not only conceptually understand their motives for securitizing a receivable portfolio, but also understand the expected results given the interaction of the portfolio characteristics, the economy, and their objectives.

Exhibits 13–2, 13–3, and 13–4 illustrate financial pro forma results given the ability to recognize a gain or loss in an asset sale. While there are "nonfinancial" motivations for selling assets, as illustrated in Exhibit 13–1, it can be seen by reviewing Exhibits 13–1, 13–2, 13–3, and 13–4 together that financial results can determine whether strategic objectives are met. This interactive review of financial and strategic objectives can affect the decision process, as the following examples illustrate.

• *Capital adequacy* is often considered the most basic motive for selling assets, given the absolute need to reduce assets while raising cash. It is also felt at times that because of the "survival need" to obtain cash, a good understanding of the financial issues is not necessary, since gain on sale is not the objective. While the first position is true, the latter one is not. As seen in Exhibit 13–2, where there is no gain or loss on sale, and in Exhibit 13–3 where a gain on sale is realized, the asset sale produces the expected improvement in the capital position, regardless of whether the cash realized is used to reduce debt or reinvest in profitable assets. However, as seen in Exhibit 13–4, when a loss on sale is realized, the capital position can decline if the cash is reinvested. In fact, even though the capital position is improved when the cash is used to reduce debt, the ongoing operational profitability and return can be considerably weakened, thus potentially weakening the viability of the bank. If the immediate need is to infuse cash and improve the capital position, then the bank may still be forced to sell the assets; however, the decision will be made with a full understanding of the potential shortfalls that need correcting. The point is that a simple goal of improving capital should not be the final consideration in opting for a program of securitization. It is simply the initial objective that is tested in deciding how to proceed.
• The financial results of the transaction are also important considerations if *funding risk management* is the key objective. Bank management must review the characteristics of their portfolio and match up the expected performance of the portfolio with expected conditions in the marketplace. If, for example, interest rates are expected to rise, then selling existing assets even at a loss may make sense, because it would permit reinvestment in new, higher yielding assets. In other words, short run losses may sometimes be the intentional result of responsible decision making.
• In seeking ways to *improve financial performance*, institutions often rely heavily upon financial pro forma statements. But while financial pro formas can be valuable, they sometimes point to an overly simplistic

EXHIBIT 13–2

Illustrative Pro forma Financial Statement Impact of Sales Alternatives (No Gain or Loss on Sale ($000))

	On-Balance Sheet Financing	Alternative I Reduce Debt	Alternative II Reinvestment
Transaction Facts			
Gross Assets Sold		$200,000	$200,000
Gain/(Loss) on Sale After Tax		0	0
Oper Inc Gain/(Loss) After Tax		(2,760)	1,471
Cash Realized		$197,240	$201,471
Assets			
Receivables	$500,000	$300,000	$300,000
Asset Reinvestment	0	0	$201,471
Total Assets	$500,000	$300,000	$501,471
Liabilities and Shareholder's Equity			
Liabilities/Debt	$480,000	$282,760	$480,000
Shareholder's Equity	20,000	17,240	21,471
Total Liabilities and Equity	$500,000	$300,000	$501,471
Income Statement			
Net Interest Income	$ 17,500	$ 10,500	$ 17,551
Servicing Income	0	2,400	2,400
Total Income	$ 17,500	$ 12,900	$ 19,951
Expenses & Charge-offs	10,175	10,175	10,175
Ongoing Operating Income Before Tax	$ 7,325	$ 2,725	$ 9,776
Ongoing Operating Income After Tax	$ 4,395	$ 1,635	$ 5,866
Income After Tax With Profit on Sale	$ 4,395	$ 1,635	$ 5,866
Ratio Analysis			
With Profit On Sale:			
Capital Ratio	4.00%	5.75%	4.28%
Return On Assets	0.88%	0.54%	1.17%
Return On Equity	21.97%	9.48%	27.32%
Ongoing Operations:			
Capital Ratio	4.00%	5.75%	4.28%
Return On Assets	0.88%	0.54%	1.17%
Return On Equity	21.97%	9.48%	27.32%

EXHIBIT 13–3
Illustrative Pro forma Financial Statement Impact of Sales Alternatives
(Gain on Sale ($000))

	On-Balance Sheet Financing	Alternative I Reduce Debt	Alternative II Reinvestment
Transaction Facts			
Gross Assets Sold		$200,000	$200,000
Gain/(Loss) on Sale After Tax		1,800	1,800
Oper Inc Gain/(Loss) After Tax		(2,760)	1,509
Cash Realized		$199,040	$203,309
Assets			
Receivables	$500,000	$300,000	$300,000
Asset Reinvestment	0	0	203,309
Total Assets	$500,000	$300,000	$503,309
Liabilities and Shareholder's Equity			
Liabilities/Debt	$480,000	$280,960	$480,000
Shareholder's Equity	20,000	19,040	23,309
Total Liabilities and Equity	$500,000	$300,000	$503,309
Income Statement			
Net Interest Income	$ 17,500	$ 10,500	$ 17,616
Servicing Income	0	2,400	2,400
Total Income	$ 17,500	$ 12,900	$ 20,016
Expenses & Charge-offs	10,175	10,175	10,175
Ongoing Operating Income Before Tax	$ 7,325	$ 2,725	$ 9,841
Ongoing Operating Income After Tax	$ 4,395	$ 1,635	$ 5,904
Income After Tax With Profit on Sale	$ 4,395	$ 3,435	$ 7,704
Ratio Analysis			
With Profit On Sale:			
Capital Ratio	4.00%	6.35%	4.63%
Return On Assets	0.88%	1.14%	1.53%
Return On Equity	21.97%	18.04%	33.05%
Ongoing Operations:			
Capital Ratio	4.00%	6.35%	4.63%
Return On Assets	0.88%	0.54%	1.17%
Return On Equity	21.97%	8.59%	25.33%

EXHIBIT 13–4

Illustrative Pro forma Financial Statement Impact of Sales Alternatives (Loss on Sale ($000))

	On-Balance Sheet Financing	Alternative I Reduce Debt	Alternative II Reinvestment
Transaction Facts			
Gross Assets Sold		$200,000	$200,000
Gain/(Loss) on Sale After Tax		(1,800)	(1,800)
Oper Inc Gain/(Loss) After Tax		(2,760)	1,432
Cash Realized		$195,440	$199,632
Assets			
Receivables	$500,000	$300,000	$300,000
Asset Reinvestment	0	0	199,632
Total Assets	$500,000	$300,000	$499,632
Liabilities and Shareholder's Equity			
Liabilities/Debt	$480,000	$284,560	$480,000
Shareholder's Equity	20,000	15,440	19,632
Total Liabilities and Equity	$500,000	$300,000	$499,632
Income Statement			
Net Interest Income	$ 17,500	$ 10,500	$ 17,487
Servicing Income	0	2,400	2,400
Total Income	$ 17,500	$ 12,900	$ 19,887
Expenses & Chargeoffs	10,175	10,175	10,175
Ongoing Operating Income Before Tax	$ 7,325	$ 2,725	$ 9,712
Ongoing Operating Income After Tax	$ 4,395	$ 1,635	$ 5,827
Income After Tax With Profit on Sale	$ 4,395	($165)	$ 4,027
Ratio Analysis			
With Profit On Sale:			
Capital Ratio	4.00%	5.15%	3.93%
Return On Assets	0.88%	−0.06%	0.81%
Return On Equity	21.97%	−1.07%	20.51%
Ongoing Operations:			
Capital Ratio	4.00%	5.15%	3.93%
Return On Assets	0.88%	0.54%	1.17%
Return On Equity	21.97%	10.59%	29.68%

course of action. Before taking final action, it is important to consider the impact of a decision on the objectives shown in Exhibit 13–1. As illustrated in the pro forma in Exhibit 13–3, assets can be sold to recognize an accelerated gain and improve the capital position of the bank. However, bank management must look beyond the immediate current-year impact. Although return on assets is improved and the greatest current-year impact on capital position appears to be realized when the cash is used to reduce debt, reinvestment may actually be the best decision. Reinvestment may have a less "dramatic" effect on the capital position but reinvestment in quality assets generates much stronger current year and ongoing operational profitability and return. An additional benefit is that more profitable assets are also generated for possible sale in the future.

As indicated above, the "decision tree" in asset securitization is multi-branched. As is almost always the case in any business, the better the information, the better informed the resulting decisions. Unless a framework for the decision is established with a clear understanding of the ultimate impact, the effort will likely either encounter snags along the way and be doomed to failure or produce results that are disastrously off the strategic mark.

WHOLE LOAN SALE VERSUS PUBLIC SECURITIZED PLACEMENT

Once the bank has determined its strategic objectives and the type of sale it wishes to execute, it must decide whether it will do a private whole loan sale or public securitized placement. When a bank, or any organization, is trying to sell its portfolio of assets receivables, it must research and analyze a number of issues before it can decide whether a whole loan sale or securitized transaction is more appropriate. Publicly placed securitized transactions have been receiving considerable press, with investor spreads over Treasury requirements of as low as 65 to 70 basis points being touted. Compared to the 195 to 225 basis point spread over Treasuries required by whole loan purchasers, the apparent 125 to 160 basis point benefit is very inviting and appears to make indepth comparisons moot. However, appearances can be misleading, and the bank considering assets sales should review economic, accounting, legal, operational, and systems issues thoroughly before proceeding. There are cost/benefit trade-offs between these factors, and any one of them can lead to success or failure.

The first, and possibly the major, issue in deciding whether to pursue a whole loan sale or securitized sale is the size of the portfolio to be sold. A certain "critical mass" or volume is needed to economically cover the significant transaction costs of a securitized sale. Although the investor spread requirement for a public, securitized sale is well below that required for a whole loan sale, the cost of developing and executing a securitized sale is considerably higher than that of a whole loan sale. The bank selling its portfolio must analyze the transaction costs (many of them being fixed) to determine if the volume of the transaction will justify a public securitized approach.

A securitized transaction has the following added transaction costs that are not found in a whole loan sale.

• *Investment Banker Underwriting Fees*—The investment banking fee is generally 0.4 percent of the collateral volume amount and tends to vary with volume. However, most investment banks with experience in this field require a minimum volume of $75 or $100 million when calculating their fee. Typically, they feel a $300,000 to $400,000 minimum fee is needed to cover their transaction expenses and underwriting risk, regardless of the size of the transaction.

• *Added Legal Expenses*—Because of the added complexity and legal liability of a public securitization, the seller/issuer can expect legal expenses of a securitization to exceed those of a whole loan sale by $75,000 to $150,000. In addition, some more complicated structures may require annual legal opinions costing $10,000 to $15,000 per year.

• *Trustee Fees*—Trustee fees, which are not required in whole loan sales, usually add $30,000 to $50,000 to the transaction, plus an annual fee of about 5 basis points of outstanding balances.

• *Rating Agency Fees*—At least one, but more preferably two ratings are required for a public sale and vary according to volume with a minimum fixed cost of $10,000 each. Standard & Poor's charges 3 basis points, with a minimum fee of $10,000 and maximum of $75,000. Moody's charges 2.5 basis points, with a minimum of $10,000 and a maximum of $55,000. For example, the cost of two ratings on a $100 million portfolio would be $55,000.

• *Credit Enhancement Fees*—As discussed in more detail elsewhere, credit enhancement to provide needed protection for the investor is usually required before the rating agencies will rate the issue at double-A or triple-A investment grade levels. While private placements and some public issues have used insurance for credit enhancement guarantees, most securitized public asset sales have obtained the necessary level of credit enhancement with a standby letter of credit from an appropriately rated LOC Bank (e.g., triple-A rated LOC bank for a triple-A rated issue). Letter of credit fees vary with volume, typically running 4 to 6 basis points of the collateral amount. In addition, the seller/issuer typically pays the legal fees for the bank issuing the LOC. These fees may range from $15,000 to $30,000. Credit enhancement insurance also varies with the amount of credit enhancement required and the attendant credit quality of the portfolio, the cost being determined by the insurance company that is used.

• *Securities and Exchange Commission Filing Fees*—For securitized transactions that are sold publicly, a 0.0002 percent SEC filing fee is charged to register the securities.

• *Accounting Fees*—While not required in whole loan sales, both publicly and privately placed securitized transactions require comfort letters from an independent accounting firm. The comfort letters attest to the validity of the portfolio selection criteria and the accuracy of the portfolio characteristics and and delinquency charge-off information. Typically, firms charge $25,000 to $40,000 for such reviews and comfort letters. In addition, annual independent audits of the portfolio and servicing systems are usually required. They cost $15,000 to $25,000 a year for typical structures and possibly higher for more complicated structures.

• *Printing and Engraving Fees*—Not required for whole loans sales, printing fees run from $30,000 for a privately placed sale to $85,000 for a public transaction.

The issues discussed above are illustrated in Exhibit 13–5. In summary, because of the additional costs of a public securitization, a bank or any portfolio seller should usually have an eligible portfolio volume of at least $75 to $100 million before attempting a public sale. Portfolios below $40 to $50 million can usually be sold more economically in a private whole loan sale to other banks, thrifts, financial services companies, insurance companies, or corporations.

In addition to the increased transaction costs of a public securitized transaction, other investments or initial costs are required. These costs usually include salaries and expenses for accounting control, information, and computer systems. As previously noted, banks have already developed the systems, procedures, and people to underwrite credit

EXHIBIT 13–5
Public Securitization vs. Whole Loan Sale Cost Comparisons ($000)

	AAA-Rated Public Placement	Whole Loan Bulk Purchase	Whole Loan B/(W) Public
Recommended Public Minimum Volume	$75,000	$75,000	
Breakeven Volume	$43,000	$43,000	
Rates:			
2–Year Treasury Rate	7.45%	7.45%	
Average Investor Spread (1)	0.85%	2.05%	
Average Yield To Investor	8.30%	9.50%	
LOC (7% LOC @ 60 Bps/Yr)	0.04%	—	
Trustee/Acct Per Year	0.05%	—	
Effective Rate Before Expenses	8.39%	9.50%	
Transaction Exp @ $75MM Volume (2)	0.62%	0.02%	
Audit & Legal Exp Per Year @ $75MM	0.06%	0.00%	
All-In Cost/Yr @ $75MM Volume	9.07%	9.52%	
Spread to Treasury @ $75MM	1.62%	2.07%	−0.45%
Transaction Exp @ $43MM Volume (3)	1.03%	0.02%	
Audit & Legal Exp Per Year @ $43MM	0.10%	0.00%	
All-In Cost/Yr @ $43MM Volume	9.52%	9.52%	
Spread to Treasury @ $43MM	2.07%	2.07%	0.00%
(1) Investor Spread Range (Bps)	70–100	190–200	
(2) Expenses @ $75MM Volume:			
Underwriting Fee	$400.0	$ 0.0	
SEC Registration	15.0	0.0	
NASD Filing Fee	5.1	0.0	
Blue Sky Registration	0.5	0.0	
Printing & Engraving	85.0	0.0	
Legal Fees	125.0	15.0	
Accounting Fees	35.0	0.0	
Trustee Fees	35.0	5.0	
Rating Agency Fees	41.0	0.0	
Misc & People Expense	25.0	10.0	
Total Exp @ Min Vol	$766.6	$30.0	
(3) Expenses @ Breakeven Volume:			
Vol Adj For SEC Reg	($ 6.4)	$0.0	
Vol Adj Rating Agency	(35.0)	0.0	
Total Exp @ Tran Vol	$725.2	$30.0	

risk, track repayment performance, and service portfolios for collections and recoveries. Therefore, they have a head start over many other companies in being able to securitize and service a portfolio for investors. However, considerable investment is still required to develop the right organization and personnel to consistently offer securitized products. The bank must establish the right accounting and computer systems to enable the organization and the asset generating business to maintain control of the process and the servicing after the sale is executed.

The bank may find it needs to create a project team by recruiting people who have the skills to develop and structure securitized transactions. It may also need to develop a dedicated staff for the settlement reporting and troubleshooting efforts needed after the portfolio is sold. If there are plans to securitize assets on an ongoing basis, then a staff familiar with the business unit generating the loans or assets to be sold should be established.

New investments in computer systems may also be needed. Exhibit 13–6 lists seller requirements for a receivable-backed transaction; it

EXHIBIT 13–6
Requirements of The Seller For Receivable-Backed Transaction

Pre-Pricing:
  Produce a tape in required format of the loan portfolio.
  Process tape of selected loans.
  Prepare statistics of loan portfolio.
Pre-Closing:
  Determine preclosing collections and deposit in the Collection Account.
  Permanently mark computer records to identify sold loans.
  Prepare a final list of sold loans.
Post-Closing Servicing & Settlement Reporting:
  Daily
    Determine daily collections.
    Deposit daily collections in the Collection Account.
  Monthly
    Determine amount of funds available to make required payments.
    Determine required payments
    Notify Trustee in event of deficiency of available funds.
    Withdraw excess funds from the Spread Account.
    Prepare monthly reports for Trustee, LOC issuer and Certificateholders.
  Quarterly
    Prepare servicing officer's certificate.
  Yearly
    Prepare annual statements for Trustee, LOC issuer and Certificateholders.
    Ensure annual accountant's report is completed.

focuses on the tasks remaining when the initial structuring and documentation has been completed and the sale is being taken to market. The tasks are divided into three phases. The first two phases, pre-pricing and pre-closing, occur in about 30 days. The third phase covers the entire life of the portfolio and involves daily, monthly, quarterly, and annual tasks. Although these requirements obviously have major implications for training and deployment of staff, they will affect in an even bigger way the development of computer systems to generate the needed information in an accurate and timely manner. The first systems requirement is to develop the ability to quickly select loans for sale, according to specific selection criteria. The systems also must have the flexibility to repeatedly analyze the portfolio using different selection criteria to allow the bank to economically test the feasibility of the selection. Once selected, the portfolio needs to be separated and electronically marked, with all cash flows being separately accounted for after the cut-off date. At that point, the cash flow is the property of the trust created to hold the assets, in which the investors own shares or certificates (i.e., grantor trust or owner's trust). If the bank wants to service the portfolio (a task for which it is eminently qualified and which generates fee-based income), systems also have to be developed to track the cash flows, delinquencies, and charge-off data to allow the generation of investor settlement reports and the distribution of cash periodically as required by the servicing agreement. A bank should typically expect to invest $250,000 to $500,000 in systems development; however, this investment can sometimes be reduced by using the investment bank's selection and analytical software. A drawback of using the investment banker's software is that the bank issuer may become dependent on a specific investment bank, thereby compromising its leverage in negotiating lower fees on future transactions.

As part of the servicing activity, the bank will have to keep track of the cash flows and determine the distribution of payments. This not only requires the systems ability to determine the amounts owed to the parties in the transaction, but requires a sophisticated network of collection and trust departments and payment distribution channels. Operating under tight schedules, the bank must collect and distribute payments (often monthly) to the investors for interest at the agreed rate and principal repayment, to the servicer for the base servicing fee, and to the letter of credit bank to cover charge-offs. The seller/servicer retains the excess servicing fee. All this requires knowledgeable people, a well integrated organization, sophisticated computer systems, and the ability to efficiently handle large volumes of cash. Although many organizations possess most of these skills, banks are uniquely qualified to efficiently transfer large volumes of cash to individual investors through wire transfers or checks.

Besides reporting on investor settlements, the seller/servicer also must file periodic Securities and Exchange Commission reports, tax returns, and annual audits of the portfolio performance and servicing activities. Periodically, the servicer will have to file with the SEC financial statements related to the activity of the trust and the underlying assets. In addition, Internal Revenue Service tax returns will have to be filed annually for the trust as well as for each investor. The servicer's systems, controls, and the performance of the portfolio will have to be audited annually by an independent auditor. The servicing bank must keep these reporting and filing requirements in mind when developing the operating and control procedures and computer systems.

REQUIREMENTS FOR A BANK TO BE A SUCCESSFUL SECURITIZED SELLER AND SERVICER

Asset Knowledge

For a bank to become a successful securitized seller and servicer of receivable assets, it has to be perceived by the rating agencies, the credit enhancer, and the investor marketplace as a capable lender with a skilled and experienced collection and servicing operation. To execute an efficient and profitable securitized transaction, the institution must have accurate information about its assets and collateral, and must thoroughly understand its servicing/collection capabilities and costs. Demonstrated knowledge and command of this information can affect the pricing of the issue and the amount of credit enhancement necessary.

The quality and type of underlying assets can influence investor comfort in many ways. Thorough knowledge of the assets not only allows a bank or any seller to provide necessary information for the investor, but also demonstrates the bank's expertise as a lender and servicer to the rating agencies and credit enhancers. In-depth knowledge of the assets and marketplace is also important for the seller to be actively involved in developing the most effective structure for a successful and economical sale. Knowledge of market characteristics, demographics, and geographic issues are important to the securitized package. For example, many investors are concerned about the geographic distribution of assets. If the assets are concentrated in a few regions, an economic downturn in a given area can lead to higher credit losses than would occur if the assets were widely disbursed. Similarly, if the portfolio is heavily concentrated in a particular type of automobile, difficulties with that manufacturer could have a negative effect on the performance of the loan portfolio.

Other characteristics of the assets are also important. The source of the asset has a crucial bearing on the portfolio's performance. Automotive loans originated *directly* through a bank branch tend to perform differently than loans *indirectly* originated through an automobile dealer. If the loans are purchased indirectly from dealers, the bank will need to demonstrate to investors that it possesses solid credit review and buying procedures. Credit card accounts originated within the bank also perform differently than those originated through a direct mail campaign or indirectly through another financial institution. In addition, indirectly originated portfolios tend to have associated fees or reserves to compensate the dealer or originator; these negatively impact the cash flow of the portfolio.

Even within indirectly originated portfolios, the variation in the product structure of the assets can be significant. This is due to the many different approaches that banks take in compensating the dealer/originator. The level of compensation is usually linked to the extent of the credit exposure assumed by the originator, which can lead to differing levels of prepayment and delinquency exposure for the bank and investor. These relationships are shown below.

Dealer/Originator		Bank Exposure		
Commission	Liability	For Credit	For Prepayment	Delinquency Traits
Low	Non Recourse	Total	Variable (1)	Low
Medium	Repurchase (90 days)	Limited	Variable (1)	Medium
High	Recourse Unconditional Guarantees	None	Variable (1)	High

(1) Varies by program from total to none

Each of these combinations has a significantly different impact on bank economics, yields, and ultimate returns. The net implication is that an investor looking at yield and historical experience alone cannot predict portfolio quality unless the mix and any shifts occurring in mix are known. By the same token, a bank seller of assets can seriously overestimate the economic benefits of a sale if it fails to consider how the above structures affect basic loan returns. The bank will have to be able to isolate such issues to: 1) evaluate the economics of the sale; 2) properly price and account for the transaction; and 3) properly carry out its investor reporting and settlement responsibilities after the sale. In summary, an institution considering a sale of its assets must be in touch with all the elements of its portfolio. Such awareness requires market familiarity and analytical effort. Moreover, systems may have to be developed to obtain the necessary information.

Asset knowledge is needed for any type of asset sale, but it is particularly important in a public securitized one. And if a bank wishes to participate in other aspects of securitization, such as credit enhancement, standby servicing, structuring, and underwriting, then knowledge of the portfolio and its assets is absolutely essential.

Credit Policies and Procedures

Credit quality is usually the factor that can make or break a sale. It determines the amount of credit enhancement required by the rating agencies to attain investment grade rating levels and status. It also affects the cost of credit enhancement, since it can bias the perceived risk of loss. Sometimes the credit quality can determine what type of credit enhancement is required (i.e., letter of credit or insurance) since different types of credit enhancers can evaluate, approach, and price risk differently. Given the importance of credit quality, it is imperative that the bank be able to analyze credit related trends and information such as delinquency and charge-off statistics for their portfolio, as well as comparative industry data. The bank's credit policy will also have to be supplied to those conducting due diligence reviews, as well as to the public accounting firm performing the audit for the investor trust. They are obviously going to be keenly interested in credit procedures. But more importantly, they will want to verify that the policies and procedures are followed by the bank's credit underwriting units. If a bank cannot demonstrate the quality and consistency of its credit underwriting, the credit quality of its entire portfolio becomes questionable. And that, in turn, will be reflected in its saleability.

Cash Flow

Cash flow is another major factor that can affect a portfolio's attractiveness to investors. The adequacy of cash flow will affect the charge-off and liquidity reserve or escrow required from the selling bank by the credit enhancer—the better the cash flow, the lower the reserve requirement. As with other factors discussed here, the more clearly the bank can discuss these issues, the more favorably the portfolio will be viewed.

Predictability and *adequacy* of the portfolio's cash flows are the two most critical factors to be considered. Predictability can be influenced by the actual contractual maturity of the individual loan, expected charge-offs, method of interest computation, and expected prepayment of the loans. Of the four factors, expected prepayment is the most difficult to predict, and some receivable portfolios, such as credit card portfolios, are more difficult to predict than others with more established payment trends, such as automobile loans. The bank interested in selling assets must be able to identify the contractual maturity and determine the predicted monthly cash flows of each loan's principal and interest. However, principal and interest cash flow concerns cannot be addressed without a sound understanding of the method of interest income recognition that is used, be it actuarial, simple interest, or precomputed (Rule of 78s). The most direct approach is to sell an actuarial portfolio, since the timing of the cash flow requirements between the seller and the investor is the most straightforward. Payments coming in during a month are pooled by the servicer and typically paid to the investor monthly. Simple interest loans add an additional layer of complexity as the date of actual receipt of payment affects the yield. In turn, the handling of excess (early) cash or shortfalls (late) cash inflows becomes more cumbersome. Lastly, "Rule of 78s" loans are still very prevalent in many states. A key attribute of these loans is a declining yield to maturity over the term. Because income has been accelerated to the beginning of the loan, a sale of such a portfolio during the term will likely result in a loss rather than a gain on sale. To simplify and standardize asset sales, from an investors perspective, these loans typically are analyzed to yield an actuarial equivalent, regardless of the type of interest being used in the loan itself. The portfolio cash flow can then be determined based on expected prepay and charge-off assumptions. Assuming that the parties involved are satisfied that cash flow is sufficiently predictable, the cash flow is then analyzed to determine if it can support the principal and interest at the pass-through rate due the investors, the servicing fees due the seller/servicer, and the predetermined charge-off coverage required by the credit enhancer.

Another major element of both credit risk and cash flow assessment is the rate risk characteristics of the loan. At one extreme, the loan is fixed rate and the originating institution has not burdened the consumer with any rate risk over the term. At the other end, a floating rate note exports all rate risk from the bank to the consumer. Most variable rate consumer notes, however, are blended, incorporating both a variable rate index to which interest payments are tied along with certain rate floors or ceilings to limit consumer exposure to volatile interest rates. These caps and floors, though, are applied differently. One approach involves setting explicit boundaries on rate fluctuations. From a cash flow perspective, this causes severe problems to an investor looking for adequacy of cash flow coverage for a variable rate funding, inasmuch as the funding will not likely be subject to the same boundaries. More typically, however, these boundaries are set implicitly by fixing the borrower's monthly payment obligation and achieving rate adjustment by changing the mix of monthly interest and principal amortization. This method increases or decreases the number of remaining payments. The problem of this approach is that, in a rapidly increasing rate environment, the incoming consumer payments needed to service the investor may be inadequate, result ing in an unsecured obligation by the seller to the investor. Thus, sound asset knowledge requires a fundamental understanding of the rate risks associated with the portfolio to be sold. Without this, severe miscalculations of the sale's economics, exposure, and financial impact can result.

Servicing

Unless a bank wants to completely sell off a particular type of asset, the asset sale will be made on a "servicing retained" basis, so the bank can earn ongoing service fee income and the excess servicing gain. However, retaining servicing rights is not an automatic right for the bank, but is something that must be earned or granted. Servicing rights are granted by the investor, who is the new owner of the assets, although in most sales the initial servicing rights are typically awarded to the seller at the time of sale. However, the servicing rights can later be forfeited by the seller/servicer if certain agreed upon responsibilities are not met. Therefore, the bank must understand the normal expectations of the servicer as well as the specific pooling and servicing agreements it has made to be sure it can perform. The penalty of missing the mark here is possible forfeiture of the servicing income stream, the right to the excess servicing cash flow, and the right to the unneeded charge-off reserve or "spread account" remaining at final maturity of the portfolio. The stakes are high!

The investor, rating agency, and credit enhancer are going to be highly concerned about servicing retention. Collectability and uninterrupted cash flow are of prime concern to the investor, since they significantly impact yield and return on investment. Therefore, next to credit quality, servicing is probably the most important element in the success of the transaction. The parties involved are going to be interested first in the financial viability of the servicer. The seller/servicer should be prepared to provide financial statements and evidence of viability and capital adequacy. During due diligence reviews and in the seller's CPA opinions, representations about the financial strength of the servicer may be required. Extensive attention will also be paid to the institution's servicing and collection resources. The bank's staff skills, the computer systems and capacity, demonstrated experience, and its servicing reputation will also be reviewed in-depth by the underwriters, rating agencies, and credit enhancer. The perceived image of the bank as a viable servicer also becomes a major factor when the issue is actually sold in the public marketplace. Regardless of the "facts" about the bank's servicing ability, the reputation of the bank in the eyes of investors can significantly affect the "spread" needed to sell the deal. That obviously can affect the economic benefit of the transaction for the selling institution. If the parties involved determine that the lack of servicing ability will be a detrimental factor in the sale, the bank may have to find a strong standby servicer or a strong contract servicer to do the servicing, with the selling bank acting as "master servicer" to retain the gain realized through the excess servicing fee. While these options may mitigate a bank's servicing weakness, they are usually expensive. That's because portfolio transfers are difficult to achieve due to differences in servicing system mechanics and procedures for nonmortgage types of receivables. Therefore, backup servicing options should be approached cautiously and as a last resort. If the bank itself is seen as a strong servicer, it will not only have the opportunity to service its own sold portfolio, but may also have additional fee income opportunities to become a standby servicer or contract servicer for a weaker institution.

Legal and Regulatory Issues

A number of other securitization issues are important for banks to understand. Many regulatory issues can impact the effectiveness of a transaction; these include Regulation D, Regulation 21A, true asset sale treatment and capitalization requirements. Legal hurdles include the need to provide legal opinions, representations and warranties (given by the seller/servicer), and loan documentation. The bank must be able to demonstrate the quality of the portfolio's documentation and compliance with legal and regulatory requirements. Collateral quality and perfection of the bank's security interest, if the asset is collateralized, must also be shown.

For commercial banks, bank regulatory issues are of a major concern. This is one disadvantage commercial banks have compared with their thrift and nonbank brethren in completing cost effective asset securitized transactions. The steps needed to comply with bank regulation can often be time-consuming and expensive. Proper structuring is critical if the transaction is to be treated as an asset sale to reduce capital requirements, and to recognize accelerated gain on sale for both regulatory accounting procedures (RAP) and generally accepted accounting principles (GAAP) purposes. To qualify as a true sale of assets for GAAP purposes, the bank simply needs to demonstrate that 1) the asset's future economic benefit has been transferred, 2) the future income to the bank can be reasonably estimated, and 3) any future recourse liability to the bank can be reasonably estimated and will be deducted from the present value of future earnings recognized as gain on sale. However, to qualify for RAP the assets have to be sold strictly on a *NONRE-COURSE BASIS*. If there is any recourse, except for a small "cleanup call" of usually 5 percent or less when the portfolio matures, the asset sale treatment for regulatory purpose will be denied and the strategic goal of reducing capitalization requirements will not be achieved. This nonrecourse requirement has led to the use of credit enhancement by a letter of credit and the development of the "spread account" structure, discussed earlier, to be held in escrow to cover a limited guarantee for defaults. Another common regulatory issue is the avoidance of an additional reserve assessment according to Regulation D, which requires a bank to hold reserves for the deposits, liabilities, or contingent liabilities the bank is carrying on its balance sheet. In structuring a transaction, the aim is to keep the transaction off-balance sheet to avoid contingent liabilities requiring a reserve. A bank also has to be concerned about violating Regulation 21A, which prohibits a bank from funding a subsidiary of the bank holding company. Under Regulation 21A, a sale may be questioned if the bank and subsidiaries of the bank holding company are intertwined in the transaction. The structure of the transaction should reflect both regulatory requirements and the bank's strategic goals.

No matter how well the institution demonstrates its proficiency in legal and regulatory compliance and documentation, it must still be prepared to provide representations and warranties. If the representations and warranties are subsequently violated, a breach will occur that can force the institution to repurchase the affected loans. In extreme cases, a breach can unwind the entire transaction. Therefore, the institution should be very familiar with what is being represented or guaranteed. It should be particularly careful to make representations and warranties that reflect the facts, rather than try to paint a prettier picture than exists. The future viability of the transaction, not to mention sizable damage awards, could be at stake. But more importantly, the bank's reputation is also on the line, which can have considerable impact on its ability to economically consummate future asset sales or even to transact sales at all.

Representations or warranties cannot be made by the bank about the credit quality of the portfolio, except as they relate to policies and procedures, general delinquency data, and specific delinquency representations for each contract sold. To warrant credit quality would be construed as recourse, which would result in the disallowance of the transaction as an asset sale for regulatory purposes.

Legal opinions that properly relate to the sale's structure complexities are also critical to the success of a securitized transaction. Where principal and interest payments are specifically identified, such as in automotive loan sales, the bank's outside counsel will have to be convinced that the transaction qualifies as a true sale for GAAP, RAP, and tax purposes. However, where the payments received are treated as a more homogeneous cash flow, such as with revolving credit card sales, the legal opinion will have to indicate that the transaction is a sale for GAAP and RAP purposes, while qualifying as a borrowing for tax purposes. Legal opinions will also be required concerning board resolutions, the bank's ability and authority to sell the assets, its lending authority in the states where the assets were generated, and officer certifications, among other things. The bank wishing to sell assets should determine what legal opinions are required before getting too far into the project. If the bank feels some of the opinions may be difficult or impossible to obtain, then it may not make sense to pursue the asset sale until that situation can be rectified.

Systems and Structuring Ability

As indicated earlier, a bank has to be comfortable that its computer systems are capable of making random selection of the portfolio according to certain criteria. Such random, accurate selection is critical to receiving favorable ratings from the rating agencies. The bank must also be comfortable with its ability to structure the transaction to meet its strategic and economic goals. It must be satisfied with its ability to play an effective role in structuring and developing the transaction to the level required or desired. The bank must also determine to what degree, if any, it wants the participation of an investment banking firm. The level of investment bank participation depends largely on the bank's ability to develop its own securitized product. Despite a commercial bank's desire to "do its own thing" in asset securitization, it should realize that securitization is complicated and difficult, and that investment banks are on the "leading edge" of this technology. As a result, banks should try to develop a balanced working partnership with major investment banks to create the most up-to-date, cost effective structures and obtain the best market distribution channels to sell the securities.

THE ROLE OF THE BANK IN PUBLIC MARKET PLACEMENTS

The role of the bank in a public market placement of a securitized asset sale can be multifaceted. Obviously, a bank can be an originator, seller, and issuer of the trust and become very involved in the structuring of the securitized transaction. A bank can also perform the roles of servicer, master servicer, or standby servicer. Additionally, a bank can be involved in the sale of the certificates or securities as a private placement agent, a member of the dealer selling group, a syndicate member, or an underwriter as comanager, lead manager, or sole manager. A bank may serve as a trustee representing the investors' interests, as a letter of credit bank providing the necessary credit enhancement with a standby LOC, or as the transfer agent for the securities. While some banks will have the expertise, resources, and financial strength to be involved in many of these areas, few, if any, will have the wherewithal to perform every role. It is, therefore, important for a bank to understand the requirements of each role and how its strengths and strategic desires might match up with them.

Originator and Issuer

The most basic role is that of an originator and issuer. Most banks originate loans or assets that they may wish to sell through public securitizations. Their level of involvement in the development of the securitized structure is largely dependent upon their desire, prior asset sale experience, and resource availability. Many elements are involved in the development of a publicly offered asset sale, as illustrated in Exhibit 13–7, the Projected Timetable for a Public Offering. The actual elapsed time is dependent on the sense of urgency, needs, abilities, and portfolio problems of the issuer. The purpose of the exhibit is to point out the many elements or tasks involved in completing a securitized transaction. While banks can get deeply involved in an issue, they should only undertake such a complicated task if they have decided to dedicate the time and resources to be successful.

While a bank may ask an investment bank to do a "turnkey" securitization, thus minimizing its involvement, most banks have the ability to participate more fully. First of all, few entities know more about lending and credit than banks. Usually, the bank is also most familiar with the demographics of its marketplace, the loan documents, security perfection issues, and systems involved in the transaction. Therefore, if a bank possesses the resources it can add value to the development of the structure. As issuer, the bank should definitely make a point of working on the development of the legal documentation, particularly the pooling and servicing agreement. This establishes its rights and obligations for

EXHIBIT 13–7
Projected Timetable for a Public Offering

Phase 1:
  Organizational meeting
  Begin drafting registration statement
  Begin discussions with letter of credit banks
  Meeting to review draft documents
  Begin discussions with rating agencies

Phase 2:
  Print registration statement and file with the SEC
  Draft and distribute Pooling Servicing Agreement, LOC Agreement and
    Underwriting Agreement
  Continue discussions with rating agencies
  Prepare drafts of various legal opinions
  Continue discussions with letter of credit banks
  Meeting to review documents

Phase 3:
  Prepare and file amendment to registration statement (including any rating
    agencies' comments)
  Review drafts of various legal documents and opinions
  Receive drafts of prospectus and comfort letters from accountants
  Receive commitment from letter of credit bank
  Finalize all opinions and documents required for the offering
  Seller provides to investment bank a tape of eligible loans for selection
  Receive comments from the SEC
  Prepare Amendment 2 to registration statement to reflect comments from
    the SEC and file amendment with the SEC
  Receive comfort letter from accounts on delinquencies and charge-off history
  Print preliminary prospectus
  Investment bank completes selection of loans to be sold and provides a
    copy to the Seller

Phase 4:
  Prepare statistics and receive confirmation from auditors of loan statistics
  Receive ratings from rating agencies
  Pricing
  Sign Underwriting Agreement
  Prepare final prospectus and file with the SEC

Phase 5:
  Receive final legal opinions
  Receive from letter of credit bank the LOC Agreement
  Closing

the asset sale and subsequent servicing. As the bank develops its experience in structuring asset sale transactions, it should be able to increase its direct involvement in developing various asset sale structures. The bank may also be able to structure asset sales for others; the constraint is the bank's willingness or ability to make the investment to create the innovative structures needed to effectively execute economic sales in a competitive investor market. Investment banking firms invest heavily in research and development activities and commercial banks will have to do likewise to be competitive.

Servicer

The nonmortgage receivables market can be expected to mature like the mortgage secondary market has over the years, resulting in the development of a wholesale receivable origination network and a wholesale-based secondary marketplace. This will obviously give banks an opportunity to perform any of the following functions: wholesale loan origination and sale, or purchase, packaging and secondary market sale of receivables-backed securities while retaining servicing rights.

Much of the economic justification for an asset sale rests with the retention of the servicing rights for the portfolio, as is the case in the more mature secondary mortgage market. Unlike the mortgage product, however, nonmortgage receivable servicing systems typically are not easily transferable between servicers. Because of this difficulty and the interruption of collections and cash flows that may occur if that is required, the financial viability and dependability of the seller/servicer is critical to the investor, the letter of credit bank providing the credit enhancement, and the rating agencies. Because of this, only the larger, stronger financial services institutions have typically been able to publicly securitize rated transactions over the last couple of years. The increasing desire by troubled financial services institutions to publicly sell and securitize their loan portfolios can, however, lead to profitable opportunities for the larger, stronger banks to generate fee-based income. Banks that can develop computer systems capable of efficiently and dependably handling "service transfers" as it is done in the mortgage banking industry, can act as master or standby servicers in transactions that need a stronger servicer to be "saleable." Such opportunities already exist, with investment banks currently indicating a need for experienced master servicers to backstop weaker portfolio sellers. Likewise, banks capable of handling service transfers could step in to take over servicing of portfolios when the original servicer defaults on the pooling and servicing agreement.

Placement and Underwriting

Many commercial banks have been involved in the private placement of their loan portfolios sold in both whole loan and securitized formats. Some banks have also been involved in public underwriting of nonmortgage securitized transactions, primarily as comanagers with investment banks. There has been an ongoing debate between commercial banks and the securities industry about whether the underwriting of securities backed by their nonmortgage receivable portfolios violates the Glass-Steagall Act, which generally separates commercial banking and underwriting activities. Banks have asserted that they have the right to sell their assets and that securitization and underwriting of those assets is a natural extension of credit origination, a position supported by the comptroller of the currency. In April 1987, the Federal Reserve Board ruled banks could underwrite mortgage-backed securities, commercial paper, and municipal revenue bonds and securities backed by consumer receivables. Public underwriting of nonmortgage securities by banks was subject to a moratorium from the second quarter of 1987 through March 1, 1988. The Securities Industry Association challenged the Fed ruling in the courts and in mid-June 1988, after the moratorium expired, the U.S. Supreme Court refused to hear the case, thus confirming the Fed ruling. As of this writing, legislation is pending for expanded banking powers that can once again change the complexion of this issue. It is difficult to predict the final outcome, but it is expected banks will be authorized to at least underwrite transactions backed by receivable portfolios, although they may have to underwrite securities through separate holding company subsidiaries.

Obviously, appropriate market and securities trading experience is important for a bank wishing to underwrite these transactions. The bank must also be registered in each state as a securities broker/dealer and have a subsidiary that is sufficiently capitalized to handle the underwriting. A more subtle requirement for successful underwriting is the need for a large enough distribution network to quickly, efficiently, and economically place the securities with investors. The larger and more complex the transaction, the more extensive the network has to be. Additionally, the distribution network must have access to investors with an appetite for the type of structure and life of the securitized asset being sold. Once a transaction is priced and taken to market, time becomes money. Rapid placement of the securities underwritten is essential to avoid big losses. A bank can mitigate its underwriting risk in several ways. It can develop a co-manager relationship with another underwriter. And it can syndicate the offering with other underwriters and dealers to create the largest possible distribution network. To properly assess its underwriting risk and potential rewards, a bank must assess its underwriting abilities and distribution network capability. In any case, assuming underwriting risk is probably not appropriate for the small, inexperienced or under-capitalized bank.

Non-Underwriting Opportunities

Non-underwriting or selling opportunities may exist for banks that do not want to underwrite. Banks that are properly capitalized and have the systems to properly provide the necessary services to the investor may act as the transaction's trustee, letter of credit bank, or securities transfer agent.

• Trustee activity provides fee income for the trust bank. Involvement as trustee will require a reputable trust organization with a strong deposit and credit rating to make the rating agencies and investors comfortable. Experience in receivable portfolio management is also helpful, and the ability to accept servicing responsibility if a transfer is necessary, due to servicer default or failure, is a definite strength. In order to protect the rights of the investors, the trustee must be able to monitor and analyze both the performance of the portfolio, to determine when the standby letter of credit is activated, and the performance of the servicer, to assure that covenants are enforced.

• Providing the standby letter of credit for the transaction requires financial strength, strong capitalization, and a credit rating, often granted by at least two major rating agencies, that is at least equal to the desired rating for the issue. For transactions done so far, this would require a triple-A rating in most cases and a double-A rating in some cases. Given this requirement, few banks are qualified to act as the LOC bank for these types of transactions; however, fee income opportunity exists for those banks that can provide this service.

• One other type of participation could be as registration and transfer agent for the securities or certificates. To date, banks typically have functioned as registration or transfer agents for their own issues. However, if the bank has the systems or transfer credentials and reputation for this type of activity, it may be able to generate added fee income opportunities in this marketplace.

CONCLUSION

Since 1985, public securitization of nonmortgage receivables has come a long way. The near future will see more banks participating as sellers, issuers, and servicers of their own assets. If expanded bank powers are obtained shortly, the industry will most likely see more banks structuring and underwriting securitized asset sales for other financial services institutions. Many banks should plan to become active in the developing wholesale receivable industry. As the industry matures other banks should consider providing related services, such as trust and letters of credit. Like the development of asset securitization itself, such increased involvement will not likely occur overnight, but will be an evolutionary process that will require preparation, experimentation, learning, success, and even failure.

CHAPTER 14

A REGULATOR'S VIEW OF SECURITIZATION RISKS

Owen Carney, Director
Investment Securities Division, Comptroller of the Currency

The securitization process has a tremendous potential to benefit the banking system by liquefying bank assets, providing more flexibility for managing various types of risk, and generating fee and spread income. By using publicly traded securities to access different sectors of the capital markets, securitization can improve systemic liquidity. Simply put, securitization of banking assets could turn out to be a very attractive form of alternative funding for traditional banking activities.

Securitization is driven by several developments, including the deregulation of bank deposit interest rate ceilings and the resulting increase in interest rate risk, regulatory capital requirements, increased competition for prime credits from investments bankers, and by competition from captive finance companies for consumer loans.

The deregulation of deposit interest rates has resulted in greater reluctance by bankers to continue in the role of the traditional intermediary, that is, purchasing short-term source funds and investing longer term at fixed rates. Securitization may allow a banker to behave like the traditional intermediary in meeting the legitimate credit needs of customers while transferring to investors many of the risks traditionally borne by the intermediary.

Securitized bank loans usually need some type of credit enhancement to make them attractive to investors. Over-collateralization is a common form of credit enhancement for mortgage-backed securities sales. The majority of asset securitization programs involving consumer and commercial loans provide some type of a limited guaranty by the selling bank or by a third party in order to insulate the investors from losses on the sold assets.

REGULATORY ACCOUNTING

It is these guarantees or recourse arrangements by the selling bank and in particular, the reporting of assets sold subject to a recourse arrangement that is a significant concern of bank regulators. Under Financial Accounting Standards Board Statement No. 77 (FASB 77) securitized bank assets can be recorded as a sale if all of the following conditions are met:

• The seller surrenders control of the future economic benefits embodied in the receivables. Control has not been surrendered if the seller has an option to repurchase the receivables at a later date.

• The seller's obligation under the recourse provisions can be reasonably estimated. Lack of experience with receivables with characteristics similar to those being transferred or other factors that affect a determination at the transfer date of the collectability of the receivables may impair the ability to make a reasonable estimate of the probable bad debt losses and related costs of collections and repossessions. A transfer of receivables shall not be recognized as a sale if collectability of the receivables and related costs of collection and repossession are not subject to reasonable estimation.

• The transferee cannot require the transferrer to repurchase the receivables except according to the recourse provisions.

We regulators did not concur with FASB 77 because we are more concerned about the seller's retention of risks than we are about the retention of benefits, and we are not convinced that the seller can reasonably estimate loss exposure, particularly for commercial loans. Today's reasonable estimate may not turn out to be so reasonable in the future. For regulatory purposes the existence of risk is much more important than a reasonable estimate of risk.

It is safe to say that the generally accepted accounting principles applicable to loan sales are easily manipulated. If sellers want to get the assets off their books they can easily have the transaction treated as a sale for accounting purposes. If, on the other hand, they wish to retain the assets on their books in order to avoid recognition of a loss on the sale they can easily structure the transaction as a financing rather than a sale.

Regulatory reporting is more certain. A nonmortgage "asset sale" will be regarded as a borrowing for regulatory reporting purposes if the seller gives the investor any recourse for losses. In this context "recourse" means any investor claims against the selling bank's capital.

In response to this regulatory policy, different forms of credit enhancement have been developed to insulate investors from losses and at the same time allow the transaction to be treated as a sale for regulatory purposes. Rather than provide investors with a claim against a selling bank's capital, these newer forms of credit enhancements depend upon internally generated cash reserves to absorb losses in the sold loan portfolios. Unfortunately, these structures only seem to work with higher rate consumer loan securitization programs.

I expect to see the emergence of other structures that are designed to remove commercial loans from the books of a selling bank and provide investors with some form of credit insurance. Commercial loan credit insurers are going to insist that bank originators adhere to rigorous credit underwriting and administrative standards.

When these new structures emerge the securitization process will continue to expand and most bankers will do well in managing the risks associated with it. However, like any other new banking activity, a small number of bankers will make the regulators' lives difficult by incurring unacceptable levels of risk. Accordingly, the regulatory focus will be on bank management's efforts to identify, measure, and control the risks arising from their own asset securitization program.

The newer, unfamiliar risks in sold and serviced loans cannot be isolated and thought of as unrelated to other risks within the banks. Loan securitization sales must be managed in the context of the overall risk to the institution in order to understand the appropriate level of risk taking within the entire institution. Integration of the securitized assets risk management control systems with the existing risk control systems within the institution is very important.

MORAL RECOURSE

The most difficult risk for bank managers to measure and control is the likelihood that they will follow the time honored practice of protecting their franchise by throwing money at problems that can adversely affect their bank's reputation. Bank managers have historically not walked away from a problem with their bank's name on it. In the market for securitized loans this type of behavior may cause a bank to repurchase troubled securitized loans when it has no legal responsibility to do so. This type of "moral recourse" is the biggest threat to management's ability to increase their flexibility through securitization, and this mind set has to change if the securitization process is to work.

There may be legitimate reasons for a bank manager to repurchase individual securitized credits. It is a standard and perfectly reasonable banking practice to consolidate a troubled borrower's loans, perhaps to waive payments and certainly to establish the best collateral position available by taking liens against all available assets. If some of the troubled borrower's loans are already securitized, a restructuring may necessitate a buy back of the securitized loan. Unfortunately, this type of troubled debt restructuring will certainly be viewed as the seller providing the investor with recourse if it involves the buy back of previously securitized loans.

Bank management's efforts to protect the bank's reputation or to enhance their collateral position by repurchasing securitized loans creates risk—the type of risk that must have additional capital support. Whatever else a selling bank's provision of moral recourse means, it means the need for additional capital support for the unrecorded off-balance sheet risk.

As an aside, securitization of loans to bank officers, directors, or major shareholders raises recourse issues that cannot be controlled, that is, immoral recourse. Loans to insiders should not be securitized.

CREDIT CONCERNS

One disturbing trend that is evident in a number of different securitization programs is an overreliance (by everyone) on collateral values. Traditional bank credit underwriting standards look to cash flow to repay loans and discourage overreliance on collateral. Pawn shops rely on collateral for repayment, whereas investors are supposed to rely on an obligor's ability to repay. The value of collateral can change dramatically. During periods of economic distress collateral values may not provide a ready source of repayment.

Other types of credit problems will occur if the promotional aspects of the securitization process—the investment banking and production considerations—compromise sound credit standards. Hopefully, the credit exposures associated with securitized loans will be controlled by experienced credit people who are operating under well thought out underwriting standards. In the event credit problems in securitized portfolios do occur, experienced credit officers will need to have adequate human and financial resources at their command to quickly resolve credit problems.

Unless management has made a conscious decision to the contrary, the credit strength of borrowers whose loans are securitized should be as strong as that of the borrowers whose loans remain on the books. Allocating lower quality loans to securitization programs will surely lead to problems, unless the process is very carefully planned and administered.

On the other hand, the rating services, the credit enhancers or investment bankers (or all three) may apply pressure on a bank originator to include its best quality loans in the securitization process. If a bank sells its best loans, one has to question what is left and the impact of these loans on the bank's financial condition. I can think of a lot of good reasons why a bank would not want to sell their best loans and only a few less noble reasons for selling top quality loans. Unless management makes a conscious decision to the contrary, the same standards of loan underwriting should apply to securitized loans as to loans remaining on the books.

Regardless of bank management's decision about the quality of securitized loans to be originated for resale, the same loan servicing standards should be applied to loans remaining on the bank's books and to sold loans.

CONCENTRATION RISKS

The securitization process may lessen a bank's dependence on local credits that share common risk characteristics and may be vulnerable to a downturn in the local economy. One only has to look to banks located in energy or agricultural dependent areas to appreciate the effect of a localized economic decline on the local banks. However, securitizing local loans and removing them from a bank's balance sheet should not completely eliminate concerns about the vulnerability of such concentrations of credit. When securitized assets are concentrated in a few kinds of borrowers, they are vulnerable to unforeseeable risks—more vulnerable than a diversified pool of securitized loans. If loans dependent on a common economic factor for repayment are to be securitized, the selling bank should exercise greater care in managing its securitization program. If investors lose their appetite for a particular type of loan or for loans originated in a certain part of the country, the costs associated with curtailing a bank's securitization program may be heavy.

Investor concentrations—the flip side of the concentration issue— is another apsect of securitized loans that should be looked at closely. Presently the market for securitized bank assets is dominated by institutional investors. Institutional investors are driven by a herd instinct. They often tend to move in the same direction at the same time; they generally have the same market timing and liquidity concerns. Accordingly, banks selling securitized loans to one class of institutional investor assume the risk that the market for their securitized assets may weaken or disappear due to an adverse systemic event affecting the class of investor who had supported the market. A bank selling assets to one type of investor must exercise more care in securitizing its assets than a bank selling to a diversified pool of investors. A concentration of investors with similar investment requirements may limit the amounts and types of assets that can be safely securitized.

FUNDING RISK

In dealing with the funding risk associated with sizable amounts of securitized bank assets sold *with recourse,* bank management should have predetermined contingency funding plans. The plans should include a worst-case scenario, based on the possibility that all the securitized loans could return to the seller at the same time and need to be funded. The degree of recourse to the seller dictates the volume of the securitized loans that can come back at any one time. The contingency funding programs should have a predictive quality and not be based solely on historical perspective. The plans should be updated frequently to reflect changing market conditions. In addition to the contingency funding plans, backup emergency funding programs are appropriate.

Loan strips and overnight loan participations are examples of sup-posedly nonrecourse securitization programs that can create funding risks. A loan strip involves the sale of a 90-day increment of a three year revolving term loan arranged under a loan agreement that technically requires a renewal every 90 days. Overnight loan participations are one day sales of longer maturity loans. The buyers of loan strips and overnight loan participations share two characteristics than can introduce significant funding risks to the selling bank. Regardless of what the loan documents say, the investors are clearly looking to the selling bank to buy back their interest in the loan when the interest matures. Also, the buyer often supplies the selling bank with other types of short-term funds, such as certificates of deposits, repurchase agreements, or commercial paper.

It is reasonable to conclude that buyers of loan strips and overnight loan participations, along with other suppliers of more traditional short-term liabilities, will stop supplying funds when they think the selling bank is experiencing funding problems. In this situation the selling bank's repurchase of loan strips or short-term loan participations will have to be funded when funds are more difficult to obtain from normal sources.

RISKS VERSUS REWARD

At some point in the securitization process bank managers must ask themselves if the risks associated with loan securitization are more than offset by the rewards. A selling bank is probably not being adequately compensated for the risks it is assuming if the pricing of the securitized assets is dictated by the pursuit of market share. When a bank is not adequately compensated, then bank management may try to improve earnings by lowering credit standards and increasing volume. If bank managers wish to avoid succumbing to this temptation, they should develop management information systems to monitor securitized loan programs and to evaluate the risks against the potential earnings in a timely and accurate manner.

Determining service costs and establishing fee schedules are among the thorniest problems faced by managers of securitization programs. It is difficult to estimate service costs with any real accuracy. Unfortunately, the costs of servicing many types of consumer and commercial loans vary considerably. The real cost of servicing a sold loan will change with the level of risk being underwritten. Problem loans can be very expensive to collect. However, there is a natural tendency to lower service expense estimates in order to realize more of the sales price as current income. Under generally accepted accounting principles, the seller must defer recogniton of an appropriate portion of sale price in order to cover expenses, if service fees cannot reasonably be expected to cover service expenses.

SERVICING RISKS

Banks also run the risk that clerical errors or computer problems will not permit economical servicing of securitized assets. Existing systems used to service retained loans are usually adequate to service loans that are originated and sold. However, because the standard operational systems were designed for a different purpose, at some point the increasing volume of sold and serviced loans can strain bank operational capabilities. Similarly, if the bank is buying loans to package and sell, the existing operating systems may not be compatible with the servicing system of the originator, and the purchasing bank may not be capable of servicing loans originated by other institutions.

Processing activity on securitized loan portfolios can become so large that operational breakdowns can result in massive out-of-balance positions in a bank's securitized loan service accounts. Such a breakdown can create tremendous liabilities to the investors who purchased securitized loans. Failure to accurately and promptly fulfill service responsibilities can trigger a technical default and thus require a transfer of servicing to a more capable servicer or, at worst, may even force the selling bank to repurchase the assets. Backup methods of servicing or transferring, or selling securitized assets should be worked out in anticipation of possible operational breakdowns.

Bankers must develop the operational capabilities to service what they sell or sell the servicing at the time they begin securitizing the assets. In order to predict servicing needs and to try to prevent operational problems, a very thorough audit of the securitization program's operational capabilities should be undertaken at the outset. Selling banks should also review their insurance coverage (e.g., errors and omissions coverage) to determine if insurance types and amounts are sufficient to protect them against errors by their own employees.

Investors will surely lose their appetite for a bank's securitized assets if significant losses are taken because of negligence by a servicer.

DUE DILIGENCE AND DISCLOSURE

There is another peril for banks attempting to securitize commercial loans. If anything goes wrong with these securitized assets, investors are likely to try to sue the selling bank—the deep pocket. An investor suffering a loss will undoubtedly claim the seller failed to disclose some material information about the borrower. Bank credit files usually contain a great deal of nonpublic information, and this poses a dilemma. Nonpublic information on commercial borrowers is often obtained in confidence. However, material information must be disclosed to investors. If the selling bank fails to disclose material information and the investor suffers a loss, the selling bank may be liable for the loss. Bank managers involved in securitizing loans to nonpublic companies will be in a difficult position when determining appropriate disclosure to investors. Selling banks, working with securities counsel, should develop a policy about disclosure of nonpublic information.

It may be possible to avoid the need to disclose information on privately held companies if the securitization process for middle market commercial loans involves a third-party guarantor. Of course, the third party supplying the guaranty will require a fee and some influence over the credit underwriting and administration processes. Is a cut in earnings and management's flexibility too high a price to pay for progress?

CHAPTER 15

THRIFT INSTITUTIONS
AS ISSUERS

Wayne Hardenbrook, Senior Vice President and Treasurer
Paul Willax, Chairman
Empire of America

BACKGROUND

For a variety of reasons, thrift institutions were early participants in the securitization of auto loan receivables. The economic difficulties of the 1980s and the pressures of deregulation taught many thrift institutions the value of managing earnings with sales of assets. Additionally, competitive pressures in the mortgage markets had begun to reduce interest rate spreads and restrict opportunities of thrifts for profitable origination and sale of mortgages. The expansion of lending powers for federal thrift institutions in the early 1980s to include auto lending, as well as other kinds of consumer lending, permitted many savings banks and savings and loans to aggressively pursue the shorter duration and higher yielding auto loans as tools to improve gap management and increase operating income. Thus, as innovations began to develop in asset securitization, a number of large thrift institutions were well positioned with both auto loan receivables portfolios and the need to find new balance sheet and income management tools.

During the first half of this decade, many larger thrifts had also already developed considerable capital market expertise. The pressures of deregulation and increasing competition had already forced many thrift institutions to seek lower-cost sources of funds and capital in the public capital markets. Many of these institutions accumulated considerable experience with the issuance of public securities through the issue of finance subsidiary preferred stocks, common stock conversions, public debt securities, and other structured financing transactions. Perhaps more important than just the security formation experience was the structure of the securities being issued. Because of the low ratings, or the lack of ratings, of many thrifts, security issues were frequently collateralized, with assets of the issuing thrift or credit enhanced with third-party credit support. This collateralization/credit support experience combined with earlier experience with securitization of mortgages gave a number of thrifts the expertise necessary to easily absorb the financial concepts of asset-backed securities and to form public issues.

Through these early public market transactions thrifts had also developed relationships with major underwriters that helped them become more familiar with capital market innovations, particularly asset-related financings. A number of thrift institutions were already considering asset-backed transactions when the Sperry Lease Finance A computer lease transaction reached the public markets in August 1985. Only five months later, Home Federal Savings and Loan Association of San Diego became the first thrift and the third issuer to sell an auto receivables-backed security. The first GMAC transaction did not take place until December 1985, followed one day later by the first auto loan receivables transaction of Western Financial Federal Savings Bank, done through a finance subsidiary. Then, in 1986, Empire of America Federal Savings Bank entered the asset-backed markets with the largest thrift auto loan receivables offering to date ($190,216,000). Western Financial became the first repeat thrift issuer and Goldome Savings Bank issued a computer leases asset-backed security, becoming the first thrift to issue an asset-backed security not backed by auto loan receivables. Thus, in a period of about 18 months, thrift institutions established market acceptance of thrift-issued, asset-backed securities.

As the asset-backed markets continue to evolve, thrift institutions will continue to be significant contributors. With the expanded powers to originate a variety of consumer lending products and the competitive pressures to find more profitable products, thrift origination of such consumer-oriented products as credit cards and auto loans will continue to grow. Provided with new sources of funding through asset-backed securities, thrift institutions will have significant opportunities to expand market presence and compete for auto loan and credit card business. These consumer lending markets are thus likely to become more competitive, with market share struggles reducing interest rates on auto loans and credit cards and narrowing interest spread opportunities in much the same manner as the thrifts' traditional mortgage market spreads have collapsed. The diminishing spread opportunities will put additional pressure on large consumer loan originators to leverage their originations through off-balance sheet growth. This situation will encourage further issuance of asset-backed securities. Additionally, as the popularity of other consumer products grows and as new products are developed, it is likely that new asset-backed security structures will ultimately be devised. Securitization of new consumer products, however, will be restrained until a track record of delinquency and loss experience can be developed to allow the financial markets to properly value the underlying assets. For this reason, it seems likely that in the near term thrift participation in the asset-backed markets will be dominated by auto loan receivables and credit card receivables.

FACTORS AFFECTING THRIFT PARTICIPATION

The universe of thrift institutions that can be active participants in the asset-backed markets will be limited by a number of factors. The first and most obvious limitation is the availability of consumer loans. Typically, small thrift institutions lack the origination and servicing capacity to generate consumer loan portfolios of sufficient size to regularly issue asset-backed securities. While smaller institutions may, over an extended period of time, accumulate adequate portfolios to support asset-backed issues, the shorter-term nature of consumer products will make it considerably more difficult to build a consumer portfolio than a mortgage portfolio. Additionally, accumulating portfolios for sale over an extended period may prove to be an unsound practice due to interest rate risk exposure. Large thrift institutions, particularly those like Empire of America that operate in multistate markets, are best positioned to develop the origination capacities necessary to provide sufficient volume for regular issuance of asset-backed securities.

Another limiting factor is the capacity to effectively service consumer products. It has been said that consumer loans do not pay off, they have to be collected. This statement is sufficiently accurate to make a highly proficient servicing and collection function critical to the success-ful operation of a consumer lending program. Poor loss or delinquency experience will negatively affect the credit enhancement costs and pric-ing of asset-backed securities. Issuance of asset-backed securities also brings with it the added servicing burdens of reporting to investors. Large thrift institutions seem most likely to be capable of developing effective servicing operations, not necessarily because of any inherently more effective management, but because size may provide the necessary capital base, and large anticipated volumes may provide the justifica-tion for establishing servicing capacities in advance of realizing any of the benefits of the products generated. While size thus seems to pro-vide an obvious advantage, smaller thrifts are not necessarily precluded from participation in the asset-backed markets. Access to active con-sumer markets providing strong originations and effective underwriting and servicing are the cornerstones to building portfolios for asset-backed security issues.

One factor that does not seem likely to be a limitation is the demand for asset-backed securities. In the three years since the first asset-backed security was issued, more than $26 billion of these securities have been issued. Total issues exceeded $20 billion by the end of 1987, with 11 of the active issues at that time having been formed by thrift issuers. To date, asset-backed securities have provided attractive investment vehicles for buyers of intermediate-term corporate debt. These securities have generally carried higher yields than corporate securities of similar maturities and ratings. The yield differential is probably due to the monthly payment structure of many of the issues and the newness of the security structures. Innovation in payment structures and greater familiarity with asset-backed securities will help to reduce this yield differential. Liquidity in the asset-backed markets should improve as these securities develop greater homogeneity and the depth of the asset-backed markets grows.

TYPES OF STRUCTURES

Asset-backed security issuance provides excellent asset/liability manage-ment tools for thrift institutions with large auto loan and/or credit card origination and servicing capacity. The variety of structures available help to provide considerable flexibility for managing operating income, on- and off-balance sheet growth, regulatory capital requirements, and cash flow. To date, two broad categories of security structures exist: financings and sales. Additionally, Empire of America Federal Savings Bank has issued a third type of related asset-backed issue. This third structure utilizes a financing subsidiary capitalized with auto loan receivables to issue low-cost market auction preferred stock.

Financing Structure: Pay-Through Bond

The financing structure is generally an asset-backed, pay-through bond. The issuing thrift creates a debt issue secured by a collateral pool of asset product. The issuer pledges but retains ownership of the assets in the collateral pool. The structure is quite similar to mortgage-backed, pay-through bond issues in that principal and interest streams from the pool of assets are used to pay the scheduled principal and interest on the bonds. Interest and principal payments on the bonds are supported by a credit support structure. The issuing institution may provide a recourse guarantee whereby they agree to replace defaulted receivables up to a specified percentage of the pool. The recourse level must be sufficient to give comfort to a rating agency, based on the loss and delinquency experience of the issuer's overall portfolio, that adequate cash flows will be available to satisfy the bond issue. The poorer the issuer's portfolio experience has been, the higher the recourse would have to be to achieve a top credit rating. An alternative to a recourse guarantee is illustrated by the approach taken by Western Financial Savings Bank in the issuance of auto loan receivable collateralized bonds.

These issues provide a surety bond guarantee for scheduled interest payments and ultimately for full principal repayment supported by over-collateralization of the bond principal. Since most thrifts do not themselves have top credit ratings, the recourse obligation or other credit enhancement structure must be supported by an institution having a top credit rating using a third-party instrument such as a letter of credit or surety bond.

The financing structure can provide a variety of strategic opportunities. For those institutions pursuing asset growth rather than off-balance sheet growth, a debt structure can provide a source of funds for asset growth and development of market presence. Because this structure provides on-balance sheet growth, the full income stream from the assets comprising the collateral pool remains in the institution's operating income; operating income reporting does not have the erratic characteristics that can result from asset sales. This advantage can be of considerable importance to publicly-owned thrifts.

Asset-backed debt issues are also good gap management tools. The cash flows on the asset collateral pool are structured to closely match the cash flow requirements on the debt issue. This structure provides an asset/liability match that has considerably less interest rate risk and provides a much better cash flow match than funding through retail or jumbo certificates of deposit. Securitizable assets, such as auto loan receivables and credit card receivables, typically have amortizing natures unlike the final maturity structure of most thrift deposits. The traditional thrift deposit sources must then only be relied upon to provide whatever overcollateralization factors there may be in the transaction. By reducing the reliance on deposit funding, the timing of cash flows to support asset growth can be more closely controlled. This reduction in the reliance on deposits to fund securitizable consumer products is particularly important in light of the difficulty of accurately forecasting deposit flows and the difficulty in raising deposits at maturities of 3 to 5 years. In addition to the obvious economic benefits of better duration matching, there may also be Federal Home Loan Bank (FHLB) duration matching benefits for thrifts issuing asset-backed debt.

For thrift institutions, there are inherent federal regulatory and income tax problems associated with consumer debt growth. Federal tax and Federal Home Loan Bank Board (FHLBB) regulations are structured to encourage thrift institutions to maintain 60 percent of their assets in "qualifying" assets. Since qualifying assets do not include most types of consumer lending, aggressive consumer lending growth can endanger satisfaction of the qualifying asset test. Western Financial Savings Bank encountered this problem as a result of their formation through merger with a commercial bank and their aggressive auto lending program; they were able to use auto loan receivable securitization to resolve the problem. Western has taken advantage of the FHLBB finance subsidiary regulations to use a special-purpose, wholly-owned subsidiary to issue asset-backed debt securities. By transferring auto loan receivables to a subsidiary, Western substantially reduces the balance of nonqualifying assets on the parent's balance sheet. This transaction allows Western to continue to consolidate the income from auto loans for income statement purposes, while improving their qualifying assets ratio for federal income tax and FHLBB regulatory purposes.

Another interesting feature of the Western transactions is the concept of a guaranteed final maturity. The guarantee is supported by the underlying credit support structure provided in the form of a surety bond. The guaranteed final maturity is structured for three years. With a top credit rating, this structure creates a security that meets the FHLB regulatory liquid asset requirement, while at the same time providing yields somewhat in excess of other qualifying corporate debt securities. It was hoped that this would prove to be an attractive security to other thrifts in their struggle to meet regulatory liquidity requirements without seriously compromising operating income. At this time, it is still an open question as to whether this format has created a more cost-effective security for the issuer. Nonetheless, the concept itself is innovative and could ultimately find applications that will improve the pricing and cost of some asset-backed securities.

Sale Structure: Grantor Trust

Asset-backed security issues can also be formed as asset sales. The sale structure typically is done using a grantor trust, which acts as the buyer of the receivables pool. Units of the trust are sold publicly as asset-backed securities. As with asset-backed debt, thrift asset-backed sale transactions derive their top credit rating through the use of credit support structures. The issuing thrift provides a level of recourse to the grantor trust sufficient to secure a top credit rating. Once again, the thrift's overall portfolio performance provides the base for the credit agency analysis and recourse requirements. Lacking a top credit rating of its own, the thrift's recourse obligation must be supported by a performance guarantee, usually in the form of a letter of credit or surety bond from a top-rated institution.

Unlike asset-backed debt, the level of recourse can impact the accounting treatment of the sale transaction. Generally accepted accounting principles (FASB 77) permit sale treatment of assets sold with limited recourse, provided that any anticipated loss under the recourse obligation is carried on the recourse guarantor's balance sheet as a liability. The Federal Reserve Board, the Federal Deposit Insurance Corporation (FDIC), and the Controller of the Currency are, however, all at odds with GAAP and require debt treatment of any transaction providing recourse of any amount. The FHLBB and the Federal Savings and Loan Insurance Corporation (FSLIC), in their attempt to rationalize and unify accounting treatments, have steadily moved toward aligning their regulatory reporting requirements with GAAP. As a result, thrift institutions regulated by these bodies are able to use a sale structure different from and somewhat simpler than the structure used by banks regulated by the Controller of the Currency. Since loan loss reserves are intended to be sufficient to meet anticipated total portfolio losses, any losses anticipated under recourse obligations should already be reflected on the balance sheets of thrifts and should not require any significant adjustment as a result of an asset sale with recourse.

Sale treatment for issuance of asset-backed securities provides most of the same asset/liability management opportunities available under debt treatment and some significant additional advantages. For many thrift institutions, off-balance sheet growth is more attractive than asset growth that may strain already burdened capital ratios. In the typical grantor trust structure, the selling institution retains the servicing responsibilities and receives a servicing fee. This allows the issuing thrift to leverage consumer portfolios by continuing to receive income on assets no longer on the balance sheet, much as mortgage banking operations leverage their mortgage portfolios. However, given the much shorter average life of consumer portfolios (1.7 years for auto loans), the leverage opportunity is obviously more restricted with consumer loans than with mortgages. Nonetheless, with sufficient origination capacity and an efficient capital market operation, it should be possible to leverage auto loan portfolios two or three times—and perhaps more—depending on the characteristics of particular pools. This leveraging opportunity is of considerable value to those thrift institutions that have yet to reach the ultimate 6 percent capital requirement, since it permits substantial growth without additional amounts of regulatory capital.

While continued leveraging of the consumer loan portfolio seems the most likely use of proceeds from asset-backed security sales, "unleveraging" of a thrift's balance sheet is another available opportunity. With the availability of alternative low-cost sources of funds or during periods of low consumer demand, proceeds from asset-backed security issuance could be used to pay down existing higher cost debt. "Unleveraging" the balance sheet would have an immediate positive impact on a thrift's capital ratios, particularly if the asset-backed sale generated a significant profit.

The ability to generate a profit from the sale treatment of asset-backed security issuance can represent a significant advantage over debt treatment. This ability creates a very useful tool for earnings management. Depending on the size of a thrift's origination capacity, this can be a very powerful, as well as useful, tool. With a large origination capacity and an efficient capital market operation, management may use timing either to maximize profits or to provide earnings when needed. For thrift institutions, maximizing profits and timing earnings would seem to be mutually exclusive goals in most cases; generally, maximization of profits occurs in periods of low rates, while the need for earnings generally surfaces under rising or higher rate conditions. Nonetheless, the capacity to time earnings makes asset sales a very attractive approach, particularly for publicly-owned thrift institutions. It would seem that, given efficiency in the origination, servicing, and capital marketing operations, and market-sensitive pricing in the consumer portfolio, profit opportunities from asset sales should be regularly available, except, perhaps, in times of extremely fast-rising interest rates. This is possible because the securitization process takes a low-credit rating asset, such as an auto loan or credit card, and creates a security with a top credit rating. Ultimately, efficient markets may reduce the spread created by credit upgrading and substantially reduce or eliminate this type of profit opportunity. While this does not seem to be an immediate prospect in today's auto lending markets, increasing competition and declining returns are already beginning to appear in the credit card markets.

Thrifts should approach projections of profits from auto loan sales with considerable caution. A number of variables have to be weighed before a "final" profit figure can be determined. The profit on an auto sale is, in simplest terms, the difference between the sale price of the auto loans and the net present value of the cash flow stream from the auto loan discounted at a rate based on the yield on the asset-backed security less a "reasonable" margin for servicing. Clearly, any change in the cash flow from what was projected will change the profit calculation. This means that, not only must projected payment and prepayment assumptions be developed, but the profit calculated at the time of sale may subsequently have to be adjusted up or down if the actual payment stream on the auto loan receivables proves to be significantly different from the projected payment stream. In general, auto loan receivable prepayments are not affected by the same types of factors as mortgage loans; in particular, auto loan receivable prepayments seem to be unaffected by changes in interest rates. Prepayment rates should be determined based on the specific characteristics of the pool in question.

An additional factor that must be considered in calculating the profit on an auto loan receivable sale is the accrual base of the receivables in the pool. Auto loans are generated under a variety of accrual methods, the most frequent being the effective interest method and the Rule of 78s method. Unfortunately, market acceptance requires that asset-backed securities be issued only under an effective interest rate method. Since the Rule of 78s method is an accelerated method of accruing a loan, conversion of Rule of 78s method loans to the effective interest method will result in a negative adjustment to income to recapture the excess or accelerated income accrued since origination. The impact of the accrual conversion is the same in a financing transaction as well. For this reason, any thrift institution that plans to issue auto loan receivable-backed securities should originate loans using the effective interest rate method.

The third major factor that can affect the calculation of profits from an auto loan receivable sale results from the indirect origination of auto loans through the purchase of retail installment agreements from auto dealers. Frequently, the thrift institution agrees to buy contracts at a specified retention rate. The dealer may then issue auto loans at any rate equal to or in excess of the retention rate. The thrift institution services the loan at the gross dealer rate and sets up a reserve for the difference between the retention rate and the dealer rate. For any such loan held in portfolio, this reserve is simply amortized over the life of the loan to create a net yield equal to the internal rate of return of the scheduled cash flows. However, at the time of the sale of a loan having an outstanding dealer reserve balance, the remaining reserve must be written off. This write-off will result in a negative adjustment to income. For all these reasons, estimates of gross profits from auto loan receivable sales should be closely reviewed for potential adjustments.

The asset-backed sale structure creates the same opportunities for qualifying asset management as the Western Financial collateralized bond transaction. Unlike the Western transaction, the asset-backed sale does not require the complication of a finance subsidiary. The size of the asset sale can be adjusted to solve or aid in meeting the qualifying asset ratio by reducing the amount of nonqualifying assets on the balance sheet. Obviously, the larger the auto loan or credit card portfolio is, the more powerful the qualifying asset management tool becomes.

Auction Rate Preferred Stock

Another asset-backed structure that is of particular interest to thrift institutions is the asset-backed auction rate preferred stock structure. Quite a few thrift institutions have already issued market auction preferred stock through wholly-owned finance subsidiaries. Because of the corporate dividend received deduction, these 49-day auction rate preferred stocks typically have dividend rates that provide a more favorable financing cost than debt issues of similar maturities and ratings. For institutions that have net operating loss carryforwards available for sheltering the income of the issuing finance subsidiary, these preferred stock issues provide low-cost funds on an after-tax, as well as before-tax basis. To date, thrifts have formed these finance subsidiaries primarily with mortgage-backed securities.

In January, 1988, Empire of America issued an auction rate preferred stock that uses auto loan receivables as finance subsidiary assets. In order to avoid federal tax treatment as debt, finance subsidiary preferred stock cannot be directly collateralized. The top credit rating of these preferred stock issues is derived from the subsidiaries being capitalized with top-rated securities and not allowing any liens to be created against these assets. Thus, in the event of default, the preferred stock owners would have first claim against the high-quality assets of the finance subsidiary. Guarantee of sufficient assets to liquidate the outstanding preferred stock and any unpaid dividends is provided by requirements for significant overcapitalization of the finance subsidiary relative to the size of the preferred stock issue. The difficulty of using auto loan receivables as assets of a finance subsidiary is the perceived lesser quality of auto loan receivables and the difficulty that probably would be encountered in liquidating the auto loan receivables in a timely fashion. This problem was resolved by having an independent special-purpose company guarantee to purchase the auto loan receivables in the event of a required redemption of the preferred stock. This third company's purchase guarantee is supported by a surety bond issued by a monoline insurance company. The purchase guarantee supported by surety bond thus resolves both the quality and liquidity concerns that accompany the use of auto loan receivables as finance subsidiary assets and allowed Empire of America to issue asset-backed securities at rates well below the rates on auto loan receivable collateralized bonds.

In addition to providing low-cost funding, the auto loan receivable-backed preferred stock structure creates the opportunity to manage qualifying asset ratios much in the same manner as Western Financial's collateralized bond issues. Since FHLBB regulations follow federal tax regulations for the purpose of determining qualifying asset ratios, the nonqualifying auto loan receivables contributed to the finance subsidiary help to reduce the nonqualifying assets on the parent's balance sheet and improve the ratio of qualifying to nonqualifying.

From a gap management point of view, there are some obvious negatives of funding auto loan receivables with average lives of 1.5 to 2 years with preferred stock that has rate adjustments every 49 days. However, the interest rate risk inherent in this structure is considerably less than the risk that accompanies the mortgage-backed transactions. As with the mortgage-backed transactions, the gross initial spread between the yield on assets and the dividend paid is substantial. In fact, depending upon loss experience and dealer reserve costs, the spread on auto loan preferred stock can be as much as 350 basis points or more. Initial spreads of this size would require upward movements of short-term interest rates of substantial proportions to make this transaction uneconomical.

Auto loan receivable preferred stock has a number of balance sheet and income statement impacts that must be considered. Finance subsidiary preferred stock is reported as a liability on the consolidated balance sheet of the parent thrift. This creates balance sheet growth and an immediate negative impact on the net worth-to-liabilities ratio. In this respect, auto loan receivable preferred stock is the same as auto loan collateralized bond issues. Unlike the bond issues, the mismatching aspect of the preferred stock transaction will increase an institution's one-year gap measurement for FHLBB reporting purposes, thus reducing the potential for the net worth matching credit. For the income statement, the preferred stock transaction has similar but more beneficial effects than the debt issue. Both transactions retain the interest income of the auto loans in gross operating income and create interest expense. The preferred stock issue, however, should create a superior net interest spread due to the lower dividend rate.

CREDIT ENHANCEMENT

There are a number of factors common to all forms of thrift-issued, asset-backed transactions. The most obvious feature of all these transactions is the need for credit enhancement. The most efficient pricing of asset-backed securities can generally be expected to be achieved with a top credit rating from one of the nationally recognized rating agencies. In order to meet rating agency criteria, two obstacles have to be overcome. The first is the relatively low credit rating of auto loan or credit card receivables.

The thrift industry's traditional mortgage loan products carry much less credit risk than either auto loans or credit cards. The higher loan-to-value ratios and depreciating nature of the underlying collateral in the case of auto loans and the lack of collateral in the case of credit cards make both investments considerably higher risks than mortgage loans. Auto loan portfolio loss experience of 2 percent or more is acceptable performance for auto lenders. These higher loss expectations are reflected in the higher rates that lenders demand on these products. The higher credit risk associated with auto loan and credit card receivables is compensated for by establishing a recourse level to the issuer of the asset-backed security. This recourse level requires the issuer to buy back defaulting loans up to a certain percentage of the pool of loans sold. The recourse percentage is set at a level sufficiently above the portfolio loss experience of the issuer to give the rating agency comfort that the potential losses will be fully absorbed by the recourse guarantee. Recourse levels to date have ranged from 5 percent to nearly 20 percent. For a regular issuer of asset-backed paper, it becomes quite important to maintain loss and delinquency experience in line with industry standards; otherwise, recourse guarantee costs may reduce the cost-effectiveness of asset-backed security issuance. It is possible to reduce recourse requirements despite poor general portfolio experience by tightening up pool selection criteria. For instance, the selection criteria might specify only receivables that have never been more than 30 days delinquent and have at least one year's seasoning. Tighter selection criteria create an obvious tradeoff, since they reduce the percentage of the portfolio available for securitization and thus compromise the liquidity of the portfolio. For the regular issuer of asset-backed securities, adequate controls on underwriting and servicing are the best avenues to low recourse levels.

The second obstacle the thrift industry generally has is the lack of top credit ratings on thrift institutions. Since a transaction will carry the rating of the institution providing the recourse guarantee, it is necessary for thrift institutions not having top credit ratings to secure a guarantor for their recourse obligation, typically in the form of a letter of credit or surety bond. The thrift institutions must also secure their obligations under the surety bond or letter of credit by providing acceptable collateral to the recourse guarantor. What constitutes acceptable collateral is a matter of negotiation between the thrift and the guarantor. Discount factors must be established to adjust for price volatility to the assets that are pledged. The actual types of assets that are permissible as collateral must also be negotiated. Typically, mortgage-backed securities guaranteed by GNMA, FNMA, or FHLMC, U.S. Treasury securities, and top-rated corporate securities are considered acceptable collateral. Each individual thrift institution can and should negotiate types and levels of collateral that best suit their existing portfolios.

A possible alternative to the recourse approach might be to create an asset pool sufficiently large to allow the establishment of an escrow or reserve account to fund loan losses. The transaction could be structured much as a collaterized mortgage obligation (CMO) with the asset-backed security receiving priority on asset pool cash flows and the issuer retaining rights to the residual or interest in the asset pool. Whether this method would produce an efficient alternative to credit-enhanced recourse cannot be accurately ascertained until such an approach has been discussed with the rating agencies. This approach may be useful for institutions that lack other types of available collateral for collateralizing the recourse agreement.

DATA PROCESSING

Another significant area of concern for the thrift issuer of asset-backed securities is data processing. The capacity to generate accurate information for portfolio experience and portfolio statistics is critical to the rating agency review and pool formation process. It is not inconceivable that an asset-backed security transaction could be rendered excessively costly or even impossible because the computer systems of a thrift cannot produce the necessary data in the format required. It is quite likely that a new issuer that does not have in-house computer programmers will find it necessary to hire a data processing firm to compile the necessary information. In addition to calculating such statistics as coupon, months from origination, scheduled payment, remaining maturity, final maturity, geographic origin, and dealer reserve, if any, it may also be necessary to perform the calculations required to convert Rule of 78s loans to the effective interest method. It would be ideal if the thrift's computer systems had the capacity to manipulate portfolio data to compile pools using various mixes of loans by coupon, geographic origin, dealer reserve, or final maturity. This capacity to create different pool mixes would allow the thrift to maximize pool configurations under varying conditions.

In addition to the system considerations that must be met to create a pool, an issuer must also consider the requirements of servicing the securities once they are issued. Servicing of auto loan receivable-backed securities can be a complex data processing exercise. Depending upon the structure of the transaction, there may be a need to maintain the identity of the cash flows on the auto loan receivables pool by separating principal, interest, past due principal and interest, and payments made in advance. Additionally, delinquencies, losses, and recoveries need to be accurately accounted for to satisfy the mechanical requirements of the recourse obligation.

MANAGEMENT CONSIDERATIONS

Finally, it is important for any potential thrift issuer of asset-backed securities to designate a project leader or coordinator. The formation of an asset-backed transaction will require the participation of thrift management from a number of areas in the organization. Typically, participants in the project will include representatives from consumer lending origination and servicing, data processing, legal, accounting, and the department responsible for capital market transactions. Coordination of all these functions is critical in order to create an asset-backed security in an efficient and timely manner. The project manager also must coordinate the activities of external parties, such as underwriters, attorneys, rating agencies, recourse guarantors, and trustees. Efficient management of these various entities is important to maintaining control over costs incurred in issuing the asset-backed security. Depending on the size of the thrift issuer and the size of the portfolio and asset pool, the issuance of an asset-backed security may require a considerable allocation of personnel. These resource allocations should be evaluated before making the commitment to issue an asset-backed security, particularly in the case of smaller thrifts where abundant managerial resources may not be available.

CHAPTER 16

SECURITIZING MIDDLE MARKET COMMERCIAL LOANS

Christopher L. Snyder, Jr., President
Loan Pricing Corporation

INTRODUCTION

By the mid-1990s, Wall Street may have discovered that the largest and most profitable source of securitized assets are the corporate and commercial loans that are today locked up on the balance sheets of the 400 principal U.S. banks.

Indeed, the asset securitization movement is already nibbling around the edges of the corporate loan portfolio.

• *Loans are being sold.* Loan Pricing Corporation (LPC) records $5 billion per week of loans originated and sold by banks. An active, liquid sales market is the first step on the way toward pooling and securitization.
• *Loan documentation is becoming more uniform.* Commercial loan documentation is often individualized and idiosyncratic. As more loans are sold, increasingly uniform standards will emerge.

When will commercial loan securitization happen in a major way? Innovation in financial markets is frequently borne of pain and suffering. Merrill Lynch's Cash Management Account (CMA), account, residential mortgage pooling, and the swaps market all spawned from severe financial pressures.

We are entering an era when commercial banks will be taken over and broken up. When this movement reaches its peak depends on the regulators and the global economy. Securitization of commercial loans will be at the epicenter of this upheaval. But banks will have to standardize their loan pricing and documentation before this can really begin to take place.

Currently the commercial loan market is the largest, most price-inefficient and most fragmented market served by the banks. (See Exhibit 16–1).

Interestingly, the commercial lending market is not very well understood by financial market analysts in general. It seems that those who know most about the huge ($600 billion assets, $100 billion credit-related revenue) market are lending officers and lending officers are not analytical people. They are deals people, and like deals people in the securities business or the insurance business, they are paid to do deals, not to think about their market. Bank regulators do think about the commercial lending market, but purely from the safety and soundness perspective of the regulator.

Other players in the financial services marketplace, who are well equipped to analyze this market and discover new approaches (like secu-

EXHIBIT 16–1
Corporate Loan Marketplace

	Annual sales	Risk 1	2	3	4	5	6	Loan volume by customer sales
	Small $0–20 mm	1	30	40	24	4	1	$100 billion
Middle market	50	3	25	25	10	4	3	70
	125	9	15	15	15	8	3	65
	250	9	15	15	15	8	3	65
Large corporate market	1000	3	20	20	15	1	1	60
	Large	15	45	45	21	5	9	140
		40	150	160	100	30	20	500

Loan volume by risk

Source: Loan Pricing Corp.

ritization), are not very familiar with the norms and peculiarities of this market.

Consequently, this chapter has two missions:

1. To explain to commercial lenders how securitization can and will change the commercial lending business; and
2. To explain the functioning of the commercial lending market to those who are interested in finding new markets to securitize.

The chapter is divided into four sections:

The first section, *Introduction to Commercial Lending*, begins with the startling fact that there are no widely recognized published prices for commercial loans. (Loan Pricing Corporation focuses on this problem.) This chapter lays out the size, industry, and risk structure of the market. It describes how lending officers function in a market without external pricing bench marks. Next, this part outlines the rough pricing contours uncovered by Loan Pricing Corporation's pricing research programs. The chapter concludes by dealing with the serious policy issues faced by the commercial lending departments as they cope with the problems of trying to establish a loan pricing policy. Commercial banking is under attack by investment bankers who bring with them an entirely different approach to negotiation. This section of the chapter outlines that clash.

The second section, *Pathways of the Commercial Banker*, deals with the solutions open to the commercial lender. They must learn to accept the axiom that loans have prices and that they must identify and sell at market if they are to survive. This recognition leads to several key management actions, including the establishment of a loan sales distribution system. This sets the stage for Part 3.

Payoffs, Pitfalls, and Profits from Commercial Loan Sales is the third section. There are five ways, in theory, to securitize commercial loans. They can be sold one at a time on an unsecured basis. They can be asset-backed or guaranteed in some fashion. Loans can also be pooled and sold, either to other banks or nonbank investors. Ways to do this are being explored now, but the field is very new and populated with bear traps and land mines that will kill off many explorers before securitization is a success in commercial lending.

This last section, *A Strategic View of the Corporate Loan Business in the 1990s: An Era of Discontinuity*, wraps up the picture and provides what turns out to be an optimistic view of what the future holds for those remaining in the commercial lending business.

INTRODUCTION TO COMMERCIAL LENDING

Middle market lenders are beginning to experience the market pressures that wholesale lenders have been facing since 1981 and that investment bankers experienced 20 years ago.

In fact, middle market lenders can learn quite a bit from the metamorphosis that investment bankers were forced to undergo in the 1970s. Twenty years ago a company dealt with, say, Morgan Stanley or Goldman Sachs because that company had always dealt with Morgan Stanley or Goldman Sachs. No more. Today, corporate finance departments on Wall Street "die on an eighth (of a percentage point)."

The biggest contrast between investment bankers and middle market lenders is that the investment bankers really know the current market price of everything they sell. So do wholesale lenders today—at least the successful ones. Knowing current market prices is a survival trait on Wall Street. It is becoming a survival trait in the middle market as well.

Research shows that loan pricing varies across market segments. Yet how many otherwise astute middle market lenders know the pricing differences between an electronics company and a beverage company with equal sales and risk characteristics? Few if any, I dare say.

This is not surprising. Commercial bankers are trained to be relationship- or deal-focused. Their orientation toward the loan negotiating process places price relatively far down the priority list. Indeed, to many bankers, the notion that loans have market prices that vary by industry, firm size, and other characteristics is an alien idea.

Exhibit 16–2 compares middle market loans to other forms of corporate debt according to complexity and creditworthiness.

A Large, Fragmented, Price-Inefficient Market

The middle market is the largest, most fragmented and least price-efficient marketplace served by commercial banks. There are approximately 45,000 borrowers with sales between $1 million and $250 million, and they borrow about $450 billion from the 400 largest banks. But even the biggest banks see only a small fraction of the total deal flow. The largest bank in the country holds less than 8 percent of the total commercial loan volume.

Consequently, no bank is in a position to map the marketplace in enough detail to produce a complete picture of current market pricing across lending segments.

EXHIBIT 16–2
Context Map: American Corporate Finance

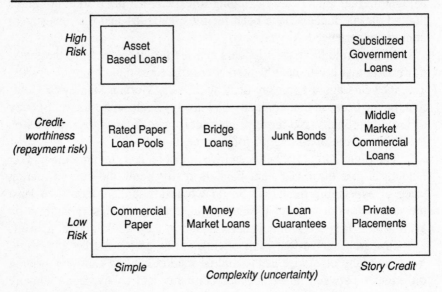

| | Simple | Complexity (uncertainty) | Story Credit |

Source: Loan Pricing Corp.

Furthermore, pricing loans is a complicated business. The all-in rate spread calculation detailed in Appendix A shows a method for calculating the true return—think of it as the return on assets (ROA)— on a commercial loan considering spread, fees, utilization, rate, and credit-related balances. Most banks have great difficulty assembling this information when they want to analyze the pricing of their deal flow or review the pricing in their loan portfolio. And then there is the problem of trying to untangle the implicit subsidies of payments for excess balances and noncredit services.

Consequences: No Pricing Policy; Linear Pricing

Consequently, loan pricing is an ad hoc affair in most banks. In contrast to the orderly credit review procedures followed in most banks, there is no efficient way to price loans systematically on the basis of risk, borrower size, industry, and so on.

The individual commercial lending officers see such a tiny deal flow that they follow "rules of thumb" in bidding for loans. That is, they try to charge the same fees and spreads without taking into account the specific nature of their borrowers other than their size. This is referred to by some analysts as linear pricing.

Because the lending officers see such a small deal flow, they enter the loan negotiation process with less practical information about the market conditions affecting the particular deal than the borrower. The borrower has shopped around and has more practical information about the loan terms he can get. Indeed, the lender is typically in the odd position of having to learn about the market from the customer. Needless to say, the customer is under no obligation to be candid.

The net of this pricing syndrome is that the lender leaves money on the table in dealing with health care or cable companies where pricing seems high, and loses deals in electronics, printing, and other sectors where pricing is lower.

Prices Banks Are Getting

Loan Pricing Surveys collect pricing data from approximately 60 banks of various size throughout the United States. Bankers price standardized loans from various industries. They are asked to estimate the price at which the loan will be made.

This survey process is similar to the methods used by the government, Moody's, and Salomon Brothers to collect financial pricing information. Most financial data that we all use—bond prices, three-month Treasury prices, and certificate of deposit prices—are collected by survey experts who are in the market every day, asking about the current market price for these instruments.

Because the middle market for commercial loans is so much less price efficient than the market for, say, corporate bonds or government debt, Loan Pricing Corporation has to collect 15 to 30 samples per item (three is the usual number in more efficient markets).

The matrix and database constructed from the middle market *Loan Pricing Survey* program provide an intriguing view of pricing patterns in the marketplace.

Exhibit 16–3 shows pricing variation across subregions. Within the Southeast, for example, pricing appears higher in the Nashville subregion than, for instance, in the Charlotte area. These pricing differentials may suggest where the interregional competition will come from.

Exhibit 16–4 shows that the all-in spread varies markedly by sales size. A facility with an average credit score to a firm with sales between

EXHIBIT 16–3
The South: Spread over Prime for 3-Year Revolver

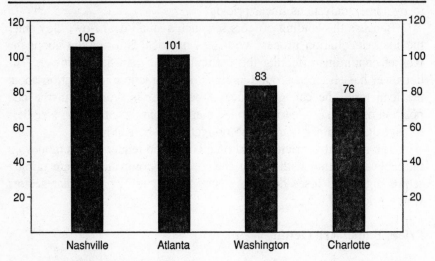

Source: Loan Pricing Corp.

$5 and $20 million averages 280 basis points above funds costs, while a $125 to $250 million sales firm will pay, on average, 214 basis points.

Spread also varies by risk score. Exhibit 16–4 shows that companies with sales between $5 million and $250 million will pay from 175 basis points to 394 basis points, depending on the risk category. And lending is becoming so competitive that a small market appears to exist even at the high-risk end of the marketplace among the special mentions and worse.

Exhibit 16–4 also illustrates a quirk in the middle market. The utilization rate of minimal-risk loans is so low—about 18 percent— that the all-in rate is actually higher (203 basis points) than the rate for modest-risk loans (195 basis points). Needless to say, lending to minimal-risk borrowers is fast disappearing as these firms turn to other sources of credit.

Pricing also varies by industry. Exhibit 16–5 shows prices for companies of the same sales and risk classes but in different industries. Three-year loans to nursing firms or surgical and medical instrument producers carry an all-in spread in excess of 260 basis points. But for radio broadcasters, ordnance producers, and hotel and motel operators the spread is under 200 basis points.

EXHIBIT 16–4
How the All-in Spread Varies

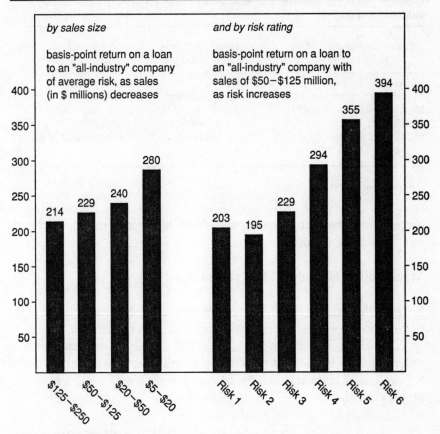

by sales size

basis-point return on a loan to an "all-industry" company of average risk, as sales (in $ millions) decreases

and by risk rating

basis-point return on a loan to an "all-industry" company with sales of $50–$125 million, as risk increases

Source: Loan Pricing Corp.

Bankers give seemingly "good deals" to some relatively unattractive enterprises. Often industries with the best pricing are those that have an element of glamour, like radio and TV receiver producers and TV broadcasters. In other cases, the industry may be easy to understand and therefore attracts so many potential lenders that the lending price is bid down. This perhaps is why retail apparel and accessories companies or auto repair and services firms enjoy relatively low rates.

Most industries are priced fairly close to the norm. Of the 130 industries followed by LPC, about 60 percent fall into this category. Approximately 6 percent carry spreads that are plus or minus 20

EXHIBIT 16–5

Loan pricing varies by industry (All-in spreads for companies of average risk (LPC risk class 3) with sales between $20 and $50 million; selected industries)

Low spread—200 basis points or less	Average spread— 225 basis points	High spread—260 basis points or higher
Radio Broadcasting	Printing	Nursing Facilities
Telephone Communications	Material Handling	Railroads
Motor Vehicles-Wholesale	Freight Forwarding	Surgical/Medical
Ordnance	Personal Services	Equipment
Hotels and Motels	Restaurants and Bars	Furnaces and Mills

Source: Loan Pricing Corp.

percent from the normal spread and about 30 percent are priced plus or minus 10 percent from the norm.

Vulnerability of Middle Market Lenders

Because they shop around, borrowers frequently enter their loan negotiation with more useful pricing information than do bankers.

Typically, the corporate treasurer has sounded out a few banks in order to get a rough idea of what he's going to have to pay. But the lender has no way of knowing what the market price is for a loan to a borrower of this particular size, credit class, and industry. Is the customer bluffing when he suggests that the price is too high?

As noted earlier, commercial bankers tend to be linear pricers. Bear in mind that this practice can cause them to leave money on the table when they underprice a facility to a company that, because of size, risk category, or industry, would be charged more by other banks. And they can lose the deal—and perhaps the entire relationship—if they're not aware that the market has bid the spread low.

All of this is very frustrating to lending officers and leads to extreme perceptions on their part. Some bankers will state outright that they are "price dictators" while other bankers, often in the same city, will lament that they have been forced into the position of being "price takers."

The obvious pricing imperfections in the middle market notwithstanding, neither perception is correct.

In contrast, those investment bankers who "die on an eighth" would never dream of describing themselves as price takers. The ethos of Wall Street is that of a "market maker."

Lessons from Investment Bankers

Investment bankers spend many late nights assembling price books or term books to present early the next morning.

Price books are impressive documents. They strive to convince the customer:

1. That the investment banker (IB) knows the market price (by showing nearby deals and using pricing matrices).
2. That the IB knows the company and industry. This is demonstrated through an exhaustive presentation of financial analysis and industry review laden with facts.

If the investment banker succeeds in his presentation, the customer is convinced that the stated price is correct. This puts the banker in a powerful negotiating position, in this respect: the customer will counter that another IB (or commercial banker) claims to be able to do the deal at a better price. The IB replies with a market-based argument: "You have accepted that we have priced the deal on market. What are the true, hidden costs to you to do the deal below market?"

At this point, the customer is forced to admit that the competing bank is in a position that will be untenable in the long run. The bank may not be able to stand by the customer in time of need.

Dissonance in Negotiating Priorities

Investment bankers lead with price. And, in fact, most borrowers put price first, too. But because of their training, middle market lenders tend to raise the topic of price last.

As middle market lending becomes more competitive, bankers will learn to lead with price and will justify it in market terms.

Importance of Pricing Data

Why is it important to know what bankers are actually getting on commercial loans? Simply stated, it's because both technology and deregulation are exposing lenders to increasing competition from nonbank competitors. This is a competition the banks are eminently suited to win.

As we enter an environment where loans are increasingly sold off the balance sheet, banks with mispriced loans will not be able to sell them at par. To the degree that the risk/return structure of a bank's portfolio is not lined up with the market, the bank will be subjected to arbitrage. And in a market-based world, it is far better to be an arbitrager than an arbitragee.

Need for Pricing Discipline

Loan pricing policy procedures at commercial banks will come to resemble credit policy procedures in terms of efficiency and rationality. In short, pricing will become a managed process.

The development of market-based loan pricing policies will go very far toward meeting two key objections that borrowers have against their bankers:

1. "My bank says it wants a relationship with me, but the only time I get my deal changed is when a competitor threatens to take me away."

2. "The bank hands me a rate on an otherwise blank sheet of paper with no justification. That's why I have to shop around."

A quarter-century ago, Walter Wriston revolutionized the relationship Citibank had with its customers by actually telling them how he set the prime rate. Showing the customer that the rate was market-based created a deep trust that stood the bank in good stead.

Given the greater sophistication of borrowers today, shouldn't Wriston's philosophy be the key to pricing? A bank that takes steps to convince the customer that its loan prices are fair with respect to the market—and will be repriced if the market changes—will instill in the customer a deep feeling of trust toward the bank that will promote an enduring relationship.

PATHWAYS OF THE COMMERCIAL LENDER

Middle market lenders today face the same competitive pressures investment bankers confronted 20 years ago when deregulation wiped out fixed commission rates. Like investment bankers of yesteryear, they must learn to negotiate deals within the context of competitively set open market prices.

Like investment bankers, commercial bankers must not succumb to the defeatist temptation to regard themselves as mere "price takers."

They must instead be "market makers," both in their own eyes and in the eyes of their customers.

The regional bank has several built-in advantages that will enable it to prosper and win in this emerging marketplace, despite a growing list of nonbank competitors.

1. *Credit analysis.* The regional bank can evaluate and monitor the credit quality of its borrowers more effectively than its out-of-town competitor.

2. *Franchises.* Middle market borrowers prefer to deal with the regional bank. In fact, they prefer to turn to banks for all debt needs— including subordinated finance—if the regional bank is prepared to offer these new credit products at market prices.

3. *Cost structure.* Studies by Loan Pricing Corporation show that local or regional banks can originate and service borrowers in their marketplace more profitably than nonregional competitors.

Preserving and strengthening this advantageous position, however, depends on banks adopting as an operating philosophy the axiom that loans must be priced to market.

Middle market lenders must learn to identify and exploit market inefficiencies missed by competitors and to design their cost structures to achieve a sustainable profit based on that strategy. In short, they must adopt market pricing as their axiom.

What Information Technology Offers Lenders

Information technology offers lenders two sets of tools: pricing databases and valuation software.

Loan Pricing Databases
Pricing databases—external pricing benchmarks—lie at the heart of the investment banker's approach to negotiating with a customer. By mutually reviewing the pricing of comparable deals, investment bankers seek to reach agreement with the customer on how a deal should be priced. In other words, IBs work to agree on the market price by surveying the market itself. Both the underwriter and the borrower come to accept the axiom that a mispriced deal eventually leads to trouble for both parties in the transaction.

This is an old idea to investment banking and a new idea to commercial lending. It is, however, well in place among wholesale lenders, and it is fast becoming reality at the middle market level.

For commercial lenders, there are three databases of importance.

1. Current prices of middle market loans by facility type, risk grade, location, and industry of borrower.
2. Current prices of leveraged buyout and acquisition bridge loans and other related forms of loans for sale.
3. Corporate bond prices to compare pricing for fixed-rate loans and subordinated loans.

Valuation Software

Investment bankers use pricing matrices or market-based pricing models to fine tune the price for a specific deal and to test the sensitivity of that price to variations in deal structure. Portfolio valuation software is used to estimate the par and current market value of a portfolio of securities or deals for sale. For middle market leaders, current information technology offers two valuation software sets.

1. Loan pricing matrices, which value individual deals by customer characteristic and type of facility.

2. Mark-to-market software, which permits the lender to value the loan portfolio and identify mispriced deals.

These information technology tools—databases and loan valuation software—are quite new and still relatively crude. But like the information tools developed years ago by Wall Street, they will evolve as their uses become widespread.

Why are these tools only now emerging for the middle market? The chief reasons are deregulation and resulting competition, cheap and widespread computer power in banks as a consequence of personal computers (PCs), and the growing population of analytically trained MBAs in corporate lending. These tools are becoming available because they are *necessary for survival* and because the knowledge and technology is in place for their use.

By adopting these tools, commercial lenders are able to undertake management actions that set the stage for stable profits growth.

Action 1: Marking the Portfolio to Market

These new information tools help commercial lending departments deal with several important pricing policy problems.

"Hallway loan pricing policy." Frequently, senior lenders must approve pricing "on the fly," with no policy guidance or strategy. How

many times each month do junior lenders seek pricing approval by informal means rather than submit each price to a mutually agreed upon set of market-based external pricing bench marks?

Catching mispriced deals in the portfolio. In helping banks mark their loan portfolios to market, Loan Pricing Corporation finds that banks routinely overprice loans to their most creditworthy customers and underprice loans to the "fallen angels" or poorer risk borrowers. LPC also finds serious mispricing by industry and facility type. Identifying and acting to correct these errors preserves relationships with better customers and boosts overall ROA.

For example, Exhibit 16–6 shows a sample of 150 loans taken from a midsized bank. The sample portfolio yields an ROA of 160 basis points on $2 million outstanding. Using the pricing matrix to mark each loan to market shows that the overall portfolio was 36 basis points "under water;" that is, if each loan were priced at market, the yearly revenue would rise by 36 basis points of $579,000.

The bank identifies the mispriced loans by segmenting the portfolio by facility type and borrower characteristic. Exhibit 16–7 shows that prime loans were priced on market, but money market (LIBOR, the London Interbank Offering Rate) loans were underpriced by 70 basis points. This is a common finding. Lending officers often underprice LIBOR option loans.

By risk grade, Exhibit 16–8 shows that high quality loans, of minimal and modest risk, were overpriced by 170 and 15 basis points, respectively. In this case, these loans were traced to borrowers whose sales have grown considerably since the loans were put on the

EXHIBIT 16–6
Mark to Market

	"Year Ahead"	
	ROA	Revenue
Bank	160	$2,515,000
Market	196	3,094,000
	(36)	$ (579,000)
Number of loans		150

Source: Loan Pricing Corp.

EXHIBIT 16–7
Mark to Market Pricing Base

	"Year Ahead" ROA	
	Prime Only	Money Market Price
Bank	230	88
Market	220	158
	10	(70)
Revenue Impact	$41,000	$(620,000)
Number of Loans	125	25

Source: Loan Pricing Corp.

EXHIBIT 16–8
Booked and Market ROA by Risk

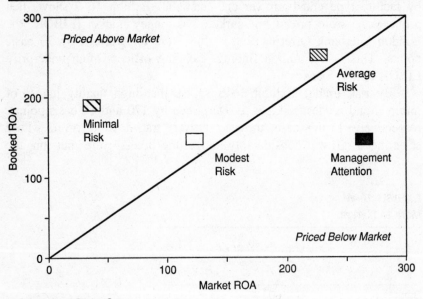

Source: Loan Pricing Corp.

books and whose financial strength had subsequently improved. Although the bank must sacrifice some revenues in the short run, the bank should slightly lower the pricing on these loans. On the other hand, poorer quality loans account for $300,000 of the revenue deficit. These loans should also be repriced or eliminated.

Exhibit 16–9 shows that the bank was doing an excellent job in pricing loans to wholesale, financial services, and heavy manufacturing borrowers. It was underpricing loans to light manufacturers and health care borrowers. (Substantial yet correctable reasons accounted for this.) Loans were overpriced to communications and retail customers.

Exhibit 16–10 groups loans by quintile according to the extent to which they were overpriced or underpriced. Note that while the portfolio as a whole was under market by $600,000, the top 20 percent were over by $350,000. The bottom 20 percent were under by $470,000.

Repricing loans is a painful but crucial procedure. To minimize the problem of the "pricing drift" inherent in its middle market portfolio, the bank must redesign its loan documentation.

EXHIBIT 16–9
Booked and Market ROA by Industry

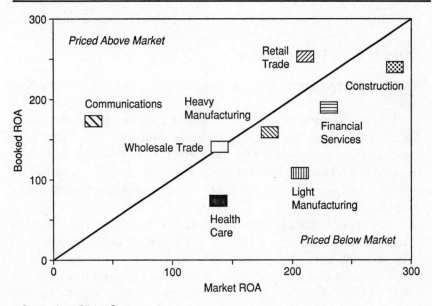

Source: Loan Pricing Corp.

EXHIBIT 16–10
Booked ROA—Market ROA

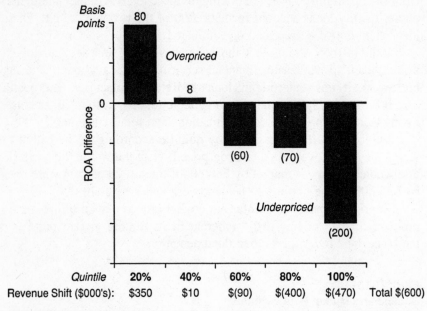

Quintile	20%	40%	60%	80%	100%	
Revenue Shift ($000's):	$350	$10	$(90)	$(400)	$(470)	Total $(600)

Source: Loan Pricing Corp.

Action 2: Loan Documentation

Most lending agreements still carry covenants of the "Thou Shalt Not" variety.

Under this approach to documentation, no automatic mechanism reprices the loan as the borrower becomes stronger or weaker. "Risk-based" lending agreements, however, which have emerged strongly in the deals market and are also appearing in specialized lending situations, provide a badly-needed adjustable pricing apparatus directly tied to risk characteristics.

A typical risk-based covenant might offer the borrower the incentive to reduce the spread on a loan if a key financial ratio changes in its favor. It might also automatically give the lender a wider spread if the borrower is not able to improve on a key financial ratio over a certain period of time. Increasingly, banks will rewrite their agreements with fewer covenants, but build in preset fee and spread changes that both insure that the bank is adequately compensated and yet give the borrower more financial flexibility. Borrowers, on the whole, are in favor of this new type of agreement.

Action 3: Negotiate Like an Investment Banker

A key contrast between investment bankers and commercial lenders is that investment bankers really know the market price of everything they are trying to sell. Investment bankers negotiate much like good real estate brokers. Rather than seek to impose a price on the transaction, the IB examines comparable deals, then strives to reach a mutual understanding with the customer on how the deal should be priced. Similarly, a good real estate broker lets the customer set the selling price for the house by encouraging the customer to review the prices of comparable houses.

Frequently, the pricing is presented in an impressively formulated "price book" or "term book," which contains:

- Financial analysis of the customer;
- Analysis and projection of the customer's industry;
- Listing of comparable deals—stressing price;
- A description of the transaction and price range.

Wholesale lenders are learning fast that their selling methods must increasingly resemble those of investment bankers. Most middle market lenders, in contrast, still view price as a threat. Rather than lead with price, they raise the question of pricing late in negotiations. Rather than develop the price by reviewing comparably structured situations with the customer, middle market lenders present the loan pricing *naked*, with little or no justification or rationale.

This method is obsolete. It invites the customer to shop around and leaves the lender with few negotiating points.

Of course, if the lender truly tries to identify the market price for the deal, it may be discovered that the price is too "skinny" to put on the bank's books. The lender may still originate and service the loan, but it must be sold. This leads to the fourth management action.

Action 4: Learn to Sell Loans—and Build Distribution

Exhibit 16–11 shows how commercial banks are redesigning their "value-added chains" to accommodate the greater pricing efficiency they are finding in the corporate lending market. Regional banks have a built-in

EXHIBIT 16–11
Current Lending Operations

Current Structure: Banks keep what they originate. This leads to inefficient portfolios.

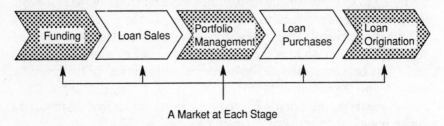

A Market at Each Stage

Future Structure: By unhinging the link between originating loans and holding loans, banks
can develop lending specialties, optimize the portfolio and price loans to market.

Source: Loan Pricing Corp.

cost advantage in originating loans—they can do it cheaper than either
the out-of-town banks or the investment banks. But in the future, many
of these loans will still be too thinly priced for the banks to hold them
on their balance sheets.

In the 1990s, stock analysts will increasingly cite strong loan sales
distribution as a key to banking success.

Just as broad, deep, liquid CD networks spelled stock market success for commercial banks in the 1960s and 1970s, so the top performing
banks of the 1980s will achieve stable profits growth by learning to find
markets for all of their assets, especially commercial loans.

But a key to the distribution network will be whether the product
is credible; and credibility in the emerging loan sales business depends
on developing a reputation for excellent credit analysis.

Action 5: Invest in Credit Analysis

Sound credit analysis has always been a necessary, if not sufficient,
condition for commercial banking success. A reputation for astute credit
analysis will go hand in hand with a reputation for skill in loan sales and

distribution. Investment banks clearly recognize this, given the numbers of bank credit officers they are hiring.

Action 6: Designing a Profitable Cost Structure

The previous discussion leads inevitably to the conclusion that commercial lending operations must change their cost structure to achieve sustained profitability.

1. *Loan origination.* Selling at market puts less stress on personality and more stress on deal structuring ability. Banks will need fewer but more highly compensated lending officers.

2. *Market research.* Investment banks or the capital markets sections of larger commercial banks must add staff analysts to prepare "term books" and to keep current on market prices.

3. *Distribution.* Some of the lending officers will be redeployed in building loan sales and distribution operations.

4. *Credit analysis.* This area must be strengthened.

5. *Back office.* Operations will be expanded to service sold loans.

These changes are underway at the so-called superregional banks. All commercial lending operations will come to recognize the need to identify and negotiate around market prices—or they will leave the market.

Conclusion: Stress Test Ahead

The speed with which these changes can be made depends on how tight credit will be in the decade ahead.

Reading today's business news, the economy appears to be testing its capacity limits. There will be labor shortages in the near term. The falling dollar is affecting export sales in a major way. We may be in for a small boom in capital and inventory investment. The Federal Reserve, in all probability, will push up the yield curve to dampen inflationary tendencies, especially in the commodity and labor markets. Open credit markets do not do well in this environment. Indeed, the junk bond market really dried up during the April 1987 inflation scare. Equity markets too, tend to fall when rates rise. Expanding loan volume coupled with the Federal Reserve Board's risk-based capital guidelines will push banks toward market pricing and loan sales. The speed of change will depend on the stress the regulators and markets place on the banks.

PAYOFFS, PITFALLS, AND PROFITS OF COMMERCIAL LOAN SALES

The size, average lending spread, fragmentation, and obvious price inefficiency of the commercial lending market makes it a tempting target for invaders.

Nonbank competitors bring with them novel business systems and different ways of defining success. The commercial lending market, of $600 billion generating nearly $100 billion in credit-related revenues and a 250 basis point median spread over the marginal cost of funds, is attracting competition from the moon.

Indeed the marketplace has been under attack since the late 1950s when commercial paper became a viable option for the largest and most creditworthy borrowers. Later, other entrants began picking away at the commercial lending franchise. Asset-based loans, private placements, and junk bonds are several of the more successful nonbank credit products.

Now commercial lenders face competition from an entirely new quarter. Some think that nearly every asset with a cash flow stream and a long-term payment history is an eventual candidate for securitization. This view raises several key questions:

- How far and how fast will the commercial lending market become securitized?
- More fundamentally, what is securitization as it pertains to commercial lending?
- Why is it being so seriously considered at this time?
- Who will benefit from changes along these lines? Who will be hurt?
- What are the regulatory and risk aspects of this move?

The Neighborhoods of Commercial Loan Securitization

Securitization converts illiquid assets—loans, mortgages, lease agreements, and so on—into liquid securities, readily traded on financial markets.

Commercial loan securitization is grouped into four "neighborhoods":

- Individual loan sales
- Asset-backed individual loan sales

- Individual loan sales backed by a guarantee
- Loan pools

Many of these things have been done by banks and nonbanks for years, but under different names. Many old timers look at this list and wonder if there is really anything new here at all, other than some esoteric jargon.

In fact, there is quite a bit that is old, but its discovery by nonbank competitors is giving these "neighborhoods" an ominous new twist.

Individual Loans

Banks have sold individual commercial loans—with and without recourse—for years. More commonly, banks "participate" loans to correspondent banks, retaining a share of the exposure and the revenue and continuing to service the loan.

Typically, only high-quality loans to "known names" could be sold, with the selling bank retaining at least a moral obligation to monitor the credit standing of the borrower. Often, the originating bank would take the loan back if it ran into difficulty, especially if the purchasing bank was much smaller.

Commercial paper emerged as a viable alternative for the largest and most creditworthy borrowers in the late 1950s.

Banks were prohibited, both by regulation and internal attitudes, from jumping on the nascent commercial paper market and making it their own. Consequently, investment banks moved into this niche and prospered. Commercial paper is today a $70 billion market. There are no technical reasons why banks had to lose this business. (Ironically, commercial paper issuers return to the bank for letters of credit to back up their commercial paper lines. Banks earn a 1/16 to 1/2 percent annual fee on these arrangements.)

Recent Developments.   Since 1984, leading banks have invested heavily in "loan sales desks." These new functions sell approximately $11 billion per month in loans. The loans fall into three categories:

- *Money market loans*—loans to highest quality borrowers who typically issue commercial paper. These money market loans are hardly distinguishable from commercial paper in terms of pricing, borrower, and purchaser. Trading slightly above commercial paper spreads, these give the borrower more flexibility and liquidity, especially when the markets are roiling over bad news. They are not directly profitable for the banks.

• *Corporate restructuring loans*—The Hawley Group deal, the Hospital Corporation of America deal, and other corporate restructuring projects require huge bridge loans to "grease the path" from the transaction to the eventual long-term financing arrangement. The *Deals Database* provided by Loan Pricing Corporation records about 50 of these large transactions each month. Commercial banks are leaders in arranging and distributing these large bridge loans. For practical purposes, these loans trade like securities. Buying syndicates are arranged among smaller banks, foreign banks, and insurance companies. Thrifts and nonbank purchaser loans are sold and resold. Distinct market pricing is evolving.

• *Special situations*—A large western bank decides to leave the wholesale lending market; another bank decides to "get out of" loans to midwestern customers because they are too costly to service. A commercial bank suffers severe losses and must trim $250 million in loans to comply with regulatory capital guidelines. All of these are special situations. Billions of dollars of loans trade each year for these purposes. It is difficult to say that any of these situations, or any of the loans, are securities in the usual sense. But this market is huge and, while individual players come and go, the market is probably fairly stable in terms of volume and pricing.

Asset-Backed Loans

Traditionally, asset-backed lending was a borrowing mechanism for smaller and weaker corporations. Receivable factors companies are an ancient and simple form of asset-based lending institution. During the 1960s, asset-based lending became more sophisticated using equipment leasing financing to underwrite the purchase of computers, railcars, construction equipment, and other forms of machinery. Though asset-based lending developed first for the least creditworthy corporate borrower, today asset-based loans are a viable alternative for all borrowers with collateralizable assets. General Electric Capital, Westinghouse Credit, and CIT are dominant examples of nonbank players in the large and growing marketplace for asset-based loans.

Traditionally, an asset-based loan was held by the originating institution and not sold. Recently, the same characteristics that make asset-based lending attractive to banks and other institutions are forming the basis for asset-backed loan sales. Basically, if the receivables or other assets pledged are widely perceived in the market to be low risk, then the act of pledging transfers the risk from the borrower to the assets. Thus, to create an asset-backed security the following characteristics must be present:

- Widely recognized high-quality, low risk, highly liquid assets
- Sufficient assets to fully collateralize the loan
- Assets must be capable of being stripped away from the business with no covenant encumbrances

How Big a Market?

How big a market potential exists for sales of individual loans backed by collateralizable assets? There is no good market data on this question but investigation suggests that it is fairly limited. There appears to be a limited quantity of high-quality assets not already involved in an existing asset-backed loan or lease—either in a bank or in a nonbank like GE Capital. Such unencumbered assets that remain are viewed by banks as security for the loans that they have already made and they would object to being placed in a subordinated position through an asset-backed loan sales scheme. Further, packaging this type of security is tricky and costly as a practical matter. There are no standard terms and conditions. Buyers of the loan would have to understand the esoterica of the secondary market for specialized corporate assets or receivables. Asset monitoring systems would have to be established by the entity that structured and sold the asset-backed loan.

Guarantees on Individual Loans

This sector of the loan sales movement shows sizable promise, and not because of innovative technology or new ideas coming from the investment banking market. If the Fed imposes capital risk guidelines in their present form, commercial banks will be driven from the loan guarantee business, and this will leave a huge vacuum.

There is, however, a second, innovative loan guarantee business. For practical purposes, it is still on the drawing boards. But if technology, innovation, and regulation come into proper alignment, this could prove to be revolutionary for commercial banking.

To keep these two loan guarantee businesses strictly separated, let's make the following distinctions:

Banks have been in the old business of loan guarantees for years. It is called the letter of credit (LOC) or standby letter of credit business. It is a large and important business that banks will lose if the regulators strictly apply the risk capital guidelines currently under discussion.

The new business of loan guarantees is based on the fact that commercial bank loan portfolios today are poorly diversified by geography and industry. If banks can learn to separate their loan origination function from their loan portfolio holding function through the development of a robust, liquid interbank secondary market for commercial loans, banks will be in a position to achieve much more stable earnings growth. This, in turn, could pave the way for a reward from the stock market in the form of higher price/earnings ratios.

The "Old" Loan Guarantee Business

This business is big. By early 1987, the 20 or so largest banks had more than $1 trillion in letters of credit and other types of guarantees on their books.

Letters of credit make good business sense for banks. The credit review and monitoring functions of commercial banks, along with their role in the payments mechanism, are a key to their franchise, enabling the banks to quickly write letters of credit with a good profit margin. The bank lends its credit rating to the letter of credit holder's transaction based on the bank's credit review. The bank analyzes the complexity of the deal and determines the true creditworthiness of the transaction. The bank earns a fee for that effort.

This business made sense for the banks and consequently it grew rapidly. Unable to lend funds to the largest and most creditworthy borrowers because the spreads were too thin, the banks could underwrite or guarantee a commercial paper line or other transaction because the LOC contingency did not appear on their balance sheet. Hence, guarantees represented pure fee income. The Fed capital guidelines may drive banks from this business unless ways can be found to harmonize the regulators' capital requirements with the reality of the marketplace.

Financial guarantees do not have to cover the entire loan exposure. After 1984, large banks began experiments with "strip sales" of commercial loans. Banks strip a 5- to 7-year loan into 30- to 90-day sections and sell each section without recourse. If the credit has not deteriorated within that period, the issuing bank takes the loan back and resells it. The purpose of this approach is to "levitate" the loan off the balance sheet of the bank and, hence, lower capital requirements accordingly. We should note that as a practical matter, the accountants have not entirely bought this scheme. It is doubtful that banks can use loan stripping to lighten capital requirements.

The "New" Business of Loan Guarantees

Congress has chosen to retain the populist tradition of American banking by deferring national banking. Instead, Congress has chosen to "Balkanize" banking by permitting the development of large regional banking groups in the country. This is permitting the development of "mega-regional banks" that may develop franchises across several states but which may not operate nationwide—at least until current banking legislation is changed.

Leaving aside questions about the wisdom of Congressional decisions in this area, the current legislative recipe creates a strong case for a secondary market among banks for middle market commercial loans. The stock market knows that middle market loan portfolios of the 400 principal commercial banks are poorly diversified by region and industry. The stock market also knows that this poor diversification causes banks to get into trouble—as energy, agriculture, and real estate loans clearly attest. The market senses that the commercial loan portfolios of most banks represent a sort of undiversified industrial "conglomerate" about which the stock market has little information and from which considerable bad earnings news has emanated over the past 15 years.

Little wonder, then, that bank stocks tend to trade at 70 percent of the price earnings ratios of the S&P 500. This means that banks pay more for capital than their industrial borrowers. This state of affairs genuinely hems the banks in.

The logical solution is for banks to separate their loan origination from their loan holding or portfolio function. In other words, banks must learn to originate and sell loans but continue to service them. And they must learn to buy and hold loans for portfolio diversification purposes that they do not originate.

These new functions require an active, liquid secondary market for commercial middle market loans. This market does not exist today.

Banks also need a secondary loan sales market for liquidity purposes. When banks start to press up against the risk capital guidelines (as they will the next time there is a surge in commercial loan demand), the fastest growing banks can stay in the game only if they can sell off loans to slower growing institutions. They can then use the cash to make new loans, retaining the servicing fees and noncredit revenues.

These two functions, portfolio diversification and asset reduction, will be called asset liquidity management. Asset liquidity management will be a key to commercial bank prosperity in the 1990s. Indeed, the banks that will be the stock market stars of the next decade will master asset liquidity skills just as the stock market stars of the 1960s and 1970s mastered the art of liability management by establishing robust distribution networks for their certificates of deposit.

The key to asset liquidity management lies in the development of a secondary market for middle market loans. And the development of a middle market loan guarantee industry may prove to be the key to that market.

It is possible that the insurance industry, not the banks, will champion the loan guarantee business. Operating under a mish-mash of state regulations, insurance companies are far freer to innovate in this area than banks.

Loan Pools

The last securitization method involves establishing pools of middle or wholesale loans. Similar in concept to mortgage, credit card, or auto loan pools, a commercial loan pool would spread the risk of individual default in a fashion that would permit the calculation of the expected value of default or creditworthiness.

Pooling is used to transfer, at least to some degree, unpriceable uncertainty into priceable risk. Some events can be shown to be members of a large and stable population that behaves in a predictable fashion. Identifying like cases and organizing them into pools is the neat technical trick discovered by life insurance actuaries and now applied to a large array of new financial vehicles. Salomon Brothers evidently has done this for their certificates for automobile receivables or cars.

Whether this information technology can be successfully transferred to commercial loans, without additional credit guarantees, is an open question.

The answer may hinge on the nature of corporate profits. Professor Frank Knight of the University of Chicago makes the distinction between risk, which can be analyzed and priced, and uncertainty, which cannot be measured and priced. The probability of auto loan default appears to be an example of poolable and priceable risk. Professor Knight states that business profits may belong to a class of events that cannot be effectively pooled. "That's what gives profits their peculiar character," he said.

Unenhanced pooling of commercial loans, in a sense, represents what banks do now. Whether they can exist outside the banking system has yet to be demonstrated.

A STRATEGIC VIEW OF THE CORPORATE LOAN BUSINESS IN THE 1990s: AN ERA OF DISCONTINUITY

The corporate lending market is facing the prospect of sudden changes in the way business is conducted. These discontinuities will profoundly change a system that has been relatively stable in structure and function for many decades.

Though corporate lending departments specialize to a degree, most are patterned after the "full service" model established before World War II. They perform their own credit analysis and spend the bulk of their resources marketing and maintaining customers and hoping to establish lucrative lead bank relationships. For the most part, they hold the loans they originate. Corporate customers strive to reduce borrowing costs by resorting to commercial paper and fostering competition among banks.

Powerful forces are creating a discontinuity with this system:

1. *Corporate bankers cannot sustain portfolios that are both profitable and safe.* Corporate lending departments are overstaffed for the 1980s. Hence, competition is unsustainably intense. Risk adjusted, the average corporate loan today is probably unprofitable. Banks must either create truly new products and enter new markets or shrink staffs on the order of 25 percent.

2. *We are entering a period of grave difficulty.* Unlike previous economic recoveries, corporate balance sheets did not improve significantly from 1982 to 1984. This factor, coupled with a mediocre profits outlook, suggests that the slightest increase in rates will place unprecedented burdens on corporate solvency.

3. *Bank earnings are becoming unpredictable.* Bank security analysts do not have enough information to analyze corporate loan portfolios. Corporate loan portfolios resemble small scale industrial conglomerates. This may partly explain the depressed price/earnings ratio of bank stocks and the interest rate floor under CDs. These trends are making bank capital and credit very expensive.

4. *New demands for corporate lending market research.* Almost overnight, corporate lenders are establishing market research functions and demanding highly specific information on corporate lending patterns, lead bank relationships, and pricing.

These discontinuities are placing great pressure on the corporate lending system. This pressure will spawn a new business. While it is impossible to pinpoint how and when the new system will emerge, it will contain three major innovations:

1. *Unhinging the Lending Function*—Corporate lending departments will become differentiated and highly specialized. The business will cleave along three major divisions: relationship management, the transaction or administrative function, and the investment or portfolio function. All but the largest departments will specialize.

2. *Technology*—An active secondary market for corporate loans will evolve. An electronic marketplace will evolve, geared to the highly individualized nature of corporate loans.

3. *Loan Portfolio Organization*—Banks will balance their corporate loan portfolios through the new secondary market. The market will establish prices based on credit risk, location, industry, size, and other corporate characteristics. Corporate loan portfolios will achieve much better risk-return characteristics than they do today.

The corporate lending business will remain vulnerable until this new system is in place. However, as the discontinuities are resolved, bank P/E's will improve, and banks will achieve sustained profitability.

This vision of the U.S. corporate lending markets in the late 1980s is by no means accepted by most lenders today. This report represents these ideas and establishes a framework for debate.

The Peril of Visions

Peter F. Drucker, the management philosopher, stated in his 1968 book, *The Age of Discontinuity*, that the economy was entering a period that would differ sharply from the past.

"The industrial world as we know it today, the principal industries—steel, petroleum, autos, agriculture—were all basically in place in 1900.... [Even] most of the major names appearing on the New York or London stock markets are companies originated by our Victorian or Edwardian great-grandfathers." But, Drucker asserted, this was coming to an end." "The economy is entering a period of discontinuity as radical as the period from 1850 to 1913."

And Drucker wrote, "If a good economist or businessman were to fall asleep in 1913 and awaken today (1968), he/she would be astonished, not at how much things had *changed*, but how much things had stayed the same."

In the half century before 1913, the economic map of the world was changing fast. Developing economic giants such as the United States, Russia, Japan, and Germany were forging ahead of the old champion— Great Britain. New industries, new nations, and a new financial system were established. Between 1913 and 1968, the world economic order did not change significantly.

Therefore, the prognosticator of 1913 could have forecast the 1968 industry structure with reasonable accuracy—just by extending trend lines. However, he would never have dreamed of forecasting continuity because his entire experience was based on a world of discontinuity.

In 1968, Drucker was warning us not to extrapolate experience. Indeed, the last 16 years have witnessed the oil crises, erosion of basis industry, and the rise of high technology and service-oriented economy.

Like the global economy of 1968, the U.S. corporate loan market of today is entering a period of discontinuity that will change the basis of business lending.

The Market for Corporate Loans

Imagine a corporate banker who fell asleep in October 1970, just before floating exchange rates and the Arab oil crisis of 1973 shattered the post-WWII world economic system. Had he awakened in 1982, and being a good banker, immediately reached for the latest banking statistics, he would have been very surprised—not because banking had changed so much, but because it had changed so little. As of 1982, all the ripping inflation, deregulation, and painful strains seem to have left few traces on the corporate loan statistics. In fact, the chief problems of 1972 were still recognized as the chief problems of 1982.

Only during 1984 through 1987 did discontinuities appear. Certainly, there had been changes in how we *thought* about corporate banking. But the basic lending process had undergone little real change.

Fundamentally, the *technology* of corporate lending is still based on the transactional computer, the telephone, and the jet plane. Because credit judgment is still more of an art than a science, banks strived for long-term banking *relationships*. The lending officer focused on the *changes* in the clients' business or management to signal shifts in creditworthiness. The corporate banker sought to attain a lead bank relationship, supplying a bundled full-service product line.

Throughout the post-WWII period, this full-service bundled relationship has been under attack as corporate treasurers sought cheaper financing routes via unbundled pricing and the commercial paper market. During this period, both the terms and pricing evolved and changed as floating rates became necessary. Until very recently, however, U.S. corporate banking was practiced under a structure bequeathed to us by the bankers of 40 years ago. But in the past 24 months, the ground on which that structure was built has shifted.

Four Discontinuities

As indicated earlier, we face at least four major discontinuities.

Discontinuity 1: Difficulty in Sustaining Portfolios That Are Both Profitable and Safe

In the 1960s, the "real" volume of corporate loans expanded dramatically. In the 1970s, the nominal volume continued to rise but the real volume trailed off.

There is considerable anecdotal evidence that corporate lending staffs continued to grow even though the market did not grow in real terms. Banks were misled by the actual dollar growth. In fact, the corporate loan market was becoming much more competitive as staffs grew.

Because of these pressures, corporate lenders find it increasingly difficult to sustain portfolios that are both profitable and safe. Hence, despite the 30 percent gain in corporate loan volume in 1984, corporate bankers perceive the future as quite competitive. They react to worsening competition by:

- Shaving rates to the bone
- Improving products

- Positioning the loan portfolios for a change in interest rates (a form of Russian roulette, with comparable odds)
- Making lower quality loans

There are numerous examples of corporate loan departments pursuing each of these actions but none of these actions deal with the basic problem that occurred during the 1970s when there were too many lenders chasing too few deals.

There are only two viable strategies available to the industry:

- Shrink staffing, probably on the order of 25 percent
- Innovate—Develop truly new markets and products to generate growth

Discontinuity 2: An Era of Grave Credit Difficulty

Business is still riding the crest of the best earnings rebound in 40 years. Yet, an examination of corporate balance sheets suggests that once this cyclical surge is over, difficulties will undoubtedly resurface. It would astound our Rip Van Winkle banker to see what slight progress corporations have made, or bankers have insisted upon, in restructuring corporate balance sheets.

Fragile Balance Sheets.   As Steven Roach, vice president of Morgan Stanley points out, despite the bull market from 1982 to 1987, manufacturing companies in the first half of the 1980s had a lower equity-to-debt ratio than in the late 1970s. Even worse, there has been an ominous shift in the composition of liabilities. After rising at an extraordinary pace during the last recession, short-term debt has risen at nearly twice the normal rate for this phase of recovery. Nor does the asset side offer relief. The current ratio (liquid assets to short-term liabilities) has never looked worse at this stage. Today, only $1 of every $4 of short-term debt service will be offset by the earnings of floating-rate assets. Despite some publicity to the contrary, only the slightest use of "swaps" or other hedging devices like futures has been used to neutralize the interest rate risks.

Consequences.   Corporate earnings are unusually sensitive to fluctuations in short-term rates. Thus, the ominous tilt in balance sheet ratios suggests that an upward surge in interest rates will place unprecedented burdens on corporate solvency. It doesn't take much imagination to see that earnings growth could be brought to an abrupt halt whenever short-term rates exceed 10 percent.

Discontinuity 3: Unpredictable Bank Earnings

The job of a stock analyst is rarely easy, especially in the late 1980s. But most have a *model* of the stocks they follow and their errors can be linked back to faulty assumptions. But in addition to the task of specifying assumptions correctly, bank stock analysts have a special problem—many believe that they do not have enough information to construct the model.

A comparison between the year ahead estimates of 250 bank stock analysts suggests that they are having real trouble forecasting bank earnings.

The problem centers in the corporate loan portfolio (certainly international loans have been a highly publicized problem, but they affect only a handful of banks). Stock analysts do not have good information about a bank's corporate loan portfolios. They do not know its industry composition, pricing terms, or commitment structure.

This crisis of information is beginning to affect the perceptions of financial market analysts. To some, it appears as though each bank is, in effect, constructing a mini industrial conglomerate. As P/E ratios suggest, investors shun conglomerates.

This discontinuity—not knowing how to predict the earnings or capital value of corporate loan portfolios—may lead to a crisis of confidence on the part of big buyers of bank stock and CDs.

A major concern relating to the big bank crises of 1984 is not just what happened, but that so few apparently knew there were problems until the events occurred. A CFO of a major company remarked in May of 1984, when Continental Illinois' funding difficulties became public, "I have a $2.5 mm CD in that institution. I didn't plan on losing any of that, I haven't told the chairman yet. I wonder what he'll say?"

Discontinuity 4: Need for Corporate Loan Market Research Information

Today, market research, market forecasts, and specialized consulting on both the market for corporate loans and the risk of those loans is becoming a major spending category.

Corporate lending departments are demanding more corporate information (like Standard & Poor's Register of Corporations that lists lead banks). Departments are urging the development of specialized loan pricing databases to better follow the weekly changes in terms and conditions. There is a fast growing need for "better" credit risk procedures and even ways to monitor creditworthiness on a "real time" basis.

A sudden change in the type or level of information required is a sure sign that an industry or market is undergoing rapid change or discontinuity.

A View of Corporate Banking in the 1990s

Economic forecasting tends to be a numbers-based exercise. But no matter how detailed or pervasive these exercises are, they rarely address the most important structural, qualitative, and technological features of the path ahead. This section of the chapter strives to *visualize* how the corporate lending market will look in the 1990s.

Human innovation, especially in the financial area, is generally borne of pain and suffering:

• The financial collapse of 1929 to 1933 yielded the Glass-Steagall Act and the Securities and Exchange Commission.
• The bank liability crisis of 1959 spawned the Eurodollar market and the negotiable CD.
• The credit crunch of August 1966 popularized floating-rate loans.
• The interest rate turbulence and deposit disintermediation from 1979 to 1982 produced negotiable order of withdrawal (NOW) accounts and deposit regulation.
• The thrift crisis gave birth to the GNMA pool market.

The four discontinuities discussed above are putting great pressure on the corporate lending system. These pressures will spawn a new corporate loan business, different in form and function in fundamental ways. Although it is impossible to specify the exact nature and timing of an event, the system will have three major innovations:

1. Separation of Origination and Portfolio Holding Functions—The corporate lending business will split into three distinct segments: relationship management; the transaction or administrative function; and the investment or portfolio function. Certainly these distinctions exist today.

But in the future, all but the very largest corporate lending departments will specialize and concentrate in one or at most two of these functions. Some departments will primarily develop and originate loans for resale, while others will compete purely on price for new business. Others will concentrate on assembling portfolios or packages of loans purchased on the secondary markets.

Departments will reap profits through specialization or economies of scale. The traditional "full-service" corporate lending department will become rare.

2. Technology—An active secondary market will appear for corporate loans. Corporate lending departments need an electronic marketplace. However, none of the existing financial marketplaces, like Telerate or Quotron, can serve this function. The highly individualized terms, conditions, and characteristics of each loan, and the need for confidentiality, require an electronic marketplace far more sophisticated than current systems. The new marketplace will more nearly resemble one of today's sophisticated global oil trading systems. Indeed, corporate loans more nearly resemble oil contracts, with their place of origin, destination, timing, shipping, quality, and financing functions. A system like that used to trade oil contracts will evolve as the electronic marketplace for corporate loans.

3. Balanced Corporate Loan Portfolios Will Emerge—Commercial banks will be big buyers as well as sellers of corporate loans. Bankers are already trading "transferable loan certificates" or "loan participation certificates." These certificates, based on standardized lending agreements, completely transfer the ownership of the loan.

Banks will find that purchasing individual corporate loans or pools of corporate loans via a new secondary market to be much better than the clumsy loan participation and syndication functions of today, and much cheaper than loan production offices (LPOs). They will strive to develop portfolios balanced by tenor, pricing, industry, firm size, geography, and a host of other characteristics. These portfolios will achieve much better risk/return characteristics than the loan portfolios of today.

The essential function of this marketplace will be to put a price on the yield, cash flow, and creditworthiness of corporate loans and loan packages. In effect, corporate loans will become securitized to the degree that they circulate on the secondary market.

Benefits

The benefits of this new corporate lending market are significant:

- The market will bear more of the credit risk. Credit judgments will be more open and competitive.
- Stock analysts will better understand banks. Bank P/E's will tend to rise and the cost of capital to the banks will moderate.
- Most significantly, corporate lending will recover the sustained profitability that has so deteriorated in the present environment.

The Vision

Had this secondary trading market for corporate loans been in place in the early 1980s, banks may have avoided the recent wave of severe credit losses and failures. In each case, the problems intensified because there was no mechanism for the marketplace to evaluate the worth of these loans. Had secondary markets existed for these instruments, investors would have aggressively sought information regarding these instruments before investing in them. This competition for better information would have led to far more energetic and informed speculation about soundness and to a trading down of the secondary market prices of these assets as the bad news began to emerge. Surely, some bad energy loans would have been made. But secondary markets are forward-looking and the reaction time would have been much shorter, as it is in today's stock, fixed income, commodities, and foreign exchange markets.

Consequently, originating institutions would have pulled back from writing this business as they saw prices fall for corporate loan pools already on their books. Had they persisted, the stock market, better able than presently to assess the portfolios of these originating institutions, would have bid down their stock prices, hence flashing a second warning to management.

A recent *New York Times* article pointed out that free market controls for banks make a "...key assumption that the public is capable of determining the quality of a bank's loan portfolio." Until the new corporate lending market is in place so that the stock market can better determine the quality of corporate loans in a bank's portfolio, it will not supply capital and the banking system, deregulated or not, will not function properly.

APPENDIX A

CALCULATION OF THE "ALL-IN" SPREAD

From each survey form filled out by a lender, Loan Pricing Coporation calculates an all-in spread net of funding costs. The formula assumes that the cost of funds equals the pricing base, except for prime-based loans that are funded at the adjusted CD rate. The spread between prime and the adjusted CD rate is assumed to be 125 points. Balances arising from commitment and utilization agreements are valued at the cost of funds rate.

The basic formula is:

$$\text{All-in spread} = \frac{[\text{Spread (rate)} * \text{Loan balance (\$)}] + [\text{Fee} * \text{Commitment (\$)}] +}{\text{Loan balance (\$)}}$$

$$\frac{[\text{COF (rate)} * \text{free balances}]}{\text{Loan balance (\$)}}$$

Making two substitutions:

- Loan balance (\$) = Utilization rate * Commitment (\$)
- Free balances (\$) = .88 * balances against commitment and usage (\$) [to account for reserve requirements and FDIC assessment]

The formula is restated as follows:

$$\text{All-in spread} = \frac{\text{Commitment (\$)} * [\text{Spread(rate)} * \text{Utilization rate} +}{\text{Utilization rate} * \text{Commitment (\$)}}$$

$$\frac{\text{Fee} + .88 * \text{COF (rate)} * (\text{Commitment balance rate} +}{\text{Utilization rate} * \text{Commitment (\$)}}$$

$$\frac{\text{Usage balance rate} * \text{Utilization rate})]}{\text{Utilization rate} * \text{Commitment (\$)}}$$

The Commitment cancels out, leaving:

$$\text{All-in spread} = \frac{\text{Spread (rate)} * \text{Utilization rate} + \text{Fee} +}{\text{Utilization rate}}$$

$$\frac{.88 * \text{COF(rate)} * (\text{Commitment balance rate} +}{\text{Utilization rate}}$$

$$\frac{\text{Usage balance rate} * \text{Utilization})}{\text{Utilization rate}}$$

PART 4

THE CORPORATE VIEW

CHAPTER 17

THE CORPORATE VIEW

Phillip L. Zweig, Senior Writer
Corporate Finance Magazine

Editor's Note: Like depository institutions, corporations and nonbank financial concerns securitize assets to liquefy their balance sheets, expand their sources of funding, and raise new capital. But they typically do not have to thread their way through the maze of regulation that confronts banks and thrifts. In the following interviews, financial officers of two giant nonbank financial concerns (General Motors Acceptance Corporation and Household Finance Corporation) and a major service company (American Airlines, the principal subsidiary of AMR Corporation) discuss recently completed transactions and the reasons behind them.

In the first public securitization of personal, unsecured consumer loans, Household Finance Corporation in November 1987 securitized $454 million in consumer credits that had been originated by consumer finance offices in 16 states. However, the loans were sold to Household Bank, the company's thrift subsidiary and the notes issued in its name. Consequently, the transaction was subject to Federal Home Loan Bank Board rules. In the first section of this chapter, R. J. Clout, vice president for borrowings of General Motors Acceptance Corporation, the automaker's captive finance subsidiary, responds to questions about GMAC's experience with securitization. GMAC was one of the first issuers of asset-backed securities and remains the largest single issuer.

SECTION 1: GMAC

ED:

How would you compare the costs or benefits of securitizing receivables with those of other financing devices?

CLOUT:

Asset-backed securities are unique among financing devices in providing certain strategic benefits, including management of asset growth and earnings and liquefication of assets.

They offer some financial benefits that are also unique. These include perfect asset/liability matching (interest rate and maturity). This is not achievable with other financing alternatives. Other benefits include the creation of a "riskless" spread and sale treatment for accounting and tax purposes.

In addition, they offer financial benefits that are available in different degrees with other financing alternatives, such as equity, but at a significantly lower all-in cost. One such benefit is increased borrowing capacity. On a regular debt transaction, GMAC finances with about a 12 to 1 debt/equity ratio. On an ABS transaction, (5 percent recourse), that ratio is increased. Another benefit is access to new sources of funds. New investors represent a permanent new source of capital. They're also cost competitive, especially on a cost of capital basis.

ED:

What kinds of constraints does securitization create for you? For example, does it in any way limit your ability to issue other kinds of debt?

CLOUT:

No constraints are caused by asset securitization. If anything, it adds to our flexibility by decreasing dependence on other forms of financing. ABSs access new investors or a different pocket within the same institution. By reducing demand for credit from other sources at the margin, GMAC should be able to pay less for traditional sources. An added benefit is the ability to sell receivables to a third party, such as the Asset Backed Securities Corporation (ABSC), thereby accessing the market with an entirely new name and often a different class of credit.

ED:

In other words, what do you give up by doing this?

CLOUT:

Very little. As the spread between the sold receivables and the cost of money is locked in at the time of sale, the seller does give up the opportunity to benefit from a decline in money costs over the life of the receivables. This, of course, assumes the receivables are not perfectly match funded.

ED:

Does securitization enable you to offer customers more attractive rates?

CLOUT:

GMAC doesn't approach the concept of securitization from this perspective, although we understand a number of institutions consider this in their analysis. The increased borrowing capacity that flows from selling receivables could allow a financial institution the opportunity to increase penetration and volume, however, and "grow" the business.

ED:

What lessons have you learned from previous issues that you would apply to future ones?

CLOUT:

Asset securitization of automotive receivables is a recent development and the learning curve continues to steepen. GMAC continues to work with selected investment banks in developing greater flexibility with respect to structures—pass-throughs and pay-throughs, fixed-rate and floating-rate transactions, market timing, and many others.

ED:

Do you think it will become a widely used technique?

CLOUT:

Yes. We definitely believe it will be widely used. In 1986, of the $10.04 billion offered, $8.26 billion (82.3 percent) involved GMAC receivables. So far in 1987, $6.62 billion of ABSs have been offered and only $2.23 billion have been GMAC collateral (33.7 percent). In all of 1986, there were nine different seller/servicers. So far in 1987, there have been 17 different seller/servicers. The introduction of credit cards and trade receivables as collateral in public transactions was also witnessed in 1987. The market is clearly broadening.

ED:

Based on your experience, what kinds of issuers would benefit most from securitization? Which ones would benefit least?

CLOUT:

Issuers with large asset portfolios and, therefore, large funding needs will benefit most. There are some initial costs in undertaking an ABS program. Once upfront costs are amortized, however, ABSs don't cost more than other types of financing alternatives.

Although this doesn't apply to GMAC, lower rated companies will also benefit because of the higher ratings possible with ABS structures. But the benefits discussed above can be useful to any issuer, even a triple-A rated one.

ABSs would least benefit holders of small portfolios who have in mind one small issue, or one small issue each year (small being less than $50 million). However, in such a case, there are other possibilities such as whole loan sales, private placements, or the use of a conduit.

ED:

Under what conditions would you do a public issue as opposed to a private one?

CLOUT:

For GMAC, it comes down to all-in cost and occasionally speed. While we can do a public ABS transaction very quickly, sometimes the private market can be faster, such as when we are notified by an investment banking agent that an investor or group of investors is looking to invest money quickly (reverse inquiry). On occasion, there also may be an advantage to completing a quiet private placement away from the public market.

ED:

Does having this option fundamentally change your financial strategy?

CLOUT:

Yes. We look at asset securitization as a permanent addition to an overall funding strategy. Factors in deciding how great a percentage of our overall financing needs will be satisfied by asset securitization will depend on 1) our asset/liability matching decisions (for example, we will intentionally mismatch a portion of a portfolio, depending on our interest rate outlook), 2) market interest rate levels and spreads among the various fixed income sectors, and 3) balance sheet management and leverage.

ED:

Do you plan to diversify the channels you use to market these securities? Put another way, do you plan to expand the investor base or the number of investment banks that underwrite the securities?

CLOUT:

GMAC is monitoring all developments in the market and maintains regular dialogue with a number of investment and commercial banks. With regard to the investor base, we feel that creation of new and dynamic structures will, of itself, broaden and diversify the investor base.

SECTION II: HOUSEHOLD FINANCE CORPORATION

This interview is with Robert W. Mitchell, vice president and treasurer of Household Financial Services.

ED:

Tell me a bit about what was going on at Household that led up to this deal.

MITCHELL:

From 1985 to 1987, Household Finance grew rapidly as a result of new products and marketing. At the same time, the thrust into consumer banking with Household Bank was expanded, and the bank grew from $700 million in assets to $3.4 billion at the end of 1987. We needed to find additional financial vehicles to help us manage the growth on the HFC balance sheet. Securitization of assets was simply one more tool to enhance the liquidity of the company.

While we completed the first issue in November 1987, the conceptual work began in November 1986, and in March 1987 we established working groups to develop the transaction. Because of the involvement of Household Bank, one complicating factor was the need for regulatory approvals.

ED:

What were some of the legal and regulatory issues?

MITCHELL:

In this transaction, HFC securitized unsecured consumer receivables into a passthrough certificate and sold the certificate to Household Bank. Household Bank actually issued the securities in the marketplace (see Appendix A, Consumer Loan Securitization Flows).

There were a lot of related party issues that had to be addressed, and we needed to obtain the blessing of the Federal Home Loan Bank Board.

ED:

What kind of issues did the Securities and Exchange Commission raise?

MITCHELL:

Nothing specifically. They were looking at the Household Finance Corporation guarantee and, obviously, that we had accurate disclosure. There was nothing unusual.

ED:

Could you tell us a little more about the underlying receivables?

MITCHELL:

They are unsecured consumer receivables. We had been making this type of loan for many years, and these were seasoned receivables. The average balance per account was about $1,800.

Historically there was no public market to sell these loans. We wanted to see if we could take an asset that historically had been illiquid and convert it into a liquid asset.

Frankly, one of objectives was to be first and to establish standards for future issues that we or others in the industry might do.

ED:

How was it offered in the market?

MITCHELL:

We broke it into two tranches, a short and long term to appeal to two different investor groups.

ED:

How was the issue priced?

MITCHELL:

One tranche was based on LIBOR (London Interbank Offering Rate) and the other tranche was based on more traditional corporate pricing. From an asset liability management standpoint, the notes were essentially match-funded with the assets since prepayment risk in the underlying loans was borne by the investors, although the prepayment patterns are highly predictable. We were able, on an overall basis, to fix the all-in rate at about 8.5 percent.

ED:

Who were the buyers?

MITCHELL:

The buyers of both tranches were basically banks, thrifts, pension funds and insurance companies, with certain of them being money market buyers, the others being medium term buyers.

ED:

Could you say something about the market acceptance? Was it fully subscribed?

MITCHELL:

It was well accepted in the market and sold quickly, even though it was roughly a month after Black Monday.

ED:

So the crash didn't affect price, structuring, or sales?

MITCHELL:

It affected pricing, especially the spread to Treasuries, but no more so than for any other instrument.

ED:

What can you say generally about how market conditions affect these issues?

MITCHELL:

I don't think you can look at securitization in isolation. Securitized deals will react to market changes in generally the same way as other bonds, with some difference because of the nature of the prepayments of the underlying assets. From the lender's perspective, the desire to issue will be driven in part by interest rate or other market considerations, but will be often driven by balance sheet management concerns as well.

ED:

What advantage did you gain in terms of price and yield in doing this? What were some of the competing yields on other forms of funding?

MITCHELL:

If you just did a straight debt issue, you could do it at a slightly lower rate. But obviously the debt would have been on the balance sheet. So from our perspective, the financing cost was reasonable—a little bit higher than a straight debt issue because it was a little bit more complex, but it met our goals of managing the balance sheet for liquidity.

ED:

Could you elaborate on some of these alternatives?

MITCHELL:

If one really needed to manage the balance sheet, frankly, just an outright sale into the market with unrelated parties could have been done. The other way you'd manage the balance sheet would be to raise the pricing on basic products and cut the volume of product you're originating. One of the things you want to do is maintain volume and market presence consistently and manage your growth by other means. Asset securitization is becoming one of the tools many companies use for that purpose.

ED:

Was some form of credit enhancement used?

MITCHELL:

Yes. HFC guaranteed 15 percent of potential write-offs so that Household Bank itself was at risk for the amount in excess of that. Other forms of enhancement, such as letters of credit, could have been used, but we knew the receivables pretty well and were comfortable with their quality and know the actual losses will be a fraction of the guaranteed amount.

ED:

Was the credit rating of the parent or the bank involved here?

MITCHELL:

It was ultimately HFC's credit rating.

ED:

What were some of the other obstacles you had to overcome in bringing this issue to market?

MITCHELL:

We had the regulatory hurdles I mentioned with the Federal Home Loan Bank Board and SEC filings.

In addition, we had to work through the structure, which had never been used before, with the rating agencies which were quite supportive. We had systems hurdles and the educational process internally. We had to explain the rationale for doing this.

ED:

What were some of the objections that came up?

MITCHELL:

Securitization allows us much more efficient capital allocation, because by liquefying the balance sheet we can free up funds for the generation of additional receivables. Secondly, Household Bank can leverage at roughly 15 to 1, and HFC is leveraged in the 7.5 to 1 area, which suggests that you can get some leverage enhancement from the transfer structure we used, even though we did not defease the assets. Profitability from the bank's standpoint was enhanced, since the bank was earning a spread and was able to match fund the assets. On the one side, it had the pass-through certificate, and on the other, the notes, which mirrored the cash flow effects from the assets. So those were key areas we had to think through. But as soon as you do an asset securitization, the other internal area you have to address is performance reporting. All of a sudden you have removed the assets from the balance sheet and retained the servicing in one legal vehicle, but added the assets in another legal vehicle. So that has a tendency to distort traditional performance measures, and you have to come up with some new approaches.

ED:

How do you assess the cooperation you got from the regulatory agencies? Are they able to deal with new concepts like this? Was there a lot of lost time?

MITCHELL:

Whenever you deal with regulatory agencies, there's a fair amount of lost time. Secondly, anytime you're attempting to come up with a new concept, there's an education process. The more complex the concept, the longer that process takes.

The regulators are paid to ensure that, in this case, Household Bank was not going to be disadvantaged.

ED:

How do you go about allaying such concerns?

MITCHELL:

Persistence is the key word. We tried to be as communicative as possible in explaining the concept, making sure they understood it, and making sure they could see the benefit to the bank.

ED:

Was this a one shot transaction or do you plan to do it on a regular basis?

MITCHELL:

What we wanted to do was to prove the concept and establish something that would be available to us on an ongoing basis. Now that we have worked out the systems and established market acceptance, we can put the package together periodically as appropriate.

ED:

Is it basically now a cookie cutter process that you can use for any group of receivables?

MITCHELL:

This one took us nine months from working group to close. We could probably cut that in half. But when you're working with these types of structures and receivables, the way financial markets change, it would be overstating it to say you have an absolute cookie cutter. You're always going to have variations.

ED:

When do you expect to do another transaction?

MITCHELL:

The second transaction was successfully marketed in June 1988.

ED:

Do other companies seem to be interested in using your structure?

MITCHELL:

Goldman, Sachs has gotten a number of inquiries from others seeking to understand the structure, and I suspect that other companies will be examining it. The real question they have to address is whether they have the systems capability to do this. You have to identify all the loans and track the payments on them.

ED:

Would you consider doing a private placement?

MITCHELL:

Certainly. That basically becomes a trade-off of the economics, the speed with which you want to get the transaction consummated, and working out the terms and conditions with the investor.

ED:

Does the consumer benefit at all from this?

MITCHELL:

The borrower is not aware the loan has been sold. The consumer benefits in a general way, in that it frees up capacity for HFC to make additional loans and creates another funding vehicle for this type of product.

ED:

Does this allow you to be more competitive, say on rates?

MITCHELL:

Only in the general sense that we've found a new financing source that helps on an overall basis to keep financing costs down. It allows us to examine the whole pricing question, but the price for any product is set by the market.

ED.

Based on what you went through with this, what do you think

is the potential for securitizing portfolios that haven't yet been securitized?

MITCHELL:

The asset securitization market has real potential. With proper systems support and creative structuring, many, many companies that previously felt they had assets on their books that were illiquid can come up with structures that will allow them to gain liquidity. The real key in this whole effort is the creativity in packaging and timing that can be brought to bear on what investors are looking for in the marketplace.

ED:

Is there a danger of the market becoming too crowded with these issues?

MITCHELL:

There's always that possibility at some point in time, but realistically, that's a long way off. The commercial paper market, for example, has grown about tenfold over the last 15 years. People 15 years ago said there was a limit to that market, but it has grown fairly dramatically. So I think there's a lot of capacity out there for securitized assets of many types.

ED:

With the benefit of hindsight, what would you do differently in putting this together? Any advice for other prospective issuers?

MITCHELL:

Don't underestimate the complexity of one of these transactions, particularly if it has never been done before. It's very time consuming, but in the long run you should take comfort in the knowledge that such deals should be able to tap entirely new sources of liquidity.

SECTION III: AMERICAN AIRLINES

This final interview is with Douglas A. Hacker, vice president for corporate finance and development, American Airlines. Mr. Hacker played a key role in a $92.6 million securitization of leveraged leases used to refinance 80 percent of the equipment cost of six McDonnell Douglas DC-9 aircraft originally leased to American in 1986. The transaction was completed in October 1987. See Appendix B for a diagram of the payments in this transaction.

ED:

> Maybe you could begin by describing how you've used securitization of leases to finance aircraft?

HACKER:

> What we've been doing has grown out of our practice of using the private placement market to fund the debt portion of leveraged leases. That's been a typical way of financing aircraft for a number of years. You've got an equity participant who's in the transaction for the tax benefits, and he generally puts up between 20 and 40 percent of the equipment cost. Then you have the debt participant who puts up the rest of the money. He's in it just for the interest return. We've been doing that using the private placement market for some time.
>
> We were looking for a way to access a new source of capital, basically using the public markets as a vehicle to market the debt portion of leveraged leases. We had done some transactions in the public market in 1983 and 1984. At that time, there were a number of constraints that were very difficult to live with in using a public debt issue to finance the debt portion of a leveraged lease. Basically, the public market was very limited. In the summer of 1986, when we felt it had become very important to open up a new source of debt for leveraged leases, we embarked upon a project to use new practices that had developed in securitization to see if that wouldn't help us market leveraged lease debt publicly.
>
> So we looked at the various models being used in securitization. Drawing from the mortgage markets, we looked at, I guess, two basic models—the pass-through and the CMO type of transaction. Now you also have the REMIC. We would have preferred to use the CMO type of structure but we weren't comfortable with certain tax risks, so we settled on a pass-through structure. That allowed us to take a lot of different leases and bundle them together to offer to public investors participations of the debt portion of a bunch of different leases.

So that's what we did when we issued these pass-through certificates through Morgan Stanley and Salomon Brothers. That's been our main experience with securitization.

Merrill Lynch did present to us another public markets vehicle, where they sold publicly the debt portion of leveraged leases on an aircraft by aircraft basis. I don't really view that as securitization. It was just basically a registered private placement. The real securitization we did in the Morgan Stanley transaction. I think we did the first of this type of lease-backed securitized debt financing.

ED:

How did the pass-through structure, as you applied it, differ from CMO structure that you were considering?

HACKER:

In the CMO structure you establish a corporate vehicle and then you offer securities of that corporation. The corporation turns around and uses the proceeds to purchase debt of the leveraged lease. So you have—if you think of the way the cash flows work— American Airlines making a rent payment to a lessor and the lessor assigning the debt portion of that rent payment, to be paid ultimately to the security holders and the debt holders. In a CMO transaction, the money is actually paid into a corporate vehicle, some shell issuer, and then that corporation turns around and distributes the money to debt holders. In a pass-through, there is no corporate vehicle. The money goes from us to a lessor, is assigned, passes through a trust, and is given to debt holders, more or less directly.

That distinction is a relatively fine one, but it actually generates a lot of real world implications. When there's a corporate vehicle in there you have to worry about the taxation of that corporate vehicle.

ED:

This was actually a refinancing of existing leases financed by banks. You basically took the banks out with this?

HACKER:

Right. We refinanced the entire debt portion.

ED:

What advantages did you achieve in terms of pricing and market acceptance over methods you used in financing aircraft in the past?

HACKER:

We are always interested in obtaining the lowest possible cost leveraged lease. To us, what that means is having a variety of alternative sources, so that at any given time we can look to various private markets, U.S. and foreign, and to U.S. public markets through a couple of structures. Having developed these various structures, we can at any point in time decide which one is the most cost effective and tap that source.

Obviously what you're trying to do is make sure that you don't use up any particular source because once that starts to happen you're going to drive your costs up. So we viewed it as a new source, providing us with flexibility and keeping us from tapping out any available market. The pricing of this transaction was very competitive with its alternatives. Considering that it was the first time it had been done, we were very pleased with its execution.

ED:

What's the advantage of this type of transaction over a leveraged lease done with bank financing?

HACKER:

Just interest rates. There's no magic to this. A bank could invest in these pass-through certificates. The end result would be no different than if a bank bought the leveraged lease debt directly. It's just a question of whether a bank will provide this type of financing with these terms, and at this type of rate. Or will an insurance company prefer to provide this type of funding through a private transaction in which they don't have the opportunity for liquidity, or would they prefer to buy publicly and remain liquid?

ED:

In terms of complexity, the time involved, or tax, legal, and accounting considerations, how did it differ from other financings?

HACKER:

It was extraordinarily complex. It took over a year to do. We also had many constituencies we had to be responsible to. We had an equity participant who was concerned about any implications this might have for his tax benefits. We obviously had to develop the structure to the point where the public would be receptive to it. This was the first time it has ever been done, so there was a lot of new ground to cover.

We also had to be mindful of changing tax law in the leveraged lease area, which hung us up a couple of times.

But we viewed it as a long-term investment. Our goal was to develop an alternative source of debt. If the first transaction wasn't entirely cost competitive or involved extra legal costs, that was something we were willing to consider as an investment. As it turned out, I think our legal fees were higher than they would have been in a standard transaction. But if you put aside the legal costs, and look at just the interest rates we received on the debt and the underwriting costs on the debt, it was very competitive. I think we can say the extra legal fees were kind of an investment in developing this structure.

ED:

What were some of the legal issues that came up?

HACKER:

I'm not a lawyer, but we had questions about whether the pass-through trust that was formed was an investment company and whether or not equity participations should be registrants. We ultimately had to get a "no action" letter from the Securities and Exchange Commission. We had to establish seven separate trusts, and we asked the SEC to allow us to use the same trustee for all of them. From a purely lease point of view, there were a number of tax issues as well.

ED:

Who were the buyers of these securities?

HACKER:

It had a fairly wide distribution—insurance companies, pension funds, investment companies, and banks.

ED:

How liquid do you expect these securities to be? Do you think they'll be widely traded?

HACKER:

It was an institutionally placed transaction. So I don't think we expect any substantial volume of trading.

ED:

What were the maturities of these securities?

HACKER:

They were structured in seven tranches, and there were six aircraft. Basically, we had 42 pieces of debt floating around. There were five serial tranches maturing in January 1, 1988, 1989, 1990, 1991, and 1992. There were two other tranches, a ten-year tranche maturing in January 1997 and a final tranche maturing in January 2006.

ED:

Did this get a triple-A?

HACKER:

It trades basically on the credit rating, of American Airlines, which for secured transactions would be an A1 A+.

ED:

Did you use any credit enhancement?

HACKER:

No. It wasn't considered because this was rated A1 A+ based on American Airlines' credit rating, and to enhance it further to make the rating higher than that wasn't an economically attractive proposition.

ED:

Does this device impose any constraints on your ability to go into the market for any other kinds of money? Are there any drawbacks for your financing strategy?

HACKER:

Not that I can think of.

ED:

How does your selection of this type of structure reflect interest rate, market, or economic conditions?

HACKER:

This is long-term, fixed-rate funding. Any time you want to do that type of funding this would be an alternative.

ED:

What lessons did you learn from this issue that you could apply to the next one?

HACKER:

The next one would be a cookie cutter. Having developed the structure, it's now kind of generic. We can use it again without a lot of changes. The next one should be quite a bit easier. We created something out of whole cloth that didn't exist before.

ED:

Are you contemplating doing another one in the immediate future?

HACKER:

I suspect we will do more of these types of transactions in 1988.

ED:

Would another airline or another company buying aircraft be able to use your structure as a cookie cutter structure?

HACKER:

Sure. It would certainly make their task a lot easier.

ED:

Is there any indication that other airlines or similar companies will use your deal as a model for their own?

HACKER:

We know that one airline looked at a variety of public structures we had pioneered and recently filed a prospectus for a public offering of leveraged lease securities based not on this transaction but on an alternative transaction—the registered private placement— we had done through Merrill Lynch that I described earlier. We know that they looked at this structure as well. They opted for that one at that particular point in time. It's important to note that you have to have quite a strong credit rating to successfully issue these types of securities. Only the top couple of airlines really have this as a viable alternative.

ED:

Is this applicable to other types of equipment, or are there peculiarities that make it useful only for financing aircraft?

HACKER:

I don't think there's anything that makes it useful exclusively for airlines. It ought to be useful for any leveraged lease debt, even the leveraged lease of a nuclear plant. It's not going to be useful for a nonleveraged lease transaction.

ED:

Based on what you've done here, what expectations do you have for the growth in the use of this method by other companies?

HACKER:

The real thing we've done here is to put pressure on traditional private placement buyers of securities. They no longer have a captive market for this type of paper. If private placement sources of money continue to be attractive, I don't expect to see tremendous growth in this type of activity. The important thing is that it's not something that's in any way similar to, say, the development of securitization of home mortgages or car loans. Aircraft leveraged leases are just a much smaller activity. It's always been an institutional market for the debt, not a retail market. I don't think it's going to expand to become a retail market because you don't get diversification through these types of transactions.

You're basically buying the credit of American Airlines. You're not getting any other airlines mixed in there or any credit diversification. That wasn't the case in home mortgages, where you get a piece of many different mortgages. It's much different than that kind of securitization. It's much more driven by circumstances.

ED:

What determines whether you would do a public issue as opposed to a private one?

HACKER:

Cost.

ED:

Do you plan to diversify your channels for marketing these securities or expand your investment banks or investor base?

HACKER:

We initially plan to continue doing this through Morgan Stanley, who worked with us to develop it. They made quite an investment of time and legal fees on their own part. We would continue with them until we had good reason to believe others could do it better.

APPENDIX A
Consumer Loan Securitization Flows

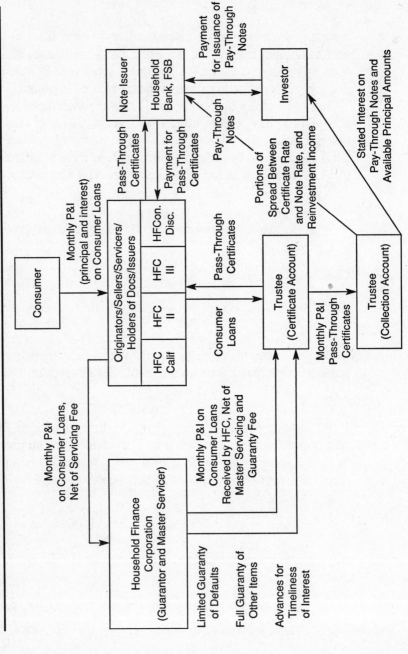

Appendix B American Airlines Lease Securitization

DIAGRAM OF PAYMENTS

Using the leveraged lease transaction for Aircraft 1 as an example, the following diagram illustrates certain aspects of the payment flows in this transaction among American, the owner trustees, the loan trustees, the trusts and the holders of the pass-through certificates.

American leases Aircraft 1 from the owner trustee for such aircraft under a separate lease. Equipment notes for such aircraft will be issued in seven series by such owner trustee and will be secured by such aircraft and by an assignment of the related lease. Rent is payable under such lease to such owner trustee; however, as a result of the assignment of the lease, American will make rental payments for Aircraft 1 directly to the loan trustee. From these rental payments the loan trustee will on behalf of such owner trustee first make payments to the trustee for each of the trusts on the equipment notes held in such trust and will pay the remaining balance to the owner participant for Aircraft 1. (Payments to the owner participant are not shown on the diagram.) The trustee for each of the trusts will distribute to the holders of the pass-through certificates of such trust payments received on the equipment notes held in such trust. The Connecticut National Bank will act initially both as trustee of the seven trusts and as loan trustee under the six lease indentures.

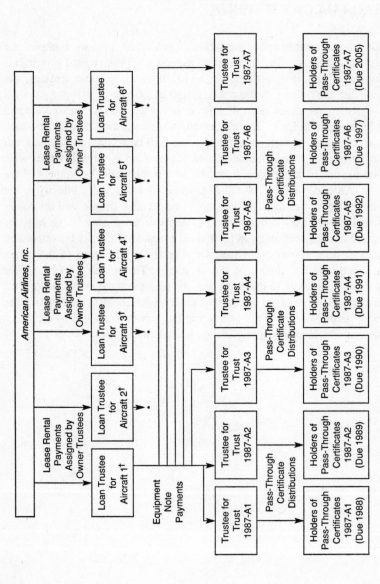

American Airlines, Inc.

Equipment Note Payments

†Payments of the balance of the lease rental payments to the owner participants for Aircraft 1 through 6 are not shown on the diagram.
*Payments related to Aircraft 2 through 6 flow in the same manner as the payments related to Aircraft 1.

Source: Prospectus. October 2, 1987.

PART 5

INVESTOR CONCERNS

CHAPTER 18

AN OVERVIEW OF
SECURITIZATION RISKS

Theodore V. Buerger, Senior Vice President
Linda S. Iseley, Assistant Vice President
Financial Security Assurance

> If you don't know you don't know, you think you know.
> —*R. D. Laing*

INTRODUCTION

There are two major types of risk inherent in every asset securitization, one of which is largely overlooked by many investors.

Before an investor buys an asset-backed security, it is obvious that he must evaluate the credit quality of the assets backing that security ("asset quality risk"). Less obvious, however, is the fact that an investor only indirectly invests in the assets underlying a transaction; he directly invests in the structure that repackages the assets. As a result, even if the underlying assets perform, the investment could still collapse if the securitization structure fails to perform ("securitization risk").

Moreover, the consequences of a structural failure can be far more severe than the consequences of a misestimation of asset quality risk. An asset quality problem can, in extreme circumstances, lead to a diminution of cash flows. But, a problem with the securitization structure can lead to a loss of rating, a complete interruption of payments, or even the invalidity of the securities themselves.

Aggravating these potentially devastating consequences is the fact that as asset-backed financings become more and more complex, the chances for a breakdown increase exponentially. Simply put, the more things that have to go right at the same time, the more likely that something will go wrong. Therefore, it is imperative that investors understand the securitization risks in every transaction and reduce these risks as much as possible.

METHODS OF RISK REDUCTION

Although the risks to investors in an asset-backed structured financing may not be eliminated, they may, as in any financing, be reduced by varying degrees. The extent of the risks and the degree to which they are addressed varies from transaction to transaction, generally as a function of the specific deal and the primary participants. In most transactions, the major asset quality risks can be effectively identified and limited through sophisticated statistical and analytical techniques.

The major securitization risks, however, cannot be so easily contained. There is no mathematical formula for analyzing and reducing these types of risk. Instead, investors are provided with an amalgam of representations, warranties, due diligence investigations, legal opinions, comfort letters, and the like to reassure themselves about the accuracy of critical facts and assumptions.

To begin, let us review these assurances and the minimum steps that investors must take in any asset securitization. Once the limitations of these assurances are understood, it will make more meaningful our discussion of specific examples in which these assurances proved inadequate.

Representations, Warranties, and Indemnities

The typical asset-backed transaction relies upon a variety of representations, warranties, and indemnities, which attempt to identify and confirm the major assumptions that must be made about the accuracy and reliability of essential, underlying information. To assess the extent to which such measures provide protection for investors, the following factors, at a minimum, should be reviewed:

1. The degree of recourse available to the maker of the particular representation, warranty, or indemnity. Although the provision may be broad, the damages payable upon a breach may be limited to a specified dollar amount or specific assets, or the recourse may expire after some limited period of time.

2. The creditworthiness of the maker of the representation, warranty, or indemnity. Triple-A securities are often issued that rely to some degree on key warranties made by entities that are less than triple-A, and sometimes even less than investment grade.

3. The extent to which representations and warranties are made on a "best of our knowledge" basis. This qualification places the risk of the unknown and the uncertain on the security holders.

Due Diligence Investigations

Various parties to the typical asset-backed transaction customarily conduct "due diligence" investigations, which address certain securitization and asset quality risks. As for the securitization risks, these investigations are intended to verify that the risks associated with the securities, including those related to the strength of the seller of the assets, have been properly disclosed in the offering materials. In the case of publicly offered securities, this type of an investigation may also provide the underwriter with a "due diligence" defense to strict liability for damages under the Securities Act of 1933. Although such due diligence investigations are standard procedure, investors will want to determine 1) how much time has been devoted to such investigations (to make certain they are not hastily done); 2) the scope of the investigation; and 3) the experience of the investment bankers and/or attorneys performing the investigation.

Legal Opinions

The major legal assumptions needed for asset securitization are customarily assessed in legal opinions rendered by independent or internal counsel. These opinions would address such concerns as "true sale," bankruptcy remoteness, valid security interests, valid obligations, and tax treatment. In addition, issues pertaining to the Securities Act of 1933, the Securities Exchange Act of 1934, and the Investment Company Act of 1940 would be evaluated.

Although legal opinions are intended to reassure investors about various securitization risks, sophisticated investors understand the lawyers' adage that "a legal opinion is only an opinion." The degree to which one should be comforted by any legal opinion is a function of a number of factors, including:

1. The caliber of the counsel rendering the opinion. Ascertain whether the counsel is independent and of sound reputation.

2. The caliber of the opinion itself. Investigate whether the opinion is one that other law firms would be willing to give.

3. The scope of the opinion. Confirm that the opinion addresses not just some, but *all* aspects of a particular risk.

4. The factual assumptions upon which the opinion is based. The reasonableness and accuracy of such factual assumptions, whether incorporated by reference or more generally relied upon, must be evaluated.

5. Whether the opinion is a "clean" opinion, stating a legal view conclusively, or a "reasoned" opinion, stating a legal view that is reasoned and defensible, but not free from doubt.

Accountants' Comfort Letters and Certificates

Certain financial aspects of asset securitizations are typically addressed by comfort letters and certificates of independent accountants. Regrettably, time and cost constraints often limit the scope of review actually performed by these accountants. In some instances, investors have questioned the degree of "comfort" actually provided by such letters, since accountants' reviews often rely on financial and other information prepared by the issuer. Audited GAAP financial statements, however, are generally considered very reliable.

Credit Enhancement

A final method of addressing risk employed in many asset-backed structured financings is the third-party guarantee, usually in the form of a surety bond or a letter of credit. Such a guarantee can provide a "deep pocket" from which to recover asset quality losses and may also provide substantial protection against securitization risks.

The level of protection provided by a guarantee may vary from first loss portfolio protection to a 100 percent guarantee of the securities. In either case, investors should understand the limitations on and the defenses to payment under the guarantee and should investigate the diligence with which various guarantors review transactions. In several early asset securitizations, the "first loss" guarantor had an indemnity from another interested party and, therefore, was said to have done very little independent review.

MAJOR SECURITIZATION RISKS

Assuming the investor has confirmed the quality and accuracy of the assurances above (or at least has identified those assurances that provide little comfort), a number of other securitization risks will still remain. It is these risks, including the reliance on so many sub-AAA rated parties, aggravated by the sheer complexity of the securitization process, that have led some experts to distinguish asset securitizations from other Triple-A debt issues. Many investors have also questioned how much is really known about the behavior of these novel financings under unfavorable circumstances.

Admittedly, the history is limited. Yet, a number of the potential risks can already be discerned by examining the experience of some of the asset-backed structured financings that were the forerunners of today's asset securitizations. Although these earlier transactions were less complex than today's securitizations, they do provide considerable insight into the securitization risks present in asset-backed financings. The seven most frequently encountered securitization risks are:

1. Risk of fraud.
2. Invalidity of contracts, agreements, or securities.
3. Legal uncertainties and changes of law.
4. Reliance on experts.
5. Financial engineering risks.
6. Property and casualty risks.
7. Risk of downgrading.

The impact of these securitization risks and their likelihood of occurrence varies from transaction to transaction. In some financings, legal risk is clearly the overwhelming concern, whereas, in other financings, the probability of a rating downgrade is the critical issue. What is true in nearly every securitization, however, is that these seven risks do not exist independently, but rather are interrelated. For example, the occurrence of fraud can trigger the withdrawal of an expert opinion, which in turn, can trigger a rating downgrade.

Set forth below is a discussion of each of these frequently encountered securitization risks. This discussion is not intended to be all-encompassing, but rather is meant to act as a general guide to certain known securitization risks faced by investors.

Risk of Fraud

Notwithstanding the efforts of sophisticated investors to reduce risk through the various methods discussed above, there is no shortage of examples in which the occurrence of fraud proved to work to the detriment of investors. In fact, the potential for fraud exists in every financial transaction. In the simplest transactions, this risk, of course, is de minimus. However, as the number of participants and complexity of a financing increase, so does the potential for fraud. As was noted in a recent article in *Institutional Investor*, "One intimidating drawback to asset-backed receivables is that they can be fiendishly complicated to re-package as securities."[1]

Fraud can arise in conjunction with any aspect of a financing, from the securitized financial assets to the underlying opinions. Witness the cases of OPM Leasing Services and Spangler Group Inc.

In what was believed to be a secured lease-backed financing, OPM's management successfully "conned 19 banks, insurance companies, and pension funds,"[2] according to the *Wall Street Journal*. As reported in the *Legal Times*, "Using forged or altered documents and in many cases referring to equipment that did not exist, OPM defrauded [these] lenders into forwarding more than $200 million to finance the purchase of computer equipment leased by OPM to Rockwell International Corp."[3]

In 1986, the Securities and Exchange Commission charged Mark E. Spangler, the head of Spangler Group Inc., with misleading investors. Spangler's firm had managed a total of more than $25 million for approximately 150 clients. According to the *Wall Street Journal*, the SEC alleged that "Spangler gave potential clients a copy of a fabricated opinion letter concerning Spangler Group's performance that was typed on Arthur Young & Co. letterhead." Spangler was barred from "ever working for

---

[1]"Whatever Became of Asset-Backed Receivables," *Institutional Investor*, April 1987, pp. 231–234.

[2]"O.P.M. Fraud Raises Questions About Role of a Criminal's Lawyer" *Wall Street Journal*. December 31, 1982, p. 1.

[3]"Trustee's Criticism of Lawyers in O.P.M. Imbroglio." *Legal Times*, May 2, 1983, pp. 20–23.

an investment advisor, brokerage firm or investment company," noted the *Journal*. "Spangler settled the SEC's administrative proceedings against him, without admitting or denying guilt, by agreeing to the sanction."[4]

Yet, even more alarming than these cases are the cases of fraud or alleged fraud involving the investors' primary line of defense against such actions—the "experts" (accountants, attorneys, and investment bankers) party to a transaction. Consider, for example, a 1987 case involving structured financings in the tax-exempt market:

> According to the *Wall Street Journal*, "About $1 billion of tax-exempt bonds underwritten by New York based Matthews & Wright in 1985 and 1986 is under scrutiny amid allegations involving fraud and possible illegal payments to public officials." The article notes that Moody's Investors Service "withdrew ratings" on eight issues after a legal opinion was "reported withdrawn amid inquiries by the Federal Bureau of Investigation and several U.S. attorney's offices." The article also states that "Matthews & Wright denies the allegations and says its own investigation hasn't uncovered any improprieties."[5]

Clearly, in these and other cases, representations and warranties, due diligence investigations, legal opinions, accountants' comfort letters, and the like all proved inadequate to contain the risk of fraud. In fact, the National Commission on Fraudulent Financial Reporting, whose mission is limited to the study of only *one* of the many types of fraud, recently reported that "No company, regardless of size or business, is immune from the possibility that fraudulent financial reporting will occur. That possibility is inherent in doing business."[6] The Commission's statement might well have been applied to the wide range of fraud possible in asset securitizations.

Invalidity

Invalidity is a legal risk addressed by legal opinions and customarily supported by representations, warranties, and indemnities. In the case of many of the more complex and innovative structured financings,

---

[4]"SEC Bars Spangler From Work As Investment Adviser," *Wall Street Journal*, June 19, 1986, p. 8.
   [5]"Ratings of Five Bonds Issued in Pennsylvania Restored by Moody's," *Wall Street Journal*, August 20, 1987, p. 33.
   [6]"Exposure Draft," The National Commission on Fraudulent Financial Reporting, April 1987, p. 5.

although a law firm may be able to render a validity opinion, the opinion 1) may result from the application of established legal principles to sets of facts that the law does not specifically address or 2) may cover situations of such recent origin that the case law or other legal precedent is limited.

If an asset-backed security is declared invalid, the issuer could have no further obligation to make payments to security holders. For example, one reason an asset securitization's exception or exemption from the Investment Company Act of 1940 is so critical is that all of the securities of an issuer may be deemed invalid if that issuer is later declared to be an unregistered "investment company" within the provisions of the 1940 Act.

Similarly, if an important transaction document is found to be invalid, the mechanics of a structured transaction may cease to function and the issuer may not have the necessary funds to make payments on its securities.

> In the celebrated Washington Public Power Supply System ("WPPSS") cases, take-or-pay contracts covering debt service on the bonds "whether or not any of the Projects are completed, operable or operating" were declared invalid. According to the *Municipal Finance Journal*, "The [Washington State] Supreme Court, shocking the bondholders and bond analysts everywhere, ruled that the take-or-pay agreements were void and that the utilities did not have to pay."[7] As a result, payments to the investors in some $2.25 billion of WPPSS securities (issued to finance two nuclear generating units known as Project 4 and Project 5) were suspended. Today, only the holders of bonds entitled to third-party credit enhancement (in the form of a surety bond) are continuing to receive payment on their securities.

> In the less known Hot Springs case, the Arkansas Supreme Court invalidated several issues of municipal bonds and the outstanding ratings of the major rating agencies were revoked in the case of bonds not entitled to 100 percent credit enhancement in the form of a surety bond or letter of credit. Fortunately, the Court later amended its order so as to apply prospectively only.

Although the validity of any security can be affected by a subsequent legal or regulatory ruling, the possibility of such a ruling is of greatest

---

[7]"What Went Wrong with WPPSS," *Municipal Finance Journal*, Winter 1984, p. 81.

concern when there is little legal precedent for the underlying opinions. This is often the case in novel structured financings in which attorneys find themselves charting unknown waters.

Legal Uncertainties and Change of Law

Ironically, legal letters and opinions, which are intended to address sources of risk at the outset of a transaction, may themselves become sources of risk over the life of the transaction.

Billions of dollars of structured financings (including many asset-backed financings) are issued in reliance on key "legal letters." These legal letters are less conclusive about the actual laws and regulations than legal opinions.

In particular, many transactions rely on a letter written by the then general counsel of the Federal Home Loan Bank Board (FHLBB) concerning the "enforceability of [transaction] provisions requiring the liquidation of collateral" in the event of a FSLIC-insured thrift's in-solvency.[8]

A great deal of reliance is placed on this FHLBB letter despite the fact that the letter opens... "as a threshold matter, it should be noted that the Federal Savings and Loan Insurance Corporation (FSLIC) will not provide commitments as to what it, in its capacity as receiver, would do in hypothetical situations with respect to receiverships of FSLIC-insured institutions." An additional risk is potential conflict with new legislation as the law develops. A case in point is HR1680, a bill that was proposed before the U.S. House of Representatives several years ago, which conflicted with the opinion of the FHLBB's counsel. Fortunately, the bill was withdrawn before coming to a vote. Yet despite risks such as these, financings have been and continue to be routinely completed in reliance on this and similar legal letters without investors clearly understanding their limitations.

Virtually every structured financing relies to some extent on legal opinions. Yet, as is the case with legal letters, such opinions are not without risk. As previously mentioned, withdrawal of a legal opinion can have very adverse effects on bondholders and can call into question their rights under the bond issue. Consider the loss of rating and the

---

[8]FSLIC ratings criteria, *Standard & Poor's Creditweek*, April 2, 1984, p. 1926.

market value decline suffered by bondholders in 1987 when, as reported in *The American Lawyer*, "Buchanan Ingersoll [a Pittsburgh law firm] withdrew its legal opinion certifying a $200 million county bond offering after learning that funds to cover the bonds were not on deposit at Mellon [Bank] when the deal closed."[9]

Even when a legal opinion is correct when written, it ordinarily does not address the likelihood or the effect of a change in law or regulation. For example, changes in the Bankruptcy Code have often affected the rights of creditors, as has consumer legislation (generally in a fashion detrimental to creditors). Such changes in law may affect many of the critical protections for investors.

Yet, even without a change in law, a correct legal opinion appropriately reflecting case history cannot anticipate changes in interpretation of law or regulation. Moreover, such changes in interpretation are not always uniform across various courts. It is not uncommon for different circuit courts to hand down different rulings. Recall the questionable Twist Cap ruling,[10] for example.

> In the case of Twist Cap, the bank had issued letters of credit to a bond trustee for a debtor's account and received a secured reimbursement obligation from the debtor. The bankruptcy trustee succeeded in enjoining the bank from honoring the letters of credit based on the theory that the debtor's obligation to reimburse the bank for payments was secured, whereas the bondholders were unsecured. The Court held that honoring the letter would result in the preferential treatment of the bank relative to other unsecured creditors.

Reliance on Experts

In an asset-backed transaction, it is common for investors to rely, sometimes to a significant extent, on attorneys, appraisers, accountants, and other experts to provide comfort letters or certificates or even to define transaction standards. The use of such experts is intended to reduce specific risks perceived in the transaction; however, that expert advice may itself become an independent risk. Consider the following.

First, if a comfort letter is withdrawn or a required accountant's

---

[9]"Buchanan's Negative Rainmaking," *American Lawyer*, October 1987.
[10]See Twist Cap, Inc. v. Southeast Bank of Tampa, 1 B.R. 284 (1979).

certificate is not delivered on a timely basis, an entire transaction may be aborted or, even worse, may proceed on the basis of undisclosed material facts. Consider the National Student Marketing case, which involved the closing of a merger in which the amount of stock to be received by stockholders of the merged company depended on the relative values of the two companies.

> In that case, the proxy statement sent to stockholders contained unaudited financial statements that were to be approved by an accountant's comfort letter at the closing. Although the comfort letter disclosed material negative adjustments to earnings, the merger was closed. The federal court held that the attorneys for the merged company violated the federal securities laws because they breached a duty to inform stockholders of the material negative information.

Second, when a specific provision of a transaction is defined in terms of an expert's current standards, investors face the risk of that expert's standards changing in a material or unforeseen way over the life of the transaction. Consider mortgage-backed bonds, which often allow substitute collateral on the basis of rating agency standards. In these instances, not only may the required levels of collateral change due to subsequent action by the rating agencies, but so may the acceptable forms of collateral. As a case in point:

> In September of 1987, a major rating agency for the first time published standards for using junk bonds as collateral. According to the *Wall Street Journal*, it also stated that it "would allow the companies that have issued mortgage-backed bonds [during 1987] to back them with junk bonds instead." The *Journal* further pointed out that "investors and some investment bankers argued that it wasn't fair to allow a substitution that investors hadn't expected, especially because corporate bonds, and especially junk bonds, are generally considered riskier than insured mortgages."[11]

In addition, almost all asset securitizations contain "permitted investments" provisions, which almost uniformly define eligible investments in terms of minimum credit ratings. Rating standards now include junk-backed bond issues.

---

[11]"S&P to Allow Firms to Back Securities With Junk Bonds," *Wall Street Journal*, September 21, 1987, p. 51.

Financial Engineering Risk

Asset securitizations are the height of financial engineering representing a delicate balance of implementation, technology, and structural techniques. When there is a breakdown in any one of these elements, the entire transaction may be jeopardized. The risk of such a breakdown can generally be referred to as "financial engineering risk."

The investor's exposure to financial engineering risk arises primarily from three sources: 1) the failure of participants to manage the transaction as agreed, 2) the failure of equipment to perform as required, and 3) the malfunction of transaction mechanics.

Transaction Management

In an asset securitization, the two parties on which investors rely most heavily throughout the life of a transaction are the servicer of the underlying receivables and the trustee charged, on behalf of investors, with monitoring and controlling the transaction. Because of the key role each party plays, it is customary that neither party be permitted to relinquish its duties before the expiration of the agreement or the succession of an acceptable substitute party.

Unfortunately, such stipulation generally fails to provide complete protection.

First, if investors wish to have a party terminated due to poor performance, it may be difficult, and perhaps even impossible, to find a substitute party willing to provide that service for the price permitted under the documents. Second, a party may be prohibited by banking or other regulation from continuing to perform its responsibilities, even though an acceptable substitute is unavailable. Third, the bankruptcy of either the servicer or the trustee may preclude an orderly transfer of responsibilities. Finally, even when such parties fully comply with the terms of an agreement, a significant level of deterioration in the quality of their performance may occur.

Highlighted below are some of the risks associated with the performance of servicers and trustees.

Servicer Risk. The servicer is the investor's chief defense against a deterioration of the asset pool. In a receivables-backed financing, for example, the servicer is the one party in a position to directly influence payment behavior on the underlying contracts. An interruption in the servicing process may not only result in payment delays to investors, but may also lead to a permanent diminution in overall credit quality. When receivables-backed transactions are structured, certain assumptions about delinquencies, defaults and recoveries are made based on historical experience. To the extent that this experience was a function of the servicing process, the structure of a transaction may indirectly rely, not only on the quality of servicing, but also on a particular servicer.

For example, many servicers of automobile contracts have extensive dealer arrangements that are fundamental to their servicing records, but which may not be easily transferable to a successor servicer. Even when dealer arrangements take the form of formal contractual agreements, it may still be very difficult for replacement services to enforce them. Other servicers, which are also manufacturers, may provide warranties on their products. The existence of such warranties can be a key factor in resale values and therefore liquidation proceeds. If this type of servicer becomes insolvent, overall portfolio cash flow may be significantly reduced because recovery rates can be a prime determinant of aggregate portfolio losses. Even when the insolvent entity fully intends to honor its warranty commitments, significant buyer uncertainty will likely remain. Witness the depressed resale market for Chrysler automobiles during its near financial collapse.

Trustee Risk. While trustee performance does not directly influence the cash generated by a pool of underlying receivables, it does affect the security of this cash once it is collected and the timeliness with which it is passed through to investors.

Therefore, most transactions have strict provisions governing trustee performance that investors will want to review. When properly constructed, these limitations can provide substantial protection. They cannot, unfortunately, eliminate the possibility of mismanagement, which is becoming an increasingly prevalent problem. Recall the recent case involving The Citizens and Southern Corporation (C&S).

> As reported in the *American Banker*, C&S "agreed to pay up to $32.6 million to settle a class-action suit brought by trust fund customers." The suit charged that the Citizens and Southern National Bank, a unit of C&S, "mismanaged an income fund designed for conservative investors."[12]

---

[12]"C&S Settles Suit, To Pay Up to $32.6 million," *American Banker*, August 6, 1987, p. 2.

In this case, the investors received some compensation; however, it came nearly three years after the initial filing of the case and several weeks into the actual trial.

Furthermore, the failure of a trustee to perform as agreed is not limited to lower credit quality institutions. There have been numerous transactions involving major money center banks, in which the banks have failed to comply with the stated terms of their trust agreements. Although even high credit quality trustees must be evaluated by investors, at least in these instances there is a "deep pocket" to sue for redress if losses result.

In fact, Standard & Poor's has taken the added measure of warning investors of this potential risk. In the April 21, 1986 *S&P Credit Week*, Standard & Poor's reports that "the risk of non-performance by a trustee or other agent of its fiduciary responsibilities should be taken into account by a bondholder" and cautions investors that a rating by Standard & Poor's "does not make an assessment of the probability that a particular trustee will misinterpret the legal provisions or ignore them in managing the financing."[13]

Equipment Failure

A typical securitized financing is extremely dependent on sophisticated and complex computer systems to monitor the payment and performance characteristics of the underlying contracts. A failure in one of these systems could easily lead to processing delays, resulting in an interruption of timely payments to investors and an inability to track the receivables pool. This latter consideration is particularly important in structured financings that contain trigger provisions based on currently reported portfolio statistics.

Clearly, the risk of equipment failure is not a new risk for servicers of receivables portfolios. In fact, most sophisticated servicers already have well-developed catastrophe plans that include, among other things, maintaining duplicate software and backup computer capacity. Assuming that such safeguards are in place, the impact of a wide-scale equipment failure should be both temporary and limited. Obviously, investors will want to verify the existence and adequacy of such contingency plans and backup systems.

---

[13]"Trustee's Role in Structured Financings," *Standard & Poor's CreditWeek*, April 21, 1986, p. 20.

Malfunctioning Structural Mechanics

Asset-backed transactions are structured by some of the most creative minds in the capital markets. Although this results in extremely innovative financings, it can also result in the occasional structure that fails to protect the participants as intended. Three common structural concerns are: 1) inadequate first loss protection, 2) ambiguous first loss protection, and 3) the release of first loss protection.

Despite the sophistication of the parties evaluating and approving the first loss level for a particular structure, the amount of first loss protection may still prove inadequate. Consider the following example.

> In the 1970s, a major insurance company provided asset-based financing using "high quality," secured agricultural loans as its protection. The transaction was structured to withstand in excess of 10 times historical losses. Unfortunately, historical losses proved to be a poor indicator of future loan performance and the insurance company suffered significant losses before ultimately withdrawing from this market.

As for the second concern, the structure of a transaction may be ambiguous enough to lead investors to believe that they have first loss credit protection greater than what is, or at least what is intended, to be provided. Recall the Fireman's Fund–Woodson case.

> Fireman's Fund wrote two guarantees with a purported combined policy limit of $12 million to back $55 million of mortgage securities issued by Woodson. The more than 2000 investors in these securities, however, believed that their investments were fully guaranteed. To settle a class action suit and maintain its reputation as a responsible guarantor, Fireman's Fund eventually repurchased the entire $55 million portfolio held by these investors. Net losses are believed to be in the $16 to $20 million range, considerably in excess of the first loss coverage originally thought to be sufficient to protect investors.[14]

Concerning the release of first loss protection, the structure of a transaction may permit excess protection that is built-up in favorable environments to be removed, diminishing the protection for investors in unfavorable environments.

> Some commercial mortgage-backed transactions rely on a form of credit enhancement known as a "top-up" policy, which allows excess protection

[14]"Fireman's Fund Agrees to Settle Lawsuit By Woodson Investors for $55 million," *American Banker*, May 16, 1985, p. 2.

(defined as any amount in excess of the minimum amount necessary to maintain a specific rating) that accumulates over time to be released, rather than requiring it to be retained for the benefit of investors. In these transactions, if the real estate market is strong for a few years, the top-up policy may be reduced, leaving investors with less protection if the real estate market weakens.

Property/Casualty Risks

The physical collateral in asset-backed transactions involving secured receivables is often subject to traditional property/casualty insurance risks. These risks may appear to be fully addressed, but appearances can be deceiving.

First, although collateral may be insured against property damage or other loss, property-casualty insurance proceeds may prove to be uncollectable. Transactions involving secured receivables (such as automobile receivables) usually require both property damage insurance and vendor's single interest insurance, but minimum quality standards for the providers of such coverage are not ordinarily specified. As a result, transactions may be structured relying on the existence of insurance from marginal entities—entities that may be noninvestment grade and unrated by A.M. Best.

Second, insurance coverage may simply be unavailable for certain risks to collateral. For example, the insurance coverage provided by many large property/casualty companies excludes asbestos risk; indeed, a number of these companies have refused to make first mortgage loans on properties with asbestos exposure. As a result, many transactions with asbestos exposure are structured without asbestos insurance. A case in point is 55 Water Street in New York City. This property, which is known to contain asbestos, was used as the collateral in a double-A rated commercial mortgage transaction, which required neither asbestos insurance nor asbestos removal.

Third, the availability of insurance coverage for some types of collateral risks is often very limited. For example, flood loss coverage is typically limited to the levels available under the National Flood Insurance Program, even though these limits can be substantially below foreseeable loss levels. Similarly, insurance coverage for special hazard losses is generally limited to amounts well below actual collateral values. In many instances, special hazard insurance totals only 1 to 2 percent of the amount of securities outstanding.

Fourth, and even more potentially calamitous, is the risk that title to collateral will prove inadequate to provide recourse to the property. Title insurance is generally limited to "real property." As a result, securitizations of personal property routinely rely on representations made by the seller about the transfer to the trustee of good and marketable title to the secured property. Once again, however, representations can be breached. Therefore, the remedies available against the representing party must be closely examined. In many instances, the only remedy available is a repurchase requirement by the seller, even though the seller may not be an investment grade institution.

Risk of Downgrading

In most financial transactions, the risk of downgrading is far more likely than the risk of default. In 1987, for example, less than 3 percent of rated high yield (nonconvertible) bonds defaulted. By comparison, nearly 20 percent of triple-B rated companies experienced a downgrade in 1987.

Asset securitizations have proven particularly vulnerable to downgradings. Because the strength of an asset-backed transaction is a function of the strength of each of the complex and diverse elements underlying the transaction, its rating is dependent upon the performance of each of these elements not only at the time of closing, but throughout the life of the transaction. If any one of these elements deteriorates, the rating on the entire issue may be jeopardized. Clearly, the potential sources of a rating downgrade in an asset securitization are as numerous as the transaction is complex.

There are a number of recent examples of structured financings that have suffered temporary or long-term rating downgrades, including Washington Public Power Supply System, Matthews and Wright and Hot Springs, Arkansas. Even within the the relatively young industry of asset-backed structured financings, downgradings are not uncommon. For example, ratings on eight GMAC auto loan securitizations totaling over $4.4 billion (roughly 47 percent of total securitized financings issued up to that time) were lowered in late 1986 in connection with the downgrading of GMAC's unsecured debt rating from double-A plus to double-A. Two additional asset-backed issues were downgraded in 1987 as a result of the downgrading of the Japanese letter of credit banks that provided credit enhancement on these transactions. In addition, many other issues have been placed on "credit watch" for potential downward ratings revision.

Fortunately, barring major events with negative financial implications (e.g. leveraged buyouts and liability suits), most rating downgrades do not exceed one full rating level. Furthermore, the impact of a downgrade on the market value of an investment is far less for higher investment grade rated issues than for lower investment grade rated ones, as illustrated in the chart at the bottom of this page.

This chart is comforting with regard to the small market value loss to be expected from modest downgrades of asset-backed financings. However, these financings are generally rated "triple A" at original issue. In fact, as noted by Anthony Dub, head of First Boston's asset finance unit, in a recent issue of *Asset Sales Report*, "The market has not made much distinction between "Aaa" and "Aa1."[15] Ironically, however, a

Expected Market Value Decline from a Rating Downgrade
September 30, 1987 for a 3-year Taxable Bond

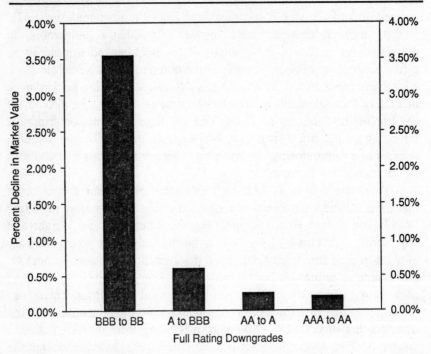

Source: Based on market prices.

---

[15]"Asset-Backed Ratings Hit," *Asset Sales Report*, August 31, 1987, p. 5.

by-product of this orientation toward highly rated asset securitizations is that there may be a liquidity problem in the secondary market with asset securitizations that are downgraded out of the double-A range. Less than 1 percent of 1987's new issue asset securitization volume (as of November 18, 1987) was rated below the double-A range at the time of issue.[16]

On the other hand, there can be a dramatic market impact when a transaction's rating is severely downgraded or withdrawn entirely. Consider the case of the Washington County, Pennsylvania, structured financing bond issues whose ratings were dropped when a legal opinion was withdrawn amid allegations of fraud. In this instance, the investor was not faced merely with the difference between two strong investment grade ratings, but rather with the difference between a rated and an unrated investment. For institutional investors with minimum investment rating requirements, such an occurrence might result in the ownership of "nonpermitted" investments. For these institutions, the loss of a rating (or in some instances the occurrence of a severe rating downgrade), may require a liquidation of investments precisely when it is least favorable to do so.

Prudent investors are aware that a deterioration in any element of an asset securitization, even those elements only indirectly related to the transaction, may potentially lead to an adverse rating development. As a result, these investors will want to, at a minimum, 1) evaluate the strength of each of the major parties to the transaction, including the originator, the servicer, the trustee, the issuer, and the credit enhancer and 2) assess the impact of each of the major opinions, contracts, appraisals, warranties, representations, and the like that are relied upon, either directly or indirectly, in the transaction.

REMEDIES AVAILABLE TO THE INVESTOR

Given the number of things that can go wrong in the new and innovative world of asset-backed financing, an investor should recognize that at some point certain investments could have problems. To prepare for those problems, investors should be aware of the available remedies.

In general, an investor's remedies will derive from the pursuit of his legal rights through either the courts or creditors' committees or both.

---

[16]"New Issue Guide," *Asset Sales Report*, November 23, 1987, p. 6.

Unfortunately, investors will quickly discover that a complex financing does not stop being complex simply because it stops functioning. In fact, just the opposite occurs—a failure tends to further complicate an investor's risks.

When a transaction fails, the first difficulty investors face is the time and expense associated with any of the available courses of action. Because of the complexity of many asset securitizations, these transactions may take years to unravel, and the attorneys' fees for litigation could easily run well into the millions. In addition, there is the concern that many aspects of these securitizations, although understood by the particular parties initially involved, may be confusing to some judges and most juries.

Complicating both of these concerns is the fact that lengthy legal documents are inherently subject to ambiguous interpretation; cases have hung on a misplaced comma. The attorneys who litigate these cases are every bit as aware of the vulnerabilities of these transactions as the attorneys who assembled the financings, and they need only find one error or ambiguity to call into question the investors' legal protections.

Worse than the legal costs and uncertainties, however, are the conflicting interests of aggrieved creditors, which can create monumental problems in litigation. Implementation of a coordinated legal and work-out strategy is often hampered, even in private transactions with only a few major investors, when the interests and temperaments of bondholders differ. In public issues, involving thousands of bondholders, attempts to take decisive action and to compromise are even more limited. Consider a recent meeting of the creditors and bondholders of the Washington Public Power Supply System's failed nuclear projects. The meeting was so large that it was held in the 5000-seat Felt Forum at Madison Square Garden!

Further aggravating the conflicts of interest are innovations in structured financings, such as the introduction of three classes of bonds with different payments priorities (so-called "senior," "junior," and "subordinated" classes). Not only must bondholders within a class of creditors agree on a work-out strategy, they must also agree on an "equitable" solution for all classes or face the prospect of interminable litigations among classes. Consequently, the rights and remedies of senior and even junior creditors can be severely limited in such "three tier" transactions.

The curtailment of the rights of creditors is not limited, however, to transactions involving multiple classes of creditors. Consider, for example, the problems investors face in bankruptcy.

> Bankruptcy is perhaps the worst position a secured bondholder can find himself in, because in addition to the obvious problems of diminished and delayed payments, investors may also face considerable restrictions of their rights due to the broad powers of the bankruptcy courts. A bankruptcy judge has the power to, among other things, disallow excess collateral, erase contingent claims and make collateral substitutions. As an illustration of this last power, recall the bankruptcy proceedings of Continental Airlines during which a bankruptcy judge replaced with airplanes the short-term receivables collateralizing certain creditors.

Because the impact of bankruptcy can be so devastating, a great deal of legal effort is often expended to make the issuer in an asset securitization "bankruptcy-remote" and "nonconsolidatable." Rating agencies have specific standards which, though changing over time, reflect the state-of-the-art in establishing these special-purpose company financing vehicles. Yet, experienced investors know that some of these provisions (e.g., nonpetition agreements) may not be enforceable, that no entity can be made truly "bankruptcyproof," and that consolidation cannot be judged by some "safe-harbor" checklist alone. Rather these issues must be resolved in court based on a host of considerations, including whether or not a particular transaction worked to the detriment of other creditors.

In short, because of these difficulties (as well as risks such as the possible attachment of assets for tax, pension, and other employee liabilities), investors simply cannot assume that structure and asset quality alone are sufficient to fully protect them when there is a real possibility of the failure of a transaction. Although an investor in a failed transaction can personally control the actions he takes to pursue his legal rights, he cannot control the actions taken by the other investors in the transaction, much less the actions taken by various third parties such as the courts. Even under the best of circumstances, an individual investor can count on being only one voice in what is often a very large crowd.

CREDIT ENHANCEMENT

By now, it may appear to the reader that the only way to fully protect against the numerous risks present in even well-structured securitizations is to obtain a 100 percent guarantee from a reputable bank or insurance company. Although this does shift both the asset quality risk and the securitization risk to the shoulders of the guarantor, not even this strategy fully eliminates the investor's need for prudent investigation and self-protection. In evaluating a particular guaranteed transaction, there are four major considerations.

Ability to Pay

If an investor is going to rely on a guarantor, the investor will obviously want to be certain that the guarantor is able to pay if called upon. Credit ratings are one of the best indicators of ability to pay. But investors will also want to take into account the risk of a guarantor's downgrading by considering, for example, the guarantor's capital adequacy, its exposure to cyclical or risky lines of business, leverage, regulation, ownership structure and exposure to risks such as leveraged buyouts and product liability.

Obligation to Pay

Although a particular guarantor may be able to honor its financial commitments, it must also have the legal obligation to do so for its guarantee to truly provide protection for investors. Accordingly, a guarantee should state that the guarantor "unconditionally and irrevocably" guarantees timely payment and that the defenses of the guarantor "including, without limitation, the defense of fraud" are expressly waived "to the fullest extent permitted by applicable law."

Secondary Market Liquidity

One of the major advantages of 100 percent guaranteed transactions is enhanced secondary market liquidity. It is easier for a new investor to assess the quality of the guarantor than to evaluate all of the risks in a structured financing in midstream with limited timely data. Even so, there are two primary considerations concerning secondary market liquidity in fully guaranteed transactions. First, guaranteed transactions with identical ratings do not always trade equally well in the secondary markets, because different guarantors have different market acceptance and recognition. Second, not all guarantors are rated by a least two major rating agencies, and the market can be less receptive to issues with only one rating.

Prepayment Risk

In all asset securitizations, whether guaranteed or not, there is the risk of prepayment. As noted by Moody's Investors Service in *Asset Sales Report*, certain pay-out triggers, such as those standard in credit card securitizations, "also act to increase call risk to investors, by retiring the security early." Moody's further points out that its ratings do not reflect the probability of occurrence of pay-out triggers.[17] Despite such events, many securitizations offer attractive prepayment characteristics. For example, prepayment rates in asset securitizations are often less sensitive to interest rate movements than prepayment rates in other investments.

Appendix A summarizes the risks investors must evaluate based on the extent to which the investment is guaranteed.

CONCLUSION

Due to the sheer complexity of asset securitization, every transaction, no matter how well-structured, thoroughly researched, and precisely documented, will still present some risks. Therefore, investors must identify these risks, analyze their magnitude, examine the ways they have been reduced and assess the effectiveness of such risk reduction devices.

Risk is an unavoidable element of any investment and can be controlled only by thoroughly understanding the investment. Given such an understanding, an investor cannot only ensure that his investment matches his risk appetite, but he can also differentiate between the quality of various investments and ensure that he is appropriately compensated for the risks he assumes.

The higher yields available from asset-backed securities are not intended to eliminate risk, but rather to compensate the investor for the numerous risks in these transactions. The reward half of this risk/reward equation is easily evaluated—asset-backed securities offer some of the highest returns for top-rated investments available in the market. In fact, triple-A securitizations often provide single-A type returns. It is the risk half of the equation that poses the real analytical challenge, but as with many challenges, the reward can be well worth the effort expended.

---

[17]"Payout Events: Good & Evil," *Asset Sales Report*, August 31, 1987, p. 6.

APPENDIX A
Investor Risks: A checklist

	Which Risks Investors Must Evaluate		
	Senior Subordinated	Partial Guarantee	100% Guarantee
Analyze Strength of Primary Participants			
Seller	*	*	—
Issuer	*	*	—
Servicer	*	*	—
Trustee	*	*	—
Guarantor	—	*	*
Determine Adequacy of Due Diligence Investigations	*	*	—
Evaluate Soundness of Reps, Warranties & Indemnities	*	*	—
Determine Adequacy of Recourse to Makers of Reps, and so on	*	*	—
Assess Validity of Key Contracts & Agreements	*	*	—
Verify Regulatory Compliance ('33 & '40 Acts, and so on)	*	*	—
Review Key Legal Opinions & Legal Letters	*	*	—
Evaluate Expert Opinions	*	*	—
Investigate Prepayment Risks	*	*	*
Analyze Risk of Downgrading of:			
Transaction	*	*	—
Guarantor	—	*	*
Review Comfort Letters & Accountants' Certificates	*	*	—
Verify Existence & Adequacy of Back-up Computer Systems	*	*	—
Identify Structural Shortfalls, including:			
Insufficient loss protection	*	*	—
Ambiguous loss protection	*	*	—
Release of loss protection	*	*	—
Evaluate Property/Casualty			
Insurance of Physical Assets			
Collectability of insurance	*	*	—
Sufficiency of insurance	*	*	—
Availability of insurance	*	*	—
Verify Title to All Collateral (valid, perfected, and so on)	*	*	—
Investigate Secondary Market Liquidity	*	*	*

CHAPTER 19

THE INVESTOR'S VIEW

Phillip L. Zweig, Senior Writer
Corporate Finance Magazine

Editor's note: Institutional investor response to asset-backed securities has been mixed, largely because of concerns about the liquidity or secondary market trading of these issues. Nevertheless, they seem to believe that this market has unlimited potential.

In the following interviews, money managers with two leading firms that have bought asset-backed securities for their portfolios talk about the pros and cons of these instruments as investments. The interviews were conducted separately with Lawrence S. Harris, senior vice president, Fixed Income Group, Alliance Capital, New York; and Christopher L. Gootkind, assistant vice president and Robert E. Pruyne, managing director, Scudder Stevens & Clark, Boston.

ED:

Maybe you could begin by telling me a bit about your firm and what kinds of funds you manage.

HARRIS:

Alliance Capital is an investment counselling firm that is a subsidiary of Equitable Life. It was started in 1971 chiefly to manage pension assets. Today it manages about $32 billion in assets, of which about $11 billion are fixed income. We manage portfolios for pension funds, endowments, and insurance companies, as well as a family of mutual funds and a family of money market funds. And we're active investing not just in the U.S. but around the world.

PRUYNE:

We are investment counsel; that's our only business. Our clientele ranges from our own in-house mutual funds to individuals and institutions on the outside. The institutions are primarily in the employee benefit area, some insurance companies, and a number of endowments. We cover the rainbow, as it were, of clientele. In terms of where we might think of using these securities, it could be in any one of those situations.

ED:

Tell me something about the makeup and philosophy of the fixed-income portfolio.

HARRIS:

A lot depends on the kind of money we're managing. The mutual fund money, as with most fixed income mutual fund money, is very much yield-oriented, because that's what fixed-income shareholders seem to want. The income is taxable, and the investors are concerned more with receiving a steady, robust level of current income than they are with total return. Clearly, they don't want to see their asset get unduly devalued. But income is the primary concern, and we try to respond to that objective. For pension or endowment accounts where they're nontaxable, they're clearly more total return-oriented, and we manage those funds in that light. We tend not to make major bets on the directions of interest rates, although we'll adjust our portfolio maturities within some circumscribed band around a market index appropriate to the client's risk tolerance.

We are active across the entire spectrum of the yield curve and in a broad range of markets to meet different kinds of objectives.

ED:

When did you start looking at nonmortgage asset-backed securities as potential investments?

HARRIS:

The first deal I can remember looking at was the Sperry lease deal. It was the first deal I was conscious of as an effort to securitize something other than mortgages. We began to pay much closer attention when securitization of auto loans began, with their shorter duration. Since then, credit card receivables and other things have been securitized. And we have been interested observers of the scene since the process began. We are very significant investors in mortgage-backed securities, and that naturally led us to asset-backed securities. We also have some understanding of the assets being securitized.

ED:

What portion of your portfolio is now made up of nonmortgage asset-backed securities?

HARRIS:

It's very small at the moment, if only because the nature of our clients' investment objectives doesn't allow us to be major players in that market right now.

It's maybe less than a half of one percent. But that's on a big asset base, and it's a fairly small market. So, I'm not sure how indicative that is of anything. For us, part of the appeal of these securities is that 1) their effective average lives are fairly short and 2) given those effective average lives, returns and yield spreads, we think, are still very attractive. When you can buy a GMAC deal with an average life of under two years and a spread of 65 to 70 basis points over Treasuries, that's got to be terribly attractive. We think there are reasons why it's attractive and that's what draws us to that market. In fact, we've designed and have begun to offer a new investment service that will include these kinds of securities in an important way.

Let me explain the background of where we're coming from. As you look along the spectrum of the yield curve there seems to be a certain discontinuity, if you will, from the standpoint of how investors participate. At the very short end of the yield curve—one year and under—the market is dominated by the money market funds, which by the nature of what they do, want to be sort of surrogate bank accounts. That is to say, when you sell somebody a money market fund for a dollar a share, it's always got to be a dollar a share. The Securities and Exchange Commission says that if you always want it to be a dollar a share, you can't invest in anything over a year to maturity. So you always have money chasing things that are a year and under. Other kinds of institutional investors tend to invest out longer on the curve. To be sure there's plenty of institutional investment money that goes into intermediate maturities—say three, four, and five years—and there's lots of money that goes out longer than that. But in that one to three or four year place on the yield curve, there's always been a void. It's too long for the money market funds and it's too short for most other investors. This was not a traditional place for investors to play, so some inefficiency has been created in the marketplace, which has begun to be exploited by these kinds of securities. And the reason I think those rates are so attractive is that they still need to lure institutional investors into that part of the yield curve where they're not used to playing. There are a lot of other securities out there that are either nominally or effectively very short and have the same sort of behavior characteristics—very short, two-year average lives. And all or most of those also trade at yield premiums to Treasuries that we think are fairly excessive, given the nature of the securities and the spreads at the farther end of the curve. And those include things like the very short tranches of collateralized mortgage obligations and very high coupon Ginnie Maes, 14s or 15s, with very high prepayment rates. Their effective average lives wind up being two years or so. Another example is very high coupon corporate bonds that may be nominally 30-year bonds but will be callable in the next year or two. So you can aggregate an array of instruments that may not nominally be that short but will act in the marketplace like they are. And they tend to be orphans, so they tend to trade at premium yields.

We are attempting to put together an investment service that invests in those things as a sort of "super-charged money market fund alternative," if you will. It's for people who want a higher yield than they can get in the money market funds and are willing to take a tiny bit of principal risk to get it. We're offering it to institutional clients. One client, a corporation, that has signed up has excess cash and is unhappy with money market returns and is trying to do better. We think it also has other applications. So that's really where the principal attraction comes for us in that segment of the yield curve.

PRUYNE:

To date, it's been fairly limited with the shorter average life of these instruments that are generally available. One of the characteristics of short-term instruments that we value highly is liquidity. We have had some concern, particularly where we've had portfolios that had relatively low short positions, so we would primarily use Treasuries and other very liquid instruments.

We do have some reserve-type accounts. These may be corporations with a large pool of reserve assets where lack of or lessened liquidity is not as important.

In the accounts we're involved with, 5 or 10 percent of the account would probably be the maximum that we've gone into to date. That's because we normally look for diversification, and a 5 percent commitment in a single instrument would be a heavy one. Typically such a commitment would be reserved for something we really had a strong feeling about in terms of liquidity as well as quality. So when we think in terms of these large reserve accounts, individual commitments might be on the order of 2 to 3 percent. And, therefore, if we had three or four commitments, we'd only get up to 10 percent or thereabout.

ED:

These are funds you manage for particular corporations?

PRUYNE:

They could be part of an employee benefit fund or corporate surplus funds. A corporation that sold a division or something has surplus to be invested. We have some funds that have dedicated particular pools of assets toward the shorter end of the maturity spectrum and have hired Scudder to manage those funds against a relatively short-term maturity structure.

ED:

What's the range of maturities and yields represented in these instruments?

GOOTKIND:

In the accounts where there's a short-term focus, most of them have been about 2 to 3 years. They may have a final maturity of five years but usually an average life of 2 to 3. For those accounts where we're using a bogie, a duration of a year and a half or so, a 2 to 3-year type bond would work very well.

ED:

How do the yields compare with other instruments in those portfolios?

GOOTKIND:

Most of these have been structured with some sort of prepayment assumptions, and if you like the assumptions, the yields have been fairly attractive. The next question would be what other instruments we have looked at in these types of accounts, and short corporate paper comes to mind. There aren't that many corporate issuers out there that do issue straight two- and three-year paper. They generally tend to borrow longer. Finance companies with shorter life assets will borrow at the shorter end, so we've seen a lot of their paper. We've also been buying some bank deposit notes in these accounts.

Given the prepayment assumptions and liquidity considerations, you should get paid a little bit more for that. They're reasonably attractive alternatives.

ED:

Have you put any kind of a cap on purchases of these instruments?

HARRIS:

No. You have to realize it's still a fairly small market. Also, as we look across the spectrum of our asset base, we just don't have that much money that would naturally find its way into that part of the yield curve. As we attempt to attract more assets for this enhanced money market program, hopefully that will grow.

ED:

Will that program be sold at retail?

HARRIS:

It will be sold principally to institutional clients of one sort or another, but we may do it in mutual fund form as well.

ED:

What concerns do you have about these instruments?

GOOTKIND:

We have concerns about the credit card deals. I don't think we've bought any of those. A lot of the large banks are basically giving these credit cards away. They've experienced losses of 5 percent plus in their portfolios. You're talking about an unsecured loan. But if you look at the loss experience on the automobile deals, it's very low. In distressed times, in economic recessions, next to their homes, people will pay off their car loans.

We've seen a few lease receivable deals but have passed on those. Liquidity is what bothers us about those. The lack of a secondary market. A $150 million Sperry lease receivable—try to find a trader who's going to bid on that in another year. I'm not sure we're going to find someone to step up to the plate very aggressively for that.

HARRIS:

There are really two sets of concerns. One is the lack of any history on how they ought to trade relative to Treasuries of comparable maturity and duration. We're not too concerned about that if only because the spreads are so wide that we feel there's not a whole lot of risk. I mean a two-year piece of paper that's trading at 70. What's the risk that it's going to 100—probably not too great. So we're not too worried about that. What we are worried about is secondary market liquidity in these things on an ongoing basis. What happens when we want to sell?

ED:

Have they been traded much in the secondary market?

HARRIS:

Yes, some, but you have very few dealers who really seem geared up to do this. It's been the same way with every new kind of security that we've seen. It takes a while for liquidity to develop. It takes a while for dealers to think that they can make money trading them. And it's a sort of chicken and egg situation. The dealers are not interested until they think they can get a lot of institutions interested in them and a lot of order flow going. But on the other hand, the institutional buyers are reluctant to get involved until the secondary market liquidity is there.

The mortgage securities market was the same way in the early 1970s when it was just developing. Two or more dealers were dominant and lots of investors were afraid of it because in those days you had concerns about the differential nature of the contract as well as monthly payments. Back offices could not accommodate it.

ED:

Do you see any differences in the secondary market trading one type of issue as opposed to another? Are some more liquid than others?

HARRIS:

It's hard to tell at this point because they're so new. The auto receivables are becoming more liquid because there's been more issuance. The credit card receivables are probably still less liquid because there are less of them out there. It's a problem that gradually resolves itself with issuance.

ED:

What characteristics make some issues more liquid or tradable than others?

HARRIS:

The most important thing—and we had the same problem in the early days of CMO creation—was to try to develop, if you will, a contract specification for the instrument that is fairly uniform from issuer to issuer. In this way the trader can know whether he's trading issue A or issue B and whether they have the same basic cash flow patterns, so that he's dealing with apples and apples. Now, every instrument is unique. There's a built-in disincentive to provide liquidity for a trader because he never knows what he's bidding on. He's got to look it up. That will continue until you reach some sort of consensus as to what this animal ought to look like from the standpoint of structure. We're pretty much there with these things. It took a while to get there with CMOs. Once the liquidity problem is overcome that disincentive goes away.

ED:

What kinds of concerns do you have about credit risk? Have they been allayed by credit enhancement?

HARRIS:

Pretty much—it's a difficult thing to judge. It will be interesting to see what happens going through the next recession. We have a large volume of data on the delinquency experience of these things that should be statistically reliable. But then we've been in an environment where people have been in pretty good shape financially. What happens if there's a recession? I don't know. That's an experience we're not going to be able to come to grips with until we live through it. But one thing that gives investors some comfort is that even though these are monthly payment vehicles, they don't have the prepayment risk you have on mortgage-backed securities that burned everybody badly in the past year. They're much shorter instruments. People don't refinance their cars when interest rates go down, so the certainty of the cash flow is much greater. And that gives investors a heightened sense of confidence.

ED:

Do you have any fundamental preferences for lease-backed, auto-backed, or credit card-backed securities? Or are they pretty much homogenous?

HARRIS:

I'm sure they're not. But I'm not sure we know enough at this point to be able to discriminate among them really intelligently. There have got to be, it seems to me, fundamental differences in the credit that we'll learn about only with the passage of time. Maybe that's why the spreads are so attractive. They're paying us to take the risk of inexperience. We can only speculate about those things. What happens in tough times? If you can only write one check, do you make it for your car payment or your credit card? Or if you think they'll take your car away, do you put it on your credit card? I don't know.

GOOTKIND:

The bulk of our analysis has been on the CARS—the auto loan receivables. One of the major reasons is that they've been the largest issues, and I think they're a little bit easier to understand. When you look at a credit card deal and you look at the underlying assets, you're talking about unsecured loans to John Doe on the street. With an auto receivable loan at least you have the underlying collateral of the automobile should something happen. And while we haven't been overly concerned that problems may arise, it certainly does make one a little more comfortable to know that it's a secured loan.

In recent months we have increased our commitments in the auto receivables deals, particularly in our short duration, lower volatility accounts.

However, we also recently made a modest commitment in the credit card receivables issues as well. While recognizing that these issues still represent unsecured loans to John and Jane Doe on Main Street, we are sufficiently comfortable with the layers of protection in most of the deals to warrant investment. The structure of the deals tends to be a little "cleaner" than that of auto receivables issues: there is a two year, interest-only period followed by rapid amortization of the collateral, usually over 11 to 13 months.

The layers of protection include a subordinated piece held by the seller or letter of credit from a high-rated bank—typically for 10 to 15 percent of the deal. Another level of protection is from "excess servicing," which is the amount left over, if any, after subtracting the coupon on the certificates, the servicing fee, the letter of credit fee and charge-offs on the loans from the yield on the overall portfolio, which typically is 16.5 to 19.5 percent. We use a "safety ratio" to determine the amount of protection. This ratio is:

$$\frac{\text{Excess servicing\% + Letter of Credit\% (or subordinated portion)}}{\text{\% charge-offs}}$$

This ratio ranges from $5\times$ to approximately $8\times$ on deals we have examined. The major risks on the card deals are if the yield on the receivables drops or charge-offs rise significantly, or both.

ED:

Was there any controversy early on about whether to invest in these securities?

HARRIS:

It wasn't terribly controversial. It had more to do with the lack of secondary market liquidity than anything else. I think there was a general level of comfort with the underlying instrument. It was more what happens when we want to sell it. In the great void out there, who's going to make us a bid and at what price?

ED:

How about the time it takes you to analyze the investment. Is that an issue?

HARRIS:

No. They're not so complicated that they create an undue analytical burden for us. I think most institutional investors are sufficiently conditioned to asset-backed securities and the unusual patterns of cash flow that come from some of these things, that the analytical process, at least from a quantitative standpoint, is not that difficult anymore. It's part of their everyday routine. The other part of the process, of course, is the credit process. In some cases you have people relying on the enhancements, and saying, well, what the heck, it's Bank of America or GMAC behind it, and how bad can it be?

GOOTKIND:

It does take a little longer. The reason is that every single issue, we feel, is different. You can talk about GMAC paper, and a three-year GMAC deal is a three year GMAC deal, but in reading the fine print of an asset-backed prospectus you really do have to look at every deal standing on its own. So from that standpoint, it does take longer. You have letters of credit if you want to look at some credit enhancements. There are letters of credit for different percentages, from different banks. There are different structures for the prepayment. You may have a guaranteed investment contract from a Morgan Guaranty. What is the diversification of the underlying loans? How big is the deal? This comes into play not just because of liquidity but also because of ERISA (Employee Retirement Income Security Act of 1974) considerations.

ED:

Can you elaborate on the ERISA angle?

PRUYNE:

The basic issue is what happens if an individual has a loan on his credit card and he is also the beneficiary of the ERISA account that owns the bond. Would that be self-dealing? It's pretty remote, but it is a possibility. Lawyers are working to establish ground rules to qualify these asset-backed securities to get around this problem. Size is one of the issues. Obviously, if any individual loan in a total pool that is used for collateral is only a drop in the bucket, then the chance of any conflict of interest becomes pretty remote. The big deals may be eligible to be bought by ERISA accounts; the smaller deals might not be.

ED:

What are your criteria for investing in these issues?

HARRIS:

We take them on a case by case basis. We haven't set any hard and fast rules. The market's new, so we try to approach each situation as a new one and see where it leads us.

GOOTKIND:

There are individual criteria we do look at but I can tell you it's a collective decision as well. It's not like you have a checklist of things and if five of them are satisfied then it's a go and if not we pass. It has to do with some of the legal considerations. They've got to qualify under ERISA for certain accounts. Then there's liquidity. We do look at credit enhancement and the credit quality of the issuer. The structure is another thing that has to do with prepayment. Then there's the final maturity: It's one thing to talk about something having an average life or a weighted average maturity of a year and a half but with a final maturity of five years, what happens with some of those tag end pieces down the road?

ED:

What kind of credit enhancements do you require and have you bought any without credit enhancements?

HARRIS:

We haven't set a hard and fast rule for ourselves. I don't think we have any now. In the earlier going, we might have used a few that didn't have them. It's not an insurmountable obstacle from our standpoint if we have some basic faith in the loan value of the collateral, or if they're overcollateralized by 20 or 30 percent. If there's enough there to protect us, credit enhancements are helpful but not absolutely necessary.

PRUYNE:

We prefer to look at the structure of the deal first and foremost.

ED:

Are there certain ratings that you won't buy? Do they have to be rated at a certain level?

HARRIS:

It depends on the nature of the portfolio we're buying them for. In some cases we're restricted. For instance, we have sizable assets invested in the high yield bond market—well over $1 billion and growing. That's because we have a lot of clients who let us do that, and we have some expertise in that area. Given total freedom, we don't necessarily cut off any place. Everything has a price, and if we can understand the credit and feel comfortable with it, it's just a matter of, 'Are we getting paid for the risk?'

PRUYNE:

Some investors may rely very heavily on ratings, but we don't look at the service ratings that closely. We're not tied to them. We rely on our own homework and assign our own ratings. We're willing to look down the quality scale, but if we're going to dip down in quality we want to be compensated in yield. Sometimes, not only in asset-backed securities but in securities generally, we tend to be a little harsher than the rating agencies. Pricing is generally a lot more closely correlated with the rating service ratings than with our own.

ED:

In descending order of priorities, what counts most?

PRUYNE:

Obviously, price in relation to a whole long list of things including: the offering price of the security relative to perceived quality, the perceived repayment schedule, and what that means in terms of how the price translates into yield, typically versus Treasuries.

ED:

Are these fairly equally distributed in pension or other types of profolios?

HARRIS:

Not necessarily. Because while we set a market risk posture for ourselves on a collective basis, we basically let portfolio managers make their own decisions about what sectors of the market to invest in. So a given portfolio manager may decide he likes this area of the market and another may not.

ED:

Have you bought private as well as public issues?

PRUYNE:

So far I don't believe we've bought any of the privates. We have bought [other] private placements but in small quantities. Most of our portfolios are actively managed. We're willing to pay a small premium—and in today's market it seems to be a very small premium—for being in publicly traded, active, and liquid issues. We buy an instrument today because we think it's undervalued and we always feel that sometime before maturity it will be overvalued and we'll sell it and go into something else. We're willing to pay a little bit of a premium, to accept a lower yield, to get that liquidity and to be able to do that in the future.

ED:

Under what market conditions do these issues make sense or not make sense for your portfolios?

PRUYNE:

The value of any bond is determined more by its price within the market than it is by the market environment itself. When we look at the bond market we're always appraising various alternative investments on the basis of "what if" questions. And the "what if" questions we pose to ourselves are, "what happens if the market goes up, goes down, or goes sideways?" And then we assign a probability to that happening.

What's most important is how the issues are priced within the marketplace as opposed to what the marketplace looks like it's doing. The fact that we've got relatively small holdings is indicative of the fact that we haven't found them to be priced terribly attractively. It's been on a very selective basis.

ED:

What impact does a rising rate environment have on your appetite or on market acceptance of these issues?

HARRIS:

I don't think it changes our view one way or the other. These things have a definite role to play at a circumscribed point on the yield curve. Certainly to the extent that we decide we want to get very defensive in our longer term portfolios, it might increase our appetite. From the standpoint of money we have available to invest in that part of the marketplace, generally it's always going to be there. If anything, higher rates may increase our appetite.

ED:

Under what conditions would you expand your position?

GOOTKIND:

I guess a change in relative value, which is what we're always looking for. I guess if we felt alternative investments in the shorter end of the market—whether it be finance paper, shorter corporate paper, short CMOs, or whatever short structures we were looking at—were all tight to Treasuries, we'd probably go into Treasuries, or we might look at these some more. There is some size—and it's large—that would satisfy our ERISA-type accounts. Oftentimes if we're buying a large piece of a deal, we'll put it into eight or ten accounts. We don't want to have to put it into some accounts where we don't have to worry about ERISA and some where we do. It's just too difficult to keep track of everything. We generally buy something we can put into any of our accounts.

ED:

Under what kind of conditions might you see a flight from these kinds of securities and a diminution of investor appetite?

HARRIS:

If we thought rates were going to go down a lot, then clearly where we have the freedom to get longer, it would be better to be longer than in these things. I think the only other thing that could drive us away is if there were some significant credit problems— like a super high rate of defaults on auto loans. It would take a horrendous economic environment for that to happen, a very low odds bet. If we move away from them, it would be less because of disenchantment with the vehicle than because there were better returns elsewhere.

PRUYNE:

When a class of securities becomes unattractive to us, it's because they have developed a special following with a specific group for some noninvestment reason. I guess the best example is in the early days of mortgage-backed securities and Ginnie Maes in particular. They had special appeal to savings institutions way back in the early 1970s. And we had no interest in Ginnie Maes at that time because they were being sold. They were a small part of the total market obviously, but they were being sold and bought by the savings institutions themselves. It wasn't until the days of disintermediation when the savings institutions were selling their holdings to raise liquidity that they interested us as general investors. If in some way, for some reason, a particular group of investors came along for which asset-backed securities were very attractive, they would, in effect, price us out of the market.

ED:

What has to happen for these issues to be more attractive to people like yourselves?

PRUYNE:

Obviously, the fastest way to increase the attraction is to raise the yield relative to the market. One of the biggest question marks in the investor's mind is uncertain cash flow. It's not like buying a Treasury bill where you put up money today and you know exactly how many dollars you'll get on some day in the future. To the extent that the underwriting community comes up with new ways of packaging that reduce the uncertainty of cash flow, then the same securities could look more attractive with the same spread.

ED:

What other things do packagers and issuers have to do to enable these instruments to achieve the kind of acceptance seen in the mortgage-backed securities market?

HARRIS:

I think there are two things they need to do. One, they need to make the format of the vehicles as standard as possible, so that it becomes pretty much a commodity product. Everybody knows about Ginnie Maes and how they work. It's got to be the same thing for these too. And beyond that, it's just a matter of beginning to attract institutional investors further in on the yield curve. The yield spreads that are available will help to do that. If we get a growing consensus that we're in a real bear market for bonds, that'll help to do it just because people will be looking for surer things, and these are surer things with nice yields. It's a long-term education process just as it was with mortgages. It'll develop slowly just like mortgages did. Maybe it'll develop even more quickly than mortgages just because we've gone through the mortgage thing already. Everybody's reached that plateau of education. It's here to stay. I think it'll grow.

ED:

What kind of hesitancies do your colleagues elsewhere express?

HARRIS:

There's a sort of knee jerk reaction on the part of a lot of people that, "gee whiz, these things are new and I'm not sure I understand them, and I have other things to do so why bother?" That's true with any new vehicle. It's not particularly endemic to asset-backed securities. It just takes time to overcome that.

ED:

What advice do you have for other institutional buyers looking at an offering for the first time?

HARRIS:

I guess the only advice I could give them is the same sort of caution we had about after market liquidity. As time passes that caution either diminishes or increases depending on what happens. These are fairly straightforward vehicles. If there are any hidden hooks we certainly haven't found them yet. I don't see any reason to particularly caution anybody against using them. They fulfill a very useful purpose.

ED:

Do you see a growth in the securitization trend and in institutional investor acceptance of these securities?

HARRIS:

I'd expect it to continue to grow. You can look at it from the issuer side and the investor side. From the investor side, it creates a continual stream of new things on the menu in which to invest. That brings with it some risk but also brings with it some opportunities and gives investors more tools. From the side of the issuers, we're going through a period where 1) financial markets are becoming more and more deregulated, and 2) given the volatility of interest rates, financial institutions, the originators, and the sellers of the underlying collateral for these things are trying more and more to eliminate interest rate risk from their balance sheets. So it seems to me that it's a natural on both sides for the process to continue to grow. Whether it's securitization of consumer-oriented receivables of one sort or another, or commercial business receivables, it's a

natural adjunct of deregulation as well. As you break down the
walls between the suppliers of capital and the demanders of capital
it seems to me that the processes can only grow.

PRUYNE:

It represents the investment banker getting closer to the commerical banking business just as the reverse is going on in many
other ways. It's part of a general trend and I would not expect it
to reverse itself.

ED:

What other questions should I be asking you about how institutional investors and fixed income managers should look at these
instruments?

HARRIS:

What you need to do is to change people's habits. We're all
creatures of habit. Fixed-income investors are used to investing at
certain points along the curve in certain types of instruments and
to change those habits takes time. But it will happen, and as it
happens liquidity develops and you have viable markets. I view the
whole thing as a positive, constructive development in the capital
markets and I would expect it to grow.

CHAPTER 20

CONCLUSION: ASSET SECURITIZATION'S ROLE IN A BETTER FINANCIAL WORLD

Lowell L. Bryan, Director
McKinsey & Co.

In my introductory chapter, I outlined the nature and growth of asset securitization—the forces and innovations driving it and the immediate benefits accruing to its players. In these concluding thoughts, I would like to suggest some broader benefits of a fully securitized world and also sketch out some likely roles that various participants in that world might play in the future.

The transition to a fully securitized world will not be automatic, despite the momentum we see in the marketplace. As I indicated in the introduction, many infrastructural issues need to be solved, though some are indeed only mechanical. Regulatory issues are more problematical, and the evolution of this new technology (at least in the United States) is unavoidably wrapped up not only with current laws separating banks and securities firms but also, in fact, with our entire credit system itself. Our traditional bank-dominated credit system is dangerously weak, and the general regulatory framework that bears on securitization has not kept pace with changes in the marketplace. These things need to be fixed before asset securitization can truly flourish.

This forum, however, is not the place to tackle those questions which I have treated in detail elsewhere.[1] To summarize, I have argued that U.S. regulators must:

1. Clean up the problems of U.S. depository institutions.
2. Encourage risk to migrate outside those institutions.
3. Allow financial holding companies to own a wider range of financial service subsidiaries.
4. Regulate those subsidiaries functionally with an eye to making the marketplace more efficient.
5. Rewrite laws and regulations specifically with securitized credit in mind.

On the assumption that these—or comparable—steps are eventually taken, and the technology of securitized assets is allowed to develop fully, how will the new system be superior to the old?

A securitized system would beat traditional lending on five counts. First, it would have better economics. Second, it would ensure better credit underwriting. Third, it would provide for better credit risk diversification. Fourth, it would make assets more liquid. Fifth, it would transfer interest rate risk to players who are better equipped to handle it than banks are. Let us review these one at a time.

First, let us look at *economics*. Our tradional credit system is very expensive, particularly for high-quality assets. Irrespective of all the other operating costs, banks, finance companies, and thrifts have substantial intermediary costs that cannot be reduced under current rules. Today, for a typical bank, these costs include about 20 basis points for required reserves, about 10 basis points for FDIC insurance, and over 1 percent in equity costs. In other words, all assets placed on a bank's balance sheet must earn a minimum net interest spread of about 1.5 percent. These costs are on top of other operating costs and loan loss reserves. In other words, a bank must earn a pretax net interest spread of approximately 1.5 percent on its loans, net of operating costs and loan loss reserves, to keep its stock price equal to

---

[1] *See* Lowell Bryan, "The Credit Bomb in Our Financial System," *Harvard Business Review*, p. 65 (January - February 1987) pp. 45-51; id. Testimony to U.S. Senate Banking Committee, October 14, 1987: "Securitized Credit: The Potential for a Sounder, More Effective Financial System," *Breaking Up the Bank: Rethinking an Industry Under Siege (Dow-Jones Irwin)*

its book value. In truth, the average commercial bank in this country has not, for the last several years, been able to meet this test. Bankers are not, on average, recovering their equity costs, which is why many bank stocks sold (as of this writing) well below book value after a five-year bull market. Cost savings are usually even higher for most finance companies, corporations, or thrifts that securitize their assets because they are generally less highly leveraged than banks. Moreover, for any lender with less than a double-A credit rating, the interest savings alone on issuing securitized assets are usually sufficient to make the entire transaction economic.

A second advantage of securitized assets is that it should only be possible to securitize loans in which the *credit underwriting* is sound (i.e., when the price charged for taking credit risk is less than the expected credit losses). To ensure sound credit underwriting, we must demand that the originator of every securitized asset deal retain at least the expected loss on the securitized loans; the system will not work unless the loan originator is motivated to underwrite the credit properly and to service the underlying loans. For most high-quality assets, this means that the originator will need to guarantee at least two or three times the expected credit loss on the asset. In other words, if the maximum expected loss on the portfolio is 1 percent, we would expect the originator to guarantee the first loss for at least that amount. This system should ensure sounder credit underwriting than the normal lending process.

This is because the originating institution has to deal with an outside credit enhancer that reviews the credit assessment skills, servicing capacity, documentation, and so on, of the originating institution before agreeing to participate. Credit enhancers are far less likely to have community or customer class biases than local commercial banks, which are likely to be overly optimistic about the health of the local economy, the creditworthiness of a local borrower, or the finance units of corporations that want to support the sale of manufactured goods. Further, credit enhancers should have strong economic incentives to work with originating institutions to improve the credit skills of originators. And finally, in the securitized asset process, a rating agency looks over the shoulder of both the originator and the enhancer. Weak creditors will either have to improve their credit skills or be foreclosed from being able to securitize their loans. The net result is that credit underwriting through asset securitization should be far sounder than under the traditional system.

This technology should also lead to *better diversification of credit risk*—particularly by banks and thrifts. Theoretically, the loan portfolio of a bank or thrift should be a good diversifier of credit risk, but experience has proven this theory false. In fact, the traditional credit system has led to two kinds of concentration of credit risk: 1) credit risk that is concentrated geographically and 2) credit risk that is concentrated among a small percentage of weak depository institutions. Let us consider geographic concentration first.

Banks originate most of their loans wherever they happen to be located. Thus, most banks in Oklahoma have loan portfolios filled with loans to independent oil and gas producers and farmers—partly because they were overoptimistic about the health of the local economy, and partly because they had few other lending opportunities. It is not surprising, therefore, that we now have a concentration of charge-offs in different regions of the country. While banks in New England and the Mid-Atlantic have been experiencing only marginal charge-offs, banks in the West North Central and West South Central regions have been charging off loans at a rate over twice the national average.

Asset securitization will cause this credit risk to be diversified. While expected losses will be retained with the originator, catastrophe credit risk will be placed with a credit enhancer, and this in turn will probably be syndicated to other credit enhancers. In the process, catastrophe credit risk will be spread from the originating institution to credit enhancers, with any residual risk borne by investors—who further spread the risk by diversifying their portfolios. If this system had been in place in the early 1980s, it would have prevented the kind of regional concentration of credit charge-offs we are seeing now.

The fourth dimension in which securitization wins over the traditional system is *liquidity*. The traditional system produces illiquid assets. Banks, thrifts, and finance companies make few short-term, self-liquidating loans these days. There is no secondary market for most loans, with the exception of the whole loan mortgage market. Once a loan is made to a borrower, the lender has limited ability to convert that loan back to cash until the borrower pays the lender back. This means that lenders can do little to adjust their loan portfolios for changing interest rate or market conditions. Since economic volatility has become a way of life, this lack of liquidity makes lenders more vulnerable than they need to be.

In contrast, securities are liquid. If a lender had more such assets on its balance sheet, it would have a far more liquid portfolio than at present. As a result, it could adjust its portfolio much more quickly to changing conditions. Other investors can, of course, either hold or sell credit securities just like any other security in their portfolios.

The fifth comparison between the traditional credit system and securitized credit is in terms of *interest rate risk*. Since 1980, interest-sensitive deposits of banks and thrifts have increased from about 50 percent of their total source of funds to about 75 percent of the total. Many commercial banks (but fewer thrifts) have responded very intelligently to the increasing market rate sensitivity of the liability side of their balance sheets by making many more floating-rate loans.

The problem is, though, that floating-rate assets do not yield good margins. As a result, in order to increase earnings, many lenders have taken significant interest rate bets of two types: 1) discretionary bets involving fixed-rate investments in the investment portfolio and, 2) fixed-rate assets generated in the course of doing banking business (i.e., the credit card book and the auto loan book on the consumer side). Banks, thrifts, and finance companies, as highly leveraged institutions, are poorly structured to take significant interest rate risk. Even modest mismatches can lead to significant losses. The level of interest rate betting by many lenders raising interest sensitive deposits and investing them in fixed-rate investments—that is, playing the yield curve—has now reached very significant proportions and has exposed them to enormous risks.

The securitized asset system lenders continue to offer fixed-rate loans to customers while choosing whether or not to take interest rate bets. If a lender chooses to securitize these loans, it can transfer fixed-rate interest risk to the end investor who is far better positioned to take that risk. For example, pension funds or mutual funds are not leveraged institutions; they are, in effect, all equity. They are properly structured and managed to take market risk; indeed, they do it all the time.

NEW ROLES IN THE NEW AND BETTER SYSTEM

For the above reasons and regulatory changes permitting, the transition to full asset securitization should provide all of us with a more effective, more efficient, and sounder financial system. It would be a system that provides the benefits of competition without endangering the soundness of the financial system.

Specifically, it would provide for: 1) more profitable roles for existing, skilled commercial banks and thrifts, 2) profitable roles for skilled nonbanks, and 3) a safer financial system.

1. *More profitable roles for existing, skilled commercial banks and thrifts.* In the traditional system, there has been one role for all depository institutions that included origination, structuring, servicing, and funding.

The United States has 14,000 commercial banks (plus 3,000 thrifts) that are trying to play that role today. Due to similarities in regulation, many of these institutions have pursued parallel strategies and have evolved similar capabilities and ways of operating. Now that the regulatory barriers, such as interstate banking laws which had long limited competition between these institutions, are either falling or are being bypassed, many institutions find themselves as head-to-head competitors with institutions with very similar capabilities. The more similar the institutional skills of those participants, the less value is being added. The public gains little from having thousands of institutions that offer the same undifferentiated product. Asset securitization changes the dynamics of this situation by creating a far greater variety of roles available to participants. For example, some participants can choose to compete in one function, credit origination, while others can choose to operate in credit enhancement or servicing. Moreover, each category of assets has the potential for these different functional roles: mortgages, credit cards, commercial loans, leasing, commerical mortgages, and so forth. Thus securitization has the potential to increase the variety of roles for financial institutions and to reduce head-to-head competition.

Despite the potential benefits, many bankers have been slow to adopt the new technology—many of them fear it. Small banks have been particularly fearful; most of them believe that it represents only a threat to them. And, at first glance, it would appear that asset securitization is only an important concern for large players. To date, except for government-guaranteed mortgage assets, almost no assets originated by community and local banks have been securitized. Is asset securitization an opportunity only for large players?

In fact, no. Ample evidence exists that small mortgage brokers and mortgage banks have been able to prosper in a securitized world. Furthermore, asset securitizaton may represent one of the main ways that community and local banks can maintain their customer franchise and survive the tidal wave of change now transforming our financial system. Many community and local banks are poor diversifiers of credit risk; securitization represents an opportunity for local banks to provide their customers with long-term, fixed-rate credit without taking undue interest rate risk. Moreover, some of the classes of securitized assets (e.g., floating-rate, mortgage-backed securities) may represent attractive investments for some local and community banks, particularly those banks in parts of the country suffering from regional recessions.

But community and local banks are too small to be effective players in securitization on their own. They need an infrastructure to join them together. But this infrastructure could evolve naturally from the national and regional correspondent banking networks that exist today.

The securitized asset system would create a large variety of new roles. Structuring, the process of actually converting the loans into cash flows and repackaging them for investors, would become a major business. We would envision that this role could be played not only by investment banks but by commercial banks that would work with their correspondents. Credit enhancement, the process of underwriting and diversifying credit risk and removing credit risk from investors, would become a major business for publicly rated foreign banks, insurance companies, and credit insurance subsidiaries of institutions that are today called bank holding companies.

Placing and trading the resulting securities would become an even bigger business than it is today as volumes continue to grow. It would probably continue to be dominated by investment banks although, regulation permitting, there would probably be a major role for some affiliates of bank holding companies as well. Finally, servicing the loans and the securities would also become an even bigger business, with the funds collection role continuing to be performed by the originating institution, and with the data processing and safekeeping roles being performed by a combination of commercial bank correspondents, service bureaus, and custodial banks.

The absolute profits earned by the entire industry from borrowers from this new system would probably decline over time because most of the direct earnings derived from simply lending out equity would be eliminated. However, the returns earned on equity form originating and servicing the loans that were converted into securities might be expected to be high, just as returns on equity from the mortgage banking business are already high. If so, stock prices would likely be high relative to book value. Moreover, successful players could earn significantly higher absolute profits than they do today because they could potentially gain so much market share from other commercial banks, thrifts, and finance companies.

2. *Profitable roles for nonbanks.* Participants in the system described will succeed based upon their ability to add value. But the roles just described, of course, would not be limited to players who are today called commercial banks and thrifts. Rather, all players would be free to compete wherever they choose, including through ownership of a riskless depository institution. They would no longer have to compete against players with unfair regulatory advantages (e.g., deposit insurance). Indeed, the distinctions between bank and nonbank holding companies would disappear.

Up until now, much of the momentum behind the securitization of assets has been from noncommercial banks: investment banks, rating agencies, finance companies, law firms, and so on. I expect these participants will continue to lead the way and prosper accordingly.

As Adam Smith observed over 200 years ago, the winners in a competitive environment will be in the companies that provide the best products at the lowest prices to their customers. The amount of value added can be increased either by making services more valuable to customers or by managing resources more effectively and efficiently to reduce cost. Fundamental profit strength will come from adding value to customers relative to competition.

3. *Provide for a safer financial system.* The final, and most important, advantage of securitized assets is that they provide the potential to limit credit defaults without resorting to massive government intervention. The FDIC, FSLIC "government safety net," while essential to protecting depositors, is the source of unsound lending practices in the country, because it permits incompetent lenders to lend money to borrowers that lack the capacity to service or repay the debt. Yet it is this very same safety net that has enabled the nation to avoid the financial crashes that plagued our economy from the nation's inception through the 1930s. The problem is that without the safety net one major default can result in a "daisy chain" of defaults through the payment system. That is, an otherwise sound institution can fail today simply because some other institution defaulted, which then leads to that institution defaulting, causing others to fail, and so forth. Presently, it would be impossible for the Federal Reserve to allow any major bank to fail because the interdependence through the payment system is such that it would bring the whole system down. It was this reality that had led to the bailouts

of such institutions as Continental Illinois and more recently, First City Bancorp of Houston.

One of the major advantages of securitization is that the special-purpose vehicles used to do the deals can be used to isolate these individual transactions from all other risks. Thus, even if a transaction is poorly underwritten, the resulting loss will not affect parties that did not participate in the transaction. In other words, while today it is the federal government that ultimately must absorb the risk of a disastrous credit decision by a depository institution, in the future the risk of a poorly underwritten securitized asset transaction can be borne by investors and credit enhancers, so there will be no need for federal bailout. Of course, this is only true to the extent that neither the end investors nor the credit enhancers in the transaction are federally insured depository institutions.

By this point the reader may wonder if there is indeed any real down side to asset securitization. As promising as the new technology is, it is not a panacea for all financial ills. Asset securitization cannot—and will not—miraculously cure the loan problems from any originator's balance sheet, including, of course, those of our nation's banks and thrifts, nor can it help out any financial institution that lacks the skills and people to compete. Many of the advantages of asset securitization exist only in potential. But it should be clear from the preceding pages that it is in the interest of all of us to help realize that potential, in whatever way we can, in the coming years.

GLOSSARY

absolute prepayment model (ABS) A model designed by First Boston to measure the percentage of original contracts in a pool that prepay each month. This measure is an absolute rate in that it measures prepayments in each month as an absolute number of contracts, expressed as a fraction of the original number. The model reflects historical experience on consumer installment sale contracts on automobiles better than the single monthly mortality model. This model is denoted absolute or ABS, referring to both the absolute measure used and the asset-backed securities it was designed to analyze.

actuarial method See effective interest.

advances Payments made by the servicer of an ABS transaction when scheduled payments due from obligors are delinquent. Advances are only made by the servicer to the extent it expects to recoup any monies from subsequent collections on the receivables.

all-in cost The issuer's total transaction cost, which includes such items as investor spread, underwriting discount and associated issuance expenses amortized over the weighted average life of the transaction.

amortization period Period during the life of a credit card asset-backed security that follows the revolving period, during which principal is paid out to investors rather than invested in additional receivables. Investors receive payments of principal and interest during this period.

annual percentage rate (APR) The rate at which finance charges are assessed on an account or loan expressed as an annual rate.

asset-backed certificates Pass-through securities representing fractional undivided interests in a grantor trust that holds receivables.

asset-backed commercial paper Commercial paper issued by a special-purpose corporation and backed by financial assets.

asset-backed notes A single tranche type of asset-backed obligations.

asset-backed obligations (ABOs) Debt instrument similar to a collateralized mortgage obligation (CMO) but backed by nonmortgage assets. ABOs can consist of one or more classes, any of which may have fixed payment schedules.

asset-backed preferred stock Preferred stock issued by a special-purpose subsidiary that purchases financial assets, such as notes, trade, or consumer receivables, from its parent or affiliate.

asymmetrical treatment Treatment of asset-backed securities as debt of the selling company for tax purposes notwithstanding removal of the assets from the selling company's balance sheet for financial reporting purposes.

average life The average number of years that each dollar of principal will be outstanding.

bankruptcy-remote entity Either an entity that is not eligible for relief under the bankruptcy code (e.g. thrifts, banks, insurance companies) or a special-purpose subsidiary of the selling company that has a separate corporate existence and is organized solely to purchase receivables and issue ABSs.

bullet maturity The maturity date of an obligation on which the entire principal amount is payable.

clean-up call An optional call by which the issuer of asset-backed securities can repurchase receivables when the principal balance of the sold receivables declines to a small percentage (5 to 10 percent) of the aggregate face amount of the securities. The purpose of the call is to minimize the administrative expense of servicing a small remaining pool of assets.

collateralized mortgage obligation (CMO) A corporate bond backed by a pool of mortgages in which the principal cash flows of the pool are channeled sequentially into one or more classes, or tranches, of bonds. Interest is usually paid currently or accrues on all tranches.

conduit or conduit issuing corporation A limited purpose corporation, generally formed by an investment banking firm, that issues securities backed by assets purchased by the conduit from unaffiliated originators.

constant prepayment rate (CPR) model   A measurement device designed to estimate the likely incidence of prepayments on an automobile portfolio. CPR measurements assume that prepayments occur at a constant rate each month as a percentage of the then-outstanding balance of the assets supporting the issue.

convexity   Refers to the market value response of a security to changes in interest rates. When the market price of a security is convex (positive convexity), the distribution of returns is biased in the investor's favor. For a given decline in yield, the investor's profit is generally greater than the loss that would be created by an equal increase in yield. "Negative convexity," on the other hand, refers to the distribution of returns biased against the investor. Negative convexity, which is typical of mortgage-backed securities, is caused by the sensitivity of prepayment rates on the underlying mortgages to prevailing interest rate levels.

credit card asset-backed securities (credit card ABS)   Asset-backed securities that are collateralized by credit card receivables or that represent ownership of a portfolio of credit card receivables.

credit card trust   A trust into which credit card accounts and receivables generated by those accounts are deposited. The beneficiary of a credit card trust consists of one or more classes of investors and the sellers of receivables. For tax purposes, the investors' interest in the trust is considered debt of the seller.

credit enhancement   A component of an asset-backed security designed to protect investors from suffering "normal" losses on the pool of assets supporting the security. Credit enhancement is usually provided by a third party in the form of a letter of credit or surety bond. Occasionally, an issuer guaranty or subordination agreement is used.

duration   A measure of bond volatility. It is computed as the weighted average time to receipt of the present value of all projected cash flows, using as weights the present value of the cash received at various times.

effective interest   Precomputed income recognition method that results in economic accrual of interest assuming all intervals between payments are equal. Payment schedules and principal/interest breakdown are known at the origination of the contract. (Also known as the "actuarial method.")

finance lease A lease transaction in which the lessee can acquire the use of equipment for most of its economic life while the lessor, through rental payments, recovers the full cost of the equipment plus a return on the investment. Since it is not a tax lease, the user is responsible for maintenance, taxes and insurance.

fixed investment trust For federal income tax purposes, a passive investment vehicle formed as a trust in which there is no power to reinvest proceeds beyond distribution dates. It has either a single class of beneficial interests or two or more classes that are incidental to facilitating direct investment in the assets of the trust.

fixed payment bond A collateralized debt security that pays off according to a guaranteed sinking fund schedule. Investors therefore bear no prepayment risk.

force placed insurance Automobile insurance purchased by a servicer and added to the cost of an automobile owner's contractual obligation when the owner fails to renew his personal insurance. It is not used in all states or even by all servicers in those states where it is used.

full payout lease A lease in which the total lease payments alone (without dependence upon guaranteed or unguaranteed residuals or purchase options) pays back to the lessor enough to cover the entire cost of the leased asset together with the cost of financing the lessor's overhead and a return acceptable to the lessor.

grantor trust For federal income tax purposes, a trust whose income is not taxable at the trust level but rather at the level of beneficiaries who receive income or principal or otherwise control the trust; a grantor trust includes a pooled investment vehicle in which investors acquire undivided beneficial interests in the trust's assets, provided it also qualifies as a fixed investment trust.

guaranteed investment contract (GIC) An agreement by a bank or other party to invest amounts in the collection account (a segregated account, typically maintained by the trustee, that holds payments received on the assets) at a specified interest rate. This agreement permits the issuance of nonmonthly and fixed pay asset-backed securities.

guaranty amount   The percentage of defaulted receivables that a guarantor is obligated to repurchase under its limited guaranty.

hell or high water lease   A lease containing a clause stating the unconditional obligation of the lessee to pay rent for the entire term of the lease, regardless of any event, change in the equipment, or other circumstance of the lease.

Investment Company Act of 1940   The statute providing for the regulation by the Securities and Exchange Commission of "investment companies"; that is, companies formed to invest in securities and pass the profits of the investments to the shareholders of the investment company. The Act is relevant to asset securitization because the broad definition of "investment company" may encompass entities traditionally utilized to securitize assets.

lease residual   The project market value of leased equipment upon the expiration of the lease.

limited guaranty   The obligation of a seller of receivables to repurchase the principal balance of receivables that it deems uncollectable, up to a certain guaranty amount.

money over money lease   A transaction in which a lease broker purchases an asset, obtains a lease, and sells or assigns, on a nonrecourse basis, the right to receive rentals for an amount that exceeds the investment in the leased asset.

monthly payment rate   A measure of a credit card portfolio's receivable turnover that is calculated as the amount of payments received during a month (including both principal and interest) divided by the amount of receivables outstanding at the beginning of the month.

mortgage-backed security   A pass-through certificate or bond backed by an interest in a pool of mortgages or trust deeds. Cash flow from the underlying mortgages is used to pay off the securities.

nonconsolidation opinion   Legal opinion that the separate corporate existence of a special-purpose subsidiary has been properly observed and would not be disregarded if the parent selling company became a debtor under the bankruptcy code.

nonrecourse   A structure by which a bank can achieve sale treatment for regulatory accounting purposes (RAP). Rather than provide recourse to investors, the bank creates a reserve account into which it deposits the difference between the contract rate on its receivables and the interest paid to investors. Amounts on deposit in the reserve account are available to reimburse the provider of credit enhancement for the ABS transaction.

operating lease   A lease in which a lessee can acquire the use of equipment for a term that is less than the equipment's useful life. The lessor often assumes the risks of ownership, which may include personal property taxes, maintenance and insurance costs. At the expiration of the initial lease, the lessor depends on the residual value to pay out its investment and realize a profit, through either renewals or sale. For financial accounting purposes, an operating lease does not meet the Financial Accounting Standards Board #13 criteria of a capital lease.

owner trust   An entity formed as a trust under state law in which ownership is represented by transferable certificates of beneficial interest, and which typically owns a leveraged asset or pool of assets.

pass-through   A trust structure used in both the mortgage and asset-backed market. Pass-through securities are established by the creation of a grantor trust into which a pool of assets are sold. Certificateholders are entitled to all cash flow from the assets, creating, in effect, an equity interest in the assets.

payment delay   The time lag between the date on which the servicer passes through payments on pool assets to the trustee and the date the trustee pays the pool investors.

pay-out event   An event that results in a termination of a credit card ABS's revolving period and the commencement of the amortization period.

pay-through   A bond structure used in both the mortgage and asset-backed market. Pay-through bonds represent an issuer liability where repayment is secured by cash flows associated with assets pledged as collateral. Pay-through structures allow for active management of cash flows.

pool factor   The fraction of a pool's original principal balance that remains at any given time.

prepayment rate   The rate at which the obligors on a given pool of receivables prepay the principal balance of those receivables, expressed according to either the Absolute Prepayment Model,

(ABS) the Constant Prepayment Rate (CPR) Model or Single Monthly Mortality (SMM) Model.

REMIC   Real Estate Mortgage Investment Conduit. A mortgage securities vehicle, authorized by the Tax Reform Act of 1986, that holds residential or commercial mortgages and issues securities representing interests in those mortgages. A REMIC may be formed as a corporation, partnership, or segregated pool of assets. The REMIC itself is generally exempt from federal income tax, but the income from the mortgages is reported by investors. For investment purposes, REMIC securities are virtually indistinguishable from CMOs.

reserve account   A form of credit enhancement, also known as a spread account, which is funded from excess finance charges on the assets in a trust and is used to reimburse any losses incurred by the third-party credit provider. Since the credit provider is not entitled to reimbursement from any other assets of the trust, the servicer or the seller, a reserve fund structure is considered nonrecourse.

residual   Cash flows resulting from the difference between the cash inflow generated by a pool of collateral and the cash outflow necessary to fund bonds that are entirely supported by the collateral.

revolving period   The period during the life of a credit card ABS in which principal received from payments on credit card receivables is reinvested in additional receivables. Investors receive only interest during this period.

roll rate analysis   A predictive technique for credit card receivables used to forecast portfolio delinquencies and losses.

Rule of 78s   Precomputed (that is, principal and interest components are known at the origination of the contract) income recognition method that results in a greater interest allocation to early periods than the effective interest method.

Sears Regulations   Treasury regulations [§301.7701-4c] that generally treat multiclass trusts as either partnerships or associations taxable as corporations for federal income tax purposes, so named for multiclass pass-through certificates issued by Sears Mortgage Securities Corporation.

Securities Act of 1933   The statute that provides for regulation by the Securities and Exchange Commission of the offering and sale of securities.

Securities Exchange Act of 1934   The statute that, among other things, imposes periodic reporting requirements upon the issuers of publicly offered securities.

senior-subordinated   Credit enhancement method in which two classes of ABSs are issued, a senior class and a subordinated class. Principal and interest payable on the subordinated class can be utilized to cover losses on the senior class.

simple interest method   Income recognition method that results in economic accrual of interest taking into account the exact number of days between payments. Collections from obligors are applied first to interest, which accrues daily, and then to principal. Thus, the principal/interest breakdown of each payment is not known until the payment is actually received.

single monthly mortality (SMM)   A prepayment measure developed by First Boston in 1977 and commonly used in the analysis of mortgages. This measure is a relative rate, in which each month's prepayments are expressed as a fraction of the loans remaining at the end of the previous month.

special-purpose corporation   A corporation organized solely to issue debt and purchase receivables, thereby isolating the receivables from bankruptcy concerns relating to the originator.

standby letter of credit   A letter of credit that is drawn upon only if the seller of receivables in an ABS transaction fails to repurchase defaulted receivables according to the terms of its limited guaranty.

stated interest   Interest payable at a rate specified by the terms of an obligation or indenture.

Statement of Financial Accounting Standards Board No. 77   Statement issued in December 1983 that sets forth generally accepted accounting principles for transfers of receivables with recourse.

strips   Specified payments of either principal, interest, or both (other than undivided interests) on an obligation, that are sold separately from the remainder of the payments on the obligation.

total return   The value an investor will receive by holding a security for a prescribed time period under a set of interest rate and pricing assumptions.

"true sale" opinion   For bankruptcy purposes, an opinion of counsel that the selling company is transferring ownership of the assets to the purchasing entity in the transaction and that in the event of the seller's bankruptcy a court would not recharacterize the transaction as a pledge of assets. This opinion is based on a multifactor analysis of the form and structure of the ABS transaction.

weighted average coupon (WAC)   The average APR of a pool of receivables as of the issue date, weighted by the principal balance of each receivable.

weighted average maturity (WAM)   The average maturity of a pool of receivables as of the issue date, weighted by the principal balance of each receivable.

Sources:

Charles M. Adelman, Cadwalader, Wickersham & Taft
Citicorp
First Boston Corporation
C. Thomas Kunz, Skadden, Arps, Slate Meagher & Flom
Salomon Brothers

INDEX